THE RĀMĀYAṆA OF TULASĪDĀSA

THE RĀMĀYAṆA OF TULASĪDĀSA

Translated from the Original by
F.S. GROWSE

Edited and Revised by
R.C. PRASAD

MOTILAL BANARSIDASS PUBLISHERS
PRIVATE LIMITED • DELHI

First Edition: Delhi, 1978
Second Revised Edition: Delhi, 1987
Reprint: Delhi, 1989, 1995, 1998

ISBN: 81-208-0205-5

Also available at:

MOTILAL BANARSIDASS
41 U.A. Bungalow Road, Jawahar Nagar, Delhi 110 007
8 Mahalaxmi Chamber, Warden Road, Mumbai 400 026
120 Royapettah High Road, Mylapore, Chennai 600 004
Sanas Plaza, Subhash Nagar, Pune 411 002
16 St. Mark's Road, Bangalore 560 001
8 Camac Street, Calcutta 700 017
Ashok Rajpath, Patna 800 004
Chowk, Varanasi 221 001

PRINTED IN INDIA

BY JAINENDRA PRAKASH JAIN AT SHRI JAINENDRA PRESS,
A-45 NARAINA INDUSTRIAL, PHASE I, NEW DELHI 110 028
AND PUBLISHED BY NARENDRA PRAKASH JAIN FOR
MOTILAL BANARSIDASS PUBLISHERS PRIVATE LIMITED,
BUNGALOW ROAD, DELHI 110 007

PREFACE TO THE SECOND REVISED EDITION

It is a pleasure to know that another edition of F.S. Growse's fascinating translation of the Hindi *Rāmāyaṇa* is called for, and this has enabled me to correct many misprints and profit by the suggestions made by my students and colleagues to whom I am greatly indebted.

For some years now *The Rāmāyaṇa* of Tulasīdāsa has been sought for with increasing fervour, and its popularity is by no means limited to India, nor are the Hindus its only readers and admirers. Many of its genuine lovers are the simple semi-educated people in India and abroad to whom Tulasīdāsa was the guardian of Indian culture at a time when not only the Hindu religion, but the whole body of Hindu culture was already under the threat of extinction. To the scholar well-versed in the Hindu scriptures, Tulasīdāsa is the defender of values which Indian literature as a whole has ever attempted to maintain, and his *Rāmāyaṇa* is, in Arnold's words, "a study of perfection, and of harmonious perfection,...and perfection which consists in becoming something rather than in having something, in an inward condition of the mind and spirit, not in an outward set of circumstances..."

It is in the light of this special function of Tulasīdāsa—the function of educator, seer and representative of a national culture of whose glories he is so thoroughly aware—that he must be considered, not just in the light of some of his obsessive themes and images to which Growse has drawn our attention in his preface. That he is primarily a votary of Rāma in the widest and deepest sense of the word no reader of his epic will dispute, but he is also a poet of revolt, as can be seen from his attitude to Rāma's treatment of Guha, the Niṣāda chief and of all 'houseless poverty' and 'poor naked wretches' dropping with hunger, faint with privations. Despite all his shortcomings as a poet, it cannot be denied that Tulasī's creativeness is sustained, culminating in a mastery of the devotional epic hardly equalled in the Indian languages.

F.S. Growse's prose translation is eminent not only for its exactness and the knowledge it shows, but also for its consistently noble and lofty tone, and amplitude of its construction which owes much to *The Rāmāyaṇa* itself. Growse was familiar with the deepest stratum of art—the images of myth, religious and poetic—which Tulasīdāsa saw as a curious treasure-trove and to which he again and again had recourse. This prose rendering of Tulasī's epic leaves the riches of the folk tradition intact and allows the reflection of mythology to shine through countless new configurations. With its frequent repetitions, its unfailing and open appeal to set effects, and its use of stereotyped turns of phrase, the poem in Growse's translation answers much the same cravings of imagination and feeling as the original Hindi *Rāmāyaṇa*, *Rāmacaritamānasa* to be exact, in which the tradition of oral poetry blends harmoniously with that of the literary epic.

R. C. Prasad

Department of English
Patna University
9.1.1987

INTRODUCTION

Dr. R. C. Prasad

There is nothing in Hindi, or in any other Indian language, comparable to Tulasī Dāsa's *Rāmacaritamānasa*. It is acknowledged not merely as the greatest modern Indian epic, but as something like a living sum of Indian culture. Second only to the *Gītā* in its influence, it has come to dominate not only the literature of the Hindi language, where even some of the *avant-garde* poets and humanists have been unable to resist its influence, but the whole field of our culture in northern India. It appears that apart from educational compulsion, the professional studies of scholars and college-teachers, and the devotion of a few most sensitive and spiritual-minded among the Hindus and men of letters, it is unusual for a young north-Indian Hindu to read the Sanskrit *Rāmāyaṇa* of Vālmīki at all. But as literature and popular religious poem, the *Mānasa* ministers munificently to the imagination and fancy of millions of people in northern India who have made the poetry of Tulasī Dāsa one of their most frequent and precious companions. The distinct infusion of the values which their mind usually associates with the 'Hindu genius', the variety of human experience gathered into its vast embrace, the boundless inventiveness and ingenuity of the author, the thrills awakened by marvellous episodes and the endless surprise of unexpected events—all add to its popularity, even though the original poems on which it is based have fallen into neglect.[1]

The *Mānasa* has apparently gone too deep. Like all normal people, the Hindus cannot saturate themselves for centuries with a book like the *Rāmacaritamānasa* and throw off the spell in a couple of generations. Tulasī for them is not just a poet believing, as did Milton, in his destiny as a poet and despising prose, he is a seer, a law-giver, a liberator. When the country was

1. The book, says Growse, "is in everyone's hands, from the court to the cottage, and is read, or heard, and appreciated alike by every class of the Hindu community, whether high or low, rich or poor, young or old."

plunged in that sinister, gloomy and morbid atmosphere which the Muslim rule had from time to time unleashed, it was Tulasī, they feel, who brought them hope and liberation. They got a new and fresh inspiration, an inspiration not only from the *Mānasa's* literary beauty but from its real religious significance. For them it is the huge gamut of religious beliefs that mount up in its cresting tide that proves this Hindu epic to be a greater book than any other written in India except the Upaniṣads and the Gītā. Tulasī is so passionately devoted to the son of Daśaratha, so intensely in love with him, that by the sheer liveliness of his poetic imagination he transforms the hero of the Solar race, first into the qualified Incarnation of Viṣṇu, and then into the Lord Himself whom even the Vedas and the Purāṇas cannot fully comprehend, in other words into the Nameless Absolute or attributeless, formless, imperceptible and unborn Brahman.

The basic religious principles of Tulasī Dāsa, so far as they can be known, are contained in the dialogue between Bhusuṇḍi and Garuṛ in the Epilogue (Uttarakāṇḍa). His religion is a religion of being wholeheartedly devoted to Rāma whose Name, itself, he says, is like a sun to dispel the darkness of ignorance. Tulasī's Rāma is Truth, Consciousness and Bliss, untouched by the night of delusion. He is the Blessed Hari, whose being is Light itself. Joy and sorrow, knowledge and ignorance, egoism and pride — these are the characteristics of a *jīva* or mortal man; but Rāma is the all-pervading Brahman; He is Supreme Bliss personified, the highest Lord and the most ancient Being. Tulasī makes Śiva describe the story of Rāma as "the cow of heaven that grants all joys to those who tend her." It is, as Śiva further says, "the pleasant clapping of the hands to scare away the birds of doubt; the story of Rāma is an axe to fell the tree of Kaliyuga."

There is utter humility, often reminiscent of the 'gentler qualities of Christian virtue', in Tulasī Dāsa's religion, the humility of losing oneself in the service of Rāma, the humility of beating down one's ego and surrendering oneself, body and soul, to the Lord Himself. It is not a religion of being friends with the Lord, as Sūradāsa's is, or His spouse, as Mīrā's is, so as to sport with Him like the Gopīs. It is a religion of universal charity and of being pure and humble and looking upon the Lord as your master, finding your heaven in His service as well as in His grace, and obeying His mind in your own soul. Essentially in keeping with the teachings of Christ and the Apostles, it is a religion in which God has a total claim on his devotees.

> Sooner may hair grow on the shell of a tortoise, sooner may a barren woman's progeny slay anyone, sooner may flowers of every description appear in the air than a creature find happiness even though hostile to Hari. Sooner may thirst be quenched by drinking of a mirage or horns sprout on a hare's head, or darkness efface the sun than a soul at odds with Râma find happiness. Sooner may fire appear out of snow than an enemy of Râma find peace. Sooner shall butter be churned out of water or oil be extracted by crushing sand than the ocean of worldly existence be crossed without worshipping Hari. This is a conclusion which cannot be set aside.

Few Catholic saints would have found these lines savouring of anything exclusively Hindu or pagan. Nor would Tulasī have found their message of humility and charity incompatible with his own. There is nothing sectarian in the Christian belief (he would have said) that a man who serves the King of kings has nothing to fear but his own shortcomings, or that the Christian magnanimous man will receive rewards beyond all human ambition. He must not, therefore, waste it on trivialities. He needs no possessions. In God he has the highest rank of all. To *serve* God is to rule.

And Tulasī Dāsa would surely have agreed with 'the man on the palliasse', who taught St. Francis Xavier the importance of poverty. "Begging," he had told St. Francis, "is only a very small part of the matter. It is good for our humility. It is good also for the charity in the hearts of others. Poverty makes a man free. People will not envy him — except for a few and they can easily satisfy their envy by imitating him. A man who is not carrying possessions has his mind free as well as his hands."[1] Tulasī, who had refused to serve Mammon, was certainly envied

1. Louis de Whol, *Set All Afire : A Novel of St. Francis Xavier* (1953), p. 35.

by some of his contemporaries, especially the Brāhmaṇas of Kāśi. But he never abandoned his humility or his potent talisman of faith in Rāma. "Rāma I adore, I adore, I adore !" he cried. "The imperishable I adore, by seeking sanctuary with whom even such guilt-stained sinners as myself are purified !"[1] And he refused to be cowed down by those who envied him but dedicated himself to his master, Hari, full of the humble realization of his entire dependence upon Him for all that he is and has and of the fact that whatever he has is derived from Rāma not entirely for himself but also in trust for his neighbours. For him here is only one thing that matters, one word, one power, one magic touch, that ends the ignorance of men and enables them to cross the ocean of birth and death.

> 'I am the servant and he my master' — without this relationship, Garuṛ, the ocean of birth and death cannot be crossed. Hold fast this doctrine and worship the lotus feet of Rāma.[2]

And again :

> 'I am That' — this unbroken mental state is the lamp's brightly burning flame. Then on the soul's experience dawns the fair light of bliss, and all distinction and error, source of rebirth, are destroyed.[3]

Where there is faith in Rāma, the mind of material objects does not lead reason astray. Where there is genuine piety, one does not fall a prey to infatuation even in a dream. Like the Sufi mystic, Jalaluddin Rumi, or like St Paul, Tulasī does not tire of stressing the value of self-loss for one seeking to attain the supreme state of final beatitude. The following passage in 'The Beautiful',[4] sums up his attitude to selfless love :

> Even though a man should be the enemy of all creation, if he comes terror-striken to me, seeking my protection and discarding vanity, infatuation, hypocrisy and trickeries

1. The Epilogue, C. 119.
2. *Ibid.*, D. 119 a.
3. *Ibid.*, C. 113.
4. See C. 48.

> of various kinds, I speedily make him the very like of a saint. The ties of affection that bind a man to his mother, father, brother, son, wife, body, wealth, house, friends and relations are like so many threads which a pious soul gathers up and twists into a string wherewith he binds his soul to my feet. Nay, he looks on all with an impartial eye and abandons all desire, grief and fear. A saint of this description *abides in my heart*[1] even as Mammon resides in the heart of a covetous man.

Rāma makes it clear that those who surrender their selfhood to God abide in his heart; they are 'deified', they have 'become' or 'been made' God. Therefore, when animated by a passionate and selfless love, they look to their centre, they see only God.[2]

Looked upon as the greatest poet of his time it would be easy to expect that there should be some signs of consciousness of this, and as a consequence some of that unpleasant self-assertion which so often makes great creative and intellectual geniuses unpopular. Tulasī, however, never seems to have had any over-appreciation of his own talents, but, realizing how little he knew compared to the whole round of knowledge, and how imperfect he was compared to the perfection of the Lord about whom he was writing, it must be admitted that there was no question of conceit having a place in his life. There are scores of passages in the *Mānasa* alone in which this humility finds expression and the poet tells us that he has sung of the glory of Rāma to sanctify his voice. "I am no poet," he declares early in his *Mānasa*, "nor am I called clever, but I sing the excellence of Rāma according to the measure of my understanding; how wondrous are the acts of Raghupati, how poor my wit, devoted to this world !" Poets like Chaucer often appear to show the same urbanity and charity but not the same humility.[3] Tulasī did not possess their courtly sophistication or their inimitable ingenuity and skill in using subtle ironies and innuendoes.

1. Italics mine.
2. F. C. Happold, *Mysticism* (Penguin Books, 1963), p. 97.
3. On several occasions, Tulasī recalls Christ's first commandment that thou shalt love the Lord thy God with thy whole soul, with thy whole heart, and with thy whole mind.

While, with characteristic humility, Tulasī considered himself scarcely more than a childish babbler and his composition clumsy and devoid of all poetic charm, his natural genius was eminently original and he added much more of his own than what he took from the *Adhyātma Rāmāyaṇa*, Vālmīki's *Rāmāyaṇa*, the *Hanuman-nāṭaka* and the *Prasannarāghava*. There can be no doubt that his *Rāmacaritamānasa* is a classical monument of the first importance for the exposition of the doctrines and the ritual of the *Advaita Vedānta* and the Rāmaite teachings of Rāmānanda's disciples. In the variety of its contents, allusions and doctrinal teachings, it is a perfect encyclopaedia of the learning of the ancient Indian sages, especially of the learning contained in the Upaniṣads, Vedānta Sūtras and the Gītā. By it we can fix the high-water mark of Vaiṣṇava ideals, for it contains the thoughts and doctrines of a poet who considered Rāma to be an incarnation of Viṣṇu and derived his doctrine of *jīva* from the Vaiṣṇava-Vedāntins, whose views he synthesized.

It is by the study of such books that one enters into the mental life of the period at which they were written, not by the hasty perusal of histories of religious thought. No student of the *Mānasa*, however, is likely to acquiesce in the belief that Tulasī was a religious bigot or that his work is limited in its appeal to those already acquainted with the Sanskrit *Adhyātma Rāmāyaṇa*, Rāmānanda's *Viśiṣṭādvaita* teachings and the Advaita Vedānta of Śaṅkarācārya. Tulasī was a liberal, who made Rāma, his hero, the sum of True Being, Thought and Bliss, the uncreated dwelling-place of wisdom, beauty and might, pervading all and all that is pervaded, undivided, infinite, entire, the Blessed Lord of never-failing power, impersonal, supreme, whom neither speech nor sense can grasp, all-seeing, faultless and invincible, disinterested, formless, everlasting, void of emotion, transcending nature, etc. Rāma is not just a sectarian hero, a Hindu god. He is the gracious Lord Himself in mortal form, the Word becomes Flesh to save the human race.

It is interesting that the Hindu theory of avatāra is essentially not incompatible with the Christian concept of the plan of redemption. The Hindu, too, looks upon God as the saviour of man and believes that He must therefore manifest Himslef whenever the forces of evil threa[illegible] [illegible]troy human values. "An avatāra is a descent of God into man and not an ascent of man into God, which is the case with the liberated soul..."[1] Making Śiva his mouthpiece, Tulasī explains why the Absolute took human form and says that Rāma "slays the Demons and sets the gods upon their throne; he defends the bounds of his own Vedic law and proclaims throughout the world his spotless glory. This is the cause of Rāma's descent." The "gracious Lord," he says further, "puts on mortal forms for the sake of the faithful." There is thus little difference between this 'gracious Lord' full of sportive wiles and the Son of God of the Puritans, for example, who was touched, as they say, with pity for the fallen race. His heart was moved with infinite compassion as the woes of the lost world rose up before Him. Thus it was that the Word became Flesh and the Divine Nature, which was pure and holy, entered as a renovating principle into the corrupted line of Adam's race, without being affected by corruption. Through the Virgin Birth, Jesus Christ became operative in human history without being subject to the evil in it. Bethlehem, like Ayodhyā, the birth place of Rāma, became a link between heaven and earth. Neither Christ nor Viṣṇu gained one perfection more by becoming man, nor did He lose anything of what He possessed as God. There was the Almightiness of God in the movement of Christ's arm as in that of Rāma. Both Christ and Rāma possessed the Infinite Love of God in the beatings of their human heart and the unmeasured compassion of God to sinners in their eyes. While God's becoming manifest in the flesh is called the Incarnation in Christian theology, the Hindus call it avatāra (descent, *avataraṇa*).

Growse has recorded the following story of Tulasī's wife who is said to have reproached the poet for his pursuit of her. According to Priyā Dāsa's gloss quoted by Growse, Tulasī, who had great love for his wife, Ratnāvalī, hastened to her when she went home to her parents without his permission. When she saw him, she was beside herself with shame and anger. "Have you," she said, "no love for Rāma ? My body is but a framework of skin and bone." Stung by his wife's reproaches, Tulasī sped at once to Kāśī, where he made his abode and began to lead an austere life, "making a rigid vow, and thirsting exceedingly for a vision." Had Ratnāvalī not greeted the poet with

1. Radhakrishnan, *The Bhagavadgītā*, p. 34.

her reproaches, as Tulasi's biographers remark, the *Rāmacaritamānasa* would never have been written. With all home ties abandoned, Tulasī was left free to go on with his great work, and during the most creative years of his life he must have applied every spare moment to the composition of his *Mānasa*. That it should be the basis in north India of the common man's knowledge of his faith to this day is of itself quite sufficient to proclaim its merit. The men who are most enthusiastic about it are those who have used it the longest and who know it the best.

Probably the most marvellous thing about the life of Tulasī Dāsa, apart from his devotion to Rāma, is his capacity for assimilating diverse tenets, Vaiṣṇava, Śaiva, advaita, *Sāṅkhya*, etc. Another marvellous thing about him was his capacity for work. He wrote twenty-two poems in all, though only twelve are considered by most scholars to be genuinely his own. This of itself would seem to be enough to occupy a lifetime without anything more. Tulasi's written works, however, represent apparently only the products of his hours at leisure. He was only forty-two when he began, on March 30, 1574, to write his longest poem at Ayodhyā, a poem written by him "in accord with all the Purāṇas, the Vedas and the Āgamas, that which is told in the *Rāmāyaṇa*...for his own soul's delight." How could Tulasī assimilate so much learning in so short a period ? It would seem as though his days must have been, like Aquinas's, at least twice as long as those of the ordinary scholar and student to accomplish so much. Yet he is, again like Aquinas, only a type of the 'monks' of the Middle Ages, of whom so many people seem to think that their principal traits were to be fat and lazy. Tulasī was not fat, as we know from his portraits. Though they reveal a little abdominal development, the last thing that would occur to anyone who knows anything about Tulasī Dāsa would be to accuse him of laziness. Clearly those who accept the popular notion of sādhus being idle spongers will never understand the poet of the *Mānasa*. The great Bhakti Movement in Hindi literature was due almost entirely to saints

We know less of Tulasī, however, than of any of the great writers of the world. There are only great mysteries, or at least mysteries, in his literary career, and the biographer is driven, with the lovers of Sūradāsa and Kabīr, to conjectural reconstruction from the shards of legend and anecdote. Even his personality is blurred beside the portraits of his European contemporaries who stand forth fresh and convincing. For this paucity of useful and trustworthy information about Tulasī's life Growse holds 'the Hindu mind' responsible. "It is a curious illustration," he says, "of the indifference to historical truth and the love for the marvellous, by which the Hindu mind has always been characterized, that although the *ṭīkā* even of the *Bhakt-Mālā* was written less than a century after the poet's death, it still gives us little trustworthy information about the real incidents of his life and supplies so much that is clearly fictitious." Part of this indifference is traceable to the Hindu's indifference to grossly material events of life. In the case of Tulasī, this indifference went deeper, for he was not only a poet but a sage as well. We have many an early proof in his writings that Tulasī the poet was at one with Tulasī the saint — that his genius, so to say, did not run against his theology or his Vaiṣṇava faith. There was no Savonarola in his soul fighting against an Ariosto or a Titian; he did not have to say *nay* to his genius. He was born to glorify Rāma or reverently recite the tales of Raghupati's excellent perfections. And of these he sang to 'quiet his conscience.' Had he raised his beautiful structures on his own life, he would also in later years have suppressed them and declared them immoral or impious. His Muse very seldom prompted the saintly, impersonal Vaiṣṇava in him to autobiographical or egotistical flights of poetic imagination.

Just as Dante's *Divina Commedia* embraces the triple worlds of Hell, Purgatory and Paradise and Milton's *Paradise Lost* sweeps across Hell, Chaos, Heaven and Earth, the scene of action in Tulasī's *Mānasa* is not just Ayodhyā or the forest to which Rāma, Sītā and Lakṣmaṇa were banished or the isle of the demons; it extends as far as the triple world of the Nāgas (Pātāla), gods (Heaven), demons and men (Earth). The world of the gods in the *Mānasa* is so close to that of men that you always find them raining flowers on the human actors below or worshipping Daśaratha's son, Rāma, who is an Incarnation of Viṣṇu. The following extract provides a good illustration of this earth-heaven proximity :

> Perceiving that the gods and Earth were afraid and hearing their loving plea, the Lord uttered these solemn words from heaven to dispel their anxiety and doubt :

"Fear not, ye sages, adepts and high gods ! For your sakes I will assume the form of man and with all my parts take human form in the noble Solar race. Kaśyapa and Aditi performed severe penance, and I promised them a boon long since. They have become manifest as Daśaratha and Kausalyā, a royal pair in the city of Kosala. In their house I shall become incarnate as four brothers, princes of the line of Raghu. I shall bring to fulfilment the word of Nārada and descend to earth with my high consort. I shall relieve the whole earth of its burden; be not afraid, O company of gods !"

When they heard the divine voice from heaven the gods were comforted and straightway returned; then Brahmā consoled Earth, and she was no more afraid but confident.

Brahmā instructed the gods each to take on earth the form of a monkey and wait on the feet of Hari, and then returned to his own sphere. All the gods departed to their several homes; they and Earth were at rest.[1]

In the *Mānasa*, too, as in the European epics, the reader has to reckon with new dimensions and unknown modes of being. There is both "an immense, an incalculable, extension in space and time," and "also — paradoxically enough — an amazing constriction, even an annihilation of space and time." Tulasī's 'fable', no less than Homer's or Milton's, involves an excellent action and great issues and is single and entire in a sense — Rāma's victory over the demons, the beginning of the hostility, its course, its consequences. Episodes like Rāma's childish sports, Viśvāmitra's visit to King Daśaratha to ask for Rāma and Lakṣmaṇa, the redemption of Ahalyā, Rāma's visit to Janaka's garden, Lakṣmaṇa's fulmination and challenge to Janaka, the breaking of the bow, the arrival of Paraśurāma and exchange of hot words between Lakṣmaṇa and Paraśurāma, Kaikeyī in the sulking-chamber, the boatman's love and the passage across the Gaṅgā, Bharata's arrival at Ayodhyā and his lamentation, the gift of the sandals, the dialogue between the sage Nārada and

1. Childhood, D. 186; C. 186; D. 187; C. 187.

Râma in 'The Forest', etc. — all lead to the central action, the episode of Mârica, Sītâ's abduction and the destruction of the demon host. This excellent central action, in the words of Arnold, appeals most powerfully to "the great primary human affections" as do all the minor episodes, or to "those elementary feelings which subsist permanently in the race, and which are independent of time." Tulasī is so inextricably caught in these episodes that the very telling of them is extremely moving and coherent. His tone is clear and sure and full of the certainty that Râma is Hari Himself even though he also suffers and acts like a human being. With love and untroubled faith, in his own voice and in that of Kākabhuśuṇḍi, he declares, "For the sake of his worshippers, Râma, the Blessed Lord, assumed the form of a king and played his most holy part as an ordinary man. Just as an actor plays upon the stage in various disguises, exhibiting characters appropriate to his dress, but himself remains the same, so, too, O king of birds, does Raghupati act his part, destroying the demons but gladdening the faithful." It is clear that Tulasī, as the narrator, is nowhere completely detached from the events he tells us about. Again and again he lets debates, arguments, long speeches interrupt the narrative and pours a whole philosophy of Advaita Vedânta into the epic story. Still when the worst has been said, the artistic unity of the work, under the circumstances, does not fall to pieces. With absolute ingenuity and artlessness he unites the conception of Râma as a man with that of Râma as an Incarnation of Viṣṇu. In fact, it is remarkable how, throughout his epic, he succeeds in doing so without much didactic elaboration and over-insistence.

In the passage I have just quoted, as in much of the *Mānasa*, the simile conveys all it is meant to convey with immediate significance and without in any way stopping the flow of narrative. Even complex images and states of mind fall simply and unerringly into place like the bits of glass in a kaleidoscope pattern.

> Lust is wind; insatiable greed is phlegm; choler is bile, that continually inflames the soul; and when these three brothers form an alliance, there comes into being a painful state of general paralysis....There are the ringworm of selfishness, the itch of jealousy, the swollen goitre of elation and despondency, the phthisis of envy at the sight of another's

> happiness, the leprosy of vice and perversity of soul, the excruciating rheumatism of egoism, the guinea-worm of hypocrisy, deceit, vanity and pride, the dreadful dropsy of greed, the fierce tertian ague of the three ambitions, the two fevers of covetousness and lack of discrimination — but why enumerate all the many diseases ?[1]

Tulasī was as aware as Castiglione and Erasmus, for example, of the power of metaphor to please while teaching. Like them, he felt that it was one of the best means of impressing the reader with an important subject-matter, *doctrina*, by means of *eloquentia*, and facilitating the retention of knowledge. The *Mānasa* abounds in vivid metaphors and displays of *ingegno* :

> Devotion to Raghupati is the season of rain; his faithful servants are the growing rice, and the two fair syllables of Rāma's Name are the months of Śrāvaṇa and Bhādra.
>
> Two sweet and ravishing syllables that are the eyes of the alphabet and the life of the faithful, easy to remember, bringing happiness to all...[2]

Though not 'brief to prick the intellect' of the reader, the following metaphors please by their 'revelation of correspondences' :

> Right thoughts are the earth and the heart a deep place therein; Veda and Purāṇa are the sea, and the saints the clouds which rain down praise of Rāma's glory in sweet, refreshing and auspicious showers. The sporting acts they tell of Rāma as man are the pure cleansing property of rain, while loving devotion...is its sweetness and coolness. That rain refreshes the rice-fields of good deeds and is the life of Rāma's faithful votaries. Its cleansing water falls on the earth of understanding and flows in one stream through the fair channel of the ears; it fills the holy place that is the Lake of the mind and settles there, a permanent source of joy and cool entrancing loveliness.[3]

1. *The Epilogue*, C. 116.
2. *Childhood*, D. 19; C. 20.
3. *Ibid.*, C. 36.

Tesauro, one of the exponents of *concettismo*, felt that the *ingegno* often leads to excesses, for once it is set in motion, it is difficult to control. Most of Tulasī's metaphors, one feels, are indeed logically expanded metaphors, but there is no dearth in the *Mānasa* of metaphors whose purpose is rather to create beauty than to develop the plot. The following metaphors, logically expanded as they are, reveal Tulasī's *ingegno* at its best :

> The glory of Rāma and Sītā is its ambrosial flood; the similes are the enchanting play of its ripples; the *caupāīs* are the lovely lotus leaves, thick-clustering; poetic skill the lustrous oyster-pearls; the elegant *chands* and *soraṭhās* and *dohās* gleam like a mass of many-coloured lotus flowers; the unequalled sense, the lofty sentiment and graceful language are their pollen and juice and fragrance; all the meritorious deeds are pretty swarms of bees; knowledge, detachment and thought are swans; allusions, inversions and other poetic devices are many kinds of beautiful fish....[1]

It is plain to see that the images are not only *leggieri* or graceful, but also *mirabile* or extraordinary. All unwittingly, Tulasī displays an interest in metaphor which corresponds to that of such seventeenth-century continental Europeans as Baltasar Gracián in Spain and Emmanuele Tesauro, Cardinal Sforza-Pallavicino, Pierfrancesco Minozzi, and Matteo Pellegrini in Italy.[2] And all unwittingly, again, he voices the same humanistic belief in the nobility of 'the form of man'[3] as Vives and Pomponazzi, Shakespeare and Browne.

Although Tulasī Dāsa is often compared with Sūradāsa, the celebrated author of *Sūrasāgara*, his superiority is now an established fact, especially in view of the really very vast range of experience that he explores. Sūradāsa's poems lack the variety and breadth of appeal and the deep understanding of Tulasī Dāsa. Both, however, stand for and typify the whole of their age. Like Wordsworth, both are burdened with the mystery

1. *Childhood*, C. 37.
2. Joseph Anthony Mazzeo, *Renaissance and Seventeenth-Century Studies* (New York and London, 1964), p. 45.
3. See *The Epilogue*, C. 116.

and the heavy and the weary weight of all this unintelligible world. Both feel the general sorrow of mankind. Both hear the still, sad music of humanity. They see the race moving in a mighty caravan of pain and tower above their contemporaries more than any other giant of Hindi literature; but their real greatness lies less in the fact that they stand out, than that they both stand on their age, rising out of it to unsurpassed heights, but never forgetting the foundation of the society to which they belonged. In this, the most vital period in Hindi literature, poetry was, in the fullest sense of the word, popular. The rhetoricians and poets of the Rīti school wrote for the court and scholars; the romantics of the Chāyāvād school often so loathed their age that they refused to understand its problems and took recourse to escapism as a cult. But Tulasī and Sūradāsa took the subjects beloved by the mass of Indain people, and made from them songs and hymns which continued to appeal to the mass and yet had deep, abiding interest for the greatest minds of their own and every succeeding age.

Whereas Sūradāsa is the poet of Love's bow, Tulasī, it seems, is pre-eminently a poet of Rāma's arms. While the *amor*-motif plays an important part in *Sūrasāgara*, the amorous sentiment has been subordinated in the *Mānasa*. While Sūradāsa is a poet of love, beauty, sweetness and other tender emotions, Tulasī ranges over the whole field of human experience and makes his poetry encompass all, or almost all, the nine sentiments, ranging from the sensitive or *śṛṅgāra* to *bhayānaka* (i.e., the sentiment of fear). Like Bhāmaha and Daṇḍin, Tulasī holds *rasa* to be one of the characteristics of an epic (*mahākāvya*) and in the episode of the meeting of Rāma and Sītā in the garden of Janaka, he expresses the aesthetic sentiment of *rati* (śṛṅgāra, love); in the episodes describing how Lakṣmaṇa robbed Śūrpaṇakhā of her nose and how the people of Laṅkā kicked Hanumān and laughed at him with loud guffaws and then set fire to his tail, we have the comic or *hāsya* (humour, *hāsa*) *rasa*; in the scene where Rāma mourns like a lover for his beloved, Sītā, we have the compassionate or *karuṇa* (grief, *śoka*) *rasa*; in several scenes described in Laṅkākāṇḍa or in the famous episode of Kaikeyī's anger, one finds vivid illustrations of the furious or *raudra* (anger, *krodha*) *rasa* : in the episodes describing Lakṣmaṇa and Hanumān's exploits in Laṅkā or in Rāma's encounter with the demons, Khara and Dūṣaṇa, in 'The Forest', the aesthetic experience of heroism (*vīra rasa*, energy, *utsāha*) is expressed; and in the episode of Śūrpaṇakhā revealing her own fearsome form in Pañcavaṭī or in that of the fight with Triśira, Khara and Dūṣaṇa when "jackals snapped; ghosts, spirits and goblins collected skulls; vampires beat time on warriors' fleshless heads while witches danced," we have the apprehensive or *bhayānaka* (fear, *bhaya*) *rasa*. The horrific or *bībhatsa* (disgust, *jugupsā*) *rasa* is experienced in reading such passages as those dealing with vultures clutching entrails and flying off and Meghanāda showering down upon Rāma ordure and pus and blood and hair and bones. Finally, the marvellous or *adbhuta* (astonishment, *vismaya*) *rasa* is encountered in Meghanāda's magic show, in Hanumān's enlarging his tail in sport and then making himself so large that he touched the sky.

Tulasī was fully conscious of the fundamental principles of artistic creation. His world of beauty does not, however, seem to be isolated at all from the everyday experiences of life. Underlying the allegory and splendid imagery of his poetry there is always a firm foundation of ideas and principles. It is these ideas and principles which prevent his poems from losing contact with the common joys and sorrows of man. In fact, Tulasī must be recognized not only as an artist who conjures up before our imagination the scriptural realm of piety, the exploits of the princes of Ayodhyā and the historic defeat of the demons of the Isle of Laṅkā but also as an independent poet who can create, out of materials derived from the *Rāmāyaṇa* of Vālmīki and the *Adhyātma Rāmāyaṇa* and the *Bhāgavata Purāṇa*, a world of ideas with a value and significance all its own.

Altogether the *Rāmacaritamānasa* is worthy of its position as the first signal work of a great literature. It outlines with a noble simplicity the image of a national genius who, by virtue of his superhuman deeds and miraculous achievements — the destruction of the country's outlaws symbolized by the various monsters and demons and of the enemy represented by the demon king of Laṅkā — is also an avatāra. While not equalling the sheer formal impressiveness of the *Mahābhārata*, it stands fitly for a human-spiritual world with which the Indian mind can efficiently cope. The supernatural is close at hand; Lord Śiva is one of the narrators of the story and the smaller deities are always either raining down flowers or beating their kettledrums; but the subject works itself out on a plane of mixed allegory and legend which an unsophisticated audience—and the poet—thoroughly accept. An intuitive tendency to portray the scenes dramatically and leave room enough for the development of dramatic elements is perceptible in the progression and form of the poem, its vivid study of character, and its sustained force and dignity.

It can be truly said that except Dante in Italy and Shakespeare in England, there is perhaps no single figure in the national and literary annals of other lands who represents for his countrymen what Tulasī Dāsa—the 'moon' of Hindi literature as a well-known couplet has it—represents for north Indians and even for those living far in to the south. He is the symbol of that essential and unbroken continuity between Purāṇic Āryāvarta and modern India which is the dominant note of Indian civilization throughout the centuries; he is, to some extent, the father of Hindi poetry and Hindi literature; the incarnation of India's genius, the interpreter of her past and the prophet of her future. He is not only the supreme poet, but the national poet of India. A religious thinker and reformer no less than a poet, he strove, like the Italian poet Dante, to translate his dream from the sphere of ideas to the sphere of facts : first, his dream of a living Hindu culture, for which he strove to "revitalize every aspect of Hindu society and culture as he found it,"[1] and then, his dream of integrating this culture into his own devotional ideology, for which he strove to "harmonize the divergent facets" of Hindu culture by standing firmly in the existing tradition, of which the Sanskrit *Adhyātma Rāmāyaṇa* is an example, and translating it into the vernacular language. "It is here," observes F. R. Allchin, "that his skill as a poet plays its part. For, for the people of a large part of north India Tulasī claims reverence comparable to that accorded to Luther as translator of the Bible into the native German. Many men have paid him their homage. His epic has been compared not only to that of Vālmīki, but to the Vedas themselves, or to the Kuran for (*sic*) the Muslim, or the Bible of the Christian. Others (including Mahatma Gandhi) have set it beside the *Bhagavad-gītā*."[2]

1. F. R. Allchin, *The Petition to Ram* (London : George Allen and Unwin Ltd., 1966), p. 18 (Introduction).

2. *Ibid.*, pp. 18 et seq.

Of Tulasī Dāsa's place among the major Indian poets there can be no question; he is as sublime as Vālmīki and as elegant as Kālidāsa in his handling of theme. Tulasī, as Nābhāji (fl. c. 1600 A.D.), the author of the *Bhaktamālā*, said, was no other than Vālmīki himself born again as Tulasī Dāsa to supply, by means of his new *Rāmāyaṇa*, a boat for the easy passage of the boundless ocean of existence. "Now again," he added, "as a blessing to the faithful, he has taken birth and published the sportive actions of the god." And time has substantiated Nābhāji's statement. Lest, however, the reader should form the impression that the *Rāmacaritamānasa* is merely a Hindi translation of the Sanskrit epic, it must here be pointed out that while Tulasī follows the course of Vālmīki's story, dividing it into seven *kāṇḍas* bearing the names that Vālmīki had given to his sections, the Hindi *Rāmāyaṇa* is essentially different from that of Vālmīki, "the copious and original source of all the poems which celebrate the deed of Rama."[1] The *uttarakāṇḍa* in the Hindi epic, for instance, bears no resemblance whatever to that of the Sanskrit work. Nor does the reader find anything in the latter resembling the conversation between Garuṛ and Kākabhusuṇḍi. A. A. Macdonell's statement, that the Hindi 'version' by Tulasī Dāsa is an important 'adaptation' of the Sanskrit epic, is therefore ill-founded.

Like the *Mahābhārata* and the *Rāmāyaṇa*, the Hindi epic too is rather a long nature poem in the grand manner, a poem in which we see the hero more in action amid woodland scenes than in the palace. Like its epic predecessors, again, it is closely connected with the religious faith of millions of people and is "the timehonoured repository of their legendary history and mythology, of their ancient customs and observances, as well as of their most cherished gems of poetry."[2] Although it belongs to mediaeval India, one feels that it actually belongs, like the *Rāmāyaṇa* and the *Iliad*, to a younger world, we enter them "as we enter a house in Pompeii — the colours may still

1. See W. Douglas P. Hill (tr.), *The Holy Lake of the Acts of Rama* (Oxford University Press, 1971), pp. xvii et seq., for a detailed examination of the points of difference between Tulasī Dāsa's poem and Vālmīki's epic.

2. Monier Williams, *Indian Epic Poetry*, Preface , iii, iv. Quoted by Ralph T. H. Griffith, *The Ramayana of Valmiki* (Varanasi : The Chowkhamba Sanskrit Series, 1963), p. vii.

seem fresh, and no mark of decay remind us of their age, but we feel that they belong not to us or ours, and a gulf of ages lies between us and our objects."[1] Both Vālmīki and Tulasī possessed the qualities of divine furor and the universality of knowledge and were in no way less learned than Homer or Virgil or Petrarch, nor were they unfamiliar with the skill of hiding their erudition, like Dante, under an allegorical exterior. Probably because a part of his wisdom consisted in an understanding of the passions, Tulasī Dāsa, like Vālmīki, was able to produce a great emotional effect in his readers, and this is the source of his power both as entertainer and as teacher. No less than Vālmīki or Kālidāsa, he could also create a world not fettered by the laws of nature, a world "which is of the very essence of joy, which is self-existent and not depending on anything else, and which brings into being a creation shining with the nine *rasas*."[2] If Vālmīki's poetry gives — as all great poetry gives — in a beautiful form a message of deep meaning and overloaded significance, the greatness of Tulasī's epic lies in its suggestion of the profoundest vision in the most perfect style.

If Kālidāsa claims merit for his power of evoking the emotions of love, pathos, heroism, and wonder, Tulasī Dāsa too merits praise for the brilliance of his descriptions and skill in evoking all these emotions in addition to those of deep personal devotion, loyalty and friendship. The reader, it is said, marvels at the vividness and precision of Kālidāsa's observations and at his skill in bringing before us scenes of Indian life in the court and forest, of the ancient *svayaṃvara*, of marriage rites, etc. He finds the same scenes depicted in the *Rāmacaritamānasa* with equal, if not greater, vividness and precision. True, the Hindi *Rāmāyaṇa* is not "the poetic reflex of the achievements" of any emperor,[3] but in the scenes where the demons torment the hermits and sages and are ultimately annihilated, it is certainly a reflex of the age, a crowning achievement of the poet who wished his contemporaries to remember that there was no reason whatever to despair. By depicting Rāma's victory over the

1. *Ibid.*, p. v. (Introduction).

2. Mulk Raj Anand, *The Hindu View of Art* (London : George Allen and Unwin Ltd., 1933).

3. *The Raghuvaṃsa*, as A. B. Keith has observed, provides the poetic reflex of the achievement of Samudragupta and Chandragupta.

band of demons, Tulasī reminds his readers of the ultimate victory of truth over the forces of evil, over Kaliyuga.

Just as the Kāvya style attains in Kālidāsa its highest pitch, so does the epic style in Hindi reach its perfection in Tulasī. If Kālidāsa, as Keith said, chooses to show us his skill in poetical artifice in the *Raghuvaṁśa*, Tulasī Dāsa chooses to do the same in the *Rāmacaritamānasa*. Tulasī is not — he never was — behind Kālidāsa in the use of a remarkable number of metres,[1] nor in the employment of alliterations, yamakas, paronomasias, onomatopoeias, etc. Kālidāsa's *forte* is declared to lie in similes, Tulasī Dāsa excels in both metaphors and similes, especially in the latter. The story of Rāma's wedding is, for Tulasī, the happy and auspicious king of seasons, spring; Rāma's departure to the forest is the intolerable heat of summer, and the tale of his journeying the burning sun and wind; the fierce war with the demons is the season of the rains, a blessing to the gods as rain is to the rice-fields; the rule of Rāma — an age of happiness, gentle conduct and greatness — is the fair autumn, pure and pleasant; the story of the virtues of Sītā, that crowning glory of womanhood, is the virtue of this water, incomparable, undefiled; the character of Bharata is its refreshing coolness, ever the same and indescribable. Viśvāmitra's love, like the clear unfathomed depth of the ocean, swells to the highest tide of ecstasy under the full-moon influence of Rāma's presence. When Rāma tosses upon the ground the two broken pieces of Lord Śiva's bow the latter is as pleased and free of care as a tired swimmer on reaching a shallow; the kings who had failed to lift up the bow are as confounded at the breaking of the bow as a lamp is dimmed at dawn of day; but Sītā's gladness can only be compared to that of the *cātaki* on finding a rain-drop in October; while Lakṣmaṇa fixed his eyes on Rāma as the *cakora* on the moon. When certain kings — all frantic degenerate fools — are inflamed with desire and want to carry off Sītā, the good ones put the whole assembly to shame and in a speech full of similes declare:

1. Of the *varṇika* metres used in the *Rāmacaritamānasa* the following may be mentioned : *anuṣṭubh, indravajrā, toṭaka, bhujaṅgaprayāta, mālinī, rathddhatā, vaṁśastha, vasantatilakā, śārdūlavikrīḍita*, and *sragdharā*. All metres other than *Caupāīs, dohās* and *soraṭhās* are called *chanda* by Tulasī, who generally uses the *varṇika* metres like *anuṣṭubh* for the composition of his *ślokas* and hymns.

"Like a crow who would rob the king of the birds of an offering; or a rat who would spoil a lion; as a man who is passionate without cause and yet wishes for peace of mind; as a reviler of Śiva who wishes for happiness and prosperity; as a greedy and covetous man who wishes for fair fame, and as a gallant who would have no scandal; as an enemy of God who wishes to be saved; such is your desire, O ye kings." Kālidāsa's similes are not more appealing than Tulasī's. Moreover, it is Tulasī, and not Kālidāsa,[1] who offers — if poets do really offer — "a solution, or suggested solution of the mysteries of life." Whereas the *Raghuvaṁśa* fails to offer any such solution, the *Rāmacarita-mānasa* eminently succeeds in doing so and brings, as W. Douglas P. Hill has rightly said, "a simple and pure gospel — good news of salvation — in homely and idiomatic vernacular straight home to the heart of the average Hindu, oppressed by the prospect of perpetual rebirth and depressed by the impossibility of the unlearned ever grasping the knowledge of the Absolute demanded by the metaphysicians of the *advaita* school."[2] The poem, Hill further maintains, not only presents the ideals of chivalry, tenderness and love, it also promises salvation to "the humblest outcaste if only he would put his trust, with love and adoration, in the Name of Rāma."[3]

What Sri Aurobindo says[4] about Hindu drama and epic is highly significant. "But to the Hindu," he says, speaking about the latter, "whose ideas of epic are not coloured with the wrath of Achilles, epic motive and character are not confined to what is impetuous, huge and untamed."[5] Tulasī, unlike the European epic poet, does not feed on the physical, grossly material features of life. Like the poets of the great Indian tradition he treats of gentleness, patience, self-sacrifice, purity, and other civilized virtues as he treats of martial fire, brute strength, revenge, anger, hate and ungovernable self-will. He excels in depicting the impetuous and the gentle, and even though his idea of epic is

1. See A. B. Keith, *Classical Sanskrit Literature* (London : Oxford University Press, 1923), p. 45.

2. *Op. cit.*, p. xix (Introduction).

3. *Ibid.*

4. *Vide Kalidasa* (Pondicherry : Sri Aurobindo Ashram, 1954), Second Series, Chap. 1.

5. *Ibid.*, p. 7.

not "coloured with the wrath of Achilles" he is endowed with competence enough to depict this wrath as movingly as any other poet in the world. He not only knows how to evoke the nine different forms of *rasa*; he also depicts martial fire in Lakṣmaṇa, brute strength and revenge in Rāvaṇa, anger in Kaikeyī and Paraśurāma, hate in the demons and ungovernable self-will in Rāvaṇa as well as in other demonic characters.

Just as Dante is the successor alike of the poets of ancient Rome and of the prophets of the Old Testament, so is Tulasī the successor alike of the Purāṇas and of the *Rāmāyaṇa* of Vālmiki. The splendour of Tulasī's art, the pregnant concision of his style, the perfect correspondence of thought with utterance also remind one of Dante. These are some of the qualities we would attribute to his native genius as well as to his study of the Sanskrit poets. (Dante, it may be pointed out, derived them from his study of the Latin poets). Both Dante and Tulasī Dāsa, however, make these qualities essentially their own, the former drawing fresh harmonies from that new Italian language which is itself the speech of imperial Rome grown to maturity, the latter from his "racy idiomatic language, larded with popular maxims and phrases, and...polished compounds and figures of speech which might well grace any text-book of Indian poetics." The *Rāmacaritamānasa*, like the *Divina Commedia*, is the first vernacular poem of modern India that can claim equality with the masterpieces of classical antiquity. It interprets like the *Divina Commedia*, again, "an epoch of abiding significance in the history of man." While the Italian poem interprets it, not only by rendering intelligible the intellectual, political, and religious heritage of the later Middle Ages, but also by the poet's unique revelation of the passions and motives of his contemporaries, the *Rāmacaritamānasa* interprets the period[1] allegorically and from the Vaiṣṇavite angle of a poet who "attempted to reconcile the Advaita Vedānta point of view with the Rāmaite teachings of Rāmānanda's disciples." The men and women he has created in his epic stand out — as in the *Divina Commedia* — from its cantos with an actuality, a dramatic power of delineation that even Kālidāsa or Shakespeare can hardly surpass. And, though faith, hope and love in Rāma is professedly Tulasī's

1. It marked the zenith of Muslim power in India.

subject, his poem is a treasury, again like Dante's *opus magnum*, of the most faithful and delicate transcripts from external nature: Janaka's garden planted with ornamental trees of every kind and overhung with many-coloured creepers, Rāma and Lakṣmaṇa emerging from the shade of the arbour, like two spotless moons from a riven cloud and the two gallant champions looking like a white lotus and a dark, with their hair parted like a raven's wing on their comely head, and here and there bedecked with bunches of flower-buds.[1] Both Dante and Tulasī Dāsa are the poets of what Francis Thompson called love's "possible divinities and celestial prophecies"; they are the poets of Eternity when they see "bound by love into one volume what is dispersed in leaves throughout the universe" and find desire and will brought into perfect harmony with "the love that moves the Sun and the other stars."

It is to "the otherness of mental for spiritual realities," says G. Wilson Knight, that the source of all poetry can be traced. These, he further says, "are 'nothing' until mated with earthly shapes," for creation is nothing but an offspring of this union between 'earth' and 'heaven', the material and the spiritual.[2] The source of Tulasī Dāsa's work too is rooted in the otherness of spiritual realities which are mated with earthly shapes. Rāma's character, based though it is on the oral and written traditions of the country, is born of this union. Rāma is *Puruṣottama* — the 'Higher Self,' 'beyond the perishable and imperishable', 'the former being the world, or the totality of all existence, and the latter being the seed from which the universe manifests itself endlessly.' He exemplifies 'the two spirits' of the world, one emerging in front of action and the other continuing motionless "in that perpetual silence from which the action comes and in which all actions cease and disappear into timeless being—Nirvāṇa."[3] In Rāma these two realities meet and in Him their opposition is reconciled. He is the Logos and Everlasting I Am, both Absolute Knowledge and Absolute Love.

1. There are many such transcripts in the *Divina Commedia* : the fireflies gleaming on the hillside at nightfall after the long summer day, the quivering of the sea at dawn, the appearance of the stars at the first fall of evening, the song of the skylark, etc.

2. G. Wilson Knight, *The Wheel of Fire*, 1930.

3. C. K. Handoo, *Tulasidāsa* (Orient Longmans, 1964), p. 193.

Viewed from the angle of characterization, Tulasī and Homer are poles apart. For Homer the tale was the thing, for Tulasī it was Rāma's character and his glory, might and power. And this explains Homer's thin and accidental characterization as well as the fact that Tulasī's characters are all distinct people with varying human relations, conflicts, motives of action and impulses. Both Homer and Tulasī thumb-nailed well; but whereas Homer afterwards lost heart, Tulasī did not. Nausicaa, for instance, appears dramatically and shapes, as T. E. Shaw has pointed out, "for a few lines, like a woman — then she fades, unused."[1] Neither Sītā nor Mantharā ever fades in the *Rāmacaritamānasa*, or is a silent witness to the main action of the epic. The central family standing out in Homer's epic includes "the sly cattish wife, that cold-blooded egotist Odysseus, and the priggish son who yet met his master-prig in Menelaus."[2] Tulasī's heroes and exemplars were different people.

Both Homer and Tulasī appear to have loved the rural scene as only simple citizens can. No farmers, they had learned the points of a good greenwood tree. They were surely neither land-lubbers nor stay-at-home nor ninnies. But whereas Homer's pages are steeped in a queer naiveté, Tulasī is quite sophisticated and subtle.[3] Yet there is a dignity about both which compels respect and baffles us, they being neither simple in sensibility nor primitive socially. Homer sprinkles tags of epic across his pages; Tulasī borrows a great deal from the *Vālmīki* and *Adhyātma Rāmāyaṇa* and the *Hanumannāṭaka*.

Like the Homeric poems, Tulasī's epic is a picture of a heroic age (Rāmarājya) on which the poet looks back as far-off in the past, but for his idea of which he often draws not on his own days, as Homer did, but on the Purāṇas and the Sanskrit *Rāmāyaṇa*. The gods and goddesses of the *Rāmacaritamānasa*, like

1. *The Odyssey of Homer* (New York : Oxford University Press, 1956), Translator's Note.

2. *Ibid.*

3. He is the author of 'the best poetry' in Hindi. About the best poetry, according to A. C. Bradley, "there floats an atmosphere of infinite suggestion. The poet speaks to us of one thing, but in this one thing there seems to lurk the secret of all. He said what he meant, but his meaning seems to beckon away beyond itself, or rather to expand into something boundless which is only focussed in it" (*Oxford Lectures on Poetry*, 1909). The *Rāmacaritamānasa* is full of the atmosphere of infinite suggestion.

the deities of the *Iliad*, are men and women, stronger and fairer than mortals, able to work wonders and to take any form they please, but not all-powerful or all-wise. From time to time they rain down flowers before Rāma enters the pavilion in Janaka's city; the goddesses appear, disguised as women, to witness Sītā's marriage; when Sītā sets her foot within the lists all beholders are fascinated by her charms, particularly the gods who in their delight sound their kettledrums and rain down flowers amidst the singing of the *apsarās* ; after Sītā lets fall the wreath upon Rāma's breast :

"Gods, seraphs, saints, men and dumb creatures expressed
Their victorious joy as each other they blessed;
The nymphs and goddesses, with dancing and singing,
To earth frequent handfuls of flowers were flinging."

— Childhood, C. 269

But whereas Homer's deities are often immoral, Tulasī describes his as morally faultless. True, "whoever listens to Nārada's advice, be it man or woman, is certain to become a homeless beggar" (Childhood, C. 79). But Nārada, like Bhṛgu and Durvāsā, is only an arch ṛṣi, a saint, and not a god. Indrāṇī, Śāradā, Lakṣmī and Bhavānī are said to be the wisest of all the queens of heaven, and no jealous goddesses. When the nuptial procession begins to approach the pavilion, they assume the disguise of woman's form and flock to the king's seraglio, singing delightfully with divine voice, and for joy, says the poet, there was no one who recognized them.[1] While Zeus of the Homeric poems[2] is a sensual, passionate but genial person, Brahmā, the Creator and the first god of the later Hindu triad, is a kind-hearted and all-perfect deity. When Umā begins her penance and for three thousand years eats only dry leaves of the *bel* tree, Brahmā's deep voice resounds through heavens :

"Hear me, O maiden, O mountain-king's daughter,
Soon you'll attain your desire;
So give up your suff'rings, he soon will be yours,
Lord Śiva, to whom you aspire."

— Childhood, D. 72

1. Childhood, C. 322.

2. "The moral standards of the gods," says T. A. Sinclair in his *History of Classical Greek Literature*, "are not better than those of human beings; they often seem worse" (p. 20).

Even Śiva the destroyer is a kindly deity who meditates on Tulasī's Rāma.[1] His destruction of Kāmadeva is no unkind act performed out of malice or enmity; it only exemplifies his love of man, of the law and self-control. When Kāma begins to provoke love, the stepping-stones of the law are swept away in a moment; religious laws and obligations, ceremonial observances, knowledge and philosophy, self-mortification, etc. are all panic-stricken and put to flight. Every creature in the world, animate or inanimate, forgets natural restraint and becomes subject to sensual passions. On seeing Śiva, Kāmadeva trembles, and the whole world returns to itself. Every living creature at once grows calm, as when a drunk recovers from his drunkenness. Kāmadeva, a god, is also full of the milk of divine kindness. He agrees to incur Śambhu's displeasure for the sake of the ṛṣis and gods who were being harassed by Tāraka, a demon of gigantic strength of arm and high renown. The Creator had reassured them, saying, "The demon shall die when a son is born of the seed of Śambhu, who shall conquer him in fight." It was He who had asked them to send Kāmadeva, the god of love, to Śiva to agitate his soul.

Though Homeric religion is basically different from Tulasī's, Homeric morality appears to be relatively high and akin to what Tulasī depicts in his poems. Fear of the gods, Homer appears to have believed, though powerful as far as it goes, would not go very far towards making man moral. For that he needs a moral law, independent of his religion. Tulasī, however, believes that devotion to God is enough and that the repentance of even the greatest sinner is accepted by the Lord. All virtues stem from Him, who is the lake of physical beauty, house of virtues, benefactor of the universe.[2] He is :

> "Like smoke-bannered fire for the forests of the Dānavas, with long and powerful arms, fierce bow and terrible arrows,
> With ruddy hands and feet, face and eyes the colour of red lotuses, a place of virtues and abode of beauty equal to many love gods,

1. Cf. "But Śiva his mind and his thought concentrated,
   And wholly on Rāma again contemplated."
   —Childhood, C. 82
2. *Vinayapatrikā*, 44.

Sun for the withering of the water lilies of lust, frost for
the lotus-garden of love, anger and intoxication,
Lion for the most maddened elephant of greed, banisher
of earth's load for the sake of devotees !"[1]

Although Tulasī does not appear to advocate the need of a moral law, independent of religion, Rāma, his brothers, and the warriors whom they lead are all full of what Greeks call *aidos*, the sense of honour, and *nemesis*, literally 'distribution' or that feeling which is roused in the mind by an unjust distribution — moral indignation. Rāma feels *aidos* for the opinion of his subjects. Lakṣmaṇa and Bharata feel *nemesis* when their own sense of right is shocked. In the *Rāmacaritamānasa* we find a riper moral sense than in the *Odyssey*, and a much larger number of words to express moral distinctions.

Among the epic poets of the world after Homer, the most influential and the most attractive no doubt has been Virgil, the Roman Homer, whose *Aeneid* is often described as a 'literary' rather than a 'genuine' or 'primary' epic. It is to this category of literary or secondary epics that the *Rāmacaritamānasa* also belongs. Possessed, it seems, by 'the glory of the countryside divine', both Tulasī and Virgil had an unmistakable love for nature, a love that shows itself in the sympathy which personifies inanimate things and attributes human feelings to the brute creation. While Virgil freely borrowed from Homer, Tulasī Dāsa "borrowed a great deal from the Vālmīki and *Adhyātma Rāmāyaṇas* and the *Hanumannāṭaka*...scattered through the book and delicately woven into the texture of the story, sometimes we find translations, literal or otherwise, of verses from the *Gītā*, the *Upaniṣads*, the *Bhāgavata*, the Purāṇas, Kālidāsa's plays, the Sanskrit dramas and other books."[2] While Virgil's aim was to make the glories of Greek epic live again for his countrymen in Roman guise, Tulasī speaks of his aim as follows :

> "In accord with all the Purāṇas and different secred texts, and with what has been recorded in the *Rāmāyaṇa* (of Vālmīki) and elsewhere, I, Tulasī, to gratify my own heart's desire, have composed these lays of Raghunātha in most choice and elegant modern speech."[3]

1. *Ibid.*, 46.
2. C. K. Handoo, *op. cit.*, pp. 128 *et seq.*
3. Childhood (Sanskrit Invocation).

Tulasī's aim is to "narrate the great deeds of Raghupati" and make them live again for his countrymen in his homely speech. "I declare and record it on a fair white sheet," says Tulasī, "that though my style has not a single charm of its own, it has a charm known throughout the world, which men of discernment will ponder as they read — the gracious name of Raghupati; all-purifying essence of the Purāṇas and the Vedas, abode of all that is auspicious, destroyer of all that is inauspicious, ever murmured in prayer by Umā and the great Tripurāri." And he goes on to praise his theme, clothed though it is in a vulgar tongue : "My language is that in vulgar use, but my subject is the highest, the story of Rāma, enrapturing the world."

Critics have often pointed out that it was impossible for Virgil, writing in Augustan days, to reproduce the primitive tone, of an epic born when the world was young. He could not, it is said, remain unaffected by all that had come into being in the interval — Greek tragedy, Greek philosophy, the learning and the sentiment of Alexandria. Much in the same way Tulasī Dāsa found it impossible to reproduce the tone of Vālmīki's *Rāmāyaṇa*, though his work is "no unworthy rival of its more fortunate predecessor." Whereas Vālmīki's classical Sanskrit is rich in polished phraseology, Tulasī's idiom is rough, colloquial and "in the course of three centuries has contracted a tinge of archaism."[1] Like Virgil, again, Tulasī could not remain unaffected by all that had come to being in the interval — the emergence of the vernaculars, the Vaiṣṇavites, Rāmānanda and his disciples Rāi Dāsa, Pipa and Kabīra. Each of these influences is discernible in the *Rāmacaritamānasa*; that of the vernaculars in the language of the poet;[2] that of the Vaiṣṇavites in the religious speculation, distinct and profound, which pervades the poem; that of Rāmānanda in the fact that it was he who revolutionized the worship of Rāma throughout north India.

Besides corresponding to the literary standards, the *Rāmacaritamānasa*, like the *Aeneid*, embodies the thoughts and aspirations of the age to which it was addressed. The Indian

1. See F. S. Growse's illuminating introduction.

2. The poet uses Braja Bhāṣā, Avadhī, Bundelkhaṇḍī, Māgadhī, Bhojapurī and also a few Persian and Arabic words in his poems.

Virgil knew that a story told for the story's sake would not suffice. Like the Roman poet who considered the true subject for a Roman epic to be Rome, Tulasī considered the true subject for an Indian epic to be Rāma. "The most elegant composition of the most talented poet," he said:

> "has no real beauty if the name of Rāma is not in it, in the same way as a lovely woman adorned with the richest jewels is vile if unclothed. But the most worthless production of the feeblest versifier, if adorned with the name of Rāma, is heard and repeated with reverence by the wise, who extract what is good in it, like bees gathering honey; though the poetry has not a single merit, the glory of Rāma is manifested thereby."

But whereas the interest of the *Aeneid* is national rather than personal or religious, that of the Hindi *Rāmāyaṇa* is mainly, I think, religious, which is why the "mass and the cultured classes have as much faith in it as if it were the equivalent of the Vedas, the Upaniṣads or the *Gītā*... It deals with problems of social, political and family life from the point of view of *dharma*, or righteous living, and religion."[1] It conforms to C. M. Bowra's classical prescription that :

> "An epic poem is by common consent a narrative of some length and deals with events which have a certain grandeur and importance and come from a life of action, especially of violent action, such as war. It gives a special pleasure because its events and persons enhance our belief in the worth of human achievement and in the dignity and nobility of man."[2]

Even the constant repetitions of certain stereotyped phrases in the *Rāmacaritamānasa* — such as 'lotus feet', 'streaming eyes', 'quivering frame', etc. — and prayers and invocations appear to be a heritage from the ancients whose epics are, broadly speaking, divisible into two distinct classes. Vālmīki's *Rāmāyaṇa*, like the Homeric epics and *Beowulf*, belongs to the class

1. C. K. Handoo, *op. cit.*, p. 126.
2. *From Virgil to Milton* (London : Macmillan & Co. Ltd., 1963), p. 1.

of minstrel poetry or to that of oral epics which are said to be "the mature form of improvised lays such as...were once popular in many parts of the world." The Hindi *Rāmāyaṇa* belongs to the second category : it is a written epic meant not to be heard or recited but to be read. The technique of the oral epic is largely that of improvisation and the "constant epithets, the repeated lines and blocks of lines, the copious store of synonyms and of alternative word-forms, are a heritage from improvisation." Since the Tulasian epic was not composed for recitation — though, of course, people have been reciting it — it is in some ways more closely woven than the Sanskrit *Rāmāyaṇa*. "It is also less wordy and diffuse," says F. S. Growse, "than the Sanskrit original and, probably in consequence of its modern date, is less disfigured by wearisome interpolations and repetitions...." The reason why it is more closely woven is that it belongs to the class of epics to which the *Aeneid* belongs. Although Tulasī and Virgil, too, use stock passages for recurring themes and are masters of a traditional language which often has little relation to the vernacular of their home, it is because they are consciously following Vālmīki and Homer "in the conscious conviction that they ought to do so, not because their conditions compel them to use devices which are indispensable to oral poetry and make it what it is."

The *Aeneid* is said to have dominated Roman education and literature for centuries. The *Rāmacaritamānasa* has not in any way been less popular and influential. "I have never met a person," says Grierson about the *Mānasa*, "who had read it in the original and who was not impressed by it as the work of a great genius." Like the *Aeneid*, the *Mānasa*, too, has been a "set book" for centuries of scholars and students alike and has evoked admiration from almost every writer from Nabba Dāsa to Nagendra. Just as the *Aeneid* survived both the rise of Christianity and the fall of Rome, so has the *Mānasa* survived both the decline of popular devotionalism and the division of Hindu religion into numerous cults and sects. In *An Englishman Defends Mother India*, Ernest Wood, the author, considers Tulasī's *Mānasa* to be "superior to the best books of the Latin and Greek languages," and in *Akbar, the Great Moghul*, Vincent Smith records his appreciation of Tulasī, saying, "...that Hindu was the greatest man of his age in India and greater even than

Akbar himself, inasmuch as the conquest of the hearts and minds of millions of men and women affected by the poet was an achievement infinitely more lasting and important than any or all the victories gained in war by the monarch...." Sir George Grierson was not overestimating the popularity of our poet when he said that while Kabīra's or Dādu's adherents may be numbered by hundreds of thousands, no less than ninety millions of the people of Upper India acknowledged Tulasī as their spiritual guide.

The great and complicated scheme of the *Mānasa*, though essentially different from that of the Nibelungen legend, is akin to it in an important respect. In the Nibelungen legend as well as in the *Mānasa* historical and mythical elements mingle. Insofar as the structure of the *Mānasa* is concerned, its affinity to the German epic *Nibelungenlied* cannot be overemphasized. The *Nibelungenlied* is not a mere collection of certain episodes selected from the legend, but consists of and exhausts the whole of the legendary material, thereby attaining a higher degree of unity than the *Iliad*. With slight verbal modification the remark may be made to apply to the *Mānasa* as well. The closeness with which both the poems link a crime and its punishment is characteristic of an ideal world, such as the spirit of a nation yet in its youth dreams of and desires. On the contrary the heroes of the Homeric poem, especially of the *Iliad* with their naive selfishness are nearer the level of ordinary humanity. The *Mānasa*, however, is superior to the *Nibelungenlied* as a work of art, for reasons that are, to the careful reader, obvious. The *Nibelungenlied* is admittedly a work of various hands, some of whom have arbitrarily followed their own devices while others have scrupulously adhered to the original designs of their predecessors. While, therefore, the best parts — if we refrain from considering the difference of style — may fairly compare with the noblest flowers of Tulasī's poetry, we can hardly venture to mention the name of Tulasī — or Homer — in connection with the inferior ones. Of the *Mānasa* it can be said that there is hardly any passage in it which the reader finds dull or grotesque, whereas side by side with the most beautiful scenes in the *Nibelungenlied*, we also come across many dull and sometimes even grotesque passages through which we painfully make our way.

Now the question is: Who are the poets who belong, not merely to their own race and language but to the world? T. S. Eliot gives the following answer:

> "...the true sage is rarer than the true poet; and when the two gifts, that of wisdom and that of poetic speech, are found in the same man, you have the great poet. It is poets of this kind who belong, not merely to their own people but to the world..."[1]

And Tulasī was admittedly a great poet, a world poet, who not only had the gift of wisdom but also possessed the gift of speech. He derives his status — as did Shakespeare and Goethe — not from one masterpiece, but from the total work of his lifetime. If they created two great mythical figures in Hamlet and Faust, Tulasī created the third, Rāma. It was this prerogative, like Shakespeare's and Goethe's, to have the universal, which, as Coleridge said, "is potentially in each particular, opened out to him, the *homo generalis*, not as an abstraction from observation of a variety of men, but as the substance capable of endless modifications, of which his own personal existence was but one, and to use this one as the eye that beheld the other, and as the tongue that could convey the discovery."[2] Like them, again, he had undisputed claims to greatness for the elements of *permanence* and *universality* found in his work. As regards permanence, there is no denying the fact that Tulasī's work has continued — and must continue — "to give delight and benefit to successive generations." His influence is not confined to an age only; it has continued to matter to the poets and people of every age who no doubt understand him differently and are compelled to evaluate his work afresh. And he has been — and is — important almost universally, that is, to his own race and language as to others. It is not only in the work of Dante, Shakespeare or Goethe that we find the common characteristics of *Abundance*, *Amplitude* and *Unity*. Tulasī Dāsa, too, wrote a good deal, and nothing that he has written is negligible. Like

1. "Goethe as the Sage" in *On Poetry and Poets* (London : Faber and Faber Limited, 1957), p. 207.

2. Lectures on Jonson, Beaumont, etc., 1818.

Shakespeare and Goethe, he had a very wide range of interests[1] — amplitude — as well as sympathy and understanding, and like them, what he gives us is Life itself. This is mainly due to the fundamental unity of his interests, to the fact that he is able to see the world from a particular point of view of a particular age and a particular man in that age.

I owe thanks to Messrs. Motilal Banarsidass, at whose request this revised edition of F. S. Growse's excellent translation of the *Rāmacaritamānasa* has been prepared. They encouraged me from time to time to overcome the special difficulty involved in this work that took me out of my accustomed field. Whether the offer was wisely made, and accepted, I shall not presume to say. But the years devoted to this undertaking have given me happiness in constant exertion. I have further to apologize for not revising the punctuation in Growse's text. In fact, I have not in any way undone the historical importance of this first — and in more than one sense the best — English translation of the *Mānasa*. More drastic revision of the text was neither possible to make nor desirable.

Since the reader is also aware of the immense popularity and appeal of this translation, I need not point to those passages in the present work where Growse is characteristically and eminently more acceptable than any other translator. He had a charming poetic gift, which, we must confess when all is said, he indulges now and then. The heroic spiritual subject suits his talent. His choice of words is pleasant, his prose flowing, easy to grasp, musical, with a well-marked rhythm. It is only when the text should sometimes be more correctly interpreted that he is sometimes wide of the mark. But he had undertaken to translate a work whose text had not till then been correctly determined,

1. Cf. "For the fulfilment of desires, Canto V (The Sundara Kāṇḍa) is recited in the form of a hymn... (while certain other lines) are considered to be the equivalent of the *Gāyatrī mantra*. From the point of view of righteous living, this book is used as a moral code or *Purāṇa*. It is a musical poem, because people sing it. It is also a drama, because Gōswāmī Tulasī Dāsajī started his *Rāma Līlā* on the basis of this book, which even now is performed in the same manner everywhere. Therefore the *Rāmacaritamānasa* is an epic poem, song, hymn, *mantra* and *drama*. It is to be heard, seen and read. It represents all acknowledged forms of poetry at one and the same time. No other poem in the world is full of such excellence." Quoted by C. K. Handoo, *op. cit.*, p. 128.

nor did he have anything of authentic exegetical comments to rely upon. Some of the passages therefore have been too freely translated, some incorrectly, and could perhaps hardly avoid being so; to pioneer a work is at best a severe handicap. Still this is not assuredly a dead, wooden, merely verbal translation of the *Mānasa*. The symbolism and sense of the poet's imaginings are vividly enough realized by Growse and, if we are properly attuned to the manner, by us as well. There is a graphic power in many of Growse's lines and genuine art, for example, in the translation of Tulasi's Oriental imagery into their vivid English equivalent.

Department of English *Ram Chandra Prasad*
Bhagalpur University
21.2.1978

GROWSE'S INTRODUCTION

The Sanskrit *Rāmāyaṇa* of Vālmīki has been published more than once, with all the advantages of European editorial skill and the most luxurious typography. It has also been translated both in verse and prose, and, in part at least, into Latin, as well as into Italian, French and English. The more popular Hindi presentment of the same great national Epic can only be read in lithograph or bazār print,[1] and—with the exception of a single Book—has never till now been translated in any form into any language whatever. Yet it is no unworthy rival of its more fortunate predecessor. There can, of course, be no comparison between the polished phraseology of classical Sanskrit and the rough colloquial idiom of Tulasī Dāsa's vernacular; while the antiquity of Vālmīki's poem further invests it with an adventitious interest for the student of Indian history. But, on the other hand, the Hindi poem is the best and most trustworthy guide to the popular living faith of the Hindu race at the present day—a matter of not less practical interest than the creed of their remote ancestors—and its language, which in the course of three centuries has contracted a tinge of archaism, is a study of much importance to the philologist, as helping to bridge the chasm between the modern tongue and the mediaeval. It is also less wordy and diffuse than the Sanskrit original and, probably in consequence of its modern date, is less disfigured by wearisome interpolations and repetitions; while, if it never soars so high as Vālmīki in some of his best passages, it maintains a more equable level of poetic diction, and seldom sinks with him into such dreary depths of unmitigated prose. It must also be noted that it is in no sense a translation of the earlier work : the general

1. A handsome edition of the text was issued from the press of the Baptist Mission in Calcutta many years ago; but it has long been out of print, and the only copy I have ever seen of it was the one in use at the College of Fort William in 1861. I had thus entirely forgotten the fact till reminded of it by Mr. Bate, a gentleman who has ably maintained the scholarly reputation of the Mission by his very useful Hindi Dictionary.

plan and the management of the incidents are necessarily much the same, but there is a difference in the touch in every detail; and the two poems vary as widely as any two dramas on the same mythological subject by two different Greek tragedians. Even the coincidence of name is an accident; for Tulasī Dāsa himself called his poem *The Rāma-carita-mānasa*, and the shorter title, corresponding in character to the *Iliad* or *Aneid*, has only been substituted by his admirers as a handier designation for a popular favourite.

However, the opinion that the more modern poem is a close adaptation, or *rifaccimento*, of the Sanskrit original is very widely entertained, not only by European scholars but also by Hindus themselves. For, among the latter, an orthodox pandit is essentially *homo unius libri*, to whom the idea of comparative criticism is altogether strange and unintelligible. Whatever is written in the one book, to which he pins his faith, is for him the absolute truth, which he positively declines to weaken or obscure by a reference to any other authority. If he can understand Vālmīki's Sanskrit, he despises Tulasī Dāsa as a vulgarian and would not condescend to read a line of him; if he knows only Hindi, he accepts the modern poem with as implicit faith as if it were an immemorial śāstra, and accounts a quotation from his *Rāmāyaṇa* as an unanswerable argument on any disputed topic. Thus, in all probability, the only educated Hindus who have much acquaintance with both poems are the professors and students of Government colleges, whose views have been broadened by European influence. It may, therefore, be of interest to show a little more at length how great is the divergence between the two poems.

In both, the first Book brings the narrative precisely to the same point, *viz.*, the marriage of Rāma and Sītā. With Tulasī Dāsa this is much the longest book of the seven, and forms all but a third of the complete work; in the Sanskrit, on the contrary, it is the shortest but one, even after including the first four cantos, which are obviously a late addition. They give a table of contents and explain how Vālmīki learnt the story from Nārada and taught it to Kuśa and Lava; thus corresponding in no respect with Tulasī Dāsa's introduction. The actual poem commences at once, without any prelude, with a description of

Ayodhyā and its King Daśaratha and his ministers, and of his longing for an heir; and tells how Ṛṣyaśṛṅga, Vibhāndaka's son (whose previous adventures are recorded at length) was invited from the palace of his father-in-law, Lomapāda, the king of Campā, to direct the ceremonies of a great sacrifice, which the childless Daśaratha resolved to celebrate, in the hope of obtaining his desire. The gods, being at that time sorely distressed by Rāvana's persecution, had fled to Visnu for succour; and he, in answer to their prayer, became incarnate in the four sons that were born to the king, while inferior divinities took birth as bears and monkeys. The four princes are named by Vasistha. They grow up, and the king is thinking where to find suitable brides for them, when Viśvāmitra comes, and, after a long colloquy, takes away with him Rāma and Lakṣmaṇa to protect him at the time of sacrifice from the demons that persistently assail him. On the way they pass by the Aṅga hermitage, where the god of love had been reduced to ashes by Siva—a legend to which very brief allusion is made,—then through the forest of Tārakā, whom Rāma meets in battle and slays, but not till her genealogy has been fully recorded. He is then invested by the saint with certain heavenly weapons and magical powers, and, arriving at Viśvāmitra's hermitage, he slays the demons Mārīca and Subāhu. Being told of Janaka's bow-sacrifice he resolves to attend it; and as he crosses the Śoṇa and the Gaṅgā on his way thither, Viśvāmitra entertains him with a prolix account of his own descent from King Kuśa, of the birth of Gaṅgā, the legend of the sons of Sagara and his sacrifice, and how his descendant Bhagīratha brought down the Gaṅgā from heaven and concludes with the genealogy of the kings of Viśālā. As they draw near to Mithilā, Rāma delivers Gautama's wife Ahalyā, whose legend is given with all its circumstances. He is welcomed by Janakā and by Ahalyā's son, Śatānanda, and the latter makes a long speech of eight hundred lines, in which he gives a complete history of the contention between Viśvāmitra and Vasistha, with an account of Triśaṅku and Śunaḥśepha and Ambarīṣa and of Viśvāmitra's final promotion to Brāhmanical rank. Janaka shows Rāma the bow in its case, and he then and there takes it up and snaps it in pieces. The royal suitors had all tried in vain, and after fruitlessly besieging the city, with intent to carry off Sītā by force, had returned discomforted to their own realms. Envoys are despatched to Ayodhyā for King Daśaratha; Kuśa-dhvaja, Janaka's brother, is also summoned from Sāṅkāsya; and then in full conclave Vasiṣṭha proclaims Rāma's pedigree, after which Janaka recites his own. The fourfold nuptials then take place, a hundred thousand cows being given to the Brāhmaṇas in the name of each of the brides, and many precious gifts being bestowed in dowry. Daśaratha then takes his way home with his sons and daughters, but is met by Paraśurāma with Viṣṇu's bow, which Rāma strings at once, and the son of Bhṛgu acknowledges his supremacy. They then reach Ayodhyā, whence Bharata soon departs with his uncle, Yudhājit, on a visit to his mother's father, Kekaya.

On comparing the above sketch with my translation of the corresponding portion of the Hindi poem, it will be seen that the two agree only in the broadest outline. The episodes so freely introduced by both poets are, for the most part, entirely dissimilar; and even in the main narrative some of the most important incidents, such as the breaking of the bow and the contention with Paraśurāma, are differently placed and assume a very altered complexion. In other passages where the story follows the same lines, whatever Vālmīki has condensed — as, for example, the description of the marriage festivities — Tulasī Dāsa has expanded; and wherever the elder poet has lingered longest, his successor has hastened on most rapidly.

In the seventh, or last, Book, the divergence is, if anything, still more marked. It consists with Vālmīki of 124 cantos, the first 49 of which are occupied by a dialogue between Rāma and the Ṛṣi Agastya, who relates the story of Rāvaṇa's birth and his conquest of the world. In the 50th canto Rāma dismisses his monkey followers to their homes : and in it only in this one passage and in occasional reference to the glory and happiness of Rāma's reign that there is any coincidence with the Hindi 'Sequel'. The remainder of the Sanskrit poem relates the exile of Sītā and the Aśvamedha sacrifice; after which Rāma and his brothers ascend to heaven. All these topics are totally omitted by Tulasī Dāsa, who substitutes for them the story of Kākabhuśuṇḍi and a series of laboured disquisitions on the true nature of Faith.

The earliest notice of our author, as, indeed, of all the other celebrated Vaiṣṇava writers who flourished about the same period, *viz.*, the 16th and 17th centuries A.D., is to be found in the *Bhakta-Mālā*, or 'Legends of the Saints,' one of the most difficult works in the Hindi language. Its composition is invariably ascribed to Nābhā Ji, himself one of the leaders of the reform which had its centre at Bṛndāban; but the poem, as we now have it, was avowedly edited, if not entirely written, by one of his disciples named Nārāyaṇa Dāsa who lived during the reign of Shāhjahān. A single stanza is all that is ordinarily devoted to each personage, who is panegyrized with reference to his most salient characteristics in a style that might be described as of unparalleled obscurity, were it not that each such separate portion of the text is followed by a *ṭīkā*, or gloss, written by one Priyā Dās in the *Sambat* year 1769 (1713 A.D.) in which confusion is still worse confounded by a series of the most disjointed and inexplicit allusions to different legendary events in the saint's life. The poem has never been printed, and though it is of the very highest repute among modern Vaiṣṇavas, and is, therefore, not rare in MS. either at Mathurā or Bṛndāban, it is utterly unintelligible to ordinary native readers. The text of the passage referring to Tulasī Dāsa is, therefore, here given, and is followed by a literal English translation :

॥ मूल ॥

कलि कुटिल जीव निस्तार हेत बाल्मीक तुलसी भयो ॥
त्रेता काव्य निबंध करिव सत कोटि रामायण ॥
इक अक्षर उद्धरै ब्रह्महत्यादि करि जिन होत परायन ॥
अब भक्तनि सुख दैन बहुरि बपु धरि लीला बिस्तारी ॥
राम चरन रसमत्त रटत अह. निस ब्रतधारी ॥
संसार अपार के पार को सुगम रूप नौका लियो ॥
कलि कुटिल जीव निस्तार हेत बाल्मीक तुलसी भयो ॥

Translation of the text of Nābhā Jī.

For the redemption of mankind in this perverse Kali Yuga, Vālmīki has been born again as Tulasī. The verses of the *Rāmāyaṇa* composed in the Tretā Yuga are a hundred crores in number; but a single letter has redeeming power, and would work the salvation of one who had even committed the murder of a Brāhmaṇa. Now again, as a blessing to the faithful, has he taken birth and published the sportive actions of the god. Intoxicated with his passion for Rāma's feet, he perseveres day and night in the accomplishment of his vow, and has supplied, as it were, a boat for the easy passage of the boundless ocean of existence. For the redemption of man in this perverse Kali Yuga, Vālmīki has been born again as Tulasī.

॥ टीका ॥

तिया सो सनेह बिन पूछैं पिता गेह गई
भूली सुधि देह भजे वाही ठौर आए हैं ॥
बधू अति लाज भई रिसि सों निकसि गई
प्रीति राम नई तन हाड़ चाम छाए हैं ॥
सुनी जब बात मानो होय गयो प्रात वह
पाछे पछितात तजी कासीपुरी धाए हैं ॥
कियो तहाँ बास प्रभू सेवा लै प्रकास
कीनों दृढ़ भाव नैंन रूप के तिसाए हैं ॥
सौंच जल सेस पाय भूतहू बिसेस कोऊ
बोल्यो सुख मानि हनुमान जू बताए हैं ॥
रामायन कथा सो रसायन है काननि कों
आवत प्रथम पाछैं जात घृना छाए हैं ॥
जाय पहिचान संग चले उर आनि आए
बन मधि जानि धाय पाय लपटाए हैं ॥
करैं सीतकार कहि सकोगे न टारि मैं तो
जाने रससार रूप धर्‌यो जैसे गाये हैं ॥
मांगि लीजै बर कहि दीजे राम भूप रूप
अतिही अनूप नित्त नैंन अभिलाखिये ॥
कियो लै संकेत वाही दिन ही सों लाग्यो हेत
आई सोई समै चेंत कब छबि चाखिये ॥
आये रघुनाथ साथ लछिमन चढ़े घोरे
पट रंग बारे हरे कैसे मन राखिये ॥
पाछैं हनुमान आय बोले देखे प्रान प्यारे
नैकु न निहारे मैं तो भले फेरि भाखिये ॥
हत्या करि बिप्र एक तीरथ करत आयो
कहै मूख राम भिक्षा डारिये हत्यारे को ॥
सुनि अभिराम नाम धाम में बुलाय लियो
दियो लै प्रसाद कियो सुद्ध गायो प्यारे कों ॥

भई द्विजसभा कहि बोलि कै पठाए ग्राप
कैसें गये पाप संग लैके जेये न्यारे कों ॥
पोथी तुम बांचो हिये सार नहीं सांचो ग्रजू
तातें मत काचो दूर करै न ग्रंध्यारे कों ॥
देखि पोथी बांच नाम महिमाहू कही सांच
ग्रैपै हत्याकरै कैसे तरे कहि दीजिये ॥
ग्रावै जौ प्रतीत कहो योही याके हाथ जेवें
सिवजू को बैल तब पंगति में लीजिये ॥
थार में प्रसाद दियो चले जहां पन कियो
बोले ग्राप नाम के प्रताप मति भीजिये ॥
जैसी तुम जानों तैसी कैसेंकै बखानों ग्रहो
सुनिकै प्रसन्न पायो जै जै धुनि रीजिये ॥
ग्राये निस चोर चोरी करन हरन धन
देखे श्यामघन हांथ चाप सर लिये हैं ॥
जब जब ग्रावै बान सांधि डरपावै वे तो
ग्रति मंडरावै ग्रैपें बली दूरें किये हैं ॥
भोर ग्राय पूछैं ग्रजू सांवरो किसोर कोन
सुनि करि मौन रहै ग्रांसू डारि दिये हैं ॥
दई सबै लुटाय जानी चौकी रामराय दई
लई उन्हें दीछा सीछा सुद्ध भये हिये हैं ॥
कियो तन बिप्र त्याग लागि चली संग तिया
दूरही तें देखि किया चरन प्रनाम है ॥
बोले यों सुहागवती मारचो पति होउ सती
ग्रब तो निकल गई ज्याऊं सेवो राम है ॥
बोलि कै कुटुंब कही जो पै भक्ति करो सही
गही तब बात जीव दियो ग्रभिराम है ॥
भये सब साधु ब्याधि मेटी लै बिमुख ताकी
जाको बास रहै तो न सूझे स्याम धाम है ॥
दिल्लीपति पातसाह ग्रहदी पठायो लैन
ताकों सो सुनायो सू वे बिप्र ज्यायो जानिये ॥
देखिवे की चाहै नीकें सुख सों निबाहैं ग्राप
कहि बहु बिनय गहि चले मन ग्रानिये ॥
पहुंचे नृपति पास ग्रादर प्रकास कियो
उच्च ग्रासन लै बोल्यो मृदू बानियें ॥

दीजै करामाति जग ख्याति सब मात किये
कही झूठ बात एक राम पहिचानिये ॥
देखें राम कैसो कहि कैदि किये किये हियें
हूजिये कृपाल हनूमान जू दयाल हो ॥
ताही समय फैलि गये कोटि कोटि कपि नये
लोचें तन खेंचें चीर भयो यों बिहाल हो ॥
फोरें कोट मारें चोट किये डारें लोट पोट
लीजे कोन ओट जानि मानों प्रलै काल हो ॥
भई तब आंखें दुखसागर को चाखें अब
वेई हमें राखें भाखें वारों धन माल हो ॥
आय पाय लिये तुम दिये हम प्रान पावें
आप समझावें करामात नेकु लीजिये ॥
लाज दबि गयो नृप तब राखि लीयो कह्यो
भयो घर रामजू कौ बेगि छोड़ दीजिये ॥
सुनि तजि दियो और करयो लैके कोट नयो
अबहू न रहै कोऊ वामें तन छीजिये ॥
कासी आय वृन्दावन आय मिले नाभाजू सों
सुन्यौ हो कवित्त निज रीझि मति भोजिये ॥
मदन गोपालजू कों दरसन करि कहि
सही राम इष्ट मेरे दृष्टि भाव पागी है ॥
वैसोई सरूप कियो लै दियो दिखाय रूप
मन अनरूप छबि देखि नीगी लागी है ॥
काहू कही कृष्ण अवतारोजू प्रसंस महा
राम अंस सुनि बोले मति अनुरागी है ॥
दसरथ सुत जानो सुन्दर अनूप मानों
ईसता बताई रति बीस गुनी जागी है ॥

Translation of the gloss (or supplement) by Priyā Dāsa.

He had great love for his wife : without asking his leave she went home to her father's; he forgot all about himself and hastened there too. She was greatly ashamed, and went away in anger, saying : "Have you no love for Rāma ? My body is but a framework of skin and bone." When he heard these words, it was, as it were, the daybreak; he felt compunction and left her and sped to the city of Kāsi. There he made his abode, worshipping the lord publicly, making a rigid vow, and thirsting exceedingly for a vision.

A certain ghost, who had secured the remainder of the water he had used in washing,[1] was grateful and told him of Hanumān. "A recitation of the *Rāmāyaṇa* has a special charm for his ears; he will be disguised in mean attire, but is always the first to come and the last to leave." Thus recognizing him as he left, he went with him in full confidence, and in the wood, knowing him to be in truth the god, ran and embraced his feet, crying with a shout of joy: "You shall not escape me." Perceiving his intense devotion, he assumed the form in which he is famous, and said : "Ask of me what you will." "I am ever craving to behold with my very eyes the incomparable beauty of King Rāma." He told him the place for meeting. From that day forth he was longing till the time came, thinking: "When shall I behold his beauty ?" Raghunātha came, and with him Lakṣmaṇa, both mounted on horseback, in green raiment (like huntsmen). Why should he notice them ? Afterwards came Hanumān and said : "Have you seen your dear lord ?" "I did not give them even a glance ; turn now and speak to them again."

A Brāhmaṇa, who had committed a murder, came on a pilgrimage, crying: "For the love of Rāma, give an alms even to me, a murderer." On hearing the delightful name, he called him into his own house, and gave him of the offerings to the god, and purified him and sang the praises of his Beloved. The Brāhmaṇas sat in conclave and summoned him before them, saying : "How has his guilt been remitted that you could thus take and eat with him apart ?" "Read your books, their real meaning has not penetrated your heart; therefore your faith is dull and your blindness has not been removed." "We have read and examined our books; the virtue of the name is truly as you have said; but can a murderer be absolved ? Please explain that." "Tell me how I may convince you." They said : "If Śiva's bull will eat from his hand, then will we receive him into our company." He gave him of the temple offerings in a dish, and they returned to the place where he had made the vow. There he cried : "Saturate their souls with the glory of thy name; thou knowest how the matter stands, what can I say ?" On hearing those words he graciously accepted the offering; there was a joyous shout of Victory ! Victory !

Some thieves came by night to thieve and plunder his goods, but beheld a cloud-dark form with bow and arrows in his hand. Whenever he approached with ready shaft, they were afraid; and though they went round and round, they could not get rid of this watchman. At daybreak they came and asked him : "Sir, who is this dark-complexioned lad of yours ?" On hearing this question, he remained silent and wept; then gave away all that he had, knowing that Rāma himself had been the watchman. They were initiated and received instruction, and became pure of heart.

---

1. A ghost is supposed to suffer from perpetual thirst and to be glad to secure even a drop of water, however impure the purpose for which it has been used.

A Brâhmaṇa had died; his wife was following him to the pyre. She saw him at a distance and made him obeisance. He addressed her as a happy wife. She replied : "My husband is dead, and I am about to perish with him." "The word has passed my lips; I will restore him to life; worship thou Râma." Then he called her kinsfolk to his word, and he restored the man to the delights of life. They all became saints when he had taken away their sinful frowardness : none can see heaven in whom passion still lives.

The emperor of Delhi sent an officer to fetch him, explaining, "It is he, you must know, who brought the Brâhmaṇa to life again." "He is anxious to see you," they said, "so come; all will be well." They spoke so courteously that he agreed and went. They arrived before the king, who received him with honour, gave him an exalted seat, and said in gracious tones :"Let me see a miracle; it is noised throughout the world that you are master of everything." He said : "It is false; know that Râma is all in all." "How is Râma to be seen ?" he said, and threw him into prison. He prayed within himself : "O gracious Hanumân, have pity upon me." That very moment thousands upon thousands of sturdy monkeys spread all over the place, clawing bodies, and tearing clothes, and great was the alarm. They broke open the fort, wounding the men, destroying everything; where could one fly for safety ? It seemed as though the end of the world had come. Then his eyes were opened by this taste of a sea of calamities, and he cried: "Now I wager all my treasure it is he only who can save me." He came and clasped his feet : "If you give me life, I live ; pray speak to them." "Better watch the miracle a little." The king was overwhelmed with confusion. Then he stopped it all and said : "Quickly abandon this spot, for it is the abode of Râma." At the word he quitted the place and went and built a new fort, and to this day anyone who abides there falls ill and dies.

After returning to Kâsi he came to Bṛndâban and met Nâbhâ Jī and heard his poetry, and his whole soul was filled with delight. On visiting the shrine of Madan Gopal he said : "Of a truth Râma is my special patron; I would fain see him." Then appeared the god to him in that very form; and he was glad on beholding his incomparable beauty. It was said to him : "The Kṛṣṇa Avatâr is of greatest renown; Râma was only a partial incarnation." On hearing this he said : "My soul was full of love for him when I took him only for the son of Daśaratha and admired his incomparable beauty; now that you tell me of his divinity, my love is increased twentyfold."

Professor Wilson, in his most valuable and interesting *Essay on the Religious Sects of the Hindus*, gives the following notice of Tulasī Dāsa, and adds that he had derived it from the *Bhakta-Mālā* : "Having been incited to the peculiar adoration of Rāma by the remonstrances of his wife, to whom he was passionately attached, he adopted a vagrant life, visited Banaras, and afterwards went to Chitrakūṭa, where he had a personal interview with

Hanumān, from whom he received his poetical inspiration and the power of working miracles. His fame reached Delhi, where Shāhjahān was emperor. The monarch sent for him to produce the person of Rāmā, which Tulasī Dāsa refusing to do, the king threw him into confinement. The people of the vicinity, however, speedily petitioned for his liberation as they were alarmed for their own security : myriads of monkeys having collected about the prison and begun to demolish it and the adjacent buildings. Shāhjahān set the poet at liberty and desired him to solicit some favour as a reparation for the indignity he had suffered. Tulasī Dāsa accordingly requested him to quit ancient Delhi, which was the abode of Rāma; and in compliance with this request the emperor left it and founded the new city, thence named Shāhjahānabād. After this Tulasī Dāsa went to Bṛndāban, where he had an interview with Nābhā Jī; he settled there and strenuously advocated the worship of Sītā Rāma, in preference to that of Rādhā Krsna."

On comparing this sketch with the literal translation of the text from which it was derived, it will be seen that it is not very closely in accord with it. It omits many particulars and adds others, and was probably taken not from the genuine Hindī poem itself, but from some prose adaptation,[1] of which, in consequence of the difficulty of the original, there are very many in existence.

It is a curious illustration of the indifference to historical truth and the love for the marvellous, by which the Hindu mind

1. I was afterwards able to verify this conjecture, as Mr. Leonard, the Assistant Secretary of the Calcutta Asiatic Society, was kind enough to lend me his copy of Price's *Hindi and Hindustāni Selections*, a work to which Professor Wilson refers more than once in the course of his essay. It was published in Calcutta in 1827, and has long been out of print. I find that as many as 50 pages of it are occupied with extracts from the *Bhakta-Mālā*; but with the exception of some 18 stanzas from the *mūl* of Nābhā ji, all the rest is in simple narrative prose; and the compiler in his introduction specially mentions that the work itself was rarely to be met with in the Lower Provinces, and that his extracts were taken from a copy in Mr. Wilson's library. Sanskrit and Hindi being two languages, as distinct as Latin and Italian, the above remarks were never intended (as a reviewer wrongly supposed) to detract, in any way from the peculiar merits of one of the greatest Sanskrit scholars that England has ever produced and to whose works no one is more indebted than myself.

has always been characterized, that although the *ṭīkā* even of the *Bhakta-Mālā* was written less than a century after the poet's death, it still gives so little trustworthy information about the real incidents of his life and supplies so much that is clearly fictitious. That it was his wife who first persuaded him to exchange an earthly for a divine love and to devote himself to the service of Rāma may well be accepted as a fact. As to the other legends — of the ghost who introduced him to Hanumān, through whom he obtained a vision of Rāma and Lakṣmaṇa ; of the murderer whom he recognized as cleansed of his crime by the repetition of the holy name; of the widow on her way to the funeral pile, whose husband he restored to life; of the emperor's requiring him to perform some miracle and, on his refusal to produce the god to whom he ascribed all his power, throwing him into prison, from which he was delivered by Hanumān's monkey host; of the emperor's thereupon abandoning a spot which Rāma had made so peculiarly his own; of the thieves who were prevented from breaking into the poet's house by Rāma himself acting as watchman; of his visit to Bṛndāban and his interview with Nābhā Jī; and finally of his persistence in preferring the worship of Rāma to that of Kṛṣṇa, though the latter assured him in person that there was no difference between the two — all these legends, as given in the *Bhakta-Mālā*, whatever their foundation, are still popularly accepted as verities and are indissolubly connected with the poet's name. A few further facts of more prosaic character may be gathered from his own works and from tradition; thus we learn from the prologue to the *Rāmāyaṇa* that he commenced its composition at Ayodhyā in the *Sambat* year 1631, corresponding to 1575 A.D., and that he had studied for some length of time at Soron. He was by descent a Brāhmaṇa of the Kanaujiya clan, and in the *Bhakta-Sindhu* — a modern poem of no great authority, the writer when at a loss for facts being, as it seems, in the habit of supplying them out of his own imagination — it is stated that his father's name was Ātmā Rāma and that he was born at Hastināpura. Others make Hājipur, near Chitrakūṭa, the place of his birth. The greater part of his life was certainly spent at Banaras, though he also passed some years in visits to Soron, Ayodhyā, Chitrakūṭa, Allahabad, and Bṛndāban. He died in the *Sambat* year 1680 (1624 A.D.).

A complete copy of the *Rāmāyaṇa* in his own handwriting was once in existence at Rājapur, but it was stolen about the year 1800 by a devotee, who on being pursued threw it into the river. It was eventually recovered by a net, but not till it had been greatly damaged by the water; Book II, the Ayodhyā, which forms the centre of the volume, being the only part that remained legible. This fragment is still in the temple; but as every pilgrim is expected to make an offering of a cover for it, it is now enveloped in some 50 wraps and is quite lost to sight. The Mahārājā of Banaras is said to have employed a copyist to consult it before publishing his edition, which in that case represents the standard text; and a commentary written by Mahant Rām Charan in *Sambat* 1862, and published by Naval Kishore of Lucknow, professes to have been undertaken after 'handling' the original MS., which possibly was then complete. The 'handling,' however, may have been only from a motive of veneration and not for critical purposes.

In addition to his great work Tulasī Dāsa composed at least six other poems, all of them having the one object of popularizing the cultus of his tutelary divinity. They are the *Rāmagītāvalī* (which is one of the text-books in the Government examination for a Degree of Honour), the *Dohāvali*, the *Kabit-sambandha*, the *Vinaya Patrikā*, the *Satsai* and the *Rāmāgyā*. All of these have been published, either at Lucknow or Banaras, within the last few years, and all now for the first time, excepting the *Vinaya Patrikā*, which was printed in good type by Sri Lallū Jī for the use of the college of Fort William as far back as the year 1826; but copies of this first edition are now very scarce. The list is not unfrequently extended by the addition of the following minor works, as to the genuineness of which there is considerable doubt, *viz.* the *Rāma-Śalākā*, the *Hanumān Bāhuka*, the *Jānakī Maṅgal*, *the Pārvatī Mangal*, the *Karkā Chhand*, the *Rora Chhand* and the *Jhulnā Chhand*. An autograph MS. of the *Rāmāgyā* was preserved in the temple of Sītā Rāma at Banaras, which Tulasī Dāsa had himself founded, till the Mutiny, but was then lost.[1]

1. For the information as to this and the Rajapur MS. I am indebted to Pandit Bhān Pratāp Tiwārī, of Chanār, who also tells me that he has in his possession a manuscript of the poem which professes to be copied from an original dated *Sambat* 1700; that is, only 20 years after the author's death. This he would gladly lend for collation, if a critical edition of the text—which is much required — should ever be undertaken. At present the best edition is Rām Jasan's, Banaras, 1883.

His theological and metaphysical views are pantheistic in character, being based for the most part on the teaching of the later Vedantists as formulated in the *Vedānta-Sāra* and more elaborately expounded in the *Bhagavad Gītā*, which is the most popular of all Sanskrit didactic poems. The whole visible world, as they maintain, is an unreal phantasm, induced by ignorance or illusion, and it is only by a concession to conventional speech that it can be said to exist at all. The sole representative of true existence is the supreme spirit, Brahman, conceived as absolute and unchangeable unity; invisible, eternal and all-pervading, but having no relation to the world — since that would involve a notion of dualism — and for the same reason void of cognition, will, activity and all other qualities; a potentiality, in the ordinary use of language, rather than an actual entity. All phenomena, whether material or spiritual, including even the gods of Vedic mythology, are simply fictions of the mind. But the worship of the inferior divinities and compliance with the external ritual of religion, are considered to purify and prepare the intellect for the reception of higher truths. They are therefore salutary and even necessary practices during the early days of the soul's progress towards perfection. If a man is overtaken by death before he has advanced beyond this preliminary stage, he is born again either into this or into a higher world in some different form, the dignity of which is determined by the aggregate merit or demerit of all his actions in all his previous births.[1] The highest reward for devotion to any special god is the exaltation of the soul to his particular sphere in heaven. But this blessedness is not of permanent duration; on the expiry of a proportionate period the burden of mundane existence has again to be undergone. It is only on the attainment of perfect knowledge that final emancipation is complete and the individual soul is absorbed for ever into Impersonal :

> "A spriritual star — wrought in a rose
> Of light in Paradise, whose only self
> Is consciousness of glory wide diffused."

1. The absence of all recollection of acts done in former states of existence is not an objection to the theory of transmigration; for the continuity is not one of consciousness, but of that tendency or disposition which is the separate nature of each individual.

Except to a theosophist, the promise of such an ultimate destiny is not a very attractive one, nor is it conducive to popular morality. For good deeds and evil deeds and the god that recompenses them, all alike belong to the unreal, to the fictitious duality, the world of semblances; while the so-called Supreme Being is no proper object of worship, being a mere cold abstraction, unconscious of his own existence or of ours, and devoid of all attributes and qualities. To correct this practical defect and supply some intelligible motive form withstanding temptation and leading a pure and holy life, the supplementary doctrine of Bhakti, or Faith, was developed. Some one of the recognized incarnations of the Hindu Pantheon was no longer regarded as a partial emanation of the divinity, but was exalted into the complete embodiment of it. A loving devotion to his personality was then enjoined as a simple and certain method of attaining to endless felicity; not the transitory sensual delights of Indra's paradise, nor the mere unconsciousness of utter extinction, but the conscious enjoyment of individual immortality in the immediate presence of the Beatific Vision.

The late introduction of this crowning dogma of Faith in an incarnate Redeemer and its marked similarity to Christian ideas have induced several scholars to surmise that the Brāhmaṇas borrowed it from the early Christian communities in Southern India. The notion is favoured — if not, indeed, originated — by the fact that in the *Bhagavad Gītā* it is Kṛṣṇa who figures as the embodiment of the Supreme Being, and both in the name and in the legends of Kṛṣṇa there is a superficial resemblance to the name of Christ and to some of the incidents recorded of Him in the Gospels. As I have shown more fully elsewhere, there is no historical basis for the supposed connection, while the similarity of name is demonstrably accidental. The doctrine appears to have grown up as a natural sequel to the purely indigenous school of thought in which we find it established, and an exact parallel can be traced in the history of Buddhism, where the nihilism of Nirvāṇa was practically abrogated by the gradual deification of its teacher.[1] In selecting Rāma as his ideal of the

1. In a Chinese inscription, of the year 1021 A.D., that has been discovered at Bodh Gaya, he is thus addressed : "O great master, merciful to the people, sympathizing with all creatures, although thou dost not manifest thyself, still thou art a most efficacious God."

divine in preference to Kṛṣṇa, Tulasī Dāsa has certainly improved upon the teaching of the *Bhāgavata*.

The tendency of modern scientific thought is setting strongly in favour of the Vedantist theory; as declaring the existence from all eternity of a personal God to be simply unknowable, and referring all phenomena to a strange mysterious energy, or will, that pervades all nature, that produces all work done on the face of the earth, and is probably at the roof of life itself; invisible and insensible, and exhibited only in its effects. Such a theory — as we see from our author's own case — is by no means incompatible with a belief in a divine incarnation : the difficulty is to establish by historical proof that such and such a character — Rāma or Kṛṣṇa or whoever it may be — was really born out of the ordinary course of nature, really performed the marvellous acts ascribed to him for the deliverance of the saints, the overthrow of the wicked and the establishment of righteousness, and having accomplished them was again taken up into the heaven from which he came. The whole of Tulasī Dāsa's *Rāmāyaṇa* is a passionate protest against the virtual atheism of philosophical Hindu theology. The problem that confronted him is the very same that now most exercises the thought of the nineteenth century. If the Supreme Being is a personal God, he must be limited by the conditions of personality, and can neither be omniscient nor omnipotent. If, on the other hand, the Deity is an omnipresent, all-pervading impersonality, how can any special relation be developed between such an abstraction and the individual soul ? The difficulty is one that has its root in the nature of things; and no solution of the mystery can be found but in the recognition of faith and reason as two distinct human faculties, with the infinite and the finite as their separate provinces. In the words of Saint Ambrose *non in dialecticâ complacuit Deo salvum facere populum suum.* God would not be adorable if he were not incomprehensible : and a religion that does not transcend man's understanding is not, strictly speaking, a religion at all. A just discrimination of good and evil and a sound code of morality are not beyond the compass of natural intelligence : but the rites and mysteries of religion can only be learnt by a direct revelation from God and through the action of His grace. Their acceptance by faith, even when they seem to conflict with reason, is a part of our earthly probation and a meritorious confession of our dependence on the Supreme. The final purpose of the Incarnation, like the idea of any revelation whatever from God to man, is above comprehension. The fact of the divine message having been sent may be reasonably established by historical evidence, but the tenor of the message transcends argumentative discussion, and demands nothing short of implicit and absolutely unquestioning *ex hypothesi*, submission. For the dogmas of revealed religion must, be incomprehensible mysteries. If they were ascertainable by the ordinary processes of reason it would not be consistent with the economy of the universe to communicate them by the special vehicle of revelation. A professedly revealed religion, which is demonstrable and intelligible throughout, stands self-convicted as a human invention.

The following passage from Book VII of the *Bhagavad Gītā*, as freely rendered by Mr. Edwin Arnold in his *Song Celestial*, is a very explicit summary of the accepted Vedantic doctrine:

"There be those, too, whose knowledge, turned aside
By this desire or that, gives them to serve
Some lower gods with various rites constrained
By that which mouldeth them. Unto all such—
Worship what shrine they will, what shapes in faith—
'Tis I who give them faith. I am content.
The heart thus asking favour from its God,
Darkened but ardent, hath the end it craves,
The lesser blessing; but 'tis I who give.
Yet soon is withered what small fruit they reap:
Those men of little minds, who worship so,
Go where they worship, passing with their Gods:
But mine come unto me. Blind are the eyes
Which deem the Unmanifested manifest,
Not comprehending Me in my true self.
Imperishable, viewless, undeclared,
Hidden behind my magic veil of shows,
I am not seen by all; I am not known —
Unborn and changeless — to the idle world.
But I, Arjuna, know all things which were,
And all which are, and all which are to be,
Albeit not one among them knoweth Me."

The words "Blind are the eyes Which deem the Unmanifested manifest" emphatically condemn the worship of any incarnation, on the ground that it involves an inadequate conception of the Deity. Tulasī Dāsa, on the other hand, insists that they derogate from the divine perfection, who divest it of personality and reduce it to an abstraction. Against such theologians he hotly protests as when he cries (*VII Chand* 5) — "Let them preach in their wisdom who contemplate thee as the Supreme Spirit, the Uncreate, inseparable from the universe, recognizable only by inference and beyond the understanding; but we, O Lord ! will ever hymn the glories of thy incarnation." Nor does he want supporters even in this nineteenth century, who give the same answer to the old question 'Can the attribute of Personality be ascribed to the absolute ?' Thus Lotze, in his *Outlines of the Philosophy of Religion*, argues as follows : "If all the predicates of unconditionateness are to be valid for the highest being then one condition of this validity lies precisely in the addition of a last formal predicate, *viz.*, that of personal existence. All hindrances of perfect personality we can imagine as not existent in the Infinite Spirit. On this account we conclude with the assertion — which is exactly the opposite of the customary one — that Perfect Personality is reconcilable only with the conception of an Infinite Being; for finite beings, only an approximation to this is attainable."

The introductory portion of the first Book of the *Rāmāyaṇa* is curious as containing the author's vindication of his literary style as against his critics, the pedants. They attacked him for lowering the dignity of his subject by clothing it in the vulgar vernacular. However just his defence may be, it has not succeeded in converting the opposite faction : and the professional Sanskrit pandits who are its modern representatives, still affect to despise his work as an unworthy concession to the illiterate masses. With this small and solitary exception the book is in every one's hands, from the court to the cottage, and is read, or heard, and appreciated alike by every class of the Hindu community, whether high or low, rich or poor, young or old. The purity of its moral sentiments and the absolute avoidance of the slightest approach to any pruriency of idea — which the author justly advances among his distinctive merits — render it a singularly unexceptionable text-book for native boys. For several years I persistently urged its adoption upon the Education

Department,[1] and — thanks to Raja Siva Prasad — extracts from it have been introduced into our primary schools; while it has always been prescribed as the principal test in the civil examinations for High Proficiency and a Degree of Honour. It is equally well adapted for these apparently incongruous purposes : for a Hindu child generally grasps at once the familiar idiom, and finds no great difficulty in even the most crabbed passage; while, on the other hand, both the terminology and the syntactic collocation of the words are in the highest degree perplexing to the European student, and severely try his knowledge of the language. As has been said of Spenser in the *Faerie Queene*, Tulasī Dāsa never scruples on his own authority to cut down or alter a word, or to adopt a mere corrupt pronunciation, to suit a place in his metre, or because he wants a rhyme. His treatment of words, on occasions of difficulty to his verse, is arbitrary in the extreme. He gives them any sense and shape that the case may demand. Sometimes he merely alters a letter or two; sometimes he twists off the head or the tail of the unfortunate vocable altogether. Such vagaries, being unconsciously regulated by the genius of the language, are no more puzzling to a Hindu than the colloquialisms of Sam Weller or Mrs. Gamp are to an English reader of Dickens. But they would seem inexplicable mysteries to any Anglo-Indian official, who knew only the language of the Courts and had never studied the vernacular of the people. For such neglect there was formerly much excuse, in the absence both of a dictionary and a grammar; but the latter want was most admirably supplied in 1876 by Mr. Kellogg, of the Allahabad American Presbyterian Mission, in a work that is to a remarkable degree both lucid and exhaustive; while Messrs. Hoernle and Grierson's new *Comparative Dictionary* is not only more scientific ih method and elaborate in execution than any similar work that has ever before been attempted by Indian philologists, but it is further supplemented by a special Index to the *Rāmāyaṇa* which exhibits every single word in the poem, and refers to all

1. A writer in the *Calcutta Review* expressed his astonishment at my proposal. But he falls into the error which has wrecked so many well-intentioned schemes in this country, that of measuring Indian tastes and requirements by a purely English standard. Manuals of history, geography and physical science are all very well in their way, but correct information by itself is really the least part of education.

the passages in which it occurs. As yet only one part of this gigantic work has appeared, and some years must elapse before it is completed. Mr. Bate's dictionary, to which I have already referred, is scarcely intended for very advanced students, but it will be of much use to beginners, since it gives in alphabetical order all the archaic forms of inflection, which at the outset are found so perplexing.

The second Book is more generally read than any other part of the poem, and is the most admired by Hindu critics. The description of King Daśaratha's death and the different leave-takings are quoted as models of the pathetic, and in a public recital there is scarcely one in the audience who will not be moved to tears. The sentiments that the poet depicts, and the figures that he employs to illustrate them, appeal with irresistible force to the Hindu imagination; and, if for no other reason than this, they would be interesting to the English student for the insight they afford into the traditional sympathies and antipathies of the people. The constant repetition of a few stereotyped phrases — such as 'lotus feet,' 'streaming eyes', 'quivering[1] frame' — are irritating to modern European taste, though they find a parallel in the stock epithets of the Homeric poems, and a still more striking one in Klopstock's *Messiah*, where similar expressions are for ever recurring in wearisome reiteration. Everybody wonders and weeps and smiles and embraces everybody else and dissolves in tears, while every hair on their body stands on end; the last two performances being so specially Tulasīan, that it ceases to be an exaggeration to describe the eyes of his *dramatis personae*, in the words of Crashaw, as

> Two walking baths, two weeping motions,
> Portable and compendious oceans.

Again, the curiously artificial similes derived from the — frequently fabulous — habits of different birds and plants, which (like the oft-repeated refrain of a popular song) never fail to elicit the applause of an appreciative audience, only repel a

1. The *pulak*, which I generally translate by 'quivering' or 'throbbing', means strictly the bristling of the hair upon the body, which is a sign of violent mental agitation. The Munshi, with whom I read in Calcutta some twenty years ago, always, I remember, rendered it by 'horripilation', a frightful word, which would destroy all the poetic effect of the most impressive passage, but which he greatly admired on account of its sesquipedalian proportions.

foreigner as frigid and unmeaning conventionalities. Such are the perpetual allusions to the lotus, that expands in the day and closes at evening; to the lily, that blossoms in the night and fades at sunrise; to the rice crop, that luxuriates in the rain, and to the *javāsa* plant, that is killed by it; to the *cakvā*, that mourns its mate all through the hours of darkness; to the *cakor*, that is never happy except when gazing upon the moon; to the *cātak*, that patiently endures all the buffeting of the storm, in the confident expectation that the cloud will at last let fall the one auspicious drop for which it thirsts : to the swan, that knows how to separate milk from the water with which it has been mixed; and to the snake, that carries a precious jewel in its head, of which it is always afraid of being robbed. In Shakespeare's time, who was contemporary with Tulasī Dāsa, many equally strange pieces of natural history were popularly accepted even in Europe, and were similarly worked up into poetical commonplaces. As, for instance, the maternal affection of "the kind life-rendering pelican;" the belief that the chameleon lives upon air; that the adder is deaf; that the swan sings before it dies; that crocodiles weep when they have done wrong; that bear's cubs are born formless and are licked into ursine shape by their mother; that some snakes have stings in their tail; and that the toad carries a jewel in its head which is an antidote to poison.

In spite of all drawbacks, the Hindi *Rāmāyaṇa* has many passages that are instinct with a genuine poetic feeling, which appeals to universal humanity, and which it is hoped will be dimly recognized even through the ineffectual medium of a prose translation. The characters also of the principal actors in the drama are clearly and consistently drawn; and all may admire, though they refuse to worship, the piety and unselfishness of Bharata : the enthusiasm and high courage of Lakṣmaṇa; the affectionate devotion of Sītā, that paragon of all wife-like virtues; and the purity, meekness, generosity and self-sacrifice of Rāma, the model son, husband and brother, 'the guileless king', high, self-contained and passionless' — the Arthur of Indian chivalry.

In the later Books the narrative is generally more rapid than in the earlier part of the poem, and several incidents are so casually mentioned that, without the explanatory references to the Sanskrit *Rāmāyaṇa*, which I have given in the notes, a literal rendering would convey no meaning to the ordinary reader.[1] It is to some extent a literary defect that the role of poet is so often dropped for that of theologian; and the frequent hymns to Rāma, who is apostrophized under every conceivable name that can help to realize to the mind the mystery of incarnate divinity, soon becomes wearisome. But the object that Tulasī Dāsa had in view is his sufficient excuse. By the course that he has adopted, fitting his special doctrines of faith, individual immortality and the like into the familiar framework of ancient legend, instead of inculcating them by a more strictly didactic method, he has succeeded in popularizing his views to a far greater extent than any of the rival Hindu Reformers, who flourished about the same period. It was their object also to simplify the complications and correct the abuses of existing practice, but the only result of their preaching was to establish yet another element of dissension and augment the disorder which they hoped to remove. Tulasī Dāsa alone, though the most famous of them all, has no disciples that are called after his name. There are Vallabhāchāris and Rādhā Vallabhis and Malūk Dāsīs and Prān Nāthis, and so on, in interminable succession, but there are no Tulasī Dāsīs. Virtually, however, the whole of Vaiṣṇava Hinduism has fallen under his sway; for the principles that he expounded have permeated every sect and explicitly or implicitly now form the nucleus of the popular faith as it prevails throughout the whole of the Bengal Presidency from Hardwar to Calcutta.

In the year 1876, when I published the first instalment of my translation, I was still at Mathura, in a congenial atmosphere of Hindu associations. After my transfer to Bulandaśahar in 1877, I laboured under the serious disadvantage of writing in a thoroughly Muhammadanized district, where it was almost as difficult to obtain any assistance on subjects connected with Hindi literature or scholarship as it would have been in England. But by that time the familiarity I had acquired with my author was sufficiently long and intimate to enable me to complete my task unaided.

At the outset I was under the impression that as a translator, there was no one at all in the field before me; but after making

1. Of the two current recensions of the older poem, the one generally followed by Tulasī Dása is the Bengal, which is the text given by Gorresio in his handsome edition.

some little progress in the second book, I discovered that there was already in existence for that particular section of the poem an English version, published in 1871, by Adālat Khān, a Muhammadan Munshi of the College of Fort William in Calcutta. I at once procured a copy of it, and it is only proper to acknowledge that it was of considerable assistance to me. It does not, however, encroach very largely upon the ground that I had intended to occupy. The Munshi appears to have written solely with a view to lighten the labours of his own pupils and of others who, like them, were preparing for a special examination. Despite not a few misapprehensions of the sense, such persons will probably find it quite as useful for their purpose as my translation, if not more so. But in the attempt to secure literal accuracy, and also, no doubt, from the fact that English was not the mother tongue of the translator, the language employed is throughout so curiously unidiomatic that in many places it is absolutely unintelligible without a reference to the original, and this the general reader would not be in a position to make. ...

The uncouthness of the Munshi's style will give some idea of what is certainly the main difficulty that has to be encountered in a prose translation from Hindi verse. No one who has not had practical experience in the matter can fully appreciate the amount of thought that has to be expended on almost every sentence before the peculiarities of Oriental expression can be adapted to the requirements of English idiom. Without the most delicate handling it is impossible to avoid either a sacrifice of accuracy in the letter, or a misrepresentation of the spirit by a baldness of rendering, which suggests only images of the ludicrous and grotesque, while the sentiments of the original in their native dress are felt to be both natural and pathetic.

Postscript.

Under the patronage of Mr. Grierson, an enterprising publisher of Patna (Babu Rama Din Sinh of the Kharg Vilasa Press, Bankipore) has now published a text of the *Rāma-carita-mānasa*, which is an exact reproduction of the original MSS. This must be a work of the highest interest to all Hindi scholars; but it may be surmised that the variations from the received text are of more importance from the philological than from the literary point of view.

BOOK I

CHILDHOOD

CHILDHOOD

Sanskrit Invocation

I REVERENCE Śāradā and Gaṇeśa, inventors of letters and their significance, of poetic sentiments and metres, too, and of all blessings. I reverence Bhavānī and Śaṅkara, the incarnations of faith and trust, without whom not even the adept can see God, enshrined in his heart. I reverence, as the incarnation of Śaṅkara, the all-wise and eternal *guru*, through whom even the crescent moon is everywhere honoured.[1] I reverence the king of bards[2] and the monkey king, of pure intelligence, who ever sport with delight in the holy forest of Rāma and Sītā's infinite perfection. I bow to Sītā, the beloved of Rāma; the queen of birth, of life and death; the destroyer of sorrow; the cause of happiness.

I reverence the Lord Hari, whose name is Rāma, who is supreme over all causes; to whose illusive power are subject the whole universe and every supernatural being from Brahmā downwards; by whose light truth is made manifest, as when what appeared to be a snake turns out a rope; and by whose feet as by a bark those who will may pass safely over the ocean of existence.

In accord with all the Purāṇas, the Vedas and the Āgamas, and with what has been recorded in the *Rāmāyaṇa* (of Vālmīki) and elsewnere, I, Tulasī, to gratify my own heart's desire, have composed these lays of Raghunātha in most choice and elegant modern speech.

1. The crescent moon, being one of Śaṅkara's (*i.e.*, Śiva's) constant symbols, is honoured on his account, though in itself imperfect : while the full moon is honoured for its own sake.

2. The king of bards, Vālmīki, the reputed author of the Sanskrit *Rāmāyaṇa*. The monkey king is of course Hanumān, and the two are brought together more on account of the close similarity of name than for any other reason, *Kavīśvara* and *Kapīśvara* differing only by a single letter.

Soraṭhā 1-5

O Gaṇeśa, of the noble elephant head ; the mention of whose name ensures success, be gracious to me, storehouse of wisdom, abode of all good qualities ! Thou, too, by whose grace the dumb becomes eloquent, and the lame can climb the steepest mountain, be compassionate to me, O thou that consumest as a fire all the impurities of this iron age. Take up thy abode also in my heart, O thou that slumberest on the milky ocean, with body dark as the lotus, and eyes bright as a budding water-lily. O spouse of Umā, fair of hue as the jasmine or the moon; home of compassion, who showest pity to the humble; show me his grace, O destroyer of Kāmadeva. I reverence the lotus feet of my *guru*, that ocean of benevolence, Hari incarnate, whose words are like a flood of sunlight on the deep darkness of ignorance and infatuation.[1]

Caupāi 1

I reverence the pollen-like dust of the lotus feet of my *guru*, bright, fragrant, sweet and delicious; pure powder of the root of ambrosia, potent to disperse all the attendant ills of life; like the holy ashes on the divine body of Śambhu, beautiful, auspicious, ecstatic. Applied to the forehead as a *tilak*, it cleanses from defilement the fair mirror of the human mind and gives it the mastery of all perfections. By recalling the lustre of the nails of the reverend *guru's* feet, a divine splendour illumines the soul, dispersing the darkness of ignorance with its sun-like glory. How blessed he who takes it to his heart ! The mental vision brightens and expands, the night of the world with sin and pain fades away, the actions of Rāma[2], like diamonds and rubies, whether obvious or obscure, all alike become clear, in whichever direction the mine is explored.

1. The persons addressed in this stanza are Gaṇeśa, Sarasvatī, Nārāyaṇa, Śiva, and the poet's own spiritual instructor, or guru.

2. The simple actions are compared to rubies, which may be picked up on the surface of the ground; the mysterious actions to diamonds, which have to be dug out of a mine.

Dohā 1

By applying this magic ointment as it were to the eyes, the aspirant acquires both holiness and wisdom, and is able to understand his sportive career when on earth—on mountain, or in forest—and all the treasures of his grace.

Caupāi 2

The dust of the *guru's* feet is a soft and agreeable collyrium, like ambrosia for the eyes, to remove every defect of vision. With this having brightened the eyes of discernment, I proceed to relate the acts of Rāma, the redeemer of the world. First I reverence the feet of the Brāhmaṇas, potent to remove the doubts engendered by ignorance. In fair and loving words, I reverence the whole body of saints, mines of all goodness; whose good deeds resemble the produce of the cotton plant in its austerity, purity, and manifold usefulness, and in its hiding the faults even of those by whom it has been most roughly treated, and who thus are worthy of reverence and win the honour of the world. Their congregation is all joy and felicity, like the great *tīrtha* Prayāga endowed with motion: for devotion to Rāma is as the stream of the Gaṅgā; contemplation on Brahmā as the Sarasvatī;[1] and ritual, dealing with precepts and prohibitions for the purification of this iron age, as the sun-god's daughter, the Jamunā. The united flood of the Triveṇī is represented by the legends of Hari and of Hara, filling all that hear with delight : the sacred fig-tree, by faith firm in its own traditions; and *Prayāga itself, by the assembly of the virtuous.* Easy of access to all, on any day, at any place, curing all the ills of pious devotees, is this unspeakable, spiritual chief *tīrtha*, of manifest virtue and yielding immediate fruit.

Dohā 2

At this Prayāga of holy men, whoever hears and understands with joyful heart and bathes with the utmost devotion, receives even in this life all the four rewards.[2]

1. A subterranean stream which is traditionally believed to join the Gaṅgā and the Yamunā at Prayāga, thus accounting for the name 'Triveṇī', which signifies a meeting-place of three rivers.

2. The four rewards are *kāma*, *artha*, *dharma*, *mokṣa*, that is, pleasure, wealth, religious merit and final salvation.

Caupāi 3

In an instant behold the effect of the bath; the crow becomes a cuckoo and the heron a swan. Let no one marvel at hearing this, for the influence of good company is no mystery. Vālmīki, Nārada and the jar-born Agastya[1] have told its effect upon themselves with their own lips. Whatever moves in the water, or on the earth, or in the air; every creature in the world, whether animate or inanimate, that has attained to konwledge, or glory, or salvation, or power, or virtue, by any work, at any time or place, has triumphed through association with the good; neither the world nor the Veda knows of any other expedient. Intercourse with the good is attainable only by the grace of Rāma and without it wisdom is impossible : it is the root of all joy and fortune; its flowers are good works and its fruit perfection. By it the wicked are reformed : as when by the touch of the philosopher's stone a vile metal becomes gold. If by mischance a good man falls into evil company, like the gem on the hood of a serpent, he still retains his noble character. Brahmā, Viṣṇu, Mahādeva, poets and scholars, all shrink from expounding the pre-eminence of a saint : for me to tell it is, as it were, for a vegetable seller to expatiate on the merits of a set of jewels.

Dohā 3a-3b

I reverence the saints of equable temperament, who have neither friend nor foe, like a gracious flower which sheds its

1. Vālmīki confessed to Rāma that he had once been a hunter and taken the life of many innocent creatures, till he fell in with the seven Ṛṣis, who converted him and taught him to express his penitence by constantly repeating the word *māra, māra*. As this contains exactly the same letters as the name Rāma, it acted as a spell and advanced him to the highest degree of sanctity.

Similarly Nārāda confessed to Vyāsa, the author of the Purāṇas, that he was by birth only the son of the poor slave-girl, and had become a saint simply by eating the fragments of food left by the holy men who frequented his master's house.

Agastya also declared to Mahādeva that by birth he was the meanest of all creatures, and had only attained to miraculous powers by the influence of good company.

fragrance alike on both the folding hands.[1] O ye saints, whose upright intention, whose catholic charity, and whose ready sympathy I acknowledge, hear then my child-like prayer, be gracious to me and bless me with devotion to the feet of Râma.

Caupāi 4

Next, in all sincerity, I would propitiate those wretches[2] who without cause return evil for good; for whom a neighbour's loss is gain; who rejoice in another's ruin and grieve over his prosperity; who are as an eclipse to the full-moon glory of Hari and Hara; who become as the valiant Sahasrabāhu to work another's woe; who have a thousand eyes to detect a neighbour's faults but, like flies on *ghī*, settle on his good points only to spoil them; fierce as fire, implacable as the god of hell;[3] rich in crime and sin as Kuvera is in gold; who ruin all like Ketu at his rising, and as dead asleep as Kumbhakarṇa[4] to everything good; if they can do any injury, as ready to sacrifice themselves as hailstones that melt after destroying a crop. Regarding them as Śeṣa himself, I reverence those scoundrels who with a thousand tongues maliciously proclaim the faults of others; and like Pṛthurāja,[5] with ten thousand ears, tell and hear of others' sins; like the thousand-eyed Indra, too, ever delighting in much strong drink and in hurling harsh words like thunderbolts.

Dohā 4

I know when the wicked hear of benefit done to neutral friend or foe, they burn with jealousy; but I fold my hands and entreat them piteously.

1. Though the right hand is the one by which it has been plucked, and the left that in which it is held and preserved.
2. In the following lines the poet defends himself by anticipation against possible objections and roundly abuses the whole army of critics.
3. Yama, the Hindu Pluto, is here called Mahiṣeśa, from *mahiṣa* a 'buffalo', that being the animal on which he is represented as riding.
4. Râvaṇa's gigantic brother, Kumbhakarṇa, obtained as a boon from Brahmâ, that whenever he had satisfied his voracious appetite the slumber of repletion might be of the longest and deepest, and that he might only wake to eat again.
5. It is not related that Pṛthurâja had really ten thousand ears, but only that he prayed that he might be as quick to hear whatever redounded to the glory of God as if his ears were so many.

Caupāī 5

Though I for my part have made my supplication, they will not depart from their ways. However carefully you may bring up a crow, will it ever give up eating meat ? I propitiate at once the feet of saints and sinners, who each give pain, but with a difference : for the first kill by absence, while the second torture by their presence : as opposite as the lotus and the leech, though both alike are produced in water. The good and the bad thus resemble nectar and intoxicating drink, which were both begotten by the one great ocean:[1] each by its own acts attains to pre-eminence; the one in honour, the other in dishonour; compare with the good, ambrosia, or the moon, or the Gaṇgā; and with the bad, poison, or fire, or the unholy river Karmanāśā. Their merits and demerits are known to all; but whatever is to a man's taste that seemeth him good.

Dohā 5

The good aim at goodness, and the vile at vileness; nectar is esteemed for its immortalizing virtue, poison for causing death.

Caupāī 6

Why enumerate the faults and defects of the bad and the virtues of the good ? Both are like the boundless and unfathomable ocean. Hence, only a few virtues and vices have been mentioned, for unless they are recognized, one cannot

1. The churning of the ocean is one of the commonplaces of Hindu poetry, and the allusions to it in the *Rāmāyaṇa* are innumerable. With Mount Mandara as a churning-stick, the great serpent Vāsuki as a rope, and Nārāyaṇa himself in tortoise form as the pivot on which to work, the gods and demons combined to churn the milky ocean. Thus were produced from its depth the moon; the sacred cow, Surabhi or Kāma-dhenu; the goddess of wine, Vāruṇī; the tree of paradise, Pārijāta, or Kalpataru; the heavenly nymphs, the Apsarās; the goddess of beauty, Lakṣmī or Śrī; and the physician of the gods, Dhanvantari. The cup of nectar which the latter held in his hand was seized and quaffed by the gods; while the poison, which also was produced, was either claimed by the snake gods or swallowed by Mahādeva; whence comes the blackness of his throat, that gives him the name of *Nīlakaṇṭha*.

accumulate the former or shun the latter. For God hath created both, but it is the Vedas that have distinguished one from the other.[1] The heroic legends (such as the *Rāmāyaṇa* and the *Mahābhārata*) and the Purāṇas also, no less than the Vedas, recognize every kind of good and evil as creatures of the Creator: pain and pleasure; sin and religious merit; night and day; saint and sinner: high caste and low caste; demons and gods; great and small; ambrosia and the happy life; poison and death; the visible world and the invisible God; life and the lord of life; wealth and poverty; the beggar and the king; Kāśī and Magadha;[2] the Gāṅgā and the Karmanāśā; the desert of Mārwār and the rich plain of Mālwā; the Brāhmaṇa and the butcher; heaven and hell; sensual passion and asceticism—the Vedas and the Āgamas have made distinction of every variety of good and evil.

Dohā 6

The Creator has endowed the universe consisting of things animate and inanimate with virtues and defects; a saint like the swan extracts the milk of goodness and rejects the worthless water.[3]

Caupāi 7

When the Creator grants men this faculty of judgment they abandon error and become enamoured of the good; but conquered by time, temperament, or the law of action, even the good, subject to illusion, may fall from virtue; but Hari's votaries get rid of sorrow and sin and rise from their fall to bring blameless glory instead. If, on the other hand, the bad through intercourse with the good do good, their inherent badness is not effaced. An impostor of fair outward show may be honoured on account of his garb, but in the end he is exposed and does not succeed, like Kālanemi, or Rāvaṇa, or Rāhu.[4]

1. "I did not know sin, but by law."—*St. Paul.*
2. Magadha (Bihar) is taken as the opposite to Kāśī, in consequence of its being the birthplace of Buddhism.
3. To the swan (*rājahaṁsa*) is ascribed the fabulous faculty of being able to separate milk from water, after the two have been mixed together.
4. Kālanemi by assuming the form of an ascetic imposed for a time upon Hanumān, as Rāvaṇa did upon Sītā : and even Viṣṇu, at the churning of the ocean, was at first deceived by Rāhu, who appeared like one of the gods.

The good are honoured, notwithstanding their poor guise, like Jāmbavān or Hanumān. Bad company is loss, good company is gain; this is a truth known to all and recognized both by the world and the Vedas. In company with the wind the dust flies heavenwards; if it joins low-flowing water, it becomes mud and sinks. According to the character of the house in which a parrot or *mainā*[1] is trained, it learns either to repeat the name of Rāma or to abuse. With the ignorant, soot is mere refuse; but it may make good ink, and be used even for copying a Purāṇa; while water, fire, and air combined become an earth-refreshing rain-cloud.

Dohā 7a-7d

The planets, drugs, water, winds, clothes, all are good or bad things according as their accompaniments are good or bad; and men of judgment can observe this distinction. Both lunar fortnights are equal as regards darkness and light; but a difference in name has been wisely made, and as the moon waxes or wanes the fortnight is held in high or low esteem. Knowing that the whole universe, whether animate or inanimate, is pervaded by the spirit of Rāma, I reverence with folded hands the lotus feet of all gods, giants, men, serpents, birds, ghosts, departed ancestors, Gandharvas, Kinnaras, demons of the night —I pray ye all be gracious to me !

Caupāī 8

By four modes of birth[2] are produced eight million four hundred thousand kinds of creatures inhabiting the air, the water and the earth. With folded hands I do obeisance, recognizing the whole world as pervaded by the spirit of Sītā and Rāma.

1. Also called *sārī* or *sārikā*. The *mainā*, a black- bodied small bird with a yellow beak, is able to talk like a parrot; *Gracula religiosa*.

2. The four *ākaras*, or modes of birth, are named *piṇḍaja*, or viviparous; *aṇḍaja*, or oviparous; *svedaja*, born in sweat, like lice; and *udbhija*, produced by sprouting like a tree. The 84 lakhs of species are divided as follows : 9 lakhs of aquatic creatures, 27 lakhs of those attached to the earth, 11 lakhs of insects, 10 lakhs of birds, 23 lakhs of quadrupeds is and 4 lakhs of men. The literal meaning of *ākara* being a mine, *khāni*, which has the same primary signification, is used for it in *Caupāī* 44.

In your compassion regard me as your servant, and dissembling no longer, be kind and affectionate. I have no confidence in the strength of my own wisdom, and therefore I supplicate you all. I would narrate the great virtues of Raghupati, but my wits are poor and his acts unfathomable. I am conscious that I have no skill or capacity; my intellect in short is beggarly, while my ambition is right royal; even though my intellect is exceedingly mean, my aspiration is pitched too high; I am thirsting for nectar, when not even buttermilk is to be had. Good men will pardon my presumption and listen to my childish babbling, as a father and mother delight to hear the lisping prattle of their little one. Perverse and malignant fools may laugh, who pick out faults in others wherewith to adorn themselves. Everyone is pleased with his own rhymes, whether they be tasteful or very insipid; but those who are pleased when they hear another's voice are good men, of whom there are few in the world; there are many enough in the world, my friend, like the rivers, which on getting a rainfall swell out a flood of their own, but barely one like the generous ocean, which swells on beholding the fulness of the moon.

Dohā 8

My lot is poor, my ambition high, but I am confident of one thing, that the good will be gratified to hear me, though fools will laugh.

Caupāī 9

Yet even the mockery of fools will be beneficial to me; the crow calls the *koil's* voice harsh. The goose ridicules the swan, and the frog the *cātak*; so the low and vile abuse pure discourse. Those who have taste for poetry but no love for Rāma's feet will find pleasure in jeering at my verses. If my homely speech and poor wit are fit subjects for laughter, let them laugh; it is no fault of mine. To those who are truly devoted to the Lord's feet but whose understanding is poor, the tale will seem insipid enough when they hear it, but to the true and orthodox worshippers of Hari and Hara the story of Raghubara will be sweet as honey. The singer's devotion to Rāma will by itself be sufficient embellishment to make the good hear and praise the melody. Though no poet, nor clever, nor accomplished; though unskilled in every art and science; though all the elegant devices of letters and rhetoric, the countless variations of metre, the infinite varieties of sentiment and style, and all the defects and excellences of verse, and the gift to distinguish between them are unknown to me, I say what is true and record it on a fair white sheet.

Dohā 9

That though my composition has not a single charm of its own, it has a charm known throughout the world, which men of discernment, whose judgment is pure, will ponder as they read.

Caupāī 10

It contains the gracious name of Raghupati, all-purifying essence of the Purāṇas and the Vedas, abode of all that is auspicious, destroyer of all that is inauspicious, ever murmured in prayer by Umā and the great Tripurāri. The most elegant composition of the most talented poet has no real beauty if the name of Rāma is not in it : in the same way as a lovely woman adorned with the richest jewels is vile if unclothed. But the most worthless production of the feeblest versifier, if adorned with the name of Rāma, is heard and repeated with reverence by the wise, who extract what is good in it, like bees gathering honey; though the poetry has not a single merit, the glory of Rāma is manifested thereby. This is the confidence which has possessed my soul; is there anything which good company fails to exalt ? Thus smoke forgets its natural pungency and in incense yields a sweet scent. My language is that in vulgar use, but my subject is the highest, the story of Rāma, which brings felicity to the world.

Chand[1] 1

Though rapturous lays befit his praise, who cleansed a world accurst,
Yet Tulasī's rivulet of rhyme may slake a traveller's thirst.
How pure and blest on Śiva's breast show the vile stains of earth !
So my poor song flows bright and strong illumed by Rāma's worth.

1. The *chands* are generally somewhat enthusiastic outbursts, in which the oft-repeated rhyme is a little apt to run away with the sense. The better to indicate their special character, one-half of the 62 that occur in this book will be rendered metrically. The first line always repeats some emphatic word from the last line of the preceding stanza.

Dohā 10*a*-10*b*

From its association with the glory of Rāma, my verses will be very dear to everyone. Any wood that comes from the Malaya sandal-groves is valued; who considers what kind of wood it is ? Though a cow be black, its milk is white and very wholesome, and all men drink it; and so, though my speech is rough, it tells the glory of Sītā and Rāma, and will therefore be heard and repeated with pleasure by sensible people.

Caupāī 11

So long as the jewel remains in the serpent's head, the ruby on the mountain top, and the pearl in the elephant's forehead, they are all without beauty; but in a king's diadem or on a lovely woman they all become exceedingly beautiful. Similarly, as wise men say, the outpourings of a good poet originate at one place (in the poet's own mind) but exercise their charm elsewhere (on the mind of the admirer); for it is in answer to pious prayer that Sarasvatī leaves her heavenly abode and speeds to earth; without immersion in the fountain of Rāma's deeds all labour and trouble count for nothing. An intelligent poet understands this, and sings only of Hari, the redeemer, and his virtues. To recount the doings of common people is mere idle beating of the brow, which Sarasvatī loathes. Genius is, as it were, a shell in the sea of the soul, waiting for the October rain of inspiration; if a gracious shower falls, each drop becomes a lovely pearl of poetry.[1]

Dohā 11

Then dexterously pierced and strung together on the fair thread of Rāma's adventures, they form a beautiful chain to be worn on a good man's pure breast, where it glows with the beauty of their devotion.

Caupāī 12

Men born in this grim iron age (*Kaliyuga*) are outwardly swans, but inwardly as black as crows; walking in evil ways, abandoning the Veda,[2] embodiments of falsehood, vessels of

1. "The wise liken the heart of a poet to the sea, his intellect to the shell containing pearls and goddess Sarasvatī to the star called Svāti (the modern Arcturus, the fifteenth lunar asterism considered as favourable to the formation of pearls). If there is a shower in the form of beautiful ideas, lovely pearls make their appearance in the form of poetic effusions".

2. By the Vedā, to which Tulasī Dāsa so frequently appeals, must be understood not the original Veda itself, with which he had absolutely nothing

impurity, hypocrites, professing devotion to Rāma, but slaves of gold, of passion, and of lust. Among them I give the first place to myself, a hypocrite, alas ! of the very first rank; but were I to tell of all my vices, the list would so grow that it would have no end. I have therefore recounted but a very few, but a word is enough for the wise. Let none of my hearers blame me for offering so many apologies; whoever is troubled in mind by them is more stupid and dull of wit than I am myself. Though I am no poet, and have no pretensions to cleverness, I sing as best I can the excellence of Rāma. How unfathomable his actions, how shallow my poor world-entangled intellect ! Before the strong wind that could uproot Mount Meru, of what account is such a mere flock of cotton as I am ? When I think of Rāma's infinite majesty I tremble as I write.

Dohā 12

For Sarasvatī, Śeṣa-nāga, (the thousand-headed serpent-god), Śiva and Brahmā, the Śāstras, the Vedas, the Purāṇas, all are unceasingly singing his perfection, yet can but say, 'Not thus, not thus'.

Caupāī 13

All know the power of the Lord to be thus unutterable, yet none can refrain from attempting to describe it. The Vedas account for it by saying that there are many different modes of effective worship (and that hymning the glory of the Lord even for a little while enables man to get across the ocean of mundane existence). There is one God, desireless, formless, uncreated, True Being, Consciousness and Bliss, the supreme spirit, the all-pervading, whose shadow is the world; who has become incarnate and does many things, only for the love that he bears to his faithful people; all-gracious and compassionate to the humble; who in his mercy ever refrains from anger against those whom he loves and knows to be his own : restorer of the past; protector of the poor;[1] all-good, all-powerful, the lord Raghurāja.

in common, but only the Upaniṣads, which are also popularly quoted as of Vedic authority. They are brief speculative treatises, over 200 in all, in a discursive and rhapsodical style and of an ultra-Pantheistic tendency. Though attached to the end of the Vedas, they are for the most part of much later date.

1. *Gharīb nawāz*. This is the first Persian word that has occurred in the poem.

In this belief the wise sing the glory of Hari, and their song thus becomes holy and meritorious. I, too, bowing my head to Râma's feet, am emboldened to sing his fame, following a path which has been made easy by the divine bards who have trodden it before me.

Dohā 13

As when once a king has a bridge built across a broad stream, an ant, very tiny as it is, is able to cross without exertion.

Caupāī 14

In this manner re-assuring my mind, I undertake to recount Râma's charming stories, as they have been reverently told by Vyâsa and the other top-ranking poets, whose lotus feet I adore, praying, Fulfil ye all my desires ! I reverence also the poets of these latter days, who have sung of Raghupati, bards of high intelligence, who have written in Prakrit and the vulgar tongue. All who have been in time past, or who now are, or who hereafter shall be, I bow to all in the utmost good faith and sincerity. Be propitious and grant this boon, that in assemblies of good men my song may be honoured ! If the good and wise will not honour it, the stupid poet has had all his labour in vain. The only fame, or poetry, or power, that is of any worth, is that which, like the Gaṅgā, is good for all. The disparity between Râma's glory and my clumsy speech makes me hesitate; but by your favour all will turn out well: for even coarse cloth, if embroidered with silk, becomes beautiful. Be kind enough to think of this, and my style will then match the excellence of my theme.

Dohā 14*a*-14*c*

If poetry be simple and its theme spotless fame, it is esteemed by the wise, and when enemies hear it, they forget their natural hostility and repeat the strain. But such verses cannot be composed without genius, and genius I have none; so again and again I beg of you to bear with me while I sing the glory of Hari. The great poets are like the swans sporting in the Holy

Lake of the Acts of Raghubara; look on me as a well-meaning child and make allowances.

Soraṭhā 14*d*-14*f*

I reverence the lotus feet of the great sage (Vālmīki) who composed the *Rāmāyaṇa*, which, though containing an account of the demon Khara, is yet very soft and charming, and though faultless, is yet full of references to Dūṣaṇa.[1] I reverence the four Vedas which are like a boat in which to cross the ocean of birth and death, without ever dreaming of weariness, while recounting Rāma's unsullied glory. I reverence the dust on the feet of Brahmā, creator of this ocean-like world, from which have been produced men, good and bad; as of old from the same source came at once nectar, the moon, and the cow of plenty, Kāmadhenu, and also poison and intoxicating liquor.

Dohā 14*g*

Reverencing with folded hands gods, Brāhmans, philosophers, and sages, I pray, 'Be gracious to me and accomplish all my fair desires.'

Caupāī 15

Again, I reverence Sarasvatī and Gaṅgā, both holy and enchanting streams; the latter cleanses the sin of him who bathes in it and drinks of its holy waters, while the former destroys the ignorance of him who speaks or hears of its glory. I adore as

1. In Hindi poetry it is considered a beauty if a phrase is so worded as to be capable of two or more different interpretations. It is sufficient to note this peculiarity once for all; but there are an immense number of passages in which, though the meaning which I have adopted seems to me, on the whole, the one most appropriate to the context, it by no means follows that other interpretations are not, from the grammarian's point of view, equally correct. Thus, the line rendered as above would literally stand thus—Rough, soft, beautiful, faultless, full of faults. And this conveys the general meaning which I have expressed. But there are two plays upon words; for *sakhara*, ordinarily 'rough', and therefore contrasted with *sakomal*, 'soft', is also intended to bear the meaning 'relating to the demon Khara'; and similarly *dūṣaṇ sahit*, 'full of faults,' can be forced into meaning 'with the demon Dūṣaṇ.

I would my *guru*, and my natural parents, Śiva and Pārvatī, protectors of the humble, daily benefactors, servants and courtiers in attendance on Sītā's lord and in every way Tulasī's true friends; who, in their benevolence and considering the degeneracy of the times, have themselves composed many spells in a barbarous language, incoherent syllables and unintelligible mutterings, mysterious revelations of the great Śiva.[1] By his patronage I may make my story an agreeable one, and by meditating on Śiva and Pārvatī may relate Rāma's adventures in a way that will give pleasure. It is only by his grace that my verse can be beautified, as a dark night by the moon and her company of stars. Whoever in a devout spirit, with intelligence and attention, hears or repeats this lay of mine, he shall become full of true love for Rāma, and, cleansed from worldly stains, shall enjoy heavenly felicity.

Dohā 15

Whether I am awake or dreaming, if Śiva and Gaurī grant me their favour, all that I say shall come true as to the effect of my song, though it be in the vulgar tongue.

Caupāī 16

I reverence the exceedingly holy city of Ayodhyā and the river Sarjū, which wipes out the sins of the Kaliyuga. I salute also the inhabitants of the city, for whom the Lord had no little affection; seeing that he ignored all the sin of Sītā's calumniator and set men's minds at rest.[2] I reverence Kauśalyā, eastern heaven, from

1. The allusion is to the magic spells and mystical formularies of the Tantras, which are for the most part mere strings of uncouth and utterly unmeaning words, such as *Om, Aiṅ, Hrīm, Srīm*, and again *Aṅ, Hūṁ Phaṭ*, two mantras recited during the ceremonies of the Durgā Pūjā. They all purport to have been revealed by Śiva himself to Pārvatī.

2. The calumniator was a washerman, whose wife had gone away, without asking his permission, to her father's house and had stayed there three days. On her return her husband refused to take her in, saying—'Do you think I am a Rāma, who takes back his Sītā after she has been living for eleven months in another man's house ?' When this came to Rāma's ears, he showed his respect for the delicacy of his subjects by dismissing Sītā, and instead of punishing the washerman, promoted him to honour. This incident

which glory was diffused over the whole world; whence Raghupati arose as a lovely moon, giving joy to the world, but blighting like a frost the lotus leaves of vice. To King Daśaratha and all his queens, incarnations of virtue and felicity, I make obeisance in thought and word and deed, saying, 'Be gracious to me as to a servant of your son, O parents of Rāma, that come of greatness, ye in whose creation the creator surpassed himself.'

Soraṭhā 16

I reverence the King of Avadh, who had such true love for Rāma's feet that, when parted from the Lord of compassion, his life snapped and parted too like a worthless straw.

Caupāī 17

I do reverence to Videha and his household, who had the greatest affection for Rāma's feet; though he concealed his devotion under royal state, yet it broke out as soon as he saw him. Then, next, I throw myself at the feet of Bharata, whose rule of life and vows cannot be described; whose soul like a bee thirsting for sweets was ever hovering round the lotus feet of Rāma. I reverence too the lotus feet of Lakṣmaṇa, cool, comedy and source of delight to their worshippers, whose glory is as it were like a staff to bear the spotless banner of Rāma's renown. Thou who to remove the terrors of the world didst become incarnate in the form of the thousand-headed serpent for the sake of the universe, be ever propitious to me, O son of Sumitrā, ocean of compassion, storehouse of perfection. I bow also to the lotus feet of Ripusūdana (i.e., Śatrughna), valiant and chivalrous companion of Bharata; and to the conqueror Hanumān, whose glory has been told by Rāma himself.

would naturally find a place in the 7th canto of the poem; and from the allusion to it here, it may be presumed that Tulsī Dās originally intended to relate it. But by the time he had written so far, the enthusiasm of the devotion had waxed too great to allow of his admitting that such an insinuation of evil had ever been made against the immaculate Sītā.

Soraṭhā 17

Yea, I reverence the Son of the Wind, of profound intelligence, like a consuming fire to the forest of evil-doers, in whose heart Rāma, equipped with bow and arrows, has established his home.

Caupāi 18

The monkey king, the king of bears and demons, Aṅgada and all the monkey host, I throw myself at the benign feet of them all; for, though contemptible in appearance they yet found Rāma, I worship all his faithful servants—whether birds, beasts, gods, men or demons—all his unselfish adherents. I reverence Śukadeva, Sanaka and his brethren and all devotees, Nārada, and all high sages, who are wise and proficient in the spiritual lore, putting my head to the ground and crying: 'My lords, be gracious to your servant.' I propitiate the lotus feet of Janaka's daughter, Jānakī, mother of the world, best beloved of the Fountain of Mercy by whose grace I may attain to unclouded intelligence. Again, in thought and word and deed I worship the all-worthy feet of Raghunātha; the glance of whose lotus-eyes, like an arrow from the bow, rejoices his votaries by destroying all their misfortunes.

Dohā 18

I reverence the feet of Śīta and Rāma, who dearly love the afflicted and who are truly inseparable, as a word and its meaning are inseparable, and as a wave cannot be distinguished from the water of which it is composed, difference being only in the name.

Caupāī 19

I adore the name of Rāma as borne by Raghubara,[1] the source of all light, whether of the fire, or the sun, or the moon; substance of the triune god; vital breath of the Veda; the passionless; the incomparable; the source of all good; the great spell muttered by Mahādeva and enjoined by him as necessary to salvation even at Kāśī. By confessing its power, Gaṇeśa obtained the first

1. For there are two other Rāmas besides Rāmacandra, *viz.*, Paraśurāma and Balarāma.

place among the gods;[1] by its power, though he muttered it backwards, the great poet Vālmīki attained to purity; by repetition, after she had heard from Śiva that it was equal to a thousand names, Bhavānī was able to join her husband;[2] while he, Mahādeva, in his delight on beholding her simple faith, assumed the woman, making that ornament of her sex the ornament of his own body. Again, it was by the power of this name that the poison swallowed by Mahādeva was converted into nectar.

Dohā 19

Devotion to Rāma is for Tulasī Dās like the rainy season; his noble devotees are the growing rice and the two glorious consonants in Rāma's name are like the months of Śrāvaṇa and Bhādra (July-August).

Caupāi 20

Two sweet and ravishing syllables, the eyes as it were of the alphabet and the life of the devotee, easy to remember, delightful to one and all, a gain in this world and felicity in the next; most delightful to utter, to hear, or to remember; as dear to Tulasī as the inseparable Rāma and Lakṣmaṇa. My love is inflamed as I speak of these mystic syllables, as naturally bound together as

1. According to the legend, the gods were disputing among themselves as to which of them should be accounted the greatest. To settle the matter Brahmā proposed that they all should race round the world. They started accordingly, each on the animal which he most delighted to ride; and Gaṇeśa being mounted, as was his custom, on nothing better than a rat, was of course soon left far behind. In his distress the sage Nārada appeared to him and suggested that he should write the word Rāma in the dust and pace round that, for in it was virtually included all creation. Thus he did, and returned to Brahmā who at once awarded him the prize.

2. One day when Śiva had finished eating, he called to his wife Pārvati to come and take her food too before it got cold. She pleaded that she had not yet finished repeating, according to her daily wont, the thousand names of Viṣṇu : whereupon her husband instructed her that it would suffice if she said the mere name of Rāma once, for that had as much virtue as all the thousand. She at once believed him and complied; and the god was so pleased at her ready faith that in her honour he assumed the Ardhanāri or half male, half female form.

Brahman and the individual soul; twin brothers like Nara and Nārāyaṇa; preservers of the world: redeemers of the elect; bright jewels in the ears of beauteous Faith; pure and beneficent as the sun and the moon; like sweetness and contentment; the inseparable attributes of ambrosia; like the tortoise and serpent, supporters of the world; like the bee and lotus of a pious soul; and as sweet to the tongue as Hari and Balarāma were sweet to Yasodā.

Dohā 20

Like a royal umbrella and jewelled diadem over all the other letters of the alphabet gleam the two consonants in Rāma's name.[1]

Caupāi 21

A name may be regarded as equivalent to what is named, the connection being such as subsists between master and servant. Both name and form are two attributes of the Lord; they are unspeakable and uncreated, known only by right understanding. They are sometimes wrongly distinguished as greater and less, but the wise will understand my explanation of the difference between them. See, now, the form is subordinate to the name, for without the name you cannot come to a knowledge of the form; if the very form be in your hand, still without knowing the name it is not recognized; but meditate on the name without seeing the form, and your soul is filled with devotion.[2] The mystery

1. The allusion is to the form the letters *r* and *m* take when written above the line.

2. To the European reader all this panegyric of the Divine name will probably at first sight appear extravagant and absurd. but from the Hindu point of view it is reasonable enough, and *mutatis mutandis*, may be paralleled by many similar expressions in the writings of Catholic theologians, as for example the following :—

Sancta oratio, brevis ad legendum, facilis ad tenendum, dulcis ad cogitandum, fortis ad protegendum. —*Thos. á Kempis.*

Suo sanctissimo nomine, quod quinque literis constat, confert quotidie veniam peccatoribus. —*P. Pelbert.*

Nomen tuum devote nominari non potest sine nominantis utilitate. *S. Bonaventura.*

Nomen solum sufficit ad medendum; nam pestis tam efficax nulla sic haeret, quae ad nomen non cedat continuo. —*Ricardus de S. Laurentio.*

of name and form is unutterable; but delightful to those who understand it, but it cannot be expressed, the name acting as a witness between the material and immaterial form of the deity, and being a guide and interpreter to both.

Dohā 21

Place the Name of Râma on your tongue, like a jewelled lamp on the threshold of the door, and there will be light, as you will, both inside and out.

Caupāī 22

As his tongue repeats this Name, the ascetic wakes to life, his thoughts free from passion and all detached from the world; he enjoys the incomparable felicity of God, who is unspeakable, unsullied, without either Name or form. Those who would understand mysteries, by repeating this name understand them; the religious who repeat this Name absorbed in contemplation, become workers of miracles[1] and acquire the power of rendering themselves invisible and the like; those who repeat it when burdened with affliction are freed from their troubles and become happy. Thus there are in the world four kinds of

Spiritus maligni diffugiunt, audito nomine, velut ab igne.—*S. Bridget.*

Omnes daemones verentur hoc nomen, et timent, qui audientes statim relinquunt animam de unguibus quibus tenebant eam.—*S. Bridget.*

Gloriosum et admirable est nomen; qui illud retinent, non expavescent in puncto, mortis.—*S. Bonaventura.*

Nomen plenum est omni dulcedine et suavitate divina—*Honorius.*

1. The miraculous powers that can be acquired by perfect saints, or siddhas, are reckoned as eight in number, and are called *aṇimā*, *mahimā*, *garimā*, *laghimā*, *prāpti*, *prākāmya*, *īśitva*, and *vaśitva*. These words denote the faculty—1st, of becoming infinitely small; 2nd, becoming infinitely great; 3rd, of becoming infinitely heavy; 4th of becoming infinitely light; 5th, of obtaining whatever one wishes; 6th, of doing whatever one wishes; 7th, of absolute supremacy; 8th, of absolute subjugation. Compare the four gifts of beatitude as enumerated by Catholic theologians : *viz.*—1stly, Agility, by which the soul can in an instant descend from the height of heaven to earth; 2ndly, Brightness, by which (according to St. Augustine) each blessed soul is so much more luminous than the sun as the sun is brighter than any other celestial body; 3rdly, Subtility, by which the soul can penetrate a mountain in the same way as a ray of light passes through a crystal; and 4thly, Impossibility, by which it is exempt from suffering, disease, or death.

Rāma-worshippers, all four meritorious, holy, and noble; but of these four sages they are the most dear to the lord who wisely rely upon his Name. His Name is mighty in the four Vedas and in all the ages of the world, but in this fourth age especially there is no other hope.

Dohā 22

Free from all sensual passions and absorbed in devotion to Rāma the soul disports itself like a fish in the ambrosial lake of the love of the Name.

Caupāī 23

The Supreme may be regarded either as impersonal or as personal ; under either aspect it is unspeakable, unfathomable, without beginning and without parallel. To my mind the Name is greater than both, for it has prevailed to bring both under its sway. My friends must not take this as an exaggeration on my part, for I say it confidently and with sincere devotion. This dual distinction of the Supreme is like the two kinds of fire, which is either potential in the wood or visible externally; each is in itself unapproachable but is easily approached by means of the Name: and therefore I say that the Name is greater than either Brahma or Rāma. For the one immortal, true, sentient, complete, and blissful Brahma is all-pervading; yet though such an immutable lord is in our very soul, the whole creation is in slavery and wretchedness, till he is revealed in definite shape, and is energized by the Name; as a jewel is not valued till it is so called.

Dohā 23

Thus the power of the Name is infinite and transcends the Supreme, and in my judgment is greater than Rāma too.

Caupāī 24

From the love that he bore to his followers, Rāma took the form of man and by himself enduring misery secured their happiness. By incessantly and devoutly repeating his Name, all the faithful may attain to felicity. Rāma himself redeemed only one woman, the ascetic's wife;[1] but his Name has converted the sinful hearts of millions of sinners. To gratify the Ṛṣi Viśvāmitra, Rāma wrought the destruction of Suktu's daughter Tāṛakā with her son Mārīca and his army; but as the sun puts an end to night, so his Name has scattered all crime and pain and despair. In his own person Rāma broke the bow of Śiva, but his glorious Name has broken the fear of death;[2] the Lord himself restored to life only the forest of Daṇḍaka,[3] but his Name has sanctified countless generations; the son of Raghu destroyed many demons, but his Name has destroyed all the evil of the Kaliyuga.

Dohā 24

Raghunātha granted the bliss of final release to Śavarī and the vulture Jaṭāyu[4] and his other righteous servants; but his Name, precious theme of the Vedas, has delivered innumerable wretches.

Caupāī 25

Rāma, as all men know, extended his protection to Sugrīva and Vibhīṣaṇa; but his Name has protected countless supplicants, shining forth gloriously in the world and Veda. Rāma assembled a host of bears and monkeys, and even then had no little trouble to build his bridge; his Name can dry up the

1. Ahalyā, the wife of the Ṛṣi Gautama, having been seduced by the god Indra, was cursed by her indignant lord, and doomed to remain alone and invisible in the forest for thousands of years, till Rāma should come and redeem her.

2. Here is a play upon words which cannot be preserved in the translation, for in the first half of the couplet the word *bhava* is to be taken as a name of Siva, while in the second half it means life or rather death, since, according to Hindu ideas, all conscious life is merely a preparation for inevitable death. Compare Milton's expression : "This earthly load of death called life, which us from life doth sever."

3. Dandaka is the name of the pathless forest near the Godāvarī, where Sītā was stolen away by Rāvana.

4. The bird Jaṭāyu stopped the chariot in which Sītā was being carried off by Rāvana and was mortally wounded by the giant, but lived long enough to give Rāma tidings of his beloved. In return for his faithful services Rāma and Lakṣmana themselves performed his funeral rites.

ocean of life; meditate thereon, O ye faithful. Rāma slew Rāvaṇa and all his family, in battle, and returned with Sītā[1] to his own city, a king to Avadh, his capital, while gods and saints hymned his praises; but his servants, if only they affectionately meditate on his Name, have no difficulty in vanquishing the whole army of error, and absorbed in devotion live at ease without even a dream of sorrow.

Dohā 25

The Name is greater than either Brahma or Rāma and blesses even those that bless. This Mahādeva knew when he selected it from the hundred *crores*[2] of verses in the *Rāmāyaṇa.*

Caupāī 26

By the grace of this Name the blessed god of curst attire, even the great Śiva, acquired immortality; by the power of this Name Śukadeva, Sanatkumāra, and all saints, sages, and ascetics have enjoyed heavenly raptures : Nārada too acknowledged its power, himself as dear to Hara and Hari as Hari is dear to the world; by repeating this Name Prahlāda, through the Lord's grace, became the crown of the faithful.[3] Dhruva in his distress repeated the Name of Hari, and was rewarded by a fixed and incomparable station in the heavens;[4] by

1. Sugrīva, the monkey chief, as told at full length later on in the poem, assisted Rāma in his search for Sītā; and Rāma rewarded him by installing him as sovereign of Kiṣkindhā in the place of his brother Bāli. Similarly, Vibhīṣaṇa was made king of Laṅkā in the room of Rāvaṇa.

2. Of these hundred crores it is said that Śiva distributed 33 crores to each of the three worlds. The one crore that remained over he similarly divided into three sets of 33 lakhs each; the odd lakh into three sets of 33 thousand each; the odd thousand again into three sets of three hundred each; the odd hundred into three sets of thirty-three each, and finally the one remaining *śloka* into three sets of ten letters each. The two letters that remained over, being the two consonants in the name of Rāma, he kept for himself, as containing the gist of the whole matter.

3. Prahlāda, the pious son of the impious Hiraṇyakaśipu, who was destroyed by Viṣṇu in the Narasiṁha avatār, was made equal to Indra for life and finally united with Viṣṇu.

4. Dhruva, the son of Uttānapāda, being slighted by his step-mother, left his home with the determination of winning himself a name in the world.

meditating on his holy Name Hanumān won and kept the affection of Rāma; by the power of Hari's Name Ajāmila[1] and the elephant and the harlot all three obtained salvation; why further extend the list ? not even the incarnate Rāma could exhaust it.

Dohā 26

In this Kaliyuga the Name of Rāma is as the tree of paradise, the centre of all that is good, meditating whereon Tulasī Dāsa, who was but a vile hemp-stick, has become the sacred *tulasī* plant.

Caupāī 27

In all four ages of the world, in all time, past, present, or future; in the three spheres of earth, heaven and hell; any creature that repeats this Name becomes blessed. This is the verdict of the Veda, Purāṇas and all the saints—that love of Rāma is the fruit of all virtue. In the first age, the Lord is propitiated by contemplation; in the second age, by sacrifice; in the Dvāpara age, by ritual worship; but in this vile and impure

By the advice of the seven Ṛṣis, he devoted himself to the service of Visnu and was finally exalted by the god to the heavens, where he shines as the pole-star.

1. According to the history given in the 6th Skandha of the Śrī Bhāgavata, Ajāmila was a Brāhmana of Kanauj, of most dissolute and abandoned life. By a happy chance the youngest of ten sons whom he had by a prostitute was named Nārāyaṇa, and the father when at the point of death happened to summon him to his side. But the god Nārāyaṇa, thus casually invoked himself came in answer to the call and rescued the guilty soul from the demons that were about to carry it off to hell.

The story of the elephant is given in the 8th Skandha of the same Purāna. An alligator had seized him by the foot while bathing, and though he struggled desperately for 2,000 years, he was unable to rid himself of his enemy, and at last was deserted by all his wives and children. He then began to give himself up for lost; but reflecting on the pertinacity of the alligator, he came to the conclusion that the creature must be the embodiment of all the sins he had committed in previous existences and that God alone could save him. He therefore addressed a fervent prayer to Nārāyaṇa, who thus invoked by name came down from heaven and with his discus Sudarśan cut off the alligator's head and delivered the suppliant.

The 8th chapter of the 11th Skandha gives the story of the penitent prostitute, Piṅgalā.

iron age (Kaliyuga), where the soul of man floats like a fish in an ocean of sin, in these dreadful times the Name is the only tree of paradise, and by meditating on it all the world's disquiet is stilled. In these evil days neither good deeds, nor piety, nor spiritual wisdom is of any avail, but only the Name of Rāma : his Name is as it were the wisdom and the might of Hanumān to expose and destroy the Kālanemi-like[1] wiles of Kaliyuga.

Dohā 27

As Narasiṁha was manifested to destroy the enemy of heaven, Hiraṇyakaśipu, and protect Prahlāda, so is Rāma's Name for the destruction of the foes of the gods and protection of the faithful.

Caupāī 28

By repeating this Name. whether in love or hatred, in action or in repose, bliss is diffused all around. Meditating upon it and bowing my head to Raghunātha, I compose these lays in his honour; he will correct all my defects, whose mercy is mercy inexhaustible. Thou art my good lord, I thy poor servant; bear this in mind and graciously protect me. The world and scripture alike declare these to be the characteristics of a good master, that he hears prayer and acknowledges affection. Rich or poor, villager or citizen, learned or unlearned, pure or impure, good poet or bad poet, all according to their ability extol their king as being good, amiable, and gracious, lord of incomparable compassion; and he hears and accepts their honest attempts, recognizing in their words both

1. Kālanemi was the uncle of Rāvaṇa, who commissioned him to kill Hanumān.. Accordingly, he assumed the garb of a devotee and retired to a magic hermitage, where he was soon after visited by Hanumān. The latter accepted the hospitality of the holy man as he took him to be, but before eating went to a pond close by to bathe. As soon as he put his foot in the water, it was seized by a crocodile, which, however, he soon killed; when from its dead body sprung a beautiful nymph long under a curse, who informed him of Kālanemi's true character. Hanumān thereupon threw his tail round the demon's neck and strangled him. The incident is related in Book vi, dohās 55, 56.

devotion and a measure of ability. This is the way with earthly kings, and Rāma is their crown: he is satisfied with simple piety, though in one who is duller and feebler of intellect even than I am.

Dohā 28*a*-28*b*

Yet will the merciful Rāma regard the love and zeal of his foolish servant; for he made a ship out of rock and wise ministers out of monkeys and bears. Everyone calls me Rāma's servant and I say so too, and Rāma is exposed to ridicule, in that he, being such a lord, has such a servant as Tulasī Dāsa.

Caupāī 29

My presumption is indeed very sad and villainous enough to disgust hell itself; I am quite aware of this and tremble to think of it; but Rāma has never for a moment taken my sins into account. Nay, the lord heard them and with his own eyes attentively considered my faith, and thereupon applauded my devout intentions. Though my story is spoilt by the telling, Rāma is satisfied and accounts it good, since the will is good. The lord is not mindful of a chance fault, but on every occasion he considers the purpose of the heart. Thus the very crime for which he like a huntsman killed Bāli was in turn the sin of Sugrīva, and again of Vibhīṣaṇa; but in their case Rāma did not dream of censure, but honoured them both at his meeting with Bharata and commended in open court.

Dohā 29a-29c

The monkeys too that scrambled up in the boughs of the tree under which the lord sat, even these he made equal to himself, Nowhere, says Tulasī, is there a master so generous as Rāma. O Rāma, thy goodness is good to all, and if so, then good to Tulasī also. Thus declaring my merits and defects and again bowing my head to all, I proceed to tell the glorious acts of Raghubara, by the sound of which all the sin of the Kaliyuga is effaced.

Caupāi 30

The engrossing tale that Yājñavalkya related to the great sage Bharadvāja as they conversed I shall repeat at length; let all good souls hear it and rejoice. It was first of all composed by Śiva and graciously revealed to Umā, and again declared to Kākabhuśuṇḍi, known to be chief among the votaries of Rāma. From him Yājñavalkya received it and he recited it to Bharadvāja. These listeners and reciters were of equal virtue and had an equal insight into Hari's sportive actions. Their intellect comprehended all time, as it were a plum in the palm of the hand. Other intelligent votaries of Hari have also in different ways heard, understood and spoken.

Dohā 30a-30b

As for myself, I heard the story from my *guru* at Sūkarakhet (*i.e.*, Soron),[1] not understanding it, when I was quite a child and had no sense. How could such a dull creature, being both ignorant and eaten up with the impurities of the Kaliyuga understand so mysterious a legend and a dialogue between such sage interlocutors ?

Caupāī 31

But my *guru* repeated it over and over again, till at length I understood as much as could be expected; and I now put it down in the vulgar tongue, to enlighten myself; with a heart inspired by Hari and using all the little sense, judgment, and ability that I possess. The story that I have to tell clears my own doubts as it does every other error and delusion, and is a raft on which to cross the ocean of existence. The story of Rāma is a resting-place for the intellect; a universal delight; destroyer of the foul stains of the Kaliyuga; an antidote to the venom of passion; a stick to enkindle the fire of wisdom; the cow of plenty in this iron age; an elixir to make good men

1. Soron, the modern name, is a corruption of Śūkara-grāma(Boar-town). The place is still much frequented by pilgrims, the principal concourse being on the festival of the Varāha (or Boar) avatār, Sūkara-grāma=Sūar-gawn—Sūarān=Soron.

immortal; a terrestrial stream of nectar; a destroyer of death; a snake to devour toad-like error; the annihilator of hell, like as Pārvatī on behalf of gods and saints annihilated the army of demons; like as Lakṣmī was born of the sea, so conceived in the assembly of saints; immovable as the earth that supports all the weight of creation; like the Jamunā, to put to shame the messengers of death; like Kāśī, the saviour of all living creatures; as dear to Rāma as the sacred *tulasī*; as sincerely beneficial to Tulasī as his own mother Hulasī, as dear to Siva as the daughter of Mount Mekal (*i.e.*, the Narmadā), bestower of all perfection and prosperity; like Aditi, gracious mother of all the gods; the perfect outcome of love and devotion to Raghubara.

Dohā 31

The story of Rāma is the river Mandākinī and the pure heart is Mount Citrakūṭa, while sincere affection is the forest where Rāma and Sītā disported themselves.

Caupāī 32

The acts of Rāma are the delectable wishing stone:[1] or a fair jewel for the bridal adornment of saintly wisdom; His perfection is the joy of the whole world, fraught with the blessing of virtue, wealth, and eternal salvation: a true teacher of wisdom, asceticism and spiritual contemplation; the physician of the gods to heal the fearful diseases of life; the very parent of devotion to Sītā and Rāma; the seed of all holy vows and religious practices; the destroyer of sin, of affliction, and of sorrow; our loving guardian in this world and the next; the valiant minister of wisdom, its king; a very Agastya[2] to drink up the illimitable ocean of desire; a lion-cub in the forest of life to slay the wild elephants of lust, anger, and sensual impurity; as dear to Śiva as the presence of a highly honoured guest; as an abundant shower to quench the forest fires of poverty; a potent spell against the venom of the

1. A fabulous gem which, it is said, fulfils all the desires of the possessor.

2. As Agastya was one day worshipping by the sea-side, a wave came and washed away some of his altar furniture, whereupon in three draughts he drank the whole ocean dry.

world; effacing from the forehead the deep brand of evil destiny; dispelling the darkness of error like the rays of the sun; like a shower on a rice-field refreshing the aridity of prayer; like the generous tree of paradise granting every desire; like Hari and Hara, accessible to all servants and bringers of joy; like the stars in the clear autumn sky of the poet's mind; like the richness of life enjoyed by Rāma's faithful votaries; like the perfect felicity that is the reward of virtue; like the assembly of the faithful in benevolence and composure; like a swan in the pure lake of the believer's soul; like the abundant flood of Gaṅgā's purifying stream.

Dohā 32a-32b

Rāma's perfect merit is like a strong fire to consume the dry wood of schism and heresy, evil practices and worldly deceit, hypocrisy and infidelity prevailing in this Kaliyuga. His acts are like the rays of the full moon that bring joy to all, but are specially consoling to the souls of the pious like the lily and the partridge.

Caupāī 33

All the questions that Bhavānī asked, with Saṅkara's replies thereto, I now proceed to repeat in substance, with agreeable diversity of style. No one is to be astonished if he should happen not to have heard any particular legend before. A philosopher, on hearing for the first time any marvellous acts, will feel no surprise, reasoning thus with himself; I know well that there is no limit in the world to the stories about Rāma, for he has in various forms become incarnate, and verses of the *Rāmāyaṇa* are some thousand millions in number; his glorious acts are of myriad diversity, and have been sung by sages in countless ways.[1] So indulge no doubts, but listen reverently and devoutly.

1. "Truth has never been grasped on all sides nor has ever been embraced entirely by the mind of man; and no one can gaze attentively on that truth which is always old, without discovering there beauties that are always new." These words of Abp. Dechamps express in abstract form the very same idea that the Hindu poet has presented in the concrete.

Dohā 33

Rāma is infinite, his perfections infinite, and his stories of immeasurable expansion; men of enlightened understanding will therefore wonder at nothing they hear.

Caupāī 34

Having in this manner banished all doubt, I place on my head the dust from the lotus feet of my *guru*, and with folded hands making a general obeisance, that no fault may attach to my telling of the story, and bowing my head reverently before Śiva, I proceed to sing of Rāma's excellent glory. In this *Saṁvat* year of 1631, I write with my head at Hari's feet, on Tuesday, the ninth day of the sweet month of Caita, in the city of Avadh, on the day when the scriptures say Rāma was born; when the spirits of all holy places there assemble, with demons, serpents, birds, men, saints, and gods, and there offer homage to Raghunātha, while the enlightened keep the great birthday festival and hymn Rāma's high glory.

Dohā 34

Many a large crowd of devotees bathes in the all-purifying stream of the Sarjū and murmurs Rāma's name, while his dark and beautiful form is imprinted on their hearts.

Caupāī 35

The Vedas and the Purāṇas declare that sin is washed away by the mere sight or touch of this holy river as well as by bathing in or drinking of its water. Its immeasurable grandeur is indescribable even by the pure intelligence of Sarasvatī. The city, exalting to Rāma's heaven,[1] beautiful, celebrated through all worlds, is so all-purifying that countless as is the number of animate species that result from the four modes of birth, yet every individual that is freed from the body at Avadh is free for ever. Knowing it to be in every way charming, a bestower

1. The compound may also mean—giving a home to Rāma—and probably both meanings are intended.

of all success and a mine of every blessing, I there made a beginning of my sacred story, which will destroy in those who hear it the mad frenzy of lust; its mere name—lake of Rāma's acts—serves to refresh the ear, while the soul like an elephant escaping from a forest on fire with lust, plunges into it and gains relief; delight of the sages, as composed by Sambhu, holy and beautiful; consuming the three ill conditions of sin, sorrow and want; putting an end to the evil practices and impurities of the wicked world; made by Mahādeva and buried in deep lake of his own soul till at an auspicious moment he declared it to Umā; thus Siva looking into his own soul and rejoicing gave it the excellent name of Rāma-carita-mānasa.[1] And this is the blessed legend that I repeat: hear it, good people, reverently and attentively.

Dohā 35

Now meditating upon Umā and upon him who has a bull emblazoned on his banner (*i.e.* Mahādeva) I explain the context, showing how it is a lake and in what manner it is formed, and for what reason it has spread through the world.[2]

Caupāī 36

By the grace of Śambhu a bright idea has come into the poet Tulasī's mind regarding the Rāma-carita-mānasa, which he will state as well as he can, subject to the correction of those good people whose attention he invites. The heart is as it were a deep place in a land of good thoughts, the Vedas and Purāṇas are the sea, and the saints are as clouds, which rain down praises of Rāma in sweet, grateful and auspicious showers; the sportive

1. From this it will be seen that the name which Tulasī Dāsa himself gave to his poem was not '*the Rāmāyana,*' but '*the Rāma-carita-mānasa*' a name, which may be interpreted to mean either the lake or the soul of Rāma's acts. In the stanza above translated the word is first taken in the one sense and then in the other, and as there is no English word with the same double signification, some obscurity is unavoidable.

2. The words may also bear the following secondary meaning; I relate the whole history, showing how the great soul became incarnate, and why it dwelt in the world.

actions related of him are like the inherent purity and cleansing power of rain-water; while devotion, which is beyond the power of worlds to describe, is its sweetness and coolness. When such a shower falls on the rice-fields of virtue, it gives new life to the faithful, and as its holy drops fall to the earth they are collected in the channel supplied by the ears, and flowing into the lake of the soul fill it and then settle down permanently, cool, beautiful and refreshing.

Dohā 36

This pure and lovely lake has four beautiful *ghāṭas*, *viz*. the four charming dialogues contrived by divine wisdom.

Caupāī 37

The seven Books are its beautiful flights of steps, which the eyes of wisdom delight to look upon : the unqualified and unsullied greatness of Raghupati may be described as its clear and deep expanse; the glory of Rāma and Sītā as its ambrosial flood; the similes as the pretty play of its ripples; the *caupāīs* as its beautiful lotus leaves thick-clustering; the elegance of expression as lovely mother-of-pearl; the *chands*, *soraṭhās*, and *dohās* as many-coloured lotus flowers : the incomparable sense, sentiment, and language as the pollen, filaments and fragrance of the lotus; the exalted action as beautiful swarms of bees; the sage moral reflections as swans; the rhythm, involutions, and other poetical artifices as diverse graceful kinds of fish; the precepts regarding the four ends of life, the wise sayings, the thoughtful judgments, the nine sentiments (or *rasas*),[1] the prayers, penance, abstraction and asceticism, of which examples are given, are all beautiful living creatures in the lake; eulogies on the faithful, the saints and the holy name are, like flocks of water-birds; the religious audience are like circling mango groves, and their faith like the spring season; the expositions of all the phases of devotion and of tenderness and generosity

1. The nine poetical sentiments are the Śṛṅgāra-rasa, or erotic; the Hāsyarasa, or comic; the Karuṇa-rasa, or elegiac; the Bīra-rasa, or heroic; the Raudra-rasa, or tragic; the Bhayānaka-rasa, or melancholic; the Bībhatsa-rasa, or satiric; the Śānta-rasa, or didactic; and the Adbhuta-rasa, or sensational.

are like the trees and canopying creepers; self-denial, morality and holy vows are their flowers, and wisdom their fruit; the love for Hari's feet as the sound of the Vedas : and all other stories and episodes as the parrots and cuckoos and many kinds of birds.

Dohā 37

The hearer's emotion is some grove, garden or parterre, where sportive birds symbolise his delight and Piety the gardener pours a stream of devotion from (the water-pot of) his beauteous eyes.

Caupāī 38

Those who sing these lays with careful heed are like the vigilant guardians of the lake; the men and women who reverently hear them, these excellent people are like its owners. Sensual wretches are like the cranes and crows that have no part in such a pond nor ever come near it; for here are no prurient and seductive stories like snails, frogs and scum on the water, and so the lustful crow and greedy crane, if they do visit it, are disappointed. It is very difficult to get to this lake, and it is only by the favour of Rāma that one reaches it. For bad company makes much steepness and difficulty in the road; their evil sayings are so many tigers, lions and serpents; the various entanglements of domestic affairs are vast insurmountable mountains; sensual desires are like a dense forest full of wild delusion; and unsound reasoning is a raging flood.

Dohā 38

For those who have no provision of faith (necessary for such a long journey), nor the company of saints, nor fervent love for Raghunātha, for them this lake is inaccessible.

Caupāī 39

Again, if any one laboriously makes his way to it, but becomes over-powered by sleep and feverishness, strange torpor and numbness settle on his soul, and though he is on the spot, the luckless wretch makes no ablution. Having neither bathed in the lake nor drunk of it he goes away in his pride, and when some one comes to inquire of him he abuses it. But no difficulties deter those whom Rāma regards with affection. They reverently bathe, are relieved from the fierce flames of sin, sorrow, and pain, and being sincerely devoted to Rāma will never abandon it. If, my friend, you would bathe in this lake, be diligent to keep company with the good. As for myself, having thus with the mind's eye contemplated it, my poetical faculty has become clear and profound, my heart swells with joy and rapture and overflows in a torrent of ecstatic devotion. My song pours on like a river flooded with Rāma's bright renown; like the river Sarjū, fountain of bliss, with piety and theology for its two fair banks; a holy stream rejoicing the pious soul (*or* born of the Mānasa lake,) sweeping away all worldly impurities like trees and roots on its bank.

Dohā 39

The three kinds of hearers[1] in the assembly are like the towns, villages, and hamlets on the river-side; while the company of saints is like the incomparable city of Avaḍh, full of all that is most auspicious.

Caupāī 40

The glorious Sarjū, that river of great renown, has united with the Gaṅgā of devotion; and the magnificent river Sona, pure as the warlike prowess of Rāma and his brother, has joined them as a third. Between the two, the Gaṅgā stream of devotion shines clear in its wisdom and self-control, while the combined flood destroying the triple curse of humanity is absorbed in the mighty ocean of very Rāma. The united stream of the Mānasa-born Sarjū and the Gaṅgā purifies the pious listener, while the various tales and episodes interspersed here and there are the groves and gardens on its opposite banks; the details of the marriage and wedding procession of Umā and Śiva are like the innumerable fish in the water; the joy and gladness that attended

1. *Viṣayi*, the worldly; *mumukṣu*, seekers after salvation; and *mukta*, the self-realized and liberated.

Rāma's birth are like beautiful swarms of bees and the ripple of the lake.

Dohā 40

The childish sports of the four brothers are like the goodly lotus buds of many hues; the virtuous deeds of the king and queen and their family are bees and water-birds.

Caupāī 41

The charming story of Sītā's marriage-choice like the bright gleam of the flashing river; the many ingenious questions like the boats on the stream; the appropriate and judicious answers like the boatmen; again, the argumentative discussions show like crowding travellers; the wrath of Bhṛgunātha like the rushing torrent; Rāma's noble words like the firmly arranged *ghāṭas*; the wedding festivities of Rāma and Lakṣmaṇa like the grateful swell of the tide; the thrill of pleasure that spreads through the delighted audience like the ecstatic feelings of the virtuous bathers; the auspicious preparations for marking Rāma's forehead with the *tilaka* like the crowds assembled on holidays; and like water-moss is Kaikeyī's evil counsel, the cause of many calamities.

Dohā 41

Like prayers and sacrifices effectual to subdue all the countless misfortunes are Bharata's virtuous acts; while the corruptions of the world and sinful men and slanderers of whom the story tells are like the filth in the water and the cranes and crows.

Caupāī 42

This river of glory is beautiful in all six seasons, exceedingly bright and holy at all times. The story of the marriage of Śiva to the daughter of the snowy mountains (Himālaya) is like the winter; the glad rejoicings at the Lord's birth are like the dewy season; the account of the preparations for Rāma's wedding are like the delightful and auspicious spring; Rāma's departure to the forest is like the intolerable heat of summer and the story of his rough journeyings like the blazing sun and wind; his encounters with fierce demons, by which he gladdens the hosts of heaven, are like the rains, that refresh the fields; the prosperity of his reign, his meekness and greatness are like the clear, bountiful and lovely autumn;[1] the recital of the virtues of Sītā, that jewel of faithful wives, is as the undefiled and excellent water; the amiability of Bharata as its unvarying coolness.

Dohā 42

Their looks and words at meeting, their mutual love and laughter, the true fraternal affection of the four brothers, are the water's sweet fragrance.

Caupāī 43

My woeful state, humility and modesty correspond to the singular lightness of good water, which is anything but a defect. This marvellous lymph works its effect by the mere hearing, quenching the thirst of desire and cleansing the soul of impurity; it resuscitates true love to Rāma and puts an end to all the sin and sorrow of the world; draining life of its weariness; comforting with true comfort; destroying sin and pain and poverty and error; dispelling lust and passion and frenzy and infatuation, and promoting pure intelligence and detachment from the world. Those who reverently drink or bathe in this stream, from their soul is effaced all sin and distress; those who do not cleanse their heart in it are wretches whom the world has ruined, turning back, hapless creatures, like a panting deer that has seen a river in a mirage !

Dohā 43*a*-43*b*

Thus I have declared to the best of my ability the virtues of this excellent water, and having plunged my own soul in it, and ever remembering Bhavānī and Śaṅkara, I proceed with my delectable story. Now laying the lotus feet of Raghupati on my heart and thus securing his gracious patronage, I will sing the meeting of the two great sages and their auspicious discourse.

1. The six Hindu seasons to which allusion is here made are Hemanta, winter; Śiśira, the early spring; Basanta, the Spring; Grīṣma, the hot weather; Varṣā, the rains; and Śarat, the autumn.

Caupāī 44

At Prayāga lives the saint Bharadvāja, devoted beyond measure to Rāma's feet, a self-restrained ascetic full of sobriety and benevolence, supremely skilled in divine knowledge. In the month of Māgha,[1] when the sun enters the sign of Capricorn, every one visits this chief of holy places; gods, demi-gods, *kinnaras*, and men in troops, all reverently bathe in the triple flood and worship the lotus feet of Mādhava while they have the happiness of touching the imperishable fig-tree. At Bharadvāja's hallowed hermitage—so charming a spot that even the saint loved it—is ever a concourse of seers and sages come to bathe at the holiest of all holy places; and having with gladness performed their ablutions at break of day, they converse together on the glories of Hari,

Dohā 44

discussing the nature of the Absolute, religious observances and the classification of primordial entities; and declaring faith in God to be the epitome of wisdom and spiritual detachment.[2]

Caupāī 45

After thus bathing every day in the month of Māgha, they again return each to his own hermitage, and every year there is a similar rejoicing when the saints meet for the annual ablution. On one occasion, when the bathing time was over, and all the holy men had left, Bharadvāja clasped by the feet and detained the supremely wise saint Yājñavalkya, and having reverently laved his lotus feet and seated him on a pre-eminent throne, he with religious ceremony extolled the saint's glory, and finally

1. January-February.

2. This couplet sums up the characteristics of the principal systems of Hindu philosophy : the Vedānta being chiefly concerned with and indeed defined as, *Brahma Jijñāsā*, 'an inquiry into the nature of God; the Mīmāṁsā being a system of ritualism and Vedic observances; the Sāṅkhya 'a synthetic enumeration' of the primary germs, or elements, out of which creation has been evolved; and the later eclectic Vaiṣṇava school declaring that the only one thing needful is *bhakti*, 'religious faith'.

thus addressed him in mildest of tones, "Sir, I have a great doubt, while in your grasp are all the mysteries of the Veda; I am afraid and ashamed to speak, but if I speak not, I lose a great opportunity.

Dohā 45

This, sir, is a maxim of all the sages, and is also declared by the Vedas and Purāṇas, that there is no sound wisdom in his breast who conceals aught from his ghostly father.

Caupāī 46

Remembering this, I expose my ignorance—take pity, my lord, on your faithful servant and dispel it. The might of Rāma's name is immeasurable, so tell the saints, the Purāṇas and the Upaniṣads; the immortal Śambhu, who is the Lord Śiva, the perfection of wisdom and goodness, is ever repeating it; though all the four groups of animate beings in the world attain to salvation if they die in his city Kāśī, yet O king of saints, it is by the virtue of Rāma's name; and therefore Śiva in his compassion enjoins its use. I ask of you, my lord, who is this Rāma, be gracious enough to instruct me. There is one Rāma, the prince of Avadh, whose acts are known throughout the world, who suffered infinite distress by the loss of his wife, and waxing wrath slew Rāvaṇa in battle.

Dohā 46

Is it this Rāma, my lord, or another, whose name Tripurāri is ever repeating? You are the abode of Truth and omniscient; ponder the matter well and tell me.

Caupāī 47

Tell me the whole history in full, my master, so that my overpowering perplexity may be solved." Said Yājñavalkya with a smile, "The sovereign power of Raghupati is known to you; you are a votary of his in word and thought and deed; I understand your stratagem. Wishing to hear the marvellous tale of Rāma's perfections, you have questioned me with an affection of great simplicity. Listen then, my son, with devout attention while I repeat the fair legend, which vanquishes every monstrous error, as dread Devī vanquished the demon Mahiṣâsura, but which is drunk in by the saints as the light of the moon by the *cakor*. When a similar doubt was suggested by Bhavānī, Mahādeva expounded the matter :

Dohā 47

and I now repeat, as well as I can, the converse held by Umā and Śaṁbhu; hear, O sage, both its time and occasion, so that you may cease to despond.

Caupāī 48

Once upon a time, in the Tretāyuga,[1] Śambhu visited Agastya the seer, with him went the mother of the world, the faithful Bhavānī. The seer made obeisance, for he recognized them as the sovereigns of the universe, and recited the story of Rāma, with which Mahādeva was delighted. The seer then asked him about true faith in Hari; and Śambhu instructed him, for he saw him to be deserving. In such converse the mountain-lord Mahādeva passed some days there, conversing with Agastya about Rāma's perfections, but finally took his leave and returned home with the daughter of Dakṣa. Now at that time there had become incarnate, in the family of Raghu, Hari the destroyer of the burdens of the world, who at his father's word sorrowfully left the throne and wandered, immortal god though he was, in the Daṇḍaka forest.

Dohā 48*a*

Śiva kept pondering as he went, 'How can I obtain a sight of him ? for every one knows that the lord has become incarnate secretly; if I visit him, every one will know who he is.'

Soraṭhā 48*b*

In Śaṅkara's heart was a great tumult, but Satī did not comprehend the mystery; says Tulasī, the hope of an interview filled his soul with agitation and his eyes with wistfulness.

1. *i.e.*, the second age of the world.

Caupāī 49

'Rāvaṇa', he thought, 'has obtained the boon of death at the hand of man only and the lord has willed Brahmā's word to come true. If I do not go to meet him, I shall ever regret it'. But all that he could do he could not hit upon a plan. At the very time that he was thus lost in thought, the ten-headed Rāvaṇa, taking with him the vile Mārīca, all at once assumed the form of a false deer and treacherously in his folly carried off Sītā, not knowing the extent of the Lord's great power. When Rāma returned with his brother from the chase and saw the empty hermitage, his eyes filled with tears. Like a mortal man distraught by the loss of his mistress, he wanders through the forest in search of her, he and his brother; and he who knows neither union nor bereavement manifested all the pangs of separation.

Dohā 49

Rāma's acts are most mysterious; only the supremely wise can comprehend them; the dull of wit and the sensual imagine something quite different.

Caupāī 50

Then it was that Śambhu saw Rāma, and great joy arose in his soul. His eyes were filled with the vision of the ocean of beauty, but it was no fitting time to make himself known, and he passed on, exclaiming : 'Hail, Supreme Being, Consciousness and Bliss, that redeems the world ! 'But as he went on his way with Satī, his whole body thrilled with delight; and in Satī's soul, when she observed her lord's emotion, a great doubt arose, —'To Śaṅkara, the universally adored and sovereign lord, gods, men and saints all bow the head; yet he has made obeisance to this prince, - saluting him as the Supreme God, and is so enraptured with his beauty that it is only to-day he has felt what love is.

Dohā 50

What ! the omnipresent and unbegotten God, the creator, who has neither parts nor passions, and is no respecter of persons, whom not event he Veda can comprehend,[1] has he taken bodily form and become man?

Caupāī 51

According to what Śiva says, though Viṣṇu in heaven's behalf assumes a human shape, he remains all-wise : yet here, as if quite at a loss, he is hunting for his wife, the fountain of wisdom, the lord of Lakṣmī, the vanquisher of demons. Still Śambhu's words cannot be untrue, nor can his knowledge be gainsaid. Thus an infinite doubt has come into my mind, and there is no way of solving it.' Although Bhavānī did not speak out, yet Mahādeva, who can read the heart, knew her thoughts, and said, "Listen to me, Satī! you are just like a woman, but you should not entertain these doubts; this is that Rāma, my own chosen deity, whose story was sung by the seer Agastya; in whom I exhorted the sage to have faith, and who is ever worshipped by illumined sages.

Chand 2

Seers and sages, saints and hermits, fix on him their reverent gaze,
And in faint and trembling accents Holy Scripture hymns his praise.
He, the omnipresent spirit, lord of heaven and earth and hell.
To redeem his people, freely has vouchsafed with men to dwell."

Soraṭhā 51

Though Śiva spoke thus time after time, his exhortation made no impression upon her; and at last Mahādeva, recognizing Rāma's deceptive power, said with a smile:

Caupāī 52

"As the doubt in your mind is so great that it will not leave you till you have put the matter to the test, I will stay here in

1. The reference is to such texts as the following in the Upaniṣads; "From whom words turn back, together with the mind, not reaching him'" (Taittirīya, II, 9). "The eye goes not thither, nor speech, nor mind" (Kena, 1, 3). "Unthinkable, unspeakable" (Māṇḍūkya, 7). The proceeds of Christian theology is similarly negative and agnostic : it sets forth what God is not, rather than what He is; since it is impossible for the lower nature to know the higher.

the shade of this fig-tree till you come back to me, after having evolved some device by which to satisfy your overpowering doubt." So Satī went off at Śiva's bidding, saying to herself—'Come now, what shall I do?' while Śambhu reflected,—"There is mischief in store for Satī; her doubts will not yield to my arguments; truly no good can ever be brought about against the will of fate; whatever Rāma has ordained will come to pass, so why spin out any longer discussion ?' So saying, he began to repeat Hari's name, while Satī drew nigh to the Lord, the abode of bliss.

Dohā 52

After many an anxious thought she assumed the form of Sītā and went and stood on the same route along which the king of men was coming.

Caupāī 53

When Lakṣmaṇa saw Umā in her disguise, he was much astonished and puzzled. Wise as he was, he was tongue-tied and looked very grave; The sagacious brother knew the power of the Lord. He, the heavenly king, detected the deceit: for he sees all things alike and knows the heart, the all-wise lord Rāma, the very thought of whom destroys ignorance. Yet even him Satī attempted to deceive—see how inveterate woman's nature is. But Rāma, acknowledging the effect of his own delusive power, with a sweet smile and folded hands saluted her, mentioning both her own name and that of her father, and added, 'Where is Mahādeva, and why are you wandering alone in the forest?'

Dohā 53

When she heard these simple but profound words, she was utterly ashamed; awe-struck, she returned to Mahādeva, filled with distress.

Caupāī 54

'I would not listen to Śaṅkara, but must go and expose my folly to the notice of Rāma; now what answer can I give ?' Her heart's distress was most grievous. Then Rāma, perceiving her vexation, manifested in part his glory, and as Satī went on her way she beheld a marvel. In front of her were Rāma, Sītā and Lakṣmaṇa. When again she looked back, there too she saw the Lord with his brother and Sītā in beauteous apparel. Whichever way she turned her eyes, there was the Lord enthroned with adepts and illumined sages ministering to him. Innumerable Śivas and Brahmās and Viṣṇus, each excelling in majesty, bowing at his feet and doing homage: all the host of heaven with their different attributes,

Dohā 54

Satī too and Sarasvatī and Lakṣmī in marvellous multiplicity of form, according to the various appearances assumed by their lords, Brahmā, Viṣṇu and Mahādeva,

Caupāī 55

each separate vision of Rāma was attended by all the gods and their wives, and by the whole animate creation with all its multitudinous species. But while the adoring gods appeared in diverse dresses, there was no diversity of form in Rāma. Though she saw many Rāmas, and with him an oft-repeated Sītā, it was always the same Rāma, the same Lakṣmaṇa, and the same Sītā. Satī was awe-stricken at the sight: with fluttering heart and unconscious frame she closed her eyes and sank down upon the ground. When she looked up again she saw nothing, and again and again bowing her head at Rāma's feet, she returned to the spot where Mahādeva was waiting for her.

Dohā 55

When she drew near, he smiled and asked if all were well, saying, 'Tell me now the whole truth, how did you put him to the test ?'

Caupāī 56

Satī remembered the power of the Lord and in her awe concealed the matter from Śiva, saying: 'O sir, I tried no test, but like you, simply made obeisance. I was confident that what you said could not be false.' Then Śaṅkara perceived the truth by contemplation and understood all that Satī had done, and bowed to the might of Rāma's delusive power, which had been sent forth to put a lying speech into Satī's mouth. 'The will of heaven and fate are strong;' thus he reflected, in great distress of mind; 'as Satī has taken Sītā's form, if now I treat her as my wife, my past devotion will be all lost, and it will be a sin to me.

Dohā 56

'Satī is too pure to be abandoned, yet to love her any more would be criminal.' He uttered not a word aloud, but in his heart was sore distressed.

Caupāī 57

At last, having bowed his head at Rāma's feet and meditated on his name, he thus made a resolve in his mind, 'So long as Satī remains in this body, I will never touch her.' With this firm determination he turned homewards repeating his Rāma rosary, and as he went there was a jubilant cry in heaven, 'Glory to thee, Mahādeva, for thy staunch devotion; who other but thou, O lord most strong in faith, would make such a vow ?' Satī was troubled when she heard the heavenly voice and tremblingly asked Śiva, 'Tell me, O true and gracious lord, what was the vow?' But though she asked once and again he told her not.

Dohā 57a

Then Satī guessed of herself, 'The all-wise has discovered it all, though I attempted to deceive him; silly and senseless woman that I am.

Soraṭhā 57b

Water and milk if mixed together are both sold as milk; and, see, it is just the same with love. The introduction of a drop of acid, or of a lie, at once causes a separation and spoils the taste.

Caupāī 58

Deep in thought and reflecting on what she had done, no words could express her infinite sorrow, and she kept saying to herself, 'The gracious but impenetrable Śiva has not openly mentioned my offence, but my lord has abandoned me.' Thus disturbed in soul by Śaṅkara's sternness and thinking of her sin, she could say nothing, but all the more smouldered within like a furnace. When Mahādeva saw her so sorrowful, he began to amuse her with pleasant tales, relating various legends all the way till he came to Kailāsa. Then recalling his vow, he seated himself under a fig-tree in the lotus posture of meditation and by an immediate control of all his members passed into a long and unbroken trance.[1]

Dohā 58

Meanwhile, Satī dwelt in Kailāsa, sorrowing grievously: not a soul knew her secret, but each day that she passed was like an age.

Caupāī 59

Ever growing more sick at heart, Satī thought : "When shall I emerge from this sea of trouble ? I who put a slight upon Rāma and took my husband's word to be a lie. The Creator has repaid me and has done as I deserved. Now, O God, think not thus within thyself that I can live without Śaṅkara. The anguish of my heart is beyond words; but I take comfort when I remember Rāma whom men call the lord of compassion, and whom the Vedas hymn as remover of distress. Him I supplicate with folded hands. May this body of mine be speedily dissolved.

1. Literally translated, the above passage would stand thus :—"Vṛṣaketu, perceiving that Satī was distrest, began to amuse her with pleasant tales, relating various legends all the way till Viśvanātha arrived at Kailāsa. Then recalling his vow, Śambhu seated himself under a fig-tree in the attitude of contemplation and by an immediate control of all his members Śaṅkara passed into a long and unbroken trance." As the use of many different names, Vṛṣaketu, Viśvanātha, Śambhu, and Śaṅkara—all to designate the same person, viz., Mahādeva—is likely to perplex an English reader. I have in this and similar passages omitted them and simply substituted the personal pronoun.

If my love for Śiva's feet is unfeigned, and my vow (to remain devoted to him) is true, in thought, word and deed, then

Dohā 59

do thou, O all-seeing Lord, hear my prayer and speedily devise a plan by which I may die without pain and avoid this intolerable woe."

Caupāī 60

Thus sorrowing and weighed down by grievous and unutterable pain, Dakṣa's daughter had passed eighty-seven thousand years, when the immortal Śambhu awoke from his trance and began to repeat Rāma's name. Then Satī perceived that the lord of the universe had returned to consciousness and went and did homage to his feet. He gave her a seat in his presence and began reciting the divine praises. Now at that time Dakṣa was reigning, and the Creator seeing him to be thoroughly fit had made him a king of kings. But when he had obtained great dominion he waxed exceeding proud. Never was a man born into the world whom kingship did not intoxicate.

Dohā 60

Dakṣa called all the sages together and they began to prepare a great sacrifice, and the gods who accept oblations were all courteously invited to attend.

Caupāī 61

Kinnaras, serpents, adepts, Gandharvas, all the gods and their wives, except Viṣṇu, Brahmā and Mahādeva, proceeded thither in their chariots. Satī saw the strangely beautiful procession going through the sky, with the heavenly nymphs singing so melodiously that any saint's meditation would be broken by the sound of it, and she asked Śiva its reason ; whereupon he explained. Then was she glad when she heard of her father's sacrifice and thought: "If my lord will allow me, I will make it an excuse for going to stay a few days with him." It was such sore pain to leave her lord, that she long dare not speak, remembering her transgression; but at last with soft and timid voice, overflowing with modesty and affection, she said :

Dohā 61

'There is great rejoicing at my father's house; with my gracious lord's permission I will duteously go and see it.'

Caupāī 62

Said he, 'It would please me well; but there is a difficulty, as you have not been invited. Dakṣa has summoned all his other daughters, but has left you out on account of his quarrel with me, for he took offence at my behaviour in Brahmā's court, and that is why he slights me to this day. If you go without being asked, there will be loss of temper, love and honour. One may go, no doubt, without an invitation to the house of a friend, or master, or father, or confessor; but no good can result from going where an enemy is present.' Thus Śambhu warned her over and over again; but fate was too strong, she would not be convinced. Said the Lord,—'To go unasked, in my opinion, is not right.'

Dohā 62

When Mahādeva saw that no amount of talking would make Dakṣa's daughter stay, he appointed his principal attendants as her escort and bade her farewell.

Caupāī 63

When Bhavānī reached her father's house, no one greeted her for fear of Dakṣa ; only her mother met her kindly and her sisters received her with a smile. Dakṣa uttered not a word of salutation and burned with rage to see her. When Satī went to look at the sacrifice, she could nowhere find anything for Śambhu : then Śaṅkara's words came back into her mind, and her heart so burned within her at the slight upon her lord, that the former pain she had felt was not to be compared to her present emotion. There are grievous pains in the world, but nothing so bad as a family slight. The more she thought of it, the more furious she grew, though her mother tried hard to pacify her.

Dohā 63

This insult to Śiva could not be borne; her heart refused to be pacified: and sharply reproaching the whole assembly, she cried, in wild accents :

Caupāī 64

"Hear, all ye guests and enlightened sages, who have talked over this slight upon Śaṅkara. Speedily shall ye reap your due reward, and dearly shall my father rue it. Whenever blasphemy is heard, spoken against the saints, or Śambhu, or Viṣṇu, the ordinance is either to tear out the blasphemer's tongue, if it is in your power, or else to close your ears and run away. The universal spirit, the great Lord, Purāri, the demon's foe, father of the world and friend of all, he it is whom my besotted father has reviled. Therefore this body of mine, begotten of his seed, I hasten to abandon, and impress on my soul the image of him who bears the moon as his crest and a bull as his device." As she thus spoke, the sacrificial flames consumed her body; a great cry of lamentation went up from the hall of sacrifice.

Dohā 64

When Śambhu's attendants heard of Satī's death, they began to destroy all the sacrificial offerings: but the great sage Bhṛgu, seeing the destruction, came and saved them.

Caupāī 65

When Śambhu heard the news he was wroth and sent Vīrabhadra, who went and scattered the sacrificial offerings and requited all the gods as they deserved. Dakṣa's act is famous throughout the world as an example of hostility to Śambhu; and as the story is so well known, I have related it in brief. Satī at her death asked this boon of Hari, that in every successive birth she might show her love to Śiva. On this account she was born in the form of Pārvatī, as the daughter of King

Himālaya. From the time that she entered the house of the Monarch of mountains, it was pervaded by fortune and prosperity, and hermits made their homes all about it, in fit places assigned them by the king.

Dohā 65

Strange trees of many kinds, with never-failing flowers and fruits, appeared on the beautiful hills, and mines of jewels discovered themselves.

Caupāī 66

All the rivers flowed with the purest water; birds, deer and bees were all equally joyous; every animal forgot its instinctive antipathies and dwelt lovingly on the mountain, which was as glorified by Girijā's coming as a man is glorified by the spirit of faith. Every day was some new delight in the king's palace, and Brahmā and all the gods vied in singing its praises. On hearing the news, Nārada went to visit the mountain king, who received him with high honour and bathed his feet and led him to a throne. The queen too bowed her head before him and sprinkled the whole house with the water sanctified by his use. Then the king spoke much of his good fortune and summoned his daughter also to his presence and said,

Dohā 66

"Thou who knowest all time, past, present, or future, and who hast traversed the whole universe, tell me, best of sages, after well considering the matter, what there is good and what bad about my daughter."

Caupāī 67

The sage replied with a smile, in gentle but profound tones, "Your daughter is a mine of perfection, beautiful, amiable and intelligent, whether she be called Umā, or Ambikā, or Bhavānī; a maiden rich in every quality that endears a wife to a husband. Her conjugal happiness will be firm as a rock, and she will bring renown to her parents; she shall be worshipped throughout the whole world, and in her service shall be fruition of every desire. Through her name women shall be enabled to walk the path of wifely duty, though it be like the edge of sword. Such, O king, are thy daughter's merits; but you have now to hear two or three drawbacks. A person who has neither beauty nor dignity, without father or mother, an ascetic with no thought for any one,

Dohā 67

a mendicant recluse with matted hair, a celibate with naked body and hideous accoutrements—such a one shall be her lord, as I read by the lines on her palm."

Caupāī 68

When the parents heard the sage's words, and knew they must be true, they became sad; but Umā rejoiced. Not even Nārada could understand, for all seemed affected alike, though their feelings were so different.[1] All Girijā's attendants, and she herself and her father and her mother Mainā, were trembling and had their eyes full of tears; but Umā cherished the Nārada's words in her heart, saying, 'They cannot be false' : and her love for Śiva's lotus feet revived, but she feared it would be difficult to find him! But as it was no fitting time for a disclosure, she suppressed her emotion and went back to the bosom of her playmates. They and the parents were distressed by the thought of the sage's infallible utterance, and the king, with an effort, cried aloud,—"O sir, tell me what remedy to devise."

Dohā 68

Said the sage—"Hear, O Himavant ! What fate has written on the forehead, nor god nor demon, man, serpent, nor saint, is able to efface.

Caupāī 69

Yet I will tell you one mode of escape which, by the help of heaven, may avail. Umā's bridegroom will infallibly be such

1. That is to say, they all shed tears, but the parents wept for sorrow and Umā for joy.

a one as I have described to you; but all the bad points that I have enumerated I find to exist in Śiva. If a marriage with him can be brought about, every one will account his vices as virtues. Though Hari takes a serpent for his couch, the wise account it no fault in him; though fire and the sun devour anything they come across, no one therefore calls them blind; though its stream flows in one place pure and in another sullied, no one would call the Gaṅgā impure. The powerful, my friend, can do no wrong, like the sun, fire, or the Gaṅgā.

Dohā 69

The fool who in the pride of knowledge presumes to copy them, saying 'it is the same for a man as for a god,' shall be cast into hell for as long as the world lasts.[1]

Caupāī 70

Even though they know that wine is made with Gaṅgā water, yet saints will never taste it; but the wine, if mixed with the Gaṅgā, becomes, pure; and herein is seen the difference between God and the soul.[2] The lord Śambhu is all-powerful and an alliance with him is in every way auspicious. But it is

1. A similar doctrine is inculcated in the Xth Book of the Bhāgavata Purāṇa : "The transgression of virtue and the daring acts which are witnessed in superior beings must not be charged as faults against those glorious persons. Let no one but a superior being ever even in thought practise the same. Seeing, then, that the saints are uncontrolled and act as they please, how can there be any restraint upon the Supreme, when he has voluntarily assumed a body". Granted those reasonable limitations which the Hindu mind, with its tendency to exaggeration, was unfortunately so prone to neglect, the sentiment is essentially true and is recommended by Catholic theologians. Thus Cardinal Newman writes—"It never surprises me to read anything unusual in the devotions of a saint. Such men are on a level very different from our own, and we cannot understand them. I hold this to be an important canon in the lives of the saints, according to the words of the apostle—'The spiritual man judges all things, and he himself is judged of no one.' But we may refrain from judging, without proceeding to imitate. The saints are beyond us, and we must use them as patterns, not as copies.

2. The meaning is wine, though made of Gaṅgā water, is still impure but the Gaṅgā itself is always pure, even though wine may have been poured into it.

hard to propitiate him; yet if penance is undergone, he is quickly appeased. If then, your daughter will practise penance, Tripurāri will be able to erase the lines of fate; and though there may be many bridegrooms in the world, the only one for her is Śiva, and none else. He answers prayer, relieves the distress of the faithful, is full of compassion and a delight to his servants; unless he is propitiated, no one will attain his heart's desire, though he practise infinite penance and authority."

Dohā 70

So saying, and with his thoughts fixed on Hari, Nārada gave Girijā his blessing and added, 'O king, fear no more; all will turn out well.'

Caupāī 71

Having thus spoken, the sage returned to Brahmā's court. Hear now the end of the story how it came about. Mainā finding her husband alone said to him, "My lord, I do not understand the sage's meaning. If the bridegroom and his house and family are unobjectionable and such as befit our daughter, then arrange the marriage; but if not, let her remain a maiden: for, my lord, Umā is as dear to me as life. If she does not get a spouse worthy of her, everyone will say the mountain-king is himself a mere block. Remember this, and so marry her that there may be no heart-burning hereafter." With these words she laid her head at his feet. The king affectionately replied, "Sooner shall fire break out in the moon than Nārada's word be gainsaid.

Dohā 71

Put away all anxiety, my dear, and fix your thoughts on the good God who has created Pārvatī and who will protect her.

Caupāī 72

Now, if you have any love for your child, go and thus admonish her, 'Penance is the means of approach to Śiva, and there is no other way of escaping sorrow. Nārada's words are pregnant and full of deep meaning; Mahādeva is in fact beautiful and accomplished; realize this and doubt not, he is in every way irreproachable." When she heard her husband's words she was glad of heart and rose and went at once where Umā was. On seeing the girl her eyes were filled with tears, and she affectionately took her in her lap and again and again pressed her to her bosom; but could not say a word for the choking in her throat. Then the mother of the universe, the all-wise Bhavānī, her mother's delight, said softly :

Dohā 72

"Listen, mother, to the dream I am about to tell you; a fair and noble Brāhmaṇa prince has thus instructed me :

Caupāī 73

'Go, mountain-maid, and practise penance, reflecting that Nārada's words are infallibly true. Your parents, too, are pleased with the idea, for penance is full of peace and puts an end to pain and sin. By the power of penance the Creator makes the world; by the virtue of penance Viṣṇu redeems the world; by virtue of penance Śambhu destroys it. It is by the virtue of penance that the Great Serpent supports the burden of the earth, and in short the whole creation, Bhavāni, depends upon penance; do you then practise.'" On hearing these words her mother was astounded, and sent for the king and declared to him the vision. Then, after consoling her parents in every possible way, Umā in gladness of heart commenced her penance; while they and all their loving dependants grew sad of face, nor could speak a word,

Dohā 73

Then came Vedaśiras[1] the sage and instructed them all; and when they had heard of Pārvati's glory they were comforted.

1. Vedaśiras, a son of Mārkaṇḍeya and Mūrdhanyā, was, by his wife Pīvarī, the Progenitor of the Bhārgava Brāhmaṇas.

Caupāī 74

But Umā, cherishing in her heart the feet of her dear lord, went into the forest and began to practise penance. Though her delicate frame was little fit for such austerities, she abandoned all food and became absorbed in prayer, her devotion so growing day by day that all bodily wants were forgotten, and her soul was wholly given to penance. For a thousand years she ate roots and fruit, and then for a hundred years she lived on vegetables; for some days her only sustenance was water and air, and on some she maintained a yet more absolute fast. For three thousand years she ate only dry leaves of the *bel*[1] tree that had fallen to the ground, and at last abstained even from dry leaves, whence she acquired the name of *Aparṇā* ('the leafless'). At the sight of her emaciated frame, Brahmā's deep voice resounded through the heavens,—

Dohā 74

"Hear, daughter of the mountain king ! your desire is accomplished; cease all this intolerable penance; Tripurāri will soon be yours.

Caupāī 75

Though there have been many anchorites both resolute and wise, not one, Bhavānī, has performed such penance as this. Submit now to my commands, knowing them to be ever true and eternally hold. When your father comes to call you, cease to resist and go home with him; and when the seven sages meet you know this to be the test of the heavenly prediction." When she heard Brahmā's voice thus speaking from heaven, Girijā was thrilled with delight. Now with her we have done for a time while we turn to Śambhu. From the day when Satī's spirit left the body he became a rigid ascetic, ever telling his beads in Rāma's name, and attending the public recitations in his honour :

1. The tree *bel* (*Aegle Marmelos*) is specially sacred to Śivā.

Dohā 75

Even he, Śiva, pure Consciousness and Bliss, the abode of joy, exempt from lust, frenzy and delusion, wandered about on earth with his heart fixed on Hari, the joy of the whole world,

Caupāī 76

now instructing saints in wisdom, now expounding Rāma's praises and though himself the all-wise and passionless lord god, yet saddened by the sadness of a bereaved disciple. In this way a long time passed, while his love for Rāma daily increased. Then the generous and merciful god full of grace and benignity, seeing his steadfastness and affection, and the unchangeable stamp of devotion on his soul, became manifest in all his glory and lauded him highly, for none other had ever accomplished such a vow. In diverse ways he instructed him, telling him of Pārvatī's birth and of her virtuous deeds, all at full length, in his infinite compassion.

Dohā 76

"Now, Śiva," he said, "if you have any love for me, listen to my prayer: go and wed the mountain-maid and do as I ask you."

Caupāī 77

"Though it is not what I approve," said Śiva, "yet when a master makes a request it must not be refused. I must needs bow to your order, for obedience is the highest duty. If a man would prosper, he must do, without thinking as he is told by his parents, or his confessor, or his superior; you are in every way my benefactor, and I bow to your commands." The lord was pleased when he heard Śaṅkara's words so full of faith, wisdom, and religious feeling, and said, "Hara, your vow has been accomplished, attend now to what I have told you." So saying he vanished, but the vision remained impressed in Śaṅkara's soul. Then came the seven Ṛṣis to visit him, and he addressed them thus in pleasant wise :

Dohā 77

"Go ye to Pārvatī and make trial of her love, and then send her father to fetch her home and remove all his doubts."

Caupāī 78

When the seers saw Gaurī, she seemed to them like Austerity personified, and they cried, "Hear, O daughter of Himâcala! Why practise such grievous self-mortification ? Whom do you worship and what do you desire? Why not tell us the whole secret truly." When Bhavānī heard their speech, she replied in strangely moving terms, "I greatly shrink from telling my secret, for you will smile at my folly when you hear it; but my soul is stubbornly set and refuses to hear instruction, though I am like one building a house upon the water, or as one who would fly without wings, relying only on the truth of Nārada's prophecy. See, O saints, the extent of my madness. I long for the unchangeable Śaṅkara as my husband."

Dohā 78

The Ṛṣis laughed on hearing her speech, and said : "You are a true daughter of the parent rock; but tell me who has ever listened to Nārada's instructions and had a home?

Caupāī 79

"Did he not advise Dakṣa's sons, and they never saw their father's house again ? It was he, too, who ruined Citraketu's family, and also Hiraṇyakaśipu's.[1] Whoever listens to Nārada's

1. It was by Nārada's advice that the sons of Dakṣa were dissuaded from multiplying their race and scattered themselves all over the world in the hope of acquiring knowledge. Not one of them ever returned, and the unhappy father, thus deserted by all his children, denounced as a curse upon Nārada that he, too, should always be a homeless wanderer on the face of the earth.

King Citraketu was childless, though he had a thousand wives. At last, by the blessing of a saint, one of them bore him a son; but when the child was a year old they all conspired together and poisoned it. The king was weeping sorely with the dead child in his arms, when Nārada

advice, be it man or woman, is certain to become a homeless beggar. Seemingly pious, but deceitful at heart he would make every one like himself. And now you are led away by his words, and are longing to marry an incorrigible ascetic, a worthless, shameless, tattered wretch, with a necklace of serpents and human skulls, and without either family or house or even clothes, Tell me now—what pleasure is to be had from such a bridegroom as this ? Better forget the ravings of the impostor. For he married Satī only because other people suggested it, and soon abandoned her and left her to die.

Dohā 79

And now he never gives her a thought, but goes about a-begging, and eats and sleeps at his ease. What respectable woman could ever stay with such a confirmed solitary ?

Caupāī 80

To-day if you will heed our words, we have chosen an excellent bridegroom for you, so handsome and honourable, so pleasant and amiable, that even the Veda hymns his praise—the faultless and all-perfect lord of Lakṣmī, who dwells in the city of Vaikuṇṭha. Such is the husband as we shall bring you."

came and after much persuasion consented to restore it to life. It at once sat up and began to speak, saying that in a former state of existence. it had been a king, who had retired from the world into a hermitage. There one day a woman in charity gave him a cake of fuel, which he put on the fire without perceiving that there were in it a thousand little ants. These innocent creatures all perished in the flames, but were born again in a more exalted position as Citraketu's wives; while the woman who gave the fuel, and the hermit who used it, became the mother and the child, whom inexorable fate had thus punished for their former sinful inadvertence. After finishing this explanation the child again fell back dead, and Citraketu, giving up all hope of an heir, abandoned the throne and began a course of penance.

When Kayādhu, the wife of demon-king Hiraṇyakaśipu, was about to bring forth, she received instruction from the sage Nārada, whose words reached even to the ears of the child in her womb. Accordingly from the moment he was born he devoted himself to the service of Viṣṇu, and thus provoked his impious father to the acts of persecution which resulted in his own destruction and the extinction of his royal line.

On hearing this Bhavānī smiled and replied, "You spoke truly when you said that I inherit a rock-nature, and would sooner die than yield. Gold, again, is another product of the rock that cannot be changed by any amount of burning. Nor will I change my faith in Nārada's word : whether my house be full or desolate, I fear not : whoever doubts the word of his spiritual adviser must never dream of obtaining either happiness or riches.

Dohā 80

Mahādeva may be full of faults, and Viṣṇu all-perfect; but the heart concerns itself only with object it happens to fancy.

Caupāī 81

If, reverend Sirs, I had met you earlier, I would have submitted to your advice and obeyed you; but now that I have given my life for Śambhu, it is too late to weigh his merits and defects. If you are firmly resolved upon making a match, you need not stand idle ; the world is full of young men and maidens : but as for me, though I hold out for a million lives, I will either wed Śambhu or remain a virgin. I will not ignore Nārada's admonition, even though Mahādeva himself bid me do so a hundred times ! I, who am styled the mother of the world, fall at your feet and bid you return home; your time is lost." When the sages beheld her devotion, they cried, "Glory, glory to Bhavānī, mother of the world!

Dohā 81

United as Māyā to the god Siva, the parents of the universe!" Then bowing their heads before her feet and thrilling with rapture, they left.

Caupāī 82

And sent King Himavant, and with many entreaties brought Girijā back. When they returned to Śiva and told him Umā's whole history, he was delighted to hear of her affection, and they went gladly home. Then the all-wise Sambhu, firmly directing his intention, began a meditation on Rāma. Now at that time was a demon Târaka, of gigantic strength of arm and high renown, who had subdued the sovereigns of every region and robbed the gods of all their happiness. Knowing neither age nor death, he was invincible; and the powers of heaven were vanquished in innumerable battles. At last they all went and cried to the Creator, and he seeing them so dismayed,

Dohā 82

re-assured them, saying, "The demon shall die when a son is born of the seed of Śambhu, who shall conquer him in fight.

Caupāī 83

Having heard what I say, devise a plan by which such a lord may arise and assist you. After Satī quitted the body at Dakṣa's sacrifice, she was born again as the daughter of the Himālaya, and has been practising penance in the hope of obtaining Śambhu to husband. He, on the other hand, has left all and sits absorbed in contemplation. Though it will be a difficult business, yet listen to what I propose. Send Kāma, the god of love, to Śiva to agitate his soul, and then I will approach with bowed head and arrange the marriage, and in this way your object will be attained." All exclaimed that the plan was good, and heartily applauded it. Then came the god with the five arrows and the fish-standard.

Dohā 83

And they told him their distress. He heard, and after reflecting a little replied with a smile, "Śambhu's displeasure will work me no good.

Caupāī 84

Yet I will do you this service. The scriptures say charity is the highest of virtues, and one who gives his life for another is ever the praise of the saints." So saying he bowed, and took his leave, he and his attendant,[1] with his bow of flowers in

1. Kāmadeva's attendant is Ṛturāja, or Vasanta, the spring season.

his hand. And as he went, Māra thought to himself,—'Śiva's displeasure will surely be my death.' Therefore he hastened to exhibit his power, and for a time reduced to subjection the whole world. If Love is provoked, the stepping-stones of the law are swept away in a moment; religious vows and obligations, self-control, ceremonial observances, knowledge and philosophy, virtuous practices, prayer, penance, self-mortification—the whole army of sound discretion took to flight in terror.

Chand 3

Virtue's grand force is routed in panic and dismay,
And in dark nooks of holy books her champions skulk away.
Great god of fate ! in this dread state what saving power is nigh ?
'Gainst man's one heart Love's fivefold dart wins easy victory.

Dohā 84

Every creature in the world, animate or inanimate, male or female, forgot natural restraint and became subject to Love.

Caupāī 85

In every heart was a yearning for love: the tree bent its boughs to kiss the creeper; the overflowing river ran into the arms of the ocean; lakes and ponds effected a meeting. And when such was the state of inanimate creation, what need to speak of iiving creatures? Beasts on land and birds in the air, under the influence of love, were unmindful of time and season; all were agitated and blind with desire, and the swan[1] regarded neither night nor day. Gods, demons, men, *kinnaras*, serpents, ghosts, witches, goblins and imps were all at once enslaved by love; even saints and hermits, sages and ascetics, became again sensual under his influence.

Chand 4

When saints and hermits own his sway, why speak of serf and thrall,
God's whole creation, recreant grown, swore love was all in all;
Each jocund dame, each amorous swain, found heaven in love's embrace
Two hours sped past, love still stood fast and reigned in Brahmā's place.

1. The male and female *cakva* (swan, or rather Brahmani duck) are doomed for ever to nocturnal separation, and are said to pass the night on the opposite banks of a river, vainly calling to each other to cross. During Love's brief triumph the curse was for once removed.

Sorațhā 85

None could remain self-possessed, for Love had stolen their hearts; they alone could hold their own against him to whom Rāma extended his protection.

Caupāī 86

For two hours this triumph lasted, till Kāmadeva drew nigh to Śambhu. On seeing him Love trembled, and the whole world returned to itself. Every living creature at once grew calm, as when a drunkard recovers from his drunkenness. When Love looked on Śiva, the invincible and unapproachable god, he feared; though he was ashamed to return, yet could hardly do anything. Then, resolving to die, he formed his plan of attack. Forthwith lusty Spring stepped forth, and every tree broke into blossom; wood and grove, lake and pond, every quarter of the heaven, lake and even the deadest soul quickened at the sight.

Chand 5

At love's touch the dead were quickened, blossomed all the wood so dark,
While a breeze soft, cool and fragrant, fanned the love-enkindled spark,
Laughs the lake with many a lotus, hum the bees with drowsy sound,
Swans and parrots chatter gaily, gladly dance the nymphs round.

Dohā 86

Though he tried every trick in a myriad ways, yet he and his army were defeated; Śiva's unbroken trance still continued, and Love grew furious.

Caupāī 87

Spying a mango tree with spreading boughs, he in a rage climbed up into it; then fitted a shaft to his flowery bow, and in his great passion taking aim and drawing the string home to the ear, he let fly and lodged the five arrows in his breast. Then the trance was broken and Śambhu awoke. In the lord's soul was great agitation; he opened his eyes, and looking all round saw Kāmadeva in the mango tree. At his wrath the three worlds trembled. Then Śiva unclosed his third eye, and by its flash Kāmadeva was reduced to ashes. A grievous cry went up through the universe from the gods in their dismay, from the demons in exultation; the rich were sad when they remembered love's delights, while saints and hermits felt relieved of a thorn.[1]

Chand 6

The saints were freed from torment: but Rati swooned for woe,
And in sad guise with weeping eyes at Śiva's throne fell low,
Sore wailing and lamenting her dear lord's hapless fate:
Till quick to pardon spoke the god in words compassionate;

Dohā 87

"Henceforth, Rati, your husband's name shall be called *Anaṅga* (the bodiless), and thus etherealized he shall pervade all things. But hear how you will again find him hereafter.

Caupāī 88

When Kṛṣṇa becomes incarnate in the family of Yadu to relieve the world of its heavy burden, your husband shall be born again as his son (Pradyumna); my words shall not fail." On hearing this prophecy of Śaṅkara's, Rati retired. I now turn to another part of my story. When Brahmā and the other gods heard these tidings they first went to Vaikuṇṭha, and thence, with Viṣṇu, Brahmā and all the rest, into the presence of Śiva, the gracious Lord, and each of them separately sang his praises. Then the gracious power whose crest is the moon and whose standard a bull, said, "Tell me, ye immortals, why ye have come." Said Brahmā, "My lord, you can read our hearts, but as ordered I speak.

Dohā 88

In the hearts of all the gods, O Śaṅkara, is this one earnest desire; we would fain with our own eyes see your marriage rites performed.

1. With this whole narrative compare that in the *Kumārasambhava* of Kālidāsa.

Caupāī 89

O destroyer of the pride of love, so act that we may feast our eyes on this glad event ! In granting a husband to Rati after Kāmadeva had been consumed you have done well, O sea of compassion, in punishment remembering mercy; the great have ever an easy temper. Accept her now after the interminable penance that she has endured." On hearing Brahmā's speech and perceiving its purport, he exclaimed joyfully, "So be it !" Then the gods sounded their kettle-drums and rained down flower and cried,—"Glory, glory to the King of heaven !" Then, perceiving it was the proper time, the seven sages came and were despatched by Brahmā to the Himālaya where first they sought Bhavānī and addressed her in mild but deceptive terms:—

Dohā 89

"You would not listen to us, but rather took Nārada's advice; now again has your vow proved vain, for Kāma has been consumed by Mahādeva."

Caupāī 90

Bhavānī replied with a smile,—"O wisest of sages, you have said well. Your words—'Love has been consumed by Mahādeva' —imply a belief that until this day Śambhu was liable to change. But I know him to be from everlasting an ascetic, faultless, loveless, passionless : and if, knowing him to be such as he is, I have served him devotedly in thought, word and deed, so gracious a lord (be assured, O high sages) will bring my vow to true fruition. Your saying that Hara has destroyed Love betrays great want of judgment. Fire, my friend, has an unalterable nature, and ice cannot exist near it; brought near it must inevitably perish; and so must Love in the presence of Mahādeva."[1]

1. The line thus translated stands in the original *Asi Manmatha Maheśa kī nāī.* There is an entirely different reading in some copies *jimi Sampāti nij packch ganwāī*, 'like as Sampāti lost his wings'; 'Sampāti was the brother of Jaṭāyu, and in his pride flew so high into the heaven that his wings were consumed by the heat of the sun. See Book IV, *Dohā* 27.

Dohā 90

On hearing this speech and seeing her love and confidence the sages were delighted and bowed the head before her, and went to King Himācala.

Caupāī 91

They told him the whole history. When he heard of Love's annihilation he was very sad, but was again comforted when told of Ratī's promised husband. After pondering on the majesty of Śambhu, he reverently summoned the wise sages, and at once had the day fixed according to Vedic prescription, selecting an auspicious date, and planet and hour. Then he gave the letter to the seven sages, humbly falling at their feet, and they took it to Brahmā, who could not contain himself for joy on reading it, but at once proclaimed it aloud. The whole company of heaven was delighted : there was music and a shower of flowers, and in every quarter festive preparations were commenced.

Dohā 91

All the gods began adorning their different vehicles on which they ride abroad; auspicious omens were seen and Apsarās sang for joy.

Caupāī 92

Siva's attendants began to dress their lord for the wedding, arranging his serpent-crest and crown of matted locks; with snakes for his ear-rings and bracelets of snakes for his wrists; his body smeared with ashes, and a lion's skin about his loins; the moon on his brow, the lovely Gaṅgā on the crown of his head, his eyes three in number, and a snake for his Brāhmaṇical cord;[1] his throat black with poison; a wreath of dead men's skulls about his breast. In such unblest attire was arrayed the gracious abode of all blessings ! With trident in hand he advanced riding upon a bull, while the drums beat and instruments of music were played. The female divinities all smiled to see

1. *i. e.*, the sacred thread.

him, and said, "The world has no bride worthy of such a lover!" Viṣṇu and Brahmā and all the company of heaven followed in the procession, each on his own carriage. "The gods make a fine sight, but still the procession is not worthy of the bridegroom!"

Dohā 92

So cried Viṣṇu with a smile and then summoned all the heavenly warders—"March separately, each with his own retinue.

Caupāī 93

Friends, this sorry procession is unworthy of the bridegroom! Will you expose yourselves to ridicule when you go into a strange city ?" The gods smiled to hear this speech, and marched separately, each at the head of his own followers. Mahādeva smiled to himself and thought, 'Hari's humour never fails.'[1] But taking it as a most friendly suggestion, he sent Bhṛṅgī to bring all his attendants. On receiving Śiva's order they all came and bowed their heads at his lotus feet. Then Śiva laughed to see the host in their motley attire, riding every kind of vehicle; some with monstrous heads, some with no head at all; some with many hands and feet, and some with none; some with great eyes, some with no eyes; some very stout, some very slim.

Chand 7

All, stout or slim, or foul or trim, in gruesome panoply,
With skulls for wine-cups filled with blood, from which they quaffed
with ghee :
With head of dog; or ass, or hog, a host no tongue can tell,
Ghosts, goblins, witches, every kind denizen of hell.

Soraṭhā 93

All the ghosts went singing and dancing with wonderful contortions, such as never were seen, and uttering all sorts of outlandish cries.

Caupāī 94

Like bridegroom, like procession—an extraordinary sight as it went along the road. There King Himācala erected a pavilion

1. *i.e.*, he has a predilection for indulging in sarcasm.

more splendid than tongue can tell; and every hill in the world, small and great, more than man can count, and every wood and sea, river, stream and lake, all were invited to attend; and assuming forms of exquisite beauty, with all their retinue, male and female, they flocked to the palace singing songs of gladness. First of all the king had built a number of guest-chambers, and so tastefully arranged them, that, after a glance at the beauty of the city, the Creator of the world seemed a contemptible architect.

Chand 8

Little seemed the world's Creator, and his skill of nothing worth :
Lake and fountain, grove and garden, shone more fair than aught on earth,
Wreaths and arches, flags and banners, made each house a goodly show:
Gallant youth and lovely maidens set a sage's heart all aglow.

Dohā 94

The city in which the great Mother became incarnate surpassed description; joy, prosperity and abundance were ever on the increase there.

Caupāī 95

When news came that the marriage procession was close at hand, the stir in the city and the brilliancy of the decorations grew more and more. With numerous carriages and all due equipment the heralds started for the formal reception. When they saw the army of gods they were glad of heart, and yet more so when they beheld Hari. But when they perceived Śiva's retinue, every beast they rode started back in panic. The elders summoned up courage and stood where they were, but the children all fled for their lives, reaching home straight, and when their parents questioned them they could only reply trembling all over,—"What can we say ? It is beyond telling; it is no marriage procession, but the army of Death; the bridegroom, a maniac, is mounted on a bull, with snakes and skulls and ashes to adorn him.

Chand 9

Skulls and snakes and streaks of ashes, matted locks and body bare.
Witches, imps, and frightful goblins, and appalling ghosts are there.
Happy man who sees such horrors nor dies at once of fright !"
So from house to house they babbled on Umā's wedding night.

Dohā 95

The fathers and mothers smiled, for they recognized Śiva's familiars, and reassured the children in every possible way, saying,—"Don't be afraid; there's nothing to fear."

Caupāī 96

The heralds brought in the procession and assigned them all magnificent guest-rooms. And Mainā, having prepared an elegant festal lamp, and lustrous water in a golden bowl, proceeded gladly to move it round over Śiva's head while her attendants sang songs of glad welcome. When they saw his terrible attire, the women feared greatly and ran inside the house all of a tremble. Mahādeva advanced to the guest-room and Mainā, sorely grieved at heart, called her daughter, and in the most loving manner took her in her lap, while her lotus eyes overflowed with tears, "To think that the Creator should have made you so beautiful, and then give you such a raving fool for a husband !

Chand 10

How can God send such a raving groom for such a lovely bride ?
What a thorn bush is our wishing-tree, the fruit for which we cried !
From mountain-top, in sea or fire, I'll cast me down with thee;
Welcome disgrace, so they be gone; this wedding ne'er shall be."

Dohā 96

All the ladies were distressed when they saw the queen so sad, who in her deep affection for her daughter began to weep and make great lamentation,—

Caupāī 97

"What harm had I done to Nārada that he should make my home desolate and give Umā such advice, to undergo penance to win a mad husband ? In good sooth he is fancy-free and passionless, an ascetic who wants neither money, nor house, nor wife, and therefore in destroying another's home he has neither shame nor compunction; for what does a barren woman know of the pangs of child-birth ?" When Bhavānī saw her mother's distress, she answered thus placidly and discreetly, "Be not troubled, my mother, with these thoughts, for God's plans are unalterable. If fate decrees me a mad husband, then why should anyone be blamed? Mother, can you blot out the handwriting of the Creator? Then refrain from profitless reproaches.

Chand 11

Cease from profitless reproaches, nor in vain bemoan my fate,
I must go where'er my destined joys and sorrows for me wait."
Hearing Umā's pious answer, all her ladies felt surprise.
Much they talked of God's injustice, while the tears bedewed their eyes.

Dohā 97

On hearing the news, just then came Himālaya with Nārada and the Seven Seers right speedily to the palace.

Caupāī 98

Then Nārada instructed them all, and recited in full the story of Pārvatī's former life, saying,—"Hear, O Mainā ! my words are true; your daughter is Bhavānī, mother of the world, the everlasting female energy; without birth or beginning; Śambhu's immortal spouse and inseparable half; the creator, supporter, and destroyer of the universe; who at will assumes the semblance of human form. First she was born in Dakṣa's house, Satī by name, of excellent beauty. Then as Satī she married Śaṅkara, and her story is famous throughout the world, how once, while returning home with Śiva, she met the sun of Raghu's lotus line (*i.e.*, Rāma), and in her infatuation was not obedient to Śiva, but was beguiled into assuming the form of Sītā.

Chand 12

For the crime of this assumption she was widowed many a day,
Till in the fire before her sire her sins were burnt away.
Now born your daughter, for her lord in penitence she stayed;
And Śiva aye shall be her lord; know this, nor be dismayed."

Dohā 98

On hearing Nārada's words the sadness of all was dispersed, and in a moment the story he had told spread from house to house throughout the city.

Caupāī 99

Then Mainā and Himavant were overjoyed and again and again did homage to Pārvatī's feet. All the people of the city, whatever their age, men and women alike, were equally delighted. Festive songs began to sound in the streets; golden vases were displayed; meats were dressed in various ways according to the rules of culinary science. But the banquet table in the palace inhabited by the great mother Bhavānī was altogether beyond description. The marriage guests—Viṣṇu, Brahmā and all the heavenly orders—were courteously entreated and took their seats line after line. Then the skilful servers began to serve and the women, when they found the gods dining, began to jest and banter in pleasant strains.

Chand 13

In pleasant strain with dark refrain they hint at love's delight;
Charmed with the song, the gods sit long, nor heed the waning night,
With growing zest each jovial guest prolongs the festive hour:
At last they rise; each bids adieu and seeks his separate bower.

Dohā 99

Again the sages went and reminded Himavant of the wedding day; and he, seeing the time was fit, sent and summoned all the gods,

Caupāī 100

whom he courteously addressed, and assigned to each an appropriate seat. An altar was prepared according to Vedic ritual, while the women chanted festal strains; and a divinely beautiful throne was erected, the handiwork of a god, beyond description. Then Śiva, after bowing to the Brāhmans, took his seat, remembering in his heart his own lord, Rāma. Then the high sages sent for Umā, who was brought in by her maidens, richly adorned. All the gods beholding her beauty were enraptured. What poet in the world could describe such loveliness ! The divinities who recognized in her the universal mother, the spouse of Mahādeva, adored her in their inmost soul—Bhavānī, the crown of beauty—whose praises would still be beyond me even though I had a myriad tongues.

Chand 14

A myriad tongues were all too few to sing her matchless grace:
When gods and muses shrink abashed, for Tulasī's rhyme what place ?
With downcast eyes the glorious dame passed up the hall, and fell,
Bee-like, at Siva's lotus feet, the lord she loved so well.

Dohā 100

At the injunction of the sages, both Śambhu and Bhavānī worshipped Gaṇeśa. Let no one be perplexed on hearing this, but know well that the gods are without beginning.

Caupāī 101

The whole marriage ceremony was performed by the sages in accordance with Vedic ritual, and the father, with *kusa* grass in his hand, took the bride and gave her to Śiva. When the two had joined hands, all the great gods rejoiced: the sages uttered the scriptural formulae, and the cry went up of "Glory, glory, glory to Śaṅkara !" All kinds of music began to play, and flowers were rained down from heaven. Thus was accomplished the marriage of Hara and Girijā amidst general rejoicing. The dowry given defies description—men-servants and maid-servants, horses, carriages, elephants, cows, raiment, jewellery, things of all sorts, and wagonloads of grain and golden vessels.

Chand 15

Thus great and more the dowry's store that King Himācala brought;
Yet falling low at Siva's feet he cried that all was nought.
The gracious lord cheered his sad sire in every way most meet,
Then Mainā came, most loving dame, and clasped his lotus feet :

Dohā 101

"Umā, my lord, is dear to me as life itself; take her as one of your servants, and pardon all her offences; this is the boon I beg of your favour."

Caupāī 102

After Sambhu had in every possible way reassured his wife's mother, she bowed her head before his feet and went home, there called for Umā, and taking her into her lap gave her this excellent instruction, "Be ever obedient to Śaṅkara; to say 'My lord and my god' is the sum of all wifely duty." At these words her eyes filled with tears, and again and again she pressed her daughter to her bosom, "Why has God created woman in the world, seeing that she is always in a state of subjection, and never can even dream of happiness ?" Though utterly distracted by motherly love, she knew it was no time to display it, and restrained herself. Running to her again and again, and falling down before her to clasp her feet in a transport of affection beyond all words, Bhavānī said adieu to all her companions, and then again went and clung to her mother's breast.

Chand 16

Still clinging to her mother's breast she cheered her weeping train,
Then with her handmaids sought her spouse, yet oft looked back again.
'Midst beggar's blessing, richly bought, forth rode the royal pair:
The glad gods rained down flowers, and sounds of music filled the air.

Dohā 102

Then went Himavant most lovingly to escort them, till with many words of consolation he on whose banner is blazoned the bull bade him farewell.

Caupāī 103

Then he came speedily to the palace, called all the hills and lakes, entreated them courteously with words and gifts, and allowed them to depart. They proceeded each to his own realm, and Śambhu arrived at Kailāsa. How shall I tell its delights when thus occupied by Sambhu and Bhavānī, the father and mother of the world, and their attendants ? They began to indulge in amorous dalliance, and every day some new pleasure. Thus a length of time passed and was born their six-headed son (Kārttikeya), who vanquished the demon Tāraka in battle. His birth is sung by all the sacred books and his deeds are known throughout the world.

Chand 17

All the world knows the story of the birth and the glory of Mahādeva's six-headed son;
And this is the cause why so briefly I pause on the generous deeds he hath done.
Man or maid, who shall tell, or sing true and well, how Śiva took Umā to wife,
Shall be happily wed, and, with blessinsg bestead, live at ease all the days of his life.

Dohā 103

The amorous doings of Girijā and her beloved are an ocean-like depth that not even the Vedas can cross; how then can a dull-witted clown such as Tulasī Dāsa succeed in describing them?

Caupāī 104

When the sage Bharadvāja had heard all this pleasant and delectable history of Śambhu's doings, he was delighted and longed to hear yet more. With overflowing eyes and every limb thrilling, he was so mastered by love that his tongue could not utter a word. On seeing his condition the great sage was pleased: "Blessed is thy birth, he said, to whom Gaurī's lord is dear as life. He who loves not Śiva's lotus feet can never dream of pleasing Rāma : a guileless love for Viśvanātha's (Śiva's) feet is the surest sign of faith in Rāma. For who is so faithful to Rāma as Śiva, who for no fault thus put away his wife Satī and made a vow, the pledge of unswerving fidelity ? And whom does Rāma hold more dear than Śiva ?

Dohā 104

So far I have told you of Śiva's deeds, knowing well the secret of your heart, that you are a true servant of Rāma, without any variableness.

Caupāī 105

I understand that you are virtuous and true; listen therefore while I proceed to recount Rāma's adventures. I cannot say how glad I am at this meeting with you to-day. Though Rāma's deeds are immeasurable, and not a myriad serpent kings could recount them all, yet I repeat the tale as it has been revealed, after fixing my thoughts on the god with bow in hand, who is the lord of the queen of speech. For Sarasvatī is like a puppet, and Rāma the manager who holds the hidden strings. When he finds a true believer, he graciously sets her to dance in the courtyard of the poet's fancy. To that gracious Raghunātha I bow before commencing the recital of the story of his most blameless perfection. Of all mountains the most beautiful was Kailāsa, where Śiva and Umā eternally dwell.

Dohā 105

Adepts, penitents, ascetics, gods, *kinnaras*, anchorites, and all pious souls came there to dwell and adore Mahādeva, the root of all joy.

Caupāī 106

But enemies of Hari and Hara, who had no love for religious discipline, could never even in a dream find their way to the place. On this mountain was an enormous banyan tree, which no time nor season could rob of its beauty; ever stirred by soft, cool, fragrant breezes and a shade from the hottest sun; a tree famous in sacred song[1] as Mahādeva's favourite haunt. Once on a time the lord went to rest beneath it, and in an excess of delight spread with his own hands his tiger-skin on the ground and there sat at ease; his body as fair in hue as the jasmine or the moon, his arms of great length, a hermit's cloth wrapt about his loins, his feet like lotus blossoms, and his toe-nails like gleams of light to dispel the darkness of faithful souls; his face more splendid than the brilliance of the moon in autumn : and his decorations, serpents and streaks of ashes.

Dohā 106

With his twisted coils of hair for a crown; with the Gaṅgā on his head; with full-orbed eyes like the lotus, and with the crescent moon on his brow; the blue-throated god shone forth in all his brilliancy.

1. *i.e.*, the Vedas.

Caupāī 107

So sat the enemy of Love, as it were Quietism embodied. Then Pārvatī, who is the great mother Bhavānī, approached, seeing her time. In recognition of her love he received her most courteously and enthroned her on his left side. Joyously she sat beside him and recalled her former life; and reckoning on his augmented attachment she spoke being fain to hear the salutary tale,—"O lord of the universe, my lord Purāri, your greatness is known throughout the three worlds; things moving or motionless, serpents, men and gods, all do homage to your lotus feet.

Dohā 107

You are the lord of all power and of all knowledge; the centre of art and science; the great storehouse of meditation, of wisdom and of asceticism; and your name is as the tree of life to the afflicted.

Caupāī 108

If, O essence of bliss, I have found favour in your sight, and you know me to be your own devoted servant, then, my lord, disperse my ignorance by reciting to me the story of Rāma. How can he who dwells beneath the tree of paradise know aught of sorrow that is born of want? Consider, O moon-decked lord, and relieve my mind of this perplexity. The saints, who preach salvation, declare that Rāma is the uncrested god; Śeṣanāga, Sarasvatī, the Veda, the Purāṇas, all sing his praises; you too, night and day, great conqueror of Love, reverently repeat his name. Is this Rāma the son of the King of Avadh, or some other uncreated, passionless, invisible Being ?

Dohā 108

If a king's son, and so distraught by the loss of his wife, then how the Supreme God ? When I compare his acts that I see with the eulogies that I hear, my mind is completely distracted.

Caupāī 109

Instruct me, my lord, with regard to him who is the passionless, all-pervading, almighty god. Be not wroth at my ignorance, but do what you can to remove it. In the wood, though I was too awe-stricken to tell you, I beheld the majesty of Rāma, yet my mind was so dull that I did not understand, and I reaped a just reward. Again today I am in doubt, and with clasped hands I beg of you to compassionate me: be not angry, nor say you have been taught already; the past is past; my infatuation is gone, and I have a hearty longing to hear the sacred story of Rāma's virtuous deeds. Declare it, O glory of the serpent king, great lord of heaven.

Dohā 109

Laying my head in the dust, I do homage to your feet and with folded hands entreat you to tell me all Raghubara's excellent glory, as extracted from scripture and philosophy.

Caupāī 110

Though a woman is not entitled to initiation, yet am I your servant in thought and word and deed; further, the saints do not forbid mystic instruction to a woman in great distress, and it is in extreme distress that I call upon you, heavenly king, for an account of Rāma. First, weigh well and declare to me the cause why the invisible Brahman assumed a visible body. Then, my lord, tell me of his incarnation and his pretty actions when a child, and how he wedded Jānakī, and for what fault he was exiled from his father's kingdom, and what he did when living in the forest, and how he slew Rāvaṇa, and how he amused himself when he recovered the throne, tell me all about him, most amiable Śaṅkara.

Dohā 110

Then tell me, gracious lord, of his marvellous acts, and how with all his subjects the jewel of Raghu's line passed to his own abode.

Caupāī 111

Next tell me, my lord, what it all means; explaining to me in full detail what is the intelligence that so absorbs the wisest sages; what is faith and wisdom and supreme knowledge and detachment from the world. Tell me also, O lord of purest understanding, the many other mysteries connected with Rāma; and if there be anything which I have omitted to ask, be kind enough not to suppress it. You, as the Vedas say, are the great teacher of the three worlds; what can other poor creatures know?" When Śiva heard Umā's winning and guileless speech he was glad; the whole of Rāma's acts thronged in upon his soul, his eyes were bedewed with tears and his very limbs thrilled with rapture; for the vision of Rāma entered his heart, and his ecstatic joy was beyond measure.

Dohā 111

For a brief space Mahādeva was lost in blissful contemplation; then he recovered himself and began with great joy to tell the tale of Rāma.

Caupāī 112

"He who knows not Rāma cannot distinguish between the false and the true, as a rope is mistaken for a snake; while as a dream vanishes away on awakening, so is it with those who look well and make sure. I reverence the child Rāma, most easy of access to all who repeat his name. Come to me, O home of bliss and bane of woe, as when thou usedst to sport in Daśaratha's courtyard." After thus doing reverence to Rāma, Tripurāri began his mellifluous speech,—"Blessed, blessed are you, O daughter of the mountain-king, there is no such benefactor as thou art. Thou hast asked for Rāma's history as potent as the Gaṅgā to sanctify the world; and it is on the world's account that thou hast asked, being thyself full of love for Rāma's feet.

Dohā 112

By the grace of Rāma, O Pārvatī, not even in sleep can doubt, error, delusion, or distress enter into your mind; this I know well:

Caupāī 113

but you have so put forward this old doubt as to benefit all who speak or hear. For the ears that hear not Rāma's story are mere snake-holes; the eyes that have not seen his true vision are like the false eyes in a peacock's tail; the heads that have not bowed at the feet of Hari's priest are of no more worth than bitter pumpkins. They whose heart is not inspired with faith in Hari are mere animated corpses; those who sing not his praises are like croaking frogs; and hard and impenetrable as a thunderbolt is their breast who hear his deeds and take no delight in them. Listen, O Girijā, to the mysterious deeds of Rāma, which are to gods a delight and to demons a delusion?

Dohā 113

Who is the good man that will not listen to the story of Rāma, which is like the heavenly cow, that fulfils every desire of the gods who tend it.

Caupāī 114

The story of Rāma is like the delightful clapping of the hands to frighten away the birds of doubt, or like an axe to fell the tree of the Kaliyuga; listen reverently, O daughter of the mountain-king. How sweet is the name of Rāma, and his ways and his deeds; his lives and his actions are declared by the scriptures to be beyond number. And as there is no end to Rāma, so the legends about him and his glory are endless: yet, seeing the greatness of your love, I will attempt to tell them to the best of my ability and as the scriptures have revealed. Your inquiries, Umā, are most becoming and profitable, such as the saints approve, and I too am pleased to hear: but, Bhavānī, there was one thing I did not like, though you spoke under the influence of a delusion; for you said,—'Is there some other Rāma whom the Vedas hymn and sages love to contemplate?'

Dahā 114

It is the vile wretches, whom the demon of delusion has in his clutch who utter and listen to such lies : heretics, who are the enemies of Hari and know no difference between truth and falsehood.

Caupāī 115

It is the ignorant, unlearned and blind reprobates, the mirror of whose mind is clouded by a film of sensuality, the lewd, treacherous and desperately perverse, who never even in a dream visit the assembly of the sages—it is they who utter doctrines repugnant to the Veda, with no understanding of loss or gain ; their glass is dim, their eyes are naught : how then can such hapless wights see the beauty of Rāma ? Unable to distinguish between the material and immaterial, they jabber many lying words, and under Hari's delusive influence go utterly astray in the world; for whom no words are too strong. Windy, devilish, drunken, they can utter nothing to the purpose, and are so intoxicated with a strong delusion that no one should give ear to their ravings.

Soraṭhā 115

Being thus assured in your heart, discard all doubt and worship Rāma's feet. Listen, O daughter of the Mountain-king, and the sun of my words shall disperse all the mists from your soul.

Caupāī 116

There is no difference between the personal and the impersonal, so declare saints and sages, the Vedas and the Purāṇas. The formless, invisible and uncreated Immaterial, out of love for the faithful, becomes materialized. How can this be ? In the same way as water is crystallized into ice. But how can He be subject to sensual delusion whose very name is like the sun to disperse the darkness of error ? In Rāma, who is the Supreme Being, Consciousness and Bliss and the sun of the world, the night of delusion can have no part whatever; and in the lord, who is himself true light, there can be no dawn of understanding ; neither joy nor sorrow, neither knowledge nor ignorance; neither personal piety, nor the sins of vanity and pride; but Rāma is the omnipresent Absolute, the blissful Lord of all, the most ancient Being;

Dohā 116

the Great Spirit, the glorious fount of light; the Revealed, the Incomprehensible, the jewel of the family of Raghu, my own lord !" So saying Śiva bowed the head.

Caupāī 117

"The ignorant do not perceive their own error, but, senseless that they are, attribute their delusion to the lord; like simple folk, who, seeing a clouded sky, say that the sun itself is dim, or who gaze at the moon through their fingers and fancy they see it doubled. Delusion, O Umâ, affects Râma in the same way as smoke, or a cloud, or dust affects the brightness of the sky. The five objects of sense, the organs of sense, the gods of sense, as well as the soul, are all in their degree possessed of intelligence;[1] but the great enlightener of them all is the eternal Râma, the lord of Avadh. Whatever in the world is susceptible of enlightenment Râma enlightens; every delusion is subject to him: in him centre all knowledge and virtue; and by his truth the dulness of material creation shines bright as the Ideal, the senses contributing to the deception.

Dohā 117

Though false as the silver in the oyster-shell and moisture in the sun's rays, yet no one, at any time, past, present or future, can rid himself of the delusion.

Caupāī 118

And such is the world in its dependence on Hari: though unreal, it can cause pain; in the same way as a man who dreams that his head is cut off, is in pain till he awakes. None can declare his beginning or his end, though holy scripture has hymned him as best it could. He moves without feet,[2] he hears without ears, and works in manifold ways, yet without hands. Without a mouth he enjoys all tastes, and without a voice is the

1. Even inanimate nature has an unconscious intelligence : reason, order and activity pervade the material universe, the mineral as well as the animal and vegetable kingdoms.—*Mivart*.

2. None hath beheld him, none,
Seen above other gods and shapes of things,
Swift without feet and flying without wings.
—*Swinburne*.

aptest of speakers; he can see without eyes, touch without limbs, and without a nose catch every scent. His actions are thus in every way supernatural, and his greatness is utterly beyond description.

Dohā 118

He whom the Vedas and men of wisdom have thus sung, and whom the saints love to contemplate is no other than the Lord God, son of Daśaratha, King of Kosala, who loves his votaries.

Caupāī 119

By the might of his name I exalt to the regions of the blessed any creature whom I see dying at Kāśī; he is the sovereign of all creation, animate and inanimate, my lord Raghuvara, who reads the secrets of all hearts. By repeating his name even involuntarily the most abandoned of sinners burns up the accumulated crimes of many previous existences; and by those who devoutly meditate upon him the ocean of life is as easily crossed as a puddle in the road. Rāma, O Bhavānī, is the Supreme Spirit, and the erro to which you gave utterance on this point was most improper. Such doubt, when entertained in the heart, destroys knowledge, sobriety and every virtue." On hearing Siva's luminous exposition, the whole structure of heresy fell to pieces; her love and devotion to Raghupati grew strong, and her sore incredulity passed away.

Dohā 119

Again and again, clasping her lord's lotus feet and suppliantly folding her lotus hands, her whole soul overflowing with affection, Girijā thus spoke and said,—

Caupāī 120

"My grievous delusion, like the feverish heat of autumn, has yielded to the moon-like spell of your voice. In your compassion you have resolved all my doubt, and I now understand the reality of Rāma.By my lord's mercy my distress is all gone, and I am made glad by his favour. Now regarding me as your own immediate servant, though I am but a poor ignorant woman, if

I have really found grace in your sight, reply to those my former questions. If Rāma be the Absolute, pure Consciousness, immortal, untouched by aught and yet ever abiding in the city of the hearts of all, why did he take the form of a human being? Declare and explain this to me." On hearing Umā's very modest prayer, and perceiving her sincere desire to be instructed in Rāma's history,

Dohā 120*a*

the all-wise Śaṅkara, the enemy of Kāmadeva, was glad of heart, and lavishing many a word of praise on Umā, was thus pleased to speak,—

Sorațhā 120*b*-120*d*

"Listen, Bhavānī, while I recite in auspicious strains the Rāma-carita-mānasa, or the unsullied Lake of Rāma's deeds, as of old Bhuśuṇḍī[1] declared it in the hearing of Garuḍa, the king of birds. I shall tell you later the manner of their exalted converse, after which you shall hear of Rāma's incarnation and his all-glorious and sinless deeds. Infinite are the names and virtues of Hari; his stories and his forms beyond number or measure I tell them as best as I can; listen, Umā, with respect.

Caupāī 121

Listen, Girijā, to the grateful tale of Hari's great and holy acts, as they have been recorded in the Vedas and the Āgamas. The cause of Hari's incarnation is not to be dogmatically defined; for to my mind, Bhavānī, Rāma is beyond the grasp of intellect, or soul, or speech; yet, as saints and sages, the Veda and the Purāṇas have partly and to the extent of their capacity explained the matter, so I, fair dame, will now declare to you the cause as I understand it. Whenever virtue decays, and evil spirits, waxing strong in pride, work inequity beyond the telling, to the confusion of Brāhmaṇas, cows, gods and earth itself, the

1. Kāka-bhuśuṇḍī, originally a Śudra of Ayodhyā, was by virtue of his birth in that holy place and the intercession of a saint of Ujjain born again as a Brāhmaṇa. His exclusive devotion to Rāma could not suffer him to listen to the Ṛṣi Lomas when he made Brahman the theme of his discourse, and the sage was so annoyed that he changed him for a time into a crow (*Kāka*). His story is told at length in Book VII.

compassionate Lord assumes various bodily forms and relieves the distress of the faithful;

Dohā 121

slays the demons; reinstates the gods; maintains the way of salvation; and diffuses the brightness of his glory throughout the world. Such are the motives of Rāma's incarnations.

Caupāī 122

Singing his glory, Rāma's votaries cross the sea of birth and death, and it is for their sake only that the compassionate Lord assumes a body. The causes of Rāma's incarnations have been many and various, each more wonderful than the others. I will relate one or two of his previous births, if, Bhavānī, you are prepared to give me your devout attention. Hari had once two loving doorkeepers, the famous Jaya and Vijaya. Both brothers, in consequence of a Brāhmaṇa's curse, were born again in the form of the malignant demons Hiraṇyakaśipu and Hiraṇyākṣa, who became celebrated throughout the world as the tamers of the pride of the king of heaven. Assuming the form of a Boar, he triumphed in battle over the first illustrious hero and dest oyed him, and again, in the Narasiṁha avatār, slew the second; the fame of the faithful Prahlāda is widespread.

Dohā 122

Then the evil spirits went and took birth as demons, strong and mighty in battle, Kumbhakarṇa and Rāvaṇa, who, as all the world knows, subdued even the gods.

Caupāī 123

Though slain by the deity, they did not win salvation for the Brāhmaṇa had doomed them to three births. They then were once the cause why the cherisher of the faithful assumed a body, and at that time his parents, Kaśyapa and Aditi, were incarnate as Daśaratha and Kauśalyā of glorious memory. Thus in one aeon he descended from heaven and wrought saving deeds on earth. In another aeon, seeing the gods distressed and waging ineffectual battle with Jalandhar, Śambhu warred against him times without number, but could not subdue the valiant demon, for the exceeding virtue of his wife protected him against Purâri's every attack.

Dohā 123

By a stratagem the Lord broke her vow of chastity and accomplished the purpose of the gods. When she discovered the deception, then in her wrath she cursed him.

Caupāī 124

And Hari did according to her curse; for though the Lord God, he is full of playfulness and of mercy. So Jalandhar was born as Râvaṇa, and being killed in battle by Rāma attained to high glory. This then was one cause of his birth and the reason why Râma then assumed a human form. Each avatār[1] has its legend, which the poets have sung in various ways and according to tradition. "On one occasion it was Nārada's curse that caused him to become incarnate for his sake." At this saying Girijā was astounded,—"Nârada is a wise sage and a votary of Viṣṇu's; what was his reason for uttering a curse ? What offence had Lakṣmī's lord committed ? Tell me the whole story, Purâri; it is passing strange that a saint should have fallen a prey to delusion."

Dohā 124*a*

Then answered Mahādeva with a smile,—"No one is enlightened or deluded; man is ever such as Raghupati will have him to be."

Soraṭhā 124*b*

I sing the glory of Rāma; listen devoutly, O Bharadvāja. And said Yājñavalkya, do thou, O Tulasī, put away the intoxication of pride and worship Raghunātha, the destroyer of birth and death.

Caupāī 125

In the Himālaya mountains there is a very sacred cave close to the holy Gaṅgâ. Seeing this pure and delightful retreat, the

1. *i.e.*, incarnation.

divine seer Nârada was greatly pleased; and as he gazed upon the beauty of the rocks and the forest glades he was filled with passionate love for God, and as he thought upon Hari the curse[1] was lifted and his spotless soul fell all at once into a trance. When the king of heaven saw the sage's state he feared, and, summoning Kāma, addressed him courteously—"Go, I beg, with your assistants to do me service." He then, the god of love, went off very gladly; but in Indra's mind was great alarm, for he thought,—'The saint would rob me of my kingdom.' All the world over, a gallant or a miser is as much afraid of interference as is a thievish crow.

Dohā 125

Like a wretched dog that on seeing a lion runs away with the dry bone it has in its mouth, for fear it should be taken from him, so was Indra in his shamelessness.

Caupāī 126

When the god of lòve reached the sage's retreat, his deceptive power created false spring. All the trees broke out into many-coloured blossoms, there was a murmuring of cuckoos and a humming of bees. A delightful air, soft, cool and fragrant, sprang up, fanning the flame of passion; while Rambhā and the other heavenly nymphs, all well skilled in the arts of the peerless Archer, began to sing songs in every variety of measure and play all kinds of games, ball in hand. When Love saw himself so well supported, he was glad and again manifested his creative power in diverse ways; but his devices had no effect upon the sage; and guilty Love began to tremble for himself. Who dare trespass on his bounds who has the great Ramāpati for a guardian?

Dohā 126

In dire dismay both Kāmadeva and those who helped him confessed themselves defeated, and went and clasped the holy man's feet and in accents of the deepest humility begged forgiveness.

1. The curse had been pronounced by Dakṣa.

Caupāī 127

There was no anger in Nārada's heart, who in friendly terms replied to Kāmadeva and reassured him. Then, bowing the head at his feet and obtaining his leave, they both retired, the god and his companion; and repairing to Indra's court there related all their own doings and the sage's clemency. As they listened to the tale all were amazed, and bowing the head to Hari extolled the sage. Then went Nārada to Śiva, greatly proud of his victory over Love, and told him all Love's doings. In acknowledgment of his affection Mahādeva gave him good advice,—"O great sage, again and again I beg of you never to repeat to Hari this story that you have now told me : should it happen to be brought forward, keep it as dark as possible."

Dohā 127

Good as Śiva's advice was, it did not please Nārada. Hear, Bharadvāja, what strange thing happened and see the omnipotence of Hari's will.

Chaupāī 128

What Rāma wills to have done is done, and there is no one who can alter it. As Śambhu's words did not please the saint, he went straight to Brahmā's court, and, to the accompaniment of the famous lute that he had in his hand, sang right through the excellent song of Hari's praises. Then he passed on to the milky ocean, where abides Viṣṇu, the glory of revelation. In great joy rose Lakṣmī's lord and ran to meet him, and side by side they sat together. Said the sovereign of the universe with a smile,—'Reverend sir,'tis long since you last did me this honour.' Then Nārada declared the whole story of Love's doings, though Śiva had beforehand cautioned him; the delusive power of Raghupati is so strong that there is no man living who can resist it.

Dohā 128

Then spoke the great god, with a stern look, but in flattering terms,—"Self-delusion and the intoxicating arrogance of love shall perish at the remembrance of your doings.[1]

1. Śiva's speech is so ambiguously worded that it really conveys a censure, while Nārada interprets it as a compliment. The hidden meaning

Caupāī 129

Know, O sage, that the mind of him alone is susceptible to infatuation who is devoid of wisdom and self-governance; but what pain can Love cause to one so steadfast in asceticism as yourself ?" Said Nārada in his pride,—'It is all your favour, my Lord.' The Compassionate Lord saw into his heart and thought within himself,— "Pride like a huge tree has sprouted in his soul : I must at once tear it up by the roots: ever to relieve my servants is the vow that I have made. I will surely contrive some sportive device on behalf of the sage." Then Nārada bowed his head at Hari's feet and took his leave, swelling with pride; while Viṣṇu set his Māyā[1] into operation. Listen now to his strange contrivance.

Dohā 129

He fashioned on the road a city with an area of eight hundred square miles, more perfect even than Viṣṇu's own capital, in its manifold architectural beauties,

Caupāī 130

and inhabited by such graceful men and women that you would take them all to be incarnations of Kāmadeva and Rati. The king of the city, by name Śīlanidhi, had companies of horses, elephants and troops beyond number; his royal pomp like that of a hundred Indras; himself a centre of power, policy and magnificence. His daughter, Viśvamohinī, was so beautiful that even Lakṣmī would be put to the blush, and by Hari's delusive power was in every way so exquisite that no words could describe her. As the princess was selecting a husband, innumerable princes came as suitors, The sage, too, came to the fairy city and began making inquiries of the people. When he had heard all that was going on, he proceeded to the palace, where the king most respectfully gave him a seat.

is: Hereafter when you reflect upon this incident and all its consequences, you will take a lesson by it and be more humble, remembering your weakness; but the more obvious meaning of the words and that in which Nārada took them is: By meditating on your triumph over Love, other men will triumph too.

1. *i.e.*, his deluding potency, his magic power.

Dohā 130

And then brought the princess for him to see, saying,—'Tell me, good sir, after consideration, all that is good or bad about her.'

Caupāī 131

When Nārada beheld her beauty, he forgot his vow of continence and continued long gazing at her. The auspicious marks on her body quite fascinated him; yet he would not in words express his heart's delight. "Her bridegroom must be one of the immortals, invincible in battle, reverenced by all creation; such a one must Śīlanidhi's daughter wed." But, though he calculated her fortune thus correctly, he kept it to himself, and after saying something or other to the king, to the effect that his daughter would be of good fortune, he went away full of anxiety, considering,—"What scheme can I devise now, so as to make her marry me ? No time is this for prayers or penance; O God, how am I to win the girl ?

Dohā 131

On this occasion I must make myself exceedingly charming and beautiful, so that the princess may be pleased when she sees me and give me the wreath of victory.

Caupāī 132

I will ask Hari for the gift of beauty; but in going to him there will be much delay. I have no friend who desires my weal as Hari does; this is an opportunity for him to help me." So he offered up a fervent prayer and the merciful Lord appeared before him. The sage's eyes brightened at the sight and his heart rejoiced that his purpose would be accomplished. He then with the utmost humility told his tale, and added,—"O, my Lord, be gracious and assist me. Bestow on me beauty equal to your own; for in no other way can I get possession of her. Make haste to accomplish my success; for I am your slave." When the Compassionate saw the mighty influence of the deception he had wrought, he smiled to himself :

Dohā 132

"Listen, O Nārada; I will assuredly bring about your highest good—that and naught else; nor shall my words prove untrue.

Caupāī 133

Hear, ascetic sage; if a stick man, distracted by his disease, ask for food that will harm him, the physician will not grant it. In the same way will I act as is best for you." So saying the Lord vanished. The sage was so infatuated by the power of illusion that he did not understand Hari's obscure speech, but hastened at once to the spot where the marriage arena had been prepared. The royal suitors were seated rank upon rank, each with his retinue in grant attire. The sage thought joyfully within himself,—'My beauty is such that she will never leave me to wed another.' But the merciful God, the saint's true friend, had made him hideous beyond all description. Everyone recognized him as Nārada and bowed the head, knowing nothing of what had taken place.

Dohā 133

"Now there were there two of Siva's henchmen who knew the whole secret. Dressed like Brāhmaṇas, they seemed to be spectators of the show, walking here and there and looking about.

Caupāī 134

"Both went and sat down in the same rank with the sage so proud of his beauty; and in their Brahmanical attire they attracted no notice. They uttered sarcastic words so that Nārada might hear, 'Hari has given this man such excellent beauty that the princess will be charmed with his appearance and will certainly wed him, taking him for Hari[1] himself.' The sage was so utterly subjugated by passion that Śambhu's servants could laugh and jeer as they liked, and though he heard their subtle jeers, his intellect was too bewildered to understand them. No one perceived the transformation save only the princess, who, on beholding him just as he was with his monkey face and deformed body, was quite disgusted at the sight,

1 The word also signifies 'monkey'.

Dohā 134

" and with her attendant maidens glided like a swan through the long line of kings with the wreath of victory in her lotus hands.

Caupāī 135

"She would not let her eyes rest for a moment on the spot where Nārada was sitting, swollen with pride. The sage in his anxiety kept fidgetting about, and Śiva's attendants smiled to see his plight. Then entered the gracious Lord, in form as a king, and gladly the maiden cast on him the garland. Thus Lakṣmī's lord carried off the bride, to the despair of the assembled kings. The sage was much disturbed; in his infatuation his reason was quite gone, like a diamond dropt out of a hole in a bag. Then said Śiva's attendants with a smile,—'Get a glass and look at yourself'; and having so said both ran away in great alarm. The sage looked at his reflection in the water. When he saw himself, he was furious and cursed them with a dreadful curse:

Dohā 135

'Go false and guilty pair, and become demons of the night. Be this your reward for mocking me; mock again a saint, if you dare.'

Caupāī 136

"Looking again into the water he saw himself in his proper form; yet still he was not content at heart, but his lips quivered with rage, and in haste he betook himself to Viṣṇu. 'Shall I curse him or kill myself, seeing that he has made a mock of me throughout the world?' On the way the conqueror of demons met him, and with him Rāma and the princess. With a smile and in gentle tones he said,—'Where goes the sage like one distracted?' On hearing these words, his anger rose, and infatuation utterly mastered his reason,—'You never could bear to look upon another's prosperity; your envy and deceit are notorious; at the churning of the ocean you drove Śiva mad and made the gods quaff the poisoned cup.

Dohā 136

"'Intoxicating liquor was the demon's share, and the poison was for Mahādeva; but for yourself Ramā and the *Kaustubha* jewel! You have ever been self-centred and deceitful and eternally treacherous in your dealings.

Caupāī 137

"Utterly self-willed, with no one to restrain you, and bent on doing whatever comes into your mind; confounding the good and exalting the bad; with a heart incapable either of surprise or pleasure; trying every one with your tricks, without the slightest consideration and in mere lightness of heart. Neither good deeds nor bad in any way affect you, nor has any one up to the present ever succeeded in restraining you. Now for this fine treat that you have given me you shall receive a due return. Be born in the form in which you cheated me ! This is my curse. And as you have made me like a monkey, you shall have monkeys for helpmates; and in the same way as you have sorely wronged me, so shall you be distressed by the loss of your wife.?'

Dohā 137

"The lord gladly accepted the curse and humbly begged Nārada's forgiveness thus working the will of the gods, and in his compassion withdrew the influence of his deceptive power.

Caupāī 138

"When Hari lifted the spell of his illusion, there appeared neither Ramā nor the princess; then in dire dismay the sage clasped the feet of Hari, ever ready to heal the sorrows of a suppliant, crying,— 'May my curse be made of no effect.' Said the gracious god,— 'It is my will,.' Said the sage,—'I have spoken many injurious words; how shall my guilt be expiated?' 'Go and repeat Śaṅkara's hundred names, and your soul will at once be relieved. There is no one so dear to me as Śiva; never let your faith in this truth be shaken. He on whom Śiva will not show mercy shall never know true love to me. Think on this as you wander through the earth; my illusion shall haunt you no more.'

Dohā 138

"Having thus reassured the sage, the Lord disappeared, and Nārada took his way to Paradise,[1] chanting Rāma's praises as he went."

Caupāī 139

"Śiva's attendents saw him walking on the road, rejoicing and in his right mind. In great alarm they drew near, and clasping his feet made their supplication : 'O great sage, we are not Brāhmaṇas, but servants of Mahādeva, and have reaped the fruit of our great sin: in your mercy remove the curse.' Said the compassionate Nārada,—'You must both be born as demons of vast power, majesty and strength; but when you have subdued the universe by the might of your arm, Viṣṇu shall take the form of man, and dying in battle at his hand you shall attain to salvation, nor ever be born again.' After bowing their head at his feet, both went their way and in due course were born as demons."

Dohā 139

"In one aeon this was the reason why the lord became incarnate, to gladden the gods, to comfort the saints, and to ease earth of its burdens."

Caupāī 140

"Thus Hari's lives and acts are many and various, but all of them glorious, beneficent and wonderful. Aeon after aeon he has manifested himself and wrought many excellent works; and on each occasion high sages have sung his acts in holy strains of choicest verse, relating marvellous histories of diverse kinds, which the wise hear without any amazement. For as Hari is infinite so are there infinite verses about him, which are heard and repeated by scripture and the faithful. The delightful adventures of Rāmacandra could not all be sung in ten thousand aeons. This story that I have now told, Bhavānī, shows how Hari's deceptive power can infatuate even saints and sages. He, the lord, is sportive, gracious to suppliants, accessible to his servants, and a remover of all sorrow."

1. Satyaloka or the seventh paradise, the abode of Brahma.

Soraṭhā 140

"There is neither god, man, nor sage whom unreality has not infatuated. Reflect upon this and worship the great master of the unreal.

Caupāī 141

"Hear, O daughter of the Himālaya, yet another reason, which I will proceed to relate at full length, why the uncreated, the impersonal, the formless Brahma became king of Kośala. The Lord, whom you saw roaming in the forest with his brother in hermit's garb; at whose doings, Bhavānī, when you were Satī, lost your sense, and still to this day the shadow of this disease pursues you; the recital of his adventures will heal all your sickness. All his sportive acts in that incarnation I am now about to tell as best I can." O Bharadvāja, on hearing Śaṅkara thus speak, the modest and affectionate Umā smiled for joy, while her lord continued to relate the cause of the incarnation.

Dohā 141

I am now about to tell you the same story; listen, great sage, with attention, the glorious story of Rāma can cleanse all the stains of the world and bring man to heaven.

Caupāī 142

Manu, Svāyambhuva and Śatarūpā[1] of whom was born the whole human race, were a wedded pair: even to this day the fame of their virtue and conjugal fidelity is celebrated in the scriptures. Their son was King Uttānapāda, who begot Hari's faithful votary,Dhruva. The younger son, by name Priyavrata, is mentioned with praise both by the Vedas and Purāṇas. Their daughter, Devahūti, became the devoted wife of Kardama the sage and in her womb the eternal Lord God, in his mercy and compassion, planted Kapila, the author of the Sāṅkhya philosophy, the divine exponent of the theory of entities. This Manu reigned a long while, upholding in every way all God's commandments.

1. *i.e.*, the son of the self-existing.

Soraṭhā 142

But in a palace complete detachment from worldly affairs is impracticable, Old age came upon him, and he thought with grief,—'My life has been spent without any true devotion to Hari."

Caupāī 143

Then perforce he resigned the throne to his son, and with his queen repaired to the forest, to Naimiṣa, famous among all holy places as specially sacred and liberal of success. Glad of heart, King Manu sought the spot where dwelt the company of saints and sages; and as the resolute pair passed along the way they appeared to be incarnations of Wisdom and Faith. On reaching the bank of the Gomatī, they bathed with delight in the clear stream; and there the inspired saints and sages came to meet them, recognizing in the king a champion of virtue. Devoutly the sages took them to visit each different shrine, and with emaciated bodies, clad in hermit's robes, they were ever in the assembly of the faithful listening to the Purāṇas.

Dohā 143

Husband and wife devoutly repeated the twelve-syllabled charm[1] with their whole soul firmly fixed on the lotus feet of Vāsudeva.

Caupāī 144

Meditating on the Supreme Brahman, True Being, Consciousness and Bliss, they lived on leaves and fruit and roots. Then, doing penance for Hari's sake, they gave up roots and fruit for water only. Ever in their hearts was an endless craving to see with their eyes the Supreme Lord, impersonal, indivisible, without beginning or end, whom mystics contemplate: whom the Vedas define as the unutterable,[2] the pure spirit, without attributes and beyond all comparison, as part of whom are produced many a Śambhu, Brahmā, and Viṣṇu. "Yet so great a god", they thought,

1. The twelve-syllabled charm is *Om Namo Bhagavate Vāsudevāya.*
2. "Not thus, not thus.".

"submits to his own servants, and for their sake assumes in sport a body. If this be true, as the scriptures have declared, our desire will be accomplished."

Dohā 144

In this way they spent six thousand years, living only on water; and then seven thousand, living only on air.

Caupāī 145

Next, for ten thousand years they even gave up air and remained, each of them, standing on one leg. Now Brahmā, Hari and Hara saw this interminable penance and repeatedly came to Manu and tempted them in many ways, saying,—'Ask your boon'; but for all their persuasion they were too steadfast to move. Though their bodies were reduced to mere skeletons, there was not the least pain in their soul. Then the omniscient lord knew that the king and queen were his servants and had this single object in practising such austerities. A solemn voice full of ambrosial grace sounded in the sky, saying: 'Ask, ask a boon!' It was a voice so glorious that it would quicken the dead. As it dropped upon the ears and entered their hearts, their bodies became again as comely and stout as if they had only that day left their home.

Dohā 145

As the ambrosial voice rang in their ears, they quivered and thrilled. Falling on the ground in an irrepressible transport of love, Manu thus spoke,—

Caupāī 146

"Hearken, O thou that art the tree of paradise and the Heavenly Cow to thy servants; the dust on whose feet is ever worshipped by Brahmā, Hari and Hara, accessible to the faithful, bringer of every joy, protector of suppliants and Lord of all creation. If, O friend of the friendless, I have found favour in thy sight, then in thy mercy grant me this boon; let me with mine own eyes behold thee in that form in which thou dwellest in Śiva's breast, which the saints desire to see; the swan in the lake of Bhuśuṇḍī's soul; the sum and the negation of all attributes; the theme of the Veda: do me this grace, O thou that healest the woes of every suppliant." This gentle, submissive and affectionate speech of the wedded pair went to the heart of the generous and merciful god; and the sovereign of the universe manifested himself.

Dohā 146

In hue as the blue lotus or the sapphire; dark as a rain-laden cloud; of such lustrous form that myriads of Loves were put to shame when they saw it.

Caupāī 147

With a face perfect in beauty like the autumnal moon; with lovely cheeks and chin and dimpled neck, red lips and gleaming teeth, and a nose and smile more radiant than a moonbeam; eyes bright as a lotus bud and a glance to fascinate the heart; curved eyebrows surpassing in charm Love's bow; a sect mark glistening on his forehead; golden fish-shaped earrings in his ears and a bright crown on his head; crisp curling hair like a swarm of bees; on his breast the Śrīvatsa[1] and a long wreath of sweet wild flowers, and jewelled adornments about his neck; a waist like a lion, a comely Brāhmaṇical thread, and exquisite clasps upon his arms, long and round as an elephant's trunk; with a quiver at his side and bow and arrow in his hand;

Dohā 147

his yellow garments more lustrous than the lightning; his body charmingly dimpled, and his navel like a bee hovering over the dark eddies of the Yamunā;

Caupāī 148

his lotus feet beautiful beyond description, haunted by the bee-like souls of the saints. On his left side shines in equal glory the Primal Energy, queen of beauty, mother of the world; of whose members are born countless Umās and Ramās and Brahmāṇīs, all alike perfect; by the play of whose eyebrows a world flashes into existence, even Sītā, enthroned at Rāma's side.

1. Viṣṇu is said to have a mark or curl, Śrīvatsa, on his breast.

As Manu and Śatarūpā beheld this vision of Hari in all his beauty, gazing fixedly with open eyes, they adored his incomparable magnificence, nor could be satiated with the sight. Overcome with delight and transported out of themselves, they fell prostrate clasping his feet with their hands. But the gracious lord putting his lotus hand upon their heads quickly raised them up.

Dohā 148

Then said the compassionate Lord, "Be assured that I am pleased with you. Ask now whatever boon you will, regarding me as the giver of all good."

Caupāī 149

On hearing the lord's words, Manu folded his hands in prayer, and taking courage gently spoke,—"O Lord, we have seen your lotus feet, and our every object has been accomplished. Yet one longing remains, and I know not whether to describe it as easy or difficult of attainment. It is easy, my master, for you to give; but so far as my meanness is concerned, it is difficult. Like a beggar who has found the tree of paradise but trembles to ask for too good fortune, not realizing its full power, so my heart is troubled by doubt. O my god, you read all hearts and know what I wish; grant my desire."— "O king, hesitate not, but ask of me; there is nothing I would not give you."

Dohā 149

"O gracious lord," said Manu, "I will declare honestly the crowning boon: for can anything be hid from you? I would have a son like you."

Caupāī 150

On seeing his love and hearing his sincere words, said the Compassionate, "So be it! Where can I go to find my own equal?" "I myself, O king, will be born as your son." Then, seeing Śatarūpā with her hands still folded, he said, "O lady, ask whatever boon you please." "O my lord," she replied, "the boon my husband has wisely asked is what I too should most desire. But it is great presumption; though in your clemency you have confirmed it. You are father of all the gods, the lord of the world, the supreme spirit, the omniscient; and therefore my mind doubts; and yet the Lord's words cannot fail. O Lord, the bliss that is enjoyed and the future state that is attained by your own servants—

Dohā 150

in your mercy grant to me even that bliss, that liberation, that faith, that devotion to your feet, that insight, and that mode of living."

Caupāī 151

Hearing this speech, so soft and profound and charming and sweet, the ocean of grace gently replied, "Fear not; whatever your mind desires that I have granted. O mother, your supernatural wisdom by my favour shall never fail." Then again spoke Manu, worshipping his feet, "I too have another petition, my lord. Is there any one who will not call me fool for devoting myself to your feet simply on account of a son? As a snake's hood without a jewel, or a fish without water, so is my life dependent upon you !" Begging this boon, he remained clasping his feet till the All-merciful said, "Be it so : now, as I order, go and dwell at Indra's capital.

Soraṭhā 151

There, my friend, enjoy yourself freely; and again, when some time has passed, be born as the King of Avadh, and I will be your son.

Caupāī 152

Voluntarily assuming human guise, I will manifest myself in your palace, my friend, and with every element of my divinity incarnate will do great deeds for the happiness of my votaries. Blessed are they who listen reverently; quitting the vain conceits of self they shall pass over the ocean of life. Even this Māyā, the Primal Energy, by whom the visible world was created, that self-same shadow of me here present, shall also become incarnate. I will accomplish your desire; true is my promise, true, aye ! true." Again and again thus saying, the blessed lord of grace vanished from sight, and the wedded pair, full of faith in the All-merciful, stayed for a while at the hermitage, and then, when their time was come, passed painlessly out of the body and took up their abode in Amarāvatī, the city of the immortals.

Dohā 152

Such was the sacred legend which Śiva related to Umā. Hearken now, O Bharadvāja, to yet another cause of Rāma's incarnation.

Caupāī 153

Listen, sage, to the holy and ancient tale as it was narrated by Śambhu to Girijā. There is a world-famous principality called Kekaya, and Satyaketu was its king. A champion of religion; a storehouse of political wisdom; great in glory, magnificence, virtue and power. He had two gallant sons, staunch in war, repositories of all virtues. The elder and the heir to the throne was named Pratāpabhānu, and the other Arimardana, of unequalled strength of arm and like a rock to stand the brunt of battle. The sympathy between brother and brother was perfect, and their mutual affection without either flaw or disguise.[1] To the elder son the king resigned the realm and withdrew into the woods to devote himself to religion.

Dohā 153

When Pratāpabhānu became king, his succession was proclaimed throughout the land. He looked after his subjects with utmost care as the Vedas enjoined, and not a speck of sin was allowed anywhere.

1. I read this couplet as follows : *Bhāihi bhāihi param samīti, sakal-dosh-chhal-barjita prīti* : the penultimate syllable of *samiti* being lengthened *metrigratia*. Such a license is of frequent occurrence; but in this particular instance it appears to have troubled the copyists, who have made various substitutions all more or less injurious to the sense.

Caupāī 154

The prime minister, Dharmaruci, a second Śukra,[1] was as devoted to the king as he was wise. With a prudent counsellor, a valiant brother, himself an embodiment of glory and daring in war, with a countless host of horse and foot, and chariots and elephants, and fighting men beyond number, all eager for the fray, the king might well rejoice as he inspected his army 'mid the clash of tumultuous music. Having fixed an auspicious day, he marched forth with a special force, bent on universal conquest. In all his numerous battles, wherever they took place, the pride of kings was abased; all the seven continents were reduced by the might of his arm, and their princes escaped only on payment of tribute. At that time Pratāpabhānu became the sole monarch of the whole round world.

Dohā 154

Having thus subdued the whole world by the might of his arm, he re-entered his capital and devoted himself in turn to business, duty, love and other delights.

Caupāī 155

The grateful earth, invigorated by Pratāpabhānu's sway, became a glorious cow of plenty, and all his subjects, both men and women, happy and free from all annoyance, grew in virtue and beauty. The minister Dharmaruci, devoted to Hari's feet lovingly instructed his lord in state policy; nor did the king ever fail in due reverence either to his spiritual teacher, or the gods, or the saints, or his departed ancestors, or the Brāhmaṇas. All the duties which are enjoined upon kings in the Veda he performed with reverence and delight. Every day he made large offerings and heard the scriptures read, both the Vedas and the Purāṇas; and he constructed many baths and wells and tanks, flower gardens and beautiful orchards, handsome monasteries and temples, and also restored every ancient shrine.

Dohā 155

For every single sacrifice enjoined in the Vedas or the Purāṇas the king in his zeal performed a thousand.

1. The regent of the planet Śukra (Venus) is the preceptor of the Daityas, or Titans.

Caupāī 156

In his heart there was no aiming after advantage, but being a man of supreme wisdom and discernment, he dedicated to God the whole merit of all his thoughts, words, and actions. One day he mounted his gallant steed and went, with his retinue equipped for the chase, into a dense forest of the Vindhyācala mountains and killed many fine deer. As he ranged the wood, he spied a wild boar, showing amid the foliage like Rāhu with the moon in his clutch; its orb too large to be contained in his mouth, though his rage will not suffer him to entirely disgorge it. The monstrous boar with its splendid tusks, as I have described them, and its enormous limbs of immeasurable bulk, grunted when he heard the tramp of the horse. It, too, at the sound of the horse approaching pricked up its ears and watched alertly.

Dohā 156

On seeing the huge boar, resembling some purple mountain-peak, the king whipped up his horse and rode on with speed, challenging it at the same time, "Now you can't escape!"

Caupāī 157

When it saw the horse coming on with speed, the beast took to flight swift as the wind, keeping close to the ground as it went, and ever regarding the shaft which the king had at once fitted to his bow. Taking steady aim he let it fly; but the boar evaded it and escaped, and rushed on now well in sight, and now altogether hidden, while the king in much excitement followed closely on his track. At length it ran far into a dense thicket impenetrable by horse or elephant. Though alone in the wood and distressed by his exertions, still the king would not abandon the chase; till the boar seeing him so determined slunk away into a deep cave. When the king perceived that there was no getting near him, he was quite sad; but he had lost his way in this hunt through so great a forest.

Dohā 157

Hungry and thirsty and exhausted with fatigue, the king and his horse sought desperately for a stream or pond, and were half dead for want of water.

Caupāī 158

As he wandered through the forest, he spied a hermitage where dwelt a king in the disguise of a hermit. He had been despoiled of his kingdom by Pratāpabhānu, and had deserted his army and fled from the field of battle, knowing that his adversary's star was in the ascendant and his own in the decline. Too proud to make terms with the king, too much mortified to go home, nursing his wrath in his heart, he, like a beggar, though a prince, took up his abode in the wood in the garb of an anchorite. He at once recognized King Pratāpabhānu as he drew near; but the latter was too tired to recognize him, and looking only at his dress took him to be a holy man, and alighting from his horse saluted him; he was, however, too astute to declare his name.

Dohā 158

Seeing the king to be faint with thirst, the hermit pointed out to him a fine lake, where he bathed and drank, both he and his horse, with much gladness.

Caupāī 159

Rid of all his weariness, the king was quite refreshed. The hermit took him to his own hermitage and, as the sun had now set, showed him where he might rest; but yet enquired of him in courteous tones, "Who may you be, and why, handsome youth as you are, do you risk your life by wandering alone in the forest? You have all the marks of a great sovereign, and at the sight of you I am quite moved." "Know then, reverend sir", said the king, that I am the minister of King Pratāpabhānu; I lost my way while hunting and by great good fortune have been brought into your presence. To get a sight of you was no easy matter, and I am satisfied that something good is about to befall me." "My son," said the hermit, "it is now dusk, and your city is some two hundred leagues away.

Dohā 159*a*-159*b*

The night is dark, the forest dense, and the road not easy to find. Tarry then here for today and start tomorrow at dawn." SaysTulasī— Fate is furthered in its own way; either you go to meet it, or it itself comes and leads you away to safety.

Caupāī 160

"Very well, my lord, I obey your command;" and so saying the king tied up his horse to a tree and came and sat down. With many flattering speeches he did homage to his feet, extolling his own good fortune, and at last in modest and winning terms put the question,—"Regarding you, my lord, as a father, I make bold and beg of you to look upon me as your son and servant and to declare to me your name." Now the king did not recognize him, but he recognized the king, and was as false and crafty as the king was simple minded; moreover, being an enemy, and at the same time both a warrior by caste and a prince he was bent on accomplishing his own ends, whether by fraud or by right. In his enmity he was grieved to see the king's prosperity, and his heart within him burned as with the fire of a furnace; but on hearing the prince's simple words he controlled his resentment and was glad at heart,

Dohā 160

And uttered yet another soft but false and scheming speech,—"My name now is Bhikhāri,[1] for I am a homeless beggar."

Caupāī 161

Said the king,—"Those who are repositories of wisdom like you, with whom all self-conceit has been extinguished, ever conceal their own personality, and are in every way blessed, though their outer garb be wretched. That is why saints proclaim aloud in men's ears that it is the poor whom Hari holds most dear. A poor and homeless beggar, such as you are, is an anxiety to Brahmā and Śiva. But whatever you may be, I reverence your feet and beg of you to grant me your grace." When he saw the king's simple affection he waxed all the more confident, and won him over in every way, using words with a still greater show of friendliness. "Hearken, O king," he said, "while I relate the truth of the matter. I have for a long time dwelt here.

Dohā 161a

And till now neither has anyone come to see me, nor have I made myself known to any; for worldly honour is like a fire, and penance a forest for it to consume."

1. *i.e.*, Mendicant; literally, a beggar.

Soraṭha 161b

(Says Tulasī :—"Fools are deceived by fair appearances, but not wise men : though a peacock is fair to look upon and its voice is pleasant,[1] yet it feeds on snakes.")

Caupāī 162

"That is why I remain hidden in the world, and, save Hari, have no care whatever. The Lord knows everything without being told; so what is to be gained by conciliating the world ? But you are so good and sensible that I cannot but love you in return for the faith and confidence you have placed in me: and if I were to keep anything from you, my son, it would be a very grievous sin on my part." The more the hermit talked of his detachment from the world, the more trustful grew the king; till at last the false anchorite, seeing him completely in his power, said, "My name, brother, is Ekatanu" (one-body). The king bowed and asked further, "Tell me, I pray, the meaning of this name, for surely I am your servant."

Dohā 162

"At the first dawn of creation I was born, and my name was Ekatanu (one-body), for this reason that I have never taken any other body.

Caupāī 163

"Marvel not in your mind, my son; for nothing is too difficult for penance. By the power of penance Brahmā created the world; by the power of penance Viṣṇu is the great redeemer; by the power of penance Śiva works destruction; and to penance there is nothing in the world impossible." The king, as he listened, was charmed, for he commenced relating ancient stories : many legends of pious deeds and holy lives; examples

1. The peacock's voice can scarcely be called pleasant in itself, but may be so by association as a sign of the coming rains. Thus Cowper :

"Sounds inharmonious in themselves and harsh,
Yet heard in scenes where peace for ever reigns,
And only there, please highly for their sake."

[The lines here translated have also been interpreted differently and are said to mean that not merely fools but even clever men are taken in by a fair appearance; look at the beautiful peacock; though its notes are sweet and ambrosial, it feeds on shakes.]

of asceticism and divine wisdom; tales of the birth, preservation, and destruction of the world, and innumerable other marvellous narratives. The king, as he listened, yielded completely to his influence, and proceeded to tell him his true name. Said the ascetic, — "O king, I knew you; though you tried to practise a trick upon me, I took it quite in good part.

Soraṭhā 163

"Hear, O king, it is a political maxim that a king should not declare his name everywhere; and when I observed your excellent sagacity I conceived a great affection for you.

Caupāī 164

"Your name is Pratāpabhānu, and your father is king Satyaketu. By the grace of my *guru*, O king, I know everything, but considering it harmful to myself, I do not say all I know. Ah, my son, when I beheld the simplicity of your nature, your faith and trustfulness, and your knowledge of state-craft, there sprang up an affection for you in my soul, and I told you my own story as you asked me. Now I am well pleased with you ; doubt not, but ask whatever you will." On hearing these fair words the king was delighted, and clasping his feet entreated him suppliantly, "O gracious sage, by the sight of you the four objects of human desire have all come within my grasp. Yet, as I see my lord so gracious, I will ask an impossible boon and be happy for ever.

Dohā 164

May my body be free from old age, death and bodily pain; may I never be conquered in battle : may earth rid of every foe—be all under my sole sway, and may my empire last for a hundred aeons."

Caupāī 165

"So be it, O king," said the anchorite; "there is, however, one difficulty; hear what it is. Even time shall bow down before you, with the sole exception of the race of Brāhmaṇas. By the virtue of penance a Brāhmaṇa is ever powerful, and there is none who can deliver from his wrath. If you can reduce him to your will, Brahmā, Viṣṇu and Mahādeva will also be at your command. But against a Brāhmaṇa might is of no avail : with both arms raised to heaven I tell you this solemn truth. Hearken, O king, if you escape a Brāhmaṇa's curse, your destruction shall never be." On hearing his promise the king was delighted,—"Then, my lord, my destruction will never be; by your favour most gracious lord, I shall be for ever blessed."

Dohā 165

"May it be so", said the false and guileful anchorite, and added with crafty intent,—"If you let anyone know of your straying away and meeting with me, that will not be my fault.

Caupāī 166

"For I warn you, sir, that it is most inexpedient to repeat the matter : if it come to a third pair of ears, I tell you true it will be your ruin. If you divulge this secret, or if a Brāhmaṇa curse you, you are undone, O Pratāpabhānu. When Hari and Hara are angry wretched man has no other way of escape." "True, my lord," said the king, clasping his feet; "who can deliver from the wrath of a Brāhmaṇa or a spiritual director? The *guru* can save from Brahmā's anger, but if the *guru* himself be enraged, there is none in the world that can save. If I do not follow your advice, I have not the slightest doubt that I shall perish; but there is only one thing that I fear; the curse of a Brāhmaṇa is something most terrible!

Dohā 166

"Tell me of your grace in what way I can win over the Brāhmannas; for except you, my gracious lord, I have no other friend."

Caupāī 167

"Hearken, O king," said the hermit, there are diverse expedients among men, but hard to put in practice and of doubtful issue. There is, however, one very simple plan, though even this involves a difficulty. Its contrivance depends on me, and for me to go to your city is impossible; for to this day from the time I was born I have never entered the house or village of any man. But If I do not go, your object will not be accomplished; here is a dilemma." The king replied in gentle tones,—"It is, my lord, a maxim of scripture that the great show kindness to the small; thus mountains ever bear tiny grasses on their head; the fathomless ocean bears on its front the floating foam, and the earth on its head bears the dust."

Dohā 167

Thus saying and clasping his feet, the king cried,—"Be gracious, O my lord, ever compassionate to the faithful in distress, and endure this trouble for my sake.

Caupāī 168

Perceiving that the king was altogether under his influence, the hermit, the arch-deceiver, said, — "Hearken, O king, I tell you truly there is nothing in the world I cannot do, and as you show yourself in thought, word and action to be devoted to me, I will assuredly accomplish your object for you. The power of magical schemes, penance and spells works only when secrecy is maintained. If, O king, I act as cook and serve, without anyone knowing me, then whoever partakes of the food so prepared shall become amenable to your orders; and, further, anyone who eats in his house will, I tell you, be in your power. Go now and carry out this scheme, O king, and persevere in it for a year,

Dohā 168

and everyday entertain a new set of a hundred thousand Brāhmaṇas with their families; while I, as long as the vow lasts, will provide the daily banquet.

Caupāī 169

"In this way, O king, there will be very little trouble, and all the Brāhmaṇas shall be reduced to your will. They again will perform sacrificial services and ritual worship and thus the gods, too, will easily fall under your sway. And I will give you a sign. I will not come in this dress, but by my own magic I will steal away your family priest, and by the virtue of penance will make him look like myself and keep him here for the year; while I in his form will manage everything for you. The night is far gone, so now take rest; on the third day we will meet again. While you are asleep I, by my penitential power, will convey you home, both you and your horse.

Dohā 169

"I shall then come in the form I have told you, and you will recognize me when I send for you privately and remind you of all this."

Caupāī 170

The king, as ordered, retired to his couch, while the arch-deceiver took his wonted seat. Deep sleep came upon the weary king; but what sleep for the other, distraught with care? Then came to him there the demon Kālaketu, who had assumed the form of the boar that had led the king astray, a great friend of the hermit king, and skilled in manifold ways of deceit. He had a hundred sons and ten brothers, unmatched in villainy, and a torment to the gods; but they had all before this been killed in battle by the king, who saw the distress they had caused to the Brāhmaṇas, sages and powers of heaven. The wretch, nursing this old quarrel, combined with the hermit king in devising a plot for the destruction of his enemy. The prince, overmastered by fate, knew nothing of it.

Dohā 170

A spirited foe, even though he be alone, is not to be lightly regarded. To this day Rāhu, though he has nothing left but his head, is able to annoy both sun and moon.

Caupāī 171

When the hermit king saw his ally, he rose in great joy to meet him, and told his friend the whole story. The demon was glad and said,—"Hear, O king, I am ready to settle your enemy if you will take my advice. Free yourself of all anxiety and sleep quietly here : without taking any medicine God has cured your complaint, I will sweep away the enemy, root and branch, and in four days will be back again." Having thus cheered the hermit king, the arch-deceiver went away in his wrath, and conveyed to the palace Pratāpabhānu still asleep, both him and his horse; the king he put to bed beside his queen, and the horse he tied up in the stable.

Dohā 171

He then carried off the king's family priest, and by supernatural power depriving him of his senses, kept him in a mountain cave,

Caupāī 172

while he himself assumed the form of the family priest and went and lay down on his luxurious couch. At daybreak the king woke and was astonished to find himself at home. Much impressed with the hermit's power, he rose and went out unperceived by the queen, and mounting his horse rode off to the woods without any of the people in the city knowing it. When it was noon he returned, and in every house there was rejoicing, with music and singing. When he saw the family priest, he looked at him in amazement, recalling all that had happened. The three days seemed like an age, so absorbed was he in expectation of the false hermit's coming. At the appointed time the priest came and reminded the king in detail of all that had been agreed upon.

Dohā 172

The king was delighted to recognize the *guru* (in the priest's form), for he was too infatuated to have any sense left, and at once invited a hundred thousand Brāhmaṇas with their families.

Caupāī 173

The priest superintended the cooking, and in accordance with sacred prescription concocted the six flavours in the four different ways,[1] preparing a most seductive banquet, with sauces and condiments more than any one could count. After dressing a great variety of meat, the wretch introduced into the dish some pieces of a Brāhmāṇa's flesh. He then summoned all the Brāhmaṇas to the feast and washed their feet and politely showed them to their places. But as soon as ever the king began to serve the food, a voice came from heaven,—"Arise, arise, all ye Brāhmaṇas and return to your homes; though the loss be great, yet taste not the food; there is a Brāhmaṇa's flesh in the dish!" Up rose all the holy men, believing the heavenly voice; while the king, distraught and ulterly confounded, over-mastered by fate, could not utter a word.

Dohā 173

Then cried the Brāhmaṇas in a fury, regardless of what must follow,—"Go, foolish king, take birth as a demon, yourself and all your household!

Caupāī 174

"O vile Kṣatriya, you invited all this Brāhmaṇical company here simply to destroy us; God has preserved our honour, and it is you and your race who are undone. You shall perish in the midst of four days, nor shall there be one left to offer libations to your ghost." When the king heard the curse he was terror-stricken. Again a voice came from heaven,—"The Brāhmaṇas have uttered this curse without due consideration, the king has committed no crime." All the Brāhmaṇas were astounded when they heard the heavenly voice. The king hastened to the kitchen; there he found neither food nor the Brāhmaṇa cook, and he turned away in deep thought, declared the whole history to the Brāhmaṇas, and in his terror and distress threw himself upon the ground.

Dohā 174

"Though you, O king, are guiltless, what is fated will fail not; the past is unalterable; a Brāhmaṇa's curse is a terrible thing."

1. The six flavours are 'the sweet,' *madhur*; 'sour,' *amla*; 'salt,' *lavaṇa*; 'pungent,' *kaṭu*; 'bitter,' *tikta*; and 'astringent,' *kaṣāya*. The four ways in which food can be taken are *bhakṣya*, by mastication; *bhojya*, by deglutition; *coṣya*, by sucking, and *lehya*, by lapping.

Caupāī 175

So saying, all the Brāhmaṇas went their way. When the people of the city heard the news, they were sore distressed and blamed Fate, who had begun upon a swan and ended in making a crow. The demon conveyed the family priest to the palace and told the hermit all the tidings. Then the wretch despatched letters in all directions; a host of princes came in with their troops, and with blast of trumpets beleaguered the city. Day after day there were battles of various kinds; all his champions fell in fight, after performing valiant feats, and the king with his brother bit the dust. Not one of Satyaketu's family escaped, for a Brāhmaṇa's curse can never fail of accomplishment. Triumphing over their foe, the chiefs refounded the city, and then, crowned with victory, returned to their own states.

Dohā 175

Hearken, Bharadvāja![1] Whoever incurs God's anger, for him a grain of dust becomes as vast as Mount Meru, a father like the god of death, and every rope a snake.

Caupāī 176

Hearken, sage; in due time this king, with his household, was born as a demon with ten heads and twenty arms, a formidable hero, by name Rāvaṇa. The king's younger brother, Arimardana, became his younger half-brother, the world-famous Vibhīṣaṇa, the all-wise votary of Viṣṇu. As for the king's sons and servants, they were born a fierce demon crew; wretches, taking various shapes at will: wicked, monstrous and devoid of knowledge; merciless, injurious, criminal—a torment to all creation beyond what words can tell.

Dohā 176

Though born in the incomparably pure and holy house of Pulastya,[1] yet on account of Brāhmaṇas' curse they all were of hateful mien.

1. The patriarch Pulastya was the father of Viśravas; and the latter, by three handmaids, who had been given him by Kubera, begot (1) Rāvaṇa and Kumbhakarṇa, (2) Vibhīṣaṇa, and (3) Khara and Śūrpaṇakhā.

Caupāī 177

The three brothers practised various penitential austerities, severe beyond all description; the Creator drew nigh to witness them, and said,—"Son, I am well pleased, ask a boon." The Ten-headed suppliantly clasped his feet and cried,—"Hear, O lord of earth, I would die at the hand of none save man or monkey." Brahmā and I granted him his boon, saying,—"So be it; you have done great penance." Then the lord went to Kumbhakarṇa, and was astonished to behold him; he thought, "If this wretch continues to eat perpetually, the whole world will be laid waste." So he sent Sarasvatī to turn his head, and he asked for six month's slumber.

Dohā 177

Next Brahmā went to Vibhīṣaṇa and said,—"Son, ask a boon:" and he asked for perfect love of the lotus feet of the Blessed Lord.

Caupāī 178

After granting them these boons Brahmā departed, and they went home rejoicing. Now Maya had a daughter by name Maṇḍodarī, of exceeding beauty, a jewel of womankind, whom her father brought and made over to Rāvaṇa, well aware that he would be king of the demons. Delighted at having won so lovely a wife, he next went and married off his two brothers. In the middle of the ocean is a three-peaked mountain, by Brahmā's contrivance most difficult of access. Here the demon Maya had constructed a vast palace of gold and jewels, more beautiful and charming than Bhogavatī, the city of the serpent kings, or Indra's capital Amarāvatī, and called it Laṅkā, a name famous throughout the world.

Dohā 178*a*-178*b*

The deep ocean was its moat, washing its four sides; and its four massive walls were of gold, set with jewels in a way that defies description. In every aeon the Demon King, whom Hari predestines, lives there with his army, as a mighty and puissant chief.

Caupāī 179

Formerly there had dwelt great demon warriors, but all had been slain in battle by the gods; and now by Indra's commission it was occupied by a million guards of Kuvera's. Rāvaṇa happened to hear of this, and at once marshalled his army and went and besieged the place. When the Yakṣas saw the vast host of fierce warriors, they all fled for their lives. Thereupon Rāvaṇa inspected the whole city, and was so highly pleased with it that all his trouble was forgotten. Seeing that it was not only a beautiful, but also a naturally impregnable, site, he fixed the capital there and assigning quarters to his followers according to their several deserts, made them all quite happy. Upon one occasion he sallied forth against Kuvera, and carried off his aerial car Puṣpaka as a trophy.

Dohā 179

Again, in a sportive mood, he went and lifted up Kailāsa, and after thus testing the prowess of his men of war, waxed yet more jubilant than before.

Caupāī 180

His happiness and prosperity, the number of his sons, his troops and his allies, his conquests, his might, his intelligence and renown, all these grew more and more, in the same way as avarice grows with gain. Thus, too, his brother, the stalwart Kumbhakarṇa, was a champion without a match in the world. After drinking his fill he slept for six months, and at his waking the three worlds trembled. If he had taken a meal every day the whole world would soon have been stript bare. He was unspeakably staunch in fight, and there were numberless such brave warriors as he. His eldest son was Meghanāda, who held the first place among the world's champions: before whom none could stand in the battle; who was ever harassing the city of heaven.

Dohā 180

Many other demons were there, each by himself capable of subduing the whole world, such as the hideous Kumukha, the dauntless Akampana, Kuliśarada with teeth like thunderbolts, the fiery Dhūmaketu, and the huge Atikāya;

Caupāī 181

Putting on any form at will, skilled in every kind of black magic, without ever a thought of piety or pity. One day the Ten-headed was seated in court and reviewed his innumerable retainers, sons and grandsons, friends and servants, troops of demons, more than anyone could count. On seeing the host, he swelled with pride, and in fierce tones said,—"Hearken, all ye demon troops ! The hosts of heaven are my enemies. They dare not stand up in open fight, but flee away at the sight of my great army. There is one way of effecting their death, which I will declare; now listen to it. Go ye and put a stop to the feasting of Brāhmaṇas, to every sacrifice, oblation and funeral rite;

Dohā 181

Emaciated with starvation and rendered weak, the gods will forthwith come out to meet me, and whether I slay them or let them go, they will be equally in my power."

Caupāī 182

Again he sent for Meghanāda and exhorted him to yet greater courage and resentment,—"The strong and warlike gods, who venture to confront you, you must vanquish and bring here in chains." Up rose the son to perform his father's commands. In this manner he ordered all, and himself sallied forth, mace in hand. As he marched the earth reeled, the heaven thundered, and pains of premature labour overtook the pregnant spouses of the gods. The gods themselves, on hearing of Rāvaṇa's wrathful approach, sought safety in the caves of Mount Meru. As he approached in turn each of the eight quarters of the globe, he found it deserted by its guardian. Again and again he shouted the challenge to battle and vehemently scoffed at the gods, and mad with lust of blood traversed the whole universe in search of a foeman, but nowhere did he discover one.

The sun and moon; the wind; Varuṇa and Kuvera; fire, time and death, and every divine power; Kinnaras, saints, men, gods and serpents, all were pertinaciously pursued. From one end of God's creation to the other, every living creature, whether male or female, was made subject to Rāvaṇa. All in turn do his bidding and crouch suppliant at his feet.

Dohā 182*a*-182*b*

By the might of his arm he subdued the whole universe and left not a single soul free, but acting on his own counsel exercised dominion over the whole round world. And many were the lovely and noble dames he wedded after conquest, daughters of gods and Yakṣas and Gandharvas and men and Kinnaras and Nāgas.

Caupāī 183

Whatever order he gave to Indrajit was carried out in less time than it took to order. Now hear how the other chiefs acted to whom he gave commands. The whole demon host, villainous at heart and foul of aspect, the torment of heaven, were ready for any outrage, disguising themselves by the assumption of various forms and acting in every way contrary to the Veda, in order to eradicate religion. Wherever they find a cow or a Brāhmaṇa, they at once set fire to the city, town or village; pious observances are no longer anywhere in existence; no respect is paid either to scripture or Brāhmaṇa or spiritual instructor; there is no faith in Hari, no sacrifice, no prayer, nor alms-giving, and no one would ever dream of listening either to Veda or Purāṇa.

Chand 18

At a hint of prayer or of penance, of sacrifice, vigil or fast,
Not a moment's rest, but he hied on its quest, with a vow
it should be the last.
The world was sunk in lawlessness; all holy sounds
were banned;
To read a sacred text was death, or exile from the land.

Soraṭhā 183

The fearful oppression that the demons wrought is beyond description. Bent on mischief, there was no limit to their ill-doing.

Caupāī 184

The wicked flourished, thieves and gamblers, and those lechers who coveted their neighbours' goods and wives, those who honoured neither father and mother nor the gods, and those, too, who exacted service of better men than themselves. For people who act in this way, Bhavāni, resemble demons. Seeing the general persecution of religion, earth was terror-stricken and dismayed,—'the weight of mountains, lakes and seas is nothing so heavy as this one tyrant. She saw all faith perverted, and yet for fear of Rāvaṇa could say nothing. Deeply she pondered and then took the form of a cow and went to the spot where the gods and saints were gathered together, and with tears declared to them her distress. There was no help to be had from anyone of them.

Chand 19

Gods and sages and heavenly minstrels, flocked they all to
Brahmān's throne;
With them Earth, a horned heifer, making sad and piteous
moan.
Pondered Brahmā in his wisdom.—'All vain is help of mine,
But a lord immortal is thy Lord; be he my help and thine.'

Sorathā 184

"Take courage, Earth," said Brahmā. "and remember Hari's feet. The Lord knows the distress of his servants, and will put an end to this cruel oppression."

Caupāī 185

All the gods sat in counsel and thought,—"Where can we find the Lord that we may make our cry to him ? Said one,—'We must go to Vaikuṇṭha; said another,—'His home is in the ocean. Nay, this is the way of the Lord, he is ever manifest to a faithful and loving soul.' Now, Girijā, I too was present in the assembly and took occasion to say briefly,—"Hari is omnipresent everywhere alike, but, as I well know, is revealed by love. Tell me any place, time or quarter of the heaven where the Lord is not. Present in all creation, animate or inanimate, passionless and unbiased, he is revealed like fire by love." My words were approved by all, and Brahmā exclaimed,—'Well said, well said.'

Dohā 185

Brahmā was glad at heart to hear my words and thrilled with delight, while his eyes filled with tears, and clasping his immortal hands he thus composedly and deliberately chanted his praises :

Chand 20

"To the King of heaven be all glory given, refuge of creation in distress and care.

Priests and cows befriending, hell's brief triumph ending, best beloved of Lakṣmī, Ocean's daughter fair.

Heaven and earth's upholder, who, than all men bolder, dares to scan the secret of thy strange mysterious way ?

Ever kind and loving, humble souls approving, may thy gracious favour reach now to me, I pray.

Spirit all-pervading, fleshly sense evading, hail Mukunda immoral, lord of blissfulness supreme,

Ever pure and holy, whom the Queen of Folly has no power to tangle in her world-deluding dream.

Glory, glory, glory theme of endless story, sung by saints and sages in an ecstasy of love.

Daily, nightly gazing on the sight amazing, source of every blessing, Hari, lord of heaven above.

Triune incarnation, who at earth's creation, wert alone presiding, and other aid was none ;

Though in prayer unable, and my faith unstable, O great sin-destroyer, hear our hapless moan.

Life's alarms dispelling, all disasters quelling comfort of the faithful, be our succour now ;

All the gods implore thee, falling low before thee, with unfeigned submission of body, soul and vow.

Lord God Bhagavān, Veda and eke Purāṇa, Śāradā and Śeṣanāga, and all the saintly throng,

Find the theme too spacious, only know thee gracious, hasten then to help us in our hour of wrong.

In all grace excelling, Beauty's chosen dwellihg, ark on life's dark ocean, home of all most sweet,

Gods and saints and sages, now this tempest rages, fly in consternation to clasp thy lotus feet."

Dohā 186

Perceiving the alarm of the gods and Earth, and hearing this devout speech, a solemn voice came from heaven that removed all their doubt and anxiety,—

Caupāī 186

"Fear not, Indra and ye saints, sages and gods ! For your sake I am about to assume the form of a man, with every element of my divinity incarnate in the glorious Solar race. For the severe penance practised by Kaśyapa and Aditi I granted them the full boon they asked. In the form of Daśaratha and Kauśalyā they have taken royal birth in the city of Kosala. In their house I shall become incarnate as four brothers, the pride of the family of Raghu. I will fulfil all that Nārada predicted, by myself descending from heaven with my eternal spouse, and will remove the whole of earth's burden." On hearing the heavenly voice in the air the gods turned and were consoled, and Brahmā exhorted Mother Earth, who forgot her fears in hopefulness.

Dohā 187

Brahmā proceeded to his own realm after thus instructing the gods,—'Go and worship Hari upon earth in form as monkeys."

Caupāī 187

All the gods went to their several homes, and with Earth had rest. All the orders that Brahmā had given they executed gladly and without delay. Taking birth on earth as monkeys of incomparable strength and power, all mighty warriors with rocks and trees and claws for weapons, they waited patiently for Hari's coming swarming in every mountain and forest and divided among themselves into orderly troops, I have told you of their noble acts, and now you must hear of that which was interrupted before. The king of Avadh was named Daśaratha, the jewel of the line of Raghu, well skilled in the Vedas, virtuous and wise, a defender of the faith, a sincere votary of Viṣṇu.

Dohā 188

Kauśalyā and his other loving queens were all of chaste

behaviour, faithful and affectionate to their lord, and full of humble devotion to Hari's lotus feet.

Caupāī 188

One day the king was sad that he had no son, and going in haste to his *guru's* abode touched his feet and made many entreaties. He told him all his joys and sorrows. Vasiṣṭha in reply comforted him in every way,—"Take courage, you will have four sons, who will be famous throughout the three worlds and rid the faithful of all their fears." Then Vasiṣṭha summoned Sage Śṛṅgī to perform a sacrifice for the birth of a son. The sage devoutly offered the oblation, and the Fire-god appeared with the offering in his hand and cried in gracious tones,—"I am pleased more than I can say; whatever Vasiṣṭha has imagined in his heart is all granted for your good. Take this oblation, O king, and divide it in such proportions as is proper.

Dohā 189

Then the Fire-god vanished, after telling them all of all that had to be done. The king was transported with ecstasy and could not contain himself for joy.

Caupāī 189

He at once sent for his beloved wives, and Kauśalyā and the rest came to him. To Kauśalyā he gave half of the offering, and of the remaining half he made two portions, one of which he offered to Kaikeyi; what remained he again divided into two, which he placed in the hands of Kauśalyā and Kaikeyī and they gave them to Sumitrā, to her great delight. In this manner all the queens became great with child, and they grew glad of heart with exceeding joy. From the day that Hari was conceived in their womb the whole world was filled with happiness and prosperity, and the queens shone resplendent in the palace, full of beauty, virtue and glory. Some little time was thus happily spent, till the day arrived for the Lord to be revealed.

Dohā 190

Auspicious was the conjunction of the planets in an auspicious house; auspicious the moment; auspicious the day of the week and of the month; and full of delight was all creation, animate, and inanimate, when Rāma, source of all delights, was born.

Caupāī 190

On the ninth day of the sweet and holy month of Caitra; in the bright lunar fortnight; under Abhijit,[1] his favourite constellation; on a seasonable day neither hot nor cold, a holy time of rest for all; with soft, cool, fragrant breezes blowing; midst the delight of gods and heartfelt rapture of the saints; while the woods were full of blossoms as the hills bright with gems, and every river flowed a stream of nectar. When the Creator saw the time so fit, all the gods had their chariots equipped and came forth. The bright heaven was crowded with the host of them; troops of Gandharvas chanted heroic lays; flowers were rained down by handfuls; the sky resounded with the beat of kettle-drums; serpents, saints and gods hymned his praises, and each in his own fashion tendered him service.

Dohā 191

Thus meekly did all the gods return each to his dwelling-place when the Lord was revealed, who is the abode of the world, and in whom all the world finds rest.

Chand 21

From Kauśalyā's blessed womb the great god at last has
   come, in response to a lost world's plaint,
And she gazes with what joy on the face of her dear boy.
   that would rapture the soul of a saint.
A vision of delight, with his eyes so large and bright, and
   this body as a cloud dark and grand,
But the garland on his breast and his four arms confest
   Kharāri, with a weapon in each hand.
With fingers locked in prayer she cries,—"How may I dare,
   O lord god immortal, thy boundless praise to tell,
Far above the world's confusion and reason's vain intrusion,
   whom all the scriptures witness incomprehensible.

1. *i.e.*, the 21st *nakṣatra*, or lunar asterism.

Whom saints and holy sages have hymned through all the ages, the fountain compassion, the source of every grace,
Who aye with Lakṣmī reignest, thou, even thou, now deignest to be my son and succour thy sore-tried chosen race.
Though we know by revelation, heaven and earth and all creation, in each hair upon thy body may be found,
In my arms thou sweetly dreamest, O mystery supremest, far beyond the comprehension of a sage the most profound."
Smiled the lord at her devotion and would fain have set in motion the magic that dazzles the crowd,
Telling all he had done and the triumphs he had won that his mother of her son might be proud.
But hurriedly she cried,—"My soul is terrified by these marvels, disperse them from my sight;
Let me see thee as a child, disporting free and wild, for in this is my greatest delight."
She spoke and he obeyed, and at once in fashion made as an infant began to cry.
Know that all who sing this lay, and in faith to Hari pray, shall in peace rest for ever when they die.

Dohā 192

For the sake of Brāhmaṇas, and cows and gods and saints he took birth as a man, in a body formed of his own will, he who is beyond all form, or quality, or perception of the senses.

Caupāī 191

On hearing the delightful sound of a baby's cries, all the queens came in agitated haste; their glad handmaids ran hither and thither and all the people of the city were drowned in joy. When Daśaratha knew he had a son born, his joy was like that of the blessed in heaven; with his soul full of love and his body quivering with delight he sought to rise, but could not till he had collected himself,—"The lord, whose very name it is bliss to hear, has come to my house." Thus rejoicing at heart the king summoned minstrels to play their music, and next summoned the *guru* Vasiṣṭha, who came to the court with a train of Brāhmaṇas. He went and gazed upon the peerless babe, but its beauty and grace were beyond words to tell.

Dohā 193

Then after performing the Nāndīmukha *Śrāddha*[1] he completed all the ceremonies of birth,[2] and the king made offerings to the Brāhmaṇas of gold, cows, raiment and jewels.

Caupāī 192

The city was full of flags and banners and triumphal arches arranged in a manner that defies description. Flowers showered from heaven and every soul was rapt in bliss. There was a concourse of troops of women who had come running in their ordinary dress just as they were at the time, with golden vases and salvers laden with things of good omen, singing as they entered the king's court. After passing their offerings round and round over the child's head, they strew them on the ground, and again and again throw themselves at his feet, while bards and minstrels, singing men and choristers chant the spotless perfections of Raghunātha. Everyone made an offering of all that he had, and no one kept what was given him ; while musk, sandal and saffron were thrown about in such profusion that the city streets were muddy with perfumes.

Dohā 194

In every house there was music and the jubilant shout,—"the fountain of beauty has been revealed;" and all the men and women in the city were rejoicing everywhere.

1. The *Nāndī-mukha Śrāddha* is a commemorative offering to the Manes preliminary to any joyous occasion, such as initiation, marriage, &c., in which nine balls of meat are offered to the deceased father, grandfather, and great-grandfather : to the maternal grandfather, great-grandfather, and great-great-grandfather; to the mother, paternal grandmother, and paternal great-grandmother.—*Monier Williams.*

2. The father performs the *jātakarma saṁskāra* when the navel-string is cut. The ceremony consists in touching the child's tongue with *ghī*, etc. with prayers specially meant for the occasion.

Caupāī 193

Kaikeyī and Sumitrā too gave birth to lovely sons. At that time the joy, the auspiciousness, and the crowds were more than Sarasvatī or the Serpent King could describe. The city of Avadh was as resplendent as it were Night going to meet the Lord. The sun, abashed at the vision, faded into twilight, where the dusky clouds of incense were shot through with red gleams of *abīr* : the piles of jewels in the temples were like stars, and the golden pinnacle of the palace as the gracious moon, while the murmuring sound of Vedic recitation in the royal house was like the evening song of garrulous birds. Gazing upon the spectacle the sun forgot himself, and a whole month passed without his knowing it.

Dohā 195

The day was a month long, but the mystery was noticed by none. While the sun in his chariot stood still at gaze, how could there be any night ?

Caupāī 194

There was not one who observed the mystery, and at last the sun set still chanting Rāma's praises. The gods, saints and Nāgas too, who had witnessed the spectacle, returned home, congratulating themselves on their good fortune. I will even tell you of a deception I practised myself; listen, Girijā, for I know your steadfast faith. Kākabhusuṇḍi and I were there together in human form, without anyone knowing it. Full of rapture, love and delight, we roamed about the streets in ecstatic unconsciousness. Only one on whom rests the mercy of Rāma can attain to the knowledge of these acts of ours. On that occasion the king granted everyone his heart's desire, whatever it might be that he had come for, bestowing on them elephants, chariots, horses, gold, cows, jewels and all sorts of apparel.

Dohā 196

All were satisfied from their very heart and invoked blessings upon him, saying, — 'May all the boys live long,' those lords of Tulasī Dāsa.

Caupāī 195

In this manner some days were spent and day and night passed by unnoticed till the king, knowing the time had come for naming the children, sent for the wise seer, and after reverently greeting him thus spake,—"Holy father, be pleased to declare the names upon which you have secretly determined." "Their names are many and marvellous; I will tell them, O king, to the best of my ability. The store-house of delights, the ocean of joy, by a drop of which the three worlds are gladdened, the very home of bliss, the comforter of the universe, has for his name RĀMA ('delight'). The bearer and supporter of the world is named Bharata ('the supporter'), while he whose very thought brings victory over the foe is celebrated in the Veda by his name Śatrughna ('destroyer of enemies')."

Dohā 197

For the auspicious, the beloved of Rāma, the support of the whole world, was reserved by the *guru* Vasiṣṭha the noble name of Lakṣmaṇa ('of auspicious appearance').

Caupāī 196

After naming them the *guru* pondered in heart and said,—"O king, your four sons are the very Veda itself; the saint's treasure; the believer's all in all; the darling of Śiva, who is delighted with their childish sports." Even from his childhood Lakṣmaṇa knew his dear lord and adored the feet of Rāma; while the affection of the two other brothers, Bharata and Śatrughna, grew also as between master and servant. In both pairs one was dark, the other fair; and their mother, as she gazed upon their loveliness, would break a blade of grass to avert the evil eye. Though all four were full of amiability, beauty and intellect, yet Rāma was a higher joy; his kindliness of heart was like the bright moon, which manifested itself in the radiance of a most winning smile; while now in the cradle, and now on her lap his mother fondled him and called him her own dear darling.

Dohā 198

The omnipresent god, who has neither passion nor quality, nor sensation of pleasure, and who is from everlasting, lay a babe in Kauṣalyā's arms, overcome by devout affection.

Caupāī 197

With all the beauty of a myriad Loves; dark of hue as the dark-blue lotus or a heavy rain-cloud; the glistening nails on his rosy feet like clustered pearls on the leaves of the lily; the print of the thunderbolt, the flag and the elephant-goad distinctly to be seen; the tinkling of his anklets enough to charm a sage; with girdled waist and dimpled body and deep navel, such as no one could believe who had not seen; with long arms covered with many jewels and lovely set of tiger's claws upon his breast; with necklace of gems and sparkling amulet, and soul-ravishing print of the Brāhmaṇa's feet[1] with shell-marked neck and exquisite chin, and a face flushed with the beauty of all the loves; with well-matched teeth and ruddy lips and nose and fore-head-mark beyond description; with beautiful ears and charming cheeks and lisping prattle most dear and sweet; with eyes dark and full as the lotus, and heavy brows and a fair pendant on his forehead; with lustrous curling hair that his mother dressed with loving care; with his body clothed in little yellow drawers, crawling on knees and hands upon the ground; neither scripture nor Śeṣanāga could do justice to his beauty, nor without a vision could any one imagine it.

1. Rāma is here identified with Viṣṇu, of whom the following legend is told in the *Bhāgavata Purāṇa* :—The patriarch Bhṛgu, being in doubt which of the three gods, Brahmā, Viṣṇu or Śiva, was the greatest, determined to put the matter to the test. He first went to Brahmā and entered his court without making any obeisance, an affront at which the god showed himself exceedingly indignant. He then went to Śiva and, treating him with a like want of respect, excited a yet more furious storm of passion. Lastly he went to Vaikuṇṭha, where finding Viṣṇu asleep in the embraces of his spouse Lakṣmī, he struck him roughly on the breast with his foot to awaken him. The god started up, but seeing the sage, at once prostrated himself before him, and took and gently rubbed his foot with his hands, hoping it had not been hurt by striking against him. Thus Bhṛgu learnt that in mercy and magnanimity, the highest attributes of the godhead, there was no other power that could be compared to Viṣṇu.

Dohā 199

The all-blissful Lord, who transcends all illusion, intellect, speech and perception of the senses, became subject to the perfect love of his parents and sported like an innocent babe.

Caupāī 198

In this way Rāma, the father and mother of the universe, delighted the people of Kosala; and they who love their god, O Bhavāni, show themselves like his earthly parents. But his enemies, struggle as they may, will never extricate themselves from the bonds of birth and death. The delusive power that has subdued all life, whether in animate or inanimate creation, trembles before the Lord, who with the play of his eyebrows forces it to dance like a puppet. If we leave such a Lord, whom else can we supplicate? Neither in thought, word nor deed be overwise; god is merciful only to those who pray. Thus the Lord played his childish tricks, to the delight of all the people of the city; and now his mother would take and dandle him on her knees, and now put him down and rock him in his cradle.

Dohā 200

So lost in love that day and night succeeded one another unobserved, while in her fondness for her son she kept singing of his childish acts.

Caupāī 199

One day his mother, after washing and dressing him, put him to sleep in his cradle, and prepared to worship the Blessed Lord, her partron divinity. When the service was over and she had made her oblation, she returned to the place where she had dressed the food; but when she came there she beheld Rāma in the act of eating. In a great fright she ran to the nursery and there found the child again sleeping; but coming back once more she still saw the boy. Then she trembled and was much disturbed in mind, for she saw two children, one here and one there, and was utterly bewildered; saying, — 'Are my senses at fault, or is this a miracle ?' When Rāma saw his mother's distress, he broke out into a merry laugh,

Dohā 201

And displayed to her his whole marvellous form, indivisible; with a myriad worlds gleaming on each individual hair of his body;

Caupāī 200

with countless suns and moons, Śivas and Brahmās; with many mountains, rivers, oceans, lands and forests; with time, destiny, merit, demerit, nature and every power there manifested, even though unknown by name. When she beheld the mystic vision she stood terror-stricken, with hands, clasped in prayer; for she saw both the life which Māyā sets in motion and the faith that sets it free. With quivering body and speechless mouth she closed her eyes and bowed her head at his feet. Seeing his mother thus overpowered with amazement, Rāma again assumed the form of a child. But her terror left her not, while she hymned his praises, saying,—'I have regarded the father of the world as my own offspring.' Again and again Hari exhorted his mother,—'See, my mother, that you tell this to no one!'

Dohā 202

Again and again did Kauśalyā meekly reply with folded hands,—'See you too, my lord, that the magic power of yours never again affects me.'

Caupāī 201

Hari indulged in every kind of childish amusement, to the great delight of his attendants; and after a little time all the brothers grew to be big boys, gladdening every one about them. Then the *guru* came to perform the tonsure and again the Brāhmaṇas received large offerings. The four boys run about and divert themselves in all sorts of charming ways; and the Lord, whose thoughts, works and acts transcend every human sense, plays in Daśaratha's courtyard. If the king when at dinner called him, he would not leave his playmates and come, till Kauśalyā herself went for him, when he would toddle along with her as fast as he could. He whom the Vedas declare to be incomprehensible, of whom Śiva could find no end, is picked up by his mother and carried off in a pet, and his father with a smile takes him on his lap, though grimy all over with dust.

Dohā 203

Quickly glancing here and there at his meals, as soon as he got a chance, he would run away mischievously with a scream of joy, stuffing his mouth full of rice and curds.

Caupāī 202

His innocent, charming childish sports have been sung by Sarasvatī, Śeṣanāga, Śambhu and the Vedas, and he whose soul does not warm to them has been brought into the world by God to no purpose. When the brothers were all grown up, the *guru* and their father and mother invested them with the sacred thread, and Rāma went to his *guru's* house to study. Iṇ a short time he mastered all knowledge. The four Vedas are but the breath of his mouth, and for him to study was a joke indeed. When they were proficient in scholarship and politeness and morality they began to practise all princely sports. With bow and arrow in hand they showed so fair that all creation was ravished at the sight, and as the brothers passed along the road every man and woman paused to gaze at them.

Dohā 204

Rāma was gracious to all; and not a soul in Kosala, man or woman, young or old, but held him dearer than life.

Caupāī 203

Taking his brothers with him as companions, Rāma would go to hunt in the woods. There selecting for death the noblest game, he every day brought and showed it to the king; and each beast, slain by his shaft, after death went straight to heaven. Taking his meals in company with his younger brothers, ever obedient to his parents' commands, the gracious Lord omitted nothing that could please the people. He gave his mind to hear the Vedas and Purāṇas and then himself taught his brothers. Rising at break of day, he first saluted his parents and the priest, and then, after obtaining their sanction, busied himself with work in the city. The king was glad of heart when he saw his mode of life.

Dohā 205

The all-pervading, indivisible, passionless, unborn, who is without attributes, or name, or form, performs many wonders for the sake of the faithful.

Caupāī 204

I have now sung all these his doings; now hearken attentively to the remainder of my story. The great and wise sage Viśvāmitra had chosen a fair hermitage in the forest, where he gave himself up to prayer, sacrifice and meditation. But he feared the demons Mārīca and Subāhu exceedingly, for on beholding the sacrifice, they rushed at him and did violent outrage. The saintly son of Gādhi was pained and full of thought,—'There is no killing these accursed demons without Hari.' Then he reflected,—"The Lord has become incarnate to relieve earth of its burdens. I have now an excuse for going to visit him and after entreaty made will bring back with me the two brothers. Now I will feast my eyes on the sight of him who is the abode of all knowledge, piety and goodness."

Dohā 206

His manifold longing brooked no delay on the journey, and after bathing in the stream of the Sarju he proceeded to the king's court.

Caupāī 205

When the king heard of the sage's arrival, he went to meet him with a retinue of Brāhmaṇas, and prostrating himself reverently on the ground before him,took and seated him on his own throne : then washed his feet and offered him religious honours, saying,—"There is no one so blessed as I am to day; and had various kinds of food prepared for him. The great sage was highly pleased. Next, the king brought his four sons into his presence. On seeing Râma the sage forgot his detachment from the world and was as enraptured with his lovely face as is the *cakor* with the full moon. Then said the glad king,—"Reverend sir, this favour is unparalleled; with what purpose have you come ? Tell me, and I will not delay to accomplish it." "There is a crew of demons that trouble me, and I am come to you, O king, with a request. Let me have Raghunātha and his brothers: the demons' death is all I desire.

Dohā 207

Give them, O king, gladly, without any unwise doubts; for you it will be a meritorious and honourable act, and it will also turn out well for them."

Caupāī 206

When the king heard this unwelcome speech, his heart beat fast and all the brightness of his face grew dim,—"In my old age I have begotten four sons; O sir, you have spoken without due reflection Ask of me land, cow, wealth and treasure, and I will gladly give you all I have, at once. Nothing is dearer than the life of the body; but even that I would give in a minute. All my sons are dear to me as my own soul and, sir, I cannot spare you Râma. What is this pretty little boy of mine against a fierce and terrible demon ?" On hearing the king's word so fraught with love, the wise sage was glad of heart. Then Vasiṣṭha much exhorted him, and the king's doubts were dispelled. Obediently he sent for the two boys and pressed them to his heart and fervently exclaimed,—"My two boys are my very life; but you, holy sir, are now their only father."

Dohā 208*a*

The king entrusted the boys to the seer, again and again blessing them. Then they went to their mother's apartment and bowed the head at her feet.

Soraṭhā 208*b*

Glad to relieve the saint of his alarm, the two lion-hearted heroes set forth, oceans of compassion, resolute of purpose, the whole world's champions.

Caupāī 207

Bright-eyed, broad-chested, long of arm, dark of hue as the lotus or the *tamāla* tree; with quiver at side pendent from a yellow sash, and in either hand arrows and a comely bow, so marched the two brothers, one dark, the other fair, the treasure that Viśvāmitra had acquired. "I recognize," he thought, "the lord god Brāhmaṇya-deva[1] in the child who thus on my account has left his own father." So thought the sage; and as he went he pointed out Tārakā, who on hearing his voice rushed up in a fury. With a single arrow the Lord took her life, but recognizing her submission gave her a place in his own realm. Then, the seer knew he had found his lord, but yet instructed him, the all-wise. As they travelled they felt neither hunger nor thirst; such were their incomparable strength of body and glorious vigour.

Dohā 209

After taking the Lord to his own hermitage he made over to him every kind of weapon, and devoutly gave him herbs and roots and fruit to eat, knowing him to be ever gracious to men of holy life.

Caupāī 208

At daybreak Raghurāī said to the sage,—"Go and make ready the sacrifice, and fear not." The brotherhood began preparing the oblation, while he remained to guard the sacrificial fire. On hearing of this, the demon Mārīca rushed up in a fury with his army to disturb the sage. Rāma struck him with a headless shaft, and he fell a hundred leagues beyond the sea. Then he slew Subāhu with an arrow of fire, while his brother routed the whole demon host. When they had thus slain the demons and restored peace to the Brāhmaṇas, the whole company of gods and sages began to hymn their praise. There Raghurāī stayed a few more days and showed kindness to the hermits, who devoutly repeated to him many legends of the Purāṇas, though he knew them all before. Then the sage respectfully informed him,—"There is a sight, my lord, which is

1. Brāhmaṇya-deva is one of the epithets of Viṣṇu. [These lines are often interpreted differently : "I have now realized," he thought, "that the Lord is the devoted friend of Brāhmaṇas..." or that "the Lord is a votary of the Brāhmaṇas..."]

worth your going to see." When Raghunātha heard of the ordeal of the bow, he gladly accompanied the noble sage. On the way he spied a hermitage without bird, deer, or any living creature near it, and observing a remarkable stone, inquired of the sage about it, who in reply told him the whole story in detail.

Dohā 210

"Gautama's consort," he said, "was by a curse turned into a hard rock, and is patiently longing for the dust of your lotus feet. O Raghubīra, have mercy on her."

Chand 22

At the touch so sweet of his hallowed feet, she awoke from her long unrest,
And meekly adored her sovereign lord, awaiting his high behest.
With speechless tongue, limbs all unstrung, and eyes that streamed with tears,
She fell at his feet in rapture meet, far blest above all her peers.
Then bolder grown by the favour shown with a faith that himself had given,
She dared to raise her hymn of praise,—"Great Spirit, high lord of heaven,
Save me, O save, thy succour I crave, holy god, sinful wretch though I be,
Rāvaṇa's conquering foe, joy of all else below who toil upon life's troubled sea.
Though the sage cursed me sore in the ill days of yore, now I hold it a blessing most sweet,
For my own eyes have seen my Redeemer, and I ween Śiva only my rapture could mete.
Witless and weak, one only boon I seek; as the bee within the lotus loves to stay,
May my soul upon thy feet, O my god, I thee entreat, dwell in rapture never ending night and day;

Holy feet, the adoration of the lord of all creation, and
source of the stream divine,
Which on Śiva's head descended, this day have condescended
to rest and on this vile head of mine."
Thus full of jubilation, with oft-renewed prostration, did
Gautama's long lost bride,
With the boon she most had craved, thus graciously
vouchsafed, return to her husband's side.

Dohā 211

Thus the benevolent lord Hari is compassionate beyond our deserts. Worship only him, O foolish Tulasī Dāsa, and cease from all wrangling and hypocrisy.

Caupāī 209

Rāma and Lakṣmaṇa accompanied the sage to the world-purifying Ganges. Both the lord and his younger brother reverently saluted it, and Rāma was delighted beyond measure, as the son of Gādhi told him the legend how the heavenly stream had come to earth. Then the Lord and the seers performed their ablutions and the Brāhmaṇas received manifold gifts. The hermits' champion went on his way rejoicing, and quickly drew near to the city of Videha. When Rāma beheld the beauty of the city, he and his brother were delighted at the many ponds and wells and rivers and lakes, with water of ambrosial purity and jewelled flights of steps; where the hum of bees, drunk with nectar, made a delicious sound and birds of all kinds were softly cooing: as the lilies expanded their many-coloured petals, and a cool, soft, fragrant breeze was ever delightful.

Dohā 212

On all four sides the city was bright with flower-gardens, orchards and groves, the haunt of innumerable birds and full of fruits and flowers and beauteous leaves.

Caupāī 210

The beauty of the city was indescribable; wherever one went there was something to charm the soul. Handsome bazārs and gorgeous balconies all studded with jewels, as though the Creator had fashioned them with his own hand; thriving bankers and traders, the very Kuveras of wealth, sitting with all their various goods displayed; fine squares and beautiful streets, that were constantly sprinkled with fragrant waters; magnificent temples to all the gods, as bright as if they had been painted by Kāmadeva himself; all the people of the city, both men and women, prosperous, well-dressed, virtuous, pious, intelligent and accomplished. But Janaka's palace was such a masterpiece that the gods tired themselves with looking at it, and the mind was quite overcome by the sight of the Fort, for it seemed to have appropriated to itself all that was most beautiful in the world.

Dohā 213

With glistening white walls and doors of gold with gems set in different devices, the exquisite mansion where Sitā dwelt was far too lovely for words to describe.

Caupāī 211

All the city gateways were most massive with panels of adamant, and were thronged with feudatory princes and their retinues of dancers, panegyrists and bards. The vast and well-built stables were at all hours of the day crowded with horses, elephants and chariots : and the ministers, generals and warriors all had residence in the same style as the king. Outside the city, by lake or river, the multitudinous princes had pitched their different camps. On seeing a fine mango grove, a most agreeable and convenient spot, the descendant of Kuśika (Viśvāmitra) exclaimed,—"This is just what I like, let us stay here, Raghubīra." "Very well, my lord," answered the gracious god; and there they alighted with all their hermit train. When the king of Mithilā heard the tidings that the great sage Viśvāmitra had arrived,

Dohā 214

taking with him his ministers and many gallant fighting men and noble Brāhmaṇas and the chief of his kinsmen,[1] in this fashion the king went forth rejoicing to meet the prince of sages.

1. The words rendered, 'the chief of his kinsmen,' may also be taken to mean 'his *guru* (Śatānanda) and his kinsmen .

Caupāī 212

Bowing to the ground, he made obeisance, and the sage gladly gave him his blessing. Then the king respectfully saluted all the Brāhmaṇas and congratulated himself on his good fortune. After making many inquiries as to his health and welfare, Viśvāmitra led the king to a seat, and at that very time arrived the two brothers who had gone to see the garden, one dark, the other fair; in childhood's tender bloom, the joy of all beholders, ravishing the senses of the whole world. When Raghupati came, all rose and Viśvāmitra seated him by his side. All were charmed at the sight of the two brothers; their eyes filled with tears and their body thrilled with rapture, and the king especially was beside himself with joy[1] on beholding Rāma's sweet and lovely appearance.

Dohā 215

Though feeling himself overwhelmed with love, the king discreetly composed himself, and bowing his head at the sage's feet, said in suppressed accents choking with emotion—

Caupāī 213

"Tell me, my lord, who are these two lovely children ? Are they the glory of a saintly family, or the bulwarks of a kingly line ? Or are they the twofold manifestation[2] of the Supreme Spirit, whom the Vedas declare to be unutterable ? My mind, ordinarily free from worldly attachment, wearies itself with gazing upon them, as the *cakor* in gazing upon the moon. Therefore, sir, I beg you to tell me the truth and to conceal nothing. My love grows with looking, and my soul perforce is withdrawn from divine contemplation." Said the sage with a smile,—"You have spoken well, O king; your word is always true; there is not a living creature that does not love these boys." Rāma smiled to himself on hearing this. "They are the sons of Daśaratha,

1. This line *Bhayau Videha videha bisekhi*, contains a play upon words which cannot be preserved in a translation. A literal rendering would be; particular Videha (*i.e.*, Janaka, the king of Videha) became really *videha* (*i.e.*, without a body).

2. The two manifestations are *nirguṇa and saguṇa*, the bodiless and the embodied.

the glory of the line of Raghu, and the king has sent them to help me.

Dohā 216

They are Râma and Lakṣmaṇa by name, these two noble brothers and they are as strong as they are good and beautiful; all the world will bear witness that they protected my sacrifice and vanquished all the demons in battle."

Caupāī 214

Said the king,—"O sage, when I behold your feet I cannot tell how richly I am rewarded for any former good deeds. And these pretty twins have conferred a happiness upon you, the supremely happy. Their innocent affection for each other is beyond description, a delight to the inmost soul. Hear me, sir," cried the king in his rapture, "it is like the natural union between the universal soul and the soul of man." Again and again the king gazed at the Lord with a thrill of emotion and heart bursting with devotion. Then with courteous phrase and bowed head he escorted the sage to the city and there assigned him apartments, which were bright and cheerful at all times of the day; and finally, after further homage and proffers of service, the king took his leave and returned to the palace.

Dohā 217

When Râma, the jewel of the house of Raghu, and the hermits had taken food and rested a little, he went and sat down by his brother's side : now it still wanted an hour to sunset,

Caupāī 215

And Lakṣmaṇa had at heart a great longing to go and see Janaka's city; but again, for fear of the Lord and respect for the sage, he said nothing out loud, but was smiling to himself. Râma understood what was passing in his mind, and being ever considerate to his followers was glad and with a most modest and submissive smile, after begging permission of his *guru* to speak, said,—"Sir, Lakṣmaṇa wishes to see the city, but out of respect for you is hesitant to speak out. If you will allow me,

I will show him the place and quickly bring him back again." The sage replied most affectionately,—"O Rāma, how can you do aught but good; the guardian of the bridge of religion, the loving benefactor of all faithful servants ?

Dohā 218

Go, blessed pair of brothers, in whom all joy is stored, and see the city; bless the eyes of all the people by showing them your beauty."

Caupāī 216

After doing homage to the sage's lotus feet they went off, these two brothers, gladdening the eyes of the whole world. When the children in the market-place saw their exceeding beauty their eyes and their very soul fastened greedily upon them. Clad in yellow apparel, with belt and quiver at their side, with graceful bow and arrows in hand, a lovely pair, one dark, the other fair of hue, with sandalwood *tilak* to match their complexion; with lion-like waist and long arms, and breast adorned with strings of elephant pearls, with shapely ears and lotus eyes, and moon-like face to assuage the three kinds of plain; with golden flowers for earrings, so beautiful as to steal the heart of every beholder; with a bewitching glance and fair arched eyebrows and a star on the forehead that seemed beauty's own stamp;

Dohā 219

with jaunty cap on comely head, with black curly locks the two brothers were all-beautiful from head to foot and exquisite in every limb and feature.

Caupāī 217

When the citizens heard the news that the princes had come to see the city, they all left their business and started off like beggars to pillage a treasury. When they beheld the easy grace of the two brothers, they were enraptured and their eyes were rewarded. The maidens peeping from the windows of the houses at once fell in love with Rāma's beauty, and in amorous strain addressed one another,—"They surpass in beauty a thousand loves: neither among gods, nor men, nor demons, nor serpents, nor deified sages has beauty such as theirs ever been heard of. As for Viṣṇu with his four arms, Brahmā with his four heads, and Purāri with his five faces and wondrous attire, and all the other gods, there is not one in the whole universe whose beauty, my friend, can be compared to theirs.

Dohā 220

Of tender age, the very homes of beauty, equally lovely whether dark or fair, as though a myriad Loves had been lavished on each individual limb of their body.

Caupāī 218

Tell me, friend, is there any one in human form who would not be enchanted at the sight of such beauty ?" Said one in gentle loving tones,—"Hear, my dear, what I have been told. This pretty pair of young cygnets are the two sons of King Daśaratha. They have protected the sacrifice of sage Viśvāmitra and slain in battle the invincible demons. The lovely child with dark complexion and lotus eyes, who quelled the pride of Mārīca and Subāhu and bears the bow and arrows in his hand, is the sweet son of Kauśalyā, by name Rāma. The fair youth in gallant attire, who also has bow and arrows in his hand and follows Rāma, is named Lakṣmaṇa and is his younger brother. Sumitrā, you must know, is his mother.

Dohā 221

After accomplishing the Brāhmaṇa's (Viśvāmitra's) purpose and on the way setting free the sage's wife, the two brothers have come here to see the tournament." On hearing this all the ladies were delighted.

Caupāī 219

Said a maiden, after regarding Rāma's beauty, "Here is a bridegroom worthy of Jānakī. If the king does but see him, he will abjure his vow and insist upon a marriage with them." Said another, "The king knows who they are and has received both of them and the sage, with all honour. He has not, however, gone back from his vow, but mastered by fate persists in his folly." Another said, "If God is good and is certain to reward every man according to his deserts, then here is the bridegroom Jānakī will wed. About this, my dear, there can be no doubt. When such a union is brought about by destiny, every one will be satisfied. O friend, I am deeply moved by the thought that if this marriage takes place he will come again some time;

Dohā 222

Otherwise there is no chance of my seeing him; it is only a long accumulation of merit in previous existences that is rewarded by such intercourse."

Caupāī 220

Said another,—"Friend, you have spoken well; this is a marriage that will please everyone." Said another,—"Śiva's bow is hard to bend, and this dark prince is of delicate frame; it is really a most unfair test." Hearing this, another soft-voiced maiden said,—"I have once and again heard say of them that though slight in appearance their strength is great. Touched by the dust of his lotus feet, the guilty Ahalyā attained salvation: and he will never rest till he has broken the bow; this is a belief out of which I am no-how to be cheated. When the Creator fashioned Sītā, he predestined for her this dark-complexioned bridegroom." On hearing these words all were glad and softly exclaimed,—"May it indeed prove so!"

Dohā 223

In their gladness of heart the bevy of fair-faced bright-eyed maidens shower down flowers, and wherever the two brothers went there was all the joy of heaven.

Caupāī 221

Now they reached the eastern quarter of the city, where the lists had been prepared for the tournament. In the midst of a fair and spacious paved area a spotless altar had been gorgeously adorned, with a broad golden platform all around for the reception of the princes, and close behind another circular tier for the spectators, of somewhat greater height and elegantly decorated, where all the people of the city might come and sit. Close to this was another large and beautiful gallery of glistening white, painted in diverse colours, whence ladies might view the spectacle with due decorum, according to their family rank. The children politely show the two lords all the preparations, and with pleasant voice keep telling them what this is and that is;

Dohā 224

thus, in their affection, finding a pretext for frequently touching their lovely person: while they thrill all over with delight as again and again they gaze on the two brothers.

Caupāī 222

When they perceived that Rāma was won by their devotion, they lovingly explain the different places, each according to his own fancy calling away the two brothers, who in their kindness are ever ready to come. Rāma shows Lakṣmaṇa everything, still talking in light and merry tone; and he, in obedience to whose fiat Māyā in a moment of time created the entire universe, out of compassion to his faithful people, feigns amazement at the sight of the arena of the contest of the bow. When they had seen all the show, they returned to their *guru* in alarm at being so late: and he, by whose awe Terror itself is dismayed, thus manifests the transcendent virtue of devotion. With many kind and courteous phrases they reluctantly take leave of the children;

Dohā 225

and meekly and submissively, with mingled awe and love, they bow the head at the *guru's* feet: nor sit down till they obtain his permission.

Caupāī 223

When it was dusk the sage gave the word, and all performed their evening devotions, and in the recital of sacred legends spent two watches of the solemn night. Then the sage retired to his couch, and the two brothers began to shampoo his feet; they whose lotus feet the holiest of men longing to behold practise all kinds of penance and meditation, even they, these two brothers, mastered by love, affectionately shampooed their master's lotus feet. At last when the sage had so ordered again and again, Rāma himself retired to rest, while Lakṣhmaṇa pressed his feet to his heart and reverently caressed them with emotions of exquisite delight. Again and again the Lord said,—'Sleep, dear brother,' and at last he lay down, but with the divine feet still in his lap.

Dohā 226

When the night was spent and he heard the first sound of cock-crow, Lakṣmaṇa arose; and next, before the sage, woke the lord of the universe, the all-wise Rāma.

Caupāī 224

After performing all the customary rites of purification and going to bathe, they bowed before the guru, and by his permission went out to gather flowers, as befitted the time. As they went they spied a beautiful garden of the king's where reigned perpetual Spring, planted with ornamental trees of every kind, and overhung with many coloured creepers, so rich in bud and fruit and flower that in its abundance it put to shame even the trees of paradise; while the peacocks danced responsive to the music made by the feathered choir of cuckoo, *koel*, parrot and partridge. In the midst of the garden a lovely lake shone bright with jewelled steps of varied designs: its pure expanse gladdened with many-coloured lotuses and the cooing of water-birds and the hum of bees.

Dohā 227

Both the lord and his brother were delighted at the sight of the lake and the garden. What a charming pleasance must that have been which pleased even Rāma.

Caupāī 225

Enraptured they looked all about them, and with the gardeners' permission began to gather leaves and flowers. At that very time Sītā too came there having been sent by her mother to visit the shrine of Girijā. With her came all her young and lovely companions, singing glad songs. Now Girijā's shrine was close to the lake, beautiful beyond description, the delight of all beholders. When she and her attendants had bathed in the pool, she approached the goddess with a glad heart and after adoration paid with much devotion begged of her a handsome and well-matched bridegroom. One of her attendant damsels, who had strayed away to look at the flower-garden, chanced to see the two brothers and returned to Sītā, quite love-smitten.

Dohā 228

When her companions observed what a state she was in, her body all in a tremble and her eyes full of tears, they all gently asked her to tell them the cause of this rapture.

Caupāī 226

"Two princes," she said,"of tender age and charming in every way, have come to see the garden; one dark of hue, the other fair, but how can I describe them? Voice is sightless and eyes are dumb." All the damsels were delighted at her speech, and perceiving the intense longing in Sītā's bosom, one of them exclaimed,—"My dear, they must be the king's sons, who, as I hear, arrived yesterday with the sage, who completely fascinated with their beauty and stole away the hearts of all the women in the city. Every one is talking of their loveliness; we really must see them; they are worth seeing." These words were most grateful to Sītā, whose eyes were restless with longing. With her kind friend to lead the way, she followed, nor did any one know that it was an old love.

Dohā 229

Remembering Nārada's words, she was filled with holy devotion, and anxiously turned her gaze on every side, like a startled fawn.

Caupāī 227

When he heard the sound of the golden bangles on her hands and feet, Rāma thought within himself, and then said to

Lakṣmaṇa,—"Imagine Love triumphant over the whole world to be now sounding the kettledrum of victory." So saying he agani looked in that direction, and like the moon on the *cakor*, flashed Sītā's face upon his sight. His eyes became as immovably fixed as though Nimi, the winking god, had fled in confusion from his wonted post. Beholding her beauty he was enraptured; but his admiration was all within, and utterance failed him. As though the great Architect, after creating the world, had put before it in visible form all the skill with which he had fashioned it; or as if the Beautiful had been beautified into a temple of beauty and illuminated by a sudden flash of torchlight; but all the similes of the poets are stale and hackneyed; where can I find any likeness to Videha's daughter?

Dohā 230

Dwelling in heart on Sītā's beauty and reflecting on his own good fortune, the pure-souled Lord thus addressed his brother in terms appropriate to the occasion,—

Caupāī 228

"Dear brother, this is the very daughter of king Janaka, for whom the tournament has been ordained. Her maidens have brought her to worship Gaurī, and a train of light marks her path through the garden. At the sight of her divine beauty, my ordinarily placid soul is agitated. God alone knows why! But of a truth, brother, the throbbing of my lucky side betokens good fortune. It has always been a mark of the race of Raghu that they never set their heart on evil courses; and thus I am confidently assured that all will be well; for I have never even in a dream looked upon another man's wife to long after her. And rare, indeed, in the world are the men who neither turn their back upon the foe in battle nor covet their neighbour's wife, and from whom no beggar meets a rebuff".

Dohā 231

Thus discoursing to his brother, and with his heart enamoured of Sītā's beauty, like a bee sucking honey from the lotus, he drank in the loveliness of her face.

Caupāī 229

Sītā kept looking anxiously all around, wondering where the princes had gone. Wherever fell her fawn-like glance, it seemed a rain of glistening lotus flowers. Then her companions pointed out to her under the shade of the creepers the two lovely youths, the one dark, the other of fair hue. Her eyes, on beholding their beauty, were filled with longing and with the gladness of one who has found a long-lost treasure. Wearied with gazing upon Rāma's charms, her eyelids ceased to move and being overpowered by love, as is the partridge when it sees the autumnal moon, she lost all body-consciousness. Receiving Rāma into her heart by the pathway of vision, she craftily closed upon him the doors of her eyelids. When her companions saw her thus overcome, they were too much abashed to utter a word.

Dohā 232

At that moment emerged the two brothers from the shade of the arbour, like two spotless moons from a riven cloud.

Caupāī 230

Two gallant champions, the perfection of beauty, like a white lotus and a dark, with their hair parted like a raven's wing on their comely head, and here and there bedecked with bunches of flower-buds; their forehead bright with the *tilak* and beads of perspiration, and their graceful ears adorned with ornaments; with arched eyebrows and curly locks, and eyes bright as a lotus bud, with lovely chin and nose and cheeks, and a gracious smile enslaving every soul — such beauteous features as I could never describe; they would put to shame a myriad Loves. They wore a string of jewels on their breasts and had exquisitely dimpled necks like the conch, and mighty arms like the trunk of some young elephant in whom Kāmadeva had become incarnate. Said one, "With the flowers and cup of leaves in his left hand, the dark-hued prince, O my sister, is beautiful indeed!"

Dohā 233

As her companions gazed upon the jewel of the Solar race, with his lion-like waist and bright yellow attire, very abode of bliss and amiability, they lost all self-consciousness.

Caupāī 231

Yet one wise maiden summoning up courage, grasped Sītā by the hand and said,—"You can at any time meditate upon Gaurī; why not now look at the princes ?" Then the modest Sītā unclosed her eyes and saw before her the two lions of the house of Raghu. As she gazed on Rāma, all beautiful from head to foot, and remembered her father's vow, she was greatly troubled. When her companions saw her thus overcome they all cried as if in alarm, — "It is getting late;" and one added with a meaningful smile, — "We must come again at this time to-morrow." On hearing this clever hint Sītā was abashed and said, as if in fear of her mother,—"It is late, indeed." Then summoning up resolution, she fixed the image of Rāma in her heart and turned to go; but again she thought how entirely it all depended upon her father.

Dohā 234

Pretending to look back at a deer, or a bird, or a tree, she turned her head again and again, and each time that she beheld the beauteous Raghubīra her love was augmented not a little.

Caupāī 232

Considering how hard it was to break Śiva's bow, she went sobbing silently on her way, and kept in her heart the image of the darkhued prince. When the Lord perceived that she was going, he drew in his heart with the indelible ink of love a charming sketch of her infinite beauty and virtue and blissful devotion. Again she returned to Bhavānī's shrine, and after embracing her feet, thus prayed with clasped hands,—"Glory, glory, glory to thee, O daughter of the mountain-king, as fixed in thy gaze on Śiva's face as is the partridge on the moon; O mother of Gaṇeśa and Kārttikeya; great mother of the world; whose body is lustrous as the lightning; of whom there is neither beginning nor middle nor end; whose infinite majesty is a mystery even to the Veda; cause of the birth, continuance and ultimate destruction of all being; enchantress of the universe; delighting in thy own supremacy:

Dohā 235

Among all faithful wives who adore their husbands as gods, thy name, O mother, holds the first place ! Thy immeasurable grandeur is more than a thousand Śāradās and Śeṣanāgas could tell.

Caupāī 233

The fourfold rewards of life are easy of attainment by thy servants, O granter of boons, beloved of Tripurāri; and all, O goddess, who adore thy lotus feet, are made happy, whether they be gods or men, or sages. Thou knowest full well my heart's desire, for in the heart of man thou ever dwellest : there is no need that I declare it aloud to thee." So saying, Sītā embraced her feet. Bhavānī was moved by her humility and devotion; the image smiled and a wreath dropped. Reverently Sītā clasped to her bosom the divine gift, and Gaurī herself with a heart full of joy thus spoke,—"Hearken, Sītā; my blessing is effectual; your heart's desire shall be accomplished. Nārada's words are ever truth itself; the bridegroom upon whom your soul is set shall, indeed, be yours.

Chand 23

The dark-complexioned prince, upon whose innate beauty your soul is set, shall indeed be your husband. The All-merciful and omniscient Lord is aware of your fidelity and love." On hearing Gaurī pronounce this blessing, Sītā and her companions were glad of heart, and in their delight (says Tulasī) returned again and again to the temple to adore the goddess.

Soraṭhā 236

Finding Gaurī so gracious, Sītā was more glad of heart than words can tell. As an auspicious omen, her left side, the seat of good fortune, began to throb.

Caupāī 234

The two brothers returned to their *guru*, inwardly praising Sītā's loveliness, and Rāma related to Viśvāmitra all that had taken place being simplicity itself and utterly devoid of all guile.

The sage took the flowers and performed his devotions, and then imparted his blessing to the two brothers, saying,—"May your desire be accomplished." Rāma and Lakṣmaṇa were glad at the words. Then, after taking his meal, the saintly sage began the recital of sacred legends. When the day was spent, they first asked his permission and then went out to perform their evening duties. The glorious moon arose in the eastern sky, and its orb reminded Rāma of Sītā's lovely face; but afterwards he thus reasoned within himself,—"The queen of night is not to be compared with Sītā;

Dohā 237

for she was born of the restless ocean, with poison for a brother, and by day she is dim and obscure, how then can such a poor feeble creature be matched with the lovely Sītā.

Caupāī 235

She waxes and wanes, brings sorrow to love-sick maids, and is devoured by Rāhu when she crosses the latter's orbit; she causes anguish to the *cakvā* and withers the lotus; O moon, thou are full of faults. It is a great sin and highly improper to compare Janaka's daughter to thee." Thus, finding in the moon a pretext for extolling Sītā's beauty, he returned to the *guru*, the night being now far advanced, and after bowing himself at his feet and obtaining his permission he retired to rest. When the night was over, Raghunāyaka arose and, looking towards his brother, thus began to say,—"See, brother, the day has dawned to the delight of the lotus, the *cakvā* and all mankind." Then said Lakṣmaṇa in gentle tones and with folded hands, meant to reveal the glory of the Lord:

Dohā 238

"At the dawn of day the lilies fade and the brilliance of the stars is dimmed, so at the news of your coming all the princes wax faint;

Caupāī 236

For bright though they be as the stars. they cannot overcome the night-black bow. The lotus, the *cakwa*, the bee, and every bird — all rejoice over night's defeat; and so, O lord, all your votaries will be glad when the bow is broken. Sunrise is an easy triumph over darkness : the constellations retire and light flashes upon the world. O Raghurâî, the sun in its rising figures forth to all the kings your own majesty, and your mighty arms are as it were the pass in the eastern mountain through which is manifested the spectacle of the broken bow." The Lord smiled to hear his brother's speech. The All-pure then performed the daily rites of purification and bathed and, after observance of the prescribed ceremonies, presented himself before the *guru* and bowed his comely head at his feet. Then Janaka summoned Satânanda and sent him in haste to Visvâmitra. He came and declared his sovereign's message and also called for the two brothers.

Dohā 239

After reverently saluting Śatānanda, the Lord went and sat down by his *guru*, who said,—"Come, my son, Janaka has sent for us.

Caupāī 237

Let us go and see Śītā's nuptials, and who is the happy man whom heaven will honour." Said Laksmana,—"His will be the glory, my lord, upon whom your favour rests." The sages were glad to hear this seemly speech, and all with much effusion gave their blessings. Then the gracious god, attended by all the saintly throng, sallied forth to witness the tournament. No sooner had they reached the arena than the news spread all over the city, and every one put away his work and came thronging in, men and women, young and old, and even children in arms. When Janaka saw the enormous crowd he gave orders to his practised servitors,—"Go round at once to all the people and marshal them to their proper seats."

Dohā 240

With gentle and courteous words they respectfully seated them all both men and women, according to their respective rank, whether noble, burgher or churl.

Caupāī 238

Then there arrived the royal princes, looking as though Beauty herself dwelt in their persons, graceful and accomplished champions, one dark, the other fair, but both charming : resplendent in the assembly of princes like two full moons in a circle of stars. Every spectator seemed to see in the person of the Lord the reflection of his own disposition. The princes beheld a gallant warrior, as Heroism incarnate; the wicked kings trembled at the sight of the Lord, as a visible presentment of the Terrible; the demons in their princely disguise thought they saw the image of Death : while the citizens regarded the twin brothers as the glory of manhood, a delight to the eyes.

Dohā 241

The women beheld them with joy, each according to her own attitude towards him, as though a bright vision of the Erotic in utterly incomparable form.

Caupāī 239

By the learned the Lord was seen in his divine majesty with many faces and hands and feet and eyes and heads. And how did he appear to Janaka's family group ? Like a noble kinsman and friend. The queen, no less than the king, regarded him with unspeakable love like a dear child; to mystics he shone forth as Absolute Truth, the placid radiance of unruffled Quietism; while to the pious the two brothers, appeared as their own chosen deities, granting perfect bliss. But as for Sītā, when she gazed on Râma, her love and joy were unspeakable; if she could not utter the emotion of her heart, how can any poet declare it ? Thus according to the ruling passion of each individual spectator, were the Kosala princes seen by each.

Dohā 242

Resplendent in the midst of the royal assembly in their contrasted beauty, the princes of Kosala ravished the eyes of the whole universe.

Caupāī 240

Both were endowed with such facile grace of form that a myriad Loves were all too mean a comparison; with beaming faces that would put to shame the autumnal moon, and irresistibly charming lotus eyes; with glances so unspeakably winning that they would rob Love of all his pride; with rounded cheeks and ears adorned with trembling earrings; with beautiful chins and lips and sweet voice; with smiles more radiant than the moonbeams, and arched eyebrows and delicate noses; broad brows with glittering *tilak*, and clustering locks with which no swarm of bees could vie; with yellow turbans on their shapely heads, dotted here and there with flower-buds; with exquisite necks, marked with a triple line, enclosing as it were the bliss of the three spheres of creation.

Dohā 243

They were adorned with well-wrought necklaces of elephant-pearls[1] and *tulasī* garlands on their breasts; with the shoulders of a bull and the gait of a lion, and arms long and powerful.

Caupāi 241

By their sides quivers slung from a yellow brace; they were equipped with arrows in their hands and bows on their strong left shoulders; with the yellow sacred thread round their necks, and, in short, with beautiful forms from head to foot, beauty all over. Everyone who saw them was made happy, nor could for a minute take his eyes off them. Janaka, too, rejoiced to behold the two brothers. Then went he to the sage and clasped his lotus feet, and differentially related to him all the past history of the bow,[2] and showed the hermits the place marked out for the games. Wherever the two gallant princes went, all men's eyes were dazzled; each saw Rāma looking towards himself, without understanding that it was a special miracle. The sage told the king the arrangements were perfect, and the king was thereby highly gratified.

Dohā 244

There was one tier of seats bright, spacious and beautiful above all the rest. and here the Rājā seated the sage and the two brothers.

1. The *kuñjara-maṇi* as it is here named, or more commonly *gaja-mukta*, is a pearl supposed to be found in the projections on the forehead of an elephant.

2. Notice how Tulasī Dāsa departs from the sources of the story. The past history of the bow is related in both *Vālmīkīya Rāmāyaṇa*, Bālakāṇḍa, 66, 8-26 and *Adhyātma Rāmāyaṇa*, Bālakāṇḍa, 6, 58ff.

Caupāī 242

At the sight of the Lord all the kings were in despair, like the stars at the rising of the full moon; for they felt inwardly assured that beyond all doubt Rāma would succeed in bending the bow; or even if he did not break the massy beam, that Sītā would still bestow upon him the garland of victory. And so thinking, sir, they turned homewards, abandoning all glory of victory and pride of strength. There were other kings, blind and insolent fools, who mocked at such words and cried,—'To break the bow and win the bride is a difficulty,[1] but unless it be broken how can the bride be won ? Should Death himself for once come forth against us, him too would we vanquish in our battle for Sītā." Hearing this there were other kings who smiled, good, pious and sensible men, and said,—

Soraṭhā 245

"Rāma will certainly marry Sītā, to the discomfiture of those proud princes; for who can conquer in battle Daśaratha's gallant sons ?

Caupāī 243

Why thus scoff and throw away your lives to no purpose; imagined sweets stop no man's hunger. Listen to this my solemn warning: be inwardly assured that Sītā is the mother, and Rāma the father of the universe, and feast your eyes to the full on their beauty. These two brothers, so lovely, so gracious so full of every excellence, have their home in Śambhu's heart. Why, when you have a sea of ambrosia at hand, should you leave it to run upon your death in pursuit of a mirage ? But do ye what seemeth you good : we have today reaped our life's reward." So saying, the good kings turned to gaze with affection on the picture of incomparable beauty; while in heaven the gods mounted their chariots to behold the spectacle, and showered down flowers and uttered songs of joy.

1. The word *avagāha* in this line is explained in glossaries by *athāha* 'unfathomable,' as if from the root *gāh*, to dive into. Rather, however, it seems to be for *avagrāha* (as *kohi* for *krodhi*), meaning an impediment or difficulty.

Dohā 246

Then — seeing the fitness of the time — Janaka, sent to summon Sītā; and obediently she came, with all her lovely and accomplished attendants.

Caupāī 244

Her loveliness is beyond description. Seeing that she is the Mother of the world, the perfection of all grace and goodness, all similes seem to me unworthy of her and appropriate only to mortal women. In describing Sītā, to what can she be likened, or what can the poet name that will not rather do her dishonour ? If I should liken her to other women, where is there on earth a maiden so lovely ? If I look to the denizens of heaven, Sarasvatī is a chatterer; Bhavānī has only half a body; Ratī is in sore distress on account of her disfleshed lord; and as for Lakṣmī, the twinbirth of poison and strong drink, how can Sītā be compared to her ? Even though the ocean of ambrosia were the Beautiful, and the tortoise Grace, the rope being Fascination, and Mount Meru the amorous sentiment, while Love with his own lotus hand played the part of churner;

Dohā 247

Even then, though Lakṣmī the source of all beauty and bliss, had thus been born, still the poet would shrink from saying that she could be compared to Sītā.

Caupāī 245

She came and her wise maidens escorted her, singing sweet-voiced songs. The mother of creation was she, of incomparable beauty; her delicate frame veiled in a fair white robe, and with a profusion of brilliant and tasteful ornaments, with which her maidens had bedecked her every limb. When she set her foot within the lists, all beholders, men and women alike, were fascinated by her charms; the gods in their delight sounded their kettledrums and rained down flowers midst the singing of the *apsarās*. The wreath of victory sparkled in her hands as she cast a hurried glance on the assembled kings, with anxious heart looking for Rāma. Not a king but was love-smitten. But by the sage sat the two brothers and on them she fell with her greedy eyes as upon a rich treasure.

Dohā 248

Shrinking into herself from awe of the reverend fathers and at the sight of so large a company, she turned her eyes upon her attendants, though at the same time she drew all Rāma into her soul.

Caupāī 246

Not a man or woman, who beheld the beauty of Rāma and the loveliness of Sītā, could close his eyes for a second : but all thought with dismay of the king's vow and in their heart made supplication to Brahmā,—"O God, rid Janaka of his obstinacy and make him right-minded as myself. Let the king have no hesitation about breaking his vow and giving Sītā in marriage to Rāma: the world will approve, and we all shall be pleased; but obstinacy, if persisted in, will at the last be as a consuming fire in his bosom." All were absorbed in the same ardent desire, saying,—"The dark youth is the match for Sītā." Then Janaka summoned the bards, who as they came proclaimed his state and dignity, and bade them go and declare his vow. Filled with great joy, the bards went off.

Dohā 249

They cried aloud, "Hearken, all ye princes : we announce to you Videha's vow, and with upraised hands call heaven to witness it.

Caupāī 247

Though your mighty arms be as the moon, yet Śiva's famous bow is as terrible and unyielding as Rāhu. When Rāvaṇa and Bāṇāsura saw it — albeit sturdy champions — they looked at the bow and crept silently away. Here is now the great god's massy beam, and whoever in this royal assembly shall today bend it shall be renowned in heaven and earth and hell, and at once without hesitation shall receive in marriage the hand of the king's daughter." When they heard the vow, all the kings were full of eagerness — insolent warriors, savage of soul — and girding up their loins they rose in haste, bowing their heads, ere they commenced, before their patron god. With flushed face and many a close look, they essay the divine bow: but though they put forth all their strength in a thousand different ways they cannot move it. Those, indeed, who had any sense at all did not go near it.

Dohā 250

After straining at the bow — those foolish kings — without being able to stir it, they retire in confusion, as though it had gathered strength by in turn absorbing the force of each successive warrior.

Caupāī 248

Then ten thousand princes, all at once, attempted to raise it, but it was not to be moved and yielding as little as a virtuous wife at the words of a gallant. All the kings appeared as ridiculous as an ascetic who has no religion. Their mighty glory and renown and heroism were utterly worsted by the bow, and with much confusion of face and sadness of heart they went and took again each his own place in the assembly. When Janaka saw the kings thus dismayed, he cried aloud as it were in anger,—"Hearing the vow that I had made, many kings have come from diverse realms, with gods and demons in human form, stalwart heroes, staunch in fight.

Dohā 251

A lovely bride, a grand triumph and splendid renown are the prize, but God, it seems. has not created the man who can break the bow and win it.

Caupāī 249

Tell me now who was dissatisfied with the guerdon or, refused to try his strength on Śiva's bow, but let alone lifting and breaking, sirs, there was not one of you who could stir it even a grain's breadth from the ground. Now let no proud warrior wax wroth if I declare that there are no heroes left on earth.

Give up all hope and turn your faces homewards: it is God's will that Sītā is not to be married. If I break my vow, all my religious merit is gone; the girl must remain a maid; what can I do ? Had I known, sirs, that there were no men in the world I would not have made myself a laughing-stock by recording such a vow." All men and women who heard Janaka's words and looked at Jānakī were sad: but Lakṣmaṇa was furious: his eyes flashed, his lips quivered and his brows were knit.

Dohā 252

But for fear of his brother he could not speak, though the taunt pierced his heart like an arrow. Yet at last, bowing his head at Rāma's lotus feet, he thus spoke in dignified tones:

Caupāī 250

"May there never be repeated in any assembly, where even the lowest of the house of Raghu is present, such a scandalous speech as that now uttered by Janaka in the presence of the jewel of the *Raghu race*. Hearken, thou sun of the lotus-like solar race; I state the simple truth, without any vain boasting; if only I have thy permission, I will lift the round world with as much ease as marble, and will break it in pieces like an ill-baked potter's vessel, and tear up Mount Meru like a potherb. Before thy infinite majesty, O my lord god, what is this wretched old bow ? Only give me an order and see what an exhibition I will make. I will take up the bow as though it were a lotus stalk and will run off with it a hundred thousand miles to convince you!

Dohā 253

Inspired by thy presence, my lord, I will snap it like a mushroom stem; and if I don't, I swear by thy holy feet, I'll never take bow and quiver in hand again."

Caupāī 251

As Lakṣmaṇa thus spoke in his wrath, earth reeled and the elephants of the quarters trembled.[1] The whole assembly and all

1. An elephant, according to the Purāṇas, stands as supporter and guardian at each quarter. The quarters are eight in number.

the kings were struck with terror; Sītā was glad of heart and Janaka was ashamed; while the sage and Rāma and all the hermits were enraptured and quivered all over with excitement. Then Rāma with a sign checked Lakṣmaṇa, and lovingly made him sit beside him, while Viśvāmitra, perceiving the fitness of the time, spoke in gentle and affectionate tones—"Up Rāma, break this bow of Śiva's and relieve Janaka, my son, of his affliction." On hearing the *guru's* words he bowed his head at his feet, and without joy or sorrow in his soul rose and stood upright in all his native grace, lordly in gait as a young lion.

Dohā 254

As Raghubara ascended the stage, like the sun climbing the mountains of the east, the hearts of the saints expanded like the lotus, and their eyes were glad as bees at the return of day.

Caupāī 252

The dark hopes of the kings vanished like the night, and like the serried stars their vaunts waxed feeble: the arrogant shrivelled up like the lilies, and the false slunk away like the owls; sages and gods, like the *cakwā*, were relieved of their distress and rained down flowers in token of homage. After affectionately reverencing the *guru's* feet and asking permisssion of the holy fathers, the lord of all creation strode forth, with the tread of a majestic elephant, lovely and proud. As he moved, every man and woman in the city quivered all over their body with delight, worshipping the spirits of their ancestors and the gods, and recalling their own past good deeds, saying,—"If my virtuous acts be of any avail, O father Gaṇeśa, may Rāma snap the bow as it were a lotus-stalk."

Dohā 255

After affectionately gazing upon Rāma, Sītā's mother bade her attendants draw near, and thus spoke with loving anxiety,—

Caupāī 253

"Maidens, every one is bent on seeing the spectacle, and as for saying what would be for my good, there is no one who will tell the king plainly:—These are two mere boys; this excessive obstinacy for yours is wrong; Rāvaṇa and Bāṇāsura could not touch the bow, and the kings with all their pride were conquered by it; how then give it into the hands of these boy-princes ? Can a cygnet carry off Mount Mandara ? All the king's good sense is clean gone: Ah, girls, god's ways are inscrutable!" A sharp-witted maiden gently answered, "O queen, the glorious are never to be lightly regarded. Consider the weakness of Agastya and the boundlessness of ocean; yet he drained it dry, and his fame has spread through the world. Again, the orb of the sun is small to look at, but — at its rising — darkness is expelled from heaven and earth and hell.

Dohā 256

Very short is the spell that overpowers Brahmā and Viṣṇu and Mahādeva and all the gods; and a mere goad governs the mightiest and most furious elephant.

Caupāī 254

Love, too, though his bow and arrows are but of flowers, has brought the whole world under subjection. Put away your doubts, lady, and hearken to me, — Rāma will assuredly break the bow." She took heart at these words of the maiden, her despondency ceased, and she loved him all the more. Then Śītā with her eyes fixed on Rāma, implored with anxious heart each god in turn, praying to them in her inward soul, — "Be gracious to me, O Mahādeva and Bhavānī, and reward my service by kindly lightening the weight of the bow. O divine Gaṇeśa, granter of boons, it is with a view to today that I have done your service, Hearken to my oft-repeated supplication, and reduce the weight of the bow to a mere trifle."

Dohā 257

Oft glancing at Raghubīr's form, and taking courage from her heaven-ward prayers, her eyes were filled with tears of love, and her whole body was in a tremor.

Caupāī 255

With fixed gaze she devoured his beauty, and then, as she remembered her father's vow, her soul was troubled—"Alas, my father, for your cruel resolve, made without any regard to good or evil consequences; not a minister but was afraid to give advice — the more the pity — in the great conclave of counsellors. Here is a bow as firm as adamant, and there a little dark-hued prince of delicate frame. O god, how can I maintain my faith?— Is it possible for a delicate *siris* flower to transpierce a diamond? The judgment of the whole assembly has gone astray; now, O bow of Śambhu, thou art the only hope left me; impart thy own heaviness to the crowd, and grow light thyself at once at the sight of Rāma." So great was the agitation of Sītā's soul that an instant of time passed as slowly as an age.

Dohā 258

As she looks, now at the Lord, and now at the ground, her tremulous eyes so glisten, as it were love's two fish disporting themselves in the orb of the moon.

Caupāī 256

In her lotus mouth her bee-like voice lies bound; for modesty, like night, allows it not. In the corner of her eye stood a tear-drop, like a miser's buried hoard. Abashed by the consciousness of extreme excitement, she yet summoned up courage and confidence, "If there is any truth in me at all and I am sincerely enamoured of Raghupati's lotus feet, then the Blessed God, who dwells in the hearts of all, will make me Rāma's handmaid; for wherever there is true affection of soul to soul, union will follow beyond a doubt." With her eyes fixed upon the lord she recorded this loving vow; and he, the most merciful, comprehended it all. After looking at Sītā he cast a glance at the bow, as Garuḍa might glance at a poor little snake.

Dohā 259

When Lakṣmaṇa perceived that the glory of his race had his eye fixed upon Hara's bow he thrilled with excitement, and striking the earth with his foot, cried thus aloud,—

Caupāī 257

"O ye elephant warders, ye tortoise, serpent and boar, hold fast the earth with a will that it shake not, for Rāma is about to break the great bow; hearken to my order and be ready." When Rāma drew near to the bow, men and women supplicated the gods and recalled the merit their past good deeds had won. The doubts and errors of the crowd, the arrogance of the foolish kings, the proud pretensions of Parasurâma, the terror of all the gods and saints, the distress of Sītā, the regrets of Janaka, the burning anguish of the queens, were all heaped together on the bow as on a raft, while Rāma's strength of arm was the boundless ocean that had to be crossed, and with no helmsman to steer them.

Dohā 260

Rāma first looked at the crowd, who all stood dumb and still as painted pictures; then the gracious Lord turned from them to Sītā, and perceived her yet deeper concern;

Caupāī 258

He perceived her to be so terribly agitated that a moment of time seemed an age in passing. If a man die of thirst for want of water, when he is once dead, of what use to him is a lake of nectar ? What good is the rain when the crop has withered ? or what avails regret when a chance has once been lost ? Thinking thus to himself as he gazed at Jānakī, the Lord was enraptured at the sight of her singular devotion, and after doing a reverential obeisance to his *guru*, he took up the bow with most superlative ease; as he grasped it in his hand, it gleamed like a flash of lightning; and again as he bent it, it seemed like the vault of heaven. Though all stood watching, before any one could see him grasp it, he had lifted it from the ground and raised it aloft and drawn it tight, and in a moment broken it in halves; the awful crash resounded through the worlds.

Chand 24

So awful a crash re-echoed through the worlds that the horses of the Sun left their course and strayed, the elephants of the four quarters trumpeted, earth shook, the great serpent, the boar and the tortoise tottered. Gods, demons and sages put their hands to their ears, and all began anxiously to consider the cause: but when they learnt that Rāma had broken the bow, they uttered shouts of victory.

Sorathā 261

The whole crowd of those deluded kings who had gone on board 'the Siva's bow' were drowned in the waves of Rāma's might.

Caupāī 259

The Lord tosssed upon the ground the two broken pieces of the bow, and at the sight the multitude rejoiced. Viśvāmitra's love, like the clear unfathomed depth of ocean, swelled to the highest tide of ecstasy under the full moon influence of Rāma's presence. There was a jubilant noise of music in the sky; heavenly nymphs danced and sang; Brahmā and all the gods and deified saints and sages praised and blessed the hero and rained down wreaths of many-coloured flowers; the *kinnaras* sung melodious strains; and the shout of 'Victory, Victory' re-echoed throughout the world. The noise that followed the breaking of the bow defies description. Everywhere the people in their joy kept saying,—"Rāma has broken the great bow."

Dohā 262

Bards, minstrels and rhapsodists raised their loud-voiced paeans, and all the people poured out lavish offerings of horses, elephants, money, jewels and raiment.

Caupāī 260

There was a clash of cymbals, tabors, conches, clarions, sackbuts, drums, kettledrums and all kinds of music; and in every place were choirs of women singing auspicious strains. The queen with her attendants was as glad as a parched rice-field at a fall of rain; Janaka was as pleased and free of care as a tired swimmer on reaching a shallow; the kings were as confounded at the breaking of the bow as a lamp is dimmed at dawn of day; but Sītā's gladness can only be compared to that of the *cātakī*[1] on finding a rain-drop in October; while

1. The *cātakī* (cuculus melanoleucos) is fabled never to drink, except it be such drops of rain as fall in the month of October, when the sun is in the same longitude as Arcturus (*Svati*), a time of the year when a shower is

Lakṣmaṇa fixed his eyes on Rāma as the *chakora* on the moon. Then Śatānanda gave the word and Sītā drew near to Rāma.

Dohā 263

Graceful in motion as a swan, and of infinite beauty in every limb; and with her came her fair and sprightly companions singing songs of good omen.

Caupāī 261

Resplendent in their midst as the Queen of grace among the Graces, she held in her lotus hand the fair wreath of victory, enriched as it were with the spoils of world-wide triumph. With modest air, but rapture in her soul, her interior devotion was withdrawn from sight. As she drew near and beheld Rāma's beauty, she stood motionless like a painted picture, till a watchful attendant roused her, saying,—'Invest him with the ennobling wreath.' At the word she raised the wreath with both her hands, but was too much overcome by emotion to garland him; till as the lotus, flower and stalk, shrinks at the moonlight, so her hand and arm drooped in the glory of his moon-like face. At the sight of his beauty her handmaids broke into song, while Sītā let fall the wreath upon his breast.

Soraṭhā 264

When the gods saw the wreath of victory resting on his breast, they showered down flowers; and the kings all shrank into nothing, like lilies at the rising of the sun.

Caupāī 262

Both in the city and in heaven there were sounds of music; the bad were saddened, and the good were glad. Gods, kinnaras, men, serpents and saints uttered blessings and shouts of victory. The heavenly nymphs danced and sang, and flowers fell in constant showers. In every place were Brāhmaṇas muttering Vedic texts, and rhapsodists reciting lays of praise. Earth, hell and

a very rare occurrence. The same precious drops if they fall into the sea, are transmuted into pearls, a belief to which allusion is made in Caupāī 11.

heaven were pervaded with the glad news,—'Rāma has broken the bow and will wed Sītā.' The men and women of the city light votive torches and, regardless of their substance, scatter gifts in profusion. Sītā by Rāma's side was as resplendent as if Beauty and Love had met together. 'Embrace your lord's feet,' whispered her companions, but in excess of fear she dared not touch them.

Dohā 265

She touches them not with her hands, remembering the fate of Gautama's wife; and Rāma smiled inwardly at this proof of her supernatural devotion.

Caupāī 263

Then, as they looked on Sītā, the kings were inflamed with desire, and waxed wroth of soul — frantic, degenerate fools — and sprang up — the wretches — and donned their armour and began a general chorus of abuse,—"Come now, let us carry off Sītā and overthrow and bind fast these two princes ! Though he has broken the bow, he has not yet gained his end; for who shall marry Sītā while we still live ? If the king give them any assistance, we will rout him in battle as well as the two brothers." When the good kings heard these boasts, they said, "Shame herself is ashamed to hear this company of princes! Your might and dignity, your heroism and greatness and honour have all gone the way of the bow! Is that the might of which ye now boast, or have ye since acquired something new ? Was it not thus that ye reckoned afore, when God so blackened your faces ?

Dohā 266

Cease from envy and arrogance and folly; feast your eyes upon Rāma; and be not like a moth in the fierce flame of Lakṣmaṇa's wrath.

Caupāī 264

Like a crow who would rob the king of the birds[1] of an offering; or a rat who would spoil a lion; as a man who is passion-

1. The king of the birds — Garuda — is here called *Vainateya*, that is to say the son of Vinatā.

ate without cause and yet wishes for peace of mind; as a reviler of Siva who wishes for happiness and prosperity; as a greedy and covetous man who wishes for fair fame, and as a gallant who would have no scandal; as an enemy of God who wishes to be saved; such is your desire, O ye kings." When Sītā heard the tumult, she was afraid, and with her companions went away to the queen, while Rāma composedly joined the *guru*, talking to himself of Sītā's love. Sītā and the queen were much distressed saying,—"What is it God would have now ?" And at the sound of the voices of the kings Lakṣmaṇa looked helplessly up and down. For fear of Rāma he could not speak.

Dohā 267

With fiery eyes and knitted brows he cast a furious look at the kings like a lion's whelp moved to excitement on seeing a herd of wild elephants.

Caupāī 265

Seeing the tumult, the women were all agitated and joined in reproaching the kings. Then it was[1] that the sun of the lotus race of Bhṛgu (Parasurāma) arrived, for he had heard of the breaking of the bow. At the sight of him the kings all cowered down, as a quail shrinking beneath the swoop of a hawk. Of pallid hue and well bestreaked with ashes; with the three horizontal lines sacred to Siva conspicuous on his broad forehead; with the hair on his head bound in a knot; and his moon-like face flushed with the furnace fire of smouldering wrath; with frowning brows and eyes inflamed with passion; he casts a quick and furious glance around. With bull-like shoulders and mighty chest and arms; with a fair sacred thread and string of beads and deerskin with an anchorite's dress about his loins and two quivers slung by his side; with bow and arrows in his hand, and sharp axe upon his strong shoulder.

Dohā 268

In his saintly attire and savage mien he was a figure beyond description, as though the Heroic sentiment had taken the form of a hermit; so he drew near to the kings.

1. In the *Adhyātma Rāmāyaṇa*, 'the sun of the lotus race of Bhṛgu' appears later, after Daśaratha has already left Janaka's city (see Canto 7). Vālmiki follows this sequence of events.

Caupāī 266

When they beheld Bhṛgupati's ghastly figure, they all rose in consternation, each mentioning his own and his father's name, and fell prostrate on the ground before him; and even he on whom he cast a kindly glance thought his life had come to an end. Then came Janaka and bowed his head before him and called for Sītā also to pay him homage. He bestowed upon her his blessing, and her glad companions escorted her back to her own apartments. Next came Viśvāmitra to greet him, and placed, the two boys at his feet, saying,—"These are Rāma and Lakṣmaṇa, Daśaratha's sons." He admired the well-matched pair and blessed them, with his eyes long fixed upon Rāma's incomparable beauty, which would humble the pride even of Love himself.

Dohā 269

Then he turned to Videha and said, "Why all this crowd ?" He asked as though he did not know, while his whole body was bursting with passion.

Caupāī 267

Janaka told him the whole history and the reason why the kings had assembled. After hearing his reply he again looked away and spied the fragments of the bow lying on the ground. In a mighty passion he cried in furious tones,—"Tell me, Janaka, you fool, who has broken the bow ? Show him to me at once, or this very day I will overthrow the whole of your dominion." In his excess of fear the king could give no answer: the wicked suitors were glad of heart; gods, sages, serpents and all the people of the city were full of anxiety and profound alarm; Sītā's mother was lamenting,—"God has now undone all that had just been done so well;" and when Sītā heard of Bhṛgupati's temper, she felt half a minute pass like an age.

Dohā 270

Seeing the people's consternation and Jānakī's anxiety, the imperturbable Raghubīr thus spoke and said,—

Caupāī 268

"My Lord, the bow has probably got broken by some one of your servants. What are your orders ? Why not tell me?" At this the furious sage was yet more incensed and cried,—"A servant is one who does service, but he who does the deeds of an enemy must be fought. Hearken, Rāma, whoever it was who broke Śiva's bow is as much my enemy as was Sahasrabāhu ! Separate him from among the assembly, or else everyone of these kings shall be killed." When Lakṣmaṇa heard the sage's threat, he smiled and said to him in a tone of contempt,—"O sir, I have broken many a bow as a child, and you were never before thus angry; why were you so fond of this bow in particular?" Paraśurāma replied in a fury,—

Dohā 271

"Ha ! death-doomed princeling ! Is there no stopping your tongue ? Would you compare to a common bow the great bow of Śiva, that is famous throughout the world ?"

Caupāī 269

Said Lakṣmaṇa with a smile, "I thought, holy sir, that all bows are alike. What gain or what loss can there be in the breaking of a worn-out old bow ? Rāma by mistake took it for a new one, and directly he touched it, it snapped in two: but it was no fault of his; why then, reverend sir, be so angry for no cause?" He answered, with a glance at his axe, "Fool, have you never heard of my temper ? I do not slay you because, as I say, you are but a child. You in your folly take me for a mere recluse; and from my childhood an ascetic I am, but also a fiery one and the terror of the whole Kṣatriya race, as is known throughout the world. By the might of my arm I have made earth kingless, and time after time have bestowed her upon the Brāhmaṇas. See here the axe, you king's son, with which I lopped of Sahasrabāhu's thousand arms.

Dohā 272

Do not bring distress upon your father and mother: my cruel axe has ripped up even unborn infants in the womb."

Caupāī 270

Lakṣmaṇa replied with a quiet smile,—"Ah ! holy sir, you think yourself a great warrior indeed, and keep brandishing your axe before me, as if with a mere puff of breath you could blow away a mountain ! But I am not a tender little gourd that droops as soon as it sees a finger raised against it. When I perceived your axe and bow and arrows, I spoke a little haughtily; but now that I see by your sacred thread that you are of the Bhṛgu's line, say what you like and I will bear it patiently. In our family there is no waging battle against gods or Brāhmaṇas, or devotees, or cows; for to slay them is a crime, and to be overcome by them a disgrace; and therefore I must throw myself at your feet, even though you strike me. Your curse is as awful as ten million thunderbolts, your axe and bow and arrows are therefore unnecessary.

Dohā 273

Pardon me, O great and reverend sage, for anything improper that I said when I first saw you." The glory of the Bhṛgu's race cried furiously in his deep toned voice,—

Caupāī 271

"Hearken me, son of Kuśika[1] ! This child is demented; a perverse and death-doomed destroyer of his own house; a dark spot on the moon-like brightness of the Solar race; utterly ungovernable, senseless and reckless! Another moment and he shall be a mouthful in the jaws of death, and I loudly protest it is no fault of mine. Take him away, if you would save him, and teach him my glory and might and the fierceness of my temper." Said Lakṣmaṇa,—"So long as you live, O sage, who else can tell your fame so well ? With your own mouth you have many times and in many ways declared your own doings. If you are not yet satisfied, tell them over again, and do not distress yourself beyond endurance by putting any restraint upon your passion. But if you are really a resolute and dauntless warrior, sworn to valour, there is no honour to be got by abuse.

1. The son, or rather grandson, of Kuśika is Viśvāmitra.

Dohā 274

Heroes perform valiant deeds in fight, but do not themselves publish them. Cowards finding a foe before them in the battle talk very large.

Caupāī 272

Nor would you terrify me with your repeated cries of Death." On hearing Lakṣmaṇa's impudent speech he closed his hand upon his terrible axe, "After this let no man blame me; this sharp-tongued boy deserves his death. I have spared him long on account of his being a child, but now of a truth he is as good as dead!" Said Viśvāmitra, "Pardon his offence; the wise regard not the faults or merits of children." "My axe is sharp and I am pitiless in my wrath; he is moreover guilty and has injured my *guru*. Yet though he dares to answer me, I will still spare his life, though solely out of regard for you, Viśvāmitra. But for you I would have slain him with my terrible axe, and thus easily have paid my *guru* his due."

Dohā 275

Said the son of Gādhi, smiling to himself, "Everything looks green to the sage's eyes.[1] Though Rāma has today broken the bow as though it were a stick of sugarcane, still the sage has not the sense to understand."

Caupāī 273

Said Lakṣmaṇa,—"Is there anyone, Father, ignorant of your honour ? It is notorious throughout the world. You have well paid the debt you owed to your father and mother[2] ; but it was

1. The allusion is to a popular saying,—'A man who loses his eyesight in the month of Sāvan thinks everything is always green.' *Hariarī*, green, may also be taken as two words *Hari* and *ari*, 'an enemy to Viṣṇu', a light in which it would be the height of folly for Paraśurāma to regard Rāma, since Rāma was himself an incarnation of Viṣṇu, as also was Paraśurāma. The double interpretation was probably intended by the poet.

2. Every Hindu is said to be in debt by nature to three persons, *viz*., his father, his mother and his *guru*. The two first debts had been paid by Paraśurāma in a notable fashion; for he had restored his mother Reṇukā to

a great distress to you to be still in debt to your *guru*. You have now transferred the account to me, but the interest by lapse of time has become very heavy. So you must bring forward the original creditor, and then, sir, I will at once open my purse." When he heard these insolent words he grasped his axe, and all the people cried,— "Alack, alack !" "O Bhṛgubar, you still keep showing me your axe, but, regicide as you are, I only spare you on account of your being a Brāhmaṇa. You have never yet met a real staunch fighting man, and, most reverend sir, you are a great man only in your own house." They all cried out,— "How very wrong!" and Rāma gave Lakṣmaṇa a sign to be quiet.

Dohā 276

When Rāma saw that Lakṣmaṇa's words had added fuel to the fire of the noble Bhṛgupati's wrath, the sun of the house of Raghu quenched it with the flood of admonition,—

Caupāī 274

"My lord, have compassion on a child, and wreak not your wrath on such an unweaned infant : if he had any idea of your glorious power, how could he be so foolish as to put himself on an equality with you ? When a child commits any naughtiness, its *guru* and father and mother are in raptures at it. Have pity then on the boy, who is really one of your servants; for thus it becometh a sage, so patient and wise as you are." On hearing Rāma's words he cooled down a little but again Lakṣmaṇa said something with a smile, and seeing him smile he flushed all over with rage,—"Rāma, your brother is too wicked! Though fair in outward hue, he is black at heart, and it is not mother's milk but poison that his lips have sucked! Perverse by nature, he neither takes after you nor regards me."

life again after he had first cut off her head in obedience to his father Jamadagni's order; and again when his father had been slain by Sahasrabāhu, he avenged him by the slaughter of the whole Kaṣtriya race. It now remained for him to satisfy his *guru*, Mahādeva, for the outrage Rāma had done him in breaking his bow.

Dohā 277

Said Lakṣmaṇa with a smile,—"Hearken, O sage, passion is the root of sin; those who are under its influence do unseemly things and set themselves against everyone.

Caupāī 275

I am one of your followers, reverend sir; put away your wrath and show mercy. Anger will not mend the broken bow. Pray sit down, you must be tired of standing. If you were so very fond of it, devise a plan for getting it mended and call in some skilful workman." Janaka was frightened at Lakṣmaṇa's words,—'Be quiet! Such impudence is not right!' The citizens all shook and trembled to think so small a boy could be so naughty. As Bhṛgupati heard his fearless words his whole body was on fire with rage, and his strength failed him, and in a condescending manner he said to Rāma,—"See if you can manage this little brother of yours; so fair without and foul within, he resembles a golden jar full of poison!"

Dohā 278

At this Lakṣmaṇa smiled, but Rāma gave him a look of reproof and submissively approached the *guru*, putting away all petulance of speech.

Caupāī 276

Clasping his two hands together and speaking in most modest, gentle and placid tones, he said,—"Hearken, my lord, you were born a sage; pay no heed then to the words of a child. Boys are like wasps : no wise man will ever trouble himself about them. Nor is it he who has done the mischief; I, my lord, am the offender. Be pleased, your reverence, to visit everything on me, your servant, whether it be favour or anger, death or bonds. Tell me quickly the means, O king of sages, by which your passion may be assuaged." Said the sage,—"O Rāma, how can my passion be assuaged ? Your brother has today set me at nought, and yet I have not struck off his head with my axe : what then have I done in anger ?

Dohā 279

When they hear of the fierce doings of my axe, the proudest queens are seized with untimely pains of labour; my axe is still here, and yet I see this princeling, my enemy, alive.

Caupāī 277

My hand moves not, though passion consumes my heart and my regicide axe has become blunted! Fate has turned against me; that is why I find my nature changed: for when was I ever pitiful before? Today by heaven's will I have suffered intolerable pain!" On hearing this, the son of Sumitrā laughed and bowed his head. "Even your pity is like a blast of wind and the words you speak would strip a tree of its blossoms. If a sage's body is thus parched even by pity, God help him when he is angry." "See now, Janaka, keep this child away; he is bent in his folly on visiting the realms of death! Why do you not at once take him out of my sight, this little prince; so small to look at and yet so wicked ?" Lakṣmaṇa laughed and said to the sage,—'Shut your eyes and you will see nothing.'

Dohā 280

Then said Paraśurāma in tones of fury to Rāma,—"Wretch, after breaking Śiva's bow do you now teach me ?

Caupāī 278

It is you who have egged your brother on to utter these sarcasms, and your humility and folded hands are a mockery. Give me my satisfaction in combat, or forswear your name of Rāma. You enemy of Śiva, have done with your hypocrisy and fight me, or I'll slay you and your brother too!" Flushed with passion, he raised his axe on high, but Rāma only smiled and bowed,—"Though the fault is Lakṣmaṇa's, your wrath is against me; it is sometimes a great mistake to be good and upright; for everyone is afraid of the crooked. Rāhu attacks not the crescent moon. Cease, O great sage, from your wrath." Said Rāma, "Your axe is in your hand and my head is in front of you; do anything, sir, that will tend to pacify you, for I am your servant.

Dohā 281

And how can a servant fight his master ? O holy Brāhmaṇa, restrain your wrath; whatever the boy may have said, after looking at your dress, he meant no harm by it.

Caupāī 279

For seeing you armed with axe and bow and arrows, the child took you for a warrior and challenged you; for though he knew your name, he did not recognize your person, and answered you according to his lineage.[1] If you had come as a Religious, he would have put the dust of your Holiness's feet upon his head. Forgive the error of one who did not know you; a Brāhmaṇa's heart should be all mercy. What equality, my lord, can there be between you and me ? We are as far apart as head and feet. My poor name is simply Rāma, but you have the long name of Rāma-of-the-Axe. I have only one string to my bow, while you have all the holy nine.[2] In every way I am your inferior; as a Brāhmaṇa, pardon my offence."

Dohā 282

Again and again did Rāma address his namesake, calling him by his titles of 'Sage' and 'Holy Brāhmaṇa', till Bhṛgupati exclaimed in his rage :—"You are as perverse as your brother.

Caupāī 280

You persist in taking me for a Brāhmaṇa; I will tell you now what kind of a Brāhmaṇa I am. My bow is my sacrificial ladle, my arrow the oblation, and my wrath the blazing fire; armies fully equipped with horses and chariots and elephants and footmen are the fuel, and mighty kings are the victims for oblation whom I have cut in pieces with this axe; thus have I celebrated countless sacrifices of war all over the world. To you my glory is unknown, and you address me contemptuously, taking me for a mere Brāhmaṇa. Now that you have broken the bow, you are swollen with pride, and you put yourself forward in your

1. *i.e.*, as a man of his lineage would answer.

2. *Guṇa* which is the name for a bowstring, means also virtue; and the cardinal virtues are said to be nine in number though the list is a variable one.

arrogance as universal conqueror." Said Rāma, —"O sage, think before you speak. Your wrath is excessive, but my fault is a trifling one. The old bow broke at a touch. What reason have I to be proud ?

Dohā 283

Hear the truth, O Bhṛgunāth; you say I set you at nought when I treat you with the respect due to a Brāhmaṇa; but is there any warrior to whom I would bow my head in fear ?

Caupāi 281

Any god, demon, king or warrior, whether my equal in strength or my superior, who will challenge me to combat, him would I gladly meet, or even Death himself ! For one who is born a Kṣatriya and yet shirks the battle is a disgrace to his lineage and a contemptible wretch. I state what is only a characteristic of my race and make no idle boast; there is not a descendant of Raghu who would fear to meet in battle even Death himself; but so great is the power of Brāhmaṇical descent that he fears you, who fears none else." On hearing this calm and profound speech of Rāma's, the eyes of Paraśurāma's mind were opened :—"O Rāma, take and draw this bow of Viṣṇu's and let my doubts be ended." As he gave it, the bow strung itself of its own accord; then was Paraśurāma amazed at heart.

Dohā 284

He acknowledged the power of Rāma and felt a thrill of excitement. His heart bursting with love, he thus spoke with clasped hands :—

Caupāī 282

"Glory to the Sun of the lotus race of Raghu, to the fire that consumes the serried ranks of the demons; glory to the friend of gods, Brāhmaṇas and cows; glory to the dispeller of the delusions induced by pride, ignorance and passion; glory to him whose piety, amiability, and compassion are fathomless as ocean; glory to him who is unrivalled in the art of speech, the rewarder of service, the all-beautiful of form, more gracious of person than a myriad Loves! How can I with one tongue declare his praise, who is as it were the divine swan in the holy lake of Mahādeva's soul ? In my ignorance I have said much that was unseemly; but pardon me, ye two brothers, mercy's shrine." Still repeating as he went :—'Glory, glory, glory, to the mighty Rāma,' Bhṛgupati withdrew to the forest to practise penance. The wicked kings were self-dismayed and trembled, and slunk away — the cowards — in all directions, without a word.

Dohā 285

The gods sounded their kettledrums and rained down flowers upon the Lord; and all the people of the city rejoiced, now that the thorn of fear and error had been extracted from their heart.

Caupāī 283

There was a tumultuous clash of instruments of music and a display of all things pleasant and auspicious. Troops of fair-faced, bright-eyed maidens joined in song with voices of exquisite melody. Janaka's delight was beyond description, as that of a born beggar who has found a treasure; and Sītā, relieved of her fears, was as glad as a young partridge at the rising of the moon. The king made obeisance before Viśvāmitra, saying :— "It is by my lord's favour that Rāma has broken the bow. These two brothers have gained me my purpose; tell me now, reverend sir, what it becomes me to do." Said the sage :— "Hearken, wise king; the marriage was dependent on the bow, and took effect directly the bow broke; this is well known to everyone, whether god, man or Nāga.

Dohā 286

Still, go and perform according to family usage whatever practices are prescribed in the Veda, after consultation with the Brāhmaṇas and elders and your own *guru*;

Caupāī 284

And despatch a herald to the city of Avadh to invite king Daśaratha. The king responded gladly, "'Tis well, gracious sir," and sent a messenger to Avadh that very moment. Then he summoned all the burghers, who came everyone of them, and humbly bowing before him received the order :—"Decorate all the markets and streets and temples and shrines in all four quarters of the city." They returned in joy, each to his own house. Then he called up his own servants and instructed them :—"Have all kinds of pavilions made and erected." They obeyed in all gladness and sent word to the different artificers who were skilful in the construction of canopies and triumphal arches; and they, after invoking Brahmā, set to work and made pillars of gold in the shape of plantain trees,

Dohā 287

With leaves and fruit of emeralds and ruby flowers. It was such a gorgeous show that the Creator was quite disconcerted at the sight!

Caupāī 285

The bamboo rods they encrusted with emeralds and so like in form and colour[1] that no one could tell them from real; and betel leaves they fashioned in gold so bright and glistening that no one could look at them. Then they worked up the leaves into wreaths, with strings of beautiful pearls inserted here and there, and after much cutting and engraving and inlaying made lotuses of mosaic with rubies, emeralds, diamonds and turquoises. Bees, too, they made and birds of varied plumage, which buzzed and whistled in the rustling breeze; and on the pillars they sculptured figures of the gods all standing erect with things of good omen in their hands. All manner of squares were drawn on the ground and filled in with diverse devices made of elephant-pearls[2] of exquisite beauty.

1. Another reading, instead of *saras, sabaraṇa*, is *saral sa-parva*, straight and knotted.'

2. For *sindhura* 'an elephant,' another reading is, *sindur*, 'vermilion' 'but this cannot be correct, since the *chauks* or squares, to which reference is here made, are always marked out with some *white* material, ordinarily flour, though in a king's palace strings of pearls might be substituted,

Doha 288

There were also made most lovely mango-leaves of graven sapphires with blossoms of gold, while clusters of emerald fruits glistened on silken cords.

Caupāī 286

Next, they made charming festoons, as though they were Love's own nooses, and many golden vases with silken flags and banners and waving *cauris* and elegant lamps all studded with gems. It is impossible to describe the various pavilions and in particular the one intended for the royal bride. What poet would have the hardihood to attempt its description ? The canopy for Rāma, the bridegroom, the centre of all beauty and perfection, flashed its radiance through all the three worlds. In every house throughout the city there was the same splendour as in Janaka's palace. Whoever then saw Tirahuta felt that there was nothing in the fourteen spheres[1] to compare with it. The prosperous appearance of the very meanest house was enough to fascinate even the king of heaven.

Dohā 289

For the magnificence of the city wherein dwelt the goddess Lakṣmī, in disguise as a woman, was more than even Śāradā or Śeṣanāga could tell.

Caupāī 287

When the heralds arrived at Rāma's sacred birthplace, they rejoiced to see the beauty of the city. At the royal gate they sent in word, and King Daśaratha at once summoned them to his presence. With a profound salutation they delivered the letter, and the king in his joy rose to receive it. As he read it his eyes filled with tears, his body quivered all over, and his heart seemed bursting. With Rāma and Lakṣmaṇa in his heart

1. The fourteen spheres are as followe, *viz*. first, seven above the earth —Bhū-loka, Bhuvar-loka, Svar-loka, Mahar-loka, Jan-loka, Tapa-loka, and Satya-loka, and seven beneath the earth—Atal, Bital, Sutal Rasātal. Mahātal, Talātal, and Pātāl.

and their dear letter in his hand, he could not utter a word either good or bad. At last, taking courage, he read the letter, and all the court rejoiced to hear the sure tidings. Now Bharata was playing about, and on hearing the tidings he, nay, the two brothers, came and with the utmost modesty and affection asked,—"Father, where has the letter come from?

Dohā 290

Is all well with my two dear brothers ? Tell me what country they are in." On hearing these loving words the king again read the letter.

Caupāī 288

On hearing it the two brothers felt a thrill of irrepressible joy, and the whole court was charmed to see Bharata's holy devotion. Then the king seated the messengers close by him and said in sweet and winning tones :—"Tell me, friend, are the two boys well ? Have you really seen them with your own eyes?" "One is dark, the other fair; both are equipped with bow and quiver, and are of tender age, and with them is Viśvāmitra the sage." Said the king again and again in his overpowering love, "You know them, it is clear ; tell me now of their state ; for ever since the sage took them away with him I have had no definite news of them until today. Tell me, how did Janaka recognize them ?" At these fond words the messengers smiled and replied,

Dohā 291

'Hearken, O jewel and crown of kings ; there is no man so blessed as you, who have for sons Rāma and Lakṣmaṇa, who are the glory of the universe.

Caupāī 289

There is no need to ask your sons who they are. They are lion-hearted heroes who illuminate the three spheres. Before their glory and renown the moon is dim and the sun is cold. Why say, my lord, how they were recognized ? Does one take a lamp in his hand in order to see the sun ? The countless kings at Sītā's marriage, great warriors as they were, all shrunk away one after the other ; for not one of them could stir Śambhu's bow, but all failed, those mighty princes. The power of the haughtiest champions in the three worlds was crushed by it. Though Sarāsura could lift Mount Meru, even he had to confess himself beaten, and retired after pacing around it ; and he who in sport uplifted Kailāsa (i.e., Rāvaṇa) was worsted in this assembly.

Dohā 292

Then Rāma, the jewel of Raghu's line (hearken, O sovereign lord) snapped the bow with as little effort as an elephant would put forth in breaking the stalk of a lotus.

Caupāī 290

At these tidings Paraśurāma came in a fury, and after much brow-beating gave Rāma his own bow to test his strength, then suppliantly retired to the woods. Nor is Rāma more conspicuous in his unequalled might than is the all-glorious Lakṣmaṇa, at sight of whom the kings tremble, as an elephant before a young lion. No one who sees your two sons, sir, can regard anything else on earth." At this eloquent and affectionate speech of the heralds, so loving, grand and heroic, the king and his court were much moved, and began to offer them lavish gifts ; but they closed their ears, crying,—"Not so, not so;" and all were charmed to see their integrity.

Dohā 293

Then the king rose and went and gave the letter to Vasiṣṭha, and after relating all the circumstances to the *guru*, sent courteously for the messengers.

Caupāī 291

After hearing them the *guru* was highly pleased and said, "To a good man the world is full of happiness. As rivers run into the sea, though it has no greed for them, so joy and prosperity come unasked and of their own accord to a virtuous soul. Strict in the performance of your duties to your *guru* and to

Brāhmaṇas and cows and gods, and your queen Kausalyā no less devout than yourself, you have no equals for piety in the whole world, either now or in the past, nor hereafter shall have. Whose merit, O king, can be greater than yours, who have a son like Rāma ; nay four heroic sons, all equally obedient, religious and amiable. Happy, indeed, are you for all time. Prepare the marriage procession to the sound of music.

Dohā 294

And proceed quickly." On hearing the sage's commands the king bowed in assent, and hastened to the palace, after assigning apartments to the heralds.

Caupāī 292

Then he called all the ladies of the court and read aloud to them Janaka's letter. All rejoiced greatly at the news. He then told them all the verbal message ; and both himself and the queens were as enraptured with delight as a peacock at the sound of approaching rain. The *guru's* wives in their joy invoked the blessings of heaven, and the queen-mother was completely overwhelmed with ecstasy. They take the dear letter from one another, and press it to their bosom to cool as it were their burning heart. Again and again before he turned to the door, the king repeated the glory and the exploits both of Rāma and Lakṣmaṇa, adding,—"It is all by the sage's good favour." Then the ladies sent for the Brāhmaṇas and joyfully made them offerings, for which the holy men returned their blessings.

Soraṭhā 295

Next, they called together the beggars and lavished a myriad gifts upon them. "May the four sons of the Emperor Daśaratha live for ever !"

Caupāī 293

Thus they cried as they left, attired in garments of many colours. There was a jubilant clamour of music, as the news spread among the people, and auspicious rites began to be performed in every house. The fourteen worlds were filled with joyous excitement at the marriage of Raghubīr with the daughter of Janaka. When they heard the glad tidings, the citizens were enraptured and began decorating the roads and houses and streets ; for though Avadh in itself was always a charming place, and clean and pure as being Rāma's home, yet as the natural outcome of its love it garnished and adorned itself still more with charming festal decorations. Silken flags and banners and graceful *cauris* crested the gay bazar : and at every turn were golden jars and festoons of netted pearls and heaps of turmeric, *dūba* grass, curds, rice, and garlands of flowers.

Dohā 296

Every citizen decorated his house and made it auspicious. The streets were duly watered, and every square was filled in with some tasteful design.

Caupāī 294

Troops of matrons, assembled at different places, had practised all the sixteen kinds of female adornment[1] and were brilliant as the lightning, with moon-like faces and fawn-like eyes, and beauty enough to humble the pride of Rati; singing auspicious strains with voice so melodious that the cuckoo was put to shame on hearing the sweet sound. How is the king's palace to be described ? The pavilion they set up would dazzle the world. Everything beautiful and of fair omen was displayed, and every kind of music was heard. Here were rhapsodists, glorifying the race in song ; here were Brāhmaṇas muttering Vedic spells ;

1. The sixteen *sringāra*, or modes of female adornment, are specified in the following rhymes :-

Prathama ang-suchi ek bidhi—Majjan dutiya bakhāni,
Amal basan pahirau tritiya—Yā ak chāri sujāni.
Pancama kesa-sanvāriyo—Sastahin māng-sindūra.
Bhāl-khauri saptama kahat—Aṣṭama cibuk til pura,
Mehndi kar pad racan nava—Dasma argaja anga.
Gyārah bhūhan nag-jatit—Bārah puṣpa prasanga.
Basrāg mukh terahi—Caudah rangiyo dānt.
Adhar-rāg gani pancadasa—Kajjal ṣodas bhānt.

while lovely women carolled joyous songs, ever dwelling on the names of Rāma and Sītā. The joy was so great that the palace was too small for it, and it overflowed on all four sides.

Dohā 297

What poet can describe in full the magnificence of Daśaratha's palace, in which Rāma, the glory of all the gods, had taken birth ?

Caupāī 295

The king then sent for Bharata and said, "Go and prepare horses and elephants and chariots and start at once for Raghubīr's marriage procession." When they heard this order, both brothers were full of excitement. Bharata sent for all the chief officers and issued his commands, and they joyfully arose and hastened to perform them. First they set gorgeous saddles on the horses. Of different colours were the gallant steeds, but all well-proportioned and mettlesome, touching the ground with their feet as lightly as though it were red-hot iron. I cannot tell all the various breeds ; they would race the wind and outstrip it. The princes who mounted them were all like Bharata, graceful and gorgeously attired, with bow and arrows in hand and well-filled quiver at their side.

Dohā 298

Slender, elegant and lithesome youths, but expert warriors all; and with each rider were two footmen well skilled in sword-play.

Caupāī 296

Full of high resolve, the warriors, all staunch in fight, sallied forth and halted outside the city, putting their well-trained steeds through all their paces and rejoicing in the clash of tabor and drum. The charioteers had made their cars equally gorgeous with flags and banners and jewelled adornments, with elegant *cauris* and tinkling bells, so as to outdo in splendour the chariot of the Sun. Innumerable were the black-eared horses[1], which

1. A horse to be fit for sacrifice must have black ears.

the grooms yoked to these chariots, and all were so beautiful and richly caparisoned that even a sage would be enraptured at the sight ; skimming the surface of the water like dry land nor sinking even hoof-deep; so marvellous was their speed. After preparing their equipment of armour and weapons, the charioteers gave word to their masters.

Dohā 299

Each mounted his chariot, and the marriage procession began to form outside the city. All, whatever the object on which they were bent, were met by auspicious omens.

Caupāī 297

On the magnificent elephants were set splendid canopies wrought in a manner beyond all description. As the mighty elephants moved, the bells clanged like thunder from the clouds in the pleasant month of Śrāvana. And other vehicles were there of many kinds; elegant *pālkīs* and sedans and coaches, wherein were seated companies of noble Brāhmaṇas, incarnations as it were of all the hymns of the Veda. The genealogists and bards and minstrels and rhapsodists were mounted on other cars according to their rank; while mules and camels and oxen of every breed were laden with all sorts of baggage; there were also millions of porters with burdens slung across their shoulders. But who can enumerate such an endless list of things and the great company of servants, each with his own set of appliances?

Dohā 300

All were glad and fearless of heart, and were quivering with excitement in every limb, saying,—"When shall we feast our eyes with the sight of the two heroes, Rāma and Lakṣmaṇa?"

Caupāī 298

The elephants' bells clanged with a fearful din; on all sides were heard the rumble of the chariots and the neighing of the horses; the drums would drown a tempest's roar, and no one could hear himself speak or anyone else. At the king's gate was such an enormous crowd that a stone thrown there would be trodden into dust. Women mounted on the upper story viewed the sight, with festal torches and salvers in their hands, and carolled melodious songs in an ecstasy of joy beyond description. Then Sumanta made ready two chariots and yoked them with steeds that would outrun the horses of the Sun, and brought them in all their beauty before the king — not Śāradā herself could do them justice — the one was for the royal retinue, but the other was still more splendid.

Dohā 301

This the king first caused Vasiṣṭha to mount, and then himself ascended, with his thoughts fixed upon Hara, his *guru*, Gaurī, and Gaṇeśa.

Caupāī 299

By Vasiṣṭha's side the king shone forth as Purandara beside the *guru* of the gods.[1] After performing every ceremony prescribed either by family usage or the Veda, and inspecting whatever had been done, he sallied forth to the blast of the conch shell, after obtaining the permission of his *guru*, and with his thoughts fixed on Rāma. The beneficent gods rejoiced to see the procession and rained down flowers. There was a confused uproar, horses neighing, elephants trumpeting, and drums beating, both in the sky and on the line of march. Women and goddesses alike broke out in songs of joy, while tuneful clarions played in sweet accord.

There was an indescribable clamour of bells, both large and small. Servants on foot leapt and danced as if challenging attack; the jesters practised all kinds of buffoonery, provoking laughter with facetious songs.

Dohā 302

Gallant princes make their steeds curvet to the measured beat of tabors and kettledrums, and accomplished dancers note with surprise that they never make a step out of time.

1. *i.e.*, Vṛhaspati.

Caupāī 300

But it is useless attempting to describe the procession. Every omen that occurred was fair and auspicious. On the left a blue-necked jay was picking up food as if to announce the very highest good fortune; on a fair field on the right were a crow and a *mongoose* in the sight of all; a grateful breeze breathed soft and cool and fragrant; a woman was seen with a pitcher and child; a fox showed himself winding about; and in front a cow was suckling its calf; a herd of deer came out on the right, an indication of everything good; a white-headed kite promised all success; also a *śyāmā* bird perched on a tree to the left; a man was met bearing curds and fish and two learned Brāhmaṇas with books in their hands.

Dohā 303

Every good and auspicious omen, and every bestower of desired reward, seemed all to have met at once as if to prove their truth.

Caupāī 301

Every good and aupicious omen was ready at hand for him whose glorious son was the Absolute made personal, a bridegroom like Rāma, matched with such a bride as Sītā, and with the pious Daśaratha and Janaka for the two parents. When they heard of the marriage, all the good omens began to dance and cry, "Now at last the Creator has really made us to be what our names denote." In this manner the procession set forth, with noise of horses and elephants and beat of drums. When Janaka, the glory of the Solar race, heard of its approach, he had all the rivers bridged, and at different stages had convenient rest-houses erected, which vied in splendour with the city of heaven and were supplied everything that one could desire—beds, food and linen. Ever discovering some new charm, all the travellers forgot their own home.

Dohā 304

Perceiving that the glorious procession was close at hand, and hearing the beating of drums, a deputation went out to meet it, with elephants and chariots and foot and horse.

Caupāī 302

Brimming golden vases and trays and platters and costly dishes[1] of every kind, laden with cakes as sweet as nectar and of indescribable variety, with much luscious fruit and in short, everything of the best, did the king iu his gladness send as an offering. Ornaments, wearing apparel, jewels of all kinds, birds, deer, horses, elephants, carriages of every description, well-omened spices, delicious perfumes—these, too, did the king send, and there was a train of porters with their baskets full of curds and parched rice and other light *entremets.* When the deputation saw the wedding guests, their soul was full of rapture and their body quivered with excitement; while the guests, no less charmed by the preparations made for their reception, beat their drums.

Dohā 305

Some on both sides enthusiastically galloped forward to meet one another, like oceans of bliss that had burst their bounds and come together.

Caupāī 303

The nymphs of heaven rained down flowers and sang, the glad gods beat their drums. The presents were all set before the king, with a humble and affectionate address. The king graciously accepted them and bestowed them in charity on the poor. Then with religious honours and hymns of praise the escort conducted him to the guest-chambers. The cloths spread as carpets for King Daśaratha to tread upon were so gorgeous that the god of wealth on seeing them could boast no longer. The apartments assigned were most beautiful and supplied with every kind of comfort. When Sītā knew that the procession had reached the city, she manifested her greatness to a slight extent, and with thoughtful heart called up the eight Siddhis, or wonder-working spirits, and sent them to arrange for the king's reception.

1. For *bhājan* ('dishes') some copies read *bhojan* or 'food,' but incorrectly, as the context shows.

Dohā 306

Obedient to her command, they repaired to the reception-hall, taking with them every kind of luxury and comfort and the joys and delights of heaven.

Caupāī 304

Each wedding guest on going to see his apartment found it a veritable paradise; no one, however, had an inkling of the mysterious power that had been exerted, but took it all as Janaka's doing. Rāma alone knew it for Sītā's influence and rejoiced at this recognition of her love. When the two brothers heard of their father's arrival they could not contain themselves for joy, but were too modest to speak to their *guru,* though they longed greatly to see their sire again. Viśvāmitra perceived their humility, which filled his soul with contentment, and took the two brothers to his bosom with quivering body and eyes bedewed with tears. They went then to Daśaratha's mansion, like thirsting travellers who have spied a pool.

Dohā 307

When the king saw the sage approaching with the two boys, he rose in joy and advanced to meet them, like one who feels his footing in a deep flood of bliss.

Caupāī 305

He prostrated himself before the sage again and again, sprinkling on his head the dust of his feet. Viśvāmitra clasped the king to his bosom and blessed him and enquired after his welfare. Then the two brothers prostrated themselves. The king on seeing them could not contain himself for joy, but took his boys to his heart, and forgetting the intolerable pain of the past seemed like a dead man restored to life. Next, they bowed their heads before Vasistha's feet, who also embraced them in an ecstasy of love; and in turn they saluted all the Brāhmanas and received their welcome blessings. Bharata and his younger brother Śatrughna greeted Rāma, who raised them to their feet and embraced them. Lakṣmaṇa rejoiced to see the two brothers (Bharata and Śatrughna) and greeted them with the utmost affection.

Dohā 308

The all-merciful and gracious Lord had an appropriate greeting and honour for all, whether citizens, or attendants, or kinsmen, beggars, or ministers, or friends.

Caupāī 306

When the wedding guests saw Rāma, they had a sense of rare fulfilment, and their demonstrations of love were beyond all telling. Beside their royal father the four boys seemed as incarnations of the four great ends of life. All the people of the city were delighted beyond measure at the sight of Daśaratha and his sons; the gods showered down flowers and beat their drums; the nymphs of heaven danced and sang. Śatānanda with the Brāhmaṇas and ministers of state and the rhapsodists and bards and players and minstrels, who had come in deputation, after duly reverencing the king and the marriage guests, received permission to return. The whole city was exceedingly delighted that the procession had come before the day fixed for the wedding, and was supremely happy, praying God to lengthen the days and nights;—

Dohā 309

"Rāma and Sītā are the perfection of beauty, and the two kings the perfection of virtue!" Thus would say all the people of the city wherever they happened to meet.

Caupāī 307

The princess of Videha is the incarnation of Janaka's merit and Rāma of Daśaratha's. None has equalled them in devotion to Siva, nor has anyone obtained such a reward as they have. There has been none like them in the world, nor is, nor ever shall be. We all too, are storehouses of everything that is good, seeing that we have been born into the world as Janaka's citizens and have beheld the beauty of Jānakī and Rāma; who is so superlatively blessed as we are? And we have yet to see Rāma's wedding, of all sights the best worth seeing." So, too, sweet-voiced maidens whispered to one another:— "This marriage, my dear, will be a great treat. God has brought about an event of signal felicity in lodging those two brothers in the guest-chambers of our eyes.

Dohā 310

Many and many a time will Janaka lovingly send for Sītā, and the two brothers, beautiful as a myriad Loves, will come to fetch her.

Caupāī 308

There will be all kinds of hospitable entertainments. Who, sister, would not rejoice in such a father-in-law? Everyone in the place will be delighted at the sight of Rāma and Lakṣmaṇa. Now two other princes, my friends, have come with the king, who are a match even for them; one dark, the other fair, but beautiful in every limb, so says every one who has seen them." Said one in reply, "I saw them today, and thought God must have made them with his own hands. Rāma and Bharata are so much alike that neither man nor woman could without looking close tell one from the other; while again Lakṣmaṇa and Śatrughna are also one in appearance, perfectly beautiful in every limb from head to foot; the soul would fain express its rapture, but language fails it, for there is nothing comparable to them in all the three spheres of creation."

Chand 25

No poet, however ingenious, says Tulasī Dāsa, could find aught comparable to them; for so unbounded is their strength, their courtesy, their knowledge, their amiability and their beauty, that they have no peers but themselves. All the women in the city, spreading out their garments, made prayer to Brahmā,—"May all four brothers be married here, and may we sing their wedding songs."

Soraṭhā 311

Said the damsels to one another with streaming eyes and quivering body:—" Friends, the two kings are of such boundless religious merit that for their sake Mahādeva will bring it all about "

Caupāī 30)

Thus they all expressed their desire, while their hearts overflowed with rapture. When the kings, who had come to witness Sītā's betrothal, saw the brothers, they all rejoiced and returned to their own homes, extolling Rāma's high and spotless fame. In this fashion several days were spent, to the joy alike of citizens and guests. At length the auspicious day arrived, in the cold season, in the pleasant month of Agahana. The Creator himself had carefully fixed the date, when the sign of the zodiac, the age of the moon, the conjunction of the stars and the day of the week were one and all propitious. Of this he sent word through Nārada, and it was the very same that Janaka's wise men had calculated. All the people on hearing this fact declared their astrologers to be very gods.

Dohā 312

It was towards sunset,[1] the clearest and most delightful hour of the day, that the Brāhmaṇas apprised Videha's king that the auspicious time had arrived.

Caupāī 310

The monarch said to the family priest, "What is now the cause of delay ?" At once Śatānanda summoned the ministers,

1. The word *dhenu-dhūli* stands for the more common *go-dhūli* for *go* and *dhenu* are identical in meaning—and denotes the unfortunately very brief period of the day during which the Indian climate is thoroughly enjoyable. Professor Monier Williams in his Sanskrit dictionary explains the words as follows : " 'dust of the earth'; a period of the day in the hot season when the sun is half risen; in the cold and dewy seasons when the sun is full but mild; and in the three other seasons, sunset; originally, a time at which mist seems to rise from the earth." I have always myself considered that the first part of the compound was used in its more ordinary sense of 'a cow,' and that *go-dhūli* would be literally rendered dust of cows,' not 'dust of the earth.' The word is still current in village use, and when I have been moving about in the district in the cold weather I have heard it applied by the country-people to the hour of sunset, when the cattle were all coming home from pasture, and raising dense clouds of dust along the narrow lanes, a fact to which the speaker was evidently referring, and which I think, is the more correct explanation of the etymology.

who all came bearing festal vases ; conchs, drums, and tabors sounded; all decked their vases in auspicious wise; graceful damsels sang songs, and holy Brāhmaṇas muttered Vedic texts. In this manner they went with all ceremony to fetch the guests and came to their apartments; and on beholding the king of Kosala's retinue it seemed to them that Indra was of much less glory. "The hour has come, be pleased to start." At this the drums gave a thundering beat. After consulting his *guru* and performing the family rites, the king and the sage sallied forth with all their host.

Ḍohā 313

Brahmā and all the other gods, on beholding the pomp and magnificence of Avadh's king, began to extol him with a thousand tongues and declare their own life to have been wasted.

Caupāī 311

Seeing the auspiciousness of the hour, the deities rained down flowers and beat their drums. Śiva and Brahmā and all the host of heaven mounted their chariots and came in crowds to see Rāma's wedding, their heart and every limb throbbing and quivering with excess of love. They were so charmed with Janaka's city that their own realms seemed to them as little worth. They gazed with astonishment at the pavilions and all the marvellous decorations; at the men and women so beautiful and well-formed, so good and amiable and intelligent, before whom all the gods and goddesses seemed like the stars at the rising of the full moon. Above all was Brahmā astounded at finding his own handiwork nowhere.

Dohā 314

But Śiva thus admonished them all, "Do not give way to such astonishment; recover yourselves and reflect that this is the marriage of Sītā and Raghubīr.

Caupāī 312

The mere mention of whose name destroys all that is accursed in the world; in whose hand are the four great ends of human life; such are Sītā and Rāma", said Love's destroyer. When Śambhu had thus admonished the gods, he again urged on his noble bull. The gods saw Daśaratha march forth with a heart full of joy and a thrill of rapture. The crowd of sages and Brāhmaṇas who accompanied him seemed like incarnate gods ministering to him. In the midst shone forth the beautiful boys, like the final Beatitude manifested in its four phases.[1] As they gazed on the noble pair, of golden and sapphire hue, the gods were moved with violent love, and especially were they delighted at the sight of Rāma, and glorified the king and rained down flowers.

Dohā 315

Again and again as Umā and Mahādeva fixed their gaze upon Rāma, all-perfect in beauty from head to foot, they felt a thrill of joy and their eyes filled with tears.

Caupāī 313

On his body, dark as a peacock's glistening neck, his bright raiment outshone the lightning; his wedding adornments of every kind were most exquisitely fashioned : his face more lustrous than a cloudless autumn moon; his eyes more brilliant than the lotus; his beauty, in short, so marvellous that no words can describe how it moved the soul. By his side shone forth his charming brothers, making their mettlesome steeds plunge and bound on the way, as also did all the attendant princes; while the family bards recited the glories of their line. As the king of the birds noted the action of the horse that Rāma bestrode, he blushed for shame; for its beauty was beyond all telling, as it might be Kāmadeva himself in equine disguise.

Chand 26

As though Kāmadeva himself in his love for Rāma had assumed an equine disguise of such resplendent beauty as to charm

1. The four grades or phases of *apavarga*, *i.e.*, final beatitude, are *sālokyata*, residence in the same heaven as god; *sārūpya* being in the same form as god; *sāmīpya*, being in actual contact with god; and *sāyujya*, complete absorption into god.

the whole world with his youth and vigour and form and points and paces! A saddle flashed its splendours on his back, thick set with pearls and rubies; the bridle too and band gleamed bright with jewels that dazzled the gaze of men, saints and gods.

Dohā 316

Obedient in every movement to the will of its lord, the gallant steed paced on, as beautiful as a peacock that dances in response to a thunder-cloud, whose dark mass is irradiated by the stars of heaven and the fitful lightning.

Caupāī 314

But not Śāradā herself could do justice to the noble steed that Rāma rode. Śaṅkara was enchanted with his beauty and congratulated himself on having fifteen eyes! When Hari affectionately gazed on Rāma he and Lakṣmī were both equally charmed; while Brahmā rejoiced to behold his beauty, and regretted that he had eight eyes. Kārttikeya exulted greatly, for he enjoyed the sight with no less than twelve eyes.[1] When the all-wise Indra looked at Rāma, he thought Gautama's curse a great blessing; and all the gods broke out in Indra's praise, saying :—'Today there is no one like him.'[2] All heaven was delighted at the sight of Rāma, and there was joy above measure in the court of both the kings.

Chand 27

Great was the joy in both the royal courts; the air resounded with multitudinous kettledrums; the gods rained down flowers and shouted in their joy, "Glory, glory, glory to Raghu's noble son." In this manner, when they learnt that the procession was approaching, all sorts of music began to play, and the queen gave orders to her handmaids to prepare the auspicious materials for the lustral rite.

Dohā 317

With many lights and torches and festal preparations of every kind, a bevy of graceful dames proceeded joyously to celebrate the lustral rite.

1. Since he had six heads he was half as well off again as Brahmā.
2. The reason being that Indra has a thousand eyes.

Caupāī 315

With fawn-like eyes and face of moon-like brightness, each one was beautiful enough to rob Rati of all self-conceit. Attired in costly garments of different colours, covered all over with ornaments and rendered beautiful in every limb, they sang more melodiously than the cuckoo to the music of the bells on their wrists and girdles and feet, as they moved, with all the undulating grace of a wild elephant. All kinds of music played, and there were rejoicings both in heaven and in the city. Indrāṇī, Śāradā, Lakṣmī, Bhavānī and all the wise and pure goddesses disguised themselves as lovely maidens and flocked to the king's seraglio, singing delightfully with divine voice; and for joy there was no one who recognized them.

Chand 28

In their ecstatic joy as they went to receive the bridegroom with melodious song and sweet music, who could tell who was who ? The gods showered down flowers and everything was delightful. As they gazed upon the bridegroom, the source of bliss, they were all glad of heart, their lotus eyes overflowed with tears and their every limb quivered with rapture.

Dohā 318

The joy in the heart of Sītā's mother on beholding Rāma's gallant appearance was more than a thousand Śāradās and Śeṣanāgas could tell in a hundred aeons.

Caupāī 316

Restraining her tears out of regard for the auspiciousness of the event, the queen with gladness of heart performed the lustral rite, and diligently completed the entire ceremony in accordance with Vedic prescription and family usage. The five kinds of music and the five sounds[1] were accompanied by festal

1. The five kinds of music are as follows: the *tāntrī*, or sitāra; the *tāla*; and *jhānjh*, or cymbals; the *nagārā*, or kettledrum; and fifthly, the *turahī*, or trumpet, fife or other wind instrument. The five sounds are those produced by the chanting of the Vedas, songs of the bards, the shouts of triumph, the blowing of conches and music.

chanting, and rich carpets of different sorts were spread upon the ground. After the lustral rite and the oblation Rāma proceeded to the pavilion. So great was the splendour and magnificence of Daśaratha and his retinue that Indra was put to shame by it. From time to time the gods rained down flowers, while the Brāhmaṇas repeated the appropriate propitiatory texts.[1] There was so much jubilation on the earth and in heaven that no one could hear himself speak, much less any one else. In this manner Rāma entered the pavilion, where the libation was offered and he was conducted to his throne.

Chand 29

When the bridegroom was seated on the throne and the ceremony of waving festal lamps around his head was performed, all rejoiced at the sight, scattering around him jewels and raiment and ornaments in profusion, while women sang festal songs. Brahmā and all the other gods disguised as noble Brāhmaṇas witnessed the spectacle, and as they gazed on the glorious sun of the lotus race of Raghu, reckoned it the happiest moment of their life.

Dohā 319

The barbers and makers of leaf-plates and singers and dancers, who gathered up the offerings that had been scattered about Rāma,[2] bowed their head and invoked blessings upon him from a heart bursting with joy.

1. The prayer, or propitiatory text, ordinarily known by the name of *sānti*, is as follows : *Om Sanno Mitraḥ sam Varuṇah sanno bhavatvaryamā sanna Indro Vṛhaspatiḥ sanno Viṣṇur urukramaḥ namo Brahmaṇe na maste Vāyo tvameva pratyakṣam Brahmāsi tvam eva pratyakṣam Brahma vadiṣyāmi ṛtam vadiṣyāmi satyam vadiṣyāmi tan mām avatu tad vaktāram avatvavatu mām avatuvaktāram. Om Sāntis sāntis sāntiḥ.*

2. The custom of distributing pieces of money among the crowd is still kept up by rich Muhammadan families at wedding festivals, and special coins for the purpose were struck by Jahangir and others of the Delhi Emperors. These are called *nisār*, while the word used by Tulasī Dāsa here and in many other places, is *nichhāvari*. The resemblance is so close that the Hindi might easily be a corruption of the Arabic. But it seems improbable that such a thoroughly Indian custom should not have an indigenous name; and, further, the derivation of *nichhāvari* would appear to be from the Sanskrit

Caupāī 317

Janaka and Daśaratha joined most affectionately in the observance of every custom, whether religious or secular; and the royal pair were so glorious a sight that the poet, searching for a suitable analogy and finding nothing, must acknowledge himself defeated and admit that they were comparable only to themselves. The gods beheld the two fathers with intense delight and rained down flowers and sang their praises: "Since Brahmā first created the world, we have seen and heard of many marriages, but never till this day have we seen a match so perfect in all respects, and two such well-matched fathers." At the sound of this voice from heaven, so gracious and yet so true, there was on both sides a marvellous access of love. Janaka led the way with due honours to the pavilion, offeirng libations and unrolling a carpet as he went.

Chand 30

Beholding the beauty of the manifold decorations of the pavilion, even the sages were enchanted; but the wise Janaka with his own hands conducted them all to their seats. Paying the same honour and respect to Vasiṣṭha as to his own patron divinity, he received his blessing; but the supreme devotion with which he greeted Viśvāmitra was of a kind that surpasses description.

Dohā 320

Next, with great joy the king did homage to Vāmadeva too and the other seers, and gave them all exalted thrones and received their blessing.

root *kship*, 'to throw,' with the prefix *ni*, 'down.' Mr. Bate, in his Hindi Dictionary, forms it from *niyam plus kshay plus var*: but this can scarcely be accepted as a very plausible explanation. Any how the word does not look like a foreign importation. As to the etymology of *nisār*, I must leave Arabic scholars to speak; but if there is no connection between the two words, the coincidence in sound and meaning is at least curious. Should there be no earlier authority than Tulasī Dāsa for *nichhāvari* it might be a mere adaptation, such as has converted *intikāl* into *ant kāl*; *bil ijmāl* into *Brij māl*, and has helped to popularize many other unintelligible terms of legal pharaseology.

Caupāī 318

Again he did homage to the lord of Kosala, taking him to be the peer of Mahādeva, yea, none other; with folded hands in humble phrase extolling him and enlarging on his own marvellous good fortune. Then to all the wedding guests he paid the same homage in every respect as to the bridegroom's father, and assigned them all appropriate seats. How can I with my one tongue describe all the festal ceremonies ? With gifts and compliments and profuse apologies Janaka honoured all his guests. Brahmā, Viṣṇu, Mahādeva, the eight guardians of the quarters[1] and the god of day, who knew Raghubir's glory, disguised themselves as learned Brāhmaṇas and were delighted spectators of the festivities. Though Janaka recognized them not, he paid them homage as gods and led them to exalted seats.

Chand 31

Who could tell who was who, when there was no one who could answer even for himself. As they gazed on the bridegroom, the root of joy, bliss was diffused on all sides. When he saw the gods, the all-wise Rāma assigned them what seats they fancied; and the heavenly powers were delighted to behold the gracious manner of their lord.

Dohā 321

As the partridge drinks in the light of the moon, so their bright eyes reverently drank in the beauty of Rāma's face with the utmost rapture.

Caupāī 319

Perceiving that the hour had come, Vasiṣṭha called, and Śatānanda came with ready obedience. "Go now and quickly bring

1. The guardians of the eight quarters of the world are Indra, of the east; Agni, of the south-east; Yama, of the south; Nirriti, of the south-west; Varuṇa, of the west; Vāyu or Marut, of the north-west; Kuvera, of the north; Īśāna or Śiva, of the north-east. Some lists substitute Sūrya, 'the sun' and Soma, 'the Moon,' for Nirriti and Īśāna : others again mention the Sun and Moon and the Six Planets.—*Monier Williams.*

the bride." On receiving this order the sage went gladly, and on hearing his message the queen with all her attendants was delighted, and sent for the Brāhmaṇa ladies and the elders of the tribe, and with songs of joy perfomed all the family rites. The noble goddesses, who were disguised as mortal women, were all so amiable and lovely, in the first bloom of their youth,[1] that the ladies were charmed to see them, and, though not recognizing them, held them more dear than life. Again and again the queen did them honour accounting them equals of Umā, Ramā and Śāradā. After dressing Sītā and forming a procession they joyously conducted her to the pavilion.

Chand 32

Reverently and with auspicious pomp her attendant ladies conducted Sītā, each of them of lovely form and superbly adorned, moving with the voluptuous grace of a young elephant. At the sound of their melodious strains the sages forgot their meditations, the god of love and the cuckoos were abashed; while the bells on their anklets and gleaming girdles rang out with the cymbals and a delightful accompaniment as they moved.

Dohā 322

Among her maidens Sītā shines forth in native loveliness, like Bliss personified among the Graces.

Caupāī 320

Sītā's beauty is indescribable, so great is it and so little my wit. When the wedding guests saw her approach, so exquisitely charming and altogether divine, they all did homage to her from their inmost soul. At the sight of her, Rāma was filled with

1. Ancient Hindus had a perfect mania for classifying and defining, and have invented divisions and sub-divisions of every conceivable group of objects, with a definite technical name for each variety. Thus the word in the text, here translated 'in the bloom of youth, is *syāmā* which is strictly defined 'as a woman from eight to sixteen years of age, resembling in complexion the blossom of Priyaṅgu and its slender stalk in shape.' There are many other varieties of the fair sex that have their distinctive marks specifie dwith equal minuteness.

love, and Daśaratha and his sons were glad of heart beyond all telling. The gods greeted her with a shower of flowers and the sages gave their blessings in auspicious wise; there was a confused noise of singing and playing and general rejoicing throughout the city. In this manner Sītā arrived at the pavilion, while the great sages joyously recited the set forms of prayer and the two family *gurus* performed all the due rites and ceremonies.

Chand 33

After performing the ceremonies, the *gurus* directed the glad Brāhmaṇas to worship Gaurī and Gaṇeśa. The gods in visible form accepted the homage and gave their blessing, which they received with joy. Whatever dainty dish or condiment any holy man fancied at any time was at once supplied him by the table attendants in plates and pitchers of gold. Having reverently and dutifully performed all family rites in accordance with the Sun-god's prescription, and offered homage to the gods, they conducted Sītā to her glorious throne. None can imagine the mutual love with which Sītā and Rāma regarded each other; it exceeds all sense, or intelligence, or speech, or perception; how then can the poet express it?

Dohā 323

At the time of the burnt-sacrifice, the Fire-god in person most graciously accepted the oblation, and all the Vedas in the guise of Brāhmaṇas expounded the marriage formularies.

Caupāī 321

What words can describe Janaka's illustrious queen-consort, Sītā's mother, in whose composition the Creator had combined the perfection of glory, piety, happiness and beauty? At the appropriate time the sages summoned her, and she came responsive to the summons with her attendant maidens. Then shone forth Sunayanā at Janaka's left as Menā beside Himālaya. With their own hands the glad king and queen took and placed before Rāma golden vases and costly jewelled trays full of holy water and delicious perfumes. The sages with auspicious voice recited the Vedas and at the proper time the heavens rained flowers, while the father and mother of the bride looked on in rapture and began to wash the holy feet.

Chand 34

Their whole frame quivering with rapturous love, they began to lave his lotus feet; while both in heaven and in the city there were singing and music and shouts of victory bursting forth and overflowing in all directions. The lotus feet that ever gleam in the lake of Śiva's bosom; by meditating upon which for a single moment every impurity of the soul and defilement of this wicked world is removed; by whose touch the sage's sinful wife attained salvation; whose honey[1], as the gods declare, ever rests on Śambhu's head; on which the bee-like soul of sages and ascetics ever dwells ere they reach the heaven of their desire; these holy feet are washed by Janaka, midst the glad acclaim of all. The two family priests join the hands of the bride and bridegroom and recite their descent. The mystic union is completed, and at the sight Brahmā and all gods and men and sages were full of joy. As the bride's parents gazed on the gracious bridegroom, both their soul and body were raptured with delight; and having completed every family and scriptural observance the glorious monarch gave his daughter to her lord. As Himālaya gave Girijā to Mahādeva, and as Ocean gave Lakṣmī to Viṣṇu, in like manner did Janaka bestow Sītā on Rāma, and the world was glorified anew. After stationing the happy pair on one spot (the bride so fair of hue, the groom so dark) and performing the sacrifice with all due rite, and tying the knot, the circumambulation commenced.

Dohā 324

At the sound of the huzzas and minstrelsy and the recitation of the Veda and the auspicious chanting and the music, the all-wise gods were delighted and rained down flowers from the trees of paradise.

1. *i.e.*, the Ganges.

Caupāī 322

The bride and bridegroom with measured paces performed the circumambulation, while all present feasted their adoring gaze on the spectacle. The beauty of the happy pair is not to be described; whatever comparison might be suggested would fall short of the reality. The lovely images of Rāma and Sītā were reflected in the jewelled pillars, and sparkled like incarnations of Kāmadeva and Rati, who had come to witness Rāma's glorious wedding and, from mingled curiosity and bashfulness, at one moment showed themselves openly and at another retired out of sight. All the spectators were enraptured and, like Janaka, forgot all about themselves. Joyously the sages bade them pace the circle round; the rite was accomplished and the marriage offerings made. Rāma applied the vermilion to Sītā's forehead, a scene so charming that it was beyond all description; and his arm seemed like a serpent thirsting for ambrosia, as it decorated her moonlike face with the red powder that filled his lotus hand. Then by Vasiṣṭha's direction the bride and bridegroom took their seat together.

Chand 35

When Rāma and Jānakī took their seat on the high throne, Daśaratha's soul was rejoiced and his frame quivered with emotion, as again and again he fixed his gaze upon them and saw as it were his own virtue like the tree of paradise blossoming anew. There was rejoicing all over the world at the news of Rāma's wedding. How can their blessed happiness be described? I have but one tongue in my head, while the joy had no bounds. Then Janaka, having received Vasiṣṭha's order, provided all things necessary for the marriage ceremonial, and summoned the three maidens, Māṇḍavī, Śrutakīrti and Urmilā. After affectionately performing every rite, the king gave first to Bharata in marriage the beautiful and accomplished daughter of Kuśaketu. Then next with all due honour Janaka bestowed upon Lakṣmaṇa Jānakī's lovely younger sister; and finally gave away to Ripuśūdan the bright-eyed and charming Śrutakīrti, no less amiable than beautiful. As bride and bridegroom modestly gazed on each other and noticed the contrast[1], they were glad of heart; while everyone delightedly applauded the beauty of the scene, and the gods rained down flowers. All equally beautiful, though diverse in hue, they shone resplendent in the pavilion, as though the four states of life with their several lords had met in one living soul.

Dohā 325

The king of Avadh gazed with delight on his four sons and their brides, as though that jewel of monarchs had in them realized the four ends of life[2] together with the four religious duties.

Caupāī 323

All the princes were married with the same ceremonies as those I have described for Rāma. The enormous dowry was beyond description; the whole pavilion was full of gold and jewels. Shawls, robes and silks of all kinds in the greatest profusion and of immense value; elephants, chariot, shorses, menservants, and cows with gilded horns and hoofs, as beautiful as the cow of plenty; things so many that no one could count them, nor credit their number if he had not seem them[3]. At the sight the guardians of the spheres broke out into praise of the dowry, and Avadh's king received it all most graciously. To everyone who asked was given whatever he desired, and what remained over was taken to the guests' quarters. Then with folded hands and bated breath Janaka courteously entreated all the bridegroom's party.

1. Rāma and Bharata being dark were married to Jānakī and Māṇḍavī who were fair; while the fair bridegrooms, Lakṣmaṇa and Śatrughna, were wedded to the dark brides, Ūrmila and Śrutakīrti.

2. The *char phal, i.e.*, the four fruits or ends of life, are as has been explained, before *Dharma*, *Artha*, *Kāma*, and *Mokṣa*, which are here compared to Daśaratha's four sons. The four brides are likened to the *chār kriyā*, or four methods of religion, which are either *Sevā*, *Śraddhā*, *Tapasyā* and *Bhakti*, that is to say, obedience, piety, penance and faith; or, according to another enumeration, *anuṣthāna*, religious ceremonial; *udyoga*, diligence; *rati* love; and *virati*, detachment from the world.

3. For comparison, see *Adhyātma Rāmāyaṇa*. 6, 76-77; *Vālmīkīya, Rāmāyaṇa*, 74, 3-7.

Chand 36

After courteously entreating all the guests with high ceremony, gifts, apologies and compliments, he joyfully proceeded with much devotion to do his worshipful homage to the saintly throng. With bowed head he propitiated the gods, and thus, with hands folded in prayer, addressed them all, "Gods and saints desire only love; can Ocean's wants be satisfied by a libation of a few drops?"[1] Again with folded hands Janaka and his brother spoke to the king of Kosala, with winning words full of love and amiability : "O king, I am greatly ennobled by your alliance; know that my realm and all that I have is freely yours to command. Take these girls as your handmaids and graciously protect them, and pardon me my sin and presumption in inviting you." The jewel of the Solar race in turn paid the bride's father all the highest honours; their courtesy was past all telling, and the love that overflowed their hearts. The deities rained down flowers as the monarch proceeded to the guest-chamber, amid the crash of kettledrums, the muttered recitation of the Veda, and glad rejoicings both on earth and in heaven. Then by the sage's command and singing auspicious strains as they went, the fair ladies of the court conducted to the nuptial chamber the bridegrooms and their brides.

Dohā 326

Again and again did Sītā gaze on Rāma with modest mien, but full of confidence at heart; and her eyes, athirst with love, outshone the fish in Kāmadeva's blazon.

Caupāī 324

Dark in hue and full of native grace, his beauty put to shame a myriad Kāmadevas; his lac-stained feet gleamed like some lotus, the haunt of bee-like saintly souls; his pure and lustrous yellow loin-cloth outshone the rising sun or lightning-flash; and the little bells on his waistbelt made delicious tinkling; long were his arms and clasped with glittering bangles his yellow sacred

1. Yet though it derives no benefit from such a scanty offering, it both demands and accepts it.

thread set him off to perfection; his signet ring would ravish all hearts; lustrous were all his many wedding adornments and the stars and collars on his broad breast; over his left shoulder a yellow shawl with fringes of gems and pearls; with lotus eyes and bright pendants from his ears and a face the very storehouse of beauty; lovely brows and charming nose and on his forehead a most bewitching spot, while on his head the auspicious marriage-crown shone glorious with knotted pearls and gems.

Chand 37

The knotted gems and the nuptial crown and his comely person ravished all hearts; and not a woman or goddess in heaven or earth who did not break a blade of grass[1] at the sight of his beauty. After scattering about him jewels and raiment and ornaments they waved the festal lamps about his head, singing auspicious songs, while the gods rained down flowers, and bards, minstrels and rhapsodists declared his glory. When the bride and bridegroom entered the nuptial chamber, great was the joy of the attendants, who with festive songs and in most lovingwise began to perform the customary observances. Gaurī herself taught Rāma, and Śāradā told Sītā how to perform the ceremony of the interchange of morsels;[2] and all the ladies of the gynaeceum were so taken with the merry sport that they reckoned it the happiest moment of their lives. When Jānakī saw in the jewels on her fingers the image of the all-beautiful, she dared not move her eyes or lithesome arm for fear of losing his presence. The rapture of delight, the ecstasy of love surpassed all telling; only those happy dames could comprehend it who escorted the bride and bridegroom to the guest-house. Then might be heard on all sides blessings and great exultation in heaven and on earth and a universal shout of joy : 'Long life to the four happy couples!' Hermits, saints and sages, the gods too on beholding their lord, sounded their kettledrums and returned in gladness, each to his own realm raining down flowers and crying, 'Victory.'

1. Either involuntarily from agitation and bashfulness, or as a charm to avert the evil eye, or to show how little they valued anything in the world in comparison with his beauty.

2. This is the popular ceremony of *lahakauri* performed by the bride and bridegroom, who exchange small portions of rice-milk in the nuptial chamber.

Dohā 327

Then the four princes with their brides came to their father, and such was the glory, the felicity and the rapture that it seemed to overflow the guest-chambers like a torrent.

Caupāī 325

Again, there was a magnificent banquet of varieties of dishes, to which Janaka invited all the visitors. Carpets of priceless cloth were spread as the king sallied forth with his sons. After reverently washing his guests' feet, he seated each according to his rank. First Janaka washed the feet of Avadh's lord with a loving devotion past all telling; then he washed Rāma's lotus feet, feet ever enshrined in Mahādeva's heart; and, also with his own hands, washed the feet of the three brothers, regarding them as Rāma himself. To all the king assigned appropriate seats, and then gave his orders to the cooks, who with due ceremony set out the dishes, made all of jewelled leaves stitched together with golden pins.

Dohā 328

The quick and obsequious cooks passed round, and in a moment every guest was supplied with rice and condiments and fragrant butter, and everything luscious and savoury and nice.

Caupāī 326

After making the five oblations,[1] they began to eat listening with great delight to abusive songs. There were confections of many kinds, sweeter than nectar or than words can tell, which the well-trained waiters handed round, and such an infinite variety of sauces that no one could remember all their names, with food of the four kinds mentioned in the sacred books and an indescribable variety of each kind, and seasoning of the six flavours, and each flavour exhibited in a countless number of dishes. As the banquet proceeded, scandalous jests were bandied about in

1. The five vital airs to which oblations are made are *prāna*, *apāna*, *samāna*, *vyāna* and *udāna*.

pleasant tones, and not a man or woman but heard his name brought in. Louder and broader grew the raillery of the festive hour, and the king and the whole assembly were moved to laughter as they listened. In this manner they all feasted and in the end punctiliously rinsed the mouth.

Dohā 329

And with due honour Janaka offered *pān*[1] to Daśaratha and all his guests, and the glorious king then happily retired to his own apartment.

Caupāī 327

There was ever some new festivity in the city, and the whole day and night seemed gone like a moment At early dawn the glorious king woke up, and mendicants began to chant his praises. As he gazed upon the gallant princes and their brides, the rapture of his soul was beyond all telling. After performing his morning devotions he went to his *guru* with his heart full of love and exultation, and clasping his hands in prayer bowed before him and said with a voice of mellifluous sweetness : "Hearken, king of sages, it is by your favour that today my toils have been rewarded. Now, holy father, summon the Brāhmaṇas and present them all with cows with costly adornments." On hearing these words the *guru* applauded the king, and sent to summon the whole saintly throng.

Dohā 330

Then came Vāmadeva, the divine seer, and Nārada and Vālmīki and Jāvāli and Viśvāmitra and all the other great sages and ascetics.

Caupāī 328

The king prostrated himself before them all and worshipped them, and then affectionately conducted them to seats of honour. Next, he sent for 4,00,000 cows, all as gentle and beautiful as the cow of paradise, and after decorating them in every possible way bestowed them with great joy upon the

1. *i.e.*, betel leaves.

sages, with many a phrase of studied humility, declaring it to be the happiest day of his life. On receiving their blessing the king, the pride of the Solar race, rejoiced, and next sent for all the begging fraternity and gave them, according as each desired, gold, or apparel, or jewels, or horses, or elephants, or chariots. They all went off loudly telling and singing his praises :'Glory, glory, glory to the lord of the Solar race.' Such were the rejoicings at Rāma's wedding that not even Śeṣa could describe with his thousand tongues.

Dohā 331

Again and again the king bowed his head at Viśvāmitra's feet and said, "All this happiness, O king of sages, is the result of your benignant regard."

Caupāī 329

King Daśaratha spent the whole night extolling Janaka's affection[1] and amiability and magnificence; everyday on rising he asked permission to return home, but each time Janaka would lovingly detain him. There was constantly some new fete in his honour, and everyday a thousand different kinds of entertainment. The rejoicings in the city never flagged, and no one liked to think of Daśaratha's departure. In this manner many days were spent, and the guests were fast bound by the cords of love, till Viśvāmitra and Śatānanda went and told Videha's lord, "You must now let Daśaratha take his leave, even though you cannot part with your love for him." The king replied, "It is all very well, lord," and summoned his ministers, who came and bowed the head crying, "Long live the king!"

Dohā 332

"Make it known in the gynaeceum," said Janaka, "that Avadha's lord wishes to depart." At these words the ministers, Brāhmaṇas, courtiers and the king himself were greatly moved.

Caupāī 330

When it was noised in the city that the guests were leaving, everyone anxiously asked his neighbour if it were a fact. When

1. The line, which I translate, stands thus : *nrip sab rāti sarahāt biti*. Another reading is *nrip sab bhānti sarāh bibhūti*.

they heard they were actually going, all were as unhappy as a lotus that fades in the evening. Every place where the visitors had put up on their arrival was crowded with parting presents,[1] fruits and confections of every kind, and dishes too various for description. A multitude of porters laden with wearing apparel[2] and cooks beyond number were sent by Janaka with a hundred thousand horses and twenty-five thousand chariots all exquisitely finished throughout, with ten thousand elephants in rut duly caparsioned, at sight of which earth's guardian elephants would feel ashamed of themselves, besides wagons full of gold and raiment and jewels; buffaloes also and cows, and many other articles of various kinds.

Dohā 333

The dowry, moreover, given by Videha's king was immeasurable and beyond all telling; and Indra, had he seen it, would have thought the riches of the universe as nothing in comparison.

Caupāī 331

When all his gifts had been thus arranged, Janaka despatched them to Avadh. On hearing that the guests were about to start, all the queens were as unhappy as fish when water falls. Again and again they clasped Sītā to their bosoms and blessed and exhorted her, saying : "May you ever be beloved by your husband, and with him live a long and happy life; this is my blessing. Be obedient to your new father and mother and *guru*, and regarding your lord's displeasure[3] do as he bids." Her sweet-voiced companions, too, with their overpowering affection reminded her of woman's crowning duty. Again and again after thus duly admonishing them the queens clasped the four brides to their bosom, and time after time, in the midst of their maternal embraces, exclaimed, 'Why has Brahmā created women ?'

1. The word *sidh* probably stands for *sidhya*, 'auspicious', though it might be for *sidhu*, wine.

2. For *basan* 'wearing apparel,' some copies read, *basah*, 'oxen.'

3. In this line *rukh* may be the Persian word meaning 'face'; but it is more probably the Sanskrit *rush*, displeasure.'

Dohā 334

That very moment came the joyous Rāma, the glory of the Solar race, with his brothers, to Janaka's palace to bid him farewell.

Caupāī 332

All the people of the city, both men and women, ran to see the four brothers so naturally lovely. Said one, "Today they are about to go, and Janaka has completed all the preparations for their departure; so feast your eyes on their beauty for the last time. All four princes have been most welcome visitors; who can say, friend, what we have done to deserve that god should bring our eyes such guests! Like a dying man who is given ambrosia, or as one who has been hungry all his life and discovers the tree of paradise, or as one of the damned in hell who approaches Hari's feet, so am I after seeing them. Gaze upon Rāma's beauty and treasure his image in your heart, as it were the jewel in a serpent's hood." In this manner the princes gladdened the eyes of all as they proceeded to the palace.

Dohā 335

The ladies of the gynaeceum rose in their joy as they beheld their exquisite beauty; and the mothers of the brides, in token of their delight, waved the lustral lamp around their heads and scattered gifts.

Caupāī 333

Full of love at the vision of Rāma's beauty, they affectionately fall at his feet again and again, nor are conscious of shame, so rapt is their soul in devotion and involuntary attachment beyond all description. After bathing him and his brothers and rubbing their bodies with cosmetics, they lovingly entertain them at a banquet of the six flavours. Then seeing that the time had come, Rāma said to them in the most amiable, loving and modest tone: "The king is desirous of starting for Avadh and has sent us to take leave of you. O mother, be pleased to give me your commands and ever regard me with affection as your own child." At these words the queens grieved sore and were too overcome by love to speak a word, but clasped their daughters to their bosom and then meekly gave them to their lords.

Chand 38

With humble submission Sunayanā committed Sītā to Rāma, crying again and again with folded hands, "Ah, my son, you, I ween, are all-wise, and to you are apparent the thoughts of all men. Know that Sītā is dear as life to the king and myself, nay, to all her kinsfolk and all the people of the city; consider her amiability and her affection and accept her as your own servant.

Soraṭhā 336

You are the fullness of desire, the crown of wisdom, the beloved of the universe, quick to recognize merit in your votaries, destroyer of evil, Rāma the all merciful."

Caupāī 334

So saying, the queen still clung to his feet and her voice seemed lost as it were in the quicksand of love. On hearing her most affectionate address, Rāma showed her the highest honour, and with folded hands begged her leave to depart, and again and again made obeisance to her. When he had received her blessing, he bowed once more and then with his brothers took his leave. Treasuring up his sweet and gracious image in their hearts, all the queens at first seemed paralyzed by excess of love, but summoning up courage they called their daughters and again and again gave them a maternal embrace: then leading them a few steps would take them to their arms yet again with ever-growing mutual love. Time after time they left their attendants for yet one more last embrace, as a heifer not yet weaned from the cow.

Dohā 337

All the men and women in the palace, the attendants and all, were so oveprowered by emotion that it seemed as though they had made the city of Videha the very home of piteousness and lovers' partings.

Caupāī 335

The pet parrots and *mainas* that Jānakī had kept in golden cages and taught to speak, cried in distress, 'Where is the princess?' and, on hearing, which of them was not robbed of all peace of mind ? When birds and beasts were thus distressed, how can the feelings of the people be told? Then came Janaka with his brother (Kuśa-dhvaja) overflowing with love and his eyes full of tears. As he gazed upon Sītā, all his courage deserted him and his eminent asceticism lasted but in name. As he clasped Jānakī to his bosom the stronghold of his stern philosophy was broken down. All his wise counsellors remonstrated with him, and seeing the unfitness of the time he recovered himself, and again and again taking his daughter to his heart, he ordered a gorgeous *pālki* to be got ready.

Dohā 338

The whole court was overpowered with emotion, when the king, perceiving that the auspicious moment had arrived, seated the brides in the palanquins, with his thoughts intent upon Gaṇeśa and his consort, Siddhi.

Caupāī 336

The monarch gave his daughter much advice and instructed her in the whole duty of women and in family customs. He bestowed upon her many men-servants and maid-servants and all her own favourite attendants. As she went on her way the citizens were in distress, but good signs and auspicious omens betokened all happiness. Brāhmaṇas and ministers with all their retinue joined company to escort them. The wedding-guests made ready their chariots and elephants and horses, and there was a tumultuous noise of music, appropriate to the hour. Then Daśaratha called up all the Brāhmaṇas and gratified them with gifts and compliments, and putting the dust of their lotus feet upon his head, rejoiced — great king as he was — to obtain their benison. As he set forth on his way with his thoughts on Gaṇeśa, every omen of good occurred.

Dohā 339

The gods rained down flowers, the heavenly nymphs sang for joy, as the king of Avadh set forth for his capital amidst the clash of jubilant music.

Caupāī 337

Courteously the king dismissed the burghers and reverently bade all the mendicants approach and bestowed upon them ornaments and clothes and horses and elephants, and affectionately cherishing them made them stand up before him. After again and again reciting his praises, they turned home, treasuring Râma in their hearts. Though Kosala's lord spoke time after time, Janaka in his exceeding love would not turn back. Once more said the king in gracious tones, "I beg you to turn back, sire; you have come a great distance." At last he dismounted and remained standing, his eyes overflowing with love's torrent. Then said Videha's lord with folded hands and in a voice fraught with the ambrosia of affection :"How can I fitly express my unworthiness, on whom my lord has conferred such high honour?"

Dohā 340

Kosala's king in return showed the profoundest respect to the father of the bride and his retinue; and as they embraced with mutual courtesy their heart could not contain the love they felt.

Caupāī 338

Janaka bowed his head to the assembly of sages and received a blessing from them all. Next he reverently saluted his sons-in-law, the four brothers, each a treasure of beauty, amiability and accomplishments; and clasping his gracious lotus hands he cried in accents begotten of love, "O Rāma, how can I tell thy praise; swan of the Mānasa lake of the sages and Mahādeva's souls; for whose sake ascetics practise their asceticism; devoid of anger, infatuation, selfishness and pride; the all-pervading Absolute, the invisible, the immortal, the supreme spirit, at once the sum and negation of all qualities; whom neither words nor fancy can portray; whom all philosophy fails to expound; whose greatness the Vedas declare to be unutterable, and who remainest the selfsame in all time, past, present, or future?

Dohā 341

O source of every joy, thou hast revealed thyself to my material vision; for nothing in the world is beyond the reach of him to whom God is propitious.

Caupāī 339

Thou hast exalted me in every way, and recognizing me as one of thy servants hast made me thy very own. Not ten thousand Śāradās and Śeṣanāgas, though they kept up their count for a myriad ages, could tell all my good fortune or thy perfections; know this, O Raghunath; yet I have somewhat to say — for I have this ground of confidence that thou art easily appeased by the slightest evidence of affection — and therefore time after time I implore with folded hands that never may my soul be deluded into deserting thy feet." On hearing these excellent words, the true fruit of devotion, even Rāma, in whom all pleasure ever dwells, was pleased and with gracious courtesy saluted his father-in-law, holding him equal to his own sire, or Viśvāmitra, or Vasiṣṭha. Next he bowed himself before Bharata and affectionately embraced him and gave him his blessing.

Dohā 342

Then the king embraced and blessed both Lakṣmaṇa and Śatrughna, and, overpowered with love for one another, they again and again bowed their heads.

Caupāī 340

At last, after many courtesies and flattering speeches, Rāma and his brothers proceeded on their way. Then went Janaka and clasped Viśvāmitra by the feet and put the dust of his feet on his head and eyes. "Hearken, O lord of sages, now that I have seen you, I am persuaded that nothing is beyond my attainment. Such bliss and glory as the sovereigns of the universe might desire, though they would be ashamed to express their longing, has all, my lord, been brought within my reach, for all prosperity follows upon seeing you." After again and again humbly bowing the head, the king received his blessing and took leave. The marriage procession set forth to the sound of music, and the whole assemblage, great and small, were all enraptured and, as they gazed upon Rāma and feasted their eyes upon him, were happy for life.

Dohā 343

Halting from time to time at convenient stages on the road, to the great delight of the people, the procession, on an auspicious day drew near to Avadh.

Caupāī 341

'Amidst the beat of kettledrums and clamour of many tabors and sackbuts and conches and a din of horses and elephants, and clash of cymbals and drums and sweet-tuned clarions, when the citizens heard the procession coming, they were all in a tremor of delight, and everyone began to decorate his own house and the markets and streets and squares and gates of the city. The whole roadway was watered with perfumes : on every side were festal squares filled in with elegant devices; the show in the bāzār was beyond all telling, with wreaths and flags and banners and canopies. Trees of the areca-nut and the plantain and the mango, the *maulasarī*, the *kadamba*[1] and the *tamāla*, were transplanted all laden with fruit, and grew into fine trees as soon as they touched the soil, being set in jewelled screens of exquisite workmanship.

1. *Bakula*, or *maulasarī* (*Mimusops elengi*) is noted for its fragrant flowers and bark rich in medicinal properties. *Kadamba* (*Nauclea cadamba*) is a fruit tree, with orange-coloured fragrant flowers.

Dohā 344

In house after house festal vases of every kind were made and ranged in order, and Brahmā and all the gods were delighted as they gazed upon the city of Rāma.

Caupāī 342

At that time the king's palace was so resplendent that the god of love was distracted by the sight of such magnificence. It was as though everything auspicious and of good omen and all beauty, all plenteousness and prosperity and joy and felicity and gladness had come in bodily form to visit King Daśaratha. There was a universal longing to get a sight of Rāma and Jānakī. Troops of damsels were crowding together, each exceeding in loveliness the Lovegod's consort, all with festal offerings and torches, and singing, as it were so many Sarasvatīs. The rejoicings in the palace at that glad time are beyond all description. Rāma's mother Kauśalyā and the other queens were too overcome with love to think about themselves.

Dohā 345

Many were the gifts they bestowed upon the Brāhmaṇas, after worshipping Gaṇeśa and Mahādeva, and were as rejoiced as Poverty would be on finding the four great prizes of life.

Caupāī 343

Each royal mother was so overcome with love and delight that her feet refused to walk and the whole body was paralyzed. Intensely yearning for a sight of Rāma, they all began preparing the lustral lamps. Instruments of music were played in various modes, as the glad Sumitrā arranged her auspicious offering of turmeric, *dūba* grass, curds, sprigs and flowers, betel, areca nuts and well-favoured roots, rice, blades of wheat, yellow pigment, parched grain, and bunches of the graceful *tulasī* in embossed golden vases, so exquisitely beautiful that they seemed like nests made for Love's own birdlings. The auspicious offerings and the perfumes were beyond all telling; there was nothing of good omen which each one of the queens had not prepared.

With lustral lights arranged in various devices, they sing for joy melodious festal strains.

Dohā 346

With golden salvers in their lotus hands, laden with these auspicious offerings, and their body quivering with emotion, the queens went forth with joy to perform the lustration.

Caupāī 344

The sky was darkened with the fumes of the incense, as though overhung with Śrāvaṇa's densest thunderclouds: the gods rained down garlands of flowers from the tree of paradise which seemed to the beholders as cranes in graceful flight; the lustrous jewelled festoons resembled the rainbow; the maidens on the house-tops, now in sight and now out of sight, were like the fitful flashes of lightning; the beat of the drums was as the crash of thunder; the beggars as clamorous, as the cuckoos and the frogs and peacocks; the sweet perfumes were as copious showers of rain, and all the people of the city like the freshened pastures. Seeing that the time had arrived, the *guru* gave the word, and the glory of Raghu's line made his entry into the city, mindful at heart of Śambhu and Girijā and Gaṇeśa, and exulting greatly, he and all his retinue.

Dohā 347

Every omen was auspicious; the gods beat their drums and rained down flowers, while the goddesses danced for joy and sang jubilant songs of triumph.

Caupāī 345

Bards, minstrels, rhapsodists, skilled dancers and players chanted his glory that irradiates the three spheres. In all ten quarters of the world might be heard loud shouts of victory intermingled with the religious intoning of the Vedas. All kinds of music played, and gods in heaven and men on earth were alike enraptured. The magnificence of the procession was past all telling, and the joy was more than heart could contain. The citizens made a profound obeisance to the king, and were right glad to see Rāma. They scatter around him jewels and vestments, with their eyes full of tears and their body all tremulous with excitement. Happily the women waved their lustral lights, rejoicing greatly to behold the four noble princes; but when they lifted the fair curtains of the palanquins and saw the brides, they were still more glad.

Dohā 348

In this manner, to the delight of all, they arrived at the palace gate, where the queens happily waved the lustral lights over the princes and their brides.

Caupāī 346

Time after time they performed the ceremony[1] in a rapture of love that is beyond all words. They scattered around in boundless profusion gold and silver ornaments and gems and silks of every kind, and as they gazed on their four sons and their brides, the queens were overwhelmed with the bliss of heaven. Again and again as they regard the beauty of Rāma and Sītā, they joyously considered their lives to be blessed indeed. As her companions look again and again into Sītā's face, they sing and exult over their good fortune. Every moment the gods rain down flowers, amidst dancing and singing and obsequious homage. Seeing four such charming couples, Śāradā looked up all her similes, but not one would do, all seemed unworthy, and she could only stand and gaze enchanted with their loveliness.

Dohā 349

Having performed all the ceremonies prescribed by the Vedas or family usage, they conduct their sons and their brides to the palace; sprinkling lustral water, spreading carpets in the way, and waving torches.

1. *i. e.*, of waving the festal lamps about the heads of the princes and their brides.

Caupāī 347

After seating the brides and their grooms on four thrones so magnificent that they seemed as if wrought by Love's own hands, they proceeded reverently to lave their sacred feet and to do them homage — all holy as they were — with incense and lights and oblations in accordance with Vedic ritual. Time after time they pass the torch around and wave over their heads gorgeous fans and whisks and scatter profuse gifts; for each royal mother was as full of exultation as a devotee who has obtained beatitude; or a man sick all his life who has gotten an elixir; or a born beggar who has found the philosopher's stone; or a blind man restored to sight; or a dumb man endued with the gift of speech; or a warrior victorious in battle.

Dohā 350a-350b

Greater by hundred million times than their joy was the rapture of the queens, when Râma and his brothers returned home married. As the royal matrons performed the customary ceremonies, the brides and their grooms were embarrassed, but Râma smiled to himself on beholding their joy and delight.

Caupāī 348

In due fashion they did homage to the gods and the spirits of their ancestors, and every imagination of the heart was satisfied. Humbly they begged of all the highest boon, namely, the prosperity of Rāma and his brothers, and the gods unseen conferred their blessing. The queens in their joy took them to their bosom, while the king sent for all who had joined in the procession and gave them carriages and raiment and jewels and ornaments. Then, on receiving permission, and still cherishing the image of Râma in their heart, they returned in joy each to his own abode. All the people of the city, both men and women, were clad in festal robes, and in every home was a noise of jubilant music. Anything that a beggar begged was at once bestowed upon him by the glad king, and every attendant and every minstrel band was overwhelmed with gifts and compliments.

Dohā 351

All profoundly bowing invoked blessing upon him and sang his praises, as the monarch with his *guru* and the Brāhmaṇas retired to the palace.

Caupāī 349

Under Vasiṣṭha's directions he reverently performed every ceremony prescribed either by usage or the Veda. The queens, on seeing the throng of Brāhmaṇas, thought themselves most highly favoured and respectfully rose to greet them. After bathing their feet and doing them all due homage, the king feasted them at a banquet and loaded them with affectionate civilities and gifts. Grateful at heart, they blessed him at parting. To the son of Gādhi he paid special homage, saying:—'My lord, there is no man in the world so blessed as I am;' and with many other flattering speeches both he and his queens took of the dust of his feet. Next he gave him a splendid apartment within the palace, where the king and his royal consorts alike could wait upon his every wish. Again he adored his lotus feet with the greatest humility and devotion.

Dohā 352

The princes and their brides, the king and his royal consorts, again and again did homage to the *guru's* feet and received the holy sage's blessing.

Caupāī 350

With deep devotion in his heart the king placed before him his sons and all the wealth that he possessed and begged him to accept them. But the great sage asked only for the accustomed offering, and invoking upon him every blessing set out with joy on his homeward way, with the image of Rāma and Sītā impressed upon his heart. Then were summoned the Brāhmaṇa dames and the elders of the tribe and bestowed on them fair robes and ornaments; and next the younger ladies of the house,[1] who too were presented with dresses such as each most fancied. Every person with any claim to be remembered received from the jewel of kings suitable remembrance according to his taste, while more dear and honoured friends were overwhelmed with courtesies. The gods, who witnessed Raghubīr's marriage, rained down flowers as they applauded the spectacle.

Dohā 353

And with beat of drum returned each to his own city; all highly delighted and talking to one another of Râma's glory with irrepressible rapture.

Caupāī 351

The monarch showed everyone all possible honour, and with a heart filled with gladness proceeded to the ladies' apartments, and then gazing upon the princes and their brides took them to his bosom in a rapturous embrace and with a joy beyond all telling. Seating his little daughters in his lap in a most affectionate manner, he again and again caressed them with gladness of heart. All the ladies of the harem were charmed at the sight, and their soul was filled with happiness and exultation, while they listened with delight to the king's account of the marriage and his praises of King Janaka's virtue and amiability, and the kindness of his reception and the magnificence of his wealth. The king told it all like a hired encomiast, and the queens were enraptured to hear the tale.

Dohā 354

After bathing with his sons, the king summoned the Brāhmaṇas, his *guru* and his kinsmen, and entertained them at a sumptuous banquet till five hours of the night were spent.

1. The *suasini* in a Hindu marriage takes much the same place as a bridesmaid in the west; and the word might be so translated, were it not that it is essential for the *suasini* to be herself married and with her husband alive.

Caupāī 352

Lovely women sang joyous songs, and the night was one of exquisite happiness. As they rose from their seats, all were presented with *pān* and decorated with beautiful and sweet-scented garlands; then after one more look at Rāma and bowing their heads they received the royal permission to retire each to his own abode. The display of love and rapturous delight and the beauty of the court at that time was more than could be told by a hundred Śāradās or Śeṣanāgas or by the Veda, or Brahmā, or Mahādeva, or Gaṇeśa; how then can I tell of it, any more than an earthly serpent could support the world on its head? After showing everyone the highest honour, the king in gentle tones addressed the queens :—"The brides are but children, and have come to a strange house; watch over them as closely as the eyelids guard the eyes.

Dohā 355

Go now and put them to bed, for they are tired and sleepy." And so saying he retired to his own bed-chamber with his thoughts intent on Rāma's feet.

Caupāī 353

On hearing the king's kindly words, they made ready the bed, which was of gold and set with gems, with various rich coverings as soft and white as the froth of milk, and pillows finer than words can tell. In the jewelled chamber were sweet-scented garlands, and a beautiful canopy flashing with lustrous gems which defied description; no one who had not seen it could imagine it. When they had prepared this exquisite couch, they took up Rāma and lovingly laid him down upon it, who again and again had to tell his brothers to leave him before they too retired to rest. On seeing his dark little body, so soft and delicate, the fond mothers cried :—"How, my son, could you slay on the way the terrible monster Tāḍakā?

Dohā 356

How were you able to slay those fearsome demons, those fierce warriors, who in battle held no man of any account, the vile Mārīca and Subāhu and all their host?

Caupāī 354

It was by the sage's favour, I vow, my son, that God averted from you countless calamities, while you and your brother protected the sacrifice; and by your *guru's* blessing you acquired all knowledge. At the touch of the dust of your feet the hermit's wife attained salvation: the whole world is filled with your glory. In the assembly of the princes you broke the bow of Śiva, though less flexible than a tortoise-shell or thunderbolt or mountain peak; you have won universal glory and renown and Jānakī for your bride, and have now with your brothers returned home married. All your actions are more than human and it is only by Viśvāmitra's good favour that you have prospered. To-day my birth into the world has borne fruit, now that I see your moon-like face, my son. The days that were spent without seeing you, God ought not to take into account at all."

Dohā 357

Rāma in most modest words reassured the royal dames, and meditating on the feet of Śambhu and his *guru* and all Brāhmaṇas, he closed his eyes in sleep.

Caupāī 355

Even in sleep his pretty face gleamed like a red lotus, half closed at eventide. In every house women kept vigil and jested with one another in auspicious wise. The city was so brilliant, nay, so brilliant the night itself, that the queens cried, "See, dear friends, see". The matrons slept with the beauteous brides enfolded in their arms, as lovingly as a serpent would clasp to his bosom the precious jewel from inside its head. At the holy hour of dawn the lord awoke, ere cocks had well begun to crow. Minstrels and bards, proclaimed his praises and the citizens flocked to the gate to do him homage. The four brothers saluted the Brāhmaṇas, the gods, their *guru* and their father and mother, and gladly received their blessing and while the queens reverentially gazed upon their face, advanced with the king to the door.

Dohā 358

Pure as they were in themselves, they performed all the customary ablutions and bathed in the sacred river. Then the four brothers completed their morning devotions and returned to their father.

Caupāī 356

The king on seeing them clasped them to his bosom. Then at his command they gladly seated themselves. The whole court was rejoiced at the sight of Rāma, and accounted their eyes supremely blessed. Then came Vasiṣṭha the sage and Viśvāmitra and were conducted to exalted thrones. Father and sons reverently touched their feet, and both the holy men rejoiced as they gazed on Rāma. Vasiṣṭha related sacred stories, while the monarch and his queens listened. He told with joy in diffuse strain of all the doings of Gādhi's son which surpass even the imagination of the sages. Cried Vāmadeva :—"The tale is true; its fame has become renowned through the three worlds." All who heard were glad, and in Rāma and Lakṣmaṇa's heart there was exceeding joy.

Dohā 359

Thus passed the days in perpetual delight, happiness and festivity; and the whole of Avadh overflowed with bliss that was ever on the increase.

Caupāī 357

After calculating an auspicious day, they loosened the string on the wrist[1] with no little festive merriment. The gods, beholding the constant succession of delight, were in raptures and begged of Brahmā that they might be born at Avadh. Viśvāmitra was always wishing to take leave, but was persuaded by Rāma's affectionate entreaties to stay on. Day after day, seeing the king's

1. A few days before marriage the wrist is bound round with a piece of cloth containing particles of different things that are supposed to possess a hidden virtue; and this is not taken off again till after the marriage is completed.

devotion and the excellence of his nature, the great sage was loud in his praises. When he asked permission to go, the king was greatly moved and with his sons stood before him in the way, saying :—"My lord, all that I have is yours; I and my sons and my wives are your servants. Be ever gracious to these boys, O sage, and allow me to see you." So saying the king with his sons and his queens fell at his feet, and speech failed his tongue. The Brāhmaṇa invoked upon him every kind of blessing and set forth amidst a display of affection that is past all telling, Rāma and his brothers lovingly escorting him till they received orders to return.

Dohā 360

The moon of Gādhi's race went on his way rejoicing and inwardly praising the beauty of Rāma, the devotion of the king and the magnificence of the marriage festivities.

Caupāī 358

Vāmadeva, the wise *guru* of the house of Raghu, again related the story of Gādhi's son. As he listened to the sage's high fame, the king thought to himself how efficacious his own good deeds had been. At his command the crowd dispersed, while the king and his sons entered the palace. Everywhere the glory of Rāma's wedding was sung, and his holy fame was diffused through the three worlds. From the day that Rāma brought his wife home, all bliss made its home at Avadh. The rejoicings attendant on the lord's marriage were more than the tongue of the serpent king could tell, but knowing the praises of Rāma and Sitā to be a mine of auspiciousness and the very life and salvation of the race of poets, I too have tried to sing them, in the hope of thus sanctifying my song.

Chand 39

For the purpose of sanctifying his voice has Tulasī told of Rāma's glory; but the acts of Raghubīr are a boundless ocean that no poet can cross. All pious souls that devoutly hear or recite the auspicious festivities that accompanied Rāma's investiture with the sacred thread and his marriage shall by his and Vaidehi's favour attain to everlasting felicity.

Soraṭhā 361

Whoever with love and reverence hears and listens to the tale of Râma and Sītā's wedding shall be happy for ever, for Râma's praises are an unfailing joy.

[*Thus endeth the book entitled* CHILDHOOD, *composed by Tulasī Dāsa for the bestowal of pure wisdom, continence and contentedness: being the first descent into 'the Holy Lake of Rāma's Acts, that cleanses from every defilement of the world.*]

BOOK II

AYODHYĀ

AYODHYĀ

Sanskrit Invocation

May he in whose bosom shines resplendent the daughter of the mountain-king; on whose head is the river of the gods; on whose brow lies the crescent moon; on whose throat is the poison-stain; on whose breast lies the Serpent King; whose adornments are streaks of ashes; the chief of divinities; the eternal lord of all; the complete, the omnipresent, the moon-like Śiva, the Lord Śaṅkara; may he protect me!

May he who neither rejoiced when anointed king, nor was saddened by painful exile in the woods; the holy son of Raghu of the lotus face; may he ever vouchsafe to me success and prosperity. Him I adore, with his body dark and soft as the lotus, with Sītā enthroned on his left side, with a graceful bow and arrows in hand, even Rāma, the lord of the race of Raghu.

Dohā

Cleansing the mirror of my soul with the dust of the lotus feet of the holy *guru*, I sing Rāma's spotless glory, the giver of the four rewards.

Caupāī 1

From the time when Rāma returned home wedded, there was a constant succession of joys and delights. The fourteen spheres were like the great mountains, where clouds of virtue fell in showers of happiness; wealth, affluence and prosperity were bounteous rivers, which overflowed into Avadh as into the ocean; while the noble citizens, men and women alike, were its brilliant pearls, all precious and of perfect beauty. The magnificence of the capital was beyond description; it seemed the *chief d'oeuvre* of the Creator.[1] Gazing on Rāmacandra's face, fair as the moon, the people were perfectly happy; the queens and all their attendants were enraptured to see their hearts'

1. *i.e.*, the final work of God.

desire bear fruit; and still more enraptured was the king, as he heard tell and saw for himself Rāma's beauty and accomplishments and amiability.

Dohā 1

In every heart was one desire, which they expressed in their prayers to Mahādeva: "O that the king in his own lifetime would entrust Rāma with the regency."

Caupāī 2

One day King Daśaratha sat enthroned in court with all his courtiers. Himself the embodiment of every virtue, he was delighted beyond measure to hear of Rāma's renown. All kings were solicitous for his patronage, and the very gods desired his friendship. No man was so blessed as Daśaratha in the three spheres of the universe, or in all time—past, present or to come. Words fail to describe his blessed state, who had for his son Rāma, the source of every bliss. The king happened to take a mirror in his hand, and looking at his face in it, set his crown straight. Close to his ear was a white hair like old age whispering, "O king, make Rāma regent, and thus fulfil the purpose of your life!"

Dohā 2

Having thus considered and settled it in his mind, the king on an auspicious day and at a fitting time, his body quivering with emotion and his soul full of joy, went and declared his intention to his *guru*.

Caupāī 3

Said the king, "Hearken, lord of sages, Rāma is now perfect in every accomplishment. Servants, ministers and the whole body of citizens, whether my enemies or friends or indifferent to me, all hold Rāma as dear as even I do, and regard him as a glorious incarnation of my lord's blessing. The Brāhmaṇas and their families, reverend sir, have the same love for him as you have. They, who put on their heads the dust of their *guru's* feet, obtain as it were the mastery over all dominion. There is no man my equal; but all that I have flows from the worship of your holy feet. I have now a desire at heart; it can only be accomplished, my lord, by your good favour." The sage was pleased to witness his sincere devotion and said: "O king, give me your commands.

Dohā 3

Your name and glory, O king, ensure fulfilment of every wish; on every desire of your soul, O jewel of kings, success follows naturally."[1]

Caupāī 4

When he saw the *guru* so amiably disposed, the king replied smilingly in gentle tones: "My lord, invest Rāma with regal powers; be pleased to direct the necessary arrangements to be made. Let this happy ceremony take place in my lifetime, that the eyes of all people may be gladdened by the sight. By my lord's blessing Śiva has brought everything happily to pass, but I have still this one desire at heart. It will then be a matter of no concern whether I remain in the body or depart hence, if I have nothing on this score whereof to repent." When the sage heard Daśaratha's noble words, he experienced the greatest delight. "Hearken, O king," he said, "the lord whose averted face all creatures lament, and to whom one must pray for removal of all distress, has been born your son, even the holy and compassionate Rāma.

Dohā 4

Haste, O king, and delay not, but at once make all the preparations. Happy and auspicious indeed the day when Rāma is proclaimed regent!"

Caupāī 5

Happily the king proceeded to the palace and summoned his servants and his minister, Sumantra. They bowed their heads crying, 'All hail,' and the king then declared to them the glad news: "To-day to my great joy the *guru* has charged me to install Rāma as heir to the throne. If the proposal seems good to the council, prepare with gladness to impress the royal mark on Rāma's brow." The minister rejoiced to hear these

1. Another interpretation: "The object of your heart's desire, O jewel of monarchs, is accomplished even before you entertain the desire."

gracious words, which fell like a shower of rain on the young plant of his desire. With clasped hands he made his petition: "O lord of the world, live for ever; the deed you propose is good and beneficent; haste, my lord, let us have no delay." The king was delighted to hear his minister's assent, like a creeper that spreads apace when it has once obtained the support of a strong bough.

Dohā 5

Said the king: "Whatever orders the great sage Vasistha may give with regard to Rāma's coronation, see that you carry out with all speed."

Caupāī 6

In gentle accents the glad sage spoke and said: "Bring water from all holy places, and all kinds of herbs, roots, fruits and flowers (enumerating by name every auspicious variety) with whisks of different sizes, apparel of all sorts, both of wool and silk and every other material, with jewels and all the auspicious things that there are in the world, that are fit for a king's installation." Then after instructing them in all the forms prescribed in the Vedas, he said: "Erect in the city a number of pavilions, and plant the streets in every quarter with fruit-bearing[1] mangoes and trees of betel-nut and plantains, and fashion bright and beautiful squares filled with precious jewels, and have all the bāzārs speedily decorated, and do reverence to Ganesa and your *guru* and your family god, and diligently serve the Brāhmaṇas, the very gods on earth.

Dohā 6

Make ready flags and banners, triumphal arches and vases, horses too, and chariots and elephants." All were obedient, to the holy sage's words and busied themselves each in his own special work.

Caupāī 7

Whatever the order that anyone had been given by the high sage, that he regarded as the very first thing to be done. The

1. For *sa-phala*, 'fruit-bearing', some MSS. read *panasa*, 'the jack-fruit or *Artocarpus intregrifolia*'.

king worshipped Brāhmaṇas, saints and gods, and did everything to promote Rāma's prosperity. On hearing the glad news of Rāma's installation, all Avadh resounded with songs of jubilee. Good omens declared themselves in the body, both of Rāma and Sītā, by a sudden quiver of the lucky side, and they said affectionately to one another, "This betokens Bharata's return. We have greatly missed him for many a long day. The omens assure us of a friend's approach, and in the whole world there is no one so dear to us as Bharata: this good omen can have but one meaning." Everyday Rāma was as lovingly anxious about his half-brother (Bharata) as a turtle for its eggs in the sand far away.

Dohā 7

At that time the ladies of the palace were as delighted to hear these most glad tidings as the waves of the sea swell with delight on beholding the moon in its glory.

Caupāī 8

First they took care that those who brought the news were richly rewarded with jewels and robes; then with a body all quivering with emotion and soul full of love, they proceeded to make all festal preparations. Sumitrā filled in a lovely square with exquisite gems of every kind, and Rāma's mother, drowned in joy, sent for a crowd of Brāhmaṇas and loaded them with gifts. Then she worshipped the local divinity and the gods and the serpents, and vowed them future sacrifices, praying; "In your mercy grant me this boon, that Rāma prosper." Auspicious strains are chanted by moonfaced, fawneyed damsels, with voice as sweet as the notes of the cuckoo.

Dohā 8

On hearing of Rāma's investiture as regent, all good women rejoiced and began diligently to make festal preparations, thinking God to be gracious to them.

Caupāī 9

Then the monarch summoned Vasiṣṭha and sent him to Rāma's apartments to inform him of the coming event. When

Raghunātha heard of the *guru's* arrival he came to the door and bowed his head at his feet, and after reverently sprinkling lustral water, conducted him in and paid him honour in the sixteen[1] prescribed modes. Then after again with Sītā clasping his feet, Rāma thus spoke, his lotus hands folded in prayer: "For a lord to visit his servant's house is a source of great joy, a cure for all distress; yet it had been more fitting, sir, and more in accordance with custom, had you kindly sent to say you wanted me. Since my lord has graciously waived his prerogative, my house has to-day become highly blest. Let me know, holy sir, your orders; and I will carry them out, for it is a servant's joy to serve his master.

Dohā 9

On hearing these words, steeped in affection as they were, the sage extolled Raghubīra: "O Rāma, glory of the solar race, it is like you to speak thus"

Caupāī 10

After praising Rāma's high qualifications and amiable character, the great sage with much emotion explained: "The king has prepared for a royal installation, and wishes to invest you with regal powers. To-day, Rāma, you should devote yourself to ascetic practices that God may bring the matter to a happy issue." Having thus admonished him, the *guru* returned to the king; while Rāma's heart was all amazement: "My brothers and I were all born together, and together have we eaten

1. The 16 modes of showing honour are as follows : (1) *āsana*, a seat; (2) *argha*, lustral water; (3) *pādya*, water for the feet; (4) *snāna*, a bath; (5) *ācamana*, water for rinsing the mouth; (6) *gandhākṣata*, perfumes and rice, the former only being offered to Viṣṇu, the latter to Mahādeva; (7) *vastra*, raiment; (8) *dhūpa*, incense; (9) *dīpa*, lights; (10) *naivedya*, temple offerings; (11) *mukhahasta-jala*, water for the face and hands; (12) *tāmbūla*, betel-leaf; (13) *pūgī-phala*, betel-nut; (14) *dakṣiṇā*; a gift; (15) *pradakṣiṇā*, circumambulation; and (16) *nīrājana*, lustration. As some of these ceremonies take place at the reception of a guest and some at his departure, they would never be all performed at once. But here, as in many other paralleled phrases, a definite number, the highest that could under any circumstances be predicated of the subject, is used to express merely the general idea of completeness.

and slept and played in childhood; the piercing of our ear-lobes,[1] the investiture with the sacred thread, our marriage, in short all our rejoicings have taken place together. This is the one flaw in a spotless line that the eldest only should be enthroned without his younger brothers." These gracious regrets on the part of the Lord remove all unworthy thoughts from the minds of his votaries.[2]

Dohā 10

Then at that moment came Lakṣmaṇa steeped in love and rapture, and was welcomed with words of affection by the moon of the lily-like Solar race.

Caupāī 11

There was a noise of music of every kind, and the revelries in the city were beyond description. All prayed for Bharata's return, that he might come quickly and like them enjoy the spectacle. In every street, lane, house, market and place of resort, men and women were saying to one another, "When will tomorrow come and the auspicious moment in which God will accomplish our desire; when, with Sītā by his side, Rāma will take his seat on the golden throne and all our wishes be gratified." They were all saying: "When will tomorrow come?" But the envious gods prayed that difficulties might arise; the rejoicings at Avadh pleased them as little as a moonlight night pleases a thief. The gods humbly called in Sarasvatī and again and again threw themselves at her feet:

Dohā 11

"O mother, regard our great distress and make haste to relieve it! If Rāma refuses the throne and retires into the forest, all will be well with us."

Caupāī 12

On hearing the gods' petition, she stood still thinking sadly: "I am like a winter's night to a bed of lotuses." The gods

1. One of the sixteen sacraments incumbent on a Hindu.

2. If Rāma had at once and gladly accepted the proffered dignity, it might have been urged by objectors that he had taken an unfair advantage of his brother Bharata's absence.

seeing her hesitate cried yet once more: "O mother, not the least blame will attach to you; for Raghurāī — you know his nature well — is exempt from sorrow as from joy; and (as for his people) they, like all other creatures, have their share in pain or pleasure, under the law of necessity: go therefore to Avadh and befriend us gods." Again and again they clasped her feet, till she yielded and set out, though still thinking to herself: "The gods are a meanspirited crew; though they dwell on high, their doings are mean; and they cannot endure to see another's prosperity." Again, reflecting on the future, that the ablest poets would seek her favour,[1] she became cheerful of heart and flew to the city of Daśaratha, as if she were some intolerably inauspicious aspect of the planets.

Dohā 12

Now Kaikeyī[2] had a wicked handmaid, by name Mantharā. Her mind Śāradā first perverted, and made her a very storehouse of meanness and then went her way.

Caupāī 13

When Mantharā saw the city decorated, the joyous festivities, the music and the singing, she asked the people: "What mean these rejoicings?" When she heard of Rāma's inauguration, her soul was afire and she plotted, wicked wretch that she was, how that very night to defeat it; like a crafty hill-woman, who has spied a honeycomb hanging from a tree and schemes how to get hold of it. So she went crying to Bharata's mother. "What is wrong now?" the queen smiled and said. She gave no answer, but drew a deep sigh and, like a woman, began shedding a flood of tears. Said the queen laughing: "You were always an impudent girl, and Laksmana, I suspect, has been giving you a lesson." Even then the wicked handmaid uttered not a word, but breathed hard like some venomous serpent.

Dohā 13

Said the queen with a nervous smile: "Is Rāma not well, or

1. If Rāma goes into exile, his adventures will form an inexhaustible theme for the poets of all time, who will therefore be always invoking my aid and propitiating my good will.

2. Bharata's mother.

the king, or Bharata, or Laksmana, or Satrughna?" These words tortured the heart of the hump-backed girl.[1]

Caupāī 14

"Why, O mother, should anyone give me a lesson, and who is there to encourage me in any impudence? With whom again is it well today if not with Rāma, whom the king is now associating with himself on the throne? Providence has been very gracious to Kausalyā; and after seeing her, who else can have any pride left? Why don't you go and see all the magnificence, the sight of which has so agitated me? Your son is away and you take no heed, making sure of your influence with the king, and not observing his treachery and wiliness—so drowsy are you and so anxious for your bed and pillow." On hearing this affectionate address, the queen—who knew well her malicious mind—cried: "Peace, have done. If ever you speak to me again in this way, you mischief-maker, I will have your tongue pulled out by the roots!"

Dohā 14

But remembering that the one-eyed, the lame and the hump-backed are ever crooked and vile, more especially if they be women to boot, and slaves, Bharata's mother smiled and added:

Caupāī 15

"O sweet-tongued Mantharā! I have said all this to you by way of advice and am not the least bit angry. If what you say is true, it is the best and happiest of days. It has ever been the custom in the Solar race that the eldest-born should be the lord, and the younger brothers his servants. If Rāma is really to be crowned tomorrow, ask of me, girl, what you will and I will give it you. There is no difference between Kausalyā and the other royal mothers. Rāma is equally fond of all: in fact, he bears a special affection towards me, as I have often tested. If I am born again, God in his goodness grant that Rāma and Sitā be

1. Because the fact that the queen asked, first of all, about Rāma's welfare showed her intense love for him.

again my son and daughter ! Rāma is dearer to me than life; why then should you be troubled at his being crowned king?

Dohā 15

I adjure you in Bharata's name to tell me the truth without any deceit or concealment; declare to me the reason why you should grieve at such a time of gladness."

Caupāī 16

"I have spoken once," said Mantharā, "and I am satisfied; yet now I'll have a second tongue and speak out a little. I deserve to have my head smashed on the funeral pile, wretch that I am, since I offend you by my well-meant words. Those who make the false appear true are the people who please you, my lady; while I offend you. Henceforth I too will speak only as my mistress pleases, or else will remain silent day and night. God has given me a deformed body and made me a slave: we must all reap as we have sown and take as we have given. Whoever is king, what do I lose ? Shall I cease to be a servant and become a queen now? It is only my worthless character that I cannot bear to see your disgrace, and hence I gave utterance to a word or two; but pardon me, mistress, it was a great mistake on my part."

Dohā 16

On hearing these subtle and agreeably deceitful words, so deep and crafty, the queen, being only a weak-minded woman and under the influence of a divine delusion, really believed her enemy to be a friend.

Caupāī 17

Again and again in kindly terms she questioned her, like a fawn bewitched by the song of a huntress. Her reason went astray as fate would have it so; and the slave-girl rejoiced at the success of her scheme : "You ask, but I am afraid to reply, now that you have given me the name of mischief-maker;" thus spoke the malignant star[1] of Avadh, trimming and fashioning her

1. *Sāṛhasātī*, literally '7½ ,' is a name for the malignant star Saturn, whose one revolution occupies a period of 7½ years.

speech in every way to win confidence : "You spoke, O queen, of Sītā and Rāma as your friends; and true enough Rāma did love you once, but now those days are past, in time friends become foes. The sun invigorates the lotus, but burns it to ashes if it have no water : the rival queen would tear you up by the root : protect your garden and hedge it about.

Dohā 17

Thinking yourself the king's favourite and that he is quite under your sway, you notice nothing; but however fair his words, his heart is black; but you are so good-natured

Caupāī 18

Rāma's mother, on the contrary, is deep and crafty; and having found the means has furthered her own purpose. The king has sent away Bharata to his grandmother's at her suggestion, and because he is your son; for she thinks all the other queens are well disposed to her, but Bharata's mother presumes on her influence with her lord. You, lady, are a thorn in Kausalyā's side; she is too deep and crafty for you to fathom. The king has greater love for you than for anyone else and, like a rival, she cannot bear to see it. For her own ends she has worked upon the king and got him to fix a day for Rāma's inauguration. Now Rāma's promotion is in accord with the traditions of the family : all are pleased at it, and I too like it well. But I am alarmed when I consider the consequences; heaven make them recoil on her own head!"

Dohā 18

With innumerable crafty devices she planned her cunning tale, telling story after story of jealous wives, whereby to increase her resentment.

Caupāī 19

Overmastered by fate, the queen was persuaded at heart, and adjured her by the love she bore her to speak out. "What is it you would ask ? Still do you not understand : even the brute beasts know what is good or bad for them. For the last fortnight the preparations have been going on, and it is only today that you learn the news from me. I am clothed and fed in your service, and I must therefore speak the truth at any cost. If I invent a word of falsehood giving it the colour of truth, may God repay me for it! Should Rāma be crowned tomorrow, God will have sown for you a seed of woe. I draw this line on the ground,[1] O lady, and declare most emphatically that you will be like a fly in a milk-bowl. If you and your son will submit to be servants, you will be able to stay; but on no other conditions.

Dohā 19

As Kadrū tormented Vinatā[2] so will Kausalyā treat you. Bharata will be a slave in bonds, and Lakṣmaṇa will be Rāma's vicegerent."

Caupāī 20

When she heard these cutting words, Kekaya's[3] daughter could say nothing; she was all in a fever for fear : her limbs were bathed with perspiration : and she trembled like a plantain stalk. Then the humpback checked her tongue and with innumerable crafty speeches kept consoling the queen, saying, 'courage,' 'courage.' By a turn of fate the vile became a favourite, as though a beautiful flamingo should flatter an ugly crane. "Hearken, Mantharā, your words are true; my right eye is always throbbing, and every night I have some evil dreams; but in my folly I did not tell you. What can I do, friend? I am such an innocent that I cannot myself tell right from left.

1. *i.e.*, I swear and tell you most emphatically.

2. Kadrū and Vinatā were the two wives of the patriarch Kaśyapa, the former being the mother of the serpent race and the latter of the birds. A discussion arose between them regarding the colour of the horses of the sun. Vinatā insisting that it was white, and Kadrū that it was black. It was agreed that whichever of the two was proved to be in the wrong should become the servant of the other. Kadrū then contrived to fasten one of her black snakes on to the horse's back and Vinatā, taking it to be the animal's real tail, admitted herself defeated.

3. The name of Kaikeyī's father was Asvapati, but he is often called Kekaya from the country over which he ruled, supposed to be part of the Punjāb. The Brāhmana of the white Yajur Veda mentions Aśvapati, king of Kekaya, as nearly contemporary with Sītā's father, Janaka; an interesting fact noted by Prof. Monier Williams.

Dohā 20

Never to this day have I done an unkindness to anyone during my ascendancy: for what offence has heaven all at once put me to such intolerable distress?

Caupāī 21

Rather would I go and spend all my days in my father's house than live a servant of a rival wife. Whomever God creates the dependent of an enemy, it is good for him to die rather than live." Many such lamentable speeches did the queen utter, and the humpback, on hearing them, resorted to the wily ways of a woman. "Why speak thus," she said, "and feel so wretched? Your honour and wedded joy shall yet increase daily, and may he who has plotted you this misfortune in the end reap the fruit of it himself? Since your servant, my lady, first heard the bad news, I could neither eat by day nor sleep at night. I consulted the astrologers and they declared positively : 'Bharata shall be king, this much is certain.' If, madam, you will only act upon it, I can tell you a way : for the king is under an obligation to you."

Dohā 21

"I would throw myself down a well if you told me to do so, or even abandon my husband and son. When the sight of my dire distress leads you to speak, why should I not do what will be for my good ?"

Caupāī 23

Bringing Kaikeyī as a victim for the slaughter, the humpback whetted the knife of treachery on the whetstone of her heart, and the queen, like a sacrificial beast that nibbles the green sward, saw not the approaching danger. Pleasant to hear, but disastrous in their results, her words were like honey mingled with deadly poison. Says the handmaid, "Do you or do you not, my lady, remember the tale you once told me of the two boons promised you by the king ?[1] Ask for them now and relieve your

1. Aforetime Daśaratha, had marched into the south to Vijayant, a city in the Daṇḍaka forest, to wage war against its king Timidhvaja, or Sambara,

soul : the kingdom for your son, banishment to the woods for Rāma; thus shall you triumph over all your rivals. But ask not till the king has sworn by Rāma, so that he may not go back from his word. If you let this night pass it will be too late; give heed to my words with all your heart."

Dohā 22

Having thus hatched her abominable design against the queen, the wicked woman continued, "Betake yourself to the sulking-room; make all your arrangements circumspectly, and do not believe too readily."

Caupāī 23

The queen thought the humpback her best friend, and again and again extolled her cleverness, saying : "I have no such friend as you in the whole world: I had been swept away by the flood but for your support. To-morrow if God will fulfil my desire I will cherish you, my dear, as the apple of mine eye." Thus lavishing every term of endearment on her handmaid, Kaikeyī went to the dark room; her evil temper being the soil in which the servant-girl, like the rains, had sown the seed of calamity, which, watered by treachery, took root and sprouted with the two boons as its leaves, and in the end ruin for its fruit. Gathering about her every token of resentment, Kaikeyī lay down on the floor in the sulking-room; while enjoying sovereignty, she was betrayed by her own wicked mind. But meanwhile the king's palace and the city were filled with sounds of rejoicing, for nobody had an inkling of these evil designs.

Dohā 23

All the citizens were joyously making festive preparations, and the royal hall of audience was crowded with a continuous stream of people passing in and out.

who had revolted against Indra. The battle lasted till night, and Daśaratha, wounded and senseless, would have been left for dead on the field, had not Kaikeyī taken him up into her chariot, inserting her own arm in the place of its broken axle-tree, and speedily driven him away out of reach of the enemy. The grateful monarch, thus restored to life by his wife's devotion, promised to grant her any two boons she might ask; and she had prudently reserved them both till such time as she might require them.

Caupāī 24

Delighted at the news, not a few of Rāma's boy companions called on him together, and the Lord, sensible of their affection, received them graciously, and politely asked them how they fared. At his permission they roam through the palace, discussing his praises: "Is there anyone in the whole world so kind and amiable as Raghubīra? Whatever future births fate has in store for us, God only grant us this, that we may always be the servants of Sītā's lordly spouse: we ask for nothing more." This was the earnest desire of all in the city; only Kaikeyī's heart was in a flame; for who is not spoiled by evil communications? There is no profit in taking counsel with the vile.

Dohā 24

In the evening the happy king repaired to Kaikeyī's apartments, as it were Love incarnate visiting Obduracy.

Caupāī 25

He was taken aback when he heard of the chamber of wrath and could scarcely put his feet to the ground for fear. He, under whose mighty arm the Lord of heaven dwells secure, and upon whose favour all monarchs wait, was in a fever at hearing of an angry woman; see how great is the power of love. The bearers of trident, thunderbolt, and sword are slain by the flowery shafts of Ratī's spouse. Anxiously the king approached his beloved and was terribly distressed to see her condition, lying on the ground in old and coarse attire with all her personal adornments cast away, her wretched appearance according with her wretched design, as if in mourning for her instant widowhood. The king drew near and asked in gentle tones : "Why are you angry, my heart's delight ?

Chand 1

Why are you so angry, my queen ?" and touched her with his hands. She put away her lord and flashed upon him a furious glance like an enraged serpent, with her two wishes for its double tongue, and the boons for fangs, spying out a vulnerable point. Under the influence of fate, says Tulasī, the king took it all as one of love's devices.

Soraṭhā 25

Said the king again and again, "Tell me the cause of your anger, O beautiful, bright-eyed dame, with voice as melodious as the cuckoo, and gait as voluptuous as the elephant.

Caupāī 26

Who is it, my dear, who has vexed you ? Who is it with a head to spare and so enamoured of death ? Tell me what pauper I should make a king, or what king I should banish from his realm. I could slay even an immortal, were he your enemy; of what account then are any poor worms of men and women ? O my love, you know my sentiments and how my eyes ever turn to your face as the partridge to the moon. O my beloved, my life, my sons, and everything that I own, my palace, my subjects are all at your disposal. If I tell you a word of untruth, lady, a hundred curses fall on Rāma's life. Ask with a smile whatever you desire; adorn your lovely person with jewels; consider within yourself what an hour of torture this is for me, and at once, my darling, put away this unseemly attire."

Dohā 26

On hearing this and considering the greatness of the oath, the wicked queen arose with a smile and resumed her royal attire, like a huntress who sets the snare on marking the chase.

Caupāī 27

Thinking her reconciled, the king spoke again in soft and winning accent , his whole body quivering with love: "Your heart's desire, lady, has come to pass; there is joy and gladness in every house in the city; tomorrow I give Rāma the rank of Regent; so, my love, make ready for the festival." At the sound of these untoward words she sprang up with a bound, like an over-ripe gourd that bursts at a touch; with a smile on her lips, but with such secret pain at heart as a thief's wife who dare not cry openly.[1] The king could not penetrate her crafty schemes, for she had been tutored in every villainy by a master; and skilled as he was in statesmanship, the abyss of woman's ways was more than he could fathom. Again she cried with a further show of hypocritical affection and a forced smile in her eyes and on her lips.

Dohā 27

"You say, 'Ask! Ask!,' indeed; but tell me, dear husband, when has it come to giving or taking? You once promised me two boons, and yet I doubt my getting them."

Caupāī 28

The king said with a smile: "I see what you mean, you are overfond of a little quarrel. You kept my promise in reserve and never asked for its fulfilment, and as my way is, I forgot all about it. Do not tax me with the guilt of a lie, but for two requests make four and you shall have them. It is an immemorial rule in the Raghu family to lose life rather than break a promise. No quantity of sins can equal a lie; in the same way as myriads of tiny *guñjā* seeds will not make a mountain. Truth is the foundation of all merit and virtue, as the Vedas and Purāṇas declare and as Manu[2] has expounded. Moreover, I have sworn by Rāma, the chief of our house, the perfection of all that is good and amiable." When she had thus bound him to his word, the wicked queen smiled and cried, loosing as it were the bandage from the eyes of a cruel hawk.

1. On seeing her husband suffer punishment, lest she too should be made to suffer with him. Such at least seems to me the most obvious meaning of the comparison, though some of the Hindu commentators explain it differently.

2. Some manuscripts have *Manu* for *Muni*, "the saints"; but the former may well stand, as the great lawgiver in many passages of his Code insists very strongly on the merit of truth. Thus in VIII, 81-83 "A witness, who states the truth in evidence, obtains a high place in heaven and the greatest reputation on earth : such a statement is held in reverence even by Brahmā himself. By truth a witness is purified from sin; by truth justice is advanced; therefore the truth should be spoken by witnesses of every caste." I have often thought that if these four lines were printed or engraved in bold characters in the Sanskrit original and set up in our courts of justice they might have a wholesome effect.

Dohā 28

The king's desire being as a fair forest, and the general happiness as a flock of birds, at which like a Bhil huntress she sent forth the cruel falcon of her speech:

Caupāī 29

"Hear, my beloved lord, that which my heart desires; grant me for one boon the installation of Bharata as regent; and for the second (I beg with folded hands, O my lord, accomplish my desire) may Rāma be banished to the woods for fourteen years there to dwell in the ascetic garb of a perfect anchorite." At these words of the queen the king's heart grew faint, as the *cakavā* is distressed by the rays of the moon. He trembled all over, nor could he utter a sound, like a quail in the wood at the swoop of a falcon. The mighty monarch was as crestfallen as a palm-tree struck by lightning; with his hands to his forehead and closing both his eyes, as it were Grief personified, he began his moan: "My desire, that had blossomed like the tree of paradise, has been stricken and uprooted as it were by an elephant at the time of bearing. Kaikeyī has made Avadh desolate and laid the foundation of everlasting calamity!

Dohā 29

What a thing to happen at such a time as this! Trust in a woman has been my undoing; as at the time of heavenly reward for penance an ascetic is ruined by ignorance."

Caupāī 30

In this manner did the king burn within himself, and the wicked woman, seeing his evil plight, thus began : "What, then, is Bharata not your son too, but a slave as I am, bought for a price? If my words, thus like arrows, pierce you to the heart, why did you not think before you spoke ? Answer now, say either yes or no, most truthful lord of Raghu's truthful line! Refuse me the boon you promised, break your word and be publicly disgraced ! You were loud in your praises of truth and saying you would grant me the boon, imagining, no doubt, that

I should ask for a handful of parched gram! When Śivi[1] or Dadhīci[2] or Bali[3] made a promise, they gave life and wealth to keep their word." Kaikeyī's speech was as stinging as salt rubbed into a burn.

Dohā 30

The king, upholder of righteousness, took courage and opened his eyes, and beating his head gasped out: "She has pierced me in the most vital part!"

1. King Śivi (or Śaivya), the son of Usinara, had already offered ninetytwo great sacrifices, and was hoping to complete the full number of a hundred, a feat which would have exalted him to the highest dignity in heaven, when Indra, jealous of his own supremacy, determined to prevent him. Himself assuming the form of a hawk and changing Agni, the god of fire, into a dove, he chased it through the air till it flew into the temple and took shelter in Śivi's bosom, who thereupon promised that he would protect it from all harm. The hawk followed close behind and protested that the dove was his lawful spoil, and that it was unjust of the king to rob him of food which he had fairly won, and without which he would die of starvation. The king offered him anything else that he liked to name; but the hawk would be satisfied with nothing but an equal weight of the king's own flesh. Scales were brought, the dove was put in the one balance, and the monarch began to hack and hew pieces of his own body and cast in the other; but still the dove weighed heavier. At last, when all had been cut away and only his bones were left, he threw himself in. The gods then came and restored him to life and bore him off in triumph to heaven.

2. When Indra and the other gods were hard pressed by the demon Vṛtra, Viṣṇu told them that there was a great saint named Dadhīci practising penance in the Naimiṣa forest, and that if he would let them have his bones they could be made into weapons, before which no enemy could stand. Dadhīci, as soon as he heard what they wanted, at once devoted himself to death, and out of his bones the gods made thunderbolts, with which they won an easy victory.

3. King Bali, the son of Virocana, had so extended his empire that he had acquired dominion over the three worlds. Indra, to rid himself of so dangerous a rival, applied to Viṣṇu who, assuming the form of a dwarf, as the son of Kaśyapa, appeared before Bali and begged an alms. The king promised to give him whatever he asked. He said he only wanted as much land as he could pace in three steps. This modest request was granted without hesitation; whereupon he at once developed himself into a giant, and with the first stride covered the whole earth, and with the second the heaven. For the third step he planted his foot on Bali's head and crushed him down into the infernal regions, of which he became the sovereign.

Caupāī 31

He saw her standing before him, burning with wrath; her fury was like a naked sword drawn from the sheath, with ill-counsel for its hilt and relentlessness for its sharp edge whetted on the grindstone, that was the humpback. The monarch saw the sword was keen and terrible, and thought, "Is it really going to rob me of my life?"[1] but steeling his heart, he cried in suppliant tones which she regarded not: "Bharata and Rāma are as my two eyes. I tell you truly and call Śiva as my witness. O my beloved, what is this ill word that you have uttered, destructive of all order, confidence and affection? I will not fail to despatch a messenger at daybreak, and as soon as they hear the news, the two brothers will immediately arrive. Then after fixing an auspicious day and making all due preparation, I will solemnly confer the kingdom on Bharata.

Dohā 31

Rāma has no desire to reign, and is devotedly attached to Bharata. I made my plans according to royal usage, thinking only of their respective ages.

Caupāī 32

I swear a hundred oaths by Rāma that I tell you in all sincerity that his mother never said a word to me. I arranged it all without asking you, and this is how my cherished scheme has failed. Put away your displeasure, assume a festal garb; in a few days Bharata shall be regent. There was only one thing that pained me—your second petition, really an unreasonable request. Today your bosom burns with unwonted fire; is it anger, or do you jest, or is it all really true? Tell me calmly Rāma's offence. Everyone says that he is amiability itself. Even you used to praise and caress him, and I am quite perplexed at what I now hear. His pleasant ways would charm even an enemy; how then can he do anything to displease his own mother ?

Dohā 32

Have done, my beloved, with this, be it jesting or displeasure; make a just and reasonable request, that I may rejoice in the sight of Bharata's installation.

1. Or, she will rob me of my reputation for truth (my houour) or my life.

Caupāī 33

Rather might a fish live out of water, or a wretched serpent live without its head-jewel—I tell you the simple truth in all sincerity—but there is no life for me without Rāma. Consider well, my dear, my prudent wife, my very existence depends upon my seeing Rāma !" On hearing this soft speech the wicked woman blazed up like the fire on which has fallen an oblation of *ghī* : "You may devise and carry out any number of plans, but your subterfuges will not avail with me. Either grant my request, or refuse me and be disgraced; I do not want any of your circumlocutions! Rāma is a marvel of goodness, you too are good and wise, and Rāma's mother, as you have discovered, is also good—oh yes, you know them well enough! The benefit that Kausalyā devised for me is the only fruit that I now in turn give her, and this I do with a vengeance!

Dohā 33

At daybreak, if Rāma does not assume the hermit's garb and go out into the woods, my death will ensue, O king, and your disgrace; be well assured of this!"

Caupāī 34

So saying, the evil queen rose and stood erect, like a swollen flood of wrath that had risen in the mountains of sin, turgid with streams of passion, terrible to behold, with the two boons for its banks, her stern obduracy for its current, and her voluble speech for its whirling eddies, overthrowing the king like some tree torn up by the roots, as it rushed on to the ocean of calamity. The king perceived that it was all true, and that death, in fashion as a woman, was dancing in triumph on his head. Humbly he clasped her feet and begged her to be seated, crying : "Be not an axe at the root of the Solar race. Demand of me my head and I will give it forthwith, but do not kill me by the loss of Rāma, be it in any way you will, or your heart will be ill at ease all your life long!"

Dohā 34

Realizing that his disease was incurable, the king dropped on the ground and beat his head, sobbing out in most lamentable tones, "Rāma ! O Rāma ! O Raghunātha!"

Caupāī 35

The king's whole body was so broken down by distress that he seemed like the tree of Paradise that some elephant had uprooted. His throat was parched, speech failed his lips, like some poor fish deprived of water. Again Kaikeyī plied him with biting taunts, infusing as it were poison into his wounds : "If you meant to act thus in the end, what compulsion was there to say, ask, ask? Is it possible, O king, to be two things at once? To roar with laughter and pout at the same time; to be called the munificent, and yet be miserly; to live without anxiety, and yet be a king? Either break your word or show more fortitude; do not, like a woman, appeal to compassion. It is said that life, wife, sons, home, wealth, nay the whole world, all are but as a straw compared to the ocean of truth."

Dohā 35

Hearing these cutting words, the king replied : "It is no fault of yours; my evil destiny, like some demoniacal delusion, has possessed you and bids you speak.

Caupāī 36

Bharata has never dreamed of desiring the throne but by the decree of fate evil counsel has lodged in your breast. All this is the consequence of my sins that God has turned hostile at this ill hour. Hereafter beautiful Avadh shall flourish again under the sway of the all-perfect Rāma; all his brothers shall do him service and his glory shall spread through the three spheres of creation ! Only your disgrace and my remorse, though we die, shall never be effaced or forgotten. Now do whatever seemeth you good; only stay out of my sight and let your face be veiled. With clasped hands I ask but this, speak not to me again so long as I live. You too will repent at the last, O miserable woman, who aiming at the tiger have thus shot dead the cow."

Dohā 36

The king fell to the ground, crying again and again : "Why have you wrought this ruin on our house?" But the perfidious queen spoke not a word, like a funeral pile that is ever burning.

Caupāī 37

The king continued to sob out "Rāma, Rāma!", distressed like some luckless bird clipped of its wings. In his heart he was praying : "May the day never down nor anyone go and tell Rāma! Rise not, O Sun, great patriarch of the Solar race, for at the sight of Avadh your breast will be consumed with anguish." The king's affection and Kaikeyī's cruelty were both the most extreme that God could make. While the monarch was yet lamenting, day broke and the music of lute and pipe and conch resounded at his gate. Bards recited his titles, minstrels sang his praises; but like arrows they wounded the king, as he heard them. All tokens of rejoicing pleased him as little as the adornment of a widow who ascends the funeral pile. That night no one had slept, from the joyous anticipation of beholding Rāma.

Dohā 37

At the palace gate was a throng of servants and ministers, who exclaimed as they beheld the risen sun : "What can be the reason why today of all days our lord awaketh not?"

Caupāī 38

The king was always wont to wake at the last watch; to-day it strikes us as very strange. Go, Sumantra, and rouse him and obtain the royal order to commence the work." Sumantra entered the palace, but as he passed on, he was struck with awe and dismay at its appearance, as though some terrible monster were about to spring upon him and devour him; it seemed the very home of calamity and distress. Asking, but with no one to answer him, he came to the apartment where were the king and Kaikeyī; with the salutation "Live for ever" he bowed the head and sat down. On beholding the king's condition, he was much distressed, for he lay upon the ground crushed and colourless, like a lotus broken off from its root. The terrified minister dared not put a question; but she, full of evil and void of all good, answered thus:

Dohā 38

"The king has not slept all night : God knows why. He has done nothing but mutter "Rāma, Rāma," even till daybreak; but he has not told me the reason.

Caupāī 39

Go and fetch Rāma here, as soon as possible, and when you come back you can ask what the matter is." Perceiving it to be the king's wish, Sumantra went off; but he saw that the queen had formed some evil design. So anxious was he that his feet scarcely touched the ground as he wondered to himself: 'What will the king have to say to Rāma?' Composing himself as he reached the gate, when all observed his sadness and asked the cause, he reassured them and proceeded to the prince's abode. When Rāma saw Sumantra coming, he received him with the same honour that he would have shown to his own father. Looking him in the face, he declared the king's commands and returned with him. Remarking how unceremoniously Rāma accompanied the minister, the people here and there began to grieve.

Dohā 39

The jewel of Raghu's race came and beheld the king's miserable plight, like that of some aged elephant who has dropped down in terror at the sight of a lioness.

Caupāī 40

His lips became parched and his body all aflame, like a poor snake that has been robbed of the jewel in its head. Seeing the furious Kaikeyī near, like Death counting the minutes, the pitiful and amiable Raghunātha, though he now for the first time saw sorrow, and had never before heard its name even, composed himself as the occasion required and in pleasant tones asked his mother: "Tell me, mother, the cause of my father's distress, that I may endeavour to put an end to it." "Listen, Rāma," she replied, "the sole cause is this: the king is very fond of you: he had promised to grant me two boons, and I have asked for what I wanted; but he is disturbed on hearing them and cannot get rid of a scruple on your account.

Dohā 40

On the one side is his love for his son; on the other his promise; he is thus in a strait. If it lies in your power, be obedient to his commands and so terminate his misery."

Caupāī 41

She sat and spoke stinging words so composedly that Cruelty itself was disturbed to hear her. From the bow of her tongue she shot forth the arrows of her speech against the king who was like some yielding target; as though Obduracy had taken form and become a bold and practised archer. Sitting like the very incarnation of heartlessness, she expounded to Raghupati the whole history. Râma, the sun of the Solar race, the fountain of every joy, smiled inwardly and replied in guileless terms, so soft and gracious that they seemed the very jewels of the goddess of speech : "Hearken, mother; blessed is the son who loves to obey his parents' commands; a son who cherishes his father and mother is not often found in the world.

Dohā 41

In the forest I shall get more frequent opportunities of joining the hermits, which will be beneficial to me in every way, and now there is also my father's command and your approval, mother.

Caupāī 42

Bharata, moreover, whom I love as myself, will obtain the kingdom; in every way God favours me today. If I go not to the woods under these circumstances, then reckon me first in any assembly of fools. They who desert the tree of paradise to tend a castor-oil plant, or refuse ambrosia to ask for poison, having once lost their chance, will never get it again; see, mother, and ponder this in your heart. One special anxiety still remains, when I see the king so exceedingly disturbed. I cannot understand, mother, how my father can be so much pained by such a trifling matter. He is stout-hearted and an immeasurable ocean of piety[1] : there must have been some great offence on my part, that he will not say a word to me : I adjure you to tell me the truth."

1. Being so stout of heart, why should he be thus dismayed at the mere thought of losing me ? And being so pious, how is it possible that he can hesitate for a moment about keeping his word ? There must be something else in the background. I fear I have done wrong and displeased him.

Dohā 42

Though Raghubīra's words were as perfectly straightforward as possible, the wicked queen gave them a perverse twist[1] like a leech, which must always move crookedly, however smooth the water be.

Caupāī 43

Seeing Rāma's readiness to obey her, the queen smiled and said with much display of feigned affection : "I swear by yourself and Bharata, there is no other cause that I know of. There is no room for fault in you, my son, who confer such happiness both on your parents and your brother. All that you say, Rāma, is true; you are devoted to the wishes of your parents. Remonstrate, then, solemnly with your father that he incur not sin and disgrace in his old age. Having been blest with a son like you, he cannot properly disregard your advice." These fair words in her false mouth were like Gayā and the other holy places that are in Magadha : but Rāma took his mother's speech in good part, like the Gaṅgā, which in its course receives and hallows any stream.

Dohā 43

At the remembrance of Rāma, the king recovered from his spell of unconsciousness and turned on his side. Taking advantage of the opportunity, the minister humbly informed him of Rāma's arrival.

Caupāī 44

When the king heard that Rāma had come, he summoned up courage and opened his eyes. The minister supported his sovereign to a seat, where the king saw Rāma falling at his feet. In an agony of affection, he clasped him to his heart, like some snake that has recovered the jewel it had lost. As the monarch continued gazing upon Rāma, a flood of tears poured forth from his eyes, nor in his sore distress could he utter a word, but again

1. The queen thought to herself : by his praises of a hermit's life he hopes I may be persuaded to send Bharata to the woods instead of himself *or* by his ready compliance, he hopes to wheedle me out of my resolve.

and again he pressed him to his heart. Inwardly he was praying God that Raghunātha might not be banished to the forest: and remembering Mahādeva, he humbly begged, Immortal Śiva, hear my petition, O thou who art easily satisfied, compassionate and generous; recognize then in me a poor suppliant and remove my distress!

Dohā 44

As thou directest the hearts of all, give Rāma the sense to disregard my words and stay at home, forgetful for once of his filial affectien.

Caupāī 45

Welcome disgrace and perish my good name; may I sink into hell rather than mount to heaven; be it mine to support the most intolerable pain rather than have Rāma taken from my sight." Thinking thus to himself, the king spoke not a word, while his soul quivered like a fig-tree's leaf. Perceiving his father to be thus overpowered with love, Raghupati spoke again to his mother in modest and thoughtful phrase, as the place, the time, and the circumstances demanded, "Father, if I speak a little wilfully, forgive the offence by reason of my childish years. You are grieving for a very little matter; why did you not speak and let me know of this at the first? After seeing you, sire, I questioned my mother, and on hearing her explanation my fear subsided.

Dohā 45

Put away, father, the anxiety which at this time of rejoicing your affection has caused you, and give me your commands!" So spoke the Lord with heartfelt joy and a body quivering with emotion.

Caupāī 46

"Blessed is his life in this world whose father is pleased to hear of his doings. He has in his hand all the four rewards of life, who holds his parents dear as his own life. By obeying your orders, I attain the end of my existence. If, then, it be your command, I can soon come back, and after taking leave of my mother, I will throw myself once more at your feet and then start for the woods." Having thus spoken, Rāma departed, while the king in his anguish answered not a word. The bitter news spread through the city, like the sting of a scorpion that at once affects the whole body. Every man or woman that heard it was as distressed as the creepers and bushes when a forest is on fire. Wherever it was told, everyone beat his head, and so deep was his despair that he could not be consoled.

Dohā 46

Their faces grew pale, their eyes streamed, their heart could not contain their sorrow; it seemed as though the Pathetic, in battle array and with beat of drum, had marched into Avadh and taken up quarters there.

Caupāī 47

"It was a well-contrived plan, but God has spoilt it." In this fashion they kept abusing Kaikeyī : "What could this wicked woman mean by thus setting fire to a new-thatched house? She tears out her eyes with her own hands, and yet wishes to see; she throws away ambrosia and prefers the taste of poison! Cruel, stubborn, demented wretch, a very fire among the bamboo grove of Raghu's line ! Sitting on a branch of the tree, she has hacked down the stem, and in the midst of joy has introduced this tragedy ! Rāma used ever to be dear to her as life; for what reason has she now taken to such perversity? Truly say the poets that a woman's nature is altogether inscrutable, unfathomable and incomprehensible. Sooner may a man catch his own shadow in the glass than grasp the ways of a woman.

Dohā 47

What is there that fire cannot burn; what is there that ocean cannot contain? What cannot a woman do in her strength ? What is there in the world that death does not devour ?

Caupāī 48

God first ordained one thing, but now ordains something quite different, and what he would show us now is the very reverse of what he showed us then." Said some, "The king has not done well, and without consideration has granted the wicked woman her request. He has wilfully brought all this misery upon himself, and in yielding to a woman has lost all good sense and discretion." Another wisely recognized the king's supreme virtue and would not blame him, as they repeated to one another the legends of Śivi, Dadhīci, and Harīścandra.[1] Some, too, suggested Bharata's connivance, but others were distressed at the mention of such a thing; while some stopping their ears with their hands and biting their tongues exclaimed : "Such words are false; you damn yourself[2] by saying such things. Rāma is dear to Bharata as his own life !

Dohā 48

Sooner shall the moon rain sparks of fire, or nectar have the same effect as poison, than Bharata ever dream of doing anything to injure Rāma."

Caupāī 49

One reproached the Creator, who had promised ambrosia but given poison. The whole city was agitated and everyone so sad that the intolerable pain in their heart utterly effaced all the previous rejoicing. The venerable and highborn Brāhmaṇa matrons, who were Kaikeyī's dearest friends, began to give her

1. For the legends of *Śivi* and *Dadhīci* see notes on page 245.

Harīscandra, the son of Trisaṅku, was king of Ayodhyā and the twenty-eighth in descent from Ikṣvāku, the founder of the solar dynasty. In order to satisfy the claims of Viśvāmitra who wanted to make trial of his integrity, he sold his kingdom and all that he had, together with his wife Satyavatī and his only son, and hired himself out as the servant of a man who kept a burning ghat. Whenever a corpse was brought, he had to take the fee and make it over to his master. One day a woman brought her dead child and he recognized them as his own wife and son. She had no money and he was so zealous in his employer's interests that he would not allow the body to be burnt till the regular fee was paid. As the only way to satisfy his demand, she was stripping off the one poor rag that covered her nakedness, when the gods interposed and restored the king to his throne and all his former prosperity.

2. *i.e.*, you lose all the merit you have won.

advice and praise her good disposition; but their words pierced her like arrows. "You have always said, as everyone knows, that Bharata was not so dear to you as Rāma; show him, then, your wonted affection; for what offence do you now banish him to the woods ? You have never shown any jealousy of the rival queens; your love and confidence in them were known throughout the land. What wrong has Kausalyā done you now that you should launch this thunderbolt against the city ?

Dohā 49

What! will Sītā desert her spouse? Will Lakṣmaṇa remain at home? Will Bharata enjoy the dominion of the state or the king survive without Rāma?

Caupāī 50

Reflect upon this and put away your wrath from your breast, nor make yourself a stronghold of remorse and disgrace. By all means make Bharata the king's coadjutor; but what need is there for Rāma to be banished to the woods? Rāma is not greedy of royal power; he is righteous and averse to sensual pleasures. Let him leave the palace and go and live with his *guru*; ask this of the king as your second petition. A son like Rāma does not deserve banishment; what will people say to you when they hear of it ? If you do not agree to our suggestion, nothing will prosper in your hands. If this is only some jest of yours, speak out clearly and let me know. Up quickly and devise a plan to avert future remorse and disgrace.

Chand 2

Devise some plan to avert this misery and disgrace and save your family. Be instant in diverting Rāma from going to the woods, and labour for nothing else. As the day without the sun, as the body without life, as the night without the moon, so (says Tulasī Dāsa) is Avadh without its lord; I beg you, lady, to consider this."

Soraṭhā 50

Pleasant to hear and beneficial in result was the advice her friends gave; but she paid no heed to it, having been tutored in villainy by the wicked humpback.

Caupāī 51

She answered not a word, but raged with irrepressible fury like a hungry tigress that has spied a deer. Perceiving her disease to be incurable, they left her, saying as they went : "Demented wretch ! Fate has destroyed her, queen though she be; she has acted in such a way as no one has ever acted before." Thus lamented all the men and women of the city and heaped countless abuse on the wicked queen. Burning with intolerable fever they sobbed out: "What hope of life is there without Rāma?" Agonized by his loss, the people were as miserable as creatures of the deep when water fails. Great was the distress of all, whether man or woman, but the saintly Rāma went to his mother, with joy in his face and fourfold exultation in his soul, fearing no more that the king might detain him.

Dohā 51

Raghubira's mind resembled some young elephant with kingship for its chain; the news of banishment was as its breaking: at which he rejoiced exceedingly.

Caupāi 52

With folded hands the glory of the house of Raghu bowed his head blithely at his mother's feet. She gave him her blessing and clasped him to her bosom, and scattered around him gifts of jewels and raiment. Again and again his mother kissed his face, with tears of joy in her eyes and her body quivering with emotion. She took him in her lap and pressed him once more to her heart, while drops of affection trickled from her comely breasts. Her rapture of love was past all telling, like that of a beggar made all at once rich as Kuvera. Tenderly regarding his lovely features, his mother thus addressed him in sweetest tones: "Tell me, my son, I adjure you by your mother, what hour is set for the glad and auspicious ceremonies when my piety, virtue and joy will reach their climax and bring to full fruition the joy of my life,

Dohā 52

the hour for which the people long as anxiously as the thirsty cuckoo and his mate, in the season of autumn, for the rainfall of Arcturus.

Caupāī 53

Go at once, dear son, I beg of you, and bathe and take something nice to eat, such as you like, and then, dear boy, approach your father. I, your mother, protest there has been too much delay." On hearing his mother's most loving speech, which seemed as the flower of the paradisal tree of affection laden with the fragrance of delight and produced from the stem of prosperity, Rāma's bee-like soul was not distracted by the sight, but in his righteousness he distinguished the path of virtue, and thus in honeyed tones addressed his mother : "My father has assigned me the woods for my realm, where I shall have many great things to do. Give me your orders, mother, with a cheerful heart, that I too may cheerfully and in auspicious wise set out for the forest. Do not in your affection give way to causeless alarm; my happiness, mother, depends on your consent.

Dohā 53

After staying fourteen years in the woods, in obedience to my sire's command[1], I will come back and again behold your feet; make not your mind uneasy."

Caupāī 54

Raghubīra's sweet and dutiful words pierced like arrows through his mother's heart. At the sound of his chilling speech

1. *Or*, and thus making good my father's vow.

she withered and drooped like the *javāsa*[1] at a shower in the rains. The anguish of her soul was past telling, as when an elephant shrinks at the roar of a tiger. Her eyes filled with tears and her body shook and trembled all over, like a fish overtaken by the scour of a flooded river.[2] Summoning up courage, she looked her son in the face and thus spoke, in faltering accents : "My son, you are your father's darling, and it is a constant delight to him to watch your doings. He had fixed an auspicious day for giving you the sceptre; for what offence does he now banish you to the woods? Tell me, my son, the upshot of it all; who is the destroying fire of the Sun-god's line ?"

Dohā 54

Realizing what Rama wanted, the minister's son explained to her the reason. On hearing his account she was struck dumb : words fail to describe her condition.

Caupāī 55

She could neither detain him nor bid him go; either way her heart was distraught with cruel pain : as though for 'moon' one had written 'eclipse': God's hand is ever against us all. Duty and affection both laid siege to her soul; her dilemma was like that of a snake with a musk-rat.[3] "If I keep my son, it will be a sin; my past virtue will go for nothing and my friends will abhor

1. It is a prickly plant or grass on which cattle and camels feed and of which *ṭaṭṭis* are made. A popular Hindi couplet says that every creature in the world rejoices at the coming of the rains, except four, *viz.*, the *āk* and *javāsa* plants, which flourish only on dry soil, and the saltpetre manufacturer and the carter, who cannot ply their trade :

Āk javāsa āgara; chauthe gāriwān.
Jyon jyon camake bijli, tyon tyon taje parān.

2. The line, as I translate it, stands thus : *Mānjā manahu mīn kahan vyāpī.* As to the meaning of the word *mānjā*, some commentators explain it as a sickness that prevails at the beginning of the rains; or as the scum raised on the water when the rains first break; or as the juice of a plant. Another reading is *Mānjahi khāi mīnjanu māpī*, where *māpī* would be for *mātī*, drunk."

3. If it swallows the rat, it dies; if it disgorges it, it goes blind; such is the popular belief.

me. If I bid him go into exile, it will be a sad loss." In this distressing strait the queen was sore tried. Again reflecting on her wifely duty and remembering that Rāma and Bharata were both equally her sons, the prudent queen in the sweetness of her disposition summoned up courage and spoke these woeful words: "May I die, my son, but you have done well; obedience to a father's command is one's highest duty.

Dohā 55

Though he promised you the kingdom, he banishes you to the woods; for this I am not the least sad or sorry : but, without you, Bharata and the king and the people will all be put to terribie distress.

Caupāī 56

Yet, boy, if it is only your father's order, then go not; hold your mother still greater.[1] If both father and mother bid you go, the forset will be equal to a hundred Avadhs. The forest gods will be your father, its goddesses your mother and birds and deer will wait upon your lotus feet. In the evening of his life retirement to the woods is the proper thing for a king, but I am troubled at heart when I consider your tender youth.How blest the forest and how luckless Avadh if you abandon it, you, the crown of Raghu's line ! If, child, I say, 'Take me with you,' there may be some hesitation in your mind; O my son, all hold you most dear, life of our life; if you say, 'Mother, I go alone to the forest,' on hearing your words I sink down in despair.

Dohā 56

Being thus minded I do not press my suit with a show of love beyond what I really feel; agree to your mother's request; or if you go alone, at least I pray you not to forget me.

Caupāī 57

May all the gods and the spirits of your ancestors guard you, noble boy, as closely as the eyelids guard the eyes. The term of

1. For *jāni bari mātā*, the words that I translate, some copies read *jāi bā mātā*.

banishment is like the water of a lake in which the fish are your friends and relations; you are all-merciful and righteous; remember then to make your plans so that you may find them all alive when you come again. Go, then, in peace to the woods — ah! woe is me! — leaving your servants, your relatives, the whole city in bereavement. To-day the fruit of all their past good deeds has gone, and the tide of fortune has turned against them, assuming a sullen aspect." Thus with many mournful lamentations she clung to his feet, accounting herself the most hopeless of women. Cruel and intolerable pangs pierced her heart through and through, and the burden of her misery was past all telling. Rāma raised his mother and took her to his bosom and consoled her with many tender words.

Dohā 57

At that moment Sītā, who had heard the news, rose in great agitation, and having done obeisance to her mother-in-law's lotus feet, she bowed her head and sat down.

Cāupaī 58

In gentle accents her mother gave her blessing, and at the sight of her delicate frame was more distressed than ever. With drooping eyes Sītā, the perfection of beauty, model of wifely devotion, sat and thought: "The lord of my life would go to the woods, how can I merit to accompany him? Whether in the body or only in the soul, go I must; but God's doings are inscrutable." With her lovely toe-nails she traced marks upon the ground, while the music of her anklets, like the poet's honeyed song, rang out the passionate prayer: 'Never may we be torn from Sītā's feet.' Seeing her let fall a flood of tears from her lovely eyes, Rāmā's mother cried: "Hearken, my son; Sītā is very delicate; she is the darling of your father and mother and all your kindred.

Dohā 58

Her own father is Janaka, jewel of kings; her father-in-law is the Phoebus of the Solar race; her lord, the perfection of beauty and virtue, is as it were the moon of the lily-like progeny of the sun-god;

Chaupāī 59

I again have found in her a beloved daughter, amiable, beautiful and accomplished. She is like the apple of my eye, and my affection has so grown that it is only in Jānakī that I have my being.[1] I have tended her as carefully as a creeper of paradise and watered her growth with streams of affection. When she should have blossomed and borne fruit, God has turned against me, and there is no knowing what will be the end. Or ever she left her bed or seat, I cradled her in my lap, and never has Sītā set her foot on the hard ground. I cherished her as the very source of my life, and never bade her so much as even to trim the wick of a lamp. And this is the Sītā who would follow you to the woods; what are your orders, O Raghunātha ? Can the partridge, that drinks in with delight the rays of the moon, endure to fix its gaze on the orb of the sun ?

Dohā 59

Elephants, lions, goblins, and many fierce animals haunt the forest : ah, my son, is the charming tree of life fit to set in such a deadly pasture ?

Caupāī 60

God has created for the forest Kola and Kirāta women, who know naught of bodily delights. Of nature as hard as the stone insect, the woods are no trial to them. A hermit's wife again is fit for the woods, who for the sake of penance has renounced all pleasures. But how, my son, can Sītā live in the woods, who would be frightened by even the picture of a monkey ? Can the cygnet that has sported in the lovely lotus-beds of the Gaṅgā find fit abode in a muddy puddle ? First ponder this, and then, as you order I will instruct Jānakī. If she remain at home and call me mother, she will be the support of my life." Raghubīra on hearing his mother's speech, which was drenched as it were with the ambrosia of grace and affection,

1. In the original is a play upon words which it is impossible to preserve in a translation; *jāna prāṇa*, the ordinary expression for the 'breath of life,' being presented to the eye by the conjunction of *prāṇa* with the first syllable of Sītā's name Jānakī. The line thus means: "My affection has so grown that I have centred my very being in Jānakī."

Dohā 60

Replied in wise and loving terms for his mother's consolation, and began to set clearly before Jānakī all the pains and pleasures of the forest,

Caupāī 61

Speaking hesitantly as in the presence of his mother, and considering well within himself the requirements of the time : "Hearken, lady, to my instructions; nor form any different fancies in your mind. If you desire your own good and mine, agree to what I say and remain at home. My order is this : the service of a mother-in-law is in every way, madam, a blessing to a family. There is no other duty so paramount as reverential submission to a husband's parents. Whenever my mother recalls me to mind and is distracted by affectionate solicitude, do you, my beauteous wife, comfort her with old-world tales and tender speeches. I speak from my heart and confirm it with a hundred oaths : it is for my mother's sake, beloved, that I leave you here.

Dohā 61

The reward of virtue can be obtained without trouble by submission to Scripture and one's spiritual director; through their obstinacy Gālava[1] and king Nahuṣa[2] had to endure all sorts of troubles.

1. Gālava was a pupil of Viśvāmitra's. When he had completed his studies, he asked his tutor what fee he ought to pay. He was told there was no fee. However, he still persisted in asking, till at last Viśvāmitra was annoyed and, to get rid of him, said he would be satisfied with nothing less than a thousand black-eared horses. After a long search and many inquiries Gālava discovered three childless rājas who had each 200 horses of the kind that he required, and they agreed to let him have them, but only on this condition, that he got each of them a son. Gālava then went to Yayāti, whose daughter had the miraculous gift of bearing a son for any one she wished, and yet herself remaining a virgin. By her means each of the three kings became a father. The 600 horses were made over to Gālava, and he presented them to Viśvāmitra, who as an equivalent for the other 400 horses, wanting to make up the thousand, had himself two sons by the same mysterious bride.

2. For the legend of king Nahuṣa see notes to *Dohā* 227 (Ayodhyā).

Hear me, my fair and sensible one ! I shall soon fulfil my father's words and come back again. The days will quickly pass away; listen, love, to my advice. If, my spouse, you persist in your affectionate obstinacy, you will rue it in the end. The forest is exceedingly toilsome and terrible, with awful heat and cold and rain and wind; the path is beset with prickly grass and stones, and you will have to walk without protection for your feet : and your lotus feet are so soft and pretty, while the road is most difficult : and there are huge mountains, chasms and precipices, streams, rivers and watercourses, deep and impassable, dreadful to behold; while bears and tigers, wolves, lions and elephants make such a roaring that the boldest is dismayed.

Dohā 62

[1]The ground will be your bed, the bark of trees your raiment and your food wild bulbs, fruit and roots; nor think that even they will be always forthcoming every day, but only when they are in season.

Caupāī 63

There are demons of the night, who feed on men and assume all sorts of deceptive forms; the rainfall on the hills is excessive, and in short the hardships of the forest are past all telling. There are terrible serpents and fierce wild birds and gangs of goblins that steal both man and woman. The bravest shudder at the thought of the dense forest; while you, my fawn-eyed wife, are timid by nature. Ah ! lady of swan-like gait, you are not fit for the woods; people will revile me on hearing of such a thing. Can the swan that has been nurtured in the ambrosial flood of the Mânasa lake exist in the salt sea? Can the cuckoo that roves with delight through the luxuriant mango-groves, take pleasure in a jungle of

1. Yet take good hede, for ever drede that ye coude not sustain
The thorney ways, the deep valleys, the snow, the frost, the rain,
The cold, the hete, for dry or wete, we must lodge on the plain,
And us above, none other roof, but a brake, bush or twayne,
For ye must there in your hande bere a bowe ready to drawe,
And as a thief, thus must ye lyve, ever in drede and awe.

The Nut-browne Maid.

caper, bushes? Ponder this, lady fair as the moon, and stay at home; the hardships of the forest are too great.

Dohā 63

She does not reverently accept the advice of her *guru* or her husband, who with all sincerity wish her well, shall assuredly have a surfeit of repentance in the end and gain no good."

Caupāī 64

On hearing the tender and winning words of her husband, Sītā's lotus eyes filled with tears, and his soothing advice caused her a burning pain, such as the autumn moon causes the *cakavī*. In her distress no answer came to her lips : 'So great is his love that he wished to abandon me.' Perforce restraining her tears and summoning up courage, Earth's daughter embraced her mother's feet, and with folded hands thus spake : "Pardon me, lady, my great presumption; my dear lord has thought me what is all for my own good; but I look to my feelings, and conclude that no sorrow in the world is so great as separation from one's beloved.

Dohā 64

O lord of my life, abode of compassion, beautiful, bounteous and wise, the moon of the lilies of the Raghu race, heaven without you would be hell !

Caupāī 65

Dear are father and mother, sisters and brothers; dear are my companions and my many friends; but father-in-law and mother-in-law, spiritual director, generous associates and even sons, however beautiful, amiable and affectionate, nay, my lord, all love and every tie of kinship, to a woman without her husband, are a greater distress than the sun's most burning heat. Body, wealth, home, land, city, and empire are but accumulated misery to a woman bereft of her lord. Pleasure is sickness, her jewels a burden, and the world like the torments of hell. Without you, O lord of my soul, there is nothing in the whole world that would bring me joy. As the body without a soul, as a river without water, so, my lord, is a woman without her husband. With you, my lord, all are delights, as long as I can behold your face that vies in brightness with the autumn moon.

Dohā 65

The birds and beasts will be my attendants, the forest my city, and strips of bark my glistening silken dress; with my lord a hut of grass will be as the palace of the gods, and all will be well.

Caupāī 66

The sylvan nymphs and gods will graciously protect me like my own lord's parents; my simple couch of grass and twigs will with my lord become a sumptuous marriage-couch; bulbs, roots and fruit will form an ambrosial repast, and the mountains will resemble the stately halls of Avadh. Every moment as I gaze on my lord's lotus feet, I shall be as glad as the *cakavī* at the dawn. You have recounted, my lord, the numerous hardships of the forest, its terrors, annoyances and all the many discomforts; but, O fountain of mercy, all these united will not be comparable to the pain of bereavement. Consider this, O jewel of wisdom, and take me with you, abandon me not. Why make long supplication? My lord is full of compassion and knoweth the heart.

Dohā 66

Do you think, if you make me stay at Avadh, that I can survive till the end of your exile, O most beautiful, friend of the helpless, fountain of grace and of love?

Caupāī 67

As I go along the road I shall not weary, while every moment I behold your lotus feet. In every way I shall minister to my beloved, and relieve him of all the toil of the march. Seated in the shade of some tree, I shall lave your feet and rapturously fan you, and gazing on your body stained with sweat and blackened by the sun, what thought, my dearest lord, shall I have for my own hard times? Spreading grass and leaves on the level ground, your slave will all night shampoo your feet, and ever gazing on your gracious form, neither heat nor wind will ever vex me. Who will look at me when I am with my lord, except as a hare or jackal furtively regards a lioness? Am I to be dainty and delicate, while my lord roams the woods? Is penance to be your portion and enjoyment mine ?

Dohā 67

My heart will burst at the mere sound of so cruel a sentence, and never will my miserable existence survive the anguish and torture of separation."

Caupāī 68

So saying, Sītā was overwhelmed with distress, nor could endure the mere word 'separation.' On seeing her condition, Rāma made sure, 'If I insist upon leaving her, I leave her dead.' Then said the gracious lord of the Solar race: "Have done with lamentation and come with me to the woods. There is no time now for weeping; at once make your preparations for the journey." Having consoled his beloved with these tender words, he touched his mother's feet and received her blessing: "Return quickly and relieve your subjects' distress, nor forget your hard-hearted mother.[1] Who knows but God may change my lot, and my eyes may see you both again. Ah ! my son, when will arrive the happy day and moment that I shall live to see your moonlike face once more?

Dohā 68

When again shall I call you 'my child,' 'my darling', 'noblest and best of Raghu's line,' 'my own son,' and fondly bid you come to my arms that I may gaze with joy upon your features?"

1. That is to say, I must be hard-hearted, for, if not, I should die at once.

Caupāī 69

Seeing that his mother was so distraught with affection that she could not speak and was utterly overwhelmed with distress, Rāma said all he could to console her, and the pathos of the scene was beyond description. Then Jānakī touched her mother's feet and said, "Hearken, mother, I am of all women most miserable. At the time when I should have been doing you service, fate has banished me to the woods and has denied me my desire. But have done with sorrow and cease not to love me; fate is cruel, I am blameless." On hearing Sītā's words her mother was so afflicted that her state was past all telling, Again and again she took her to her breast and summoning up courage. thus blest and admonished her: "May your prosperity be as enduring as the streams of Gaṅgā and Jamunā !"

Dohā 69

When her lord's mother had repeatedly blessed and admonished Sītā, she took her leave, after again and again affectionately bowing her head before her lotus feet.

Caupāī 70

When Lakṣmaṇa heard the news, he started up in dismay with a doleful face, his body all of a tremble and his eyes full of tears, and ran and clasped his feet in an agony of affection. He could not speak, but stood and stared aghast, like some poor fish drawn out of the water, thinking within himself: "O God, what will happen? All my happiness and past good deeds are gone for ever. What will Raghunātha tell me to do? Will he keep me here, or take me with him?" When Rāma saw his brother with folded hands renouncing life and home and all, he addressed him thus — the all-righteous Rāma, fountain of grace, love and perfect bliss: "Brother, do not afflict yourself with love, but be well assured that all will be well in the end.

Dohā 70

They who unreservedly submit to the commands of their father and mother, their spiritual director or their lord, are born into the world to some purpose: otherwise their birth is in vain.

Caupāī 71

Consider this, brother, and hearken to my advice, wait upon the feet of your father and mother. Neither Bharata is at home, nor Ripusūdana, and the king is old and sorrowing for me. If I go to the forest and take you with me, Avadh would be completely desolate, and an intolerable weight of affliction will fall upon priest and parents, subjects, kinsfolk and all. Stay, then to comfort them; if not brother, it will be a great sin. The king whose faithful subjects endure distress, is of a truth a prince of hell. Regard this as your duty, brother, and stay." Lakṣmaṇa was grievously distressed on hearing this, and his body became as dead and shrivelled as a lotus that has been touched by the frost.

Dohā 71

Overmastered by love, he could make no answer, but clung in anguish to his feet: "O my lord, I am your slave and you my master: if you leave me, then what can I do ?

Caupāī 72

Master, you have given me excellent advice, but I find it impracticable, for I am a coward. Valiant leaders of men and champions of the faith can master such abstruse doctrine, but I am a mere child, nurtured by your affection ; can a cygnet uplift Mount Mandara or Meru ? I know no *guru*, nor father, nor mother. Believe me, my lord, I speak from my heart ! All the love in the world, all claims of kinship, all affection, sympathy, wisdom and skill are for me centred in you, my lord, the protector of the humble, the reader of the heart. Expound the precepts of theology to one who aims at fame and glory and high estate; I am in heart, word and deed devoted only to your feet; and am I, gracious lord, to be discarded ?

Dohā 72

The merciful Lord, on hearing the gentle and humble words of his dear brother, took him to his bosom, and seeing him so affectionately dejected thus consoled him:

Caupāī 73

"Go, brother, and take leave of your mother, and then come back at once and set out for the forest." On hearing Raghubara thus speak, he was overjoyed; his triumph was great, his sorrow all gone. He went to his mother as glad of heart as a blind man who has recovered his sight, and while he bowed his head before her feet, his heart was away with Raghunandana and Jānakī. Seeing his agitation his mother inquired the cause, and Lakṣmaṇa told her the whole story. On hearing his cruel speech she trembled like a fawn that sees the forest on fire all around it. Lakṣmaṇa reflected: "Everything goes wrong to-day: her very affection will work me harm." Timidly and hesitatingly he asked her permission to go, thinking, "O God, will she let me go or not?"

Dohā 73

After reflecting on the beauty and loving-kindness of Rāma and Sītā, and considering the king's love for them, Sumitrā beat her head and cried, "That wicked woman is at the bottom of this bad business!"

Caupāī 74

But perceiving that this was no time for grieving, she took patience and in her kindness of heart answered gently: "Your mother, child, is Vaidehī, and Rāma is your most loving father; where Rāma dwells, there is Avadh; and wherever is the light of the sun, there is day. If Rāma and Sītā go to the woods, you have no business at Avadh. A *guru*, a father and mother, brethren, the gods and master are all to be cherished as one's own life; but Rāma is dearer than life, is the soul of our soul, and the disinterested friend of all; our dearest and most honoured friends are to be accounted those of Rāma's household. Thinking thus to yourself, go with them to the woods, and receive, my son, the fruition of your existence.

Dohā 74

You have become the receptacle of the highest good fortune, and I too — ah, woe is me! — if from an unfeigned heart you have made Rāma's feet your home.

Caupāī 75

A mother indeed is she in this world who has a son devoted to Raghubara; if not, it is better to be barren, she has given birth in vain; a son who is Rāma's enemy is a curse. It is your good fortune that Rāma goes to the woods; and other reason is there none; this, my son, is the highest reward for all good deeds, to have a sincere affection for the feet of Rāma and Sītā. Never yield even in thought to lust, or wrath, or envy, or pride, or delusion; but put aside all such disorders and serve them in thought and word and deed. For you the forest is a place of joy, since Rāma and Sītā, your father and mother, will be there with you. Take heed, my son, that Rāma be put to no trouble; this is my admonition.

Chand 3

This is my behest, my son; see to it that Rāma and Sītā live at ease and in the forest forget to remember father and mother, friends and relatives and all the pleasures of the city." Having given her son such instruction and commands (says Tulasī) she again invoked upon him her blessing: "May your love for Sītā and Raghubīra be constant and unsullied and ever renewed !"

Sorațhā 75

Having bowed his head before his mother's feet, he departed with all speed with trepidation of heart, as flies a hapless deer that has broken through a perilous snare.

Caupāī 76

He went to Jānakī's lord, and his soul rejoiced to recover his dear society. After reverencing Rāma and Sītā's gracious feet, he proceeded with them to the king's palace. The citizens were saying to one another: "How goodly a plan God made and now has marred !" With wasted frame, sad soul and doleful face, they were in as great distress as bees robbed of their honey; wringing their hands, beating their heads and lamenting, like wretched birds that have been clipt of their wings. There was a great crowd in the royal hall: grief immeasurable, beyond all telling. The minister raised the king and seated him, with the welcome news that Rāma had arrived. When he saw Sītā and his two sons, the king's agitation was profound.

Dohā 76

Again and again turning his troubled gaze on Sītā and his two handsome sons, he clasped them to his bosom time after time in an agony of love.

Caupāī 77

In his agitation he could not speak; grief overmastered him and wild anguish of heart. After most affectionately bowing his head before his feet, Raghunātha arose and begged permission to depart: "Father, give me your blessing and commands; why so dismayed at this time of rejoicing? From excessive attachment, sire, to any beloved object, honour is lost and disgrace incurred." At this the love-sick monarch arose and grasping Raghupati by the arm, made him sit down: "Hearken, my son; the sages say that Rāma is the lord of all creation, animate or inanimate; that God, after weighing good and bad actions and mentally considering them, apportions their reward, and the doer reaps the fruit of his own doings: this is the doctrine of the Scriptures and the verdict of mankind.

Dohā 77

But for one to sin and another to reap its reward—the ways of God are most mysterious; who is there in the world who can comprehend them?"

Caupāī 78

The king is his anxiety to keep Rāma at home tried every honest expedient, but when he saw that he was bent on going—righteous, brave and wise as he was—he took and pressed Sītā to his bosom and gave her much most affectionate advice, telling her of all the intolerable hardships of the forest, and reminding her of the happiness she might enjoy with her parents-in-law or at her father's house. But Sītā's soul was devoted to Rāma's feet, and neither home seemed to her attractive nor the woods repulsive. Everyone else too warned her with stories of the manifold miseries to be experienced in the woods. The minister's wife and the *guru's*—prudent dames—affectionately urged her in gentle tones : "He has not sent you into exile. You should do as you are told by your parents and your *guru*."

Dohā 78

This advice, friendly and kind and gentle and judicious though it was, was not pleasing to Sītā to hear; in the same way as the *cakavi* is troubled by the light of the autumn moon.

Caupāī 79

She was, however, too modest to reply; but Kaikeyī on hearing them started up in excitement and, bringing a box of anchorite's dresses and ornaments, placed it before her and said in whispered tones ; "Raghubīra, you are dearer than life to the king; he cannot rid himself of his too great kindness and love, and will never tell you to go, though he forfeit his virtue, his honour and his hope of heaven. Think of this and act as seems to you good." Rāma was pleased when he heard his mother's advice, but her words pierced the king like arrows: "Will my miserable life never leave me?" In his distress he fainted outright, and no one knew what to do. But Rāma quickly assumed the hermit's dress and bowing his head to his father and mother went forth.

Dohā 79

Having gathered together all that was needful for the woods, the Lord set forth with his wife and brother, after doing obeisance to the feet of the Brāhmaṇas and his *guru*, and leaving them all in bewilderment.

Caupāī 80

He passed out and stood at Vasiṣṭha's door and saw that the people were consumed with the anguish of parting. With kindly words Raghubīra consoled them all and, summoning all the Brāhmaṇas begged his *guru* to grant them a year's maintenance. Many gifts he bestowed with respectful courtesy, satisfying the mendicants with largesse and civilities, and his personal friends with demonstrations of affection. Next he summoned his men-servants and maid-servants and made them over to his *guru*, saying with folded hands: "O sir, be to them as their own father and mother, and cherish them all." Again and again did Rāma with folded hands and in gentle tones address each one of them: "He is my truest friend in whom the king finds comfort.

Dohā 80

So act, O all ye thoughtful and considerate citizens, that the queens be not distressed by my absence."

Caupāī 81

When Rāma had thus exhorted them all, he cheerfully bowed his head before his *guru's* lotus feet, and invoking Gaṇeśa, Gaurī, and Mahādeva, and receiving their blessing, sallied forth. As he went, there was great lamentation and a mournful wailing throughout the city, terrible to hear. In Laṅkā there were omens of evil and in Avadh exceeding distress : while mingled joy and sorrow possessed the hosts of heaven. When his swoon had passed, the king awoke and sent for Sumantra and thus began: "Rāma has gone to the woods, and yet my life flits not; what good does it hope to get by still remaining in my body? What more grievous tortures can there be, to force it from my frame?" Then, recovering himself, he added: "Friend, take you the chariot and go;

Dohā 81

The two boys are young and delicate, and Janaka's daughter a delicate girl; take them up into the chariot, my friend, and show them the forest, and come back in a day or two.

Caupāī 82

The two brothers are brave, and Raghurāi is the very ocean of truth and staunch to his word; if they will not turn, do you with folded hands humbly entreat him: 'Send back, my lord, the daughter of Mithilā's king.' When Sītā is frightened at the sight of the forest, seize your opportunity of telling her my instructions, saying, 'This is the message sent by your father-in-law and mother-in-law; come back, daughter; there are many perils in the desert. You can stay at your pleasure now with your own father, now with your husband's parents.' In this manner try every means to bring her back; if she returns, it will be the succour of my life; if not, it will end in my death; what can I do? God is against me." So saying, the king fainted and fell to the ground in a swoon, crying: "O that you could bring them back to me, Rāma, Lakṣmaṇa and Sītā!"

Dohā 83

Having received the king's commands, Sumantra bowed his head and in haste made ready the chariot, and went to the place outside the city where were Sītā and the two brothers.

Caupāi 83

There Sumantra declared to them the king's message and respectfully made Rāma mount the chariot. When Sītā and the two brothers had mounted and driven away, they mentally bowed the head to Avadh. As the bereaved city saw Rāma set out, all the people began confusedly to follow him. The gracious Lord said everything to console them, and they turned homewards, but again came back overmastered by their affection. Avadh appeared to them as gloomy and oppressive as the dark night of Doom; the citizens looked with trembling at one another like so many wild beasts : their home seemed like the grave, their retainers like ghosts, and their sons, friends and neighbours as the angels of death. The trees and creepers in the gardens withered; the streams and lakes were fearful to behold.

Dohā 83

Thousands of horses, elephants and tame deer, the town-cattle, the cuckoos and the peacocks, the *koels*, swans, parrots, *maināS*, herons, flamingoes and partridges,

Caupāī 84

All stood dismayed by Rāma's departure, dumb and motionless like painted pictures. The whole city resembled some dense forest full of fruit in which the agitated people were as so many birds and beasts, while Kaikeyī had been fashioned by God as some wild woman of the woods, a savage Kirātin, who had set all in a fierce blaze. Unable to endure the burning pain of Rāma's departure, the people all flocked after him in panic, each one thinking to himself, "There is no happiness apart from Rāma, Lakṣmaṇa and Sītā. Everything can be had where Rāma is, and Avadh without Raghubīra is of no account." With this fixed idea, they bore him company, abandoning halls of delight that the gods might envy. For what influence can the pleasures of sense have upon men who are devoted to Rāma's lotus feet?

Dohā 84

All left their children and old men at home and followed him. On the bank of the river Tamasā Rāma made his first day's halt.

Caupāī 85

When Raghupati saw his people overpowered with love, his pitiful heart was greatly distressed. The merciful lord Raghunātha, being quickly touched by the grief of others, spoke to them many words of tenderness and affection and did his best to comfort them, instructing them much in their religious duty. But in their fondness they could not tear themselves away. As there was no means of overcoming their innate affection, Raghurāī was in a dilemma. At last worn out with grief and toil, the people fell asleep—a divine delusion helping to beguile them—and when two watches of the night were spent, Rāma affectionately addressed his Minister: "Father, drive the chariot so as to efface the tracks of the wheels: there is no other way of settling the business."

Dohā 85

Rāma, Lakṣmaṇa and Sītā then mounted the chariot, after bowing their heads before Śambhu's feet, and the minister drove it speedily hither and thither, confusing the tracks.

Caupāī 86

At day-break all the people awoke, and there was a great cry that Raghubīra had gone ! Nowhere could they find the tracks of the chariot, though they ran in all directions, crying, 'Rāma ! Rāma!' like so many merchants in terror when their ship has sunk in the ocean. One suggested to another: "Rāma left us on seeing our distress." They revile themselves and envy the fish,[1] crying: "A curse on our life away from Raghubīra: as god has robbed us of our beloved, why has he not granted us our prayer to die?" With many such lamentations they returned to Avadh, full of bitter disappointment. The anguish of parting was beyond description, and it was only the hope of his return that kept them alive.

Dohā 86

Men and women alike began to perform religious rituals and make vows to secure his return, like the miserable *cakavā* and his mate or the lotus when bereft of the sun.

Caupāī 87

Sītā with the minister and the two brothers arrived on their way at the city of Śṛṅgavera. On beholding the river of the gods, Rāma alighted and with much joy made it his obeisance. The minister, Lakṣmaṇa and Sītā saluted it also, and Rāma was as glad as any of them; for the Gaṅgā is the source of all bliss and beatitude, the author of all happiness, the destroyer of every sorrow. Myriads were the stories and legends that Rāma repeated as he gazed upon its flood, instructing his minister, his younger brother, and his bride in the majesty and grandeur of the heavenly stream. They bathed and all the fatigue of the march was removed; they drank of the holy water and their soul was gladdened. It is only in vulgar phrase that fatigue is ascribed to him by whose remembrance all the burdens of weariness are lightened.

1. That die at once when withdrawn from their natural element.

Dohā 87

Rāma, the Banner of the Solar race, is none but untainted Truth, Consciousness and Bliss, the bridge across the ocean of birth and death,[1] though he acts like an ordinary man.

Caupāī 88

When Guha, the Niṣāda, heard the news, he was glad and summoned his friends and relations, and taking a great quantity of fruit and vegetables as a present, went out to meet him with infinite joy of heart. With a profound obeisance he put down his offering before him and gazed upon the Lord with the utmost devotion. Raghuraī with his natural kindliness inquired after his welfare and seated him by his side. "The sight of your lotus feet, divine Lord, is health indeed; I am most highly favoured, as all will admit. My land, my home, my fortune are yours, my Lord; I and mine are your poor vassals. Do me the favour of entering my abode; treat me as one of your servants and I shall be the envy of all men." "All that you say, my good friend, is true; but my father has given me other commands.

Dohā 88

For fourteen years I must dwell in the forest and adopt the rules, the dress, and the food of a hermit; to stay in a village is forbidden." On hearing this, Guha was much grieved.

Caupāī 89

Seeing Rāma, Lakṣmaṇa and Sītā to be so beautiful, the citizens affectionately protested : "What kind of parents can they be, friend, who have banished such mere children to the woods?" Said one : "The king has done well to give our eyes

1. *Saṁsṛti-sāgara-setu* : The 'transmigrations'—*saṁsṛti*—through which the soul has to pass would be endless a limitless ocean (*sāgara*) from which none could escape, were it not that Rāma has given himself to be the bridge, *setu*, over the abyss. *Anuharat* here means simply 'like.' It is almost impossible to translate this and similar phrases at once literally, concisely and intelligibly; for birth and life, which Christians are taught to regard as blessings, are to the Hindu theologian a curse. Compare Milton's—

"... This earthly load
Of death called life, which us from life doth sever."

such a treat." Then the Niṣāda chief on reflection chose a beautiful simśapā[1] tree, and took Raghunātha and showed him the place, and Rāma declared it to be most excellent. The villagers after paying him their respects, returned to their homes, and Rāma proceeded to the performance of his evening devotions. Guha made and spread for him a charming bed of grass and soft fresh leaves, and brought him leaf-made bowls filled with all such fruit and vegetables as he knew to be sweet and wholesome and good.

Dohā 89

After he had partaken of the fruit and herbs with the minister and Sītā and his brother, the jewel of Raghu's line lay down to sleep, while Lakṣmaṇa rubbed his feet.

Caupāī 90

When he knew the Lord to be asleep, he arose and softly bade Sumantra the minister take rest, while he himself fitted an arrow to his bow and took up the position of a marksman at a little distance, there to keep vigil. The affectionate Guha, having summoned trusty sentinels and stationed them round about, went himself and sat down by Lakṣmaṇa, with his quiver at his back and an arrow fitted to his bow. When the Niṣāda saw Rāma asleep, his soul was troubled with excess of love, his body thrilled with emotion, his eyes flowed with tears, and he thus in tender accents addressed Lakṣmaṇa: "The king's palace is altogether beautiful, unrivalled by the dwelling of the Lord of heaven; its charming pavilions, inlaid with precious stones, seem to have been adorned by Love's own hands.

Dohā 90

Soft and luxurious are its beds, clean and superbly wrought, sweet with odorous flowers and perfumes, with jewelled lamps and appliances of every description that offer comfort;

Caupāī 91

With all kinds of coverlets and pillows, and mattresses as soft and white as the froth of milk, where Sītā and Rāma were wont

1. The *siṃśapā* is either the *aśoka*, or the *śiśama* tree.

to repose at night and put to shame with their beauty both Rati and Kāmadeva, who now sleep on a pallet, weary and naked, pitiful to behold. He whom his father and mother, his own family and all the people of the city, his companions and associates, his men-servants and maid-servants, all cherished as tenderly as their own life, is now sleeping on the bare ground; and she whose father is Janaka of world-renowned power; whose father-in-law is Daśaratha, the friend of the King of heaven, and whose spouse is Rāmacandra, is now sleeping on the ground; an adverse fate spares none. Are Sītā and Rāma fit to be exiled to the forest? Well do men say, 'Fate is supreme.'

Dohā 91

A foolish and wicked deed has the daughter of Kekaya done by bringing this trouble on Rāma and Jānakī on their day of rejoicing.

Caupāī 92

She has become the axe at the root of the tree of the Solar race, and through her wickedness she has plunged the whole world in woe." Seeing Rāma and Sītā asleep upon the ground, the Niṣāda became exceedingly sad; but Lakṣmaṇa addressed him in gentle, tender tones that were full of the essence of wisdom, detachment and devotion: "No man is the cause of another's joy or sorrow; all is the fruit of one's own actions, brother. Union and separation, pleasure, good and evil, friendship, enmity and neutrality are snares of delusion. Birth, death, all the world's entanglements, prosperity and adversity, fortune and destiny, earth, home, wealth, city and family, heaven, hell and all human affairs; all that you can see or hear, or imagine in your mind,—all is delusive and unreal.

Dohā 92

In a dream a beggar becomes a king, and the lord of heaven a pauper; but on waking the one is no gainer, nor the other a loser: this is the way in which you should regard this phenomenal world.

Caupāī 93

Reasoning thus, be not angry with anyone, nor vainly attribute blame to any. All are sleepers in a night of delusion and see many kinds of dreams; in this world of darkness they only are awake who detach themselves from unreality, and are absorbed in contemplation of the Supreme; nor can any soul be regarded as aroused from slumber till it has renounced every sensual enjoyment. Then ensues spiritual enlightenment and escape from the errors of delusion, and finally devotion to Rāma. This, my friend, is man's highest spiritual wisdom, to be devoted to Rāma in thought, word and deed. Rāma is God, the totality of good, imperishable, invisible, uncreated, incomparable, void of all change, indivisible, whom the Veda declares that it cannot define.

Dohā 93

In his mercy he has taken human form and performs human actions, out of the love he bears to his votaries and to earth and Brāhmaṇas and cows and gods. On hearing them, the snares of the world are broken asunder.

Caupāī 94

Having thus reflected, friend, give no place to deceits, but fix your affections on Sītā and Rāma's feet." While he was yet speaking of Rāma's virtues, the day dawned and the joy of the world awoke. After performing every purificatory rite, he bathed, the all-pure and wise, and asked for some milk of the banyan, and coiled the hair of his head into a knot, as did also his brother. On seeing this, Sumantra's eyes filled with tears. Sore pained at heart, with doleful face and folded hands he made this humble speech: "The king of Kosala, my lord, thus enjoined me: 'Take a chariot and go with Rāma; let them see the forest and bathe in the Gaṅgā, and then speedily bring them home again, both the brothers, Lakṣmaṇa and Rāma and Sītā too, bring them back, resolving all their doubts and scruples.'

Dohā 94

Thus spoke the king, sire; but woe is me! I will do whatever my lord commands, I swear it." Having supplicated in this manner, Sumantra fell at the Lord's feet and wept like a child.

Caupāī 95

"Have pity, my son, and so act that Avadh be not left a widow." Rāma raised the minister and thus exhorted him: "Father, you know the path of virtue. Śivi, Dadhīci and king Hariścandra, for the sake of their religion, endured countless afflictions. Rantideva[1] and wise king Bali kept their faith through many trials. There is no duty equal to truth, as the Vedas, Āgamas and Purāṇas declare. I have reached this virtue by an easy road: If I abandon it, my disgrace will be published in earth, heaven and hell: and disgrace to a man of honour is pain as grievous as a million deaths. But why say all this to you, father ? I only incur sin by answering you.

Dohā 95

Clasp my father's feet and with folded hands convey my humblest salutations and beg of him not to distress himself in any way on my account.

Caupāī 96

You, again, are equally dear to me as my father, and I implore you, friend, to do everything that will prevent the king from grieving about me." On hearing this conversation between Raghunātha and the minister, the Niṣāda and his kinsfolk were sad and Lakṣmaṇa spoke a little angrily. But Rāma stopped him, knowing it to be altogether out of place, and nervously adjured Sumantra, by the love he bore him, not to repeat his words. Sumantra then proceeded with the king's message: "Sītā is not able to bear the hardships of the desert; you should try and persuade her to return to Avadh, otherwise I shall have no prop or stay left, and must perish as inevitably as a fish out of water.

1. Rantideva, the son of Sanskṛti, was a king famous for his great liberality. He offered so many cattle in sacrifice that their blood formed a river, said to be the Chambal.

Dohā 96

She has a happy home both with her own mother and with her husband's parents, and she can live when she pleases at either, until these troubles are ended.

Caupāī 97

The piteousness of the king's entreaties and the earnestness of his affection are more than I can express." On hearing his father's message, the All-merciful tried in every way to persuade Sītā: "Only return; and the affliction of your parents, your *guru*, and all your friends and relations will be at an end." Replied Vaidehī to her husband's words, "Hear me, my most dear and loving lord; you are full of compassion and perfect wisdom; can a shadow exist apart from its substance? Where is the sunlight without the sun, or the radiance of the moon when the moon is not?" Having uttered this affectionate prayer to her husband, she turned to the minister with these winning words: "You are as much my benefactor as my own father or my father-in-law, and if I answer you, it is the height of impropriety.

Dohā 97

Yet, friend, take it not ill of me if in my grief I withstand you:[1] away from the lotus feet of my lord all my kindred are of little account!

Caupāī 98

I have seen my father's luxury and magnificence and his footstool thronged with the jewelled crowns of kings, yet though his palace be such a blissful abode, I have no pleasure there without my spouse. My lord's father is the sovereign of Kosala, whose glorious influence extends throughout the fourteen spheres, whom the king of heaven would advance to meet him and cede him half his throne; yet though he be so great and Avadh his home, and though the whole of his family be dear to me and my mother-in-law as my own mother, I could not find pleasure in a single thing for a moment, away from the lotus flowers of Rāma's feet. Though the forest road be rough, and the coun-

1. It is unmannerly on the part of a Hindu woman to open her lips before the male elders of her husband.

try mountainous, full of elephants and tigers, boundless lakes and streams, wild Kols and Kirātas, and beasts, and birds; all is delightful, if I be with the lord of my life !

Dohā 98

Fall, then, at the feet of my lord's parents and tell them humbly from me not to grieve on my account, for I am perfectly happy in the woods and content.

Caupāī 99

With the sovereign of my soul and his dear brother, stoutest of champions, bearing bow and quiver, the toilsome wanderings of the march will not trouble me at all; be not then the least anxious about me." On hearing Sītā's chilling refusal, Sumantra was as distressed as a serpent at the loss of its head-jewel. With eyes that saw not and ears that heard not, and unable to utter a word, he was completely confounded. Rāma said everything to console him, but his heart refused to be comforted. Earnestly he begged that he too might accompany him; but Raghunandana returned an appropriate answer to all he urged. "Rāma's commands cannot be withstood; Fate is against me, I can do nothing." Bowing his head before the feet of Rāma, and Lakṣmaṇa and Sītā, he turned away like a merchant who has lost his all.

Dohā 99

The very horses of his chariot, as he drove off, continued whinnying and looking back upon Rāma; and the Niṣāda at the sight gave way to his grief and beat his head and moaned:

Caupāī 100

"When even brute beasts," he cried, "are so distressed at parting, how can his subjects and his father and mother exist without him?" Having thus perforce dismissed Sumantra, Rāma went on his way and came to the bank of the Gaṅgā. When he called for the boat, the ferryman would not bring it saying: "I know your magic power: everyone says that the dust of your lotus feet is a kind of magic charm for making man. A rock on which it fell became a beautiful woman, and wood is no harder than stone! Should my boat in like manner be turned into a sage's wife, the ferry will be closed and the boat lost, which is the support of my whole family. I know no other means of living. If, my lord, you are bent on crossing the river, you must allow me first to wash your lotus feet.

Chand 4

After washing your lotus feet, I will take you on board but I will not accept any toll. I tell you the truth, O Rāma, swearing by yourself and Daśaratha — Lakṣmaṇa may shoot me with his arrows, but I will not take you across, gracious lord of Tulasī Dāsa, until I have bathed your feet!"

Soraṭhā 100

On hearing the ferryman's rude but loving words, the merciful Lord smiled[1] and looked at Jānakī and Laksmana.

Caupāī 101

Then said the Lord of grace with a smile : "Do anything to save your boat, bring water at once and bathe my feet; time has been lost; take me across." The gracious Lord thus made request of a boatman; even he by one thought on whose name mankind is transported across the boundless ocean of existence, and for whose three strides the whole universe did not suffice.[2] The Gangā rejoiced on beholding his toe-nails,[3] and the sound of his words was relieved of all anxiety. On receiving Rāma's commands, the ferryman brought a basin full of water and in an ecstasy of joy and love proceeded to bathe his lotus feet. All the gods rained down flowers and enviously praised him, saying, "Never was any one so meritorious as he !"

1. As much as to say : We thought the Nisāda-king a pattern of piety, but even he is outdone by this rude ferryman.

2. Rāma is here identified with Visnu who in the form of a dwarf outwitted king Bali.

3. From beneath which it had issued at its birth.

Dohā 101

After washing his feet, and drinking of the water, both himself and his family, and thus redeeming the souls of his fathers, he joyfully conveyed the Lord across to the further bank.

Caupāī 102

They disembarked and stood on the sands of the Gaṅgā, Sītā, Rāma, Lakṣmaṇa and Guha. The ferryman, too, got out and made his obeisance. The Lord was ashamed that he had nothing to give him. Sītā knew what was passing in the mind of her beloved and cheerfully drew a jewelled ring from off her finger. Said the All-merciful: "Take your toll." The ferryman in distress clasped his feet. "Lord," he cried, "what have I not already received this day? The fire of my sin and sorrow, poverty and all their attendant ills have been extinguished! I have laboured for a length of years, but today God has given me my wages in full. Now, gracious Lord, I ask for nothing but your favour; at the time of your return, whatever you bestow upon me I will thankfully accept."

Dohā 102

Though Lakṣmaṇa and the Lord both pressed him much, the ferryman would take nothing. The All-merciful then dismissed him with the gift of unclouded faith, best of all boons.

Caupāī 103

Then the lord of Raghu's line bathed and bowed his head in adoration to Mahādeva,[1] while Sītā with folded hands thus addressed the sacred stream : "O mother, accomplish my desire that I may return in safety with my husband and his brother and again adore you." On hearing Sītā's humble and affectionate speech, favourable response came from the holy stream: "Hearken, princess of Videha, beloved of Raghubīra! Who is there in the world who knows not your glory? They who behold

1. The word in the text is *Pārathi*, or in some manuscripts *Pārthiva*, a derivative of *prithi*, 'the earth,' meaning 'a king,' and here—it would seem—denoting Mahādeva.

you become as the sovereigns of the spheres, and all the powers of magic meekly do you service. In the petition that you have deigned to address to me, you have graciously paid me all too high an honour; yet, lady, unworthy as I am, I bestow upon you my blessing, in order to prove my utterances true.

Dohā 103

You shall return in safety to Kosala with your beloved and his brother; your every wish shall be accomplished, and your renown shall be spread throughout the world."

Caupāī 104

On hearing Gaṅgā's gracious speech, Sītā was delighted to find the divine river so propitious. Then the Lord bade Guha return home. At this his face grew pale and his bosom burned, and with folded hands and in suppliant tones he cried, "O jewel of the house of Raghu, hear my prayer. Let me remain with my lord and show him the road and do him service for a day or two, and make a shapely hut of twigs for him in the woods where he goes to stay. After that I swear by Raghubīra to do as he shall command me." Seeing his unfeigned affection, he took him with him, to Guha's delight, who thereupon called all his kinsmen and dismissed them with kind assurances.

Dohā 104

Then with his thoughts on Gaṇeśa and Śiva, and bowing his head to the Gaṅgā, the Lord with his companion and his brother and Sītā set out for the woods.

Caupāī 105

That day he halted under a tree, and Lakṣmaṇa and his attendant supplied all his necessities. At dawn, having performed his morning ablutions he proceeded to visit the king of sanctuaries—a king with Truth for his minister, Faith for his cherished consort, the god Mādhava[1] for his friend and

1. Veṇī-Mādhava is the name of the god worshipped as the tutelary divinity of the Triveṇī, the confluence of the three streams, at Prayāga.

favourite; his treasury stored with the four great rewards of life, and all holy places for his fair dominion; with an impregnable domain and magnificent forts, so strong that no enemy could ever dream of taking them; with an army of shrines of such virtue and power as to rout the whole army of Sin; with the meeting of the rivers for his glorious throne and the deathless banyan tree for his royal umbrella, dazzling even the soul of a sage; with the ripples of the Gaṅgā and the Jamunā for his royal whisks, the very sight of which disperses all sorrow and distress.

Dohā 105

His attendants are pure and holy anchorites, guerdoned with all they desire: his heralds, the Vedas and Purāṇas, to declare his immaculate perfections.

Caupāī 106

Who can describe the glory of Prayāga, a lion to destroy the elephantine monster Sin ? On beholding the beauty of this king of sanctuaries, Raghubara, the ocean of delight, was delighted, and with his holy mouth he discoursed on its greatness to Sītā, his brother and his companion. After making it an obeisance, he visited the woods and groves, dilating on their virtue with the utmost devotion. So he came to the Triveṇī—the mere thought of which confers all happiness—and after gazing upon it, rapturously bathed and paid homage to Śiva and to the divinity of the spot in all due form. Then came the Lord to Bharadvāja, and as he prostrated himself at his feet, the sage took him to his breast in an ecstasy of joy past all telling, as though he had realized the perfect bliss of heaven.

Dohā 106

The chief of sages, Bharadvāja, gave him his blessing with as much joy of heart as though God had set before him in visible form the reward of all his virtues.

Caupāī 107

After enquiring of his welfare, he conducted him to a seat and indulged his affection in doing him honour. Then he brought and presented bulbs and fruit and shoots, all sweet as ambrosia, of which Rāma, with Sītā, Lakṣmaṇa and their attendant, partook with much pleasure and content. Rāma was refreshed and all his fatigue forgotten. Then cried Bharadvāja complacent tones: "To-day my penance, my pilgrimages, and my vigils have been rewarded; my prayers, my meditations any my dispassion have to-day borne fruit; yea, all my pious practices have to-day, Rāma, been rewarded by the sight of you. There is no higher gain, no greater happiness than this; in beholding you my every desire is satisfied. Now of your favour grant me this one boon, a life-long devotion to your lotus feet.

Dohā 107

Until a man becomes wholly yours in thought and word and deed, and without reserve, he cannot even dream of happiness, despite all that he may do."

Caupāī 108

On hearing the sage's words, Rāma was embarrassed, yet revelled with delight in so exquisite a display of faith. Then proceeded he to declare unto them all in countless ways the sage's illustrious renown : "Great indeed and highly endowed is he, Holy Father, whom you are pleased to honour." Thus they bowed to one another, the sage and Raghubīra, and were filled as they conversed with indescribable happiness. When the people of Prayāga heard the news, all the religious students, ascetics, monks, hermits and anchorites flocked to Bharadvāja's hermitage to see the glorious son of Daśaratha. Rāma greeted them all; they all rejoiced that their eyes had been so highly favoured. They blessed him and returned with exceeding joy, extolling his beauty.

Dohā 108

Rāma rested there for the night. At daybreak he bathed at Prayāga, and then, after bowing his head to the sage proceeded joyfully on his way with Sītā, Lakṣmaṇa and his attendant (Guha).

Caupāī 109

Rāma had affectionately asked the sage : "Tell me, my lord, by what road we shall go." The sage replied with a smile : "All ways are easy to you," but called his disciples to go with him. They came with joy, some fifty in number, all in their boundless love for Rāma, declaring that they knew the road. The sage elected four students who in many previous existences had done many good deeds. Then, having bowed to the sage and received his permission to depart, Raghurāī went forth rejoicing. When they passed by the village, the men and women who all flocked to see them found in the sight of their Lord the fruition of their life, and sadly turning home, sent their heart after him.

Dohā 109

Courteously Rāma dismissed the students, who returned with their hearts' desire obtained; then alighted and bathed in the stream of Jamunā, dark as his own body.

Caupāī 110

The dwellers on the bank, when they heard of his arrival, left whatever they were doing and ran to see him. On beholding the beauty of Lakṣmaṇa, Rāma and Sītā, they congratulated themselves on their good fortune, and all with longing heart began diffidently to ask their name and home. The sage elders of the party had wit enough, to recognize Rāma, and related his whole history, and how he had come into the desert by his father's order. At this, they were all sad and complained : 'The king and queen have done ill.'[1] Men and women alike, on beholding the beauty of Rāma, Lakṣmaṇa and Sītā were

1. Here, in some copies is found a whole additional stanza, which is said to exist also in the Rājāpur MS. It may, therefore, have been written by Tulasī Dāsa : but if so, was probably afterwards cancelled by him. The lines contain nothing of any interest, and they fit in very awkwardly with the context. I, therefore, like most of the native editors, prefer to omit them. [Later researches confirm that the passage in question is an interpolation, and that the Rājāpur MS is not in Tulasī's own handwriting, nor does it belong to his period. Since, however, the passage is found in the best MSS, we append here the prose version of it rendered into English : "At that moment there arrived an ascetic, young, handsome and spiritually glowing, of a nature

agitated with love and pity : "What kind of father and mother must they be, friend, who have sent such children into the forest ?"

Dohā 110

Then Raghubīra earnestly exhorted his guide, who in submission to his commands took his way home.

Caupāī 111

Again with folded hands Sītā, Rāma and Lakṣmaṇa made renewed obeisance to the Jamunā, and as they went on their way their talk was all of this daughter of the Sun and her glory. Many travellers met them on the road, and exclaimed, after gazing with affection at the two brothers : "You have all the marks of royalty on your person; on seeing them we are troubled at heart, for you go your way on foot, and the astrologers, methinks, are false. The road is difficult; the mountains and forests are very great; moreover, you have with you a delicate lady. Elephants and tigers make the woods too terrible to behold. With your permission, we will accompany you, will escort you as far as you please, and then make our bow and return."

Dohā 111

As they proffered this request, their body trembled all over with excess of love, and their eyes filled with tears; but the All-merciful gently and courteously dismissed them.

unknown to the poet, attired in the garb of a recluse and devoted to Rāma in thought and word and deed. *Doha*: His eyes were wet with tears, and a thrill ran through his body when he recognized his own adored divinity. He fell prostrate to the ground in a state of ineffable rapture. *Caupāī*: Thrilling all over with emotion, Rāma clasped him to his heart, as though a destitute beggar had found the philosopher's stone; and everyone who saw them said it was as though Love and Truth incarnate were embracing each other. Next, he threw himself at the feet of Lakṣmaṇa, who raised him with a heart overflowing with affection. Then he placed on his head the dust of Sītā's feet, who gave him her blessing as a mother blesses her child. The Niṣāda chief in his turn prostrated himself before the hermit, who gladly embraced him as Rāma's devoted friend. With the cup of his eyes he drank the nectar of Rāma's beauty and was delighted like a hungry man who has found delicious food." The ascetic is said to be either Hanumān or Tulasī Dāsa himself experiencing a mystic vision.]

Caupāī 112

All the towns and villages along the road were the envy of the cities of the serpents and the gods : 'At what an auspicious moment and by what a holy man must they have been founded, to be so happy and blessed and altogether highly favoured !' Whatever spot was trodden by Rāma's feet Paradise was not to be compared to it. The dwellers by the wayside, of high desert, were the praise of the denizens of heaven, as they feasted their eyes on Sītā and Lakṣmaṇa and Rāma dark of hue as a storm-cloud. The ponds and rivers in which Rāma bathed were the envy of the lake and river of heaven; the trees under which the Lord rested were magnified by the tree of Paradise; and earth, touched by the dust of Rāma's lotus feet, deemed her blessedness fulfilled.

Dohā 112

The clouds gave him their shade, the hosts of heaven rained down flowers and regarded him with wistful eyes, as Rāma proceeded on his way looking at the rocks and woods and birds and deer.

Caupāī 113

Whenever Sīta, Lakṣmaṇa and Raghurāī passed by a village on the way, people,— young and old, man and woman—came directly they heard the news, forgetting their own private affairs, and as they gazed on their beauty, obtained the fruition of their eyes and were made happy for ever. At the sight of the two heroes their eyes filled with tears, they felt a thrill of joy, and became all-enraptured, their state of mind as indescribable as though a beggar had discovered a pile of heavenly jewels. Everyone was telling his neighbour : "Now is the time to prove the value of sight." One in his delight to see Rāma would go with him, gazing as he went; another, drawing his beautiful image into his heart by the pathway of his eyes, was utterly overpowered in body, soul and speech.

Dohā 113

One, seeing a fine shady banyan, would spread under it soft grass and leaves and cry: "Rest a little after your fatigue, and proceed again either a little later or at daybreak."

Caupāī 114

Another brought a jar full of water and tenderly besought him, "Drink, my lord !" On hearing their affectionate speech and seeing their great devotion, the compassionate and most amiable Rāma, who, moreover, perceived that Sītā was wearied, rested for a while in the shade of the fig-tree. All were enraptured with his beauty—men and women alike—and their soul was enamoured of hi incomparable loveliness. LIke a circle of partridges gazing on the moon, they fixed their rapt and blissful gaze on Rāma's face. At the sight of his body, dark in hue as a young *tamāla* tree, a myriad Loves were fascinated; while Lakṣmaṇa, all comely from head to foot, charmed the soul with his fair limbs, bright as the lightning; in his anchorite's dress, with his tightly-fitted quiver and bow, and arrows gleaming in his lotus hand.

Dohā 114

With their hair done up in a knot as a crown upon their graceful heads, with broad chest, strong arms, and large deep eyes, with face like the autumnal full moon, glistening with beads of moisture,

Caupāī 115

The loveliness of the two brothers is past all telling; for it is boundless and my wit is scant. With every faculty of mind and soul, they all gaze upon the beauteous trio; man and woman thirsting and faint with love, like deer dazed by a light. The village women drew near Sītā with tender and bashful enquiries, and again embracing her feet, in their simplicity whispered the question : "Noble lady, we have a petition, but like women, are afraid to make it. Pardon our rude manners, madam, and be not offended by our country manners. These two charming young princes, from whom emerald and gold might borrow splendour,

Dohā 115

The one dark, the other fair, but both handsome and homes of delight, with face like the autumn moon, and eyes like the lotuses of autumn,

Caupāī 116

That would put to shame a myriad Loves, say, fair lady, how stand they to you." On hearing their pleasant and loving speech, Sītā smiled to herself in modest confusion, and looking first at them and then at the earth was abashed — the pretty maid — with a double abashment. But drooping her fawn-like eyes, and with a voice sweet as the cuckoo's she lovingly replied: "The fair youth, so easy and graceful, is by name Lakṣmaṇa my younger brother-in-law; while he, the dark complexioned, with the large eyes and arms, the all-beautiful with the gentle voice :" here veiling her moon-like face with the border of her robe she looked towards her husband with knitted eyebrows, and with a side-long glance like a pretty *khanjana*,[1] by signs indicated to them her lord. All the village women were as delighted as beggars who have robbed a pile of jewels.

Dohā 116

Falling at Sītā's feet with the utmost devotion, they showered upon her every blessing: "May your happy wedded life last as long as Earth rests on the serpent's head.

Caupāī 117

May you be as dear to your lord as Pārvatī to Śiva. Yet, lady, cease not to have some regard for us: again and again with folded hands we beseech you, if you return by this road, remember us your servants, and allow us to see you." Finding them all so athirst for love, Sītā comforted them with many a soothing word, as the lily is cheered by the moonlight. Then Lakaṣmaṇa, perceiving Raghubīra's wish, gently asked the people the way. At his words they became sad, their limbs trembled, their eyes filled with tears, their joy was extinguished, and they were troubled at heart: "God has given us a treasure only to take it away again !" Then reflecting on the ways of Fate and taking courage, they fixed upon the easiest road and explained it to them.

Dohā 117

Raghunātha went on his way to the woods with Lakṣmaṇa and Jānakī, sending them off with many fond speeches, but taking their hearts with him.

Caupāī 118

Men and women alike on their way back lamented exceedingly and imputed blame to Fate, saying sadly to one another:

1. The *khanjana* is a species of wagtail.

"God's doings are all perverse. He is utterly uncontrollable, cruel and remorseless; who has made the moon sickly and spotted, the tree of paradise a lifeless block, and the ocean all salt, and who now has sent these princely boys into the wilderness. If the woods are their proper abode, then for whom has he intended ease and pleasure? If they are to wander on their way barefooted, it is to no purpose that he has invented so many kinds of carriages. If they are to lie on the ground littered only with grass and leaves, for whom has God created comfortable beds ? If he makes them live in the shade of spreading trees, why has he taken such pains to erect splendid palaces?

Dohā 118

If such lovely and delicate children wear the rough dress and matted locks of hermits, it is to no purpose that the great Artificer has made so many kinds of dress and ornament.

Caupāī 119

If they are to eat only bulbs and roots and fruit, all such delicacies of the world as ambrosia are thrown away." Said one: "They are so beautiful, they must have been spontaneously produced and not made by God at all. In all the works of God of which the Vedas speak, that either the ears can hear, or the eyes see, or the mind imagine, or the tongue tell—search and examine the whole fourteen spheres—where is there such a man, and where such a woman? When he saw them, God was so pleased that he essayed to make their match: but after much labour, nothing came of it, and thus in spite he has sent and buried them in the woods." Said another: "I am no great scholar, but I account myself supremely blessed; nay, blessed are all, in my opinion, who see them now, or have seen them, or shall see them hereafter."

Dohā 119

With such loving words their eyes filled with tears: "How can they, who are so delicate, traverse so difficult a road."

Caupāī 120

All the women were made as uneasy by their love as is the *cakavī* at evening time. As they thought upon their tender lotus feet and the hardness of the road, they were distrest at heart and cried in plaintive tones: "At the touch of their soft and rosy feet, the very earth shrinks, as shrinks our heart. If the lord of the world must send them to the woods, why did he not strew their path with flowers ? If there be one boon that we may ask of Heaven and obtain, let it be, friend, that we keep them ever in our eyes." Those people who had not come in time, and thus had missed seeing Sītā and Rāma, when they heard of their great beauty, anxiously inquired, "How far, brother, will they have travelled by this time?" They who were strong ran on and saw them, and returned with joy, having obtained the fruition of their eyes.

Dohā 120

The frail women, the children and the aged wrung their hands and lamented. In this manner, wherever Rāma went, people were smitten with love.

Caupāī 121

In every village was similar rejoicing at the sight of the moon of the lilylike Solar race. Some who had learnt by hearsay of what had been going on imputed blame to the king and queen. One said : "It was very good of the king to give our eyes such a treat." Said others among themselves in simple and loving phrase : "Blessed the father and mother who gave them birth and happy the city from whence they came ! Blessed the hill and plains, and woods, and towns, and every spot which they visit ! Even the Creator who made them is pleased — nay, is absolutely in love with them." The delightful story of Rāma, Lakṣmaṇa and Sītā thus spread over every road and forest.

Dohā 121

Thus the sun of the lotus-like Solar race gladdened the people on his way, as with Sītā and the son of Sumitrā he proceeded on his travels through the woods.

Caupāī 50

Rāma walked in front and Lakṣmaṇa behind, conspicuous in the hermit's dress they wore; and between the two Sītā shone resplendent as Illusion between the Absolute and the Jīva (i.e., the Individual Soul). Or, to describe her beauty by another fancy, she seemed like Rati between Spring and Kāmadeva; or, to ransack my mind for yet another simile, like the constellation Rohiṇī[1] between Budha and the Moon. As she went along the way, Sītā carefully planted her feet between the footprints of her lord; while Lakṣmaṇa, avoiding the footprints of them both, set his feet as he went to their right and left. The charming affection of all three was beyond all telling; how can I declare it? Birds and deer were fascinated at the sight of their beauty, and Rāma the wayfarer stole their heart.

Dohā 122

All those who beheld the dear travellers, Sīta and the two brothers, blissfully and without fatigue arrived at once at the end of the toilsome journey of life.

Caupāī 123

And to this day any soul in which the vision of the wayfarers, Rāma, Sītā and Lakṣmaṇa abides, finds the path that leads to Rāma's home, path that scarce a sage may find. Then Raghubīra, perceiving that Sītā was tired, and observing a fig-tree close at hand and cool water, there rested and took some roots and fruit to eat, and after bathing at dawn again went on his way. Admiring the beauty of the woods and lakes and rocks, the Lord arrived at Vālmīki's hermitage. He found the sage's retreat a charming spot, a lovely wooded hill with a spring of clear water, lotuses in the pond, the forest trees all in flower, with a delightful murmuring of bees drunk with sweets, and a joyous clamour of birds and beasts feeding happily and in peace together.

Dohā 123

The Lotus-eyed was glad when he beheld the bright and fair hermitage, and the sage on hearing of his arrival came forth to meet him.

1. Rohiṇī is the ninth lunar asterism personified as the daughter of Dakṣa and the fovourite wife of the Moon. Budha is the planet Mercury, their son.

Caupāī 124

Rāma prostrated himself before him, as the holy man gave him his blessing. At the sight of Rāma's beauty, his eyes were gladdened and he conducted him with all honour to his hermitage; there he gave him a choice seat as a guest dear to him as his own life, and sent for sweet roots and bulbs and fruit, of which Sītā, Lakṣmaṇa and Rāma ate. Great was the joy of Vālmīki's soul as his eyes beheld the impeccable image of bliss. Then, folding his lotus hands, Rāma thus spoke in words to charm the hermit's ears: "O king of sages, all time, past, present and future, is in your ken, and the universe is like a little plum in the palm of your hand." So saying, the Lord related to him the whole history and how the queen had banished him.

Dohā 124

"My father's promise, my mother's favour, my brother Bharata's coronation, and my own meeting with you, my lord, are all blessings that only past merit can have won for me.

Caupāī 125

In beholding your feet, O holy sir, all my good deeds are rewarded. Now, wherever it may be your order, and no anchorite be troubled — for those monarchs burn, even though there be no fire, who vex either saint or ascetic: the satisfaction of a Brāhmaṇa is the root of all happiness, while his wrath consumes a thousand generations — tell me then some place to which I can go with Sītā and Sumitrā's son, and there build a pretty hut of grass and twigs and rest awhile, kind sir." On hearing his ingenious speech, the wise seer exclaimed, "True, true! It is only natural for you so to speak, O Banner of the house of Raghu, eternal custodian of the laws laid down by the Vedas.

Chand 5

Custodian of the laws laid down by the Vedas, you, O Rāma, are the Lord of the universe, and Jānakī is Māyā,[1] who at your

1. *i.e.*, Illusion.

gracious will creates, preserves, or destroys the world. And Lakṣmaṇa is the thousand-headed Serpent King, the supporter of the world with all that it contains, living or lifeless, who on behalf of the gods has taken a kingly form and goes forth to rout the demon host.

Soraṭhā 125

Your true form, O Rāma, transcends speech and is beyond conception, all-pervading, unutterable, illimitable, undefinable even by the Scriptures.

Caupāī 126

You look on at the drama of life, and Brahmā, Hari and Śambhu are your puppets. Even they comprehend not your mysteries; who else, then, could discover you as you are ? Only he knows you to whom you have vouchsafed knowledge; and he who knows you becomes one with you. It is by your grace, O Raghunandana, that your votaries learn to know you, soothing sandal-wood of the devout soul. Your body is pure intelligence and bliss, immutable, as they know who have found you. On behalf of the saints and the gods you have taken a human body and speak and act like an ordinary king. Fools are bewildered, but the wise rejoice, as they see or hear of your doings; whatever you say or do is true, and we can only play such parts as you set us.

Dohā 126

You ask me, 'Where can I stay?' but with diffidence I ask you to tell me where you are not; then will I assign you a place."

Caupāī 127

On hearing the sage's affectionate words, Rāma was embarrassed and smiled to himself. Vālmīki, too spoke gaily in tones of honeyed sweetness : "Hearken, Rāma; I will now tell you the places where you and Sītā and Lakṣmaṇa should abide. They whose ears are like the ocean to catch the blessed streams of your traditions, and though ever replenished are never filled to the full, their heart shall be your chosen abode. They whose eyes long for your presence, as passionately as the cuckoo's for the rain-cloud, and scorning the water of river, lake or sea, quench their thirst only in your beauty, their hearts are your glorious mansion; there abide, O Raghunāyaka, with Lakṣmaṇa and Sītā.

Dohā 127

He whose tongue, like the swan in the clear hyperboreal lake of your renown, gathers up the pearls of your perfections — in his heart fix your home, O Rāma.

Caupāī 128

They who ever reverently inhale the sweet and blessed odour of the offerings to their lord; who feed upon what has been offered to you; who wear raiment and adornments first consecrated to the Lord who bow their heads when they see a god, a *guru*, or a Brāhmaṇa, and treat them with all honour and affection; whose hands are ever engaged in worshipping Rāma's feet; who have no other hope but Rāma in their heart; and whose feet ever bear them to his shrines; be their soul, Rāma, your dwelling-place. They who are ever repeating your holy name, and adoring you with their family; who perform the varied rites of oblation and sacrifice; who feast the Brāhmaṇas, and give them liberal donations; who regard their own *guru* as greater even than yourself, and serve and honour him in every way;

Dohā 128

Who ask of all but one boon, devotion to the feet of Rāma—be their hearts your temple wherein to abide, O Sītā and Raghunandana!

Caupāī 129

Who so is unmoved by lust, anger, pride or arrogance, and is without covetousness, excitement, partiality or malice without fraud, hypocrisy or heretical delusion; dwell in his heart, O Raghurāya. They who are all men's friends, and are friendly to all; to whom pleasure and pain, praise and abuse are alike; who are careful to speak what is both true and kind; who, whether sleeping or waking, place themselves under your protection and have no other way of salvation but you; in their hearts abide, O Rāma. They who look upon another man's wife as their own mother, and another man's wealth as more poisonous than poison, who rejoice to see a neighbour's prosperity and are sore distressed at his misfortune; and to whom you, O Rāma, are dear as their own life; be their hearts your auspicious abode.

Dohā 129

To whom, dear Lord, you are at once master and companion, father, mother and spiritual guide; be their heart your temple, ye brothers twain, wherein with Sītā to abide.

Caupāī 130

They who pick out all men's good points and leave their bad; who endure troubles on behalf of Brāhmaṇas and kine; and who are of note in the world for soundness of doctrine; in their heart be your chosen home. They who understand your righteousness and their own sinfulness and fix all their hopes on you, and have an affection for all your worshippers; in their heart dwell, you and Sītā. He who has abandoned caste and brotherhood, wealth, hereditary religion, worldly advancement, friend, relations, home and all, and given himself wholly to you—in his heart take up your abode, Raghurāī. To whom heaven and hell and release from transmigration are all alike, if only they can behold you bearing bow and arrows; and who in heart, word and deed are your faithful slaves—be their heart, Rāma, your tabernacle.

Dohā 130

They who never ask for anything but simply love you; in their heart abide for ever, for that is your very home !"

Caupāī 131

Such were the dwelling-places, the high sage indicated, and his loving speech pleased Rāma's soul. The sage continued : "Hearken, lord of the Solar race ! I will tell you a hermitage suitable for your present wants. Take up your abode on the hill of Citrakūṭa;[1] there you will have every comfort. It is a beautiful hill finely wooded, the haunt of elephants, tigers, deer and birds. It has a sacred river mentioned in the Purāṇas, which the wife of Atri brought there by the power of her penance.[2] It is called the Mandākinī, and is a tributary of the Gaṅgā, as quick to drown all sins as a witch to strangle children. Atri and other sages live there, engaged in meditation and prayer and wasting their body with penance. Go and bless their labours, O Rāma, and confer dignity on the mountain."

Dohā 131

All the glories of Citrakūṭa did the great sage tell and declare. The two brothers and Sītā proceeded to bathe in the sacred stream.

1. The sacred hill of Citrakūṭa is one of a small group that forms the last spur of the great Vindhya range. It is situated in the modern district of Bāndā, close to the town of Karwi and about 100 km. from Prayāga (Allahabad). A river flows at its base, now called the Paisunī (the Sanskrit Payoṣṇī, 'warm as milk'), which has some fine waterfalls before it joins the Jamunā. The Mandākinī, so frequently mentioned, is only a small tributary stream which enters the Paisunī near the village of Sītāpur, where are a number of handsome temples. The hill is about three miles in circumference, and a narrow paved path runs the whole way round. This was constructed about 150 years ago by one of the Rājās of the neighbouring state of Panna for the convenience of pilgrims performing the ceremony of circumambulation. The two principal fete days are the Rāmanavamī (Rāma's birthday) in the month of Chaitra, and the Dīwālī in Kārtika. About 32 km. from Chitrakūṭa on the bank of the Jamunā is the town of Rājapur, which was founded by Tulasī Dāsa, where he lived for several years, and where a manuscript of the Rāmāyaṇa allegedly in his own handwriting is still preserved. He imposed some curious restrictions upon the inhabitants of the place, which are still to this day religiously observed. No private houses, however wealthy the owner may be, are allowed to be built of any material but mud and wood, stone being reserved exclusively for the temples : and no barber, potter or dancing girl may live within the limits of the town; when their services are required, they have to be called in from some other village.

2. Anasūyā, the wife of Atri, was one of Dakṣa's 24 daughters. She practised severe penance for ten thousand years, and by virtue of the religious merit that she had thus acquired, she created the river Mandākinī, and by its waters maintained the fertility of the country through a ten years' drought.

Caupāī 132

Said Raghubara, "It is a lovely spot, Lakṣmaṇa; now make arrangements for our stopping somewhere here." Lakṣmaṇa then spied out the north bank and said, "A ravine bends round it like a bow, with the river for its string, asceticism and charity for its arrows, and all the sins of this evil age for its quarry, while Mount Citrakūṭa, is the huntsman of unerring aim striking at close quarters." So saying, Lakṣmaṇa showed the spot; when he had seen it, Raghupati was pleased. The gods perceived that Rāma was well content, and came with Indra at their head. In the garb of Kols and Kirātas they came and put up neat huts of leaves and grass, two of them; both prettier than words can tell, the one of larger size, the other a nice little cottage.

Dohā 132

In that lovely abode the Lord, attended by Lakṣmaṇa and Jānakī, shone forth as beautiful as Love in the dress of a hermit between Ratī[1] and Spring.

Caupāī 133

Then flocked to Citrakūṭa the immortal gods and serpents, Kinnaras and guardians of the quarters. To all the immortals Rāma did obeisance and they all gazed with joy on that most longed-for vision. Showering down flowers and exclaiming, "At length, O Lord, we have found our lord," the heavenly host in piteous wise declared their unutterable distress, and joyfully started for their several homes. As soon as they heard the news of Raghunandana's stay at Citrakūṭa, the saints sallied forth; seeing the holy company drawn near, Rāma prostrated himself before them: but they all took him to their bosom, and invoked upon him blessings,[2] knowing that they would be accomplished. As they beheld the beauty of Rāma and Sītā and Sumitrā's son, they accounted all their pious deeds to have been well rewarded.

1 Ratī is the Indian Venus.

2. Their blessing could do Rāma no good, but its fulfilment would redound to their own credit, as showing them to be true prophets.

Dohā 133

After all due honours paid, the Lord dismissed the saintly throng to practise contemplation, prayer, sacrifice and penance at pleasure in their own retreats.

Caupāī 134

When the Kols and Kirātas got the tidings, they were as glad as if the Nine Treasures[1] had come to their homes. With leaf platters full of herbs, roots and fruit, they ran like beggars scrambling for gold. Those among them who had already seen the two brothers were questioned about them by the others on the road. Telling and hearing Rāma's perfections, all came and saw him. Laying their offerings before him with profound obeisance, their love increased exceedingly as they gazed upon their Lord. Motionless as painted figures, they stood about any how, their body thrilling with emotion and their eyes filled with tears. Rāma, perceiving that they were overwhelmed with affection, spoke to them words of kindness and received them with honour. Again and again they did obeisance to the Lord, they addressed him in humble strain with folded hands :

Dohā 134

"Now, O Lord, that we have seen your feet, we have all found a protector. O king of Kosala, what a blessing for us is your arrival!

Caupāī 135

Happy that land and forest and road and hill, where thou, my lord, hast planted thy foot; happy the birds and deer and beasts of the forest, whose life has been crowned by thy sight;

1. The nine *Nidhis* or heavenly treasures of Kuvera, the god of wealth, are thus enumerated : the Padma, Mahā-padma, Saṅkha, Makara, Machchhapa, Makunda, Nila, Nanda, and Kharba; but their nature is not exactly defined, though some of them appear to be precious gems. According to the Tāntrika system they are personified and worshipped as demi-gods, attendant either upon Kuvera, who is sometimes called *Nidhīnam Adhipaḥ*, 'lord of the Nidhis,' or upon Lakṣmī, the goddess of prosperity.—*Williams*.

happy we and all our kin, who have filled our eyes with thy vision. Thou hast chosen an excellent spot to dwell in; here in all seasons of the year thou wilt live at ease. We will do thee service in every way, by driving away elephants, lions, snakes and tigers. The thickets, ravines, mountains, chasms and caves have all, my lord, been explored by us foot by foot; we will take you out to the different haunts of game, and point out to you the lakes and waterfalls and every other place. We and all our kinsfolk are thy servants; hesitate not to command us."

Dohā 135

The Lord, whom the Vedas cannot define nor the sages comprehend, in his infinite compassion listened to the words of the Kirātas, as a father to the voice of a child.

Caupāī 136

It is only love that Rāma loves; understand this, ye who are men of understanding. He charmed all the foresters by his tender loving[1] speeches. Having taken leave and bowed their heads, they set forth, and discoursing on the way of their Lord's perfections they reached their homes. In this fashion the two brothers and Sītā dwelt in the forest, delighting gods and sages. From the time that Raghunāyaka took up his abode there, the forest became bounteous in blessing; every kind of tree blossomed and bore fruit; luxuriant creepers formed pleasant and beautiful canopies; as though the tree of Paradise in all its native gracefulness had abandoned the groves of heaven. Swarms of bees made a grateful murmuring, while breezes, soft, cool and fragrant, blew refreshingly.

Dohā 136

Blue jays, koels, parrots, cuckoos, *cakavas*, partridges and birds of every description charmed the ear and ravished the soul with their varied notes.

1. *Paripoṣa*, 'abounding with,' 'fraught with,' is for the Sanskrit *paripuṣṭa*.

Caupāī 137

Elephants, lions, monkeys, boars and deer forgot their animosity and sported together. Enraptured above all were the herds of deer who beheld the beauty of Rāma as he tracked the chase. All the forests of the gods that there are in the world were envious at the sight of the forest where Rāma dwelt. The Gaṅgā, the Sarasvatī, the sunborn Jamunā, the Narmadā, daughter of Mount Mekala, and the sacred Godāvarī, every river, stream and torrent discoursed of the Mandākinī. The mountains of the rising and the setting sun, Kailāsa, Mandara, Meru, home of all the gods, the crags of Himālaya, and all the hills there be, sang the glory of Citrakūṭa. The delight of the gods was more than their soul could contain, to think it had won such renown without an effort.

Dohā 137

"Of highest merit and blessed indeed are all the birds, deer, creepers, trees and grasses of Citrakūṭa!" so cried the gods day and night.

Caupāī 138

All creatures that had eyes, who looked on Rāma, felt with delight that now they had lived to some purpose. Things without life, touched by the dust of his feet, were gladdened by promotion to the highest sphere. The woods and rocks, all charming in themselves, were so blissful, so entirely the holiest of the holy, that how can I declare their glory, when they became the abode of the infinitely blessed, and when leaving the Milky Ocean[1] and deserting Avadh, Sītā, Rāma, and Lakṣmaṇa came there to dwell? The delights of the forest would be past telling even by a hundred thousand Śeṣanāgas. How then can I describe them, any more than a common hole tortoise could uplift Mount Mandara?" In every thought, word and act Lakṣmaṇa does him service, with an amiability and devotion more than can be told.

Dohā 138

For ever gazing on the feet of Sītā and Rāma and conscious of

1. Here Sītā, Rāma, and Lakṣmaṇa are all three regarded as incarnations of Viṣṇu, whose eternal home is the Milky Ocean.

their love for him, not even in his sleep did Lakṣmaṇa dream of absent kindred, or father or mother, or home.

Caupāī 139

In Rāma's company Sītā lived so happy that she lost all memory of the city, family and home. Ever watching the moon-like face of her beloved, she was as enraptured as the partridge (at night) looking on the moon, and seeing her lord's affection increase from day to day, she was as happy as the *cakavā* in the daytime. Her heart was so enamoured of him that the forest was a thousand times as dear to her as Avadh; dear was the cottage with her love's society, dear were the fawns and birds, now her only attendants: like her husband's father and mother were the hermits and their wives, and sweet as ambrosia the wild fruits and roots. Shared with her lord, a litter of leaves[1] was a hundredfold more delightful than Cupid's own couch. How can the delights of luxury beguile him, the mere sight of whom confers the sovereignty of the spheres?

Dohā 139

Remembering Rāma, the faithful discard as no more worth than a blade of grass all the pleasures of sense; no wonder then that Sītā, Rāma's own beloved, the mother of the world, should do so.

Caupāī 140

Anything that would please Sītā and Lakṣmaṇa, that would Raghunātha do, exactly as they suggested. He would recite legends and tales of ancient times, in the hearing of which Lakṣmaṇa and Sītā took great delight. If ever he made mention of Avadh, his eyes filled with tears; as he called to mind his father and mother, his family and his brother, with all Bharata's affection and amiable attention, the compassionate Lord grew most sad, but restrained himself knowing that the time was out of joint. At the sight Sītā and Lakṣmaṇa also became distressed, like the shadow that follows a man. When Raghunandana noticed the emotion of his dear spouse and brother, being self-restrained and tender and as soothing to his votaries as sandal-wood when appli-

1. *Sāthari* is for the Sanskrit *Sastara*, 'made by strewing', a bed of leaves.

ed to the breast, he would begin to relate some sacred tale to divert them.

Dohā 140

Rāma and Lakṣmaṇa with Sītā in their leafy hut were as resplendent as Indra in Amarāvatī with his spouse Śacī and their son Jayanta.

Caupāī 141

The Lord was as watchful over Sītā and his younger brother as the eyelids over the pupil of the eye; while Lakṣmaṇa looked after Sītā and Raghubīra as zealously as ignorant fools tend their own bodies. Thus happily the Lord lived in the forest, a friend of birds and beasts and gods and pious ascetics. I have now told the story of Rāma's exile to the woods; hear how Sumantra reached Avadh. The Niṣāda returned after escorting his Lord, and came in sight of the minister and the chariot. No words can tell the distress with which he found the minister to be agonized. Crying out "Rāma, Rāma, Sītā, Lakṣmaṇa" he had fallen to the ground utterly overpowered, while the horses kept on looking to the south[1] and neighing as piteously as a bird that has lost its wings.

Dohā 141

They would neither eat grass nor drink water, but only shed floods of tears. At the sight of Rāma's horses all the Niṣādas were deeply grieved.

Caupāī 142

At length summoning up courage the Niṣāda said, "now, Sumantra, cease mourning; you are a learned man and a philosopher, submit patiently to adverse fortune." With such kindly expostulations he made him mount the chariot, whether he would or no; but he was so faint with grief that he could not drive, his heart ached so grievously for Rāma's loss. The horses reared and bucked and would not go; you would think they were wild deer put in harness, jibbing, lying down and turning to look behind

1. Hoping, as Rāma had gone to the south, to get the first glimpse of him coming back again from that direction.

them, being overcome by sore pain for Rāma's loss. If anyone mentioned the name of Rāma, Lakṣmaṇa or Sītā the horses would at once neigh and look at him. The way in which they declared their grief is indescribable like a snake that has lost its head-jewel.

Dohā 142

The sight of the minister and the horses made the Niṣāda unutterably sad. He told off four trusty grooms and with them a charioteer.

Caupā 143

After seeing off the charioteer, Guha returned, more disconsolate at the parting than words can tell. The Niṣādas drove off to Avadh, sunk every moment in deeper distress, Sumantra, tortured by regrets, a prey to woe, cried: "A curse for life without Rughubīra ! This vile body must perish at last; it lost all glory when bereft of Raghubīra and became a sink of infamy and crime: why does it not take its departure ? Ah ! fool that it is, it missed its opportunity, seeing that today my heart has not broken in twain." Wringing his hands and beating his head in remorse, he went his way like a miser robbed of his hoard of wealth, or like a warrior of high renown, some famous champion, who has had to flee from the battle-field.

Dohā 143

The minister's remorse was like that of some learned Brāhmaṇa well-read in the Vedas, a man of good repute, of integrity and birth, who has been entrapped into drinking.

Caupāī 144

Or like some well-born, virtuous and discreet lady, who is entirely devoted to her lord, but whom Fate has forced to desert him; such was the cruel torture that racked the minister's heart. His eyes were so full of tears that he could scarcely see; his ears could hardly hear; his senses were all confused; his lips were parched; his mouth was dry; the breath of life was only restrained by the bar of Rāma's promise to return; all the colour had gone from his face and he looked like one who had murdered his father and mother. His soul was so possessed with the greatness of his loss and his remorse that he might be some grievous sinner trembling as he treads the road to hell. Words would not come, but to himself he moanned: "How can I look Avadh in the face; when they see the chariot and no Rāma in it, they will shrink from looking at my face.

Dohā 144

When the agitated citizens run to question me and I have to answer them, my heart will be cleft asunder as by a thunderbolt.

Caupāī 145

When the piteous queen-mothers ask of me, O God! what shall I say to them? When Lakṣmaṇa's mother questions me, what good news shall I tell her? When Rāma's mother comes running, like a cow mindful of its now weaned calf, and questions me, I can only answer, 'Rāma, Lakṣmaṇa and Sītā have gone to the forest!' Whoever asks, I must answer so: this is the treat I shall have at Avadh. When the sorrowful king, whose life hangs upon Rāma, questions me, with what face shall I answer him, 'I have seen the princes safe to their journey's end and have come back.' When the king hears these tidings of Lakṣmaṇa, Sītā and Rāma, he will abandon his body as not worth a straw.

Dohā 145

My heart bereft of its beloved is like clay drained of moisture, but it cracks not: now I know how capable of torture is this body that God has given *me*."

Caupāī 146

Thus bemoaning himself as he went, he quickly arrived in his chariot at the bank of Tamasā. There he courteously dismissed the Niṣādas, who after falling at his feet turned sorrowfully away. The minister was as downcast on entering the city as one who had slain his own spiritual guide or a Brāhmaṇa, or a cow. He passed the day sitting under a tree, and at eventide took the opportunity to enter Avadh in the dark. He slunk into his house, leaving the chariot at the gate. All who heard the tidings came to the king's door to see the chariot, and having recognized it and observed the distress of the horses, their body melted away like hail in the sun. All the citizens were as woebegone as fish when the water sinks low.

Dohā 146

When they heard of the minister's arrival, all the ladies of the gynaeceum were agitated. The palace struck him with as much dread as a haunted chamber.

Caupāī 147

All the queens questioned him in deep agony; no answer came, his voice was all broken. With no ears to hear, nor eyes to see, he could only ask every one he met, 'Tell me where is the king.' Seeing his confusion, the handmaidens conducted him to Kausalyā's chamber. On entering, Sumantra found the king looking like a moon bereft of its lustre when all its lustre has waned. Fasting, sleepless, stript of every adornment, he lay on the ground in utter wretchedness, sighing as piteously as Yayāti[1] when he fell from heaven, his heart every moment bursting with grief, like Saṁpātī[2] falling with singed wings, fondly crying, Rāma, Rāma, Rāma', and again, 'Rāma, Lakṣmaṇa, Sītā.'

Dohā 147

The minister on seeing him cried, 'Long live the king!' and fell prostrate to the ground. At the sound of his voice the king started up hurriedly and exclaimed, 'O Sumantra, where is Rāma?'

Caupāī 148

The king clasped Sumantra to his bosom, as if a drowning man has caught hold of some support. He seated him affection-

1. Yayāti as a reward for his many sacrifices was exalted to heaven. There Indra met him, ceremoniously conducted him to the throne, and then craftily drew him out to speak of all the meritorious acts he had done. The more he boasted, the more his virtue evaporated till at last he was left without any merit at all. The gods then turned him out of heaven and Indra was able to resume the vacant throne.

2. *See* Caupāī 27 of Kiṣkindhā

ately by his side, and with his eyes full of tears asked : "Tell me, kind friend, of Rāma's welfare : where are Raghunātha, Lakṣmaṇa and Sītā ? Have you brought them back, or have they sought the forest?" At these words tears rushed to the minister's eyes. Overpowered by anxiety, the king asked again : "Give me tidings of Sītā, Rāma and Lakṣmaṇa." Calling to mind Rāma's beauty and amiability, he sorrowed yet more : "I promised him the kingdom and then imposed exile; he obeyed with soul unmoved either by joy or sorrow. Bereft of such a son I yet can live : who so guilty a monster as I ?

Dohā 148

Take me, my friend, to the place where Rāma, Sītā and Lakṣmaṇa may be. If not, I tell you the very truth, my soul will take flight at once."

Caupāī 149

Again and again the king implored him, "Friend, tell me of my most beloved sons. Hearken, comrade, contrive some means for speedily showing me Rāma, Lakṣmaṇa and Sītā." Summoning up courage, the minister gently replied, "Sire, your majesty is a scholar and philosopher, a model of courage and endurance, and a constant attendant of holy assemblies. Life and death; pleasure, pain and all enjoyments; loss and gain; the society of friends and their bereavement; all, sir, are governed by time and fate as unalterably as the sequence of night and day. Fools triumph in prosperity, and are downcast in adversity; wise men account both alike. Consider the matter wisely and take courage; the good of all depends upon you; cease vain regrets.

Dohā 149

Their first halt was by the Tamasā; their second on the bank of the Gaṅgā, where the two heroes and Sītā bathed and stayed to drink of its water.

Caupāī 150

The boatmen showed them great courtesy and they passed the night at Sṛṅgavera. At daybreak Rāma called for the milk of the fig-tree and fastened up the hair of his head into a crown-like top-knot. Then Rāma's friend called for a boat, and after putting his beloved on board, Rāma himself followed, and after him by his Lord's permission, Lakṣmaṇa too went on board equipped with bow and arrows. Seeing my distress, Raghubīra restrained his emotion and addressed me thus kindly: 'Friend, give my salutation to my father, and again and again embrace his lotus feet. There at his feet entreat him with all humility, saying, Father, mourn not for me; my banishment to the forest is pleasant and profitable to myself, and on your part is a grace, a favour, and a meritorious deed.

Chand 6

By your favour, father, I go to the forest, there to enjoy every comfort. After fulfilling your command, I shall return again in safety to behold your feet.' Next, falling at the feet of each of the queen-mothers, console and implore them to make every effort that Kosala's king may live happy.

Soraṭhā 150

Again and again clasping the lotus feet of my spiritual instructor, give him this message: 'So exhort the king that he may cease to grieve on my account.'

Caupāī 151

Beseeching all the citizens and the poeple of the household, make known to them, friend, this my petition : 'He is my best friend who ensures the king's happiness.' Say to Bharata, too, when he comes, 'Now that you have obtained the royal dignity, forget not sound polity. Cherish your subjects in word, thought and deed, and be obedient to all the queen-mothers without partiality. Fulfil your duty, brother, as a brother, and in dutifulness to father, mother and kindred, and take such care of the king, sir, that he may never grieve for me.' Lakṣmaṇa gave vent to some angry words, but Rāma checked him, and begged of me again and again, adjuring me by himself, not to mention his childishness.

Dohā 151

Sītā sent her greetings, and would have said more, but was unable; her voice faltered, her eyes filled with tears, and her body quivered with emotion.

Caupāī 152

Then it was that at a sign from Raghubara, the boatman propelled the boat to the opposite side. In this manner the Glory of Raghu's line went his way, and I stood looking on with a heart as of adamant. How can I describe my own anguish, who have come back alive, bearing Rāma's message?' With these words the minister stopped speaking being overpowered by affection, remorse and distress. When he had heard Sumantra's story, the king fell to the ground, heartbroken with grief, and in an agony of despair writhed like a fish in the scour of a turbid stream.[1] All the queens wept and made lamentation; how can I describe so great a calamity ? At the sound of their wailings, Sorrow itself grew sorrowful and Endurance could no more endure.

Dohā 152

Avadh was in a tumult at the sound of the outcry in the queens' apartments : as when a massy thunderbolt has fallen at night in some dense forest full of birds.

1. This simile, has puzzled many of the commentators who are ordinarily grammarians rather than observers of nature. It is well-illustrated and explained by a letter in the *Pioneer* of August 5, 1878, from a correspondent at Mirzapur. He writes as follows : "We observed a curious phenomenon here which seems worth recording. Early on Friday morning huge quantities of fish of every description were seen coming to the surface all along both banks of the river gasping and dying. The people living near the sides flocked down and clubbed and secured very many . . . Before many hours all the fish susceptible to whatever influence was at work seem to have perished and in the afternoon they rose to the surface and floated past in a state of decomposition. The river is in high, but not full, flood. The water, probably on account of the prolonged drought, is intensely and abnormally turbid. It is to this peculiarity that I attribute the death of the fish. The particles of earth held in suspense have impregnated gills and stopped breathing."

Caupāī 153

The breath of life flickered at the king's mouth, forlorn as a snake robbed of its jewel; all his senses as heavy smitten as the lotuses in a lake that has been drained of its water. When Kausalyā saw the king's misery—the sun of the Solar race setting as it were at noon—Rāma's mother summoned up courage and spoke in words befitting the occasion : "Consider, my lord, and remember that Rāma's exile is like the vast ocean, you are the helmsman of the good ship Avadh, and our dear ones are the voyagers, its passengers. If you have courage you will get across: if not the whole family will be drowned. Take to heart this entreaty of mine, dear lord, and you will yet see again Rāma, Lakṣmaṇa and Sītā.

Dohā 153

Hearing these tender words from his dear wife, the king opened his eyes and looked up, writhing like some hapless fish when sprinkled with cold water.

Caupāī 154

The king with an effort sat up : "Tell me, Sumantra, where is my generous Rāma ? Where is Lakṣmaṇa ? Where my loving Rāma ? Where my dear daughter-in-law, the princess of Videha?" Thus miserably moaning, the night seemed as long as an age and would never end. The blind hermit's curse[1] came back to

1. The incident to which such brief allusion is here made is told at full length in Vālmīki's *Rāmāyaṇa*, where it occupies nearly 200 lines. One day, when Daśaratha was still a youth, he was out shooting, and had taken up a position near the bank of the Sarjū, where he hoped to get a shot at some tiger or buffalo as it came down in the evening to the river to drink. Hearing a splash in the water, he let fly an arrow. From the cry that followed, he learnt to his dismay that he had shot a young hermit, who had been filling his pitcher for the use of his blind and aged parents. His dying words were to implore the king that he would carry the water to the hermitage and inform the bereaved couple of their son's sad fate. He did so, and was told that as a punishment for his crime he, too, should hereafter die of grief for the loss of a son. The time should be far distant, because the blow was dealt unwittingly, and his confession had further lightened his guilt : had he concealed the deed, he and the whole of his line had perished for ever. (See *Vālmīkīya Rāmāyaṇa*, Ayodhyākāṇḍa, 63-64.)

his mind, and he told the whole story to Kausalyā. As he related the circumstances his agitation increased : "Bereft as I am of Rāma, I have done with life and hope; why should I cherish a body that has failed to fulfil my love's engagement ? Alas, Raghunandana, dearer to me than life, already have I lived too long without you ! Ah, Jānakī and Lakṣmaṇa ! Ah, Raghubara ! the raincloud of a fond father's cuckoo-like heart."

Dohā 154

Crying 'Rāma, Rāma !' and again 'Rāma!' and yet once more 'Rāma, Rāma, Rāma !', the king's soul, bereft of Raghubara, abandoned his body and entered heaven.

Caupāī 155

Thus Daśaratha reaped his reward, both in life and death, and his spotless fame spread through countless universes. Living, he saw Rāma's moon-like face, and dying for his loss, had a glorious death. All the queens bewailed him in an agony of grief, and spoke of his beauty, his amiability, his power and majesty. They made manifold lamentation, throwing themselves upon the ground again and again. Men-servants and maid-servants sadly mourned him; and there was weeping in every house throughout the city: "Today has set the sun of the Solar race, the perfection of justice, the treasury of all good qualities." All reviled Kaikeyī, who had robbed the world of its very eyes. In this manner the night was spent in lamentations till all the great and learned sages arrived.

Dohā 155

Then the holy Vasiṣṭha recounted many legends befitting the time, and lessened their grief by the wisdom that he displayed.

Caupāī 156

After filling a boat with oil and putting the king's body in it, he summoned messengers and thus addressed them: "Hasten with all speed to Bharata, and say nothing to anybody about the king; only tell Bharata when you arrive, 'The *guru* has sent for you two brothers." On receiving the sage's orders, they ran off at once with speed that would shame the fleetest of horses. Directly these troubles had begun at Avadh, Bharata was visited with evil omens; he saw fearful visions in his sleep by night and on awaking formed all sorts of ill conjectures. He daily feasted Brāhmaṇas and gave them gifts and with elaborate ritual poured water over the emblem of Mahādeva,[1] and with heartfelt prayers implored the god for the prosperity of his parents, his family and his brothers.

Dohā 156

In this state of anxiety was Bharata found by the heralds on their arrival. As soon as he had heard his *guru's* commands he offered up a prayer to Gaṇeśa and started.

Caupāī 157

They went with the speed of the wind, urging on their horses over rivers, rocks and trackless forests. So great was his distress of mind that nothing pleased him; he thought to himself, 'O that I had wings to fly!' A moment seemed like a year. In this state Bharata drew near to the city. On entering he was met by evil omens. Gruesome noises sounded in uncanny places, asses and jackals uttered presages of ill, which pierced him to the heart as he listened. Even the lakes and rivers, groves and gardens, seemed forlorn; while the city struck him as more melancholy still. Birds, deer, horses and elephants were painful to look at, as though the loss of Rāma were some dreadful disease that had destroyed them. The citizens were as downcast as if they had all lost everything they had in the world.

Dohā 157

The citizens who met him did not speak, but bowed to him silently and passed on. For the fear and dismay in his mind, Bharata could not ask, 'Is all well ?'

Caupāī 158

The market places and streets were as dreary to behold as though the city had been the prey of a general conflagration.

1. *Śiva abhiṣeka* : a jar full of water with a small hole in the bottom is set over the emblem of Śiva, upon which the water is thus allowed to drip.

When Kaikeyī heard of her son's approach, the moon of the lotus-like solar race rejoiced. She sprang up gladly and ran with lamp in hand and met him at the door and brought him in. Bharata saw all the household as woe-begone as a bed of lotuses when smitten by the frost, his mother as jubilant as a wild hill-woman who has set the forest in a blaze. Seeing her son anxious and distressed, she asked, "Is all well at my mother's house?" Bharata assured her that all was well, and then asked after the welfare of his own family: "Tell me, where is my father and where are the other queens? Where is Sītā and where my dear brothers, Rāma and Lakṣmaṇa?"

Dohā 158

On hearing her son's loving speech, the wicked woman's eyes filled with crocodile tears, and she replied in words that pierced Bharata's ears and soul:

Caupāī 159

"My son, I had arranged everything with the help of poor[1] Mantharā, but God somehow upset my plans half-way. The king has gone to Indra's realm." On hearing this, Bharata was overcome with distress, like an elephant at the roar of a lion. Crying, "My father, my father, alas, my father!" He fell to the ground in grievous affliction, "I could not see you ere you left, nor did you, my father, commend me to Rāma." Again with an effort, he collected himself and got up: "Tell me, mother, the cause of my father's death." On hearing her son's words, Kaikeyī replied, as one who drops poison into a wound, and with a glad heart, vile wretch that she was, recounted all that she had done from the very beginning.

Dohā 159

Bharata forgot his father's death when he heard of Rāma's banishment, and knowing himself to be the cause, he was staggered and remained speechless.

1. *Bichārī* is here for the Persian word *bechārā*. The Hindu commentator explains it by *chāra rahita*.

Caupāi 160

Seeing her son's distress, she admonished him, as one who applies salt to a burn: "The king, my boy, is no fit subject for lamentation; he won glory and renown and lived happily. In his life he reaped all life's rewards, and in the end has entered the court of heaven. Regard the matter in this light and banish grief; in state assume the sovereignty of the realm." The prince shrank back at her words, as though a burning coal had touched a festering wound. Then collecting himself, he gave a deep sigh: "Wretched woman, the ruin of us all ! if this was your vile desire, why did you not kill me at my birth? After cutting down a tree you water the branches and drain a pond to keep the fish alive.

Dohā 160

Born of the Solar race, with Daśaratha for my father and Rāma and Lakṣmaṇa for my brothers, I have had *you*, mother, for a mother ! What can be done against Fate ?

Caupāī 161

When you, wretch, formed such an evil design in your mind, how was it your heart did not break in pieces ? When you asked the boon, your soul felt no pain, your tongue did not burn, nor your mouth fester ? How could the king trust you ? His hour of death had come, and God had robbed him of his senses. Not even God knows the ways of a woman's heart; such a mine is it of all deceit, crime and sin. The king was so simple, good and pious, what did he know of woman's nature ? Is there any living creature in the world who loves not Raghunātha like himself ? Yet he was your special enemy. Tell me the truth. What are you ? Whatever you may be you have blackened your own face! Up then, and get out of my sight!

Dohā 161

God has created me out of a womb hostile to Rāma; then who so guilty a wretch as I ? But it is useless for me to say anything to you."

Caupāī 162

When atrughna heard of his mother's wickedness, he burned all over, his anger was beyond control. At that very moment the humpback came up, dressed out in fine attire and many jewels. On seeing her, Lakṣmaṇa's younger brother was filled with passion like a blazing fire upon which butter has been poured. He sprang forward and struck her such a blow on her hump that she felt flat on her face and screamed aloud. Her hump was smahsed her head split, her teeth broken and her mouth streamed with blood. "Ah! my God! What harm have I done? This is an ill reward for all my services!" Then Śatrughna, seeing her so all vile from head to foot, seized her by the hair of the head and began dragging her about, till the merciful Bharata rescued her. Both brothers then went to see Kausalyā.

Dohā 162

In sordid attire, pale, agitated, with wasted frame and her soul oppressed with woe, she seemed some lovely creeper or golden lotus smitten by the frost.

Caupāī 163

When the queen saw Bharata, she sprang up in haste andran to him, but fell swooning to the ground overtaken with giddiness. At this sight Bharata was grievously distressed,and threw himself at her feet, forgetting his own condition: "Mother, let me see my father; where is Sītā, and where Rāma and Lakṣmaṇa, my two brothers? Why was Kaikeyī born into the world, or, if born, why was she not barren instead of bearing me to disgrace the family, a very sink of infamy, the curse of my home? Who in the three worlds is so wretched as I am, on whose account, mother, you have been brought to this plight? My father dead, Rāma banished, and I alone the cause of all this calamity! Woe is me, a very fire amongst the reeds, fraught with intolerable torment, anguish and offence!"

Dohā 163

Hearing Bharata speak so tenderly, his mother recovered herself and arose and lifted him up and clasped him to her bosom, while she wiped the tears from his eyes.

Caupāī 164

Simple and kind, she took him to her heart as lovingly as though Rāma himself had returned. Then Lakṣmaṇa's younger brother was also embraced, while she overflowed with sorrow and affection. All who witnessed her kindness said : "She is Rāma's mother, it is natural to her." Seating Bharata in her lap, she wiped away her tears and said soothingly, "Now, my child, I adjure you to compose yourself; reflect that the times are evil and cease to lament. Think no more of your loss and vexation; remember that the course of time and fate is unalterable. Blame no one, my son; it is God who has set himself against me. He has made me live through such distress; who knows what may be his pleasure with me now ?

Dohā 164

At his father's command, my son, Raghubīra put aside his ornaments and ordinary attire and assumed the hermit's garb of bark without either dismay or exultation.

Caupāī 165

With a cheerful countenance and a soul unmoved by anger or attachment, he did all in his power to comfort everybody. Hearing that he was off to the forest, Sītā went too; in her devotion to Rāma's feet she could not stay. Lakṣmaṇa also. when he heard the news, rose up to accompany him, and for all Rāma's persuasions would not remain behind. Then Raghupati bowed his head to all in turn and set out accompanied by Sītā and his younger brother. Rāma, Lakṣmaṇa and Sītā went thus into exile. I neither joined them nor sent my spirit after them. All this took place before my eyes, and yet — wretch that I am — life did not leave my body. I felt no shame, for all my love, with such a son, as Rāma and myself his mother ! The king knew well the time to live and the time to die, but my heart is a hundredfold harder than adamant."

Dohā 165

Hearing Kausalyā's words, Bharata and the ladies of the court made woeful lamentation; the palace seemed the very home of affliction.

Caupāī 166

Bharata, nay both brothers, wept piteously. Kausalyā clasped them to her bosom, and comforted Bharata in every way with words of prudent wisdom. With appropriate maxims from the Purāṇas and Vedas all the queens reasoned with Bharata. And he, pure, guileless and sincere, made fitting answer thus with folded hands: "The crime of slaying father, mother or *guru*; of burning cows in their stalls or a city of Brāhmaṇas; the crime of murdering wife or child; of poisoning a friend or a king; every mortal or venial sin, of thought, word and deed, as enumerated by the seers; may all these sins be mine, O God, if this, mother, was a plot of mine!

Dohā 166

May God award me the lot of those who forsake the feet of Hari and Hara and worship the abominable spirits of the dead, if, mother, I consented to this plot !

Caupāī 167

Those who sell the Veda and traffic in piety; backbiters, who talk of others' faults; the treacherous, the perverse, the litigious, the violent; the revilers of the Veda, the enemies of all creation; the covetous, the lecherous, the fickle, the boastfull[1] who covet their neighbour's wealth or their neighbour's wife; may I come to a like ill end with them if, mother, this plot had my consent. The wretches who have no regard for the example of the good, who reject the way of salvation, who worship not the incarnation of Hari and take no delight in the glory of Hari and Hara, who abandon the path of the Vedas and follow the contrary way, who by knavish disguise impose upon the world; may Śaṅkara allot me a fate like theirs if, mother, I knew of this plot.

Dohā 167

Hearing Bharata's true and honest and generous words, his mother said, "Son, you have ever been Rāma's friend in thought and word and deed.

1. For the two words *lolā*, *lawārā*, it would seem preferable to read, *lolupawārā*, if there were any manuscript to support it.

Caupāī 168

Rāma is the very life of your life, and you are dearer than life to Raghupati. The moon may drop poison, ice emit fire, fish avoid water, a sage persist in folly; but you could never become Rāma's enemy. If anyone in the world says this was of your contriving, he shall never even in his sleep have any peace or happiness." With these words his mother clasped Bharata to her heart while her breasts dropped milk and her eyes filled with tears. As they sat and made such long lamentations, the whole night was spent. Vāmadeva and Vasiṣṭha came and summoned all the ministers and nobles and did everything to console Bharata by appropriate discourse on religious topics.

Dohā 168

"Son, take heart and perform the duties of the day." Bharata arose at the *guru's* command and ordered everything to be made ready.

Caupāī 169

As directed in the Veda, he had the body of the king bathed and a grand bier prepared. Then clasping the feet of each of the queens Bharata bid them stay.[1] They stayed in the hope of seeing Rāma. Many loads of sandalwood and aloes were brought and immense quantities of sweet-scented spices. The pyre was raised on the bank of the Sarju like a fair ladder reaching to heaven. So all the rites of cremation were accomplished; the prescribed bathing, the oblation of sesamum seeds, the ceremony of the ten balls of rice,[2] which Bharata performed after due study of the Vedas, the Purāṇas and the Code or Ritual. Whatever order was given at any time by the great sage was thereupon executed accordingly a thousand times over. For his purification he gave abundant gifts—cows, horses, elephants, all kinds of carriages.

1. That is to say, he would not allow them to ascend the funeral pile with the body of the king and perish with him as Satīs.

2. One ball is offered on the first day, two on the second, and so on till the tenth, when the ceremony is complete.

Dohā 169

Thrones, jewels, robes, grain, land, money, and houses all these did Bharata take and present to the Brāhmaṇas: their every wish was gratified.

Caupāī 170

All the ceremonies that Bharata performed on his father's account were more than a million tongues could tell. Then came the great sages, after determining an auspicious day and summoned all the nobles and ministers, who went and sat down in the royal council chamber, where they sent for and summoned Bharata and his brother. Vasiṣṭha seated Bharata by his side and addressed him in words full of wisdom and piety. First, the holy man repeated the whole history of Kaikeyī's monstrous doing and extolled the king for his piety and faithfulness to his promise, who by his death had manifested his love. As he spoke of Rāma's good qualities and amiable disposition, the sage's eyes filled with tears and his body quivered with emotion. As he went on to tell of the affection shown by Lakṣmaṇa and Sītā, the lord of sages was drowned in love and grief.

Dohā 170

"Hearken, Bharata," spoke the lord of sages sorrowfully, "Fate is all-powerful; loss and gain, life and death, honour and dishonour are in God's hands.

Caupāī 171

This being so, why blame anyone, or why be angry with any without cause? Ponder this in your heart, my son; king Daśaratha is not to be mourned. Grieve rather for the Brāhmaṇa who is ignorant of the Vedas and has abandoned his faith and become absorbed in the delights of sense; grieve for the king who knows not the principles of government and to whom his subjects are not as dear as his own life; grieve for the merchant, miserly and rich, who regards not the duties of hospitality nor the service of Mahādeva; grieve for the Śūdra who insults a Brāhmaṇa, who is boastful, ambitious and proud of his knowledge; grieve again for the woman who deceives her husband, and who is perverse, quarrelsome and self-willed; grieve for the religious student who breaks his vows and obeys not the commands of his *guru*,

Dohā 171

Grieve for the householder who, overcome by delusion, forsakes the path of religion; grieve for the ascetic who is enamoured of the world and has lost his judgment and self-governance;

Caupāī 172

Grieve for the anchorite who has given up penance and takes delight in pleasure; grieve for the backbiter and the angry without a cause, the enemies of their own parents, their spiritual guide and their kinsmen: pitiable in every way is the malevolent who cherishes self and is utterly merciless; pitiable in every way is he who does not eschew guile and become a follower of Hari; but the king of Kosala is not to be mourned; his glory is manifest abroad through the fourteen spheres. There neither has been, nor is now, nor shall be hereafter, a king like your father, Bharata. Brahmā, Viṣṇu, Śiva, Indra and all the guardians of the quarters sing the virtues of Daśaratha.

Dohā 172

Tell me, my son, in what way can any one magnify him, who has such noble sons as Rāma, Lakṣmaṇa, yourself and Śatrughna?

Caupāī 173

The king is altogether fortunate; it is vain to lament on his account. Thus hearing and considering, cease from grief; obediently submit to the royal command. The king has given you the throne, and you must needs fulfil your father's word. The monarch who for the sake of his word abandoned Rāma, though in the anguish of separation from Rāma he lost his life, and thus held his word dearer than life, is a father, my son, whose word must be obeyed. Bow your head to the royal command, for in obedience lies your highest good. Paraśurāma to obey his father's order, slew his own mother, as all the world bears witness; and Yayāti's son gave him up his youth;[1] in a father's order there can be no sin nor disgrace.

Dohā 173

Those who cherish their father's words, without discussing right or wrong, are crowned with honour and glory and dwell in the palace of the king of heaven.

Caupāī 174

Then you must certainly make good the king's word; cherish your subjects and cease to grieve. He will receive comfort in heaven; for you it will be a merit and honour, and no fault. It is laid down in the Vedas, and approved by all men, that he takes the crown to whom the father gives it. Reign then, nor further distress yourself, but accept my advice as the best for you. Rāma and Sītā will rejoice when they hear of it, and no wise man will call it wrong. Kausalyā and all the queens will be happy in the happiness of the people. Rāma knows your secret thoughts and will take it quite in good part; on his return you can deliver up the throne and serve him with cheerful affection."

Dohā 174

The ministers with folded hands exclaimed: "You must needs obey your guru's command: when Raghupati returns, you may then do what is right and fitting."

1. The legend of Yayāti is thus given in the Viṣṇu Purāṇa, IV, 10 :— He was the second son of king Nahuṣa, and succeeded to his father's throne. He had two wives, Devayānī, the daughter of Uśanas (also called Śukrācārya, the preceptor of the Daityas), and Śarmiṣṭhā, the daughter of Vṛṣaparvan, king of the Dānavas. Having been cursed by Uśanas whose daughter had complained to him of her husband's infidelity, he became old and infirm before his time, but was allowed to transfer his decrepitude to anyone who would consent to take it. Four of his sons, to whom he successively applied for relief, refused to grant it, and received in consequence their father's curse, that none of their posterity should possess dominion. But when he made the same request to his fifth and youngest son, Puru, he at once consented to give up his youth and receive in exchange his father's infirmities. After some years of enjoyment Yayāti himself withdrew to a hermitage in the woods and resigned the throne to Puru, whom he appointed supreme monarch of the world, making his elder brothers his viceroys under him.

Caupāī 175

Kausalyā, too, took courage and cried: "My son, you have your father's and your *guru's* commands, which you must respect and affectionately carry out. Cease to lament, knowing it to be the will of Fate that Rāma is in banishment, the king in heaven, and you in such perplexity. You, my son," continued his mother, "are the sole refuge of your family, your people and ministers of state. Seeing God against us and the fates untoward, be of good courage. I, your mother, adjure you, obediently comply with your *guru's* command; cherish your people, relieve the affliction of your kinsfolk." The *guru's* speech and the ministers' approval had been as grateful to Bharata's hearing as sandal perfumes, but when he heard his mother's tender appeal fraught with the pathos of sincere affection—

Chand 7

when Bharata heard his mother's simple plea, he was overcome; his lotus eyes rained with tears that bedewed the fresh shoots of desolation in his soul. All who then beheld his condition entirely forgot about themselves — ah, Tulasī! — and reverently extolled him as the very perfection of true love.

Soraṭhā 175

Folding his lotus hands, Bharata, the champion of honour, stoutly made answer to them all in noble words that seemed as if dipped in nectar.

Caupāī 176

"The *guru* has given me good advice, which has been approved by ministers, people, and all. My mother, too, has given me proper commands, and I must needs bow and obey. The injunctions of a *guru*, a father or a mother, or a master, or a friend should be cheerfully performed as soon as heard, and as all for best; to deliberate whether they are right or wrong is a failure of duty and involves grievous sin. You have now given me honest advice, which it will be good for me to follow; yet, though I understand this clearly, my soul is still discontent. Hearken then to my prayer, and according to my circumstances so instruct me, forgiving my presumption in answering you; when a man is in distress good people do not reckon up his merits and demerits.

Dohā 176

My father is in heaven, and Sītā and Rāma are in the forest, and you want me to govern the kingdom; is it my gain or some unusual advantage that you expect to result from this?

Caupāī 177

My gain is to serve Sītā's lord, and of this I have been robbed by my mother's wickedness. After reflecting and searching my thoughts I find no other way of happiness than this. Of what account is a throne with all its cares, if I cannot see the feet of Lakṣmaṇa, Rāma and Sītā? Without clothes a mass of jewels is of no use; of no use is asceticism without divine meditation; of no use is any enjoyment to a diseased body; prayer and penance go for nought without devotion to Hari; without life, beauty of body is nought; and all is nought to me without Rāma. Permit me to join Rāma; for in it assuredly lies my only happiness. If again in making me king it is your own advantage that you desire, you speak under the influence of foolish affection.

Dohā 177

In your infatuation you hope for happiness from the reign of such a wretch as I, Kaikeyī's son, perverse of nature, Rāma's enemy, and lost to shame.

Caupāī 178

I tell you truly; hearken all and believed it—in a king is required a righteous disposition. If you persist in giving the crown to me, earth will sink into hell. What guilty wretch is equal to me, for whom Sītā and Rāma have been exiled ? The king banished Rāma, but died in losing him. I, the miserable cause of all this wrongdoing, sit and listen to it all unmoved. Though I see the palace with no Rāma there, yet live to endure the mockery of the world ! Holy Rāma eschews all pleasures of sense, and I, a greedy king, am hungering after enjoyment. In what words can I tell the hardness of my heart, which surpasses even adamant?

Dohā 178

That every effect is harder than its cause is no fault of mine; the thunderbolt is harder than bone,[1] and iron more stiff and unbending than the rock from which it is quarried.

Caupāī 179

If my wretched life can cling to a body born of Kaikeyī's womb, it will have a surfeit of misery: if, bereaved of my beloved, life is still dear to me, I shall have much hereafter to see and hear. Kaikeyī has banished Lakṣmaṇa, Rāma and Sītā, and for her own advantage has sent her husband to heaven — a kindly deed ! She has taken upon herself widowhood and disgrace and has caused the people sorrow and affliction, has allotted me glory and honour and dominion and has settled everybody's business. What greater blessing can I now have ? And yet you too propose to crown me king! I have been born into the world from Kaikeyī's womb, and all this is only my due ! God has fashioned all my destiny; but why should my people combine to give a helping hand ?

Dohā 179

Stricken as I am by fate, afflicted by organic disorders,[2] and then stung by a scorpion, you give me wine to drink: tell me, tell me what kind of treatment is this?

1. The thunderbolt is said to be made from the bones of the Ṛṣi Dadhīci, who devoted himself to death in order that the gods might be supplied with arms against the Kālakeya Asuras, by whom they were oppressed. When his bones had been fashioned into thunderbolts by Tvaṣṭṛ (the Vedic Vulcan) Indra hurled them against his enemies and slew their leaders, the cloud demon Vṛtra.

2. According to Hindu physicians all organic disorders of the human frame arise from derangements of the blood or one of the three humours of the body, *kapha*, phlegm, *vāyu*, wind, or *pitta*, bile. The vitiated humour which is specified in the text is wind, *vāta*.

Caupāī 180

The all-wise Creator has ordained for me everything that befits a son of Kaikeyī. That I am also Daśaratha's son and Rāma's younger brother is an honour which God has bestowed upon me to no purpose. You all bid me assume sovereignty, for kingly power is desired by all men. How and whom shall I answer ? You talk at random as the fancy takes you. Apart from myself and my unhappy mother, tell me who will say that I have acted rightly ? Excepting myself, who else is there in the whole animate or inanimate creation that does not love Sītā and Rāma as their own life ? That a universal calamity should be my great gain, this is my misfortune and no blame to any one. You are moved by anxiety, kindliness and affection, and anything you say is all for the best.

Dohā 180

Rāma's mother is so utterly guileless and bears me such great love that she speaks from natural affection on seeing how wretched I am.

Caupāī 181

The *guru*, as all the world knows, is an ocean of wisdom, and the universe is like a plum in the palm of his hand. He too is making ready for my coronation: when God is against me, everyone is against me. Except Rāma and Sīta there is no one in the whole world who will not say this was a scheme of mine, and I must listen and bear it patiently: wherever there is water, there in the end is mud. I am not afraid of the world calling me vile; I have no thought for heaven: the one consuming and intolerable anguish of soul is this, that through me Sītā and Rāma have been rendered unhappy. Well has Lakṣmaṇa reaped his life's reward who left all to cleave to Rāma; while my birth has been the cause of Rāma's banishment. Wretch that I am, why thus lament in vain.

Dohā 181

I declare before you all my grievous misery; unless I see Rāma's feet, the fire in my soul cannot be quenched.

Caupāī 182

No other remedy can I discover and who but Raghubara can understand what passes in my heart? There is only one resolve stamped upon my soul; at daybreak let me follow my lord. Although I am a guilty wretch, and all his trouble is on my account, still when he sees my suppliant mien he will in his great mercy forgive me all. Raghurāo is so meek and utterly guileless of disposition, such a home of mercy and tenderness, that he would never injure even an enemy: while I, though I have done him wrong, am his son and his servant. Be pleased, sirs, then to give me your blessing and permit me to depart, knowing it to be for my good; so Rāma will come again to his kingdom, after hearing my prayers and considering my devotion.

Dohā 182

Though born of a wicked mother, and myself evil and iniquitous, still I am confident of Raghubīra that he will know me for his own, and not abandon me."

Caupāī 183

Bharata's words pleased all, imbued as they were with the nectar of devotion to Rāma. The people suffering from the baneful poison of separation revived as if at the sound of a healing charm. The queen-mothers, the ministers, the *guru* and all the men and women in the city were agitated by the vehemence of their affection and kept on praising Bharata and saying, "His body is the very personification of devotion to Rāma; ah, my lord Bharata, how can we say otherwise, seeing that Rāma is as precious to you as your life? If any churl in his folly impute to you your mother's wickedness, the wretch, with all who are his from generation to generation, shall have their home in hell for a hundred aeons. The jewel is not infected with the guilt and villainy of the serpent (in whose head it is found), but is an antidote to poison and subdues pain and poverty.

Dohā 183

By all means let us set out to seek Rāma to the wood; Bharata has given good advice; sinking as we all were in an ocean of despair, you have held out help to us."

Caupāī 184

There was as great joy in the hearts of all as when the *cātaka* and peacock hear the rumble of a thunder-cloud. To start tomorrow seemed an excellent resolution; Bharata was to everyone dear as his own life. After reverencing the sage and bowing the head to Bharata, they all took leave and went to their several homes, praising as they went his affectionate disposition, whose life was a blessing to the whole world. Exclaiming to one another, "What a glorious idea!" they all went to make ready for the journey. Whoever was left with orders to keep watch at home felt it like his death-stroke, and one would cry, "No one ought to be told to stay: who does not desire life's best reward?

Dohā 184

Perish that property, house, happiness, friends, parents, kinsmen and all that does not lend cheerful aid to turn one's face towards Rāma's feet!"

Caupāī 185

In every house carriages of all descriptions were making ready, and the start on the morrow was a heart-felt joy. Bharata pondered on going home: "The city, with its horses, elephants, palaces and treasuries, and all its wealth, is Rāma's. If I recklessly go and leave it, in the end it will not be good for me; to injure[1] one's own lord is a deadly sin. A good servant acts for his master's interests, however much others may abuse him." So thinking, he called such faithful servants as would never dream of failng in their duty, and after declaring to them his intention and instructing them in their work, he told them off for the posts for which they were severally fit. When he had thus diligently posted the guards, he proceeded to see Rāma's mother.

Dohā 185

Understanding the ways of love, Bharata sympathized with a mother's anxiety and ordered to be got ready convenient palanquins and seated carriages.

1. *Dohāi* here would seem to be not for *duhāi*, 'lamentation,' but for *droha*, 'injury.'

Caupāī 186

The men and women of the city, like the *cakavā* and *cakavi*, were desperately anxious at heart for the dawn, when they might start. The whole night had been spent in watching, when Bharata summoned his wise counsellors and said to them: "Take all materials for the coronation, and there in the forest, sirs, invest Rāma with the sovereignty: start at once." At his word they did obeisance and speedily made ready horses, carriages and elephants. The king of sages (Vasiṣṭha) first mounted his chariot and led the way with his spouse Arundhatī and all the materials for sacrifice. A host of Brāhmaṇas renowned for their asceticism, followed in vehicles of different kinds, and next the citizens on their own conveyances all set forth for Citrakūṭa. The elegance of the palanquins in which the different queens were seated is beyond description.

Dohā 186

All the people were as eager for a sight of Rāma as a herd of elephants that makes a rush for a stream. Reflecting within brother set forth too, with his thoughts fixed on Rāma and Sītā.

Caupāī 187

All the people were as eager for a sight of Rāma as when a herd of elephants makes a rush for a stream. Reflecting within themselves that Sītā and Rāma were in exile, Bharata and his brother went on foot. The people were moved by their affection and themselves dismounted and left horses, elephants and carriages. But Rāma's mother brought her palanquin to a halt by his side and softly said, "My son, I entreat you to mount your chariot, or all your people will be sufferers; if you walk, they will all walk, and they are so wasted with sorrow that they are not fit for the journey." Obedient to her commands, the two brothers bowed their heads before her feet, and mounted their chariots and journey on. They halted the first day at the Tamasā,[1] and the second on the bank of the Gomatī.[2]

Dohā 187

Out of devotion to Rāma, some vowed to drink only milk, some to eat nothing but fruit, others to make only one meal and that at night, and they forswore all luxuries of dress and food.

Caupāī 188

After resting on the bank of the Sai[3] they started at dawn and drew near to the city of Śṛṅgavera.[4] When the Niṣāda heard the news he thought sadly to himself: "For what reason is Bharata going to the forest? He has some evil design at heart. If he had no wrong intention, why should he bring an army with him ? He imagines that if he slays Rāma and his brother, he will reign in ease and security. Bharata has not taken to heart the maxims of sound polity; there was disgrace already, and now there will be loss of life. If all the gods and demons were to combine to fight, they would never conquer Rāma in battle. What wonder that Bharata should act thus ? Poison ivy does not bear ambrosial fruit.

Dohā 188

Having thus reflected, Guha addressed his kinsmen: "Be on the alert, up and sink the boat and close the ferry.

1. The Tamasā, 'the dark-coloured' (more commonly spelt Tons) is a branch of the Ghogra (the Sanskrit Ghargharā, the roaring'), which leaves that river about 16 kms. above Ayodhyā, and after passing the town of Azamgarh falls into the Sarju [Sarayū.]

2. The Gomatī [the name meaning 'rich in cattle'] rises in a lake near Pilibhit, and after a course of 770 kms. in which it passes the cities of Lucknow, Sultānpur and Jaunpur, falls into the Gaṅgā.

3. The Sai a river in U.P., which rises about midway between the Gomatī and the Gaṅgā, and after a course of some 370 kms. falls into the former, 16 kms. below the city of Jaunpur.

4. The site of the ancient Śṛṅgavera is marked by a village bearing the same name, under the modernized form Sangraur, 35 kms. to the north-west of Allahabad. The river has changed its course, and only a small branch now flows through the old channel.

Caupāī 189

Make ready and close the ferry, equip yourselves with every instrument of death. Take up arms against Bharata, and never let him cross the Gaṅgā alive. To die in the battle and on the Gaṅgā bank; in Rāma's cause to lay down this frail body; and mean as I am to join battle with a king like Bharata; all this is a great gain for me, even if I meet my death. If I war and fight on my lord's behalf, I reap brilliant renown throughout the fourteen spheres. If I lose my life on Raghunātha's behalf, I shall have both hands full of luscious sweets. Whoever is not numbered among the just, nor counted among Rāma's votaries, is, during the time that he lives, only a burden to earth, and an axe at the foot of the tree of his mother's youth."

Dohā 189

The king of the Niṣādas thus fearlessly excited the ardour of his followers, and thinking on Rāma, called at once for quiver and bow and coat of mail.

Caupāī 190

"Hasten, brethren, to complete your equipment, and after hearing my command let no one hesitate." All cheerfully responded, "'Tis well, my lord," and mutually encouraged each other's zeal. Bowing again and again before the Niṣāda, all the gallant warriors, eager for the fray, invoking the sandals of Rāma's lotus feet, girt themselves with quiver, slung on the bow, donned their coats of mail, put helmets on their heads, and sharpened their axes and lances and spears—some so expert in the use of shield and sword that they seemed when they sprung into the air as though they had left the earth for good. When each and all had completed their full arrangements, they went and bowed before king Guha. Seeing his gallant warriors so fighting fit, he addressed them each by name with courteous phrase.

Dohā 190

"Do not play me false, brother; I have a great work to do today!" At his they cried with vehemence, "Fear not, captain."

Caupāī 191

By the power of Rāma and your might, my lord, we will leave the enemy without a single fighting-man or horse. While life lasts, we will never draw back our foot, and will make the earth one heap of corpses and skulls." When the Niṣāda lord had inspected his gallant band, he cried. "Beat the drums of war." When he had so said, someone sneezed to the left. The soothsayers exclaimed, "A prosperous issue to the battle?" One old man thought over the omen and said, "Bharata must be met, but there will be no fighting. He is going to make entreaty to Rāma. The omen says there will be no battle." On hearing this, Guha said, "The old man has spoken well; fools act in haste and repent. Unless we ascertain Bharata's temper and disposition, we may do ourselves harm by fighting without knowledge.

Dohā 191

Close up, all ye warriors, and stop the pass, and all join to discover the mystery. When we know whether he is a friend, an enemy, or a neutral, we can then lay our plans accordingly.

Caupāī 192

We shall soon test his devotion and honest intent; hatred and love can in no wise be concealed." So saying, he began to make ready a present, and sent for bulbs, roots and fruits, birds and beasts, with the finest of fish, large *pāthins*,[1] which were brought by the fishermen in basketful. When everything was arranged they went out to meet him, and had the most auspicious omens of good fortune. As soon as he saw the great sage afar off, he declared his name and prostrated himself before him. Vasiṣṭha, knowing him to be a friend of Rāma's, gave him his blessing, and told Bharata about him. He, on hearing that he was Rāma's friend, left the chariot and advanced on foot to meet him with exuberant affection. Guha declared his village, his race and his name, and making obeisance laid his forehead to the ground.

1. The *pāthin* is a kind of sheat-fish, the *Silurus Pelorius or Boalis*.

Dohā 192

But Bharata, seeing Guha about to prostrate himself, took him to his bosom with much uncontrollable rapture as though it were Lakṣmaṇa he had met.

Caupāī 193

Bharata embraced him with the very greatest affection, and the people extolled the manner of his love. There was a jubilant cry of 'Glory, Glory,' as the gods applauded and rained down flowers upon him. "Though this man is in every way vile, both custom of the world and by scriptural prescription, so that contact with his shadow requires ablution, yet Rāma's brother has embraced him in his arms and thrilled all over with delight at meeting him. One who cries 'Rāma, Rāma,' even in the act of yawning, a multitude of sins will not rise up against him. Here is one whom Rāma had clasped to his bosom and thereby purified him and all his family. If water of the Karmanāśā falls into the Gaṅgā, tell me who will refuse to pour it on his head ? Again, it is known throughout the world that Vālmīki was made equal to Brahmā simply for repeating Rāma's name backwards.

Dohā 193

Even a Caṇḍāla,[1] a Śavara, a Khaśa, a stupid foreigner, an outcast, a Kol, or a Kirāta, by repeating the name of Rāma becomes wholly pure and renowned throughout the world.

Caupāī 194

It is no wonder, it has been so for ages; who is there whom Raghubīra cannot exalt ?" As the gods told the greatness of

1. The word translated 'Caṇḍāla' is in the original *Śva-paca*, literally 'a dog-cooker,' *i. e.*, either one who feeds on dog's flesh, or who cooks food for dogs—'a dog-keeper.' A Śavara is a wild mountaineer. The Khasiya is a native of Khasa, a hill tract in Northern India. The word for 'foreigner' is Jamana, *i.e.*, Yavana, which originally denoted specially a Greek, an Ionian, and then came to mean any foreign barbarian. Accustomed as our ears are to the division of mankind into Greeks, and Barbarians, it is a little strange to find the Greek selected as the typical barbarian.

Rāma's name, the people of Avadh listened and were glad. Bharata affectionately greeted Rāma's friend and asked him of his health and welfare. At the sight of Bharata's loving tenderness, the Niṣāda was at once utterly overpowered; so great was his confusion, his love and his delight, that he could only stand and stare at Bharata. Collecting himself, he again did homage to his feet and with folded hands made this loving speech : "When I beheld his blessed lotus feet I accounted myself blessed in time past, present and to come. Now, my lord, by your high favour my prosperity is secured for innumerable generations.

Dohā 194

Reflecting on my past deeds and my descent and again considering the greatness of the Lord, any man in the world who adores not the feet of Raghubīra must be a victim of supernatural delusion.

Caupāī 195

False, cowardly, low-minded and low-born as I am, an utter outcast by the laws both of God and society; since the time that Rāma took me for his own, I have become the glory of the world." After witnessing his devotion and hearing his noble, modest speech, Lakṣmaṇa's younger brother once more embraced him. Then the Niṣāda introduced himself by name and respectfully saluted the royal dames, who received him even as they would Lakṣmaṇa and gave him their blessing : "May you live happily for millions of years." The citizens too were as glad to see him as if he had been Lakṣmaṇa and cried, "Here is one who has lived to some purpose; whom Rāma's own brother has taken to his arms and embraced." When the Niṣāda heard them thus magnify his good fortune, he was glad at heart as he showed them the way.

Dohā 195

At a signal all his attendants, having understood their master's will, went on and made ready tents under the trees and rest-houses by the ponds, gardens and groves.

Caupāī 196

When Bharat saw the city of Śṛṅgavera, he was overcome by emotion and was unnerved in every limb. As he leant upon the Niṣāda it was as goodly a sight as though embodied Humility and Love had met together. In this manner Bharata and all his host went to see the earth-purifying stream of the Gaṅgā. As he made his obeisance to the ford where Rāma had bathed, he felt as blissful as if he had met Rāma himself. The citizens bowing low gazed upon the divine stream with rapture, and after bathing prayed with clasped hands; "May our love to Rāmacandra's feet never grow less." Bharata exclaimed : "Thy sands, O Gaṅgā, are the bestowers of all happiness, the very cow of plenty to thy votaries : with folded hands I crave this boon, unfeigned devotion to the feet of Sītā and Rāma.

Dohā 196

When Bharata had thus bathed and knew that all the queens had bathed too, he received the *guru's* permission and took them to their tents.

Caupāī 197

Whenever people had pitched their tents, Bharata saw to everybody's comfort. After paying homage to the gods and obtaining their *guru's* permission, the two brothers went to visit Rāma's mother. Then Bharata, after kissing their feet, with many tender phrases did reverence to all the queens, and having left them to the dutiful care of his brother, went away with the Niṣāda. Hand in hand they went, his body fainting with excess of love as he asked his companion to show him the spot — that the fierce longing of his eyes and soul might be a little assuaged — where Sītā, Rāma and Lakṣmaṇa slept at night. As he spoke, his eyes overflowed with tears, and the Niṣāda in great distress at his speech led him at once to the place

Dohā 197

where Raghubara had rested under the sacred *śiṁṣapa* tree; there with great reverence and devotion Bharata prostrated himself.

Caupāī 198

When he spied the delectable grassy couch, he again made obeisance and reverently paced round it. He put upon his eyes the dust of the foot-prints, with an enthusiasm of devotion beyond all telling. And seeing two or three golden spangles, he placed them upon his head as relics of Sītā. With eyes full of tears and melancholy heart he thus in gentle tones addressed his companion : "They are dim and lustreless through Sītā's absence, and all the people of Avadh are equally woe-begone. To whom can I compare her father, Janaka, who was conversant at once with all philosophy ? Her father-in-law, the sun-like monarch of the Solar race, was the envy of even the lord of heaven. Her husband is the beloved Raghunātha, by whose greatness alone it is that any one is great.

Dohā 198

I gaze on the grassy couch of Sītā, that devoted wife, that jewel of good women, and my heart breaks not with emotion; surely, O Śiva, it is harder than a thunderbolt!

Caupāī 199

Lakṣmaṇa so young and comely and made to be fondled: never was there such a brother, nor is there, nor will be: so beloved by the people, the darling of his father and mother, and dear as their own life to Rāma and Sītā; the picture of delicacy, the daintiest of striplings, whose body has never been exposed to the hot wind, how can he bear the hardships of the forest? O my heart would shame for hardness a million thunderbolts! Rāma at his birth was the light of the world, an ocean of beauty, of virtue, of joy and of all perfection. His amiability was the delight of his subjects, his household, his *guru*, his father and mother, and all. Even his enemies would praise Rāma: his courtesy of speech and manner stole every heart. Not a million Sarasvatīs, not a hundred million Śeṣanāgas could reckon up all my lord's virtues.

Dohā 199

The image of bliss, the jewel of the house of Raghu, the storehouse of all auspicious delights, slept on the ground on this littered grass: how wonderful are the ways of Providence!

Caupāī 200

Rāma had never even heard of pain, the king cherished him like the tree of life, and day and night all his mothers guarded him as the eyelids guard the eyes, and as a serpent guards the jewel in its head, And now he is roaming on foot through the woods, with nothing to eat but wild roots and fruits. A curse on thee, Kaikeyī, root of all evil! Thou hast undone my best beloved: cursed be my wretched self, that ocean of iniquity, on whose account all these calamities have come to pass. God brought me to birth to disgrace my family, and my wicked mother has made me the ruin of my lord." Hearing these words, the Niṣāda affectionately implored him: "Why, my lord, make these vain laments? Rāma is dear to you, and you to Rāma; even she is blameless; the blame rests with an adverse fate.

Chand 8

The ways of an adverse fate are cruel, for it drove your mother mad! That night the Lord again and again broke out into respectful praise of you. There is no one so dearly beloved by Rāma as you. I declare this on oath: be assured that all will be well in the end, and take comfort to your soul.

Soraṭhā 200

Rāma knows the hearts of all; he is full of meekness, tenderness and compassion; of this make firm assurance in your heart; and come, take rest."

Caupāī 201

Hearing his companion's speech, Bharata took comfort and with his thoughts directed to Raghubīra went to his tent. When the citizens were informed, heavy with woe they too came to see. Having reverently paced around, they made obeisance and heaped reproaches on Kaikeyī to their hearts' content. Their eyes streamed with tears as they reproached the hostility of fate. One would praise Bharata for his devotion, another would say the king had shown the greatest love; they reproached themselves and praised the Niṣāda: who can describe their agitation and distress? In this manner they all kept vigil throughout the night and at daybreak began the passage. First the *guru* was put on a fine handsome boat, and then all the queens on another boat newly built. In an hour and a half all had crossed over; as they came to land Bharata took count of them all.

Dohā 201

After performing his morning rites and reverencing his mother's feet and bowing the head before the *guru*, he sent the Niṣādas on ahead and started the host.

Caupāī 202

He made the Niṣāda king lead the van and started all the queens in their palanquins. He summoned his younger brother to be their escort, and made the *guru* travel with the Brāhmaṇas. He himself bowed reverently to the Gaṅgā, and invoking Rāma, Sītā and Lakṣmaṇa, set forth on foot, while his horse was led by the bridle. Again and again his faithful servants cried: "Be pleased, my lord, to mount your horse." "Rāma," he answered, "has gone on foot, and are chariots, elephants and horses made for me? It would be right for me to walk on my head; a servant's work should always be the hardest." When they saw Bharata's behaviour and heard his gentle speech, all his servants melted away for pity.

Dohā 202

At the third watch of the day Bharata entered Prayāga, crying, 'O Rāma, Sītā; Rāma, Sītā!' with irrepressible devotion.

Caupāī 203

The blisters on his feet glistened like dewdrops on a lotus-bud. The whole company were distressed when they heard that Bharata had travelled that day on foot. After ascertaining that all the people had bathed, he went and did homage to Triveṇī, the threefold stream. All who had dipped in the parti-coloured flood gave alms and did honour to the Brāhmaṇas. As Bharata gazed on the commingling of the dark and white waves, his body throbbed with emotion and he folded his hands in prayer: "O chief of the holy places, bounteous of every blessing, whose power is declared in the Vedas and renowned throughout the world. I abandon my proper calling and make myself a beggar: is there anything so vile that a man in distress will not do it? As I know you to be all-wise and beneficent, accomplish the prayer of thy suppliant.

Dohā 203

I desire not wealth nor religious merit, nor sensual delights, nor deliverance from transmigration; but only that in every new birth I may persevere in love to Rāma; this is the boon I crave and nought else.

Caupāī 204

Rāma knows my wickedness; the people call me the ruin of my lord and master; through your favour may my devotion to the feet of Sītā and Rāma increase more and more every day. Though the cloud neglects her all her life, and while she begs for rain, casts down upon her thunder and hail, yet were the *cātaka* to cease her importunity, she would be despised; she perseveres in her affection, and is much honoured. Again, as the quality of gold is refined by the fire, so my vow of love to the feet of my beloved endure through all tribulation." In response to Bharata's speech there came a soft and auspicious voice from the midst of the Triveṇī: "Dear Bharata, you are altogether upright; your love to Rāma's feet is unfathomable; you distress yourself without reason; there is no one so dear to Rāma as you are."

Dohā 204

As he heard the river's[1] gracious speech, Bharata's body trembled with heartfelt gladness; the heavens resounded with shouts of applause, and the gods rained down flowers.

Caupāī 205

The inhabitants of Prayāga, aged anchorites and students, householders and celibates, were all enraptured and said to one

1. *i.e.*, Triveṇī's.

another as they met in groups, "Bharata's affection and amiability are true and genuine." Still hearing of Rāma's many charming qualities, Bharata approached the great sage Bharadvāja. When the sage saw him prostrate himself upon the ground, he looked upon him as his own good angel incarnate, and ran and raised him up and took him to his arms and gave him the blessing he desired, and made him sit down. He bowed his head and sat, shrinking into the inmost recesses of shamefacedness; greatly distressed lest the sage should ask any question. Perceiving his embarrassment the sage said, "Hearken, Bharata, I have heard everything; God's doings are beyond our power.

Dohā 205

So be not distressed at heart by the thought of what your mother has done. Son, it is no fault of Kaikeyī's; it was Sarasvatī who stole away her senses.

Caupāī 206

If you say, 'No one will excuse me;' I reply, Scripture and the practice of the world are both accepted as authorities by the wise; and your glory, my son, will be sung unsullied, while the Vedas and custom will both be honoured, for everyone admits that this is according both to custom and the Veda that he takes the throne to whom his father gives it. The truthful king summoned you to confer upon you the honour of sovereignty and its higher duties. Rāma's banishment to the forest is a monstrous wrong, which the whole world is grieved to hear of: but the queen was demented by the power of Fate, and in the end she has repented of the evil she has done. You are not the least to blame; whoever says you are, is a vile and ignorant wretch. Had you reigned, it would have been no sin, and Rāma would have been well content to hear of it.

Dohā 206

But now, Bharata, you have done still better; this proposal is in keeping with you; for devotion to the feet of Raghubara is the root of every blessing in the world.

Caupāī 207

This is your wealth and the very breath of your life; is there anyone so blessed as you ? Nor, my son, is it strange that you should act thus; you are a son of Daśaratha's and Rāma's own brother. Hearken, Bharata, in Raghupati's heart there is no one upon whom so much love is lavished as upon you. Lakṣmaṇa, Rāma and Sītā are all most fond of you; they spent the whole night praising you. I learnt what was in their mind when they came here to Prayāga to bathe; they were overwhelmed with love for you. Raghubara has as great affection for you as a fool has for a life of pleasure. And this is no great credit to Raghurāī, who cherishes all his suppliants and their kin; while you, Bharata, as it seems to me, are the very incarnation of Rāma's love.

Dohā 207

That which seems a disgrace[1] to you, Bharata, is a lesson to all of us; it is an event which inaugurates a new flood of passionate devotion.

Caupāī 208

Your spotless glory, my son, is a newly created moon; its lotuses and partridges are Rāma's servants; it is ever rising and never sets, nor wanes in the world, its heaven, but increases day by day; the three spheres, like the *cakvās* are exceedingly enamoured of it, and the sun of Rāma's majesty never robs it of splendour, but by day *as well* as night it is ever bountiful to all and Rāhu—Kaikeyī's evil deeds—cannot eclipse it. Full of the nectar of Rāma's pure love and unsullied by any stain for wrong done to the *guru*,[2] you are saturated with the nectar of faith, and have

1. Your disobedience to the wishes of your mother and the commands of your *guru* in refusing to accept the throne.

2. There is a popular legend that Vṛhaspati, the *guru* of the gods, on one occasion when he returned from his bath in the Gaṅgā, found his wife in the embraces of the Moon-god. He was not able to seize the adulterer, but threw his dripping bathing robe at him and hit him in the face, thus causing the spots that are still to be seen there. Throughout this stanza Bharata's glory is compared to a newly-created moon, which is in every respect superior to the ordinary moon which we see in the heavens. The one sets and

brought this nectar within the reach of the whole world. King Bhagīratha brought down the Gaṅgā[1], whose invocation is a mine of all prosperity. But Daśaratha's virtues are beyond all description; why say more ? He has no equal in the world.

Dohā 208

Through his devotion and modesty Rāma was made manifest, whom the eyes of Śiva's heart are never wearied of beholding.

Caupāī 209

You have created a peerless moon of glory, in which for the figure of the hare is stamped the love of Rāma. Cease, my son, from lamentation; you have found the philosopher's stone and yet fear poverty ! Hearken, Bharata; I tell no falsehood; a hermit and ascetic dwelling in the forest, I obtained a glorious reward for all my good deeds when I beheld Rāma, Sītā and Lakṣmaṇa, the fruit of that fruit is the sight of you : Prayāga and I are both highly fortunate. Bharata, I congratulate you; you have achieved universal renown." So saying the sage was overwhelmed with emotion. As they hearkened to his words, the whole assembly rejoiced; the gods applauded his goodness and rained down flowers. Shouts of 'Glory, Glory' resounded in heaven and in Prayāga, Bharata was in raptures at the sound.

wanes, the other is always on the increase; the one mainly delights only lotuses and partridges, the other is the joy of Rāma's faithful servants; the one shines only by night, the other by day as well; the one yields nectar, it is true, but none can get at it; the other is impregnated with the nectar of faith, which is brought within the reach of all, the one is branded with the marks of Vṛhaspati's indignation, the other is spotless; though Bharata too offended his *guru* by refusing to reign at his command, the one is stamped only with the figure of a hare [the man in the moon of European nurseries], the other is inscribed with love to Rāma.

1. Bhagīratha, the son of king Dilīpa, after a thousand years spent in austerities, brought down the Ganges from heaven to earth, and with its vivifying flood watered and restored to life the ashes of the sixty thousand sons of his great-grandfather, Sagara, who had been destroyed by the Ṛṣi Kapila. This was a great achievement, but Daśaratha's was a greater, by whom Rāma was begotten into the world.

Dohā 209

With his body trembling with emotion, his heart full of Rāma and Sītā, and his lotus eyes flowing with tears, he made reverence to the assembly of sages and thus spoke in faltering accents:

Caupāī 210

"In this assembly of sages and in this so holy a place, truth must needs be spoken; any oath is superfluous and vain if in such a spot I were to say anything false, no sin or vileness would equal mine. You are all wise—I speak in all sincerity and Rāma, too, knows the secrets of the heart. I am not grieved for what my mother has done, nor pained at heart lest the world deem me caitiff. I have no dread of the loss of heaven, no sorrow for my father's death, whose good deeds and renown are glorious all the world over, who had such sons as Lakṣmaṇa and Rāma, and who, as soon as he lost Rāma, dropped his fragile body; why make long mourning for the king ? But Rāma, Lakṣmaṇa and Sītā, with feet unshod and clad in hermit's dress, and wandering from wood to wood :

Dohā 210

wearing deer-skins, feeding on wild fruits, sleeping on the ground on a litter of grass and leaves, under trees, ever exposed to the inclemency of cold and heat and rain and wind.

Caupāī 211

This is the burning pain that is ever consuming my breast, so that I cannot eat by day nor sleep by night. For this sore disease there is no remedy : I have searched in mind the whole world over. My mother's evil counsel, the root of all calamity, like a carpenter fashioned an axe out of my advantage, made a handle of the ill-wood of Resentment, and fixed the term of banishment as it were a horrible spell. To me she applied this infamous contrivance and has hurled me down in wide-spreading ruin. These disasters will come to an end when Rāma returns to live in Avadh; there is no other remedy." When the sages heard Bharata's speech, they were glad and all gave him high praise :

"Son, grieve not so sorely: at the sight of Rāma's feet all sorrow will pass away."

Dohā 211

The great sages comforted him and said, "Be our welcome guest; accept such herbs and roots and fruit as we can offer, and be content."

Caupāī 212

On hearing the sages' invitation, Bharata was troubled at heart : the time was not one for feasting, and yet it would be rude to decline. At last, reflecting that a *guru's* command is imperative, he did homage to his feet and replied with folded hands : "I must needs bow to your behest, for this, my lord, is my highest duty." The great sage was pleased at Bharata's words and called up all his trusty servants : "An entertainment must be provided for Bharata: go and gather herbs, roots and fruits." They bowed the head and said, 'Certainly, my lord,' and gladly set about each his own work. But the sage thought to himself : "I have invited a distinguished guest, who should be treated like a god." At his command Aṇimā and the rest of Kuvera's attendants came and said, "What are your orders, master, and we obey."

Dohā 212

Cheerily spoke the royal sage, "Bharata and his brother and all their host are distressed by the loss of Rāma : show them hospitality and ease them of their toil."

Caupāī 213

The spirits bowed to his commands and thought themselves most highly favoured, saying one to another : "Rāma's brother is indeed a guest beyond compare." Then kissing the sage's feet, "To-day we will do such things that the whole of the king's party shall be pleased." So saying, a number of such charming pavilions were erected, that the equipages of the gods were put out of countenance at the sight of them. They were furnished with so much luxury and magnificence that the immortals beheld them longingly. Men-servants and maid-servants with every appliance were in attendance and gave their whole mind to their work. In an instant of time the spirits completed all the arrangements though no dream of heaven was ever so beautiful. First the people were assigned their quarters, all bright and pleasant and in accordance with their taste.

Dohā 213

Then, as the seer had ordered, Bharata and his family had theirs assigned them, which astonished even the Creator by their magnificence; so great the power of the holy ascetic's penance.

Caupāī 214

When Bharata beheld the sage's power, the realms of all the rulers of the spheres seemed to him as trifles. The luxuries provided cannot be described; any philosopher would forget his self-restraint on seeing them. Thrones, couches, drapery and canopies; groves and gardens; birds and beasts; sweet-scented flowers, fruits like nectar, and many a lake of limpid water; with luscious food and drinks of innumerable kinds, so that the people were quite put out of countenance by what they saw, as though they had been ascetics. Each one had as it were his own cow of plenty and tree of paradise. Indra and Śacī grew covetous at the sight: the season, spring; the breeze mild, cool, and fragrant; all the four rewards of life ready at hand; and delights of every kind, such as garlands, sandalwood and women, which people saw with mingled feelings of joy and dismay.

Dohā 214

Affluence, like the *cakvī*[1], and Bharata as her mate, by compulsion of the sage's command were prisoned together that night, as by a fowler, in the cage of the hermitage, till daybreak.

1. According to Hindu belief the *cakvā* and his female mate, the *cakvī*, are doomed for ever to nocturnal separation. Even though they may be caught and imprisoned together in one cage they cannot enjoy each other's society till the break of day. In the same way Bharata, though detained for the night by the sage's order at the hermitage in the midst of luxury, could not enjoy it by reason of his vow. Vālmīki represents him as less abste-

Caupāī 215

Then Bharata bathed at Prayāga and with his host bowed the head to the sage. Having submissively received his commands and blessing, he prostrated himself and made much supplication. Taking guides well acquainted with the road, he set out resolutely with all his company for Citrakūṭa, supported on the arm of Rāma's friend, he seemed, as he went, the very incarnation of Love. With no shoes and no shelter for his head, in the fulfilment of his loving vow and his unfeigned integrity, he asked his companion for a history of the wanderings of Rāma, Sītā and Lakṣmaṇa. In soothing accents he told it. When he saw the tree where Rāma had rested, his heart could not contain its emotion. At the sight of his condition, the gods rained down flowers, and the path that he trod grew smooth and pleasant.

Dohā 215

The clouds afforded him shade and the air breathed soft and refreshingly; Rāma's road was not so pleasant as it is now for Bharata.

Caupāī 216

All created things, whether living or dead, that saw the Lord, or were seen by him, were rendered heirs of salvation, and the sight of Bharata has now healed them of the curse of transmigration ! This was no hard task for Bharata, whom Rāma is mindful to remember. A single mention of the name of Rāma on earth makes a man safe and a saviour of others. But Bharata was Rāma's beloved and his own brother; why should he not bring a blessing on the road he treads ? As saints, sages and hermits thus reasoned and gazed upon Bharata, they rejoiced at heart. Indra was troubled by the sight of his power and thought, "In the world things turn out well for the good and badly for the bad." Then turning to his [illegible] (Vṛhaspati), "Something must be done, sir, to prevent the meeting between Rāma and Bharata.

mious, and in describing the banquet, makes mention of wine and flesh meat of various kinds—venison, wild boar, peafowl and partridges—all of which Tulasi Dāsa has omitted in concession to modern prejudices.

Dohā 216

Rāma is so modest and affectionate, and Bharata such an ocean of affection; our scheme threatens to be spoilt; we must bestir ourselves and devise some new stratagem."

Caupāī 217

Hearing the speech, the *guru* of the gods smiled, to find the thousand-eyed so blind, and said, "Leave tricks alone, it will be all trouble in vain; any deception here would be absurd. O king of heaven, any delusion practised on a servant of the lord of delusion must recoil on the contriver. I interfered once, knowing it was Rāma's wish, but any underhand work now would only do harm. Listen, O king of heaven; it is Rāma's nature never to be angry at any sin against himself, but whoever sins against one of his servants is consumed in the fire of his wrath. Popular tradition and the Vedas abound in such legends; Durvāsā[1] knows well this great trait in his character. And is there anyone so faithful to Rāma as Bharata, who is ever repeating Rāma's name and Rāma his ?

Dohā 217

Think not, O king of the immortals, to injure any votary of Raghubara's unless you would suffer the pain of disgrace in this world, sorrow in the next, and a daily increasing burden of regret.

Caupāī 218

Hearken, king of the gods, to my instruction: Rāma has the greatest love for his servants; he is pleased at any service done

1. King Ambarīṣa was a devout worshipper of Viṣṇu [with whom Rāma is here identified] and thereby excited the jealousy of the irascible sage Durvāsā, the most intolerant of all the adherents of Śiva. On some trivial pretext he cursed the king who at once fell senseless to the ground, but Viṣṇu was ready at hand to succour his faithful follower and sent his fiery discus upon Durvāsā, which chased him all over the world and up into heaven, where the gods said nothing could be done for him till he went back and humbly begged pardon of Ambarīṣa.

to a servant, while enmity to a servant is the height of enmity itself. Though he is ever the same, without either passion or anger, and contracts neither sin nor merit, virtue nor defect; and though he has made fate the sovereign of the universe, and every one has to taste the fruit of his own actions, still he plays at variations according as hearts are faithful or unfaithful. Though without attributes or form, illimitable and immutable, Rāma has yielded to the love of his votaries and taken a material form. He has always regarded the wishes of his servants, as the Vedas and Purāṇas and gods and holy men bear witness. Knowing this, refrain from crooked ways and show fitting devotion.

Dohā 218

Any worshipper of Rāma is devoted to the good of others, sorrows with the sorrowful, and is full of compassion; then fear not Bharata, O king, who is the crown of worshippers.

Caupāī 219

The Lord is an ocean of truth and a well-wisher of the gods, and Bharata obeys his orders. You are troubled by your own selfish fear; there is no fault in Bharata, it is a delusion on your part."[1] When the great god heard the words of the heavenly preceptor he got understanding and his anxiety passed away. In his joy he rained down flowers and began to extol Bharata's good qualities. In this manner Bharata proceeded on his journey while saints and sages beheld his bliss and enviously praised him. Whenever he sighed Rāma's name, it seemed like the bubbling over of love. Thunderbolts and rocks melted at his words; as for the people, their emotion is beyond description. Encamping half-way, he came to the Jamunā, and as he gazed on its water, his eyes filled with tears.

Dohā 219

As he and his host gazed on the lovely stream, the colour of Rāma's body, he was plunged into a sea of desolation, till he climbed the boat of discretion.

1. In the Sanskrit poem there is nothing that corresponds to this colloquy between Indra and Vṛhaspati. It is introduced by Tulasi Dāsa as a peg on which to hang a theological exposition.

Caupāī 220

That day he halted on the bank of the Jamunā, giving every one time for what they had to do. In the night boats arrived from all the *ghāts* in greater number than could be counted. At daybreak all crossed in a single journey. The good service of Rāma's companion pleased him greatly. After bathing and bowing to the river, he again set forth with the Niṣāda king and Śatrughna. First of all in his glorious car went the great sage, followed by all the royal retinue; after them the two brothers on foot; their dress, apparel and ornaments all of the very simplest. With them their servants and friend and the minister's son, invoking Lakṣmaṇa, Sītā and Rāma. Every spot where Rāma had encamped or rested they lovingly saluted.

Dohā 220

At the news, the dwellers by the roadside left their homes and their household work and ran after them; seeing their beauty and their love, they were overcome with joy and had their life's reward.

Caupāī 221

One said to another in affectionate tones, "Friend, are they Rāma and Lakṣmaṇa, or not ? In age, figure, complexion and beauty they are the same, dear girl, and resemble them in an equally affectionate disposition. But their dress is not the same, friend, nor is Sītā with them, and before them marches a vast host of horse and foot, elephants and chariots. Nor are they glad of countenance, but have some sorrow at heart; from this difference, friend, a doubt arises." The women were persuaded by her arguments and cried: "There is no one so clever as you." After praising her and admiring the truth of her remarks, another woman spoke in winning tones, and lovingly related the whole story, how Rāma had lost the delights of sovereignty; and again set to praising Bharata for his affectionate disposition and happy nature.

Dohā 221

"He travels on foot, feeding only on wild fruit, and abandoning the kingdom given him by his father, is going to Rāma to persuade him to return ; is there anyone at the present day like Bharata ?

Caupāī 222

To tell and hear of Bharata's brotherly love and devotion and his course of action dispels all sin and sorrow. Anything that I can say, sister, is all too little ; he is Rāma's brother ; how could he be different from what he is ? All of us who have seen him and Śatrughna have been accounted blessed among women." Hearing his virtues and seeing his forlorn state they lamented : "He is not a fit son for such a mother as Kaikeyi." One said : "It is no blame to the queen that God has been so kind to us. What are we, outcasts from the world and the Veda, women of low birth and mean livelihood, whose home is a wretched hovel in some poor village of this miserable country, that we should have such a vision, a sufficient reward for the highest religious merit ?" There was the same delight and wonder in every village, as though the tree of paradise had sprung up in the desert.

Dohā 222

At the sight of Bharata, the good fortune of the people by the wayside manifested itself in like manner, as though by the will of providence Prayāga had become accessible to the people of Laṅkā.

Caupāī 223

Hearing these praises of his own and Rāma's many virtues, he went on his way, ever meditating on Raghunātha. Whenever he spied any holy place, or hermitage, or temple, he bathed and reverently saluted it, praying in his heart of hearts for this one boon, perseverance in devotion to the feet of Sītā and Rāma. If there met him a Kirata, or Kol, or other dweller in the woods, anchorite or student, hermit or ascetic, whoever he might be, he saluted him and asked in what part of the forest were Lakṣmaṇa, Rāma and the Videhan princess. They told him all the news of the Lord, and at the sight of Bharata reaped their life's reward. If any person said, 'We have seen them safe and well,' they were counted as dear as Rāma and

Lakṣmaṇa themselves. In this manner asking courteously of everyone, he heard the whole story of Rāma's life in the forest.

Dohā 223

Halting that day, Bharata started again early the next morning, invoking Raghunātha : all who were with him being equally desirous with himself for a sight of Rāma.

Caupāī 224

Everyone met with auspicious omens; propitious throbbings in the eyes and arm ; Bharata and all his retinue rejoiced, "Rāma will be found and our sore distress will be at an end." Each indulged his own fancy, and as they marched all seemed intoxicated with the wine of love, their limbs relaxed, their feet unsteady on the ground, and the accents of their voice inarticulate from excess of emotion. Just then Rāma's guide pointed out the monarch of mountains in all its beauty, near which on the river's bank the two heroes and Sītā were dwelling. All at the sight fell to the ground with cries of 'Glory to Rāma, the life of Jānakī !' The royal host was as overwhelmed with emotion as though Rāma had come back to Avadh.

Dohā 224

Not even Śeṣanāga can describe the extent of Bharata's love at that moment; it was as far beyond the poet as the bliss of heaven is beyond a man tainted by selfishness and sensuality.

Caupāī 225

Being all unmanned by their love for Raghubara, they had gone but four miles by the close of day, then scanning land and water they halted. When the night was past, the beloved of Raghunātha sallied forth again. On the other hand Rāma, while it was still dark, awoke, and Sītā told him what she had seen in a dream : "Methought Bharata had come with an army, being tortured in body by the fever of separation from his lord; all were sad, wretched and downcast, and the queens consort were greatly altered.' On hearing Sītā's dream, the healer of sorrows became a prey to sorrow and his eyes filled with tears. "This dream, Lakṣmaṇa," he said, "bodes no good : we shall hear of something that we by no means wished." So saying, he and his brother bathed, worshipped Purāri and propitiated the saints.

Chand 9

After paying honour to the gods and reverencing the sages, the Lord went and sat down with his gaze to the north. There was dust in the air and the many birds and beasts had taken to flight in panic and were making their way to the Lord's hermitage. He stood up and looked, anxious in mind as to the cause. Then came Kirātas and Kols and told him all the news.

Soraṭhā 225

When he heard the glad tidings, his heart was full of joy and his body quivered all over, while his eyes, like the autumnal lotu , were filled with the moisture of affection.

Caupāī 226

Again, Sītā's lord became anxious and said, 'What can be the cause of Bharata's coming ?' Then came one and said : 'There is with him no small army in full equipment.' Rāma was greatly disturbed by the news; on the one hand was his father's injunction, on the other his regard for his brother. Thinking to himself over Bharata's disposition, the Lord's mind found no sure standing-point : but at last he consoled himself with the reflection : 'Bharata is said to be good and sensible.' Lakṣmaṇa saw that his lord was troubled at heart, and spoke out as he thought the occasion demanded : "I speak, sire, before I am asked; but sometimes impertinence in a servant is not impertinent. You, master, are the crown of the wise; I a mere retainer, but I say what I think.

Dohā 226

,You, my lord, are kindly and very simple-hearted, a storehouse of amiability ; you love and trust everyone, and think them all like yourself.

Caupāī 227

Foods given to the pleasures of sense are seized with infatuation on attaining power and betray their true nature. Bharata was well-taught, good and clever, and, as everyone knew, was devoted to his lord's feet; but now that he has become king, he breaks down in his course all the bounds of duty. A wicked and ill-disposed brother having spied out his time, and knowing that Rāma is alone in the forest, he has taken evil counsel and gathered together an army, and has come to make his sovereignty secure. After devising all sorts of wicked schemes, the two brothers have assembled their army and come. If he had no treacherous intent at heart, why should he want to bring chariots and horses and elephants ? But why reproach Bharata needlessly ? All the world goes mad on winning sovereignty.

Dohā 227

The Moon-god seduced his *guru's* wife; Nahuṣa mounted a palanquin borne by Brāhmaṇas ; and who fell so low as Veṇa, the enemy of established usage and Vedic injunctions?

Caupāī 228

Sahasrabāhu, Indra, Triśaṅku—all were brought to disgrace by the intoxication of kingly power.[1] Bharata has devised this clever scheme, so as not to leave himself a single enemy or shadow of obligation anywhere; but in one point he has made

1. The pride of kings and its ruinous results are here illustrated by reference to six famous mythological personages. The first is the great Moon-god, who in the wantonness of power robbed his own spiritual instructor, Vṛhaspati, of his bride Tārā, and had by her a son named Budha, the regent of the planet Mercury. For punishment, he bears for ever in his face the marks of the brand set upon him by the injured husband.

NAHUṢA was the grandson of Purūravas, the founder of the lunar race of kings, who reigned at Pratiṣṭhāna on the Gaṅgā opposite Prayāga. When Indra had temporarily abdicated his throne in heaven, Nahuṣa was selected to fill it. But not satisfied with this dignity, he demanded also Indra's queen. She agreed to receive him, if he came to her in a pālki borne by Brāhmaṇas. At his request the seven great Ṛṣis agreed to do him this service But he was so inflamed with arrogance and lust that they could

a mistake, in despising Rāma as if he had no helper ; he will discover this today with a vengeance, when he sees Rāma's

not walk fast enough for him, and at last, disgusted with his violence and abuse, they threw down the pālki and cursed him and he was turned into a serpent.

VEṆA, the son of Aṅga, as soon as he had been proclaimed monarch of the whole world, forbade any gifts to be given to Brāhmaṇas or sacrifice offered to the gods for that he was sole lord of all and none else was entitled to worship. The holy sages implored him to desist from such impiety, but he would not listen to them. They then struck him with the light blades of grass that had been consecrated by their prayers, and he immediately fell dead.

KĀRTAVĪRYA was a mighty conqueror, who, among other boons granted him by the sage Dattātreya, obtained also this one, that he should have a thousand arms; whence he is here called Sahasrabāhu. One day, when out hunting in the woods, he was hospitably entertained by Jamadagni in his hermitage. But instead of making any proper return for this kindness, he carried off his host's sacrificial cow. Jamadagni's son, Paraśurāma, was away at the time, but when he returned and heard of what had been done, he followed after Kārtavīrya and cut off his thousand arms and slew him. The king's sons, to avenge their father's death, attacked Jamadagni in this hermitage; and in consequence of this, Paraśurāma made his famous vow to extirpate the whole Kṣatriya race.

INDRA, the king of heaven, became enamoured of Ahalyā, the wife of the sage Gautama, and visited her disguised as her husband. The sage saw him as he left her room and cursed him with perpetual loss of virility. Ahalyā was changed into a stone till Rāma should come and deliver her.

TRIŚAṄKU was a king of Ayodhyā, who in his pride aspired to celebrate a great sacrifice and by its merit ascend to heaven in person. He first requested Vasiṣṭha to conduct the ceremony; but the sage saw through his motives and refused him. He then applied to Vasiṣṭha's sons, but they, thinking that he only wished to bring about a quarrel between them and their father, cursed him, so that he became a Caṇḍāla. While in this low estate he killed Vasiṣṭha's cow; and for these three sins, pride, mischief-making, and cow-killing, three great horns grew out of his forehead. He then put himself under protection of Viśvāmitra, who engaged to perform the sacrifice and invited all the gods to it. They, however, declined to come, whereupon Viśvāmitra created new gods, completed the sacrifice, and translated Triśaṅku to the skies. But no sooner had he arrived there than the gods hurled him down again : and falling headlong he was suspended midway, where he is still to be seen, as the constellation in the southern hemisphere called Triśaṅku. The saliva that dropped from his mouth forms the river Karmanāśā, which flows between Banāras and Bihār and which it is considered a pollution to touch.

indignant face in the battle." So saying, he forgot all prudence, and his whole body, so to speak, bristled with pugnacity. Touching his lord's feet and putting the dust of them upon his head, he cried in tones of natural and honest vehemence : "My lord, think it not wrong of me; Bharata has provoked me not a little; how long shall I endure to remain quiet, my lord being with me and my bow in my hand ?

Dohā 228

Am I not of warrior descent, a scion of the house of Raghu, and known throughout the world as Rāma's faithful servant ? What is so low as the dust ? Yet if stirred by a kick it rises and falls upon your head."[1]

Caupāī 229

As he stood with folded hands and sought permission, he seemed like Heroism itself aroused from slumber, binding up his hair in a knot, girding on his quiver by his side, trimming his bow, and taking arrows in hand. "Today I shall distinguish myself as Rāma's servant and will give Bharata a lesson in fighting. Reaping the reward of their contempt for Rāma, both brothers shall sleep on the couch of battle. Well is it that the whole host has come ; today I shall manifest my wrath and have done with it. As a lion rends a herd of elephants, or as a hawk clutches and carries off a quail, so will I lightly overthrow upon the field Bharata and his brother and all their host. If Śiva himself should come to their aid, in Rāma's name I would vanquish him in battle."

Dohā 229

Lakṣmaṇa spoke so furiously that the regents of the spheres, beholding and hearing his solemn oath, looked on in terror and longed to flee away.

1. The general meaning of the passage would seem to be : Bharata has given such provocation that the meanest creature in the world would resent it ; much more should I, who am a warrior by birth.

Caupāī 230

The world was panic-stricken; a voice from heaven was heard in the air, declaring the mighty strength of Lakṣmaṇa's arm : Who can tell, or who can understand, my son, your might and majesty ? But any business, whether right or wrong, should be done deliberately ; so everyone agrees. They who act rashly and afterwards repent, the Vedas say, are anything but wise." On hearing this voice from heaven Lakṣmaṇa was abashed, and both Rāma and Sītā addressed him courteously : "What you have said, brother, is sound wisdom : the intoxication of power is the worst of all. The merest taste of it maddens any king who has not been trained in the school of philosophy. But hearken, Lakṣmaṇa, in all God's creation I have never seen nor heard of anyone so good as Bharata.

Dohā 230

He would never be drunk with sovereign power, even though he sat upon the throne of Brahmā, Viṣṇu and Śiva. What ! can a few drops of sour gruel curdle the Ocean of Milk?

Caupāī 231

The sun may grow dim at midday; yea, sooner may the pure ether be absorbed in cloud; sooner may Agastya[1] be drowned in the puddle of a cow's footprint, or earth forget to be long-suffering; sooner may the buzz of a mosquito blow away Mount Meru, than pride of sovereignty, my brother, touch Bharata. O Lakṣmaṇa, I swear by you and by our father, there is none so true a brother as Bharata. The Creator has fashioned the world by mixing the milk of virtue with the water of sin; Bharata is the swan in the lake of the Solar race, who from the day of his birth has known to distinguish between the good and the evil; choosing the milk of virtue and discarding the water of vice, he has illumined the whole world with his glory." As Raghurāī thus recited Bharata's virtues and amiable disposition, he became drowned in the ocean of love.

1. Who swallowed up the ocean.

Dohā 231

The gods, hearing his speech and beholding his affection for Bharata, all applauded Rāma, saying : "What Lord is there so compassionate as Rāma ?

Caupāī 232

If Bharata had not been born into the world, who was there on earth to be the champion of all righteousness? Bharata's good qualities are more than all the poets could describe; who save you, Raghunātha, could comprehend them ?" When Lakṣmaṇa, Rāma and Sītā heard these words of the gods, they were filled with ineffable joy. Now Bharata and all his host bathed in the sacred Mandākinī. Then leaving the people on the bank and having asked permission from his mother, his *guru* and the minister, he set out to visit Sītā and Raghurāī with the Niṣāda king and his brother. As he remembered his mother's deeds he was abashed, and formed a thousand ill-conjectures in his mind : "What if Rāma, Lakṣmaṇa and Sītā, on hearing my name, should leave the place and go elsewhere ?

Dohā 232

Taking me to be my mother's accomplice, nothing that he might do would be too much; but considering me to be on his own side (or for his honour's sake) he will overlook my sin and folly, and receive me kindly as his well-wisher.

Caupāī 233

Whether he disowns me as a black-hearted wretch, or welcomes me as his servant, my only refuge is at Rāma's sandals; he is the best of masters, the fault is all his servants'. The *cātaka* and the fish are celebrated throughout the world for the thoroughness and constancy of their vows of love." With these thoughts in his mind he went on his way, his whole body rendered powerless by excessive love and diffidence; his mother's sin, as it were, turning him back, while his strong faith, like some sturdy bull, dragged him forward. Whenever he thought of Rāma's loving nature, his feet moved swiftly along the road; his course was like that of a waterfly carried about by the stream. Seeing Bharata's anxiety and affection the Niṣāda was overwhelmed.

Dohā 233

Auspicious omens began to occur, and the Niṣāda after hearing them and making a calculation said, "Sorrow will pass away and joy will succeed; but in the end there will be distress again."

Caupāī 234

Knowing his attendant's words to be all true, he went on and drew near to the hermitage. When Bharata saw the vast woods and rocks, he was as glad as a hungry wretch on getting a good meal. Like people afflicted by every calamity,[1] worn out with troubles,[2] misfortune and pestilence, who rejoice on escaping to a prosperous and well-governed country, so were Bharata's feelings. The forest where Rāma dwelt was as bright and happy as people are happy who have got a good king; with Asceticism for King Wisdom's Minister of State; with the beautiful and sacred groves for his realm; with Continence and Faithfulness for champions; and the hills for his capital; with Peace and Good will for his virtuous and lovely queens; a king perfect at all points; a suppliant at Rāma's feet, and therefore easy in mind.

Dohā 234

Sound Judgment, having conquered king Delusion with all his host, held undisputed sway in his capital : all was joy, happiness, and prosperity.

Caupāī 235

The numerous dwellings of the hermits in the woodland province were his cities, towns, villages and hamlets, and the many

1. Public calamities, or visitations of God, *īti*, are reckoned as seven in number, *viz*. droughts, floods, locusts, rats, parrots, tyranny, and invasion.

2. Trouble (*tāpa*) is of three kinds, specified as *daihika*, *daivika*, and *bhautika*, physical, spiritual and worldly.

birds and beasts of all descriptions were his innumerable subjects. The hares, elephants, lions, tigers, boars, buffaloes and wolves, a wonder to behold, forgetting their antipathies, grazed together, like a duly marshalled army complete in all its parts. The roar of the mountain torrents and the cries of mad elephants were like the din of kettle drums; the *cakavās*, partridges, cuckoos, parrots and koels made a delightful concert; swans were in their glory; the bees hummed and the peacocks danced, as though in that prosperous kingdom joy held universal sway, and there were creepers, trees and grasses, with flowers and fruit, and all these together wore a festive and delightful appearance.

Dohā 235

Beholding the beauty of Rāma's hill, Bharata's heart was filled with love, like an ascetic who is overjoyed when he completes his vow and reaps the fruit of his penance.

Caupāī 236

Then the pilot mounted a height and reaching out his hand cried to Bharata : "See, my lord, those huge trees—fig, rose-apple, mango and *tamālā*[1] in the midst of which is conspicuous a *bar* tree, so beautiful and grand that the soul is charmed at the sight, with dense dark shoots and red fruit, affording a pleasant shade in all seasons of the year, a mass of black and purple, as if God had brought together all that was lovely to make it. Under this tree, near the river, sir, where Rāma has roofed in his sylvan hut, are many grateful shrubs of *tulasī*, planted, some by Sītā's lord and some by Lakṣmaṇa, and in the shade of the banyan tree Sītā with her own lotus hands has reared a charming altar.

Dohā 236

There the all-wise Sītā and Rāma are ever wont to sit in the midst of the hermits, listening while sacred legends are read and all the Vedas, Āgamas and Purāṇas."

1. The *pākar* is the Ficus venosa; the *jāman*, the Eugenia jambolana; the *tamāla*, the Xanthochymus pictorius : the *bar*, or banyan, the Ficus bangalensis.

Caupāī 237

As he listened to his friend's speech and gazed upon the tree, Bharata's eyes overflowed with tears. The two brothers advanced reverently; Śāradā would fail to do justice to their love. When they saw the prints of Rāma's feet they rejoiced like some beggar on finding the philosopher's stone, and applied the dust to their head, heart and eyes, with as much delight as if they had found Rāma himself. Seeing Bharata's utterly indescribable condition, birds, beasts and all created things, whether animate, or inanimate were absorbed in devotion. The guide in his excitement lost the way, but the gods showed it to him and rained down flowers. Adepts (God-realized saints) and aspirants gazed in rapture and burst out into praises of his sincere affection: "Who in all the world is like Bharata, who makes the foolish sensible and the sensible foolish?"

Dohā 237

Raghubīra, the ocean of compassion, after churning the depths of Bharata's soul with the Mount Meru (Mandara) of separation, brought out from it the nectar of love.

Caupāī 238

The two fair brothers and their companion were not visible to Lakṣmaṇa, by reason of the dense shade of the forest; but Bharata could see his lord's sacred hermitage, the charming home of everything delightful. As he entered it his burning grief was assuaged, as when an ascetic is rewarded with salvation. He saw before him Lakṣmaṇa affectionately conversing with his Lord, his hair was knotted on his head, a hermi 's robe girt about his loins, his quiver slung, arrows in his hand, and his bow on his shoulder. By the altar was an assembly of saints and sages, among whom Sītā and Rāma were conspicuous in hermit's attire, with matted hair and body darkened by exposure; like Ratī and Kāmadeva in saint's disguise. He, who with one smiling glance can dispel every fevered anguish of soul, had bow and arrows ready in his lotus hands.[1]

1. The idea would seem to be that Rāma, though the benefactor of the whole world, was obliged in the forest to go armed, to protect himself against attack.

Dohā 238

In the midst of the glorious circle of saints, Sītā and Rāma shone forth as fair as Faith and the Supreme Spirit incarnate in the council-chamber of Knowledge.

Caupāī 239

He, his younger brother and their guide were so absorbed in contemplation that joy and sorrow, pleasure and pain were all forgotten. Crying 'Mercy, mercy, O lord and master !' he fell prostrate to the ground, like a log. Lakṣmaṇa recognized his loving cry and made obeisance, knowing that it must be Bharata. On the one hand he was moved by brotherly affection, but on the other was the stronger claim of obedience to his lord. Unable to embrace him and yet loth to refrain; what poet could describe Lakṣmaṇa's state of mind ? Though obedience was the weightier, and therefore he stayed, he was like a child pulling against a kite high in the air. Bowing his head to the ground, he said affectionately, "It is Bharata, O Raghunātha, who greets you." At these words Rāma started up in affectionate haste, his robe flying in one direction and his quiver and bow and arrows in another.

Dohā 239

Whether he would or no, the gracious Lord raised him up and clasped him to his bosom. Those who witnessed the meeting of Bharata and Rāma lost all self-consciousness.

Caupāī 240

How can such an affectionate meeting be described ? Their thoughts, words and actions were beyond the power of any poet to relate. The two brothers were filled with the utmost affection; self, reason, knowledge and understanding were all forgotten. Tell me, who can express such perfect love ? By what shadow can the poet's mind attain to it ? If the poet has a model, he can work out his meaning by the force of words, and players dance when they have an accompaniment; but the love of Rāma and Bharata is unapproachable, beyond the conception even of Brāhmā, Viṣṇu and Śiva how then can I describe it ? If an instrument is only strung with grass,[1] can it make sweet music ? When the gods saw the meeting of Bharata and Raghubara, they were alarmed and trembled all over; but when Vṛhaspati had spoken to them, they awoke from their folly and rained down flowers and applauded.

Dohā 240

After affectionately embracing Śatrughna, Rāma greeted the boatman; and then Lakṣmaṇa courteously greeted Bharata and did obeisance.

Caupāī 241

When he had fondly embraced his younger brother, Lakṣmaṇa next took the Niṣāda to his bosom. Then the two brothers, Bharata and Śatrughna, after reverencing all the saints and joyfully receiving from them the desired blessing in a rapture of love, placed on their head the dust of Sītā's lotus feet. As they again and again prostrated themselves she raised them up, and with a touch of her lotus hands motioned them to be seated; in her heart invoking a blessing upon them, and so absorbed in affection as to lose all self-consciousness. When Bharata saw Sītā so graciously propitious, he became free from anxiety and all fear passed away. No one made any remark nor asked any question; the soul was so full of love that it ceased to act. Then the boatman took courage and bowing with folded hands made humble petition.

Dohā 241

"Distressed by your absence, my lord, there have come with the great sage your mothers and all the people of the city, the servants, the captains and the ministers of state."

Caupāī 242

When the Ocean of amiability heard the *guru* had come, he left Śatrughna with Sītā and went off in haste that very minute;

1. I know no other instance of the use of the word *gāndara* in the sense of "grass", which is the meaning that the best Hindu commentators give it here. It ordinarily means 'a sheep.'

he who is Rāma, the steadfast, the righteous, the all-merciful. On seeing the *guru*, the Lord and his brother were delighted and fell on their faces to the ground. The holy man ran and raised them up and embraced them, and greeted both brothers with the utmost affection. The boatman trembling with emotion, gave his name and prostrated himself afar off, but the seer must needs greet him as a friend of Rāma's, as though love had been spilt upon the ground and he stopped to pick it up. Faith in Rāma is the source of all blessing; in heaven the gods applauding rained down flowers: "There is no one so utterly vile as he, nor anyone in the world equal to the great Vasiṣṭha :

Dohā 242

Yet the lord of sages on seeing him was overjoyed and embraced him before Lakṣmaṇa, so glorious in their manifestation are the effects of faith in Sītā's lord."

Caupāī 243

Finding all the people distressed, Rāma, the all-merciful, the all-wise and blessed God, gave everyone his wish in the way he most desired; in an instant he and his brother embraced them all and at once relieved the sore anguish of their pain. This was no such great thing for Rāma to do; similarly the sun is reflected at once in a thousand water-jars. All the citizens with rapturous affection embraced the pilot and praised his good fortune. Seeing his mothers as woe-begone like sprays of some delicate creeper smitten by the frost, Rāma first of all embraced Kaikeyī, softening her will by his gentleness and piety. Falling at her feet he soothed her with many words, attributing all the blame to Fate, Destiny and Providence.

Dohā 243

Raghubara embraced all the queens and comforted them, saying: "Mother, the world is subject to God; there is no one to blame."

Caupāī 244

The two brothers did homage to the feet of their *guru's* wife and also to the Brāhmaṇa ladies who had accompanied Bharata, paying the same honour to them as to Gaṅgā and Gaurī; and they with gentle voice gladly gave them their blessing. When he embraced Sumitrā, after clasping her feet, he was like a beggar who has come upon a fortune. Then both the brothers fell at the feet of queen Kausalyā and their whole body was convulsed with love; the mother took them tenderly to her bosom and bathed them with tears of affection. How can any poet describe the mingled joy and grief of such a time, any more than a dumb man can express the sweetness that he tastes? After embracing their mother, Rāma and his brother requested the *guru* to accompany them, and the citizens, with the permission of the high sage, crossed over, admiring the scenery as they went.

Dohā 244

Taking with them the Brāhmaṇas, the Minister, the queens, the *guru*, and some others chosen out of the people, Bharata, Lakṣmaṇa and Raghunātha proceeded to the holy retreat.

Caupāī 245

Sītā came and embraced the sage's feet and received the precious blessing that her soul desired. The affectionate manner in which she greeted the *guru*'s wife and the Brāhmaṇa ladies is beyond description. Again and again she did reverence to the feet of each in turn and received the words of blessing dear to her heart. When the queen-mothers looked at Sītā, they closed their eyes and shuddered to see her so delicate, like some female swan fallen into the clutch of a fowler; what a cruel thing God has done! As they gazed at Sītā, they were distressed beyond measure, that she should have to bear all that Fate had imposed upon her. Then Janaka's daughter summoning up courage, while her dark lotus eyes were suffused with tears, went and embraced all her mothers-in-law. At that hour Pity enveloped the earth.

Dohā 245

Again and again touching their feet, Sītā most tenderly embraced them; and from their heart came the loving benediction: 'May you long live a happy wedded life!'

Caupāī 246

Sītā and the queens being thus agitated by emotion, the learned *guru* bade them all be seated. First he expounded to them the impermanence of the world and spoke a little of the highest reality, and then announced the king's death. At the news Raghunātha was sore distressed; thinking he had died out of love for him, the firmest of the firm was grievously shaken. On hearing the bitter tidings, which fell upon them like a thunderbolt, Lakṣmaṇa, Sītā and all the queens broke out into lamentations, and the whole assembly was as much agitated as if the king had died only that very day. Then the great sage exhorted Rāma and directed him and all the people to bathe in the sacred stream. On that day the Lord took a vow to refrain from drinking water, and though the sage allowed them, no one else would drink either.

Dohā 246

At daybreak, according to the order given him by the sage, the lord Raghunandana reverently and devoutly performed his father's funeral obsequies.

Caupāī 247

Having performed every funeral rite as prescribed in the Vedas, he became pure, even he, the Sun to annihilate the night of sin, whose name is a fire that consumes the cotton of wickedness, and which if merely invoked is the source of all prosperity. He became pure, in like manner as, theologians say, a bather in the Gaṅgā who invokes other *tīrthas* is purified.[1] After his purification, when two days had passed, Rāma said affectionately to the *guru*: "My lord, all the people are much inconvenienced by having nothing to take but water and bulbs and roots and fruit. When I look at Bharata and his brothers, the Minister

1. In the Gaṅgā are concentrated the virtues of all holy places : anyone who bathes in it is purified, and it is therefore a work of supererogation for him to invoke any other power. He cannot make himself cleaner than he had become already; nor could Rāma, the all-pure, become purer by any act of ceremonial purification. [*Tīrthas* are holy places.]

and all the queens, a minute seems to me like an age. Return, I pray, with all of them to the city: for you are here, the king is in heaven, and there is no one left at Ayodhyā. I have said too much and have presumed greatly: but do, holy master, as you think best."

Dohā 247

"O Rāma," replied the *guru*, "bulwark of righteousness, home of compassion, it is but natural for you to speak thus: the people are wearied, let them rest for two days and enjoy your presence."

Caupāī 248

On hearing Rāma's words, the assembly was in dismay, like a ship tossed on the ocean; but when they heard the *guru's* auspicious speech, it was as if the wind had turned in their favour. Three times a day they bathed in the sacred stream, the mere sight of which destroys any multitude of sins; and ever feasting their eyes on the incarnation of blessedness, and again and again prostrating themselves before him, they looked and rejoiced. Then they went to see Rāma's hill and wood where all was good and nought evil: the torrents flowing with streams of nectar; the air so soft, cool and fragrant that it soothed every pain of mind or body; the trees, creepers and grasses of infinite variety; the many kinds of fruit, flowers and sprays; the magnificent rocks and the pleasant shade under the trees, all made the forest beautiful beyond description.

Dohā 248

The ponds were gay with lotuses, the haunt of cooing waterfowl and buzzing bees, while forgetful of mutual antipathies, beasts roamed in the forest and birds of varied plumage.

Caupāī 249

The Kols, Kirātas and Bhīls, the inhabitants of the woods, brought delicious honey sweet as nectar, and piled up leafy bowls with herbs, roots fruit and flowers daintily arranged. With humble salutations they offered them to all telling the taste, character, quality and name of each. The people offered a liberal price, but they would not accept it, and begged them for Rāma's sake to take it back, saying in gentle tones in the depth of their affection: "The good accept what they know to be of love. You are virtuous and we are mean Niṣādas; only by the grace of Rāma have we been admitted into your presence, an honour as difficult of attainment for us as for the desert of Maru to be watered by the Gaṅgā. Rāma is merciful and the Niṣāda's patron; as is the king, so should be his household and subjects.

Dohā 249

Consider this in your mind, and without more demur recognize our affection and make friends with us; accept our fruit and herbs and flowers and make us well content.

Caupāī 250

You have come to the forest as our welcome guests, though we are all unworthy to do you service. And what is it, sirs, that we offer you? Fuel and fodder are a Kirāta's tokens of friendship, and our greatest service is not to steal and run off with your clothes and dishes. Rude creatures are we, often taking life, of vile nature and vile pursuits, low-minded and low-born, who day and night commit sin, without either clothes for the body or food to satisfy the belly; how could we possibly have ever dreamt of the knowledge of virtue, but for the effectual apparition of Rāma? Since we beheld our lord's lotus feet, our sore distress and sin have both been removed." On hearing this speech, the citizens were much affected and broke out into praises of their good fortune.

Chand 10

All began to praise their good fortune and addressed them lovingly, being delighted to find in their speech and attitude such devotion to the feet of Sītā and Rāma. Everyone, man or woman, thought little of his own devotion, on hearing the language of the Kols and Bhīls; through the mercy of the jewel of Raghu's line (says Tulasī) a boat floats, even though laden with iron.

Sorathā 250

Day after day all the people felt as great delight, as they roamed through every part of the forest, as the frogs and peacocks when invigorated by a shower at the beginning of the rains.

Caupāī 251

The citizens of Ayodhyā were so absorbed in excess of love that a day was gone in a minute. Sītā, assuming as many forms as she had mothers-in-law, waited reverently upon them all with equal attention. No one but Rāma noticed the miracle; for all delusion forms part of Sītā's delusive power. Sītā won over all the queens by her services, and they being pleased gave her both instruction and benediction. Looking at Sītā and the two noble brothers, the wicked queen repented bitterly: and Kaikeyī now prays in her heart: "Is there no escape for me? Does God refuse me even death? as it is declared in the Vedas and by popular tradition, and as the poets also have sung, that if Rāma be against you, not even in hell can you find a resting place". "Now this was the question in every one's mind; "O God, will Rāma return to Avadh or not?"

Dohā 251

Bharata was so anxious and sorely agitated that he could neither sleep by night nor eat by day, as a fish sunk in the last of the mud is in trouble about water.[1]

Caupāī 252

"It was Fate in the guise of my mother that did me this injury, as when a ricefield ripening for the harvest is smitten by

1. The fish thinks to himself, 'There is now only a little mud left, in which I can just manage to live; if that too dries up, what on earth am I to do for water ?' In like manner Bharata was thinking. 'The two days are now nearly over; when they are gone and I am left without Rāma, how shall I be able to survive ?

hail. In what manner can Rāma's coronation be secured? There is nothing now left for me to do. He would certainly return if the *guru* asks him, but then the sage will only order what he knows Rāma to wish. At his mother's bidding, too, he would return, but Kausalyā would never insist upon anything. Of what account am I, who am only his vassal, and am fallen upon evil times, and have God against me. If I resist him, it would be a grievous sin; for the duty of a servant to his master outweighs Kailāsa." Without being able to settle a single plan in his mind, Bharata spent the whole night in thought. At daybreak he bathed, bowed his head to his lord, and was sitting down when he was sent for by the Ṛṣi.

Dohā 252

After saluting the *guru's* lotus feet and receiving his permission, he took his seat: while all the Brāhmaṇas, nobles and ministers of state came and assembled in council.

Caupāī 253

The great sage addressed them in words appropriate to the occasion: "Hearken, ye counsellors and you, wise Bharata! The upholder of righteousness, the sun of the Solar race, Rama, the king, the Blessed Lord, on none dependent, true to his word and guardian of the standard of morality set up by the Vedas, has taken birth for the benefit of the whole world. Obedient to the word of his *guru* and his parents; destroying the armies of the wicked and befriending the gods; in policy and devotion, in all things that pertain to this life or the next, there is no one equal to Rāma in the knowledge of what is right. Brahmā, Viṣṇu and Śiva; the sun, the moon, the guardians of the spheres, Delusion, life, Fate, and this Iron age; the sovereigns of hell, the sovereigns of earth and all the powers that be; magic and sorcery and every spell in the Vedas and the Tantras — ponder it in your heart and consider well — all are obedient to Rāma's will.

Dohā 253

If we observe Rāma's pleasure and commands, it will be well for us all; now, wise sirs, think it over, and in your wisdom do whatever may be decided.

Caupāī 254

Rāma's coronation will be agreeable to all, as a sure source of happiness and the one way to felicity. How is he to be brought back to Avadh ? Think before you speak, and upon that plan we will act." All listened respectfully to Vasistha's speech, full as it was of justice, religion and worldly wisdom; but no answer was forthcoming : every one was dumbfounded, till with bowed head and folded hands Bharata spoke: "In the Solar race there have been many kings, each greater than the others. All owed their birth to their parents, but their good or ill fortune was the gift of God. And, as all the world knows, it was through your blessing that they triumphed over their sorrows and attained complete prosperity; whatever the course of fate that you, sir, marked out for them, none could alter it; it was fixed immovably.

Dohā 254

And yet now you ask advice of me : such is my ill fate." When the *guru* heard this affectionate speech, love sprung up in his heart.

Caupāī 255

"My son, your words are true, it is all Rāma's grace: without Rāma no one can ever dream of happiness. There is one way, my son, though I am ashamed to propose it; but a wise man will sacrifice the half when he sees the whole going; do you two brothers go into exile, then Laksmana, Sītā and Rāma will come back." On hearing this welcome speech, the two brothers rejoiced and their whole body thrilled with excitement; they were as pleased at heart and as radiant all over as if king Dasaratha had been restored to life and Rāma were already enthroned. The people gained much and sacrificed little; but the queens all wept, for their pain was equal to their joy.[1] Said Bharata : "What the sage has proposed is already as good as none; he has granted me the one thing above all others that I most desired. I will stay all my life in the forest; there is nothing I should like better.

1. For, though they recovered two of their sons, they lost the other two.

Dohā 255

Râma and Sītā know the secrets of the heart, and you are omniscient and wise. If, my lord, you mean what you say, make your word good."

Caupāī 256

Hearing Bharata's words and seeing his love, the sage and the whole assembly were transported out of themselves. Bharata's vast generosity was like a sheet of water and the sage's proposal like a woman standing on its brink, anxious to cross and trying different ways, but unable to find either ship, boat, or raft. Who can describe Bharata's magnanimity ? Can the ocean be contained in a river-shell? The sage's soul was inwardly charmed with Bharata, and accompanied by the assembly went to Rāma. The Lord saluted him and led him to a seat of honour and on receiving the saint's permission all sat down. Then spoke Vasiṣṭha in well-considered words, according to the circumstances of the place and time : "Hearken, O Rāma, you are omniscient and wise, a storehouse of piety, prudence, virtue and intelligence.

Dohā 256

You dwell in the hearts of all and know their good and evil intents; now advise what will be best for your subjects, your mothers and Bharata.

Caupāī 257

Those who are in pain talk wildly, and a gambler thinks only of his own throw."[1] "On hearing the sage's speech, Raghurāī replied, "My lord, the remedy is in your own hands. To attend to your wishes will be best for all. Only give the order, and cheerfully, I assure you, whatever your commands may be, I answer for myself in the first place those instructions I will dutifully obey; and after me, each, as he has his orders, will hasten to do his service." Said the sage : Rāma, you say truly;

1. Therefore we come for advice to you, being too much excited and having too great a personal interest in the matter to judge for ourselves calmly and impartially.

but Bharata's affection has disturbed calculation; therefore I say again and again my judgment is overcome by Bharata's piety; in my opinion, Śiva be my witness, whatever will please Bharata is the best thing to be done.

Dohā 257

Listen attentively to Bharata's prayer and then reconsider the matter; and after weighing well the duties of a king and the texts of scripture, take the advice given you both by philosophers and men of the world."

Caupāī 258

Seeing the *guru's* great love for Bharata, Rāma's heart was filled with joy, for he knew Bharata to be a champion of righteousness, and in thought, word and deed his own faithful servant. In obedience to the *guru's* commands, he made this sweet, gentle and excellent reply : "I swear by you, my lord, and by my father's feet that in all the world there has been no brother like Bharata. All who love the lotus feet of their *guru* are highly blessed : so say both the world and the Veda. But who can tell Bharata's blessedness, to whom such love has been shown by you ? When I look at him, my younger brother, my senses are abashed, as I thus praise him to his face. It will be best for us to do whatever Bharata says." Having so said Rāma remained silent.

Dohā 258

Then the sage said to Bharata, "Put aside all diffidence, my son, and tell the Ocean of mercy, your own dear brother, what you really have at heart."

Caupāī 259

Hearing the sage's address, and having already received Rāma's consent, he was satisfied of the good-will both of his *guru* and his master; but seeing the weight of the whole business put upon his head, he could say nothing and remained lost in thought, as he stood in the assembly, quivering all over his body, and his lotus eyes filled with the moisture of affection : "The king of sages has already spoken for me : what more is there for me to say ? I know my lord's amiable disposition, that he never shows displeasure even to the guilty; and for me he has a special tenderness and love; even in play he never gave me an angry look. From a child I have never left his side, and never at any time has he hurt my feelings. I have observed my lord's gracious ways, for even when beating me in any game he would let me win.

Dohā 259

I am too much overcome by affection and modesty to say a word before him; to this day my eyes, thirsting for his love, have not been satiated with the sight of him.

Caupāī 260

God could not endure my fondness, and cruelly interposed an obstacle by means of my mother. In saying this now I do myself no honour. Who is made good by his own good estimation ? To get into my mind that my mother is a wretch and I myself good and upright is a thousand times worse. Can rice be produced from ears of *kodo*,[1] or the black shells of a pond give birth to pearls ? Not a shadow of blame or wrong-doing attaches to anyone; it is my ill-luck, like some fathomless ocean. Not perceiving that it is the fruit of my own sins, I revile my mother; to my own undoing I search my heart, but am beaten all round. In one matter only am I really fortunate; with Vasiṣṭha for my *guru* and Sītā and Rāma for my masters, things must come right in the end.

1. The *kodo* (Sanskrit *kodrava* is the *Paspalum frumentaceum or scrobiculatum*, which bears a small grain of inferior quality, eaten only by the door.

Dohā 260

In this honourable assembly of the saints in the presence of my lord and my *guru* and in this holy place, I speak my true sentiments; the sage and Rāma know whether my affection is sincere or feigned, and my words true or false.

Caupāī 261

The whole world bears witness to the king's death, the result of his uncompromising love, and to my mother's wickedness; the queens are so woe-begone that I cannot bear to look at them; the citizens are consumed by intolerable anguish; and I am the cause of all their troubles; and yet though I hear and feel all this, I can still endure the torment. When I heard that Raghunātha had taken with him Lakṣmaṇa and Sītā, and in hermit's robes had set out for the woods, without shoes and walking on foot—be Śankara my witness—how I survived the wound ! Again, when I saw the Niṣāda's devotion, my heart must have been harder than a thunderbolt not to break. And now I have come and with my own eyes have seen everything; surely in this life my wretched soul has borne all that can be borne. The serpents and scorpions on the road at the sight of them forget their virulent venom and savage viciousness;

Dohā 261

but to Kaikeyī, Rāma, Lakṣmaṇa and Sītā appeared as foes! And how can God spare her son, or on whom would he rather inflict intolerable pain ?

Caupāī 262

On hearing these lamentable words of Bharata's fraught with distress and love, humility and discretion, the whole assembly was lost in sorrow and anxiety, as when the frost smites a bed of lotuses. The learned sage comforted Bharata by reference to various ancient legends, and Rāma, the moon of the lilies of the Solar race, spoke thus in seemly wise: "Brother, grieve not your heart in vain; know that the ways of life are in God's hands. To my mind, brother, all the men of highest renown for virtue in all time, past, present or future, and in the three spheres of creation, fall short of you. Whoever even imagines wickedness in you shall perish both in this life and in the next. It is only fools, who have never studied in the school of philosophy and religion, who ascribe blame to your mother.

Dohā 262

Sin and ignorance and the burden of every ill are destroyed by the invocation of your name, glory is won in this world and eternal happiness in the world to come.

Caupāī 263

Be Śiva my witness; I tell you truly : the world, Bharata, depends on your support. Do not, brother, entertain evil surmises to no purpose; love and hatred cannot be hid : birds and beasts come up close to a saint, but flee at the sight of a fowler, though he tries to stop them. If beasts and birds can distinguish between friend and foe, how much more can man, whose body is a vessel of virtue and intelligence. I know you, brother, through and through. How can I do anything that would be discordant with your spirit ? The king, to keep his word, abandoned me and, to keep his vow of love, discarded life; if I now break his word, I shall be heartily grieved; and yet my respect for you is greater; the *guru* moreover has given me his commands; in short, whatever you say, that I am ready to do.

Dohā 263

Set your mind at ease; stop this timidity and speak out; I will do it at once." When they heard Rāma, the ocean of truth, speak thus, the assembly rejoiced.

Caupāī 264

But the king of heaven and all the gods were alarmed and thought that all their plans were destined to be wrecked. Though they took counsel together, nothing came of it; mentally[1] all had recourse to Rāma for protection. After again considering, they said to one another : "Rāma is moved by the faith of the faithful." Remembering the story of Ambarīṣa and Durvāsā, Indra and the gods were greatly dejected. Long time the gods endured distress, till at last Prahlāda revealed Narasiṁha.[2] They beat their heads and whispered in the ear : "Now our only chance lies with Bharata, there is no other plan, sir, that I can see. Rāma accepts service done to one of his servants; do you all with loving heart do service to Bharata and he will subdue Rāma to his own temper."

Dohā 264

When the *guru* of the gods heard this their resolve, he said, "Well done, great is your good fortune; devotion to Bharata's feet is the source of every good in the world.

Caupāī 265

The service of the servant of Sītā's lord is as good as a hundred cows of plenty. Now that you are resolved to put faith in Bharata, cease to have any anxiety: God has provided a way. Behold, O Indra, the extent of Bharata's power; Rāma has voluntarily acknowledged him to be his guide. Make your mind easy, ye gods, never fear, knowing that Bharata is Rāma's shadow." The Lord, who knows the secrets of all hearts, was disturbed when he heard the plans and fears of Bṛhaspati and the other gods. Bharata, knowing that the whole responsibility rested upon him, was raising a thousand different arguments in his mind. After much deliberation, he came to the conclusion that his happiness consisted in obeying Rāma. "He is breaking his own vow

1. If they had gone to him in person their whole scheme would have been frustrated, for Rāvaṇa would have heard of it and thus have become aware of Rāma's divinity.

2. The legends of Ambarīṣa and Prahlāda show how ready Viṣṇu (*i.e.*, Rāma) has always been to hear the prayers of his followers, and how fierce is his indignation against those who persecute them ; it was therefore useless for the gods to think of opposing Bharata; their only plan was to win him over to their side.

in order to satisfy me, and in this is showing me no little love and affection.

Dohā 265

Sītā's lord has in every way done me great and unbounded favour." Then bowing low, and with his lotus hands folded in supplication, Bharata thus spoke :

Caupāī 266

"All-merciful and omniscient lord, what now can I say myself or have others to say for me ? My *guru* is pleased and my master kind ; the imaginary torments of my troubled soul are all over. I feared disgrace, but my fear was unreasonable; it is no fault of the sun's, sir, if a man mistake the points of the compass.[1] My own ill fortune, my mother's wickedness, the odd ways of Providence, and the malignity of fate set themselves firm and combined to overthrow me; but the protector of suppliants has maintained his character. This is no strange procedure of his; it is declared both by scripture and tradition, and is no secret. The world is evil; the Lord only is good; tell me by whose goodness is he good save by his own ? Your attributes, divine Lord, are those of the tree of paradise which is never either for or against any one in particular.

Dohā 266

All who draw near to it and acknowledge that its shade relieves all cares, high or low, rich or poor, ask and obtain the fruit that they desire.

Caupāī 267

Now that I have seen the affection of my *guru* and my master, my troubles are gone and my mind is freed from doubt. Now, O Mine of compassion, do whatever will be for the good of your

1. Your mercy is as sure as the course of the sun; but even with the sun for his guide, a man may lose his way by mistaking the points of the compass; in like manner, I was alarmed through my ignorance of the course that your mercy was taking.

servant, without being a trouble to the soul of my lord. The servant who worries his master and seeks only his own advantage is a base-minded varlet. A servant's gain is to do his master's service, to get him every comfort, and not be greedy. If my lord returns to Ayodhyā, everyone will be a gainer; but obedience to orders will be a thousand times greater gain; it is the highest good in this world, and in the next it is the fruit of all well-doing and the ornament of salvation. Listen, divine Lord, to this my one request, and then do as you think proper. I have prepared and brought with me all the requisites for the coronation; if you approve, Lord, have them brought into use.

Dohā 267

Send me and my brother into the forest and give all your people their king again; or else let Lakṣmaṇa and Śatrughna return and let me accompany you :

Caupāī 268

Or all three brothers go into the woods, and only you and Sītā return. O most merciful Lord, do whatever is most pleasing to yourself. You have cast the whole burden upon me, sire, who am unversed both in politics and theology; I make all my proposals on the ground of worldly interest : but when a man is in distress he cannot reason. A servant who hears his master's orders and answers him is one that Shame herself would be ashamed to look at : and yet though I do this and am a fathomless ocean of faultiness, still my master in his kindness praises me as good. Now, O gracious Lord, that plan best pleases me which will cause my lord's soul the least vexation. By my Lord's feet I swear that I speak the truth; there is only one scheme for securing the world's happiness.

Dohā 268

If my lord cheerfully and without reserve will only give each one of us his commands, they will be reverently obeyed, and all this trouble and perplexity,[1] will be at an end."

1. *Avareva*, which I translate 'perplexity,' is explained by the Hindu commentators as meaning the same as *ghāta* or *penca*. The word is not

Caupāī 269

On hearing Bharata's guileless speech the gods were glad and extolled his generosity and rained down flowers; but the people of Avadh were overwhelmed with uncertainty, and the hermits and all the dwellers in the woods greatly rejoiced. Raghunātha maintained an anxious silence. Seeing his state, the whole assembly became disturbed. At that very moment arrived messengers from Janaka.[1] The sage Vasiṣṭha on hearing of it sent for them at once. They did obeisance and looked towards Rāma. At the sight of his dress they were sorely grieved. The great sage asked the messengers the news : "Tell me, is all well with the king of Videha ?" At this question the noble heralds with a deprecating air bowed their heads to the ground and with folded hands replied: "Your courteous inquiry, sire, makes all well;

Dohā 269

otherwise, my lord, well-being died with the king of Kosala; the whole world is in bereavement, but especially Mithilā and Avadh."

Caupāī 270

When Janaka and his court heard of king Daśaratha's death, everyone was mad with excess of grief. All who at that time saw Videha thought that name a truly appropriate one.[2] As he listened to the tale of the queen's wickedness, the monarch was as bewildered as a serpent without its head-jewel. Bharata king—and Rāma banished to the woods ! Janaka's soul was sore distressed. He enquired of all his wise men and ministers, "Consider and tell me what ought now to be done." Reflecting on the state of Avadh and the double difficulty, if he went or if he stayed, no one gave any answer. After reasoning with him-

given in Dr. Fallon's or any other Hindustani-English Dictionary that I have seen. *Anat* is for *anīti*.

1. Janaka's visit and the long discussions that follow it, which occupy almost all the remainder of this book, are the invention of Tulasī Dāsa, and find no counterpart in the Sanskrit poem.

2. *Videha*, meaning literally 'out of the body,' and Janaka being out of his mind, beside himself, as we should say, for grief.

self, the king resolved to send four clever spies to Avadh, to discover whether Bharata meant well or ill and return in haste without being seen.

Dohā 270

The spies went to Avadh, ascertained Bharata's disposition and saw what he was doing, that he had started for Citrakūṭa, and then went back to Tirahuta.

Caupāī 271

On their arrival, they reported Bharata's doings in Janaka's court to the best of their ability. The *guru*, the citizens, the ministers and the king were all profoundly moved with grief and love at the report. Restraining his emotion and glorifying Bharata, Janaka summoned his warriors, and captains,[1] and having stationed guards for the palace, city, and realm and made ready his horses, elephants, chariots and conveyances of every description, all in about three quarters of an hour, the king set out and halted nowhere on the road, but this morning at daybreak bathed at Prayāga. The host has begun to cross the Jamunā and we, my lord, have been sent on ahead for news." So saying, they bowed the head to the ground. The sage at once gave them an escort of six or seven Kirātas and allowed them to take leave.

Dohā 271

All the people of Avadh were delighted to hear of Janaka's arrival; but Raghunandana was greatly disquieted and Indra overwhelmed with anxiety.

Caupāī 272

The wicked Kaikeyī was sinking with remorse, 'to whom shall I be able to speak or whom can I blame ?' while the people were delighted with the thought that now they had got another day or two to stay. In this manner the day passed. On the morrow all bathed, and after their ablutions they all worshipped Gaṇeśa,

1. *Sāhanī*, which I translate 'captains,' is a word not given in any dictionary.

Gaurī, Śiva and the Sun; then reverenced the feet of Lakṣmaṇa's lord and offered up their prayers, the men[1] raising their joined hands, the women holding out the skirt of their dress : "With Rāma our king and Jānakī our queen, may Avadh, our capital, the centre of all delights, be gloriously re-peopled, court and all, and Rāma instal Bharata as heir-apparent. Revive us all, O Lord, with this ambrosial bliss and grant the world its life's desire.

Dohā 272

May Rāma rule in the city, assisted by his *guru*, the council and his brothers; and may we die with Rāma still Avadh's king." This was the universal prayer.

Caupāī 273

When they heard the citizens' loving prayer, the wise sages thought little of their own penance and austerities. When the people of Avadh had in this manner performed their daily devotions, with much joy they went and did obeisance to Rāma. High and low and of middle estate, men and women, all looked up to him as their own special patron, and he discreetly received them all with due honour. Everyone extolled his inexhaustible generosity : "From a child it was said of Raghubara that he cherishes all in whom he recognizes sincerity and affection; with his bright face, bright eyes and guileless ways, he is a very ocean of amiability and gentleness." Thus affectionately speaking of Rāma's good qualities, all began rapturously to magnify their own good fortune. "There are few people in the world who can have been so meritorious as we, whom Rāma has thus accepted for his own."

Dohā 273

At the time when all were thus absorbed in devotion, they

1. That is to say, in the attitude of beggars; the women holding out the skirt of their dress to catch whatever may be thrown into it, the men holding out their hands.

heard of the approach of the king of Mithilā : the Sun of the lotuses of the Solar race rose in haste, he and the whole assembly.

Caupāī 274

Raghunātha led the way, accompanied by his brothers, the *guru*, the Minister and the people. As soon as the king, Janaka, saw the holy hill, he dismounted from his chariot and saluted it. In their eagerness and excitement to see Rāma, no one felt the slightest fatigue from the toilsome journey, for their soul was with Rāma and Sītā; and who without a soul can be conscious of bodily pain or pleasure ? In this manner Janaka and his host advanced, intoxicated with the drunkenness of love. When they came near and in sight, they lovingly and reverentially began to greet one another. Janaka kissed the feet of the hermits, and Rāma with his brothers, having first reverenced the king's spiritual advisers, embraced him, and led the way for him and his army.

Dohā 274

Rāma conducted the host to the hermitage, as if it were a river of pitifulness flowing into an ocean full of the pure water of quietude;

Caupāī 275

flooding the banks of wisdom and asceticism: with sorrowful speeches for its tributary streams and torrents; with sighs and lamentations for the wind and waves that break the stout trees of resolution on its bank; with grievous anguish for its rapid current, and terror and delusion for its many eddies and whirlpools; with sages for ferrymen and wisdom for the huge boat, which in no wise could be rowed across; while the poor Kols and Kirātas of the woods are the forlorn travellers wearied with waiting. When it reached the hermitage, it was as though the ocean had been agitated with a sudden rush of waters. The two royal hosts were so overcome with grief that they had no wisdom, courage or sense of shame left. Extolling king

Daśaratha's majesty, virtue and amiability, they sorrowed like men drowned in a sea of sorrow.

Chand 11

Drowned in a sea of sorrow, they sorrowed, men and women alike, in utter bewilderment, all angrily and reproachfully exclaiming, 'What is this that cruel fate has done ?' Gods, saints, anchorites, ascetics and sages witnessed Janaka's condition, but his love — says Tulasī — was like a broad river that no one could get over.

Soraṭhā 275

When all the people and the great sages had exhausted every topic of consolation, Vasistha thus addressed Videha : "King of men, be comforted.

Caupāī 276

By the sun of whose wisdom the darkness of the world is dispelled, and in the light of whose speech sages expand like the lotus : how then can the power of delusion and the sense of self affect him? Such is the miracle wrought by love for Sītā and Rāma. There are three classes of beings, whom the Vedas term wise in their generation, the sensual, the aspirant and the saint; amongst the pious the highest honour is for him whose soul is full of love for Rāma: but without knowledge love for Rāma is imperfect, like a boat without a helmsman." When the sage had finished his exhortation to the king, all the people bathed at the Rāmaghāṭa. Everyone, men and women alike, were so agitated with grief that they spent the day without drinking water: even the beasts and birds and deer would eat nothing; much less would his own kindred think of doing so.

Dohā 276

At daybreak the royal son of Nimi[1] and the royal son of Raghu having bathed with all their retinue went and sat under the *bar* tree, sad at heart and wasted in body.

1. *Nimi* was a former king of Videha and one of Janaka's ancestors.

Caupāī 277

The Brāhmaṇas from Ayodhyā, as also those from the capital of the king of Mithilā: Vasiṣṭha, the *guru* of the Solar race, and Śatānanda, Janaka's family priest, who while on earth had explored the path of heaven, began long exhortations full of religion, morality, asceticism and philosophy. Then Viśvāmitra eloquently admonished the assembly with many a reference to legendary stories, till Raghunātha suggested to him: "Sire, everyone since yesterday has gone without water." Said the sage: "Rāma has spoken in season; two-and-a-half watches of the day are now spent." Understanding the sage's pleasure, the king of Tirahuta replied: "It is not good for us to eat bread here."[1] The king's word pleased everyone, and having obtained his permission they went to bathe.

Dohā 277

At the very moment arrived the people of the woods, bringing large baskets laden with friuts, flowers, leaves and roots of every description.

Caupāī 278

By Rāma's favour the mountain had become a granter of desires: merely to look at it removed sorrow. The ponds, streams and glades were bursting as it were with joy and love; the creepers and the trees broke out into blossom and fruit: the birds and beasts made a most melodious concert. In short, the gladsomeness of the forest was surpassing; the air, soft, cool and fragrant, was delightful to everyone; and the beauty of the scene was beyond description, as though the Earth itself had prepared Janaka's reception. When each and all of the people of the city had finished bathing and had received permission from Rāma, Janaka and the sage, they gazed with rapture on the magnificent trees and threw themselves down here and there;

1. This refers to the custom which forbids a Hindu ever to take food in the house of his son-in-law.

while leaves and fruit, flowers and roots of every kind, fresh and fair and sweet as nectar,

Dohā 278

Were courteously sent to all, in baskets full, by Rāma's *guru*; on which they made their repast, after reverencing their ancestors, the gods, their guests and the *guru*.

Caupāī 279

In this manner four days were spent, in which the people gazed on Rāma and were happy. In both camps there was this desire at heart. "It is not good for us to return without Sītā and Rāma. Life in the woods in their society is a thousand times better than heaven. If anyone, in his longing for home, would desert Lakṣmaṇa, Rāma and Sītā, his fate is an unlucky one: it is the height of good fortune for us all to dwell in the woods near Rāma, bathing three times a day in the Mandākinī, seeing Rāma, which will be a constant delight, rambling about on Rāma's hill and among the hermitages in the wood, and feeding on sweet herbs and roots and fruit, so contentedly that the fourteen years will pass like a minute, without our knowing how they go.

Dohā 279

We are not worthy of so great happiness," they all exclaimed. "What luck can be like it ?" Such was the spontaneous devotion to Rāma's feet in both camp .

Caupāī 280

In this manner as all were expressing their hearts' desire in affectionate words, which it ravished the soul to hear, Sītā's mother sent a handmaid, who ascertained that it was a convenient time and returned. On learning that Sītā's mothers-in-law were at leisure, Janaka's queen and her attendants came to visit them. Kausalyā received them with due honour and gave them such seats as circumstances allowed. On both sides there was such love and tenderness, that the most rigid thunderbolt would have melted, could it have seen and heard. Their body quivering and unnerved, their eyes full of tears, and all lost in grief, they drew lines with their toes on the ground, each a separate incarnation of love to Sītā and Rāma, or tearful Sympathy taking many forms. Said Sītā's mother, "Perverse is the judgment of God, who has used the thunderbolt for a chisel to break up the froth of milk!

Dohā 280

We hear of ambrosia but see only venom; all his doings are hard; crows, owls and cranes are everywhere, but swans only in the inaccessibe Mānasa lake."

Caupāī 281

Upon this, queen Sumitrā said sadly: "God's ways are contrary and unaccountable. He creates and cherishes, and then destroys: his purposes are as idle as child's play." Said Kausalyā, "It is no one's fault; pain and pleasure, loss and gain, are governed by fate: the effects of action are inscrutable; God only knows them, who awards its own fruit to every act, whether it be good or bad. The Lord's decree dominates over all, whether for rising, staying or falling, whether for poison or ambrosia. It is vain, O queen, to give way to sorrow; God's schemes are, as I have said, unchangeable and from everlasting. Consider the question of the king's life or death; look now, friend, and think whether it was a loss to him or gain." Sītā's mother replied: "Noblest of noble women, consort of Avadh's kings, your eloquent words are true.

Dohā 281

If Lakṣmaṇa, Rāma and Sītā stay in exile, all will be right in the end and no harm done". "But", said Kausalyā with heavy heart, "I am anxious about Bharata.

Caupāī 282

By God's favour and your blessing, my son and his wife[1] are both pure as Gaṅgā water. Though I have never yet sworn by

1. For *suta-badhu*, 'a son's wife,' might be better to read *su-bandhu*, 'good brother.'

Râma, I now invoke him to witness, friend, that I speak truly. The greatness of Bharata's generosity, goodness and humility, his brotherly affection, devotion, hope and charity, even Sarasvatī's eloquence would fail to declare; can the ocean be ladled out with a shell ? I have always known that Bharata was the glory of his house, and the king repeatedly told me so. Gold is tested on the touchstone and precious stones by the jeweller; a man's temper is tried by fortune. It is not right for me now to have spoken thus; but sorrow and love have left me little reason." On hearing these words, as pure as Gaṅgā stream, all the queens were overcome with emotion.

Dohā 282

Kausalyā composed herself and said, "Hearken to me, queen of Mithilā, and take courage. Who is able to advise you, the consort of the wisest of men ?

Caupāī 283

Having found a fitting opportunity, speak, madam, to the king as if of yourself, and suggest that he should stop Lakṣmaṇa and let Bharata go to the forest. If the king agrees to this proposal, I will then devise and carry out some proper plan. I am greatly disturbed about Bharata, for his love is so profound that if he stays at home I surmise evil." When they marked her generosity and heard her frank appeal, they were all overpowered with sympathy. There was a shower of flowers from heaven with cries of 'Glory', 'Glory;' saints, ascetics and sages grew faint with love. The queens, despite their fatigue, still looked and waited till Sumitrā made bold to say : "Lady, nearly an hour of the night is gone." At this Kausalyā graciously arose and affectionately

Dohā 283

Said, "Pray return at once to your tent ; of a truth now our help is in God and the king of Mithilā."

Caupāī 284

Seeing her affection and hearing her modest speech, Janaka's queen clasped her holy feet and said, "Lady, this modesty on your part is only natural, since you are Daśaratha's wife and Rāma's mother. Monarchs give honour to the lowest of their servants; in the same way as fire tops itself with smoke and a hill with grass. King Janaka is your servant in thought, word and deed, and Mahādeva and Bhavānī are your constant auxiliaries. Who is there on earth who can act as your supplement ? Does the sun shine brighter with the help of a torch ? After going into exile and assisting the gods, Rāma will hold undisputed sway at Ayodhyā. Through the might of his arm gods, serpents and men will all dwell in peace, each in his own place. This has all been foretold by Yājñavalkya; and the words of a sage, lady, can never be false."

Dohā 284

So saying, she fell at her feet and affectionately requested that Sītā might go with her ; permission was accorded and Sītā set out with her mother.

Caupāī 285

Sītā greeted all her dear kinsfolk in such manner as in each case was most befitting. When they saw her in hermit's dress, they were all distressed with exceeding sorrow. Janaka, on receiving the permission of Rāma and the *guru*, came to the tent to see his daughter and clasped her to his bosom, the sanctifying guest of the soul of love. His bosom swelled, like the ocean, with affection, and his royal soul resembled Prayāga ; with his love for Sītā conspicuous as the spreading banyan tree, on which the love of Rāma appeared like the child, clutched for support by the king's bewildered senses as by the sage Cirañjīva when on the point of drowning.[1] Videha was so overwhelmed by his feel-

1. The sage Mārkaṇḍeya had the presumption to ask Nārāyaṇa to show him a specimen of his delusive power. The god in answer to his prayer drowned the whole world in a sudden flood. Only the Akṣaya-baṭa, or imperishable fig-tree at Prayāga, raised its head above the waters, with a little

ings that he had no sense left ; such is the power of love for Sītā and Raghubara.

Dohā 285

Sītā could not bear to see her father and mother so overcome by affection, but calling to mind both the time and her own duty, Earth's daughter summoned up courage.

Caupāī 286

When Janaka looked at her in her anchorite's dress, he was filled with love and contentment : "Daughter," he said, "you have sanctified both families; everybody in the world proclaims your brilliant renown. The stream of your fame excels the Gaṅgā and has spread over millions of universes. The Gaṅgā has only three great sites[1] on earth, but the congregations of saints that have been made by you are innumerable." At her father's sincere and loving eloquence Sītā was abashed and shrank into herself. Again her father and mother took her to their arms and gave her kind instructions and invoked rich blessings upon her. Sītā could not speak out, but was troubled at heart: "It is not well for me to spend the night here." The queen saw her wish and explained it to the king, inwardly praising the excellence of her disposition.

Dohā 286

After again and again embracing her, they graciously bade her farewell. Having now an excellent opportunity, the discreet queen adroitly mentioned Bharata's state of mind.

Caupāī 287

When the king heard of Bharata's conduct, brilliant as gold, refreshing as sweet perfumes, consolatory as ambrosia or the soft light of the moon, he closed his tearful eyes and his body thrilled with rapture, as he broke out into ecstatic praises of his

child seated on one of its topmost boughs, that put out its hand and rescued the terrified saint as he was on the point of sinking.

1. They are Haridvāra, Prayāga, and Sāgara.

glory. "Mark me well, fair-faced and bright-eyed queen, the legend of Bharata is effectual to loosen the bonds of existence. According to my ability, I too have mastered somewhat of theology, statecraft and spiritual meditation; but whatever my ability. if I would tell Bharata's greatness, I cannot make a pretence of reaching even its shadow. Brahmā, Gaṇeśa, Śeṣanāga, Śiva, Sarasvatī, the inspired poets and the sages most renowned for wisdom, when they hear or meditate upon Bharata's acts, his glory, his vigour, his piety, his temper, his virtues and his spotless dignity, all are enraptured; it has a flavour of purity like the Gaṅgā surpassing ambrosia.

Dohā 287

His excellence is limitless and he is incomparable; I know none like Bharata but himself. Can Mount Sumeru be weighed in any balance? The wit of the whole race of poets is at fault.

Caupāī 288

He is, fair dame, as impossible to describe as it is impossible for a fish to walk on dry land. Hearken, lady; Rāma knows it, but even he cannot describe Bharata's illimitable majesty. If Lakṣmaṇa returns and Bharata goes to the forest, everyone will imagine it to be good for all: but, lady, Bharata's love for and confidence in Rāma are past all telling, Bharata is the perfection of love and devoted attachment, but Rāma is the model of impartiality. Bharata's mind has never even dreamt of all the felicities of this world and the next; only his love for Rāma's feet has brought him success. This, I consider, is Bharata's creed.

Dohā 288

Bharata would never be beguiled into thwarting an order of Rāma's; do not then in your affection give way to sorrow," said the king, and sighed as he spoke.

Caupāī 289

As the wedded pair thus affectionately discoursed of the excellences of Rāma and Bharata, the night passed like a minute.

At daybreak both the royal camps awoke and bathed and worshipped the gods. After bathing, Rāma approached his *guru*, embraced his feet, and on receiving permission spoke thus: "My lord, Bharata and the citizens and my mothers are distressed and inconvenienced by their sojourn in the woods. The king of Mithilā, too, and his retinue have been enduring hardships for many days ; be pleased to do, my lord, as seems to you good ; the happiness of all is in your hands." So saying, Rāma was greatly abashed. The sage thrilled with delight on seeing his disposition. "Without you, Rāma, the greatest bliss would seem to both the royal hosts like hell.

Dohā 289

You, O Rāma, are the soul of their soul, the life of their life, the joy of their joy. Anyone, my son, who would desert you for the sake of the pleasure of home has destiny against him.

Caupāī 290

Perish the happiness, the actions and religion, in which is no love for Rāma's lotus feet ! That piety be impiety, and wisdom unwisdom, in which love for Rāma is not supreme ! Through you men are made happy, and without you they are unhappy ; you know the heart of everyone. Your commands rule all, and every motion is thoroughly manifest to your benignity. Return now to the hermitage." The lord of sages was overpowered with love. When Rāma had bowed and retired, the *guru* composed himself and went to Janaka, and repeated to him what Rāma had said, enlarging upon his amiability, affection and excellent disposition : "Now, sire, do whatever will be for the advantage of all without prejudice to religion.

Dohā 290

You, O king of men, are the wisest among the most wise, the champion of true piety ; who save you can at this time resolve our doubts ?"

Caupāī 291

Janaka was so moved by the sage's address and by the sight

of his agitation that all his philosophy and asceticism were forgotten. Faint with love, he reasoned to himself: "I have not done well in coming here. Daśaratha ordered Rāma into exile, but himself gave the best proof of his affection; I have now sent him from one wood to another and return in triumph forsooth with increased reputation for wisdom." Seeing the agitation of the anchorites, sages and Brāhmaṇas, the king was still more overwhelmed with emotion; but considering the circumstances he made an effort, and with his retinue set forth to visit Bharata. Bharata advanced to meet him and gave him the best seat the time allowed. "Bharata, my son", said the king of Tirahuta, "you are well acquainted with Rāma's character.

Dohā 291

Rāma is devoted to truth, a zealot in performing his duty; he respects the feelings and affection of all; out of loving-kindness towards all, he endures inconvenience without murmuring; but if you have any orders to give, speak."

Caupāī 292

At this Bharata's whole frame quivered and his eyes filled with tears; but putting a strong restraint upon himself he replied: "My lord, I love and revere you as my father, and hold you as dear as my own family *guru*; father and mother I have none. Here are Viśvāmitra and the other sages, and all this assembly; you too yourself, an ocean of wisdom; I am your obedient son and servant: regard me in this light, my lord, and instruct me. In such an assembly and such a holy place that you should question me! If I am silent, I shall look sad; if I speak, I shall sound mad. Can I speak great words out of my little mouth? Pardon me, father; the facts are against me. It is declared in the Vedas, Tantras and Purāṇas, and all the world knows, that loyal service is difficult. Duty to a master conflicts with self-interest, the deaf and blind cannot show their love.

Dohā 292

Have regard to Rāma's wishes, so pious as he is, and remember that I am but a servant: do as all approve and what is best for all, but forget not the love all feel for him."

Caupāī 293

When the king heard Bharata's speech and witnessed his generosity, he and his court burst out into praises. Simple but profound; soft and delicate but severe; pregnant with meaning in a small compass; his speech was as mysterious as the shadow of a face in a glass, which no hand can grasp. The king, Bharata, the sage, and all the venerable assembly went to Rāma, by whom the gods were made as glad as the lilies by the moon. On hearing the news all the people were as distressed as fish in unaccustomed waters. The gods, seeing first the emotion of the family *guru* and then Janaka's exceeding affection, and Bharata so full of devotion to Rāma, were selfishly dismayed and began to despond. When they saw everyone full of love for Rāma, the company of heaven was unutterably apprehensive.

Dohā 293

Indra cried sadly, "Rāma is overcome by love and modesty. We must combine to devise some scheme, or else we shall be undone."

Caupāī 294

The gods invoked Śāradā in flattering terms : "Protect, O goddess, the gods your suppliants. Exert your magic influence to change Bharata's purpose and by some deceptive artifice rescue the host of heaven." When the wise goddess heard their prayer, she understood their stupid selfishness and said : "You tell me to change Bharata's purpose; you have a thousand eyes and yet cannot see Mount Meru. The illusive power of Brahmā, Viṣṇu and Śiva is exceedingly great, but it cannot see through Bharata's purpose, and yet you tell me to pervert it. What ! can the moonlight rob the moon ? Bharata's heart is inhabited by Sītā and Rāma; can darkness invade the splendour of the sun ?" So saying, Śāradā withdrew to Brahmā's heaven, and the gods were as downcast as the *cakavā* at the approach of night.

Dohā 294

The self-seeking gods were troubled at heart and devised

plots and wicked stratagems and artifices of fear, error, sorrow and vexation.

Caupāī 295

Indra practised this villainy, thinking that success or defeat was all in Bharata's hands. When Janaka approached Rāma, the glory of the Solar race received them all with honour. Then spoke Vasiṣṭha in terms appropriate to the time, the assembly and the principles of religion, mentioning the conversation between Janaka and Bharata, and eloquently repeating all that Bharata had urged. "Rāma, my son, whatever command you may give will be obeyed; this is my conclusion." Upon this Raghunātha, clasping his hands, made truthful and guileless reply in gentle tones: "In the presence of yourself, sir, and the king of Mithilā, for me to speak is altogether out of place. Whatever command you may be pleased to give I swear by yourself I am ready to comply."

Dohā 295

On hearing Rāma's oath the sage and Janaka and the whole assembly were confounded; and fixed their eyes on Bharata's face helplessly and without power to answer.

Caupāī 296

Bharata saw the distress of the assembly, and being Rāma's brother, put a strong restraint upon himself. Seeing the unfitness of the time, he subdued his emotion, in the same way as Agastya bowed down the Vindhya mountain.[1] Grief, like Hiraṇyākṣa, carried away his soul as if it were the earth; but at once from his spotless perfection like the womb of the universe came forth the mighty Boar[2] of discretion and wrought immediate deliverance.

1. Agastya is said to have compelled the Vindhya mountains to prostrate themselves before him; and when once down, they were never able to rise again. This he did to oblige the sun, who found the range so high that he could with difficulty climb it in his daily passage from east to west.

2. The allusion is the third Avatāra, when Viṣṇu in the form of a Boar rescued the earth, which had been seized by the demon Hiraṇyākṣa and carried off into the depths of the ocean.

With folded hands he bowed reverentially to all, to Rāma, the king, the *guru*, and the sages: "Pardon me if today I act most unbecomingly and with the tongue of a child speak stubborn words." As he mentally invoked the gracious Śāradā, from the depths of his soul there came to his lotus mouth a swan-like strain fraught with pure intelligence, piety and righteousness.

Dohā 296

With the eyes of discernment, Bharata saw that the whole company was faint with love; bowing low and invoking Sītā and Rāma, he thus spoke:

Caupāī 297

"My Lord, you are my father and mother, my friend, my *guru* and my master; object of my adoration, my best benefactor, reader of my heart; the kindest of patrons, the perfection of amiability, the protector of the humble; the all-learned, the all-wise; the powerful befriender of suppliants; quick to appreciate merit and to ignore demerit and wickedness; my sovereign, my god-like God; while no servant can be so bad as I am. In my folly I have come here at the head of an army, in defiance of the commands of my lord and my father. In the world are good and bad, high and low, ambrosia and immortality, poison and death; but never have I seen or heard of anyone who even in thought could cancel an order of Rāma's. Yet I have been thus presumptuous, and my Lord in his kindness has taken it as service.

Dohā 297

Out of his own grace and goodness he has made me good; my errors have become adornments and my fair fame has been spread all around.

Caupāī 298

Your mode of procedure, your gracious speech, and generosity are known throughout the world; they are sung in the

Vedas and Tantras. The cruel, the perverse, the vile, the low-minded, the outcast, the base, the ill-conditioned, the godless, the reckless, so soon as you hear that they have come before you as suppliants and have made a single prostration, are all reckoned as friends. Though you perceive faults, you never take them to heart ; and if you but hear of virtues you proclaim them in the assembly of the sages. What other master is so kind to his servants, so perfect in all points, who never dreams of reckoning up what he has done himself, and is heartily vexed at any embarrassment of his servants. He is my sovereign Lord, and there is none other, with arms upraised, I declare on oath. A beast may dance and a parrot be a clever talker; but all depends upon the music of the dancing-master and the method of the teacher.

Dohā 298

Who now has corrected his servant and treated him with honour and made him the crown of the head of the just. Who is there, save the All-merciful, who, whether we will or no, maintains our fair fame ?

Caupāī 299

Whether it was from grief and affection or from mere childishness that I came here in spite of your commands, you in your compassion have looked upon me as a friend and in every way taken it in good part. Seeing your blessed feet and knowing my Lord's natural benignity, I look upon this great assembly as a piece of good fortune, and my great sin as evidence of my Lord's kindness ;[1] for by his gracious favour he has satisfied my whole being and his compassion has exceeded everything. Out of the goodness of his own disposition my good Lord has made sure of my fidelity. I have now displayed great audacity in discarding respect for my master and this assembly and speaking boldly or humbly, just as the fancy moved me ; but pardon me, Lord, for I am in grievous perplexity.

1. The meaning would seem to be : the greater my sin, the greater his kindness in forgiving it, and the greater the assembly, the greater my glory in having so many witnesses to his love.

Dohā 299

It is a great mistake to say overmuch to a master who is loving, intelligent and good. Be pleased, my lord, to give your commands and set me all right.

Caupāī 300

I swear by the dust of my Lord's lotus feet, the glorious quintessence of truth, virtue and happiness; with an oath I protest that the desire of my soul, whether waking, sleeping or dreaming, is to serve my lord with spontaneous devotion, without any regard to self-interest, fraud, or my own ends in this life or the next. There is no duty so imperative as submission; let your servant, Lord, win this favour."[1] So saying, he was utterly overwhelmed with emotion ; his body quivered, his eyes filled with tears, and in great agitation he clasped his Lord's lotus feet. So pathetic a scene defies description. The Ocean of compassion honoured him with gracious words and took him by the hand and seated him by his side; while himself and all the assembly were overpowered by love,[2] after hearing Bharata's prayer and seeing his disposition.

Chand 12

The Lord of Raghus himself, the august assembly, the sage, the king of Mathilā, all were faint with love and silently applauded the exceeding greatness of Bharata's brotherly affection and devotedness. The gods too praised Bharata and rained down flowers, though with a heavy heart. Everyone, says Tulasī, was as distressed by what he had heard as the lotus that withers at the approach of night.

Soraṭhā 300

Seeing every man and woman in both assemblies so grieved

1. That is to say, favour him with some order, that he may show how good a servant he is, by his immediate submission to it.

2. *i.e.*, 'Raghurāū and the assembly wellnigh swooned with love...'

and downcast, Indra,[1] vile wretch, still sought his own happiness, slaying as it were the already slain.

Caupāī 301

Though king of the gods, there is no limit to his deceitfulness and villainy; he loves another's loss and his own gain; Pākaripu's[2] ways are like those of a crow—crafty, disreputable and with no faith in anyone. Having in the first instance formed an evil design and accumulated deceits he piled up trouble on the heads of all. Everyone was infatuated by the god's delusive power; their love for Rāma was so violent that they would not be separated from him. They were all distracted; with nothing settled in their mind; at one moment longing for the woods, at another anxious to return home. The people in their distress had the current of their ideas as disturbed as the

1. "Though Tulasī Dāsa constantly appeals to the authority of the Vedas, it is clear that like 999 out of 1,000 of the most educated of his countrymen in the 19th century, he had not the faintest idea of their contents; otherwise he would not have spoken thus disrespectfully of Indra, who is one of the principal Vedic divinities, while Śiva, whom he places in a much higher sphere and regards as one of the manifestations of the Supreme Spirit—while Indra and the others are mere demi-gods—is a power for whose cultus the Vedas, though searched from beginning to end, would fail to supply any authority. If a Brāhmaṇa were now to set up a temple at Mathurā or Banāras to Indra, or Mitra, or Varuṇa, or any other Vedic divinity, he would be thought as eccentric as an Englishman who should rededicate a shrine to Diana in the precincts of St. Paul's churchyard in the city of London. Perhaps more so; for the characters of the old Greek and Roman Pantheon are still thoroughly familar to modern Europeans and have considerable influence upon art and literature; while the Vedic mythology has utterly perished, and scarcely a single name in it would be recognized by any native of India except a professed pandit. Nor is this very surprising, inasmuch as the Vedas were not really composed by Hindus, nor have Hindus in any past time ever adopted them as a religious standard. To regard them in that light now is—as the founders of the Brahmā Samaj soon discovered—an impracticable absurdity. Dating from a time when neither Englishman nor Hindu had yet come into existence, they are the common inheritance of all nations of Aryan descent. Their intrinsic value is *nil*; the only interest they possess is due to the fact that they are the earliest surviving record of the first semi-inarticulate utterances of nascent humanity."—Growse.

2. *Pākaripu*, 'Pāka's enemy,' is one of Indra's names, in consequence of his having destroyed a demon called Pāka."

water at the confluence of a river with the sea. Thus wavering in mind they got no comfort in any quarter; no one told another his secret thoughts. Seeing this, the Ocean of compassion smiled to himself and said, "Indra is like a dog and young (licentious) men in his ways !"

Dohā 301

Excepting Bharata, Janaka, the sages, the ministers and the more intelligent nobles, the heaven-sent delusion took effect upon all, according to the circumstances of the individual.

Caupāī 302

The Ocean of compassion saw the people distressed by their love and by Indra's potent deception ; the assembly, the king, the *guru*, the Brāhmaṇas and the ministers, all with their hearts under the spell of Bharata's devotion ; motionless as pictures, gazing upon Rāma, nervously uttering words which they seemed to have learnt by rote. The eulogy of Bharata's love, humility, modesty and greatness is delightful to hear, but how difficult to pronounce ! Seeing only the tiniest morsel of his devotion, the sages and the king of Mithilā were absorbed in love ; how, then, can I, Tulasī, tell its greatness? It is only by the blessing of faith that the ambitious design of my heart has prospered. I am little : I know the enormous greatness of my subject, and I shrink in confusion before a crowd of other poets ; unable to utter the vehemence of my passionate love for his perfection, the motions of my fancy are like the stammerings of a child.[1]

Dohā 302

Bharata's spotless fame is as the bright moon rising in the bright sky of a faithful heart, ever intently watched by my daring fancy as by an unfledged partridge.

1. Most readers of the original will agree with the poet that his powers of expression have here been scarcely adequate to the intensity of his feelings. All this part of the poem abounds with obscure and involved passages, the precise interpretation of which is often very difficult to determine, and I cannot flatter myself that I have invariably succeeded in hitting upon it.

Caupāī 303

Bharata's magnanimity is scarce fathomable by the Vedas; wherefore, ye poets, pardon the frivolities of my poor wit. Who that hears or tells of Bharata's perfect nature does not become enamoured of the feet of Sītā and Rāma? Whoever invokes Bharata and still finds love for Rāma a difficult matter is a monster without a parallel. Seeing the state that everyone was in, the merciful and all-wise Rāma, who knows their devotion to him, being the staunch champion of religion, a master of policy, an ocean of truth and love and amiability and everything good, having considered the place and circumstances, the time and assembly, Raghurāja, the maintainer of justice and affection, delivered a speech, the quintessence of all eloquence, sweet as the moon's ambrosia at the time of hearing, and salutary also in the end: "Bharata, my brother, you are the champion of righteousness, perfectly conversant with all the laws of the world and the Vedas;

Dohā 303

For purity of thought, word and act, your only equal, dear brother, is yourself. In this venerable assembly of *gurus* and in such distressing circumstances how can all the virtues of my younger brother be told?

Caupāī 304

You know, my brother, the custom of the Solar line and the renown and the affection of our father, that Ocean of truth; the circumstances of the time and of this assembly, the reverence due to these venerable personages, and the secret thoughts of all men, whether they be indifferent, or friends, or unfriends, are understood by you, as also your own highest gain and mine and the requirements of religion. I have entire confidence in you and yet I speak as the circumstances suggest. My words, brother, in the absence of my father, have been kept straight only by the favour of the *gurus*; otherwise all my subjects, together with the citizens, the people of the palace and myself, would have been ruined. If the lord of day sets at the wrong time, tell me, will not the whole world be in confusion ? Such trouble, brother, fate had ordained ; but the sage and the king of Mithilā have averted it.

Dohā 304

Not only the affairs of the state, but our honour and fair name, our virtue, land, wealth and homes all these will be protected by the power of the *guru*, and everything will be well in the end.

Caupāī 305

My followers and yours, the palace and the forest, are both protected by his favour. The order of a father or mother, a *guru* or a master, is like Śeṣanāga, the supporter of a whole world of righteousness. Obey it yourself, brother, and let me obey it, and thus become a protector of all the Solar race. Obedience is the one means for the attainment of every success, a triple flood of Glory, Salvation, and Power. Having thus reflected, endure the grievous burden and make your people and family happy. I have distributed my afflictions amongst you all ; but upon you is the full weight of the greatest difficulty. I know your tender heart, though I speak harshly; the times, brother, are so out of joint that this will not be unjustifiable on my part. In an emergency a brother is used for a shield, in the same way as the stroke of a sword is parried by the hand."

Dohā 305

A servant is like a hand, or foot, or eye ; a master is like the head. Hearing this description of love, says Tulasī, great poets are full of admiration.

Caupāī 306

When they heard Raghubara's speech, imbued, as it were, with nectar churned up from the ocean of affection, the whole assembly became lost in an overpowering trance of love. Śāradā herself was struck dumb at the sight of them. Bharata was immensely consoled by the graciousness of his Lord and his putting away of every trouble and wrong-doing. Cheerful of aspect and with the grief of his soul effaced, he seemed like a dumb man who has received the gift of speech. Affectionately bowing again and again and folding his lotus hands, he thus spoke, "My Lord, I am as happy as if I had gone with you ; I have reaped the reward of being born into the world. Now, O merciful sire, whatever may be your order, that will I dutifully and reverently obey. But, grant me, Lord, some support, by the help of which I may struggle on to the end of the time.

Dohā 306

In compliance with the *guru's* command, sire, I have brought here water from all holy places for the purpose of your royal inauguration : what are your orders concerning it ?

Caupāī 307

I have one great desire in my heart, but for fear and shame I cannot tell it." "Tell me what it is, brother," said the Lord, and at his command he replied in affectionate and winning terms : "With your permission I would go and see Citrakūṭa with all its hermitages, shrines and woods, its birds and beasts, its ponds and streams, its waterfalls and rocks, and the spot[1] so specially marked with the print of my Lord's feet." "Certainly, brother : only obtain Atri's permission, and then wander without fear through the woods. It is the sage's blessing, brother, that makes the forest so auspicious, holy and exquisitely beautiful. In whatever place the king of seers may direct you, there deposit the holy water." On hearing his Lord's words, Bharata was glad and joyfully bowed his head to the sage's lotus feet.

Dohā 307

When the selfish gods heard this most delightful conversation

1. One of the temples of Citrakūṭa bears the name of Caraṇa-pādukā, and has been erected over a rock which is said to bear the impression of Rāma's foot. Supposing there were any truth in the legend, it would seem rather from the name that it ought to commemorate the place where Rāma gave Bharata his sandals.

between Bharata and Rāma, they praised the whole family and rapturously showered down flowers upon them.

Caupāī 308

"Blessed be Bharata and glory to Rāma, the holy Lord !" cried the gods in their irrepressible delight. The sage, the king of Mithilā and everyone in the assembly rejoiced on hearing Bharata's speech. King Videha broke out into ecstatic praises of the many virtues and affection both of Bharata and Rāma ; master and servant of equally charming disposition, their fidelity and love the purest of the pure. The ministers too and the councillors affectionately extolled them, as each best could. In both camps there was blended joy and sorrow, when they heard the conversation between Rāma, Bharata and the sage. Rāma's mother, feeling pleasure and pain equally balanced, exhorted the queens, reckoning up both good and evil. One would magnify Rāma, another would praise Bharata's amiability.

Dohā 308

Then said Atri to Bharata, "There is a fine well near the hill ; there deposit the holy water, pure, ambrosial, incomparable."

Caupāī 309

On receiving Atri's command, Bharata despatched all the water vessels, and himself with Śatrughna, Atri the sage and the saints went to the unfathomable well.[1] There he poured out the holy water on that sacred spot ; and Atri in a rapture of affection thus spoke : "Son, this has been a holy place from all eternity ; but time had obscured it, and it was known to no one, till my servants, seeing the spot to be a desirable one, made this great well for the sake of a good supply of water. By the decree of fate the whole universe has been benefited, and a merit most difficult to compass has been rendered easy. People will

1. Vālmiki makes no mention of this well. Under the name of the Bharata-kūpa, it is now one of the seven principal stations visited by the pilgrims to Citrakūṭa.

now call it Bharata's well, hallowed in a special degree by the combination in it of the water of all holy places. Everyone who lovingly and religiously bathes in it, will be made pure in thought, word and act."

Dohā 309

All then returned to Raghunātha, telling the virtue of the well; and Atri explained to him the blessed efficacy of that holy place.

Caupāī 310

The night was pleasantly spent in loving discourse on matters of religion and sacred legends until it was dawn. After performing their daily duties, Bharata and his brother, having received permission from Rāma, Atri and the *guru*, proceeded on foot with all their retinue in simple dress to roam about in Rāma's wood. Earth, in confusion of heart at being trodden by their delicate and unshod feet, smoothened herself and cleared away all the spiky grass and thorns and stones and ruts and everything rough and unpleasant. Earth made the way delightfully easy for them; they were refreshed by soft, cool and fragrant breezes; the gods rained down flowers; the clouds afforded shade; the trees gave blossom and fruit; the grass made a soft carpet; the deer with their timid glances, and the birds with their sweet song, all recognized Rāma's friends and did them homage.

Dohā 310

And what great matter is this for Bharata, Rāma's dearest brother, when an ordinary person finds the highest success easy of attainment, if he merely repeats Rāma's name when he yawns !

Caupāī 311

In this manner Bharata roamed the woods, and the sages, who saw his faith and love, were abashed. Seeing all so divine, he asked about the sacred ponds and various localities, the birds and deer, the trees and grasses, the hills, woods and orchards, beautiful and varied pre-eminently holy ; and in reply the great sage with gladness of heart gave him the history of each, with its name, virtues and spiritual efficacy. Bathing at one place, doing obeisance at another ; here admiring the beauty of the wood, here sitting down to rest as the sage directed, he meditated on Sītā and the two brothers. Seeing the nobility of his disposition, his love and faithfulness in service, the gods of the wood were charmed and gave him their blessing. The third watch of the day was half spent when he returned to gaze upon the lotus feet of his Lord.

Dohā 311

In five days Bharata visited every shrine and holy place. The last (*i.e.* fifth) day was spent in discourse on the glory of Hari and Hara until the evening.

Caupāī 312

On the morrow, after bathing, the whole assembly was gathered together—Bharata, the Brāhmaṇas and the king of Tirahuta. Rāma knew at heart that the day was an auspicious one, but in his kindness hesitated to say so. He looked towards the *guru*, the king, Bharata and the assembly, and then in confusion turned his eyes to the ground. All the spectators admired his generosity, thinking, 'Never was there a master so considerate as Rāma is !' Bharata wisely understood Rāma's wish. He stood up and, lovingly putting the greatest restraint upon himself, bowed low, and with clasped hands thus spoke : "My Lord has granted my every desire. For me he has borne every affliction and has himself experienced every kind of trouble. Now, sire, give me your royal permission to go and serve at Avadh till the appointed time.

Dohā 312

But, O merciful and compassionate king of Kosala, teach me some way by which your servant may wait patiently for your return and see your feet again.

Caupāī 313

Your citizens, your kinsmen, and all your subjects, sire, are true and real, and bound to you by ties of affection. The sorrows of this miserable life, borne by your command, are a delight; without my Lord, the highest heaven is a worthless gain. The all-wise master knows the fancies, the desires, the longings of the hearts of all his servants : the protector of suppliants will be our protector, and both in this world and the next will secure our deliverance. I have thus the most perfect confidence ; not a particle of anxiety disturbs my calculations. My own distress and my Lord's forbearance have combined to make me thus presumptuous. Pardon, my Lord, this my great offence, and shrink not from instructing your servant what to do." All who heard Bharata's humble prayer applauded it ; like a swan it had separated the milk of truth from the water of error.

Dohā 313

The all-wise Rāma, the brother of the meek, on hearing his brother's polite and guileless speech, replied in terms appropriate to the place, the circumstance and the time :

Caupāī 314

"The *guru* and the king, dear brother, take thought for you, for me and our people, whether at home or in the forest. So long as Viśvāmitra, Vasiṣṭha, and Janaka direct us, neither you nor I can dream of trouble. For us two brothers, both for me and you, obedience to our father's command is the highest object we can have, our greatest gain, our glory, our duty and our salvation. A king's good is a good thing both in the Vedas and in the estimation of the world. Whoever observes the injunctions of his *guru* or father and mother, or master, treads an easy path and never stumbles. Remember this and putting aside all regrets, go and reign at Avadh for the appointed time. The burden of the realm, the treasury, the people and the family will weigh no heavier than the dust of the *guru's* feet. Observe the instructions of the sage, your mother and the Minister, and protect your country, your subjects and your capital."

Dohā 314

A chief should be like the mouth, which alone (says Tulasī) does all the eating and drinking, and yet maintains and nourishes each separate member of the body with remarkable discrimination.

Caupāī 315

A king's duty includes everything, in the same way as every latent desire exists potentially in the mind. In various ways he consoled his brother ; but without some memento his mind would not be satisfied nor be at rest. The *guru*, the Minister and the whole assembly were like-minded with Bharata ; and Rāma, overpowered with modesty and affection, took compassion upon him and gave him his sandals, which Bharata reverently received and placed upon his head. Not these the mere foot-gear of the All-merciful, but rather twin guardians of his people's life ; a casket to contain the jewel of Bharata's love ; the two letters[1] of Rāma's name which cure all illness of the soul;[2] the folding-doors that guard the house of Raghu; the hands for holy work; the pure eyes of service and righteousness. Bharata was as glad to receive this memento as if Rāma and Sītā had themselves stayed.

Dohā 315

As he bowed and begged permission to depart, Rāma took and clasped him to his heart. Wicked Indra seizing this sad opportunity made the people weary.

Caupāī 316

But his villainy was a good thing for all ; the hope that the time of exile would soon be over was the life of their life. Otherwise the separation from Lakṣmaṇa, Sītā and Rāma would have been such a blow that all would have died of it. The mercy of Rāma solved this difficulty, and the hostile gods became ser-

1. The two letters are the consonants in the name Rāma, for a panegyric on which see Childhood, Dohā 20.

2. *Jīva jatan ke: jatan* is either *yatna* (*upacara*) or *sādhana* (attainment of mokṣa, salvation).

viceable allies. Rāma closed his arms around Bharata with a burst of affection that cannot be described. Body, mind and speech overflowed with love ; the firmest of the firm lost all firmness, and his lotus eyes streamed with tears. The assembled gods were grieved to see his condition : the sages and *gurus* who were as firm as Janaka, the gold of whose soul had been tested by the fire of wisdom, and whom the Creator had created as unimpressionable by the world as the leaves of the lotus by the water ;

Dohā 316

Even they, seeing the unparalleled and boundless affection of Rāma and Bharata, were overwhelmed in body, mind and speech, lost all reason and restraint.

Caupāī 317

If Janaka and *guru* Vasiṣṭha were dumbfounded, the emotion of ordinary persons is not worth speaking about. People would think any poet harsh when they heard him describe the parting of Rāma and Bharata; Eloquence herself, remembering the unspeakable pathos of the scene, would be struck dumb with confusion. Raghubara first embraced and consoled Bharata and then rejoiced to take Satrughna to his arms. Knowing Bharata's wishes, his servants and ministers began each to set about his own work. In both camps there were sore distress at the news, as they commenced their preparations for the march. The two brothers after doing homage to their Lord's lotus feet and submissively receiving his commands, set out on the way, bowing to the sages, the hermits and forest gods and again and again showing them respect.

Dohā 317

Lakṣmaṇa, too, they embraced, and making obeisance, placed on their head the dust of Sītā's feet, and received her affectionate blessing, the source of happiness.

Caupāī 318

Rāma and his brother bowed the head to the king with many expressions of modesty and praise : "In your kindness, sire, you have suffered great inconvenience, you and your retinue, by coming to the forest; now grant me your blessing and return to the city." The monarch mastered his emotion and departed. After reverencing the sages, Brāhmaṇas and nobles, and taking leave of them as though they were the equals of Hari and Hara, the two brothers approached their mother-in-law, and came back after kissing her feet and obtaining her blessing. Then they took leave of Viśvāmitra, Vāmadeva and Jābāli;[1] the people of the court, the citizens, the good ministers and all; with courteous speech and address, as was most befitting. The Ocean of compassion courteously dismissed them all, men and women, high, middle-class and low.

Dohā 318

With sincere affection the Lord then did homage to the feet of Bharata's mother and embraced her and escorting her to the planquin that he had in readiness, effaced all her alarm and distress.

Caupāī 319

After saluting her father and mother and the court, Sītā came back purified by the love of her beloved. Reverently she embraced all her mothers-in-law, with an affection which the poet's soul shrinks from describing. Listening to their instruction and receiving the blessing she desired of them, Sītā stood lost in the affection of the two families. Having sent for elegant palanquins, Rāma with words of consolation escorted each of his mothers to their carriage. Again and again both brothers embraced them and led each by the hand with equal affection. When the horses,

1. In the Sanskrit *Rāmāyaṇa* Jābāli is represented as being, or professing to be, an atheist. In this character he alone openly advised Rāma to return to Ayodhyā as king; for as there was no life after death, the wisest plan was to get as much enjoyment as possible out of the present life while it lasted.

elephants and different vehicles were ready, the hosts of Bharata and the king set out on their journey. Their hearts full of Rāma, Sītā and Lakṣmaṇa, all the people went disconsolate; even the bullocks, horses, elephants and cattle were out of heart and went only by force and against their will.

Dohā 319

The Lord with Sītā and Lakṣmaṇa did homage to the feet of the *guru* and his wife, and turned and came back to their leafy hut with mingled pleasure and amazement.

Caupāī 320

The Niṣāda was dismissed with honour and he departed, sorely grieved at heart to leave. The Kols, Kirātas and Bhīls, the people of the woods, turned again and again, after they had been dismissed, to make yet one more obeisance. The Lord with Sītā and Lakṣmaṇa sat under the shade of the fig-tree and sorrowed for the loss of their dear friends. Rāma, overpowered with affection, discoursed to his spouse and brother in eloquent terms on Bharata's love and generosity, and with his own blessed mouth declared that faith and devotion were in his every thought, word, and deed. At that hour the birds, deer, fish, every creature at Citrakūṭa, whether animate or inanimate, were all woe-begone. The gods seeing Raghubara's state, rained down flowers and told him of what was going on their several spheres. The Lord bowed and reassured them; they went away glad, without a particle of anxiety in their mind.

Dohā 320

With Sītā and his brother the Lord shone forth in the leafy hut as resplendent as Faith, Wisdom and Detachment incarnate.

Caupāī 321

Vasiṣṭha, the Brāhmaṇas and Viśvāmitra, Bharata and the king were all disturbed at leaving Rāma, and they paced the road in silence, counting up in their mind all Rāma's virtues. After crossing the Yamunā they passed the Gaṅgā, where Rāma's friend made every arrangement for them. Then they crossed the Sai, bathed in the Gomatī, and on the fourth day reached Ayodhyā. Janaka stayed four days in the city, settled the entire administration of the state, committed the government to the Minister, the *guru* and Bharata, and then with all his retinue set out for Tirahuta. All the people of the city, in compliance with the *guru's* directions, settled down quietly in Rāma's capital.

Dohā 321

They all fasted and prayed to see him once again, and discarding all personal adornments, pleasure and enjoyment, they lived only in the hope of his return.

Caupāī 322

Bharata exhorted his ministers and trusty servants, and they executed his orders, each in their appointed sphere. Then he spoke and gave instructions to his younger brother, and entrusted to him the care of the dowager queens. He also with folded hands spoke to the Brāhmaṇas, bowing low and using humble supplication: "Give your orders and hesitate not, to high or to low, in great matters or in small." Next, he summoned the people of the palace, of the city, and all his subjects, and set their minds at rest and appointed them places to live in. After this he with his brother, went to the *guru's* house, and prostrating himself and joining his hands in prayer, said thus: "With your permission I will now live a life of penance." The sage thrilled with rapturous affection and replied: "Whatever you think, or say, or do, is always best."

Dohā 322

On receiving his instructions and his priceless blessing, he sent for a great astrologer and fixed the day, and then devoutly placed upon the throne his Lord's sandals.

Caupāī 323

After bowing his head at the feet of Rāma's mother and the

guru, and receiving the commands of his Lord's sandals, the champion of righteousness made for himself a hut of leaves at Nandigrāma,[1] and there dwelt, with his hair gathered up into a knot on his head, dressed in hermit's garb, and his couch of grass spread in a cave in the earth, lovingly practising the austerities of religious life in food, dress, posture, fasting and prayer ; discarding in thought, word and deed, as of no more value than a broken blade of grass, all clothes and adornments and every luxury and enjoyment. The king of heaven himself envied the capital of Avadh, and the god of riches was confounded at the sight of Daśaratha's wealth ; yet in that city Bharata dwelt as indifferent as a bee in a garden of *campā* trees.[2] A man so highly blest as to be enamoured of Rāma spurns like vomit all Lakṣmī's delights.

Dohā 323

This is no such great achievement for Bharata, the very shrine of the love of Rāma ; even the *cātaka* and the swan are models in their way, the one of marvellous constancy, the other of discrimination.

Caupāī 324

Day by day his body grew thinner, but his lustre and vigour were not diminished, and the beauty of his face remained the same. Nourished by an ever-increasing devotion, his virtue waxed stronger and his soul was unclouded : as the waters decrease in the brightness of the autumn, but the reeds spring up and the lotuses blossom. His tranquillity, self-control, piety, fasting and prayer were like stars in the pure heaven of Bharata's soul : his faith like the pole-star, the return from exile the full moon, his constant remembrance of the Lord the glistening Milky Way; his devotion a fixed and unsullied moon shining ever clear amidst a galaxy of stars. All the greatest of poets

1. Nandigrāma, now contracted to Nandagāon, is a few miles from Ayodhyā.

2. Though the *campā* bears a very sweet-scented flower, it is said that no bee ever sucks it.

would shrink from describing Bharata's composure, wisdom and magnanimity, his faith, his impassibility, and the perfect splendour of his virtues ; not even Śeṣanāga, Gaṇeśa and Sarasvatī could attain to them.

Dohā 324

Ever paying homage to his Lord's sandals, his affection was greater than his heart could contain; he constantly sought their advice in the disposal of all matters of state,

Caupāī 325

His body quivering with emotion, Sītā and Rāma in his heart, their names upon his tongue, and with tears in his eyes. Rāma, Lakṣmaṇa and Sītā dwelt in the forest, but Bharata, dwelling in the palace, subjected his body to all kinds of austerities. Everyone after considering both sides said that Bharata was in every way praiseworthy. The religious were abashed who heard of his fasting and penance ; the king of saints, who saw his condition, was put to shame. Bharata's mode of life was utterly holy, sweet and charming, and the cause of every blessing ; it removes the grievous distress of this sinful age ; is the sun to disperse the darkness of the great delusion : the lion to vanquish the elephant host of sin: the pacifier of every kind of affliction; the joy of the faithful: the liberator from the burden of rebirth; the essence of the ambrosia of Rāma's love.

Chand 13

If Bharata had never been born, imbued with the ambrosia of devotion to Rāma and Sītā, then who would have practised such self-restraint and penance, such composure, patience and rigorous fasting, transcending every imagination of the sages ? Who in legendary disguise would have removed our burning sorrows and poverty, our arrogance and sin ? What poor wretch like Tulasī now in this iron age would have ventured to set Rāma before you ?

Soraṭhā 325

All, says Tulasī, who make a vow and listen with reverence to Bharata's acts shall assuredly acquire a great devotion to the feet of Sītā and Rāma and a distaste for worldly pleasures.

[*Thus endeth the book entitled* AYODHYĀ, *composed by Tulasī Dāsa for the bestowal of pure wisdom and continence being, the second descent into the Holy Lake of Rāma's Acts, that cleanses from every defilement of the world.*]

BOOK III

THE FOREST

THE FOREST

Sanskrit Invocation.

I REVERENCE Śaṅkara, the very root of the tree of righteousness, the full moon that delights the sea of intelligence; the sun that opens the lotus of asceticism, the destroyer of sin, the dispeller of darkness, the healer of distress, the most auspicious conjunction in the high heaven of wisdom, which scatters the massed clouds of delusion, proceeding from Brahmā, the destroyer of sin, the beloved of king Rāma.

I worship him, whose body resembles a rain-bearing cloud teeming with abundant delights; the yellow-apparelled; the beautiful: the hero with bow and arrows in hand and well-fitted quiver gleaming by his side: with the large lotus eyes; the long tresses of whose hair are bound into a knot on his head, all glorious to behold; the way-farer accompanied by Sītā and Lakṣmaṇa, the charmer of charmers.

Soraṭhā

O Uma, the sages, who are learned in Rāma's mysterious qualities, enjoy peace of mind; but fools, who are Hari's enemies and have no love for righteousness, reap only delusion.

Caupāī 1

I have sung to the best of my ability the incomparable and charming affection shown by the citizens and Bharata; hearken now to the all-holy acts of the Lord, that he wrought in the forest, to the delight of gods, men and sages. Once upon a time Rāma plucked some lovely flowers and with his own hands made a wreath, with which he reverently decked Sītā. As she sat in her glory on a crystal rock, the son of the king of the gods[1] took the form of a crow and wickedly thought to make trial of

1. Jayanta, the son of Indra.

Rāma's might, like an ant so imbecile of mind as to attempt to sound the depths of ocean. With its beak it bit Sītā in the foot and flew away, the foolish crow, in its utter stupidity. The blood began to flow; Raghunāyaka saw it and made ready his bow and arrow, fashioned merely of reeds.[1]

Dohā 1

The All-merciful Rāma, ever full of compassion for the humble, even he it was upon whom the wicked wretch came and played this trick.

Caupāī 2

The divine arrow, winged with a charm, sped forth; the crow in terror took to flight and assuming his proper form went to his father, who would not shelter him, as he was Rāma's enemy. He was in despair, and as panic-stricken in soul as was the Ṛṣi Durvāsā by the terror of Viṣṇu's discus. Weary and worn with fear and remorse, he traversed the realm of Brahmā, the city of Śiva and every other sphere; but no one even asked him to rest awhile; who can befriend an enemy of Rāma's ? Hearken, Garuṛ: his own mother becomes his death; his father is changed as it were into the king of hell[2]; ambrosia turns to poison; a friend does him all the harm of a hundred enemies; the Gaṅgā is converted into the Vaitaraṇī,[3] and all the world burns hotter than fire—believe me, brother—when a man opposes Rāma. When Nārada saw Jayanta's distress, being tender-hearted and good, he took pity on him and sent him straight to Rāma. There he cried, 'Save me, O thou that art the suppliant's friend !' In terror and confusion he went and clasped his feet, crying, "Protect me, O protect me, merciful Raghurāī! Thy might is im-

1. In the Sanskrit *Rāmāyaṇa* this incident of the crow forms the subject of the 38th canto of the Sundara Kāṇḍa, this being yet another evidence of Tulasī's free handling of the Rāma story. Vālmiki puts the incident into the mouth of Sītā who relates it there to Hanumān.—*Ed.*

2. *Śamana*, 'the destroyer,' here denotes Yama, the Indian Pluto.

3. The Vaitaraṇi is the Hindu Styx or river of hell, which the dead have to cross before entering the infernal regions. It is represented as an impetuous and filthy torrent, full of blood, hair and bones and every kind of impurity.

measurable, and immeasurable thy majesty; in ignorance of mind, I knew thee not. I have reaped the fruit of my own actions; now my Lord, succour me, for to thee I have come for refuge." When the Merciful heard this most piteous appeal, he dismissed him, Bhavānī, with the loss of one eye.

Soraṭhā 2

Although in his folly he had committed such an offence that death was his due, the Lord had compassion upon him and set him free. Who is so merciful as Raghubīra ?

Caupāī 3

Raghupati stayed on at Citrakūṭa and performed many exploits as grateful to the ear as nectar. At last, he thought to himself, "There will be a crowd here, now that everyone knows of me." So the two brothers with Sītā took leave of all the sages and went on their way. When the Lord drew near to Atri's hermitage, the great sage was rejoiced at the news, and quivering in every limb he sprang up and ran to meet him. On seeing him, Rāma advanced hurriedly and was falling prostrate before him, but the sage took him to his bosom. Both wept tears of affection. At the sight of Rāma's beauty, his eyes were gladdened and he reverently conducted him to his own hermitage, where doing him every honour he addressed him in gracious terms and offered him roots and fruit such as his soul relished.

Soraṭhā 3

As the Lord took his seat, the great sage, supremely wise, gazed with streaming eyes upon his beauty, and joining his hands in supplication he thus hymned his praise:

Chand 1

"I reverence thee, the lover of the devout; the gracious and tender-hearted; I worship thy lotus feet, which bestow upon the unsensual thine own abode in heaven. I adore thee, the wondrous dark and beautiful; Mount Mandara to churn the ocean of existence; with eyes like the full blown lotus; the dispeller of pride and every other vice: the long-armed hero of immeasurable power and glory; the mighty Lord of the three spheres, equipped with quiver and bow and arrows; the ornament of the Solar race; the breaker of Śiva's bow; the delight of the greatest sages and saints; the destroyer of all the enemies of the gods; the adored of Kāmadeva's foe (*i. e.*, of Śiva); the reverenced of Brahmā and the other divinities; the home of enlightened intelligence; the dispeller of all error; Laksmī's lord; the mine of felicity; the salvation of the saints. I worship thee with thy consort and thy brother, thyself the beloved younger brother of Śacī's lord.[1] Men, who unselfishly worship thy holy feet, sink not in the ocean of existence, tossed with the billows of controversy. They who in the hope of salvation, with subdued passions, ever delightedly[2] worship thee, having discarded every object of sense, are advanced to thy own sphere in heaven. I worship thee, the one, the mysterious Lord, the passionless and omnipresent sovereign, the eternal governor of the world, the one absolute and universal spirit; the joy of all men day after day. I reverently adore thee, the king of incomparable beauty, Lord of the earth-born Sītā; be gracious to me and grant me devotion to thy lotus Feet." They who reverently repeat this hymn, full of faith in thee, will undoubtedly attain to thy sphere.[3]

Dohā 4

Again, with bowed head and folded hands, the sage made supplication and cried, "Never, O Lord, may my thoughts abandon thy lotus feet."

1. This epithet is a peculiar one; but it would seem to be intended simply as a periphrasis for Upendra, 'the lesser Indra,' a well-known title of Viṣṇu, who, in the dwarf incarnation, was born as a son of Kaśyapa; Indra, here called 'Śacī's lord,' being accounted the eldest of Kaśyapa's sons.

2. *Muda* is here the instrumental case of *muda*, 'delight.'

3. The whole of this Chand is in loose and occasionally ungrammatical Sanskrit like the language of the Gāthās in Buddhist literature.

Caupāī 4

The amiable and modest Sītā clasped Anasūyā[1] by the feet with frequent courtesy. The soul of the Ṛṣi's wife was filled with joy; she gave her her blessing and seated her by her side. Then arrayed her in heavenly robes and jewels which remained ever bright and beautiful. In simple and affectionate phrase the saintly dame spoke and instructed her in matters of wifely duty. "Hearken, princess; mother, father, brethren and friends are all good in a limited degree; but a husband, Vaidehī, is an unlimited blessing; and vile is the wife who does not pay him reverence. Courage, virtue, a friend and a wife are four things that are tested in time of adversity. Though her lord be old, diseased, impotent and poor, blind, deaf, passionate and utterly vile, yet even so the wife who treats him with disrespect shall suffer many torments in hell. Her one religious duty, her one vow and penance consist in a devotion, in thought and word and deed to her husband's feet. There are four kinds of faithful wife in the world, as the Vedas, Purāṇas and saints declare. The best is so firmly settled in mind that she could not even dream of there being any other man living; the next regards another's husband as her own brother or father, or son; she who is restrained by thought of duty and consideration for her family is said in the scriptures to be a woman of low character; but reckon her the very lowest of all, who is restrained only by fear and want of opportunity. She who deceives her husband and carries on an intrigue with another man shall be cast for a hundred ages into the hell called the terrible. Who such a wretch as she, who for a moment's pleasure considers not the torment that shall endure through a hundred million lives? Without any difficulty a woman attains to salvation, if only without guile she adheres to her duty as a faithful wife; but she who is disloyal to her spouse, wherever she be born, becomes a widow while still a girl.

Soraṭhā 5a-5b

An utterly wicked woman who is faithful to her husband has

1. The interview with Atri and Anasūyā is narrated at the end of the Ayodhyā Kāṇḍa in one recension of the Sanskrit *Rāmāyaṇa*.

a happy fate when she dies; so sing the four Vedas and so too in these days sings Hari's poor friend, Tulasī. Hearken, Sītā; women will be faithful wives, if they invoke your name; for you love Rāma like your own life; these words that I say are for the good of the world."

Caupāī 5

On hearing this, Jānakī was overjoyed and reverently bowed her head before her feet. Then the gracious Lord said to the sage, "With your permission I would go to some other wood. Continue to be ever gracious to me and knowing me to be your servant, cease not your kindness." On hearing this speech of the Lord, the champion of righteousness, the wise sage affectionately replied: "O Rāma, you are he whose favour is desired by Brahmā, Śiva, Sanatkumāra, and the other gods and by all the preachers of salvation; the passionless, the kindly, the friend of the helpless, who thus modestly bespeak me. Now I understand the wisdom of Lakṣmī who turned from every other god to worship you alone. Of a truth there is none your equal: how then could your goodness be other than it is? How can I, my Lord, tell you what wood to visit? Say, master, for you read the heart." Having thus spoken, the sage strong-minded as he was, trembled in every limb and his eyes streamed with tears as he gazed upon the Lord.

Chand 2

Trembling with emotion in every limb and filled with love, he fixed his loving eyes upon his lotus face: "It is the reward of prayer and penance that I have beheld the Lord, who transcends the senses and every faculty of thought and reason." By prayer and austerity and religious observances, men attain to the crowning virtue of faith; therefore day and night Tulasī Dāsa sings the holy acts of Raghubīra.

Dohā 6a

Rāma's praises remove the pollution of the Kaliyuga, subdue the soul, are the source of beatitude; and Rāma continues gracious to all who reverently hear them.

Soraṭhā 6b

Grievous is the burden of the sin of Kaliyuga; nor religion, nor knowledge, nor meditation, nor penance avails against it. They are prudent who discard trust in all else and worship Rāma only.

Caupāī 6

The Lord of gods and men and sages, after bowing his head before the lotus feet of the sage, proceeded to the wood, Rāma first and after him his brother, in the garb of hermits all full and complete. Between the two the incarnation of Lakṣmī shone forth like Māyā between the Absolute and the Individual Soul. The rivers and thickets and precipices and mountain-passes all recognized their Lord and made the way smooth for him. Wherever the divine Raguhrāī passed, the clouds made a canopy in the heaven. As they went along the road the demon Virādha met them. While he was yet coming, Raghubīra overthrew him, then at once he assumed a beauteous form; and Rāma, seeing him sorrowing, dismissed him to his own sphere.[1] Then the All-beautiful with his brother and Jānakī visited the sage Śarabhaṅga.

Dohā 7

At the sight of Rāma's lotus face, the bee-like eyes of the sage reverently drank thereof; blessed indeed was Śarabhaṅga to have been born.

Caupāī 7

Said the sage : "Hearken, gracious Raghubīra, the swan of Śaṅkara's lake. I had taken my departure to the halls of the Creator,[2] but I heard it said that Rāma is coming into the forest. Day and night I have been watching the road; now I have seen

1. The encounter with Virādha, which is here so very baldly told, occupies more than a hundred lines in Vālmīki's poem.

2. Vālmīki represents Indra as having come with his chariot and horses to carry off the sage to Brahmā's sphere at the very time of Rāma's arrival.

my Lord and my heart is at rest. I am deficient, my Lord, in all that is good, but you have graciously acknowledged me as your humble servant. Now, Lord, I have no request to make; I have accomplished my vow, O ravisher of the soul of the faithful, to wait in expectation of the suppliant's friend till I saw you and then to discard my body. I have practised meditation, sacrifice, prayers, penance and fasting, and have received the gift of faith as a boon of the Lord. In this manner, the sage Śarabhaṅga built a funeral pyre, and freeing his heart from all attachment, sat thereon, saying:

Dohā 8

"May the Lord, whose body is dark of hue as a dark raincloud, incarnate in form as the divine Rāma, dwell for ever in my soul together with Sītā and his brother !"

Caupāī 8

When he had thus said, the sacrificial fire consumed his body, and by Rāma's grace he ascended to Vaikuṇṭha.[1] The sage was not absorbed into the divinity for this reason, that he had already received the mysterious gift of faith.[2] When the assembled Ṛṣis saw the great sage's translation, they were mightily rejoiced at heart and all broke forth into hymns of praise, 'Glory to the champion of the humble, the fountain of mercy.' Then Raghunātha went on further into the forest, and a great company of holy men with him. Seeing a heap of bones, he asked the sages about them and was moved with much compassion. "I know, but why ask, Master? You are all-seeing and know even our thoughts. These are all sages whom the demon

1. According to Vālmīki, it was not Vaikuṇṭha, but Brahmā's sphere, to which he was translated. III 9.36.

2. The reward of faith (*bhakti*) is the admission to the actual presence of the divinity in the sphere where he specially reigns. Absorption into the divinity implies the extinction of individual existence and individual consciousness, and therefore, though the *summum bonum* of many Hindu sects, it is not so of those who cherish a personal love for any particular incarnation, a love which can only be satisfied by a consciousness of the presence of the beloved.

hosts have devoured." On hearing this, Raghubīra's eyes filled with tears.

Dohā 9

With arms upraised he vowed to rid the earth of demons. Then he gladdened the sages by visiting them all in turn at their retreats.

Caupāī 9

Sage Agastya had a learned disciple named Sutīkṣṇa devoted to God; in thought, word and deed one of Rāma's faithful servants, who had never even dreamt of any other hope or divinity. When he heard of the Lord's arrival, he rushed out hurriedly, full of longing desire: "O God, will the compassionate Raghurāī be gracious to even a wretch like me ? Will the holy Rāma and his brother receive me as their own servant? I have no assured confidence of heart, no faith, nor command over self, nor wisdom of intellect; no communion with saints, no practice in meditation, prayer, or vigil, and no steadfast devotion to his lotus feet; only the promise of the All-merciful: 'He is my friend who goeth to none other.' Today my eyes will be blessed with the sight of the lotus-faced, the deliverer from the bondage of existence." The wise sage, a philosopher as he was, was so utterly overwhelmed with love that his state, Bhavānī, was beyond all description. He could not see his way either in this direction or in that, nor remember who he was, or where he was going; at one time he would turn and go back, at another would dance and sing songs of praise. The sage's love and faith waxed yet more vehement as the Lord watched him stealthily from behind a tree. Then Raghubīra, who removes all the troubles of the world, after witnessing his exceeding devotion, manifested himself in his soul. The sage was struck motionless in the middle of the road, and his body bristled like the jack-fruit with every hair on end. Then Raghunātha drew near to him, rejoicing to witness the emotion of his servant, and tried many ways to rouse him; but he neither awoke nor derived any happiness from the vision; till Rāma withdrew his kingly guise and mentally revealed himself as the four-armed god. The sage thereupon started up in alarm, like a poor snake that has been robbed of its jewel; but seeing before him the dark-hued Rāma with Sītā and his younger brother, the abode of delight, he fell like a dog at his feet, drowned in love and supremely happy. With his long arms he took and lifted him and clasped him to his bosom with the utmost affection. As he embraced the sage, the All-merciful showed forth like a *tamāla* tree embracing a tree of gold: and the sage as he gazed on Rāma's face stood so still that you would take him for a figure painted in a picture.

Dohā 10

At last the sage growing bolder at heart, after again and again clasping his feet, conducted the Lord to his hermitage and did everything in his honour.

Caupāī 10

Said the sage : "Hearken, Lord, to my humble prayer; but how can I hymn thy praises? Thy greatness is immeasurable and my wit is scant, as ineffectual as a fire-fly in the presence of the sun. I ever adore the divine Raghubīra, whose body is dark of hue as a string of lotuses, with his knotted hair for a crown and an anchorite's dress for his robe, with bow and arrows in hand and quiver by his side. A fire to consume the dense forest of delusion, a sun to animate the lotus-bed of saints, a lion against the elephant herd of demons, a hawk to scatter the bird's metempsychosis, may he ever protect us with eyes bright as the lotus; apparelled with glory; the moon of Sītā's partridge-like eyes; the swan in the lake of Śiva's soul; the broad-chested, strong-armed Rāma, him I adore. A Garuṛ to devour the snake of doubt; the queller of violence, wrangling and pain; the conqueror of death; the delight of the company of heaven; the home of compassion, may he ever protect us. At once bodiless and embodied, like and unlike, endowed with form and formless; transcending all thought, speech and perception; pure, all-pervading, faultless, illimitable, Rāma, the loosener of earth's burdens, him I adore. Garden of the tree of Paradise for his faithful people; dispeller of passion, avarice, pride and lust; the All-beautiful;

bridge to cross the ocean of life, banner of the Solar race, may he ever protect me ! With unlimited might of arm, the home of strength; the true disperser of the manifold impurities of this iron age; the shield of righteousness; the giver of delights, the assemblage of all good qualities; may he, my Rāma, ever grant us prosperity. Though he be passionless, all-pervading, eternal, and ever dwelleth in the hearts of all; yet in his character of the wood-roaming conqueror of Khara, with his brother and bride, may he abide in my thoughts. They who understand know him to be the Lord; though embodied, the bodiless ruler of the soul, the lotus-eyed sovereign of Kosala; then make thy abode in my heart, O Rāma. Never, let this claim be forgotten that I am his servant and Raghupati is my Lord." Rāma was pleased on hearing the sage's speech, and in his delight pressed him again to his bosom: "Know, O Sage, that I am highly gratified: ask any boon and I will grant it you." Said the sage: "I have never begged a boon, nor can I discern between true and false. Whatever seems good to you, O Raghurāī, that bestow upon me, for you are your servant's benefactor." "I give you steadfast faith, self-control, and wisdom, and make you a treasure-house of all virtue and knowledge." "I have received, my Lord, the boon that you have given, now grant me what I cherish.

Dohā 11

O Rāma, my Lord, with your brother and Jānakī, yourself equipped with your bow and arrows, for ever abide like the moon in the heaven of my soul."[1]

1. Tulasī Dāsa's theory as to the principle that should regulate man's prayers to Heaven is enforced by the example of the famous sages and ascetics, whom he so frequently brings before his readers and whose aspirations refer exclusively to spiritual blessings. An exact parallel is afforded by the teaching of the great English moralist of the last century as inculcated in the following lines :—

"Yet when the scene of sacred presence fires,
And strong devotion to the skies aspires,
Pour forth thy fervour for a healthful mind,
Obedient passions and a will resigned,
For love which scarce collective man can fill,
For patience, sovereign o'er transmuted ill,

Caupāī 11

'So be it !' said Lakṣmī's lord, as he joyously started on his visit to the Ṛṣi Agastya. "It is a long time since I last saw my *guru*, and since I came to live in this hermitage; now, my Lord, I will go and see him with you; I am not putting you under any obligation." The Fountain of mercy saw through the sage's subtlety, and both brothers smiled as they took him with them. Discoursing on the excellence of faith in himself, the king of the gods arrived at the sages hermitage. Sutīkṣṇa at once went to the *guru* and after prostrating himself thus addressed him: "My lord, the son of the sovereign of Kosala, the support of the world, has come to see you, even Rāma, with his brother and Vaidehi, to whom, sir, you make your prayer night and day." As soon as he heard this, Agastya started up and ran, and at the sight of Hari, his eyes filled with tears. The two brothers fell at the sage's holy feet, but he took and clasped them to his bosom with the utmost affection. After courteously enquiring of their welfare, the holy sage conducted them to a fitting seat and then again did all homage to his Lord, saying: 'There is no other man so blessed as I !' So long as the other hermits stayed, their delight was to gaze upon the source of joy.

Dohā 12

As he sat in their midst with their eyes all fastened upon his person, they looked like a bevy of partridges gazing on the autumn moon.

Caupāī 12

Then said Raghuvīra to the sage, "My lord, nothing is hidden from you: you know why I have come, and therefore, sire, there

For faith, that — panting for a happier seat —
Counts death kind nature's signal of retreat."

Detachment from the world, subjugation of the passions, love for the divinity, patience under suffering, and to crown all, an unhesitating faith are the highest boon that man can secure; the last being followed after death by the beatific vision of the godhead, a joy for all eternity, an everlasting harmony, in which God will know Himself, and all will know God.

is no need to inform you. Give me now some charm by which I may destroy the persecutors of the saints." The sage smiled when he heard the Lord's speech: "You ask me, Lord, but what do I know? By virtue of my devotion to you, O destroyer of sin, I understand a little of your greatness. Your illusive power is a spreading fig[1]-tree, its clustering fruit the countless universes, while all things animate and inanimate, are like the insects that dwell inside and think their own particular fig the only one in existence. This fruit is devoured by harsh and inexorable fate, but even he trembles in fear of you. You, sire, are the sovereign of all the spheres, and you ask of me, as though you were only a man. O fountain of mercy, I beg this boon; dwell in my heart with Lakṣmī and your brother, and grant me steadfast faith, piety, fellowship with the sages and unbroken love for your lotus feet. Though you are the Absolute, indivisible and eternal, only intuitively comprehensible, adored by the sages, yet I declare and recognize your incarnation, and again and again adore the embodiment of Brahmā and Rati. You always exalt your own servants, and this, Raghurāī, is the reason why you consult me. There is, my Lord, a very charming and holy spot called Pañcavaṭī. Sanctify the whole Daṇḍaka forest, in which it is, and relieve it of the sage's grievous curse,[2] by taking up your abode there, Rāma; and thus show mercy to all the sages. After taking leave of the sage, Rāma set out and speedily arrived at Pañcavaṭī.

Dohā 13

After meeting the king of the vultures[3] and warmly renewing

1. The word in the text is *dunri* which represents the Sanskrit *udumbara*, the *ficus glomerata*. It bears large clusters of fruit, and every single fig in every cluster is always full of insects.

2. The curse had been pronounced by Bhārgava, whose daughter Arjā had been violated by Daṇḍa, son of Ikṣvāku, who was then king of the country. His populous realm at once became a wild forest waste, inhabited only by wild beasts and demons.

3. The interview with the vulture-king Jaṭāyu, thus briefly despatched in two lines, occupies the whole of the 20th canto in the Sanskrit 'Araṇyakāṇḍa.' It was on this occasion that he made the promise to protect Sītā which subsequently cost him his life.

old friendship, Rāma stayed near the Godāvarī, where he built himself a cottage of leaves.

Caupāī 13

From the time that Rāma made his home there, the hermits lived happily and without fear. The mountains, woods, rivers and lakes were suffused with beauty and day by day grew yet more exceedingly lovely. The many birds and deer were full of joy, and the bees added a charm by their sweet buzzing. Not even the Serpent King would be able to describle the forest in which the glorious Rāma had manifested himself. One day, as the Lord was sitting at ease, Lakṣmaṇa most humbly addressed him thus: "Master of gods and men and sages and of all animate and inanimate creation; I have a question to ask of you as of my own special master. Speak, sire, and answer it for me, for I have left all to serve the dust of your feet. Explain to me knowledge, self-governance, and the delusion of Māyā; tell me what is that faith to which you extend mercy.

Dohā 14

Tell me, my Lord, all the difference between God and the soul that I may be entirely devoted to your feet and freed from grief, ignorance and error."

Caupāī 14

"I will explain the whole matter in brief; listen, brother, with attention of mind and soul. It is from egoism and distinctions between mine and thine, that the illusion is produced which has subjugated all classes of existence. The senses and the objects of the senses, as far as the mind can reach, are all a delusion, brother; understand that. Now listen to its division: they are two, *viz.*, knowledge and ignorance; the one utterly bad and calamitous, which forces the principle of life down into the pit of transmigration; the other, the power by virtue of which the world is created, being sent by God, and having no strength of itself. Knowledge, in which there is no thought of self, sees the supreme spirit equally in all things; and he, dear brother, is to be reckoned chief of stoics, who abandons fortune, and the three elements of which the universe is composed, as if of no more account than a blade of grass.

Dohā 15

That is called the individual soul which does not recognize Māyā (illusion) or God or its own true nature;[1] God is the giver of bondage and of deliverance, the head of all things, the sender forth of delusion, the one goal.

Caupāī 15

From piety springs asceticism; and from ascetic meditation knowledge; and knowledge, as the Vedas declare, is the giver of salvation. But that at which I melt more quickly, brother, is faith, which is the blessing of my votaries ; it stands by itself without other support, and is above all knowledge whether spiritual or profane. Faith, brother, is an incomparable source of happiness, and only to be acquired by the favour of a sage. But I will explain the means towards it, the easy path by which men may find me. First, an exceeding devotion to the feet of Brāhmaṇas and in every action a close adherence to scriptural prescription. Next, the fruit of this will be detachment from the world, and then will spring up a delight in my worship. The nine kinds of faith as exercised by the ears, etc., will strengthen; there will be an exceeding love in the soul for my manifestations, a great affection for the lotus feet of holy men, a persistency in prayer—in deed and in heart as well as in tongue—and faithfulness in service done to one's *guru*, father, mother, brother, spouse and god, knowing it to be really done to me. While singing my praises the body quivers, the voice trembles, the eyes flow with tears; and neither lust, pride, nor deceit, finds a place in the soul; I am ever, dear brother, at the command of such a one as this.

1. Or it may be thus translated: 'That is to be called soul, which doubts regarding itself whether it be a delusive manifestation or really God.'

Dohā 16

I take up my abode for ever in the lotus hearts of those who in thought and word and deed depend on me and worship me without desire.

Caupāī 16

On hearing the doctrine of faith and devotion[1] thus expounded, Lakṣmaṇa was exceedingly glad and bowed his head before his Lord's feet. In this manner several days were spent in discourse on asceticism, wisdom, virtue and morality. One day Rāvaṇa's sister, Śūrpaṇakhā, foulhearted and venomous as a serpent, came to Pañcavaṭī and was excited when she saw the two princes. A woman, Garuṛ, must needs look after a handsome man, whether he be brother, father or son.[2] In her excitement she could not contain herself, like the sun-stone that melts at the sight of the sun. Having assumed a beautiful form, she approached the Lord and with many smiles thus addressed him : "There is not another man like you, nor a woman like me ; there is a match that God has taken some pains to make. I have searched the three spheres, but have not found anywhere in the world a man with beauty to equal mine. And for this reason I have till now remained a virgin, but now that I have seen you I am fairly satisfied." The Lord glanced at Sītā and said in reply : "My younger brother is a bachelor." The demon's sister took the hint and went to Lakṣmaṇa. He looked to his Lord and said in gentle tones : "Hearken, fair lady, I am his servant; it is not right that you should be in subjection to anyone. My lord is the mighty king of Kosala, and whatever he does is all done at

1. *Yoga*, the word here rendered 'devotion,' is one of the systems of Hindu philosophy. Its chief aim is to teach the means by which the human soul may attain complete union with the Supreme Being. It is defined by Patañjali, the founder of the school, as 'the prevention' of the modifications of thought by the practice of self-mortification and by keeping the mind constantly unaffected by all external influence.' The final beatitude, which is held out as the reward of such devotion, consists in the cessation of all idea of self and of any distinction between matter and spirit.

2. That is to say, apparently, whatever his age may be, whether he be of the same age or old enough to be a father, or young enough to be a son.

his own pleasure. A servant who expects ease, a beggar who expects honour, a spendthrift who hopes for wealth, a profligate who hopes for heaven, or an avaricious man who expects renown, these are four dreamers, men who would expect milk from milking the air.'' Again she turned and came to Rāma, but he sent her back once more to Lakṣmaṇa. Said Lakṣmaṇa, "The bridegroom for you must be a man lost to all sense of shame!" Then in a fury she returned to Rāma, revealing herself in a shape of terror. Seeing that Sītā was frightened, Raghurāī made a sign to his brother.

Dohā 17

And Lakṣmaṇa with the utmost speed struck off her nose[1] and ears : by her hand he sent to Rāvaṇa a challenge, as it were.

Caupāī 17

Without nose and ears she was as hideous to look upon as a mountain flowing with torrents of red ochre. She went moaning to Khara and Dūṣaṇa: "A curse, a curse, I say, on your manhood and strength, brother." They questioned and she told them all. When they heard it, the demons assembled an army, and a swarming multitude of fiends rushed forth like so many winged mountains of soot, on diverse vehicles, of diverse shapes, armed with diverse weapons, terrible and beyond number. At the head went Śūrpaṇakhā in hideous guise, robbed of her ears and nose. Many fearful omens of ill occurred, but the host heeded them not, being all death-doomed. They shouted, they defied the enemy, they leaped in the air, their captains inspected the ranks and rejoiced exceedingly. Said one, 'Capture the two brothers alive and then take and kill them and carry off the bride.' The vault of heaven was filled with dust. Rāma summoned his brother and said to him, "Go, take Jānakī away to some mountain-cave; a terrible army of demons has come; remain on your guard." Obedient to his Lord's command;

1. The traditionary scene of this event is laid at Nāsika, which is supposed to derive its name from Nāsikā, 'a nose.' The suburb on the opposite bank of the river Godāvarī is still called Pañcavaṭī.

he took his bow and arrows in hand and led Sītā away. When Rāma saw that the hostile force had drawn near, he smiled as he strung his massive bow.

Chand 13

As he strung his massive bow and bound up his long hair in a knot on his head, it looked as though two snakes were entwining the summit of a sapphire rock encircled with a myriad lightning flashes. As the Lord girded up his quiver by his side and clasped the bow in his mighty arm and fitted the arrow to the string, he glared with the glance of a lion on a herd of elephants.

Soraṭhā 18

The warriors came on with a rush, shouting, 'Seize him! Seize him!' for they saw that he was alone : the demons closed round upon him, but he stood as the rising sun.

Caupāī 18

And at the sight of the Lord they could not discharge their arrows; the whole demon host was dumbfounded. Khara and Dūṣaṇa summoned their minister and said : "This ornament of the human race must be some king's son. Nāgas, demons, gods, men and saints of all sorts I have seen, conquered and slain; but in the whole of my life—mark me, my brethren all—I have never seen such beauty. Though he has made our sister hideous to behold, so incomparable a hero is not worthy of death. 'At once put away and surrender your bride and return home alive, you and your brother.' Declare to him this that I have said and quickly come back with his answer." The envoys went and gave Rāma the message. He smiled to hear them and said : "I am a warrior by caste and am hunting in this wood; wretches like you are the game that I am tracking. I am not dismayed at the sight of the enemy's strength, but am ready to do combat with death himself. Though a man, I am the exterminator of the race of demons ; and though a mere child I am the protector of the sages and the destroyer of the wicked. If there is no strength in you, turn and go home : I never kill an enemy in retreat. If you have come up to fight, show now your cunning and dexterity ; mercy shown to an enemy betrays the height of weakness." The heralds immediately went and repeated all this: Khara and Dūṣaṇa's hearts were on fire when they heard it.

Chand 4

Their hearts were on fire and they shouted: "Rush upon him and seize him, ye mighty demon warriors, with your bows and arrows, pikes, spears, scimitars, maces and axes." The Lord gave his bow one twang ; in a moment, at the awful and terrible sound the demons were deafened and dismayed, they had no sense left in them.

Dohā 19a-19b

When they recovered themselves they made a rush, for they knew the strength of their foe; and missiles and weapons of all kinds began to rain down upon Rāma. But Raghuvīra cleft these weapons in twain, making them of no more account than so many sesamum seeds, and then drawing the bowstring to his ear he let fly his own arrows.

Chand 5

Then the terrible arrows sped forth, hissing like many serpents. The holy Rāma waxed wrath in battle; arrows, of exceeding sharpness, flew forth. When they saw his shafts so keen, the demon leaders turned to flight; but the three brothers became furious : 'Whoever flees from the field, him will I slay with my own hand; let him stay then and make up his mind to die.' Weapons of diverse kinds beat upon him from the front, and the Lord perceiving that the enemy was exceedingly furious, fitted an arrow to his bow. He let fly the huge bolts ; the dread demons were cut to pieces; bodies, heads, arms, hands and feet were scattered about all over the ground. The shrill arrows struck; like mountains the bodies fell. The leaders had their frames cut into a hundred pieces, yet they stood up again by power of magic. Many arms and heads flew through the air and headless trunks ran to and fro. Kites, crows and jackals made an awful and horrible wrangling.

Chand 6

Jackals wrangled ; ghosts, goblins and demons made cups of the skulls ; more warlike devils clashed skulls together for music, and witches danced. Rughubīra's mighty arrows smote off the leaders' bodies, arms and heads ; they fell on every side, but stood up again to fight with terrible cries of 'Seize him ! Seize him !' Vultures flew away with men's entrails in their claws, goblins scampered off with hands that they had seized ; one might fancy all the children of Battle-town were flying kites. The mighty champions lay dead and vanquished, with mangled bodies. Seeing their army routed, Khara and Dūṣaṇa, with Triśira and other champions, stood at bay, and all at once demons innumerable hurled furiously against Raghubīra arrow and spear, club, axe, javelin and dagger. In the twinkling of an eye the Lord had warded off all his enemies' missiles and sent forth his own arrows, slaying all the demon leaders with ten shafts planted in the breast of each of them. Though they fell to the ground, they rose again in their valour and joined in the fray, and would not die, but made the strangest sight. The gods were afraid when they saw the demons fourteen thousand in number, and the king of Avadh alone ; till the Lord perceiving alarm of gods and sages and having power over all illusion, wrought a merry spectacle, on account of which the enemy saw each his friend as Râma, and joining battle with one another perished fighting.

Dohā 20a-20b

Crying 'Rāma ! Rāma !' as their soul left their bodies, they thus attained beatitude. In a moment the Fountain of mercy slew all his enemies by magic. The gods in their joy rained down flowers; instruments of music sounded in the air, and with cries of 'Glory ! glory !' they all departed, each in his own celestial car.

Caupāī 19

When Raghunātha had vanquished the foe in battle, gods, men and sages were all relieved of fear. Lakṣmaṇa then brought Sītā back. As he fell at the Lord's feet, he took and rapturously clasped him to his bosom. Sītā fixed her gaze upon his dark and delicate form, but so vehement was her love that her eyes could never be satisfied. Thus the blessed Rāma stayed at Pañcavaṭī, delighting gods and sages by the deeds that he did. But Śūrpaṇakhā, when she saw the death of Khara and Dūṣaṇa, went and called Rāvaṇa. In a furious rage she cried, "You have lost all thought of realm and treasure; you drink and sleep day and night and care not that the enemy is at your gate. Sovereignty without policy, wealth without religion, good works without consecration to Hari, knowledge without discretion, these all bring no fruit save trouble to the student, the doer, or the possessor. An ascetic is quickly undone by attachment, a king by ill-counsel, wisdom by conceit, modesty by drinking, friendship by want of consideration, and good sense by pride: so goes the saying.

Soraṭhā 21a

An enemy, disease, fire, sin, a master and a serpent are never to be accounted trifles." So saying, and with much lamentation besides, she set to weeping.

Dohā 21b

In her distress she threw herself down in the midst of the assembly with many tears and cries, "O Ten-headed, to think that you should live and see me thus treated !"

Caupāī 20

At these words, the assembly arose in confusion and took her by the hand and raised her to her feet and consoled her. Said the king of Laṅkā : "Why do you not tell me what has happened ? Who has cut off your nose and ears?" "The sons of Daśaratha, the lord of Avadh, very lions of men, have come to hunt in the forest. I understood that they were about: they would rid the earth of demons. Relying on the might of their arm, O Rāvaṇa, the sages roam the woods without any fear. They are mere boys to look at, but in fact resistless as Death himself, the most intrepid of archers, with many strings to their bow.[1] Both brothers are glorious with incomparable might, and have devoted themselves to the extermination of the wicked and the relief of gods and saints. Rāma—for that is his name—is the very perfection of beauty, and with him is a young girl, whom the Creator has fashioned the loveliest of the sex : a thousand million Ratis would be no match for her. It is his younger brother who cut off my ears and nose and made a mock of me when he heard I was your sister. When Khara and Dūṣaṇa were told of this, they gave him challenge; but in an instant he slew the whole of their army." When he heard that Khara, Dūsaṇa and Triśirā had been slain, the Ten-headed was on fire all over.

Dohā 22

After consoling Śūrpanakhā and bragging and boasting of his might, he went to his palace in the deepest anxiety and had no sleep all night.

Caupāī 21

"Among gods, men and demons, serpents and birds", he thought, "there is none who can withstand my servants; and Khara and Dūsana were my equals in strength; who can have killed them, unless it be God himself? If God himself has become incarnate, in order to gladden the gods and relieve the earth of its burden, then if I go and fight against him and lose my life by an arrow of the Lord's, I shall escape further transmigration; prayer will not do for one like me of demon form; this is the plan upon which I am absolutely determined. If he is only some earthly king's son, I shall conquer them both in battle and carry off the bride." He mounted his chariot and drove off unattended to the spot where

1. In the word *guna nānā—guna* is intended to be understood in its two senses of, first, a virtue, secondly, a bowstring.

Mārīca was living by the sea-shore. Hearken now, Umā, to the marvellous account of the device that Rāma invented.

Dohā 23

When Lakṣmaṇa had gone into the woods to fetch roots and fruit and herbs, the gentle and joyous god said with a smile to Janaka's daughter :

Caupāī 22

"Hearken, most lovely and amiable of faithful wives, I am about to act a fantastic human part. Abide in fire until I have completed the destruction of the demons." As soon as Rāma had finished speaking, Sītā laid her lord's feet upon her heart and entered into the fire, leaving only an image of herself, of exactly the same appearance and the same amiable and gentle disposition. Even Lakṣmaṇa did not know the secret of what the Blessed Lord had done. The Ten-headed approached Mārīca and bowed his head to him, the selfish and contemptible wretch. When a mean creature bends, it is only to give more pain, like an elephant-goad, a bow, a snake, or a cat; the friendly speech of a churl is as portentous, Bhavānī, as flowers that blossom out of season.

Dohā 24

After doing him homage, Mārīca respectfully enquired of him his business : "What is the cause, sire, that you have come so disturbed in mind and all alone ?"

Caupāī 23

The Ten-headed laid the whole matter before him and added presumptuously—the wretch—"Do you for the purpose of deception assume the form of a deer, and by this means, I shall be able to carry off the princess." He replied : "Hearken, O Ten-headed; though in form as a man, this is the Lord of all animate and inanimate creation; there is no fighting against him, sire; if he kills, you die; and if you live, it is he who gives you life. He is the prince Raghupati, who, when he went to protect the sage's sacrifice, smote me with a pointless arrow, and in an instant I was driven a distance of a hundred leagues:[1] it is not well to quarrel with him. Wherever I look, I see these two brothers, and my senses are utterly bewildered like a fly fascinated by a spider. Even if he be only a man, sire, he is a mighty hero, and opposition to him will do no good.

Dohā 25

But can he possibly be a man, who was valiant enough to slay Tāṛakā and Subāhu, who broke Śiva's bow and slew Khara, Dūṣaṇa and Triśirā ?

Caupāī 24

Think, then, of the welfare of your family and go home." When he heard this, he was furious and abused him soundly : "You fool, you take upon yourself to teach me, as if you were my master ! Tell me, where is there in the world any warrior my equal ?" Then Mārīca thought to himself, "There are nine whom it is not good to make enemies; an armed man, an accomplice, a king, a man without principle, a rich man, a physician, a panegyrist, poet or any person of special ability." Either way he saw he must die; but he reflected that Rāma would be his sanctuary. So he answered, "You will be the death of me, poor wretch; for how can I escape when smitten by Raghupati's shaft ?" With these thoughts at heart, he accompanied the Ten-headed, staunch in his devotion to Rāma's feet and with an exceeding gladness of heart that he would not show. "Today," he said to himself, "I shall behold my best beloved.

Chand 7

My eyes shall be rewarded with the sight of my best beloved, and I shall be happy. I shall imprint upon my soul the feet of the gracious Lord with Sītā too and his brother. Hari, the ocean of joy, whose very wrath confers celestial bliss, who gives himself

1. See Book I, *caupāī* 208.

up entirely to the will of his worshippers, will with his own hands fit an arrow to the string and slay me.

Dohā 26

As he runs after me to seize me with his bow and arrows, I shall turn round again and again and get a sight of my Lord : there is none else so blessed as I am."

Caupāī 25

When the Ten-headed drew near to the wood, Mārīca took the form of a deer, so beautifully spotted as to beggar description, with a body of gold, all bespangled with jewels. When Sītā saw the wondrously beautiful creature clothed with loveliness in its every limb, she cried : "O Raghubīra, hearken, kind sir, this deer has a most charming skin; I pray you, shoot it, most amiable lord, and bring me the hide." Thereupon Rāma, who understood why this was done, arose with joy to execute the purpose of the gods. Having marked the deer, he girded up his loins, took his bow in his hand and trimmed his shapely arrows. Then the Lord cautioned Lakṣmaṇa : "Many demons, brother, roam the forest. Take care of Sītā with all thought and consideration and with force too, if need arises. The deer, seeing the Lord, took to flight, but Rāma pursued with ready bow : even he, to whom the Veda cannot attain, nor Śiva is able to contemplate, hastened in pursuit of a mimic deer. Now close at hand, now fleeing at a distance, at one time in sight, at another hid, alternately showing and concealing itself and practising many a wile, in this manner it took the Lord far away. At last Rāma aimed and let fly the fatal shaft; the deer fell to the ground with a terrible cry, first calling aloud to Lakṣmaṇa, but afterwards mentally invoking Rāma. As life ebbed, he resumed his natural form and devoutly repeated the name of Rāma, who in his wisdom recognizing his inward love, granted him that liberation which even sages can scarcely attain to.

Dohā 27

The gods rained down abundant flowers and hymned the Lord's

high virtue :" Raghunātha, the suppliant's friend raises, to his own sphere even a demon !"

Caupāī 26

As soon as he had slain the monster, Raghubīra returned, the bow gleaming in his hand and the quiver at his side. When Sītā heard the agonizing cry, she said to Lakṣmaṇa in the greatest alarm : "Make haste, your brother is in some sad strait." Lakṣmaṇa answered with a smile, "Hearken, mother; he, by the play of whose eyebrows the world is annihilated, cannot be imagined as having fallen into any difficulty." But when Sītā urged him with taunting words, Lakṣmaṇa's resolution—for such was Hari's will—was shaken; he made over charge of everything to the forest and its gods, and went after the Rāhu of the moon-like Rāvaṇa. When the Ten-headed saw Sītā deserted, he seized the opportunity and drew near in the guise of an anchorite. He, for fear of whom gods and demons trembled and could neither sleep by night nor eat food by day, even that Rāvaṇa came looking this side and that, as furtively as a cur bent on thieving. After he had turned his steps, Garuṛ, to this vile course, not a particle of his majesty, or intellect, or strength of body was left in him. After repeating a variety of legends and moral sentiments, he had recourse to threats and blandishments. Said Sīta, "Hearken, reverend Father; what you say is hateful to me." Then Rāvaṇa displayed his proper form; and she was terror-stricken when he declared his name. But plucking up all her resolute courage she said : "Wretch, stay as you are; my lord is at hand. Like as a hare that would wed a lioness, so have you wooed your own destruction, O demon king." On hearing this defiant speech, the Ten-headed was furious, though in his heart he delighted to adore her feet.

Dohā 28

Then Rāvaṇa in a fury seized her and seated her in his chariot. As he took his way through the air, he was so agitated with fear that he could scarcely drive.

Caupāī 27

"Ah ! gallant Raghurāi," she cried, "sovereign of the universe, for what fault of mine have you forgotten mercy? Ah! reliever of distress, health-giving sanctuary, sun of the lotuses of the Raghu race! Ah! Lakṣmaṇa ! this is no fault of yours; I have reaped the fruit of the temper I showed." Many were the lamentations that she uttered. "My affectionate and loving lord is far away; who will tell of my calamity? That an ass should devour the oblation intended for the gods !" At the sound of Sītā's grievous lament every created being, whether animate or inanimate, was sad. The king of the vultures, too, heard her piteous cry and recognized the wife of the glory of Raghu's line, whom the vile demon was carrying away, as it were the famous dun cow that had fallen into the hands of some savage. "Fear not, Sītā, my daughter, I will slay this monster." The bird darted forth in its fury, like a thunderbolt hurled upon a mountain. "Stop, you villain ! How dare you go on thus and take no heed of me ?" Seeing him bearing down upon him like the angel of death, Rāvaṇa paused and considered, "Is it mount Maināka[1] or the king of the birds! Anyhow they both know my might, as also do their lords."[2] When he knew that it was poor old Jaṭāyu, he cried, "He shall leave his body at the shrine of my hands."[3] At this, the vulture rushed on in a fury, crying, "Hearken, Rāvaṇa, to my advice; surrender Jānakī and go home in peace; if not, despite your many arms, it will turn out thus; Rāma's wrath is like a fierce flame, and your whole house will be consumed in it like a moth." The warrior demon gave no answer. Then the vulture flew at him in a rage and clutched him by the hair and hurled him from his chariot so that he fell to the ground. Again, having sheltered Sītā, the vulture turned and with his beak tore and rent his body. For nearly half an hour the demon was in a swoon, then gnash-

1. Maināka is the only peak which is said to have retained its wings when Indra clipped those of the other mountains.

2. Maināka's lord is the Ocean, which Rāvaṇa and the other demons had churned; and Garuṛ, 'the king of the birds,' has Viṣṇu for his lord, with whom Rāvaṇa had always been at war.

3. That is to say, 'as a man goes to a place of pilgrimage in order to die there, so has he come to me to die by my hand.'

ed his teeth with rage and drew his monstrous sword and cut off Jaṭāyu's wings. The bird fell to the ground, calling upon Rāma, and doing marvellous feats of courage. The demon seated Sītā again in the chariot and drove off in haste in no little alarm. Sītā was borne through air lamenting, like a frightened fawn in the power of a huntsman. Seeing the monkeys sitting on a hill, she cried out Hari's name and dropped her scarf. In this manner he went off with Sītā and put her down in the Aśoka forest.

Dohā 29

Though he tried every kind of threat and blandishment, the monster could not succeed, and at last after exhausting all his devices he left her beneath an *aśoka* tree. With Rāma's beauteous form impressed upon her heart, as he appeared when pursuing the mimic deer, Sītā was incessantly invoking his name, "O Hari, Hari !"

Caupāī 28

When Raghupati saw his brother coming, he was seized, or appeared to have been seized, with a new and greater fear : "O brother," he cried, "have you left Sītā alone and come here in defiance of my order, though so many demons roam the forest? My mind misgives me that Sītā is not in the hermitage." Lakṣmaṇa clasped his lotus feet and cried with folded hands: "Hearken, my lord, it is no fault of mine." When he found the hermitage on the bank of the Godāvarī bereft of Sītā he was as agitated as any ordinary mortal. "Alas! Jānakī, my precious Sītā, so beautiful and amiable, so divinely pious and devoted !" Lakṣmaṇa did all he could to comfort him. As he went along, he questioned all the trees and flowers by the way : "O ye birds and deer, O ye swarms of bees, have you seen the fawn-eyed Sītā ? The wagtails, parrots, and pigeons ; the deer and fish; swarming bees and clever cuckoos : the jasmine buds and pomegranate flowers; the lightning flash, the lotus, the autumn moon; the gliding serpent; the meshes of Varuṇa, bow of Kāmadeva; the swan, the elephant and the lion can now hear themselves praised; the coconut, the *campā*, and the plantain can now rejoice, without any doubt or misgiving at heart.[1] "Hearken, Jānakī! Now that you are away, they are all as glad as if they had won a kingdom. How can I endure this cruelty at your hands; why do you not at once show yourself, my beloved ?" In this manner the Lord searched and lamented, like a fond lover distressed by separation. Rāma who has no wish unsatisfied, the perfection of bliss, the uncreated and the everlasting, acted the part of a man. Further on he saw the vulture-king lying, with his thoughts fixed on the prints of Rāma's feet.

Dohā 30

The compassionate Raghubīra laid his lotus hands upon his head. At the sight of Rāma's lovely face he felt no more pain.

Caupāī 29

Then the vulture took courage and said, "Hearken, Rāma, remover of life's troubles. My lord, this is Rāvaṇa's doing; he is the wretch, who has carried off Janaka's daughter. He took her away, sire, to the south, crying as piteously as an osprey, I have kept alive, my lord, only to see you; now, O most merciful, I would depart." Said Rāma : "Remain alive, my friend." He smiled and answered : "He, by the mention of whose name at the hour of death the vilest sinner, as the scriptures declare, attains salvation, has come in bodily form before my eyes; what need is there, sire, for me to live any longer?" Raghurāī's eyes filled with tears as he replied : "Friend, it is your own good deeds that have saved you. There is nothing in the world beyond the reach of those who devote their soul to the good of others. When you pass out of the body, friend, ascend to my sphere in heaven. What more can I give you ? You have all you desire.

1. The different objects here mentioned from the Hindu poet's stock in trade upon which he invariably draws for comparisons when he wishes to describe the charms of a lovely woman: with clustering hair like swarms of bees, teeth white as buds of jasmine, lips like the pomegranate, eyes bright as flashes of lightning, breasts swelling like cocoanuts, waist like a lion's, a gait like an elephant's &c, &c, Now that Sīta is gone, who excelled each of them in the very point on which they most prided themselves, they may again hear themselves quoted as perfect.

Dohā 31

But, friend, say nothing to my father, about the abduction of Sītā when you go there. As sure as I am Rāma, the Ten-headed himself, together with all his house, will come and tell him of it."

Caupāī 30

Dropping the form of a vulture, he appeared in all the beauty of Hari, bedecked with jewels and in gorgeous yellow attire, with dark-hued body and four mighty arms, and with his eyes full of tears he chanted that hymn of praise :

Chand 8

"Glory to Rāma of incomparable beauty; the bodiless, the embodied; the veritable source of every bodily element; who with mighty arrows has broken the might of the arm of the ten-headed demon; the ornament of the earth. With his body dark as a rain-cloud, with his lotus face and his eyes large as the lotus flower, I unceasingly worship Rāma the merciful, the mighty-armed, the dispeller of the life's terrors; of immeasurable strength; without beginning and origin; the indivisible; the one; beyond perception; the incarnate Govinda; the annihilator of duality; the sum of mystic wisdom; the supporter of the earth; an ever-lasting delight to the soul of the saints, who practise the spell of Rāma's name. I unceasingly worship Rāma, the friend of the unsensual, the destroyer of lust and every other wickedness. He, whom the scriptures hymn under the name of the passion-less Brahma, the all-pervading, the supreme spirit, the unborn; to whom the sages attain after infinite study and contemplation, penance and abstraction; he the all-merciful, the all-radiant, the unapproachable, has now become manifest for the delight of the world. He who is at once inaccessible and accessible, like and unlike, the essentially pure, the unfailing comforter, whom ascetics behold only when they have laboriously subdued their mind and senses; even Rāma, the spouse of Lakṣmī, who is ever at the command of his servants, though the lord of the three spheres, may he dwell in my heart, the terminator of trans-migration, whose praises make pure."

Dohā 32

After asking for the boon of endless faith, the vulture departed to Hari's sphere. Rāma with his own hands performed his funeral rites with all due ceremony.

Caupāī 31

The tender-hearted and compassionate Raghunātha, who shows mercy even on the undeserving, bestowed upon a vulture, an unclean flesh-eating bird, such a place in heaven as the greatest ascetics crave. Hearken, Umā; the most unblessed of men are they who abandon Hari and become attached to objects of sense.

The two brothers in their search for Sītā visited and examined many woods, tangled with creepers, dense with trees, and swarming with birds, deer, elephants and lions. As they went on their way, Rāma overthrew Kabandha, who told him the whole story of the curse. "Durvāsā[1] cursed me, but now that I have seen my lord's feet, my sin has been blotted out." "Hearken, Gandharva; those who trouble Brāhmaṇas are displeasing to me.

Dohā 33

They who without guile in thought, word and deed do service to the gods of earth, subdue unto themselves Brahmā, Śiva, myself and every other divinity.

Caupāī 32

A Brāhmaṇa, though he curse, beat and abuse you, is still an

1. The reference to Durvāsā is obscure. According to the legend as told by Vālmīki, Kabandha had been a beautiful youth by name Danu, who as a reward for penance obtained from heaven the boon of a long life. On the strength of this promise, he ventured to challenge Indra to battle, who launched his thunderbolt against him and drove his head and shoulders down into his body, which was thus made a horrible headless, shapeless trunk. To keep him from starving, since he needs must live, his arms were made a league long; and a huge mouth was opened in his belly. In the text as translated by Griffith, there is mention of a sage Sthūla-Śiras (Great-head) who had been annoyed by Danu and therefore cursed him; but the passage has rather the air of an interpolation, and does not appear in Gorresio's edition. The meaning of the word *kabandha* is 'a headless trunk'.

object of reverence; so declare the sages. A Brāhmaṇa must be revered, though devoid of every virtue and merit; but a Śūdra never, though distinguished for all virtue and learning." So saying, he instructed him in his doctrine and was pleased to see his devotion to his feet. When the beneficent Rāma had granted him beatitude, he went on to the hermitage of Śabarī[1]. When she saw that Rāma had come to her abode, she remembered the words of the sage and was glad. With lotus eyes, mighty arms, hair fastened up in a knot on their head, and a garland of wild flowers upon their breast, one dark of hue, the other fair stood the two brothers. Sabarī fell down and clung to their feet. She was so drowned in love that no speech came to her lips, but again and again she bowed her head at their lotus feet, then reverently brought water and laved their feet and finally conducted them to seats of honour.

Dohā 34

Then she brought and offered to Rāma the most delicious herbs and roots and fruit, and the lord graciously ate of them, again and again thanking her.

Caupāī 33

She stood before him with folded hands and as she gazed upon the Lord, her love waxed yet more vehement. "How can I hymn thy praises, seeing that I am a woman of meanest descent and of dullest wit : the lowest of the low and a woman to boot; nay, among the lowest of women the one who is of all most ignorant, O sinless god." Said Raghupati: "Hearken, lady, to my words : I recognize no relationship save that of faith ; neither lineage, family, religion, rank, wealth, power, connections, virtue, nor ability. A man without faith is of no more account than a cloud without water. I will explain to you the nine practices of faith; hearken attentively and lay them up in your heart. The first

1. *Śabara*, with the feminine *sabarī*, is, strictly speaking, not the distinctive name of any one particular person, but of a whole savage tribe. The word is probably connected with *sava*, 'a corpse.'

step in faith is communion with the sages; the second a love for the legends relating to me;

Dohā 35

The third—an incalculable step—devotion to the lotus feet of the *guru*; the fourth, hymning of all my virtues with a guileless purpose.

Caupāī 34

The fifth, as the Vedas have expounded, prayer and the repetition, with an assured confidence, of mystic spells: the sixth, self-governance, kindness, detachment from the world and in every action a loving and persevering piety; the seventh, seeing the whole world full of me, and holding the sages in yet greater account than myself; the eighth, contentment with what one has without ever a thought of spying out fault in others; the ninth, a guileless simplicity towards all, and a hearty confidence in me without either exultation or dejection. Verily, lady, whoever practises any one of these, whether he be man or woman, animate or inanimate, is my friend; and you have them all in the highest degree. The heavenly prize, which the greatest ascetics scarcely win, is today within your easy reach. The result of seeing me is something most marvellous; every creature at once attains its proper consummation. But tell me, lady, have you any tidings of Jānakī ? Tell me, fair dame, all that you know." "Go Raghurāī, to the lake Pampā; there make friends with Sugrīva;[1] he will tell you all. You know it already, my god Raghubīra, yet have the patience to ask him." After again and again bowing her head at the Lord's feet, she lovingly repeated the whole story of her life.

Chand 9

After repeating the whole story of her life, as she gazed on Hari's face and imprinted his lotus feet on her heart, she aban-

1. According to the Sanskrit *Rāmāyaṇa*, it was not Śabarī, but Kabandha, who directed Rāma to apply to Sugrīva.

doned her body in the sacrificial fire and became absorbed in Hari's beatific state beyond return. O men, abandon all your religious observances, which are unrighteousness, and your many sects, which yield only sorrow, and with all confidence (says Tulasī Dāsa) lovingly embrace the feet of Rāma.

Dohā 36

He granted liberation to a woman of such low descent and so altogether born in sin as even this Śabarī was : foolish indeed are they who desire peace of mind after forgetting such a lord.

Caupāī 35

When they had left this wood, they went on their way, Rāma and his brother, two lions among men, of immeasurable strength. The Lord, like a bereaved lover, kept making lamentation and discoursing in various parables. "Observe, Lakṣmaṇa, the beauty of the forest; whose heart is not moved to see it ? The birds and deer, all accompanied by their mates, seem to laugh and jeer at me. When the deer see me and would scamper away, he does cry: 'Have no fear, enjoy yourselves, for you are genuine deer, and it is only a golden deer that these people have come to look for.' The female elephants, as they take aside their lords, seem to be teaching me this lesson: 'The scriptures, however well studied, must be read over and over again; a king, however well served, is never to be depended upon; and a woman like the scriptures and the king, though you cherish her in your bosom, is never thoroughly mastered.' See, brother, how beautiful the spring is; yet to me without my beloved it is frightful

Dohā 37a-37b

Love finding me distressed by separation, powerless and absolutely alone, has made a raid upon me with the bees and birds of the forest. His spy has seen me with only my brother, and on his report the amorous god has, as it were, resolutely encamped against me with his army.

Caupāī 36

The spreading trees and tangled creepers are like so many pavilions that he has spread; the plantains and stately palms his flags and standards; that none but the stoutest could see without amazement; the many kinds of different flowering shrubs are his warriors, arrayed in all their various kinds of panoply; the magnificent forest-trees, that stand here and there, are the separate encampments of warrior chiefs; the murmuring cuckoos are his infuriated elephants, and the herons his bulls, camels and mules; the peacocks, partridges and parrots are his war horses; the pigeons and swans his Arab steeds; the partridges and quails his foot soldiers; but there is no describing the whole of Love's host. The mountains and rocks are his chariots, the waterfalls his kettle-drums, the pied cuckoos the bards that sing his praises, the garrulous bees are his trumpets and clarions, and the three kinds of wind his scouts. With an army complete in all its four branches, he goes about and exhorts every one. O Lakṣmaṇa, they who can see Love's battle-array and stand firm, are men of mark in the world. His greatest strength lies in woman; he who can escape her toils is a mighty champion indeed !

Dohā 38a-38b

Brother, there are three evils of surpassing strength, lust, wrath, and greed : in an instant they upset the souls of the wisest philosopher. The power of greed lies in desire and pride; of love in nothing but woman; while anger's power lies in harsh speech; so thoughtful sages have declared."

Caupāī 37

O Umā ! Rāma is without attributes, the lord of all animate and inanimate creation, and knows all secrets ; yet he exhibited all the distress of a lover no less than the detachment and steadfastness of a philosopher. Anger, love, greed, pride, delusion, are all dissipated by the grace of Rāma, and the only man superior to all this jugglery is he to whom the great conjuror has shown favour.[1] I tell you, Umā, what is my conclusion; the worship of Hari is real and all the world is a dream.

The Lord went on from there to the shore of the deep and beautiful lake called Pampā; its water as clear as the hearts of sages; with charming flights of steps on each of its four sides; where beasts of different kinds came as they listed, to drink of the flood, like crowds of beggars at a good man's gate.

Dohā 39a-39b

Under its dense cover of leaves the water was as difficult to distinguish as is the unembodied supreme spirit under the veil of delusive phenomena. The happy fish were all in placid repose at the bottom of the deep pool, like the days of the righteous that are passed in peace.

Caupāī 38

Lotuses of many colours were blooming; there was a buzzing of garrulous bees, both honey-makers and black bees; while swans and waterfowls were so noisy that you would think they had recognized the Lord and were telling his praises. The geese and cranes and other birds were so numerous that only seeing would be believing, no words could describe them. The charming notes of so many beautiful birds seemed as an invitation to the wayfarers. The sages had built themselves a house near the lake with magnificent forest-trees all round, the *campā* the *mālsari*, the *kadamba* and *tamāla*, the *pāṭala*, the *kathal*, the *dhāk* and the mango.[2] Every tree had put forth its new leaves and

1. That is to say, whom he has taken behind the scenes.

2. The *campā*, or *campaka*, is the Michelia campaka, a handsome tree with sweet-scented golden flowers.

The *mālsari*, called in the text by another of its Sanskrit names, *vakula* is the Mimusops elengi. Its fragrant star-shaped flowers are much used by Hindus for garlands and supply the native silversmith with a very favourite pattern.

The *kadamba* is the Nauclea cadamba, a large and handsome forest tree, which grows wild in the Mathurā district and figures in many of Kṛṣṇa's pastoral adventures.

The *tamāla* is a tree with dark and white blossoms.

The *pāṭala* is the Bignonia or Stereospermum suaveolens, a large tree

blossoms, all resonant with swarms of bees. A delightful air, soft, cool and fragrant, was ever in delicious motion, and the cooing of the cuckoos was so pleasant to hear that a sage's meditation would be broken by it.

Dohā 40

The trees laden with fruit bowed low to the ground ; like a generous soul whom every increase of fortune renders only more humble than before.

Caupāī 39

When Rāma beheld this most beautiful lake, he bathed in it with great delight, and then with his brother sat down in shade of a beautiful tree. There all the gods and sages came once more to hymn his praises and then returned each to his own home. The All-merciful rested in supreme content and addressed his brother in edifying discourse. When Nārada saw the Lord God thus sorrowing for the loss of his beloved, his soul was much disturbed. "In submission to my curse[1] Rāma endures all this weight of woe. I must go and visit so gracious a Lord, for I may never have such an opportunity again." Having thus reflected, Nārada, lute in hand,[2] approached the spot where the Lord was sitting at ease. In dulcet tones he sang his acts, affectionately dwelling upon them in all detail. As he prostrated himself, Rāma raised him up, and again and again clasped him to his bosom and asked him how he fared and seated him by his side. Then Lakṣmaṇa reverently washed his feet.

common in South India, with dark dull-crimson, exquisitely fragrant flowers.

The *kathal*, called in the text by its Sanskrit name *panasa*, is the Artocarpus integrifolia, or jack-tree. The fruit is an important article of food in South India and Ceylon.

The *dhāk*, called in the text by its Sanskrit name *palāsa* is the Butea frondosa, a tree with scarlet flower, which precede the new leaves, and when in full bloom make a striking sight, a fire on the horizon. Hence the vernacular name, *dhāk*, from the Sanskrit *dagha*, 'on fire.'

1. For the explanation of Nārada's curse see Childhood 1, *caupāī* 137.
2. Nārada is the reputed inventor of the viṇā or Indian lute.

Dohā 41

Perceiving that his Lord was graciously inclined, Nārada made much supplication and folding his lotus hands addressed him in these words:

Caupāī 40

"Hearken, most generous Raghunāyaka, beautiful and beneficent, at once unapproachable and easy of approach, grant me, my Lord, the one boon that I ask; though you know it without my asking, since you know the secrets of all hearts." "Reverend sage, you know my nature; can I ever turn away my face from anyone of my worshippers ? There is nothing I hold so dear that you, most excellent of sages, may not ask it of me. There is nothing of mine that I would refuse to a believer; never allow yourself to abandon this confidence in me." Then Nārada was glad and said : "This is the boon I presume to ask. Though the Lord has many names, each more glorious than the other, as declared in the scriptures, may the name Rāma, sire, surpass all names, exterminating the whole brood of sin, as when a fowler ensnares an entire flock of birds.

Dohā 42a-42b

May your name 'Rāma' be as the moon in the bright night of cloudless faith, and your other names as brilliant stars in the heaven of the believer's soul." Raghunātha, the ocean of mercy, said to the sage, "Be it even so !" Then was Nārada's soul rejoiced exceedingly and he bowed his head at his Lord's feet.

Caupāī 41

Seeing Raghunātha so gracious, Nārada spoke again in winning tones : "O Rāma, when you sent forth your delusive power and infatuated me—hearken, O Raghurāī—I was anxious to accomplish a marriage, why was it, my Lord, that you did not allow me to do ?" "Hearken, O sage, and I will tell you, if you will not be angry. If men will abandon all other hope, and worship me only, I always keep watch over them as a mother over her infant child. If an infant child runs to lay hold of the fire or a snake, the mother at once rescues it; when her son has grown up, the mother does not show her affection to him in the same way as before. The wise are, as it were, my grown up sons and humble worshippers my infant children. The latter are protected by my strength, the former by their own, and both have to fight against love and anger. The learned know this and worship me, and though they have acquired wisdom, still they do not forsake their devotion.

Dohā 43

Lust, wrath, greed and all other violent passions form a rushing torrent of deception; but among them all the most formidable and the most calamitous is that incarnation of vanity, woman.

Caupāī 42

Hearken, O sage, to the teaching of the Purāṇas, the Vedas and the saints: woman is like the season of spring to the forest of infatuation; like the heat of summer to dry up the pools and waterfalls of prayer, penance and devotional exercises; like the rains to rejoice the gnats[1] and frogs of lust, anger and pride: like the autumn to revive the lily-like growth of evil propensities; like the winter to distress and deaden all the lotus beds of piety; and lastly, like the dewy season[2] to foster the *javāsa* grove of selfishness. Woman, again, is like a dark and murky night; in which owls and deeds of darkness delight, or like a hook to catch the fish of sense and strength and honour and truth; so say the wise.

Dohā 44

A young and wanton woman is the root of all evil, a source

1. *Matsara*, translated 'gnats,' also means 'selfishness,' and may be intended in that sense here, as both meanings suit the context equally well.

2. *Śiśira*, 'the dewy season,' consists of the months, Māgha and Phālguna, that come between the winter and the spring.

of torment, a mine of all unhappiness; therefore, O sages, knowing all this, I prevented your marriage."

Caupāī 43

As the sage listened to Raghupati's delightful discourse, his body quivered with emotion and his eyes filled with tears. "Tell me, is there any other lord, whose wont it is to be so kind and considerate to his servants? All, who will not abandon their errors, nor worship such a lord as this, are indeed dull and witless fools." Nārada the sage reverentially enquired further: "Hearken, Rāma, versed in all mystic wisdom! Tell me, my lord Raghubīra, destroyer of the fear of birth and death, what are the marks of a saint ?" "Listen, reverend sir, and I will tell you what are the qualities of the saints, by virtue of which they hold me in their power. They have conquered the six disturbing influences;[1] are sinless, passionless, and imperturbable; have no worldly goods, but live a life of chastity and contentedness; their wisdom is immeasurable; they are without desires and temperate in enjoyment; oceans of truth, inspired bards, practised in meditation; circumspect; void of pride and arrogance; persevering and eminently wise in the mystery of salvation;

Dohā 45

perfectly virtuous, free from the troubles of the world and with all their doubts solved; who, rather than abandon my lotus feet, account neither life nor home precious;

Caupāī 44

who are abashed when they hear themselves praised, and exceedingly glad to hear the praises of others; who are always equable and calm, persistent in virtuous practice; honest and

1. According to the Sāṅkhya philosophy, there is an original eternal germ, or primal source of all things except soul, which is called Prakṛti. From it are evolved certain *vikāras*, or productive products, or modifications which occasion all the diversity of material phenomena, and which may therefore be designated 'disturbing influences.'

kindly disposed to all men; distinguished for prayer, penance, religious observances, temperance, self-denial, and performance of pious vows; for devotion to their *guru*, to Govinda and to Brāhmaṇas; for faith, forbearance, charitableness and compassion; for a rapturous love of my feet; a superiority to all material delusions; an absolute composure, discrimination, humility and knowledge; and for doctrine in strict accordance with the Vedas and Purāṇas; who never display ostentation, arrogance, or pride, nor ever dream of setting their foot on the way of wickedness; who are always either hearing or singing my acts and have no selfish object, but are devoted to the good of others; in short, reverend sir, the characteristics of the saints are so numerous that not even Śāradā or the scriptures could tell them all.

Chand 10

No, not even Śāradā or Śeṣanāga could tell them." Hearing this, Nārada clasped his lotus feet, crying, "Thus the friend of the suppliant, the all-merciful, has with his own lips declared the virtues of his votaries !" After again and again bowing his head at his feet, Nārada returned to the city of Brahmā. Blessed, says Tulasī Dāsa, are all they who abandon other hope and devote themselves to Hari.

Dohā 46a-46b

People who sing or hear the sanctifying praises of Rāvaṇa's foe, even without asceticism, prayer and meditation, are rewarded with steadfast faith in Rāma. A young woman is like the flame of a candle; let not your soul be as the moth, but discard love and intoxication, worship Rāma and hold communion with the saints.

[*Thus endeth the book entitled* "THE FOREST" *composed by Tulasī Dāsa for the bestowal of pure wisdom and continence; being the third descent into the Holy Lake of Rāma's Acts, that cleanses from every defilement of the world.*]

BOOK IV

KIṢKINDHĀ

KIṢKINDHĀ

Sanskrit Invocation

BEAUTIFUL as the jasmine or the dark-blue lotus, of surpassing strength, store-houses of wisdom, all glorious and accomplished bowmen, hymned by the Vedas, benefactors of cows and Brāhmaṇas, may they who appeared in the form of mortal men as the two noble scions of the house of Raghu, the champions of true religion, the wayfarers intent on their search for Sītā, may they grant us faith.

Blèssed are the pious souls, who ever quaff the nectar of holy Rāma's name; nectar, the product of no ocean, but of Brahmā himself, the utter exterminator of all the impurities of the Kaliyuga, the imperishable, the quintessence of the beauty of blessed Śambhu's moonlike face, the ever glorious, the remedy for all the diseases of life, the exquisitely sweet, the life of blessed Jānakī.

Soraṭhā

How is it possible not to reverence Kāśī, where Śambhu and Bhavānī dwell, knowing it to be the earthly birth-place of salvation, a treasury of knowledge and the destroyer of sin. Dull indeed of soul is the man who worships not him, who when all the hosts of heaven were in distress, drank up the deadly poison; who is so merciful as Śaṅkara ?

Caupāī 1

Rāma again proceeded on his way and drew near to the mountain Ṛṣyamūka.[1] There Sugrīva dwelt with his ministers, who, seeing them approach in all their immeasurable strength, was exceedingly alarmed and cried : "Hearken, Hanumān; assume the form of a young Brāhmaṇa student and go and see

1. The mountain Ṛṣyamūka derives its name from *Ṛṣya*, a kind of antelope.

who these two heroes are, of such remarkable strength and beauty, and when you have ascertained make some sign by which I may know also. If that wretch Bālī has sent them, I must leave the hill and flee at once." The monkey assumed the form of a Brāhmaṇa and approached them; there bowed his head and thus questioned them: "Who are you two knights of warrior mien, who roam this wood, one dark of hue, the other fair? The ground is rough for your soft feet to tread. What is the reason, my masters, that you visit this forest ? Your bodies are too delicate and exquisitely beautiful to be exposed to the intolerable sun and wind of these wild regions. Who are you ? Are you some two of the three gods or are you Nara and Nārāyaṇa ?[1]

Dohā 1

Or has the lord of all the spheres become incarnate in your human form, for the good of the world to bridge the ocean of existence and relieve earth of its burdens ?"

Caupāī 2

"We are the sons of Daśaratha, king of Kosala, and have come into the forest in obedience to our father's command. Rāma is the name of one brother, and Lakṣmaṇa of the other. With us was my young and beautiful bride, the daughter of the king

1. Nara, the original or eternal Man, the divine imperishable spirit that pervades the universe. is always associated with Nārāyaṇa, which as a patronymic from Nara, means 'the Son of the original Man.' In Manu, I, 10, Nara is apparently identified with Nārāyaṇa : the waters, it is said, being called Nārā, as produced from Nara, the eternal Spirit, or Paramātmā, which is also styled Nārāyaṇa, as having its first place of motion on the waters. In the more systematic theology Nara and Nārāyaṇa are distinct, the former being regarded as a sage or patriarch, while the latter is a god. In epic poetry they are the sons of Dharma by Mūrti, or Ahimsā, and are emanations of Viṣṇu, Arjuna being identified with Nara, and Kṛṣṇa with Nārāyaṇa. In some places Nara and Nārāyaṇa are called *devau*, 'the two gods'; or *pūrva-devau* 'the two original gods'; or ṛṣi, 'the two sages,; or *purāṇav ṛṣisattamau*, 'the two most ancient and best of sages' or *tāpasau* 'the two ascetics; or *mahā-munī*, 'the two great munīs. — *Monier Williams*, sub verbo.

of Kosala. But some demon here has stolen her away; and it is she, O Brāhmaṇa, whom we are trying to find. We have told you our affairs, tell us now your own story." He recognized the Lord and fell and clasped his feet with joy, Umā, beyond all description. His body thrilled with emotion and all words failed his tongue, as he gazed upon the fashion of their ravishing disguise. At last he collected himself and burst forth into a hymn of praise, with great joy of heart, for he had found his Lord. "I asked, sire, in my ignorance; but why should you ask, as though you were a mere man. Under the influence of your magic I wandered in error, and therefore I did not at once recognize my Lord.

Dohā 2

In the first place I was a bewildered dullard, ignorant and perverse of soul, and then my gracious Lord God himself led me astray.

Caupāī 3

Although, master, my faults are many, yet let not the Lord forget his servant. All created things are first fettered by your delusive power and then again set free by your grace. Therefore I swear by Raghubīra and know no other mode of prayer. As a servant has confidence in his master, or a child in its mother, so all dwell secure under the protection of the Lord." So saying, he fell in much agitation at his feet, and the love that filled his soul showed itself in every part of his body. Then Raghupati raised him up and took him to his bosom, while his own eyes were flooded with tears of joy. "Hearken, O monkey," he said, "do not account yourself vile; you are twice as dear to me as Lakṣamaṇa; everyone says that I have no respect of persons; any servant is beloved of me, and has a rank in heaven second to none.

Dohā 3

For he, Hanumān, is second to none who never wavers in his faith, that he is the servant of the Lord God who is manifested in creation."

Caupāī 4

When the Son of the Wind (*i.e.*, Hanumān) saw his Lord so graciously disposed, he rejoiced at heart, and every anxiety was at an end. "The king of the monkeys, sire, lives on this rock, Sugrīva by name, a servant of yours. In return for his submission you should make friends with him and set his mind at rest. He will have Sītā tracked; for he will dispatch ten million monkeys in every direction." In this manner, he told them all the particulars and took them both with him and gave them stools to sit upon. When Sugrīva saw Rāma, he thought it a great blessing to have been born. He reverentially advanced to meet him and bowed his head before his feet; and Raghunātha and his brother returned his courtesy. The monkey's mind was occupied with this thought, 'If God would only give me such allies !'

Dohā 4

Hanumān then explained the circumstances of both sides; holy fire was made a witness, and a firm alliance of mutual aid concluded.

Caupāī 5

When the alliance had been thus concluded, nothing was kept in reserve; Rāma and Lakṣmaṇa told all their adventures. Sugrīva's eyes were full of tears as he replied—"The daughter of the king of Mithilā will be recovered. One day when I was sitting here with my ministers deep in thought, I saw some one flying through the air, with a woman in his power, who was weeping piteously and crying, 'Rāma, Rāma, O my Rāma !' When she saw me, she dropped her scarf." Rāma at once asked for it; he gave it him; he pressed the robe to his bosom in the deepest distress. Said Sugrīva, "Hearken, Raghubīra; be not so distressed; take courage. I will do all I can to serve you and recover Jānakī."

Dohā 5

The Almighty and All-merciful Lord rejoiced to hear his friend's speech. "Tell me, Sugrīva, the reason why you are living in this forest."

Caupāī 6

"My lord," he said, "Bālī and I are two brothers. We inexpressibly loved each other. The son of Maya, Māyāvī by name, came to our town. In the middle of the night he shouted at the city-gate. Bālī endures no enemy to set him at defiance and sallied forth. Seeing this he fled. Now I too accompanied my brother. and when he had gone into one of the caves of the mountain. Bālī said to me: "Wait for me a fortnight, and if I do not come then, conclude that I have been killed. I waited there a whole month, Kharāri; a tremendous stream of blood then flowed out: I made sure that Bālī had been defeated and that the enemy would come and kill me too. I therefore closed the mouth of the cave with a rock and fled away. When the ministers of state saw that the city was without a master, they forced the government upon me, whether I would or no. When Bālī, who had slain the foe, came home and saw me, he was greatly set against me and gave me a severe beating, as he would an enemy, and took from me everything that I had, together with my wife. For fear of him, O merciful Raghubīra, I wandered forlorn all over the world. The curse[1] prevents him from coming here, and yet I am ill at ease in mind." When the friend of the suppliant heard his servant's tale of woe, his two mighty arms were uplifted with a convulsive motion.

Dohā 6

"Hearken, Sugrīva," he said, " I will slay Bālī with a single arrow; though he take refuge with Brahmā even, or Rudra, he shall not escape alive!

Caupāī 7

It is a grievous sin even to look on those who are not distressed at the sight of a friend's distress. They, who do not think it

1. When Bālī had slain the demon Dundubhi, who had attacked him in the form of a bull, he hurled the body away, and a drop of blood fell in the hermitage of the Ṛṣi Mataṅga who thereupon pronounced a curse upon Bālī, that if ever he came that way he should at once die.

the most natural thing possible to regard as a mere grain of sand their own mountain-like troubles, while a friend's trouble, though really no bigger than a grain of sand, seems to them as weighty as mount Meru; such men are churls, upon whom it is useless to press friendship. To restrain from evil paths and to direct in the path of virtue; to publish all good qualities and conceal the bad; to give and take without any distrust of mind; to be always ready to assist with all one's power, and, in time of misfortune to be a hundred times more affectionate than ever; such the scriptures declare to be the properties of a true friend. But one who hypocritically speaks fair words to your face, but behind your back is an enemy in the viciousness of his soul, whose mind, brother, is as tortuous as the movements of a snake, such a man is a bad friend, whom it is well to let alone. A dishonest servant, a miserly king, an adulterous wife, and a treacherous friend, are four things as bad as the stake. Cease to distress yourself, friend; I will put forth all my strength to do your buisness for you." Said Sugrīva: "Hearken, Raghubīra; Bālī is very strong and most resolute in battle," and he showed him Dundubhi's bones and the palm-trees.[1] Without an effort, Raghubīra hurled the bones away. At this exhibition of boundless strength, the affection of the monkey king was increased and he made sure of killing Bālī. Again and again the monkey king bowed his head before his feet, in the greatest delight, knowing him to be the Lord. Knowledge sprung up in his soul, and he spoke and said : "By my Lord's favour my mind is set at rest; I will abandon all delights, fortune, kinsfolk and dignities to do you service; for all these things are hindrances to faith in Rāma, as the sages declare who are devoted to the

1. This mention of 'palm-trees' would not be intelligible without a reference to the Sanskrit *Rāmāyaṇa*. There it is told how after Rāma by a slight touch of his foot had sent flying a hundred leagues through the air the giant Dundubhi's enormous skeleton, Sugrīva still doubted whether he were a match in strength for Bālī, who had hurled the body an equal distance, while it was still clothed with flesh and therefore of much greater weight. To convince him, Rāma shot an arrow from his, which cleft seven palm-trees that stood in a line one after the other, pierced the hill behind them and sped downwards to the nethermost hell, whence again it returned and dropped into the quiver at Rāma's side, from which it had been taken.

worship[1] of your feet. All the friends and enemies, joys and sorrows of the world, are effects of delusion, and not eternal realities. Bālī is my greatest friend, by whose favour I have met you, O Rāma, the destroyer of all sorrow; as when a man dreams that he has been fighting some one, and on waking and coming to his senses is ashamed of his illusion. Now, my Lord, grant me this favour that I may leave all and worship you, night and day." When Rāma heard the monkey's devout speech, he smiled and said, with his bow in his hand : "Whatever I have said is all true; my words, friend, cannot fail." O Garuṛ, Rāma, as the scriptures say, is the juggler who makes us all dance like so many monkeys. Sugrīva then took Raghunātha away with him, who went with bow and arrows in hand. Afterwards he sent Sugrīva on ahead, who went up close and roared with all his might. Bālī on hearing him, sprang up in a fury, but his wife clasped his feet in her hands and warned him: "Hearken, my lord, Sugrīva's allies are two brothers of unapproachable majesty and might, the sons of the king of Kosala, Lakṣmaṇa and Rāma, who would vanquish even Death himself in battle."

Dohā 7

"Hearken," said Bālī, "my timid and beloved wife; Raghunātha is kind and the same to all. Even if he kill me, he will still be my Lord."

Caupāī 8

So saying, he sallied forth in all his great arrogance thinking, no more of Sugrīva than of a blade of grass. The two joined combat; and Bālī with a furious leap struck him a blow with his fist, which resounded like a clap of thunder. Sugrīva at once fled in dismay; the stroke of his fist had fallen upon him as a bolt from heaven. "Did I not tell you, O merciful Raghubīra that he is no brother of mine but Death himself." "You two brothers are so much alike that for fear of mistake I did not

1. *Avarādhak*, 'a worshipper,' is for *ārādhak*, from the root *rādh*, 'to propitiate,' with the intensive prefix ā. In the Hindi glossary it is explained by *sevak*, 'a servant,' as if connected with *avara*.

shoot him." He then stroked Sugrīva's body with his hands and his frame became as of adamant, and all his pain was gone. Next he put on his neck a wreath of flowers and sent him back with a large increase of strength. Again the battle raged, while Rāma watched them from behind a tree.

Dohā 8

When Sugrīva had tried every cunning trick and put forth all his strength and had given up in despair, Rāma drew an arrow and struck Bālī in the heart.

Caupāī 9

Struck by the arrow, he fell in dismay to the ground. Again he sat up and saw the Lord standing before him, dark of hue, with his hair fastened up in a knot on his head, and his eyes inflamed as they were when he fitted the arrow to bowstring. Again and again as he gazed at him, he laid his heart at his feet and accounted his life blessed: for he recognized his Lord. Though his heart was full of affection, the words of his mouth were harsh, as he looked towards Rāma and said : "You have become incarnate, sire, for the advancement of religion, and yet you take my life as a huntsman would that of a wild beast. I forsooth, am an enemy and Sugrīva a friend; yet for what fault have you killed me, my Lord ?" "Listen, poor fool," said Rāma; "a younger brother's wife, a sister, a daughter-in-law and an unwedded maid are all alike : whoever looks upon one of them with an evil eye may be slain without any sin. Fool, in your extravagant pride you paid no heed to your wife's warning. You knew that he had taken refuge under the might of my arm, and yet in your wicked pride you wished to kill him."

Dohā 9

"Hearken, Rāma" said Bālī, "I dealt craftily with my Lord; today, guilty as I am, I obtain, sire, at my death a place in heaven."

Caupāī 10

When Rāma heard this most pathetic plea, he touched Bālī's head with his hands : "I restore the soundness of your body; retain your life." Said Bālī; "Hearken, All-merciful; the sages are born again and again and labour throughout their life, and yet even to the last Rāma never comes near them. But he, the everlasting, by the virtue of whose name Śaṅkara at Kāśī bestows heaven upon all alike, has come in visible form before my eyes; can I ever, my Lord, have such a chance again ?

Chand 1

He has come in visible form before my eyes, whose praises the scriptures are all unequal to declare, to whom scarcely the sages attain after profound contemplation accompanied by laborious suppression of the breath,[1] abstraction of soul, and control of the senses. Seeing me the victim of utter arrogance, the Lord has told me to retain my body. But who would be such a fool as to insist upon cutting down the tree of Paradise to fence about a mere acacia ? Now, my Lord, look upon me with compassion and grant me the boon I beg; whatever the womb, in which it be my fate to be born, may I ever cherish a special devotion to the feet of Rāma. O my Lord, take this my son Aṅgad and grant him like discretion, power and prosperity; grasp him by the hand, O king of gods and men, and make him your own servant."

Dohā 10

After making a fervent act of devotion to Rāma's feet, Bālī quitted his body as placidly as when a wreath of flowers drops from an elephant's neck without his knowing it;

1. The eight means of mental concentration (according to Patañjali, the founder of the Yoga system of philosophy) are *Yama*, 'forbearance,' 'restraint'; *Niyama*, 'religious observances'; *Āsana*, 'postures'; *Prāṇāyāma*, suppression of the breath,' or 'breathing in a peculiar way'; *Pratyāhāra* 'restraint of the senses'; *Dhāraṇā*, 'steadying of the mind'; *Dhyāna*, 'contemplation; and, *Samādhi*, 'profound meditation,' or rather, a state of religious trance. — *Monier Williams.*

Caupāī 11

And Rāma dismissed him to his own realm. All the citizens came running in dismay, and Tārā with dishevelled hair and tottering frame broke forth into wild lamentation. When Raghurāī saw her distress, he imparted to her wisdom and dispersed her delusion. "The body, which is composed of the elements, earth, water, fire, air and ether,[1] is of no value. The mortal frame, which you see before you, sleeps; but the soul is eternal; why then do you weep?" When true understanding had thus dawned in her mind, she embraced his feet and received the boon that she asked, a perfect faith. O Umā, the Lord Rāma dances us all up and down like so many puppets. Then he gave orders to Sugrīva and he performed all the funeral rites with due ceremony. Rāma next directed his brother to go and set Sugrīva on the throne. He bowed his head at Raghupati's feet and went forth, he and all whom Rāma had commissioned to accompany him.

Dohā 11

Lakṣmaṇa immediately summoned the citizens and the council of Brāhmaṇas, and invested Sugrīva with the sovereignty, with Aṅgad as Crown Prince.

Caupāī 12

O Umā, there is no such friend as Rāma in the world, neither *guru*, nor father, nor mother, nor kinsman, no lord. It is the way with all other gods, men and sages, to make friends for selfish purposes; but the generous Raghubīra, from mere natural kindness, made Sugrīva king of the monkeys, when he was trembling all the day and all night in such fear of Bālī that there was no colour left in his face and his heart was burnt up with anxiety. Surely he who knowingly turns from such a lord must needs be caught in the meshes of calamity ! Rāma then

1. Ākāśa, 'ether,' is the subtle and ethereal fluid, supposed to fill and pervade the universe and to be the peculiar vehicle of life and of sound — *Monier Williams*.

sent for Sugrīva and instructed him in all the principles of statecraft, and added, "Hearken, Sugrīva, king of the monkey race; I may not enter a city for fourteen years. The hot weather is now over and the rains have set in. I will encamp on the hills close by. Do you with Aṅgad reign in royal state; but remain ever mindful of my mission." Sugrīva then returned to the palace, while Rāma encamped on mount Bravarṣaṇa.[1]

Dohā 12

The gods had beforehand made and kept for him a charming mountain cave, knowing that the All-merciful Rāma would come and stay there for some days.

Caupāī 13

The magnificent forest was a most charming sight, with the trees all in flower and the swarms of buzzing bees gathering honey. From the time that the Lord came, every plant and fruit and every kind of agreeable foliage was forthcoming in profusion. Seeing the incomparable beauty of the hill, the Lord and his brother rested there. In the form of bees, birds and beasts, gods, saints and seers came and did service to their Lord. From the time that Lakṣmī's spouse took up his abode in it, the forest became a picture of felicity. There the two brothers sat at ease on a bright and glistening crystal rock, and the younger was told many a tale inculcating faith, self-governance, statecraft and wisdom. What with clouds that ever canopied the heavens and the frequent thunder, the season of the rains seemed a most delightful time.

Dohā 13

"See, Lakṣmaṇa, how the peacocks dance at the sight of the clouds, like a householder, devoted to austerity, who rejoices when he finds a true believer in Viṣṇu.

1. In the Sanskrit *Rāmāyaṇa*, the hill is called Pravarṣaṇa but the two words bear much the same meaning. The text might also be translated, remained on the hill during the early rains.

Caupāī 14

Clouds gather in the sky and thunders roar; but my darling is gone and my soul is in distress.[1] The lightning flashes fitfully amid the darkness, like the friendship of the vile which never lasts. The pouring clouds cleave close to the ground, as sages stoop beneath accumulated lore. The hills endure the buffeting of the rain drops, as the virtuous bear the abuse of the wicked. The flooded streamlets rush proudly along, like mean men puffed up with a little wealth. The water by its contact with the earth becomes as muddy as the soul when caught in the web of illusion ! Drop by drop the waters gather and fill the ponds, like as when the quality of goodness develops in a good man; and the rivers flow into the bosom of the ocean, like as the soul, that has found Hari, is at rest for ever.

Dohā 14

The green earth is so choked with grass that the paths can no longer be distinguished, like holy books obscured by the wrangling of heretics.

Caupāī 15

On all sides, there is a lively croaking of frogs, like a class of Brāhmaṇa students repeating the Vedas. All the trees put forth their new leaves, like pious souls that have come to matured wisdom. The *āka* and *javāsa* plants have shed their leaves : as in a well-governed realm the schemes of the wicked come to nought. Search as you like, the dusty footpath is no longer to be traced; like as when religion is put out of sight by passion. The earth rich with crops makes as goodly a show as the prosperity of benevolent. The fireflies gleam in the darkness of the cloudy night like a mustered band of hypocrites. The ridges of the

1. In England a cloudy sky is associated with gloomy ideas, and the bright sunshine with everything that is cheerful. But in India it is the reverse. When the clouds gather and thunder is heard, every one rejoices at the prospect of rain.

fields are broken down by the heavy rains, like women ruined by too much license. The diligent cultivators weed their land, like philosophers who rid themselves of ignorance, vanity and pride. The *cakvā* and other birds are nowhere to be seen, like virtue that fled at the coming of the iron age. However much it may rain, no grass springs upon barren ground; so lust takes no root in the heart of Hari's worshippers. The earth gleams with swarms of living creatures of every kind; so the subjects multiply under good government. Here and there weary wayfarers stay and rest, like a man's bodily senses after the attainment of wisdom.

Dohā 15a-15b

At times a strong wind disperses the clouds in all directions, like the birth of a bad son, who destroys all the pious practices of his family. Like good or bad company giving birth to or ruining wisdom, there is at times thick darkness in the day and at times bright sunshine.

Caupāī 16

Now the rains are over and the season of autumn has returned; see, Lakṣmaṇa, how exquisitely beautiful everything is. The whole earth is covered with flowering silver grass, as though the rains had exposed its old age. The rising of Canopus[1] has dried up the water on the roads, like as greed is dried up by contentment. The surface of every river and lake is as pure and bright as is the soul of the sages devoid of all vanity and delusion; drop by drop their depths are diminished, like as the enlightened gradually lose all notions of self. The wagtails know the autumn season and come out once more, like virtuous deeds in an auspicious time. There is neither dust nor mud; the earth is as brilliant as the administration of a king who is well-versed in state policy. The fish are distressed by the shrinking of the water, like improvident men of family by the loss of money. The un-

1. The heliacal rising of the constellation Agastya, *i.e.*, Canopus, takes place on the seventh day after the new moon of Bhādra, in the rainy season.

clouded sky shines as bright as a worshipper of Hari, who has discarded every other patron. Here and there falls a slight autumn shower, like the faith of one who is not yet fully persuaded.

Dohā 16

Now kings and ascetics, merchants and mendicants, leave the city and go their way with joy, like men in any of the four stages of life,[1] who cease to labour when they have once attained to faith in Hari.

Caupāī 17

Where the water is deep, the fish are as happy as men who have taken refuge with Hari and have not a single trouble. The lakes, with their flowering lotuses, are as beautiful as the immaterial Supreme Spirit when clothed with a material form. Buzzing bees murmur melodiously and birds are making a charming concert of diverse sounds; but the *cakvā* is as sad of soul to see the night, as a bad man at the sight of another's prosperity. The cātaka cries out from excess of thirst, like a rebel against Mahādeva who knows no rest. The moon by night subdues the autumnal heat of the sun, like as the sight of a sage expels sin. Flocks of partridges fix their gaze upon the moon, as Hari's worshippers gaze on Hari. Mosquitoes and gadflies are driven away by the terrors of winter, like as a family is destroyed by the sin of persecuting Brāhmaṇas.

Dohā 17

Under the influence of the autumn, earth is rid of its insect swarms as a man, who has found a holy teacher, is relieved from all doubt and error.

1. The four stages of life, through which every Brāhmaṇa should pass, are 1st that of the Brahmacāri, or student; 2nd that of the Gṛhastha, or householder; 3rd that of the Vānaprastha, or anchorite; and 4th that of the Bhikṣu, or mendicant.

Caupāī 18

The rains are over and the clear season has come, but I have had no news, brother, of Sītā. If I could only once anyhow get tidings of her, I would in an insant recover her out of the hands of even Death himself. Wherever she may be, if only she still lives, brother, I would make an effort to rescue her. Sugrīva has quite forgotten me, now that he has got back his kingdom and treasure, his city and his queen. Fool that he is, I will to-morrow slay him with the selfsame arrow with which I slew Bālī." He, by whose favour, Umā, pride and delusion are dissipated, could never even dream of being angry. Only enlightened sages can understand these actions of his, who have a hearty devotion to the feet of Raghubīra. Lakṣmaṇa, believing that his Lord was angry, strung his bow and grasped his arrows.

Dohā 18

Then, the All-merciful Raghupati instructed his brother, saying; "Only threaten our friend Sugrīva, brother, and bring him here."

Caupāī 19

Meanwhile the Son of the Wind also had thought to himself, 'Sugrīva has forgotten all about Rāma.' So he went near and bowed his head at his feet and reminded him of the four modes of making war.[1] As Sugrīva listened, he became much alarmed. "It is carnal enjoyment that has robbed me of all my understanding. Now, O Hanumān, despatch a multitude of spies, legions of monkeys, in every direction, and tell them that any one who is not back in a fortnight shall meet his death at my hands." Hanumān then summoned the envoys, and showed them all special honour, making use of threats, blandishments and motives of policy. They all bowed their head at his feet and set forth. At that very time Lakṣmaṇa entered the city. Seeing him to be angry, the monkeys all ran away.

1. The four *upāyas*, or modes of making war, are, showing dissension, negotiation, bribery and open force.

Dohā 19

He strung his bow and cried, 'I will burn the city to ashes.' Then came Bālī's son, seeing the distress of the people,

Caupāī 20

And bowed his head at his feet and made humble petition, till Lakṣmaṇa assured him he had nought to fear. But when the monkey king heard of Lakṣmaṇa's wrath, he was terribly alarmed. "Hearken, Hanumān," he said, "take Tārā with you and with suppliant prayers appease the prince." Hanumān went with Tārā and fell at his feet, and after hymning his Lord's praises, respectfully conducted him to the palace and bathed his feet and seated him on a couch. The monkey king also bowed his head at his feet, and Lakṣmaṇa took him by the hand and embraced him. "There is nothing, my lord, so intoxicating as luxury; in a single moment it infatuates even the soul of a sage." On hearing this humble speech, Lakṣmaṇa was glad and said everything to reassure him, while Hanumān told him all that had been done and how a multitude of spies had already started.

Dohā 20

Then Sugrīva with Aṅgad and the other monkeys joyfully set out, preceded by Lakṣmaṇa, and arrived in Rāma's presence.

Caupāī 21

With folded hands, he bowed his head, before his feet and cried, "My Lord, it has been no fault of mine. Your delusive power, sire, is so strong that only Rāma's favour can disperse it. Gods and men, sages and kings are mastered by their senses; and I am but a wretched animal, a monkey, one of the most libidinous of animals. A man who is invulnerable by the arrow of a woman's eye, who remains wakeful through the dark night of angry passion, and whose neck has never been bound by the halter of covetousness, is your equal, O Raghurāī. It is a virtue not attainable by any devotional exercise; it is only by your grace that one here and one there can accomplish it." Then Raghupati smiled and said: "You are as dear to me as my own brother Bharata. Now take thought and make an effort to get tidings of Sītā."

Dohā 21

While they were thus conversing, the troops of monkeys arrived of all colours and from all parts of the world, a monkey host marvellous to behold.

Caupāī 22

I myself, Umā, saw this army of monkeys ; only a fool would try to count them. They came and bowed the head at Rāma's feet and gazing upon his face found in him their true lord. In the whole host there was not a single monkey to whom Rāma did not give separate greeting. This was no great marvel for the lord Raghurāī, who is omnipresent and all pervading. They all stood as they were told, rank after rank, while Sugrīva thus spoke and instructed them : "On Rāma's behalf and at my request, go forth, ye monkey host, in every direction. Make search for Janaka's daughter, my brethren, and return within a month. Whoever comes back after that period without any news shall die at my hands."

Dohā 22

No sooner had they heard this speech than all the monkeys started at once in every direction. Sugrīva then summoned Aṅgada, Nīla and Hanumān:

Caupāī 23

"Hearken, Nīla, Aṅgada, and Hanumān, and you, O staunch and sagacious Jāṁbavān ; go ye together, all ye gallant warriors, to the south and ask every one for news of Sītā. Strain every faculty to devise some ways of accomplishing Rāma's object. The sun must be served with the back and fire with the breast, but a master must be served with the back and front alike, without any subterfuges.[1] One must discard the unrealities of the world and devote oneself to things spiritual ; so shall all the troubles connected with existence be destroyed. This is the end, brother, for which we were born, to worship Rāma without any desire for self. He only is truly discriminative, he only is greatly blessed, who is enamoured of the feet of Raghubīra." After begging permission to depart and bowing their heads before his feet, they set out with joy, invoking Raghurāī. The last to make obeisance was Hanumān. The Lord, knowing what would happen, called him near and with his lotus hands touched his head and gave him his ring off his finger for he knew his devotion : "Say everything to comfort Sītā, telling her of my might and my constancy, and come quickly." Hanumān thought this to be the crowning moment of his life, and set out, with the image of the all-merciful impressed upon his heart. Although the Lord knows everything, he observes the rules of statecraft in his character as the champion of the gods.

Dohā 23

They all went forth, searching every wood, river, lake, and mountain cave, with their soul so absorbed in Rāma's concerns that they forgot all about their own bodily wants.

Caupāī 24

Wherever they came across a demon, they took his life with a single blow. They looked into every recess of forest and hill, and if they met any hermit they all surrounded him. Overcome by thirst, they were dreadfully distressed, and losing their way in the dense forest, could find no water. Hanumān thought to

1. In this line there is no difference of reading in any of the MSS., but the precise meaning of the words is obscure and the Pandits interpret them in as many as 22 different ways. The translation given above exactly preserves the vagueness of the original. One of the alternative renderings is, 'as the flint nourishes fire in its bosom so should one serve a master;' but I do not know of any parallel passage where *bhānu pītha* is used in the sense of 'a flint.'

himself that without water to drink they would all perish. So he climbed a mountain peak and looking all round about, spied a strange opening in the ground ; with geese, herons and swans on the wing and all kinds of birds making their way into it. Then Hanumān came down from the mountain and took them all and showed them the cavern, and with him to lead the way they entered the cave without delay.

Dohā 24

A lovely grove and a lake came in sight, with many flowering lotuses and a magnificent temple, where a holy woman[1] was sitting.

Caupāī 25

From a distance they all bowed the head before her and at her request explained their circumstances. She then said : "Take water to drink and eat at will of this luscious and beautiful fruit." They bathed and ate of the sweet fruit and then all came and drew near to her, and told her all their adventures. "I will now go to Raghurāī ; close your eyes and so leave the cave; you will recover Sītā, do not fear." The warriors shut their eyes, and when they opened them again, they were all standing on the shore of the ocean. But she went to Raghunātha and came and bowed her head at his lotus feet, and made much supplication. The lord bestowed upon her imperishable faith.

Dohā 25

Then in obedience to the Lord's command she went to the Badari forest, cherishing in her heart Rāma's feet, the adoration of Brahmā and Śiva.

1. In the Sanskrit *Rāmāyaṇa*. her name is given as Svayamprabhā, 'the self-shining.'

Caupāī 26

Now the monkeys were thinking to themselves: "The appointed time has passed and we have met with no success." So they all came together and asked one another, "There is no news, brother; what are we to do?" Aṅgada's eyes were full of tears as he replied: " It is death for us either way. Here we have failed to get tidings of Sītā, and if we go home our king will slay us. After my father's death, he would have killed me, had not Rāma protected me, no thanks to him." Again and again Aṅgada told them all that they were doomed to certain death. When the monkey warriors heard Aṅgada's words, they could make no answer, tears streamed from their eyes. For a moment they were plunged in despair, but at last they all spoke and said, "Unless we get news of Sītā we will not return, O sagacious prince." So saying, the monkeys all went to the seashore, where they spread beds of *kuśa* grass and sat down. But Jāṁbavān, seeing Aṅgada's distress, gave him many instructive lessons: "My son, do not imagine Rāma to be a man ; know that he is the invisible god, unconquerable and everlasting. All we who are his servants are most highly blessed in our love for the Absolute thus made incarnate.

Dohā 26

Of his own free will has the Lord manifested himself on behalf of gods, Brāhmaṇas, cows and earth, and remains in bodily form among his worshippers, having abandoned all the joys of heaven."

Caupāī 27

He exhorted him in this wise at great length, and Saṁpāti heard him from his cave in the mountain. When he came out and saw the multitude of monkeys, he cried : " God has provided me with a feast. I will eat them all up at once ; I am dying for want of a meal these many days past. I have never yet had a good bellyful, but today God has supplied me for once and all." The monkeys trembled to hear the vulture's words: "We were right, they thought, in saying that our time to die has come !" At the sight of him they all stood up, and Jāṁbavān was mightily disturbed at heart ; but Aṅgada, after thinking to himself, exclaimed: "Glory to Jaṭāyu, there is none like him who gave up his life in Rāma's service and, blessed beyond measure, has been translated to Hari's sphere in heaven." When the bird heard these words of mingled joy and sadness, he drew near to the monkeys in alarm and after reassuring them of safety began to question them. They told him the whole history. When Saṁpāti heard of his brother's doings, he gave all glory to Raghupati.

Dohā 27

"Take me to the sea-shore," he said, "and make him an offering of sesamum seeds ; with the help of my instructions you shall recover her whom you seek."

Caupāī 28

When he had performed the funeral rites for his brother on the seashore, he told them his own history. "Hearken, monkey chiefs; we two brothers in our first youth mounted into the heaven, winging our way towards the sun. He could not endure its splendour and turned back, but I in my pride went closer. My wings were scorched by the excessive heat. and I fell to the earth with a terrible cry. A sage named Candramā[1] was moved with compassion when he saw me. and instructed me in all kinds of knowledge and rid me of my inveterate pride. 'In the Tretā age God will take the form of a man, and his spouse will be carried off by the king of the demons. The Lord will send out spies to search for her, and if you join them you will be purified. Your wings will sprout again, fear not, when you have found them Sītā.' The sage's prophecy has come true today. Hearken to my words and set about your lord's business. On the top of mount Trikūṭa lies the city of Laṅkā ; there lives Rāvaṇa in absolute security, and there, in a grove of Aśoka trees, sits Sītā, a prey to grief.

1. In the Sanskrit *Rāmāyaṇa* he is called Niśākara, the night-maker, which also, like *candramā*, is a name for the moon.

Dohā 28

I see her, but you cannot; a vulture's sight has no bounds. I am now old, or else I would have given you some assistance.

Caupāī 29

If anyone of you can leap a thousand miles across the ocean, he will do Rāma's business for him very cleverly. Look at me and reassure yourselves; see how my body has been restored by Rāma's favour. Any wretch, who invokes his name, is able to cross the vast and boundless ocean of existence, and you are his messengers; have then no fear, but, with Rāma's image impressed upon your soul, consert your plans." So saying, Garur, the vulture, left them, and their soul was in the greatest amazement. Each one boasted of his strength, but doubted whether he could leap across. Said the king of the bears, "I am now too old and not a particle of my former strength is left in my body; when Kharāri took his three strides,[1] then I was young and full of vigour.

Dohā 29

As he fettered Bali, Lord's body swelled to an indescribable size, but in less than an hour I ran right round him seven times."

Caupāī 30

Aṅgada said : "I will leap across; but I am rather doubtful about getting back again." Then said Jāṁbavān: "You are quite competent: but why should we send our leader? Hearken, Hanumān," added the king of the bears, "why is our champion so silent? You are the Son of the Wind and strong as your sire, a storehouse of understanding, discretion and great wisdom: in all the world what undertaking is there so difficult that you, my son, cannot accomplish it? And it is on Rāma's account that

1. The allusion is to Viṣṇu's incarnation as a dwarf, which was the fifth in order, that as Rāma being the seventh.

you have come down upon earth." On hearing this, he swelled to the size of a mountain with a body of golden hue and dazzling majesty, as though a very monarch of mountains, and roaring again and again like a lion, he cried, "I can easily spring across the salt abyss, and slay Rāvaṇa with all his army and uproot Trikūṭa and bring it here. But I ask you, Jāmbavān, what I ought to do, give me proper instructions." "All that you have to do, my son, is to go and see Sītā and come back with the news. Then the lotus-eyed, by the might of his own arm, taking with him merely for a show his hosts of monkeys—

Chand 2

With his army of monkeys Rāma will slay the demons and recover Sītā; and gods and sages and Nārada and all will declare his glory, that sanctifies the three spheres." Any man attains the highest beatitude who hears, sings, tells or meditates upon the feet of Raghubīra, lotus flowers which, like the bee, Tulasī Dāsa is ever singing.

Dohā 30a

If any man or woman will listen to the glories of Raghunātha, the panacea for all the ills of life, Śiva will make him to prosper in everything that he desires.

Soraṭhā 30b

Hearken, then, to his praises whose body is dark of hue as the lotus, with more than all the beauty of a myriad Loves, the fowler who sweeps into his net all kinds of sin like so many birds.

[*Thus endeth the book entitled* "KIṢKINDHĀ," *composed by Tulasī Dāsa for the bestowal of pure wisdom and continence; being the fourth descent into 'the Holy Lake of Rāma's Acts,' that cleanses from every defilement of the world.*]

BOOK V

THE BEAUTIFUL

THE BEAUTIFUL

Sanskrit Invocation

I ADORE, under his name RĀMA, the passionless, the eternal, the immeasurable, the sinless; the bestower of the peace of final liberation; the lord, whom Brahmā, Śambhu, and the Serpent-king incessantly worship; the theme of the Vedānta, omnipresent, the sovereign of the universe; the preceptor of the gods; Hari in the delusive form of man: the All-merciful; the princely son of Raghu: the jewel of kings.

O Raghupati, there is no other desire in my soul—I speak the truth and you know all my inmost thoughts—grant me, O Raghu king, a vehement faith, and make my heart clean of lust and every other sin.

I do obeisance to the home of immeasurable strength, with his body resembling a mountain of gold; the fire that consumed the demon forest; the first name in the list of the truly wise: the storehouse of all good qualities; the Lord of the monkeys, Raghupati's noble messenger, the Son of the Wind!

Caupāī 1

On hearing Jāṁbavān speak so cheerfully, Hanumān was greatly delighted, "Wait for me here, my friends, however great your discomfort, with only roots, herbs, and fruit for your food till I return after seeing Sītā; the task is one I am most pleased to undertake." So saying, he bowed his head to them all and went forth with joy, having the image of Raghunātha impressed upon his heart. There was a majestic rock by the seashore; he lightly sprang on to the top of it; then, again and again invoking Raghubīra, the Son of the Wind leapt with all his might. The mountain on which he had planted his foot sank down immediately into the depths of hell. Like Rāma's own unerring shaft, so sped Hanumān on his way. Ocean had regard for Rāma's envoy and told Maināka to ease his toil.[1]

1. Maināka is a rock in the narrow strait between Laṅkā and the main land.

Dohā 1

But Hanumān merely touched him with his hand, then saluted him and said, 'I can stop nowhere till I have done Rāma's business.'

Caupāī 2

The gods saw Hanumān going on his way and wished to try his mighty strength and sagacity. So they sent the mother of the serpent-race, Surasā by name, who came and said, "Today the gods have provided me a meal." On hearing these words, the Son of the Wind replied, "When I have performed Rāma's commission and have come back, and have given my Lord the news about Sītā, then I will enter your mouth: I tell you the truth, mother, only let me go now." But, however much he tried she would not let him go, till at last he said: 'You cannot get me into your mouth. She opened her jaws a league wide: the monkey made his body twice that size. Then she stretched her mouth sixteen leagues: Hanumān at once became thirty-two. However much Surasā expanded her jaws, the monkey made his frame twice as large again. When she had made her mouth a hundred leagues wide, he reduced himself to a very minute form and crept into her mouth and came out again. Then he bowed and asked permission to proceed. "The purpose for which the gods sent me, namely, to make trial of your wisdom and strength, I have now accomplished.

Dohā 2

Your wisdom and strength are perfect; you will do all that Rāma requires of you." She then blessed him and departed, and Hanumān went on his way rejoicing.

Caupāī 3

A female demon[1] dwelt in the ocean, who by magic caught the birds of the air. All living creatures that fly in the air as

1. In the Sanskrit *Rāmāyaṇa*, her name is given as Siṁhikā, the mother of Rāhu.

they look down upon the water, cast a shadow upon it ; and she was able to catch the shadow, so that they could not fly away; and in this manner she always had birds to eat. She practised the same craft on Hanumān; but the monkey at once saw through her trickery and slew her, hero as he was, and all undismayed crossed over to the opposite shore. Arriving there, he marked the beauty of the wood, with the bees buzzing in their search for honey, the diverse trees all resplendent with simultaneous flower and fruit, and multitudes of birds and deer delightful to behold. Seeing a lofty hill further on, he fearlessly sprang on the top of it. But, Umā, this was not at all the monkey's own strength, but the gift of the Lord, who devours Death himself. Mounted on the hill, he surveyed Laṅkā, a magnificent fortress that defies description, with the deep sea on all four sides around its golden walls of dazzling splendour.

Chand 1

Its golden walls studded with all kinds of jewels, a marvellously beautiful sight, with market-places, bazars, quays, and streets, and all the other accessories of a fine city. Who could count the multitude of elephants, horses and mules, the crowds of footmen and chariots, and the troops of demons of every size, a formidable army beyond all description. The woods, gardens, groves, and pastures, ponds, wells and tanks were all superb: and the soul of a sage would be ravished at the sight of the fair daughters, both of men and Nāgas, of gods and Gandharvas. Here wrestlers, of monstrous stature like mountains, were roaring like thunder and grappling with one another in the different courts, with shouts of mutual defiance. Myriads of warriors of huge bulk were sedulously guarding the city on all four sides; elsewhere horrid demons were banqueting in the form of buffaloes, men, oxen, asses and goats. Tulasī Dāsa for this reason gives them a few words of mention, because they lost their life by Rāma's hallowed shafts and thus became assured of entrance into heaven.

Dohā 3

Seeing the number of the city guards, the monkey thought to

himself, 'I must make myself very small and slip into the town by night.'

Caupāī 4

Thereupon he assumed the form of a gnat[1] and entered Laṅkā after invoking Viṣṇu.[2] The female demon, by name Laṅkinī, accosted him: "How dare you come here in contempt of me? Fool, do you not know my practice, that every thief in Laṅkā becomes my prey?" The monkey struck her one such a blow with his fist that she fell to the ground vomitting blood. Recovering herself again, she stood up and with folded hands made this confident petition: "When Brahmā granted Rāvaṇa's prayer, he spoke to me and gave me a sign before he left. 'When worsted by a monkey, know then that it is all over with demons.' My meritorious deeds, my son, must have been very many that I have been rewarded with the sight of Rāma's messenger.

Dohā 4

In one scale of the balance put all the bliss of heaven and the final liberation of the soul from the body, but it will be altogether outweighed by a fraction of the joy that results from communion with the saints.

Caupāī 5

Enter the city and accomplish your task, ever mindful at heart of the Lord of Kosala. Deadly poison, O Garuṛ, becomes

1. The word *masak*, which I translate 'gnat,' never, so far as I am aware, bears any other meaning. But in one glossary, with reference to this particular passage, it is explained by *bilār*, 'a cat,' only — as it would seem — because that is the animal mentioned in the Sanskrit *Rāmāyaṇa*. In both cases the poet has no sooner stated transformation than he forgets all about it; for all Hanumān's subsequent actions are described as if performed by him in his natural shape. He may be supposed to have resumed it as soon as he had passed the guard; or the words may be taken to mean "he made himself *as small as* a gnat." [*Masak* is the mosquito, not the gnat. Editor]

2. *Nara-hari* stands for the more common Nara-sinha — *hari* and *sinha* both meaning 'a lion' — and here denotes not that particular incarnation, but Viṣṇu generally.

nectar, foes turn friends, ocean shrinks to a mere puddle, fire gives out cold, and huge Sumeru is of no more account than a grain of sand for him whom Rāma deigns to regard with favour." In the tiny form that he had assumed, Hanumān entered the city with his mind concentrated on the Blessed Lord God. Carefully inspecting every separate palace, he found everywhere warriors innumerable. When he had come to Rāvaṇa's court, its magnificence was past all telling. The monkey saw him in bed asleep, but no trace of Sītā in the room. He then noticed another magnificent mansion, with a temple of Hari standing apart, its walls brilliantly illuminated with Rāma's name, too beautiful to describe, it fascinated every beholder.

Dohā 5

The beauty of the apartments emblazoned with Rāma's insignia was indescribable. At the sight of some fresh springs of tulasī, the monkey chief was enraptured.

Caupāī 6

"Laṅkā is the abode of a gang of demons, how can the pious have any home here ?" While the monkey was thus reasoning within himself, Vibhīṣaṇa awoke and at once began to repeat Rāma's name in prayer. The monkey was delighted to find a true believer. "Shall I at once make myself known to him ? A good man will never spoil any undertaking." Assuming the form of a Brāhmaṇa, he accosted him. As soon as Vibhīṣaṇa heard him, he rose to meet him, and doing obeisance, asked after his welfare, saying, "Tell me, reverend Sir, all about yourself; if a servant of Hari, you have my hearty affection; if a loving follower of Rāma, your visit is a great honour for me."

Dohā 6

Then Hanumān told him his own name and Rāma's whole history. At the recital and the recollection of his infinite virtues, both quivered all over the body, while their soul was drowned in joy.

Caupāī 7

"Hearken, Son of the Wind; my condition here is like that of the poor tongue between the teeth. Yet do not suppose, Father, that I am friendless : the Lord of the Solar race will show me favour. The sinful body is of no avail, if the soul is not devoted to his lotus feet. But now, Hanumān, I have gained confidence : for it is only by Hari's favour that one meets a good man, and it is the result of his kindness that you have so readily revealed yourself to me." Listen, Vibhīṣaṇa, to my experience of the Lord; he is ever affectionate to his servants. Say, who am I and of what noble descent; a wanton monkey, of no merit whatever, a creature the mention of whose name in the early morning makes a man go fasting for the rest of the day !

Dohā 7

So utterly mean am I; yet hearken, friend; Raghubīra has shown favour even to me." His eyes filled with tears as he recalled his perfection.

Caupāī 8

"I know of a truth that any who turns aside in forgetfulness of such a lord may well be miserable." As he thus discoursed on Rāma's infinite excellences, he felt an unspeakable calm. Vibhīṣaṇa then told him of all that had been going on and of Sītā's mode of life, till Hanumān cried: "Hearken, brother; I would fain see the august Sītā." Vibhīsana explained to him how he might succeed (what mode of procedure must be adopted) and the Son of the Wind then took his leave and proceeded on his way. Assuming the same form as at first, he went to the Aśoka grove, where Sītā dwelt. As soon as he saw her, mentally prostrated himself in her presence. She had spent the first watch of the night sitting up, haggard in appearance, her hair knotted in a single braid on her head,[1] repeating to herself the list of Raghupati's perfections.

Dohā 8

Her eyes fixed on her own feet, but with her soul absorbed

1. To twist the hair in a single braid is a sign of mourning for an absent husband.

in the contemplation of the feet of her lord. Hanumān was mightily distressed to see her so sad.

Caupāī 9

Hidden behind the leaves of a tree, he mused with himself: "Come, sir, what ought I to do ?" Just at that moment Rāvaṇa drew near, with a troop of women in various attire. The wretch tried in every way to entice Sītā, by blandishments, bribes, threats and misrepresentations. "Hearken, fair dame," he cried, "I will make Mandodarī and all my other queens your handmaids, I swear it, if you only give me one look." Sītā plucked a blade of grass, and with averted face, fondly remembering her own dear Lord, replied: "Hearken, Ten-headed: will the lotus expand at the light of a glow-worm ? Ponder this well," cried Jānakī: "Wretch, have you no fear of Rāma's shafts ? Even though absent, Hari will rescue me. Shameless monster, have you no shame ?

Dohā 9

I tell you, you are but a firefly, while the very sun is only an image of Rāma." On hearing this bold speech, he drew his sword and cried in the utmost fury:

Caupāī 10

"Sītā, you have humiliated me. I will cut off your head with this biting blade. If you do not at once obey my words, you will lose your life, my lady." "My lord's arms, Rāvaṇa, are beautiful as a string of dark lotuses and mighty as an elephant's trunk; either they shall have my neck, or if not, then your cruel sword. Hearken, you villain, to this my solemn vow. With your gleaming scimitar[1] put an end to my distress, and let the fiery anguish that I endure for Rāma's loss be quenched in night by the sharp blade of your sword: rid me," cried Sītā, "of my burden of pain." On hearing these words, he again rushed forward to slay her; but

1. The word translated 'gleaming scimitar' is *candra-hāsa*, which means literally 'deriding the moon, by reason, that is, of its own greater brilliancy.

the daughter of Maya Mandodarī restrained him with words of admonition. He then summoned all the female demons and ordered them to go and intimidate Sītā. "If she does not mind what I say in a month's time," he said, "I will draw my sword and slay her."

Dohā 10

Then the Ten-headed returned to the palace, while the demonesses, assuming every kind of hideous form, proceeded to terrify Sītā.

Caupāī 11

One of the female demons, by name Trijaṭā, was devoted to Rāma's service, prudent and wise. She declared to them all a dream, how that they for their own sake ought to show Sītā reverence. "In my dream a monkey set fire to Laṅkā, and put to death the whole demon army, and set Rāvaṇa on an ass, naked, with his head shorn and his twenty arms hacked off. In this fashion he rode off towards the south,[1] while Vibhīṣaṇa succeeded to the throne of Laṅkā. The city resounded with cries for mercy in Rāma's name, till the Lord sent Sītā among them. I warn you that four days hence this dream will assuredly be accomplished." Upon hearing her words, they were all dismayed and went and threw themselves at Sītā's feet,

Dohā 11

After which they dispersed in different directions. But Sītā was troubled at heart: 'At the end of a month[2] this vile monster will slay me.'

1. The realm of Yama, the god of Death, is supposed to be in the south. For this reason a Hindu will never, when it is possible to avoid it, have the door of his house in that direction. Muhammadans, even at the present day, are much influenced by the same superstition.

2. As appears from what follows, it is not death that she dreads, but the long interval of a month, which has to elapse before her death takes place.

Caupāī 12

With folded hands she cried to Trijaṭā : "Mother, you are my helper in distress; quickly devise some plan that I may be rid of life, for this intolerable bereavement is no longer to be endured. Bring wood and erect my funeral pyre and then, mother, set fire to it. My constancy, reverend dame, will thus be attested." Who could bear to listen to such agonizing addresses ? When she heard her speech, she clasped her feet and would fain comfort her by reciting the majesty and might and glory of her Lord. "Hearken, fair lady; there is no fire to be had at night ;" and so saying, she went away home. Sītā exclaimed : "Heaven is unkind; without fire my pain cannot be cured. I see the heaven all bright with sparks, but not a single star drops to the earth. The moon is all ablaze, but no fire comes from it, as if it knew what a poor wretch I am. Ye *Aśoka* trees,[1] that hear my prayer, be true to your name and rid me of my pain ; and you flame-coloured opening buds, supply me with fire to consume my body." A single moment seemed like an age to the monkey as he beheld Sītā thus piteously lamenting her bereavement.

Dohā 12

After pondering a while, the monkey threw down the signet ring as though a spark had fallen from the Asoka. She started up with joy and clasped it in her hand.

Caupāī 13

When she had looked at the lovely ring, beautifully engraved with Rāma's name, she was all astonishment, for she recognized it, and her heart fluttered with mingled joy and sorrow. "Who can conquer the unconquerable Raghurāī? This cannot be any trick of Māyā." All sorts of fancies passed through her mind, till Hanumān spoke in honeyed accents and began to recount Rāmacandra's praises. As soon as she heard him, her grief took flight. Intently she hearkened with all her soul as well as

1. The name Aśoka is derived from *a* 'without' and *śoka* 'pain.' The conceit cannot be preserved in an English translation.

her ears, while he related the whole story from the very beginning. "The tale you tell is like ambrosia to my ears; why do you not show yourself, friend ?" Then Hanumān advanced and drew near. She turned and sunk to the ground in bewilderment. "Noble Jānakī, I am Rāma's messenger; the Fountain of mercy himself attests my truth. I have brought this ring, lady, which Rāma gave me for you as a token." "Tell me," she said, "how can monkeys consort with men ?" He then explained how they had come together.

Dohā 13

On hearing the monkey's affectionate speech, her heart trusted him, and she recognized him as a faithful follower of the All-merciful in thought and word and deed.

Caupāī 14

On perceiving him to be one of Hari's worshippers, she felt an intense affection for him; her eyes filled with tears, her body quivered with intense emotion. "O Hanumān, I was sinking in the ocean of bereavement, but in you, my friend, I have found a ship. Tell me now of the welfare of Kharāri, I adjure you; how is he and how is his younger brother ? Raghurāī is tender-hearted and merciful, why, O monkey, should he affect such cruelty? The mere sound of his voice is a delight to his servant. Does he ever deign to remember me ? Will my eyes, friend, be ever gladdened by the sight of his dark and delicate body?" Words failed, her eyes swam with tears. "Alas ! my Lord has entirely forgotten me." Seeing Sītā thus distracted by pangs of separation, the monkey replied in gentle and respectful tones: "Lady, your Lord and his brother are both well, save that the All-merciful sorrows for your sorrow. Do not imagine, madam, that Rāma's affection is a whit less than your own.

Dohā 14

Take courage now and listen to Rāma's message." So saying, the monkey's voice failed him and his eyes filled with tears.

Caupāī 15

Then he proceeded to tell her of Rāma's forlorn condition. "Everything — says he — is changed into its opposite. The fresh buds upon the trees burn like fire; night seems as the night of death, and the moon scorches like the sun. A bed of lotuses seems a prickly brake, and the rain-clouds drop boiling oil. The trees only add to my pain, and the winds, soft, gentle and fragrant, are like the breath of a serpent. Nothing relieves my torture, and to whom can I tell it ? There is no one who can understand it. The essence of such love as yours and mine, my beloved, only my own soul can comprehend, and this my soul is always with you. Know such to be the profundity of my love." As the Videhan princess listened to Rāma's message, she became so absorbed in love that she lost all consciousness of self. Said the monkey, "Lady, compose yourself, remembering that Rāma is a benefactor to all who serve him. Reflect upon his might and, as you listen to my speech, put away all anxiety.

Dohā 15

The demon troops are like moths and Raghupati's arrows as a flame; be stout of heart, madam, and rest assured that they will be consumed.

Caupāī 16

If Raghubīra only knew, he would make no delay. Rāma's shafts, like the rays of the rising sun, will scatter the darkling demon host. I would have carried you away at once myself, but I swear to you by Rāma, I have not received his order to do so. Wait patiently, mother, for a few days more, and he will arrive with his monkeys, will slay the demons, and take you away, so that Nārada and the other seers will glorify him in all the three spheres of creation." "Are all the monkeys, my son, like you ? The demon warriors are very powerful, and so my soul is sorely disquieted." On hearing this, the monkey showed himself in his natural form, his body in bulk like a mountain of gold, terrible in battle, and of vast strength; then Sītā took courage, and he again resumed a diminutive appearance.

Dohā 16

"Hearken, mother; the monkeys have no great strength or wit of their own, but by the Lord's favour even a snake, small as it is, might swallow Garuṛ."

Caupāī 17

As she hearkened to the monkey's speech, so full of glorious faith and noble confidence, her mind became easy, she recognized his love for Rāma and gave him her blessing : "May you abound, my son, in strength and goodness; may neither age nor death affect your good qualities, and may you be ever constant in your devotion to Rāma, and may the Lord be gracious to you." Hearing these words, Hanumān became utterly overwhelmed with emotion ; again and again he bowed his head at her feet, and with folded hands spoke thus : "Now, mother, I am fully rewarded; for your blessing is known to be effectual. But hearken, madam, I am frightfully hungry and I see the trees laden with delicious fruit." "Know, my son, that this grove is guarded by most valiant and formidable demons." "I am not afraid of them, mother, if only you will keep your mind easy.

Dohā 17

Seeing the monkey so mighty and sagacious, Jānakī said : "Go, my son, and eat of this pleasant fruit, with your heart fixed on Hari's feet."

Caupāī 18

He bowed his head and went and entered the garden and having eaten of the fruit began breaking down the trees. A number of valiant watchmen were posted there; some he killed, the others went and called for help : "My lord, an enormous monkey has come and laid waste the *Aśoka* grove; he has eaten the fruit and rooted up the trees, and with many a blow laid the watchmen on the ground." On hearing this, Rāvaṇa despatched a troop of warriors. At the sight of them, Hanumān roared and thundered and overthrew the whole demon host; a few, more dead than alive, ran off shrieking. He then sent the young son, Prince Akṣa, who took with him an immense number of his best warriors. Seeing them approach, he seized a tree, which he brandished and with an awful roar swept them down with it.

Dohā 18

Some he hacked, some he crushed, some he seized and laid low in the dust; some got back and cried "My lord, this monkey is too strong for us."

Caupāī 19

When he heard of his son's death, the king of Laṅkā was furious and he sent the valiant Meghanāda. "Do not kill him, my son, but bind him; I would fain see this monkey and where he has come from." Indrajīt[1] sallied forth, a peerless champion, full of fury at the news of his brother's death. When the monkey saw this formidable warrior draw near, he ground his teeth, and with a roar rushed forward to meet him and tore up a tree of enormous size, with which he swept the prince of Laṅkā from his car. As for the valiant champions who accompanied him, he seized them one by one and crushed them by his weight. Having disposed of them, he closed with their leader. It was like the encounter of two lordly elephants. After striking him a blow with his fist, he went and climbed a tree, while for a moment a swoon came over his antagonist. But again he arose and practised many enchantments; still the Wind god's son was not to be vanquished.

Dohā 19

On the demon's making ready the magical weapon[2] that

1. Meghanāda's name was changed by Brahmā to Indrajit, after his victory over Indra.

2. The weapon had been given to Meghanāda by Brahmā with a promise that it should never fail. Hanumān therefore submits to it in order that Brahmā's promise might not be falsified.

Brahmā had given him, the monkey thought to himself, "If I do not submit to Brahmā's shaft, its infinite virtue will have failed."

Caupāī 20

He launched the magic dart against the monkey, who overthrew a host as he fell. When he saw that he had swooned, he bound him with a running noose and carried him off. Observe, Bhavānī; the messenger of the Lord, by the repetition of whose name wise men cut the bonds of existence, himself came under bondage or rather in his Lord's service submitted to be bound. When the demons heard that the monkey had been bound, they all rushed to the palace to see the sight. The majesty of Rāvaṇa's court on the monkey's arrival there struck him as being beyond all description. The gods and guardians of the quarters, standing humbly with folded hands, were all in dismay, if they saw him frown. But the monkey's soul was no more disturbed at the sight of his majesty than Garuṛ would be frightened by any number of snakes.

Dohā 20

When the Ten-headed saw the monkey, he laughed aloud and mocked him; then again he remembered his son's death and his soul grew sad.

Caupāī 21

Said the king of Laṅkā, "Who are you, monkey, and by whose might have you wrought the destruction of the grove ? What, do not you hear me ? I see you are an uncommonly bold varlet. For what offence did you put the demons to death ? Speak, wretch; as you value your life." "Hearken, Rāvaṇa; he by whose might Māyā creates every universe; by whose might Brahmā, Viṣṇu, and Śiva produce, maintain and destroy the world; by whose might the thousand-headed Śeṣa supports on his pate the mundane egg with its mountains and forests; who assumes various forms in order to befriend the gods and to give a lesson to wretches like you; who broke the stubborn bow of Hara and crushed your pride and that of the assembled kings : who slew Khara and Dūṣaṇa and Triśirā and Bāli, in spite of their matchless strength :

Dohā 21

By the slightest exercise of whose might you yourself subjugated the entire mass of creation, animate and inanimate; he it is whose messenger I am, and it is his beloved spouse whom you have stolen away.

Caupāī 22

I have heard of your daring exploits; you had a fight with Sahasrabhuja, and also gained renown in your conflict with Bāli." He heard what the monkey said, but smiled as though he heard not. "I ate the fruit, my lord, because I was hungry, and then like a monkey began breaking the boughs. Every one, master, loves his life more than aught else; those good-for-nothing fellows fell upon me, and I gave them blow for blow. To climax that all your son put me in bonds —bonds that I am in no way ashamed of — for my only object is to accomplish my master's business. Now, Rāvaṇa, I implore you with folded hands, abandon your pride and attend to my advice. Have some consideration for your own family; cease to go astray and adore him, who relieves his worshippers from every anxiety. Never fight against him, for fear of whom Death trembles exceedingly; even Death, who devours all else, gods and demons, animate and inanimate creation alike. Surrender Sītā, as I advise you.

Dohā 22

Rāma is the protector of suppliants; Kharāri is an ocean of compassion; turn to him for protection, and the Lord will forget your offences and will shelter you.

Caupāī 23

Take Rāma's lotus feet to your heart and reign for ever in Laṅkā. The glory of Pulastya, the peerless sage is stainless as the moon; do not make yourself a spot on its brightness. Unless Rāma's name be in it, no speech has any charm ; think and see for yourself, apart from pride and vanity. Without her clothes, Rāvaṇa, a modest woman, however richly adorned with jewels, is a shameful sight; and so is wealth, or dominion, without Rāma, gone at once, possessed as if not possessed at all. Those rivers, that have no perennial source, flow only after rain and then soon dry up again. Hearken, Rāvaṇa; I tell you on my oath, if Rāma is against you, there is none who can save you. Śiva, Śeṣanāga, Viṣṇu and Brahmā cannot protect you, if you are Rāma's enemy.

Dohā 23

Delusion is a root fruitful of many thorns; abandon the deadly sins of violence and pride, and worship Rāma, the prince of the Raghu race, the Ocean of Compassion, the Blessed Lord!"

Caupāī 24

Though the monkey bespoke him in such friendly wise, in words full of faith and discretion, piety and sound judgment, he laughed and replied with the highest disdain : "What a sage adviser I have found, and in a monkey too ! Wretch, you have come within an inch of Doom for daring to give me such vile counsel." "It will be contrariwise," said Hanumān; "you will acknowledge the error of your soul, I know well." On hearing the monkey's retort, he ground his teeth in a fury. "Quick, some of you, and put an end to this fool's life." The demons obeyed and rushed forward to slay him, but Vibhīṣaṇa with his ministers advanced and bowing his head before him made humble petition : "It is against all diplomatic practices sire: an ambassador must not be killed. Punish him in some other way, Sire." All exclaimed to one another, 'This is sound counsel, friend.' Rāvaṇa on hearing it replied with a laugh : "Let the monkey go then, but mutilate first.

Dohā 24

A monkey is proud of his tail," (so he went on to say) "bind it with rags steeped in oil and then set fire to it.

Caupāī 25

The poor tailless monkey can then go back and fetch his master, and I shall have an opportunity of seeing his might, whom he has so extravagantly exalted." The monkey smiled to himself to hear these threats. 'Sarasvatī, I know, will help me.' Obedient to Rāvaṇa's command, the demons began making their foolish preparations. Not a rag was left in the city nor a drop of *ghi* or oil, to such a length the tail had grown. Then they made sport of him. The citizens crowded to see the sight, and kicked him with their feet and jeered him greatly, and with beating of drums and clapping of hands they took him through the city and set fire to his tail. When Hanumān saw the fire blazing, he at once reduced himself to a very diminutive size, and slipping out of his bonds sprang on to the upper story of the gilded palace, to the dismay of the giant's wives.

Dohā 25

That instant the forty-nine winds,[1] whom Hari had sent, began to blow. The monkey shouted with roars of laughter and swelled himself so large that he touched the sky.

Caupāī 26

Of enormous stature and yet possessed of marvellous agility, he leaped and ran from palace to palace. As the city was thus set on fire, the people were at their wits' end; for the terrible flames burst forth in countless millions of places. "Alas ! Father! Mother! Hearken to my cry : who will save us now ? As I

1. In the Veda, the Maruts, or winds, are said to be sixty-three in number, forming nine Gaṇas, or troops, of seven each. In post-Vedic literature they are described as the children of Diti, either seven or seven times seven in number. After Diti's elder sons, the Asuras, had been subdued by Indra, their mother implored her husband Kaśyapa, the son of Marīci, to bestow on her an Indra-destroying son. Her request was granted; but Indra, with his weapon Vajra, divided the child, with which she was pregnant, into forty-nine pieces, which commenced uttering grievous cries, till Indra in compassion transformed them into the Maruts, or Winds. — *Monier Williams.*

said, this is no monkey, but some god in monkey form. This is the result of not taking a good man's advice; our city is burnt down as though it had no protector." The city was consumed in an instant of time, save only Vibhīṣaṇa's house; the reason why it escaped, Bhavānī, was that he who sent the envoy had also created the fire. After the whole of Laṅkā had been turned upside down and given over to the flames, he threw himself into the middle of the sea.

Dohā 26

After extinguishing his tail and recovering from his fatigue, he assumed his old diminutive form and went and stood before Jānakī, with folded hands.

Caupāī 27

"Be pleased, madam, to give me some token, such as Rāma gave me." She unfastened the jewel in her hair and gave it him.[1] The Son of the Wind received it gladly. "Salute him respectfully for me, my son," said Sītā, "and give him this message : 'my Lord, you never fail to fulfil desire and are renowned as the suppliant's friend; relieve me then from my grievous distress'. Repeat to him, friend, the story of Indra's son,[2] and remind my Lord of the might of his arrows. If he does not come within a month, he will never find me alive. Tell me, monkey, how I can keep myself alive: for you too, my son, speak of going, and it is only the sight of you that has given me any comfort : henceforth day and night will seem to me both alike."

Dohā 27

He did everything he could to comfort Sītā and inspire her with confidence, and then bowed his head at her lotus feet and set forth to rejoin Rāma.

1. In both recensions of the Sanskrit *Rāmāyaṇa*, Sītā gives Hanumān the jewel before he destroys the grove and sets the city on fire. The second interview is not mentioned at all in the up-country text.

2. The son of Indra, to whom allusion is here made, is Jayanta, who had attacked Sītā in the form of a crow.

Caupāī 28

As he went, he roared aloud with such a terrible noise that the wives of the demons, who heard it, were overtaken by premature childbirth. Crossing the sea with a bound, he arrived on this side and uttered a cry of joy for the monkeys to hear. At the sight of Hanumān, they were as delighted as if they had gained a new spell of life. "Your face is so glad and your whole body so radiant that you cannot but have accomplished Rāma's mission." All greeted him with as much delight as an expiring fish feels when it gets back into the water; and they set out with joy to rejoin Rāma, talking as they went of all that had lately occurred. When they entered Madhuvana, with Aṅgada's consent they ate its luscious fruit; and when the watchmen tried to stop them, they were beaten off with fisticuffs. They then fled,

Dohā 28

Crying out that the prince had laid waste the garden. Sugrīva rejoiced at the news. "The monkey," he thought, "must have returned, after successfully completing his master's business.

Caupāī 29

If they had not got news of Sītā, they would never have eaten the fruit of Madhuvana." While the king was thus reasoning within himself, Hanumān and his party arrived. They at once bowed the head at his feet, and he received them with all possible cordiality and asked of their welfare. "It is well with us now that we have seen your feet. By the grace of Rāma the business has turned out excellently. Hanumān has accomplishsd his lord's purpose and has saved the life of us all." On hearing this, Sugrīva again embraced him and then set out with the monkeys to where Rāma was. When Rāma saw them coming, he was greatly delighted at the completion of the business. The two brothers were seated on a crystal rock, and all the monkeys went and fell at their feet.

Dohā 29

Raghupati in his infinite compassion greeted them all with

much affection and asked of their welfare. "All is well with us, my Lord, now that we have seen your lotus feet."

Caupāī 30

Said Jāmbavān, "Hearken, Raghurāī; anyone, my Lord, on whom you show favour will always be prosperous for ever; gods, men and saints will be gracious to him; though victorious he will still remain modest and amiable, and his glory will irradiate all the three spheres of creation. By my lord's favour the task has been accomplished, and today we may well say that our life has been worth living. My Lord, to tell the whole of Hanumān's doings would be too much for a thousand tongues." Jāmbavān then proceeded to relate to Rāma Hanumān's principal exploits. The All-merciful was charmed by the recital and again in his joy clasped Hanumān to his bosom. "Tell me, my son, how Jānakī is and how she keeps life in her body."

Dohā 30

"Your name," said Hanumān, "stands sentinel over her by night and day; her contemplation of you is as a prison-gate; her eyes are the fetters for her feet; how then is it possible for her life to flit away ?

Caupāī 31

When I was leaving, she gave me this jewel from her hair." Raghupati took and clasped it to his heart, while his eyes overflowed with tears. "And did Sītā send any message also ?" "Embrace the feet of my Lord and his brother, crying, 'O friend of the poor, healer of the suppliant's pain; in thought and word and deed, I am devoted to your service: for what offence, my Lord, have you deserted me ? Of one fault I am myself conscious in that I still continue to live, though separated from you. But this, my Lord, is the fault of my eyes, which prevent my soul from taking flight. In this furnace of bereavement which is fanned by my sighs, my body is like a heap of cotton and would be consumed in a moment, but my eyes drop such a flood in self-commiseration that it cannot catch fire.' Sītā's distress is so utterly overwhelming and you are so pitiful that it is better not to describe it.

Dohā 31

O fountain of grace, each single moment seems an age ere it passes. Set out at once, my lord, and with your mighty arm vanquish the miscreant crew and deliver her."

Caupāī 32

On hearing of Sītā's distress, the lotus eyes of the Lord, the abode of bliss, overflowed with tears. "When in thought, word and deed, a believer follows in my steps, what ought he to know of misfortune ?" Said Hanumān, "There is no misfortune, my Lord, except to forget you and your worship. Of what account are the demons to my Lord, who can rout them at once and recover Sītā." "Hearken, O monkey," said Rāma, "neither god, nor man, nor sage that has ever been born into this world has been such a benefactor to me as you. What return can I make you ? There is none that occurs to my mind to match yours. Mark me, my son; I am not free from my obligation to you; I will think and see what I can do." Again and again, as the deliverer of the gods gazed upon the monkey, his eyes filled with tears and his whole body quivered with emotion.

Dohā 32

As Hanumān listened to his Lord's words and looked upon his face, he was enraptured, and in an ecstasy of love fell at his feet, crying, 'Save me, save me, O my Lord God.'

Caupāī 33

Again and again his Lord sought to raise him up, but he was so absorbed in devotion that he would not rise. (As he called to mind the Lord with his lotus hands thus placed on the monkey's head, Śiva himself was overcome with emotion; but again, composing himself, he proceeded with the charming narrative). After raising the monkey, the Lord embraced him and took him by the hand and seated him close by his side :

"Tell me, O monkey, about Rāvaṇa's stronghold of Laṅkā, and how you were able in such an off-hand way to burn down his fort." Perceiving that his Lord was so gracious, Hanumān replied in terms of singular modesty : "A monkey forsooth is a creature of singular prowess to skip about as he does from bough to bough. When I leapt across the sea, burnt down the golden city, routed the demon host and laid waste the grove, it was all done through your power, Raghurāī; it was no strength of mine, my Lord.

Dohā 33

Nothing, Lord, is difficult for him to whom you are propitious; a mere shred of cotton, were it your pleasure, could burn up the whole submarine fire."[1]

Caupāī 34

The Lord smiled much to hear these words, and recognized him as indeed a loving servant. "Ask of me a boon, my son, some choice blessing; today I will make you happy for ever." "Faith, my lord, is the greatest of blessings; of your favour grant me this else unattainable boon." On hearing the monkey's pious prayer, the Lord, Bhavānī, responded : 'So be it !' O Umā, he who knows Rāma's true nature can take pleasure in nothing but his worship : and he who takes this truth to heart has attained to the virtue of faith in Rāma. When the assembled monkeys heard the Lord's reply, they cried, 'Glory, glory, glory to the All-merciful, the All-blessed.' Raghupati then summoned the Monkey King and told him to make preparations for the march : "What need now for any delay ? At once issue orders to the monkeys." The gods, who had witnessed the spectacle, rained down showers of flowers and returned with joy from the lower air to their own celestial spheres.

Dohā 34

In obedience to Sugrīva's summons, all his hosts of captains

1. *Baḍavānala*, the submarine fire, is represented in mythology as a being with a body of flame, but the head of a mare (baḍavā) which sprang from the things of the patriarch Urva and fell into the ocean.

came in, differing in colour, but all unequalled in strength, a vast troop of monkeys and bears.

Caupāī 35

They bowed their heads before the Lord's lotus feet, those roaring bears and gigantic monkeys. Rāma beheld all the monkey host, and turned upon them the gracious glance of his lotus eyes. Each monkey chief was as much emboldened by his favour as Sumeru would be by the recovery of his wings.[1] Rāma then set out on the march exulting, and many were the glad and auspicious omens that befell him. It was only befitting that his march should be attended by favourable omens, since in him abide all glory and auspiciousness. Jānakī knew of his march, for her left side throbbed as if to tell her. Every good omen that befell her was converted into an omen of ill for Rāvaṇa. Who could adequately describe the army on the road, with the terrible roaring of the monkeys and the bears, how they marched, brandishing rocks and trees and with their talons for weapons, now in the heaven and now on earth, as the fancy moved them? They bellowed as if with the voice of a tiger; earth shook and the elephants of the eight quarters reeled and trumpeted.

Chand 2

The elephants of the eight quarters trembled, the earth reeled, the mountains tottered, and the ocean was agitated; the sun and the moon, gods, sages, Nāgas, and Kinnars, all rejoiced to know that their troubles were over. Myriads and myriads of enormous fighting monkeys pressed onwards, snapping, and snarling, singing glory to Rāma's conquering might and hymning the praises of the Lord of Kosala. The huge Serpent King could not support the burden; he staggered again and again, but each time saved himself by clutching in his jaws the hard shell of the tortoise;

1. This conceit has a very unmeaning sound when expressed in English. The allusion is to the legend which represents all the mountains as once having had wings, till they were clipped by Indra; while the word *pakṣa* which primarily means 'a wing' has also the secondary signification of favour.

as though he had mastered the stupendous theme of Raghubīra's glorious expedition, and were inscribing it on the shell of the tortoise, an imperishable holy material to be had.

Dohā 35

In this manner, the gracious Lord marched onwards, till he arrived at the seashore, where the host of bears and fighting monkeys began to devour all the fruit they found.

Caupāī 36

On the other hand, the demons had been living in great fear, ever since the time the monkey had left, after burning down the city. Every one kept at home, thinking to himself : "There is no hope of safety for the demon race ; if his messenger was so upspeakably powerful, how can the city escape when he comes himself ?" When Mandodarī was informed of what the people were saying, she was still more distressed, and with folded hands fell at her lord's feet and thus besought him, in words full of sound judgment : "O my husband, cease to oppose Hari : take my words to your heart, they are most wholesome. His mere envoy did such deeds that our matrons, on hearing them, were overtaken by premature labour; if then you desire your own welfare, call your ministers and send him back his wife. As a frosty night comes upon a bed of lotuses to shrivel it up, so has Sītā come for the ruin of your race. Hearken, my lord; unless you give up Sītā, neither Śambhu nor Brahmā can help you.

Dohā 36

Rāma's arrows are like a throng of serpents, and the demon host so many frogs; delay not, but do the best you can before they have snapped you up."

Caupāī 37

The incorrigible monster heard her prayer and laughed aloud; his arrogance is known throughout the world. "A woman is naturally cast in a timorous mould, and even in prosperity has a mind ill at ease. If the monkey army comes, the poor wretches will all be eaten up by the demons. The very guardians of the spheres trembled for fear of me; it is quite absurd for my wife to be afraid." So saying, he laughed aloud and clasped her to his heart, and then full of inordinate conceit proceeded to the council-chamber. But Mandodarī was sore troubled at heart and knew that god was against her lord. While he was sitting in court, he received intelligence that the whole army had crossed the sea. Then he enquired of his ministers, 'Tell me what you think best to be done.' They all laughed and replied, "Don't be uneasy. You have conquered gods and demons without any trouble; of what account can men and monkeys be ?"

Dohā 37

When these three, a minister, a physician and a *guru*, use fair words, either from fear or hope of reward, dominion, religion and health are all three quickly destroyed.

Caupāī 38

This was all the help that Rāvaṇa got; they did nothing but sing his praises. Perceiving his opportunity, Vibhīṣaṇa came and bowed his head at his brother's feet, then again bowing took his seat on his throne and after obtaining permission spoke thus : "As you ask of me my opinion, I declare it, gracious lord, to the best of my ability. If you desire your own welfare and glory, with a reputation for wisdom, a prosperous issue and every other happiness, turn away from the face of another man's wife as from the moon on its fourth day.[1] Though a man were sole master of the fourteen spheres, he cannot set himself to oppose the universe. However amiable and accomplished a person may be, no one will speak well of him if he shows even the slightest covetousness.

Dohā 38

Lust, anger, vanity, and covetousness are all paths that lead

1. It is a Hindu superstition that it is unlucky to see the moon on the fourth day. Hence the proverb:—

"Jo dekh chauthe kā cānda, Bāt calat, lāge pharphand."

to hell: adjure them and worship Raghubīra, whom all the sages worship.

Caupāī 39

Rāma, my brother, is no mortal king but sovereign of the universe, the fate of Fate itself, the Supreme Spirit, the imperishable and uncreated God, the benefactor of cows and of Brāhmaṇas, of the earth and of the gods; who in his infinite mercy has assumed the form of humanity, to rejoice his votaries and to break the ranks of the impious; the champion of the Veda and true religion, the saviour of the immortals. Cease to fight against him and humbly bow the head. Raghunātha relieves the distress of every suppliant. O my lord, surrender the princess of Videha and worship him with disinterested affection. The Lord has never abandoned anyone who has fled to him for protection, though he were guilty of having ruined the whole world. Know of a truth, Rāvaṇa, that it is the Lord, he who has for name 'the saviour from ever calamity,' who has now appeared among us.

Dohā 39

Again and again I lay my head at your feet, O Ten-headed, and entreat you to have done with pride, arrogance and conceit, and worship Rāma. These are the words which the sage Pulastya sent in a massage to me, and I have at once taken this opportunity of repeating them to you, Sire."

Caupāī 40

One of his wisest counsellors, Mālyavān, was greatly delighted to hear this speech. "Take to heart, my son, this admirable counsel which your brother Vibhīṣaṇa has given you." "These two wretches who thus magnify my enemies, is there no one here who will rid me of them ?" Mālyavān thereupon returned home, but Vibhīṣaṇa with folded hands spoke yet again : "In every one's breast, my Lord, so the Vedas and Purāṇas declare, either wisdom or unwisdom finds a dwelling. Where wisdom dwells, there too is every kind of prosperity : and where unwisdom, there at the end is destruction. In your breast malignant unwisdom has established herself ; you take your friends for enemies and your greatest enemy for a friend, being thus extravagantly enamoured of this Sītā, who is the very night of Death for the whole demon race.

Dohā 40

My brother, I clasp your feet and implore you to take my words in good part : restore Sītā to Rāma ; it will be to your own advantage."

Caupāī 41

Though the advice that Vibhīṣaṇa gave was sound and prudent, and supported by the authority of the Vedas and Purāṇas, the Ten-headed rose in a fury at hearing it : "Wretch, you are within an inch of your death. It is all owing to me, you villain, that you have been able to live at all ; and yet, fool as you are, you take the side of my enemies. Can you tell me, fool, of anyone in the whole world, whom I have not overcome by the might of my arm ? You live in my capital but are in love with hermits ; you had better go to them, if you want to preach." So saying, he spurned him with a kick ; but he still continued to clasp his feet. "You are as it were my father ; kill me, if you think proper ; but, O my lord, to worship Rāma would be far better for you." This is the virtue of the sages, Umā, that they return good for evil. Taking his ministers with him, he went his way through the air, crying aloud to them all :

Dohā 41

"Rāma is the very soul of truth ; your court, my Lord, is overpowered by fate ! I will now take refuge with Raghubīra ; lay no blame to me."

Caupāī 42

After Vibhīṣaṇa had left with these words, it was all over with everyone of them. Disrespect to a sage, Bhavānī, brings speedy ruin on the most prosperous undertaking. As soon as Vibhīṣaṇa had left, Rāvaṇa lost all his glory and good fortune. But he rejoiced as he went to meet Rāma, and revolved in his mind many an agreeable longing : "I am about to behold his lotus feet, so roseate, so soft, so beneficent to all who wait upon them ; at whose touch the seer's wife was delivered from the curse and the Daṇḍaka forest was sanctified ; feet that Sītā cherished in her bosom, even while they ran to seize the delusive deer ; lotus feet in Śiva's lake-like heart; how blessed am I who am now about to see them !

Dohā 42

"With these very eyes shall I this day behold the feet, whose shoes even Bharata clasped to his heart."

Caupāī 43

With such loving fancies to occupy his mind, he quickly reached the further shore of the ocean. When the monkeys saw Vibhīṣaṇa coming, they took him to be some special envoy. So they stopped him and went to their chief and told him all the circumstances. Said Sugrīva : "Hearken, Raghurāī ; Rāvaṇa's brother has come to see you." The Lord replied : "What do you advise, friend ?" The monkey king rejoined : "Mark my words, Sire ; the craft of these demons is past all telling. Why should he come thus of his own accord ? The villain's object is to spy out our secrets. My idea is that we ought to keep him under guard." "Friend," said Rāma "you have reasoned with much worldly wisdom ; but I have a vow to befriend all suppliants." Hanumān was delighted to hear these words from the Lord, the God who shows compassion on all who flee to him.

Dohā 43

"The men who spurn a suppliant, from suspicion that he may be an enemy, are vile and criminal, and misfortune will keep her eye upon them.

Caupāī 44

I would not abandon anyone who had fled to me for protection, even though he had been guilty of the murder of a million

Brāhmaṇas. Directly any creature appears before me, I bolt out the sins of all his past lives. No one who is essentially wicked can delight in my service ; if he is really a sinner at heart, how can he come into my presence ? Only a man of pure soul can find me ; I take no pleasure in hypocrisy, deceit and vice. Rāvaṇa may have sent him as a spy ; but even so, O king, we need not fear any loss. All the demons, my friend, that the whole world contains, Lakṣmaṇa could slay in a single moment. If he has come out of fear, to sue for mercy, I will protect him as I would my own life.

Dohā 44

In either case bring him here." Thus spoke the All-merciful with a smile. "Glory to the Lord of mercy," cried the monkey as he went off, taking with him Aṅgada and Hanumān.

Caupāī 45

The monkeys respectfully escorted him into the presence of the All-merciful Rāma. He beheld from a distance the two brothers, the delight of all men's eyes, the granter of every blessing ; then looking again upon Rāma's perfect beauty, he stood quite still, with all his gaze intently fixed upon the long arms, the lotus eyes and dark-hued body of the suppliant's friend, his lion-like shoulders and magnificent broad chest and his charming face, that would ravish the soul of Kāmadeva himself. With streaming eyes and trembling limbs, he at last made bold to speak in gentle tones. "My Lord, I am Rāvaṇa's brother; Champion of heaven, I have been born of demon race, with a savage temperament, as naturally prone to evil as an owl is partial to the night.

Dohā 45

I have heard of your glory and have come; Save me, save me, O my Lord; you who are the deliverer from all life's troubles, the remover of distress, the friend of the suppliant, Raghubīra."

Caupāī 46

So saying, he prostrated himself: but when the Lord saw it, he arose in haste with great delight, being pleased to hear his humble address, and took him in his mighty arms and clasped him to his breast; then with his brother seated him by his side, and to calm his votary's fears spoke thus: "Tell me, prince of Laṅkā, is it all well with you and your family ? Your home is in an evil place. How, my friend, can one practise the duties of religion, when encompassed day and night by wicked men ? I know all your circumstances, your excellence in virtue, your aversion to evil. God keep us from evil communications : 'twere better, my son, to live in hell." "Now that I have seen your feet, O Rāma, it is all well with me, since you have recognized me as one of your worshippers and have shown mercy upon me.

Dohā 46

No creature can be happy, or even dream of real inward peace till he worship Rāma, after forswearing lust, that fountain of remorse.

Caupāī 47

So long as the heart is peopled by that villainous crew, avarice, sensuality, selfishness, arrogance and pride, there is no room there for Raghunātha, with his bow and arrows and quiver by his side. The intensely dark night of selfishness, so grateful to the owl-like passions of love and hate, abides in the soul only until the rising of the sun-like Lord. Now I am well, and all my fears are over, in that I have beheld your lotus feet. None of the threefold torments of life has any effect upon him, to whom you in your mercy show favour. I am a demon, utterly vile of nature, who have never observed any pious practices, and yet the Lord, whose form even the sages cannot comprehend for all their profound meditation, has been pleased to take me to his heart.

Dohā 47

Surely I am immeasurably blessed, and Rāma's grace is most beneficent, in that I behold with my eyes those lotus feet, which even Brahmā and Śiva adore."

Caupāī 48

"Hearken, friend; I will declare to you my characteristics, as known by Bhusuṇḍi, Śambhu and Umā. If a man who has been the enemy of the whole world comes trembling and looks to me for protection, if he abjures all his pride and sensuality, guile or subterfuge, I make him at once like one of the sages. Father and mother; kinsfolk, children and wife; life and property; home, friends and establishment; in short, every object of natural affection is gathered up as the strands of a rope wherewith to attach his soul to my feet. He regards all things as alike, without any preference, and with a soul unmoved either by joy, sorrow, or fear. A sage like this is as fixed in my soul as money is in the heart of a miser. Good men like you are dear to me, and it is only for their benefit that I am constrained to assume mortal form.

Dohā 48

Virtuous and devoted believers, who are steadfast in uprightness, strict in pious observances, and who love and revere Brāhmaṇas, are the men whom I regard as my own life.

Caupāī 49

Hearken, Prince of Laṅkā; all these good qualities are yours and you are therefore very dear to me." On hearing Rāma's speech, all the assembled monkeys exclaimed, 'Glory to the All-merciful !' But Vibhīṣaṇa, on hearing such ambrosial sounds, could not contain himself : time after time he clasped his lotus feet, his heart bursting with boundless joy. "Hearken, my God, lord of all created things, friend of the suppliant, reader of men's thoughts; I had at first another wish in my mind; but devotion to my Lord's feet has come upon me like a torrent and swept it away : now in your mercy grant me such purifying faith as that which ever gladdens the heart of Śiva." "So be it," said the Valiant Lord and forthwith called for water from the sea. "It was not part of your wish, friend, but the sight of me brings reward with it all over the world." So saying, Rāma marked his forehead with the royal *tilak* : an infinite shower of blossoms rained from heaven.

Dohā 49a-49b

Thus did Raghunātha protect the humble Vibhiṣaṇa from Rāvaṇa's fiery wrath, fanned by the strong blast of his breath, and bestow on him secure dominion; and all the good fortune which Śiva had formerly bestowed upon the ten-headed Rāvaṇa for the sacrifice of his ten heads, Rāma hesitatingly gave to Vibhiṣaṇa.

Caupāī 50

Men who desert such a lord to worship any other are mere beasts without the tails and horns. All the monkeys were charmed with the Lord's amiability, who had recognized a servant and claimed him for his own. Then spoke the All-wise, who dwells in the hearts of all, assuming any form at will, though himself formless and passionless, the champion of religion, the friend of men, and the destroyer of all the demon race; "Hearken Monkey King and valiant monarch of Laṅkā; how are we to cross the deep ocean, full of alligators, serpents and different kinds of sea monsters, of fathomless profundity and absolutely impossible." "Hearken, Raghunāyaka," Vibhiṣaṇa replied, "your arrows could burn up a thousand seas, but still it would be a better policy to go and make petition to the god of ocean.

Dohā 50

For being your family priest,[1] my Lord, he will take thought and suggest some scheme, by which the whole host of bears and monkeys may cross the deep without any trouble."

Caupāī 51

"Friend," said Rāma, "you have suggested a good idea; let us try it and may fortune be with us." This invocation did not

1. King Sagara, by whose sons the bed of the ocean was dug, which is thence called Sāgara, was one of Rāma's ancestors.

please Lakṣmaṇa; he was very sorry to hear Rāma's words. "Why trust fortune, my Lord ? Give vent to your indignation and dry up the ocean. It is the one resource of a coward in soul to sit still and pray fortune to help him." Raghubīra laughed when he heard this and said : "I shall do it all the same; but never you mind." So saying, Raghurāī rebuked his brother and went to the shore of the salt sea; after first bowing his head and doing obeisance there, he took his seat on grass that he had strewn. Now after Vibhīṣaṇa had joined Rāma, Rāvaṇa sent spies of his own,

Dohā 51

Who disguised themselves as monkeys, and so watched all that was going on. In their profound admiration of the Lord's generosity and his tenderness to suppliants,

Caupāī 52

They loudly extolled his magnanimity and in the intensity of their devotion forgot their disguise. When the monkeys perceived them to be spies from the enemy, they seized them and took them to their chief. "Hearken, all you monkeys, said Sugrīva, "just mutilate them and let them go." On receiving this command, the monkeys ran and paraded them in bonds all through the camp, ill-treating them in every possible way and refusing to let them go for all their prayers for mercy, till they cried, 'We adjure you by Rāma not to rob us of our noses and ears!' When Lakṣmaṇa heard this, he summoned them all to him, and being moved with compassion, smiled and had them at once set free : "Give this letter into Rāvaṇa's hands and say, 'Read, destroyer of your race, what Lakṣmaṇa says.'

Dohā 52

Tell the fool also by word of mouth my emphatic command! 'Surrender Sītā and submit yourself to Rāma, or it will be your death.' "

Caupāī 53

The spies bowed their heads before Lakṣmaṇa's feet and set out at once, praising his generosity. Still repeating Rāma's praises, they arrived at Laṅkā and prostrated themselves before Rāvaṇa. The Ten-headed with a smile asked them the news : "Tell me, Śuka, I pray of your own welfare, and then let me hear about Vibhīṣaṇa, to whom death has drawn very nigh. The fool left Laṅkā where he was a prince; but now the wretched weevil must be crushed with the wheat. Tell me next what force these bears and monkeys muster, who have come here by command of their evil destiny though the poor old sea has been soft-hearted enough to spare their lives. Tell me finally about the hermits, whose soul trembles for fear of me.

Dohā 53

Did he meet you as a suppliant, or did he take to flight on hearing the report of my renown ? Will you tell me nothing about the enemy's might and magnificence ? Your wits seem utterly dazed."

Caupāī 54

"Of your grace, my Lord, be not wroth," said Śuka, "but take a blunt reply to a blunt question. As soon as your younger brother joined him, Rāma bestowed upon him the mark of sovereignty. The monkeys, who had heard that we were your spies, put us in bonds and ill-treated us shamefully. They were about to cut off our ears and noses when we invoked the name of Rāma and they let us go. You ask, my Lord, of Rāma's army; a myriad tongues would fail to describe it : such a host of bears and monkeys of diverse hue and gruesome visage, huge and terrible — the one who set fire to the city and slew your son is the very weakest of them all — champions with innumerable names, fierce and unyielding monsters of vast bulk, with the strength of countless elephants.

Dohā 54

Dvivida and Mayanda, Nila and Nala, Aṅgada and Gada,

Vikaṭāsya, Dadhimukha and Kehari, the malignant Niśatha, Śatha and Jāmbavān, all valiant champions.

Caupāī 55

Each of these monkeys is equal to Sugrīva, and who could count all myriads like them ? By Rāma's favour their strength is unbounded; they reckon the three spheres of creation as of no more account than a blade of grass. I have heard say, O Rāvaṇa, that the monkey captains number eighteen thousand billions; and in the whole of the army, my lord, there is not a single monkey who would not conquer you in battle. They are all wringing their hands in excess of passion : 'Why does not Rāma give us some order, either to swallow the ocean with all its fish and serpents, or at least to fill it up with piles of trees and mighty mountains, and then crush Rāvaṇa and lay him now in the dust.' This is the language that all the monkeys hold. Utterly devoid of fear, they shout and leap about as if they would make Laṅkā a mere mouthful.

Dohā 55

All the bears and monkeys are born champions, and moreover, they have the lord Rāma at their head. O Rāvaṇa, they could conquer in battle even Death himself, a myriad times over.

Caupāī 56

Not even a hundred thousand Seṣas would describe the greatness of Rāma's glory and power and wisdom. With a single shaft he could burn up a hundred seas, yet so prudent is he that he took advice of your brother and, on hearing his reply, went to the sea and humbly asked the favour of a passage." On hearing this, the Ten-headed laughed and said, "Truly he showed as much sense then as when he took monkeys for his allies. He has put faith in the words of that arrant coward, my brother, and like a spoiled child, begs of ocean what he will never get. Fool, you have been extolling a mere impostor; I have sounded the depths of my enemy's strength and understanding.

Where in the world could anyone achieve the glory of a triumph who had such a cowardly counsellor as Vibhīṣaṇa." The envoy became furious at the wretch's speech, and thought it a good time to produce the letter. "Rāma's brother gave me this letter: have it read, my lord, and much good may it do you." Rāvaṇa guffawed and took it with his left hand and told his minister, the wretch, to read it out.

Dohā 56a-56b

"Fool, submit your soul to advice, and do not bring destruction upon all your race; you cannot escape from Rāma's displeasure, even though Viṣṇu, Brahmā and Śiva be your protectors. Either abandon your pride, and, like your younger brother, fly like a bee to the lotus feet of the Lord, or like a moth you will be consumed in your wickedness, you and all your family, by Rāma's arrows of fire."

Caupāī 57

The Ten-headed, as he heard this message, was terror-stricken at heart, but smiled with his lips and cried aloud for all to hear: "He who stretches out his hands to clutch the sky only falls to the ground ; a devotee's idle talk is of small account." Said Śuka : "My lord, every word is true; be wise and abandon your natural arrogance. Cease from wrath and hearken to my advice; make an end, Sire, of your feud with Rāma. Raghubīra is exceedingly mild in disposition, though he is the sovereign of all the world. The Lord will be gracious to you directly you approach him, and will not remember even one of your offences. Surrender Janaka's daughter; this, Sire, is all I ask of you; do it." When he spoke to him of giving up Sītā, the wretch kicked him with his foot; but he bowed his head before his feet and then went to join the All-merciful Rāma, and after due obeisance, told him all that had happened. By Rāma's grace, he recovered his proper rank; for it was by the Ṛṣi Agastya's curse, Bhavānī, that he had become a demon, though still retaining the intelligence of a saint. Now, once more in the form of a sage, after again and again prostrating himself at Rāma's feet, he went his way to his own hermitage.

Dohā 57

Dullard Ocean paid no heed to Rāma's request, though three days passed; then cried Rāma in a fury: "He will do me no kindness, unless he is frightened.

Caupāī 58

"Lakṣmaṇa, bring me my bow and arrows that with my fiery darts I may dry up the deep. To use entreaties to a churl, to lavish affection upon a rogue, to deal liberally with a born miser, to discourse of divine wisdom with a man devoted to self, to speak of detachment from the world to the covetous, to tell of Hari to a man under the influence of passion or love, is all the same as sowing the sand in hope of a harvest." So saying, Rāma strung his bow, a proceeding that pleased Lakṣmaṇa mightily. The Lord let fly the terrible shaft; a burning pain ensued in Ocean's breast. The crocodiles, serpents and fish were all sore distressed. When Ocean perceived that these creatures were burning, he filled a golden dish with all kinds of jewels and humbly presented himself in the form of a Brāhmaṇa.

Dohā 58

Though you may take infinite trouble in watering it, a plantain will not bear fruit, until it has been well trimmed: similarly, believe me, Garuṛ, a mean upstart heeds neither prayers nor complements, but requires rougher treatment.

Caupāī 59

Terrified, Ocean clasped the Lord's feet : "Pardon, O Lord, all my offences. Air, wind, fire, water and earth are all, my Lord, naturally dull and slow to change. They have been produced by the delusive power that you sent forth with a view to creation — so all the scriptures declare — and as each has been fixed by the Lord's command, so it must remain, to secure its own happiness. My Lord has done well to teach me this lesson; but still it was you who first fixed my bounds. A drum, a clown, a chur , a beast, and a woman are all fit subjects for beating. By my Lord's power, I shall be dried up, the army will cross over, and my glory will be at an end; the scriptures declare the Lord's decree to be unalterable; do then at once what seemeth you good."

Dohā 59

The Lord smiled to hear this exceedingly humble speech, and said, "Tell me, my friend, some device, how the monkey host may cross over ?"

Caupāī 60

"My Lord, there are two monkey brothers, Nīla and Nala, who from childhood have been instructed by a sage. The mightiest mountains touched by them will by your favour float upon the waves. I too, remembering your majesty, will assist to the best of my power. In this manner, my Lord, you will bridge the ocean and the glorious deed will be sung in three spheres. With this arrow, Sire, slay the dwellers on my northern shore, who are vile criminals." The All-merciful, on hearing Ocean's grievance, at once removed it, the valiant Rāma.[1] At the sight of his mighty vigour Ocean rejoiced and became easy of mind, and after telling him all that had taken place, bowed at his feet and took his leave.

Chand 3

Ocean returned home and Rāma approved his counsel. These acts, which remove all the impurities of the Kaliyuga, has Tulasī Dāsa sung to the best of his ability. The excellences of Raghupati are a treasure of delight, a panacea for all doubt, a purge for every sorrow, and they who are wise of heart will abandon all

1. In the Sanskrit *Rāmāyaṇa* this curious incident is related rather more intelligibly. Ocean complains that the Ābhīras of the north are such an impure race that he cannot bear to receive into his bosom any stream of which they have drunk. Thereupon, Rāma with his fiery arrow dries up every river in their land, but creates instead a deep chasm in the ground, with a constant supply of water, and blesses the riverless region with exemption from disease.

other hope and confidence and be ever singing them or hearing them sung.

Dohā 60

The virtues of Raghunāyaka are the source of every blessing, and those who listen with reverence to their recital cross the ocean of existence without any need for a boat.

[*Thus endeth the book entitled* "THE BEAUTIFUL," *composed by Tulasī Dāsa, being the fifth descent into 'the Holy Lake of Rāma's Acts.'*]

BOOK VI

LAṄKĀ

LAṄKĀ

Sanskrit Invocation

I PAY homage to Rāma ; the adored of Love's enemy ; the dispeller of the dread of rebirth ; the lion to destroy the mad elephant, Death; the lord of ascetics; accessible only by contemplation; the store-house of all good qualities; the invincible; the passionless; the unchangeable; beyond illusion; the sovereign of the gods: the implacable destroyer of the wicked; the only guardian deity of the Brāhmaṇa race; the god incarnate in the form of an earthly king, lotus-eyed and lustrous as the jasmine.

I reverence Śaṅkara; as glistening in hue as the conch shell or the moon; the all-beautiful in person, robed in tiger's skin; bedecked with horrible black snakes for ornaments, attended by the Gaṅgā and the moon ; the lord of Kāśī ; the subduer of the flood of pollution that distinguishes the Kaliyuga; a tree of Paradise to yield fruits of prosperity; the ever adorable lord of Pārvatī; the sum of all good qualities; the vanquisher of Love.

May Śambhu, who rewards the saints with eternal beatitude, difficult even for them to obtain, and who punishes the guilty; may that same Śaṅkara grant me abundant blessing !

Dohā

O soul, why dost thou not worship Rāma, whose bow is Death and whose arrows are sharp, with whom the merest instant of time counts the same as an age and whose year is a cycle.

Soraṭhā

After hearing Ocean's suggestioh, the Lord Rāma spoke and said to his ministers : "Why now delay ? Make the bridge, that the army may pass over." Jāmbavān folded his hands and replied : "Hearken, pride of the solar race; your name, my Lord, is the bridge, by aid of which men cross the ocean of life.

Caupāī 1

What trouble then can there be about crossing this little stream ?" Hearing this, the Son of the Wind added : "By my Lord's favour a fierce subterranean fire had before now dried up the depths of the sea, but it was filled again by the floods of tears shed by the widows of his foes, and that is what makes it salt." On hearing Hanumān's ingenious conceit, the monkeys gazed with rapture on Rāma's person. Then Jāmbavān spoke to the two brothers, Nala and Nīla, and explained to them all the circumstances : "Keep your thoughts fixed on Rāma's power and build the bridge; you will find no difficulty." Next, he addressed himself to the whole monkey host : "Hearken, all of you; I have one request to make; only impress upon your soul Rāma's lotus feet; and then you bears and monkeys will find the task a mere pastime. Away with you, my sturdy monkey troops, and bring hither heaps of trees and rocks." On hearing this, the monkeys and bears set forth hurrahing, 'Glory to Rāma and all his might !'

Dohā 1

They rooted up and carried off in sport the tallest trees and hills and brought them to Nala and Nīla, who set to build the bridge.

Caupāī 2

The enormous mountains, which the monkeys brought and gave them, were handled by Nala and Nīla like mere pellets. When the All-merciful saw the charming construction of the bridge, he smiled and said : "This is a most exceedingly delightful spot : no words can tell its immeasurable dignity. I will set up here an image of Śambhu : I have a great desire at heart to do so." On hearing this, the Monkey King sent out a number of messengers to summon and bring together all the great sages. After moulding a *liṅgam* in the prescribed manner and worshipping it, "There is none other," he cried, "so dear to me as Śiva. No man, though he call himself a votary of mine, if he offend Śiva, can ever dream of really finding me. If he desire to serve me, in antagonism to Śiva, his doom is hell; he is a fool of no understanding.

Dohā 2

They who either out of attachment to Śiva dishonour me, or who serve me but dishonour Śiva, shall have their abode in the deepest hell for a full aeon!

Cāupaī 3

All who make a pilgrimage to Rāmeśvara shall, on quitting the body, go direct to my realm in heaven. Anyone who takes and offers Gaṅgā water there will be absorbed into the divine essence. To all who serve me unselfishly and with a guileless heart, Śiva will grant the boon of faith. Whoever makes a pilgrimage to the bridge that I have built will without any trouble cross the ocean of existence." Rāma's words gladdened the hearts of all, and the great sages thereupon returned to their hermitages. This, Pārvati, is Rāma's way; he is always gracious to the humble. Nīla and Nala, clever craftsmen, built the bridge and by Rāma's favour acquired brilliant renown. The rocks, which naturally sink themselves and cause other things to sink also, were like so many rafts; nor is this to be ascribed to the power of the sea, or the virtue of the stone, or the action of the monkeys;

Dohā 3

it was by the power of the blessed Rāma that the rocks made a way across the sea. How dull of soul, then, are they who leave Rāma to worship any other lord?

Caupāī 4

When they had completed the bridge and made it thoroughly secure, the All-merciful was glad of heart at the sight. The passage of the host was beyond all telling, with the clamour of the multitude of warlike monkeys. The gracious Rāma mounted a spot near the bridge and gazed upon the mighty deep. Then all the creatures of the deep showed themselves in multitudes to behold the Lord of compassion; every kind of crocodile, alligator, fish, and serpent, with bodies a hundred leagues in length and enormous bulk. After them were others, such that a single one could devour all the first swarm; while they again trembled no less before one of the swarm that followed them. They could not take their eyes off the Lord, and in the general gladness of heart all were glad at heart and blissful. You could not see the water, so thickly they covered it, as they gazed in delight on the vision of Hari. At their Lord's command, the army marched on; who can describe the magnitude of the monkey host ?

Dohā 4

The bridge was so thronged with the crowd that some of the monkeys took to flying through the air, while others crossed over on the backs of sea monsters.

Caupāī 5

When the two brothers had gazed awhile at the spectacle, the gracious Rāma smilingly advanced and crossed over with the army. The throng of monkey chiefs was more than I can number. On the far side of the ocean the Lord pitched his camp and told all the monkeys that they might go and feast on the goodly fruit and roots. On hearing this, the bears and monkeys ran off in all directions. To please Rāma every tree was laden with fruit, whether it was in season or out of season, without any regard to the time of year. They devour the sweet fruit and shake the trees, and hurl masses of rock at the city of Laṅkā. If ever they found a roving demon, they all hemmed him in and led him a pretty dance, and finally bit off his nose and ears with their teeth and so let him go, after making him hear of their Lord's great deeds. Those who had lost their nose and ears went and told all to Rāvaṇa. When he heard of the bridging of the sea, the Ten-headed started up and cried in consternation:

Dohā 5

"What ! Has he bridged the sea, with all the springs and streams[1] that fall therein, the great deep with all its waters ? Can

1. *Vana*, which ordinarily means 'a forest', must be taken here in its very unusual signification of a stream.

it be true that ocean trembles, the lord of rivers, the storehouse of the waters, the receptacle of the floods !"

Caupāī 6

Then becoming conscious of the agitation he had displayed, he turned with a smile to the palace, full of frantic imaginations. When Mandodarī heard that the Lord had come and bridged the ocean as though it were a child's play, she took her spouse by the hand and led him to her own apartment, and besought him in these humble and winning words, bowing her head at his feet and holding up the hem of her mantle:[1] "Be not angry, my beloved, but hearken to my speech. You should fight, my lord, with one whom you may be able to subdue either by wit or by strength. But the difference between you and Rāma is like that between a poor little fire fly and the sun. He who slew the stalwart Madhu and Kaiṭabha, who worsted Diti's valiant son, Hiraṇyākṣa, who put Bālī in bonds and slew Sahasrabāhu, he it is who has now become incarnate to relieve earth of its burdens. O my lord, do not fight against him, in whose hand are fate and destiny and our very life.

Dohā 6

Bow your head before Rāma's lotus feet and give him back Sītā; then resign your throne to your son and retire into the woods and there worship Raghunātha.

Caupāī 7

He is merciful to the humble, like a tiger, who will not devour a man who comes to meet him. All that you had to do you have done long ago; you have vanquished gods and demons and all creation. The sages, O Ten-headed, have laid down this rule that a king in his old age should retire to the forest. There, O my spouse, make your prayers to him, who is the creator, preserver and destroyer, even Rāma, ever gracious to the hum-

1. This with women is a sign of the greatest humility. The corresponding action amongst men is to tie a cloth round their neck.

ble; put away your carnal affections and pride, my lord, and worship him. He for whom the greatest sages perform all their labours, for whom kings leave their throne to become hermits, is this very king of Kosala, this Rāma, who has come here to show mercy upon you. Only submit to my advice, and the glory of your renown shall spread through the three spheres."

Dohā 7

So saying, she clasped him by the feet, her eyes full of tears and trembling all over. "O my lord, worship Rāma, that I may never cease to be your happy wedded wife!"

Caupāī 8

Rāvaṇa raised the daughter of Maya from the ground and began, the fool, to boast of his own might. "Hearken, my beloved, you are disturbed by idle fears; is there any warrior in the world my equal ? Varuṇa, Kuvera, the Windgod, Yama and Fate, and all the guardians of the eight quarters, have been subdued by the might of my arm. Gods, demons and kinnaras are all in my power: what cause can have arisen for these fears of yours ?" Having thus said everything that he could to comfort her, he again went and took his seat in the council. But Mandodarī knew at heart that his arrogance was due to the influence of fate. In the council he enquired of his ministers: "In what way shall we fight the enemy ?" They replied: "Hearken, demon king; why question us thus again and again ? Consider now and say what there is to be afraid of; men, monkeys and bears are our natural food !"

Dohā 8

But Prahasta, after listening to all they said, folded his hands and said, "Do not, my lord, act contrary to sound judgment; your counsellors have mighty little sense.

Caupāī 9

They have all spoken simply to please their master; but good results do not come in that way. A single monkey leaped the ocean and came hither; what he did you all know by heart. What ! was none of you hungry then, that you did not seize and devour him when he set fire to the city ? Pleasant to hear but fraught with future trouble is the advice which your counsellors have given, my lord. Come, my friend, tell me now, is he a mere man that we can devour, who has bridged the sea without any trouble, and has crossed over to Suvela with all his army ? What they say is all idle boasting. Hearken, sire, with due respect to my prayer, and do not in your arrogance account me a coward. There are multitudes of people in the world who are ready to make or listen to pleasant speeches; but few, my lord, who care either to hear or to give wholesome advice, if it sounds unpleasant. Hearken now to wise counsel; first send an envoy and, when you have restored Sītā, do your best to make friends with him.

Dohā 9

If he withdraws after recovering his bride, there will be no need of any further dispute; if otherwise, then, sire, face to face in the battle prepare for resolute encounter.

Caupāī 10

In either case, my lord, if you accept my advice, you will enjoy glory in the world." The Ten-headed answered his son in a fury: "Wretch, who has taught you to give such advice as this? From this time I have a doubt in my mind; can a bamboo root have produced su h a mere reed ?" On hearing his father's brutal and violent words, he went off home, saying these bitter words : "Good advice is as much thrown away upon him as medicine on a man doomed to die." Seeing that it was now evening, Rāvaṇa proceeded to the palace glancing with pride at his twenty arms. On the top of the Laṅkā rock was a hall with handsome court-yard, where he went and took his seat. A number of kinnaras began to sing to the accompaniment of cymbals, drums and lutes, while beauteous nymphs danced.

Dohā 10

The delights that he here enjoyed exceeded a hundred-fold

those of Indra. The most powerful enemy might threaten him, but no fear nor anxiety could disturb his repose.

Caupāī 11

Now Rāma had encamped with his valiant army to mount Suvela. There having noted one specially lofty peak, beautiful and bright above all others, Lakṣmaṇa with his own hands spread a couch of lovely flowers and fresh twigs, which he covered with a fine soft deer's skin; and here the All-merciful took his seat. The Lord's head rested on the Monkey King's breast: to right and left of him were his bow and quiver; with his lotus hands he trimmed his arrows, while the prince of Laṅkā whispered texts of scripture in his ear. The highly favoured Aṅgada and Hanumān caressed his lotus feet, while behind him Lakṣmaṇa kept watch as a sentinel, with quiver by his side and bow and arrows in his hands.

Dohā 11a-11b

Thus sat Rāma, abode of benignity, beauty and all perfection. Blessed are they who with profound devotion ever contemplate him under this form.[1] As he looked towards the east, the Lord observed the risen moon and cried to them all : "Look at the moon, like some dauntless lion,

Caupāī 12

That has its dwelling in a cave of the eastern range, pre-eminent in might, majesty and strength, rends asunder the darkness as it were the head of a wild elephant, and paces the plain of heaven, a lion-like moon. The stars strewn about the sky like pearls are the jewels of beauteous night. "But," said the Lord, "tell me, my friends, each one of you your opinion as to the spots on the moon." Said Sugrīva : "Hearken, Rāma, it is only the shadow of the earth that is seen in the moon." Another said : "When Rāhu struck the moon, its bosom became thus

1. This scene affords a very favourite subject for Hindu painters; partly, no doubt, on account of the blessing which Tulasī Dāsa here promises to those who contemplate it.

discoloured." A third suggested : "When God fashioned Rati's face, he stole from the moon a part of its essence, and this is the hole that you see in the moon's surface showing the shadow of the sky." Said the Lord : "The moon has a great liking for poison, and has given it a home in its very heart; thence darting abroad innumerable empoisoned rays, it tortures parted lovers."

Dohā 12a-12b

But Hanumān cried : "Hear me, Lord; the moon is your devoted servant, and it is your image enshrined in the moon's bosom that causes the darkness." Again the All-wise Rāma smiled to hear the speech of the Son of the Wind; then turning towards the south, the All-merciful spoke again.

Caupāī 13

"Look Vibhīṣaṇa, in the direction of the southern quarter — to the gathering clouds and the flashes of lightning. A pleasant sound of distant thunder is heard amidst the gloom; there will be some rain, think you, or a storm of hail ? Vibhīṣaṇa replied, "Mark me, gracious Lord, there is neither lightning nor gathered cloud. On the top of the Laṅkā hill there is a palace where Rāvaṇa is witnessing a performance: the royal umbrella held above his head presents the appearance of a mighty mass of cloud : the jewelled ornament in Mandodarī's ears emits the flashes, my Lord, that you take for lightning: while the incomparable music of the cymbals and drums is the pleasant sound that you hear, O King of the gods." The Lord smiled and, perceiving his arrogance, strung his bow and fitted an arrow to the string.

Dohā 13a-13b

A single shaft struck down the umbrella, crowns and ear-drops; in the sight of all they fell to the ground, and none could explain the mystery. Having performed this startling feat, Rāma's arrows returned and entered the quiver again. But Rāvaṇa and the whole assembly were much disturbed when they saw this interruption to their revel.

Caupāī 14

"There was no earthquake, nor any violent gale, nor did we see a missile of any kind," thus they pondered each to himself. "It is certainly a most alarming ill omen." When Rāvaṇa perceived that the assembly had taken fright, he smiled and invented an ingenious answer : "Even when I lost my heads, I came to no harm; now, only my crowns have dropped off; what ill-luck is there in that ? Go home all of you and go to sleep." They bowed and took their leave. But anxiety had settled in Mandodarī's bosom the moment her earring had dropped to the ground. With streaming eyes and hands folded in prayer, she said, "O lord of my life, hearken to my petition. O my husband, give over fighting against Rāma, and do not indulge your pride with the idea that he is a mere man.

Dohā 14

The jewel of the house of Raghu, believe what I say, is the omnipresent God, in whose every limb, as the Vedas declare, is the fabric of a world.

Caupāī 15

His feet are the infernal regions, his head the abode of Brahmā and in every limb there rest the other spheres; the play of his brows is the doom of fate, his eyes are the sun, his hair the dark thunder-cloud, his nostrils are the twin sons of Aśvinī, and the constant winking of his eyes the cause of day and night. His ears, as the Vedas declare, are the ten quarters of the heaven, his breath is the wind, and his articulate voice the holy scriptures. His lips are greed and his fierce teeth the god of death; his smile is Māyā; his arms the regents of the quarters; his face is the element of fire; his tongue water; and his movements the creation, preservation and destruction of the universe. The hairs on his body are the eighteen kinds of trees and bushes that grow on the earth; his bones the mountains, and the net-work of his veins the rivers; his belly the sea, and his hinder parts hell. Everything may be called a manifestation of the omnipresent Lord,

Dohā 15a-15b

Who has Śiva for his self-consciousness, Brahmā for his reason, the moon for his mind, and the great First Principle for his intelligence; who not only dwells in man, but also assumes the form of any animate or inanimate creature, the Lord God.[1] Hearken, my beloved, ponder upon this and cease to contend

1. The terminology here employed is that of the Sāṅkhya philosophy, according to which everything is evolved or produced from an original primordial *tattva*, or eternally existing essence, called Prakṛti. From it proceed seven productions, which are also producers, and thence sixteen other principles, which are productions only, not producers. Soul, *puruṣa*, the twenty-fifth essence, is neither a production nor a producer. The first production of Prakṛti is *Buddhi*, commonly called intellect or intellectual perception, and variously termed *Mahat*, from its being the *Great* source, of the two other internal faculties, *Ahaṅkāra*, 'self-consciousness,' and *Manas* or 'mind.' Third in order comes this *Ahaṅkāra*, the 'I-making faculty,' that is, self-consciousness, or the sense of individuality [sometimes conveniently termed egoism] which produces the next five principles, called *Tan-mātras*, or subtle elementary particles, out of which the grosser elements [*Mahā-bhūta*] are evolved. These are *ākāsa*, ether; *vāyu*, air; *tejas* or *jyotis*, fire or light; *āpas* water; and *pṛthivi* or *bhūmi*, earth. In addition to the five *tan-mātras*, the third producer, Ahaṅkāra, produces also the eleven organs, *viz*. the five organs of sense, *buddhīndriyāṇi*, the ear, skin, eye, nose and tongue; the five organs of action, *karmendriyāṇi*, the larynx, hand, foot and the excretory and generative organs; and an eleventh organ standing between these two sets called *manas* 'the mind,' which is an internal organ of perception, volition and action. Thus the eight producers, *viz*, Prakṛti, Buddhi, Ahaṅkāra, and the five tan-mātras, with the five grosser elements and the eleven organs, constitute the true elements of the phenomenal world; the most important — after the mere unintelligent original germ, *Prakṛti* — being *Ahaṅkāra*. (*See* Monier Williams' *Indian Wisdom*). It is tolerably clear that these categories were in the mind of Tulasī Dāsa at the time of writing, but he has employed them in a loose and popular way. Thus *mahan*, which is strictly a synonym for *Ahaṅkāra* seems in the text to stand rather for *Prakṛti*. In Rāma Jasan's edition of the text the words are wrongly divided. As is frequently the case with native Sanskrit scholars when commenting on Hindi literature, the editor would seem to have read the passage too exclusively by the light of Sanskrit authorities. *Prakṛti* may be explained as non-extended energy; unconscious life moving on towards consciousness; a latent ego destined to put forth conscious thought when the conditions of the environment allow of it. With increase of power, there comes an increased *Ahaṅkāra*, self-consciousness, or development of the ego into a personage, individual, self-balanced, master of its resources, characteristic, *sui generis*, himself.

against the Lord; cherish a devotion to Rāma's feet, and then my happy estate shall never fail."

Caupāī 16

He laughed when he heard his wife's warning and said, "Wonderful, indeed, is the power of ignorance! The poets have truly described woman's nature. There are eight faults from which she is never free at heart: imprudence, falsehood, fickleness, infatuation, timidity, want of judgment, impurity, and illiberality. You have proclaimed all the manifestations of the enemy and tried to frighten me with your alarming story; but, my dear, I see through it at once and perfectly understand your kindness. I recognize your cleverness, my dear, for in this way you have exalted my power. Your words, fair dame, are obscure but they are auspicious when understood, though they sound alarming."[1] Then Mandodarī was inwardly assured that her husband's infatuation was the fated forerunner of his ruin.

Dohā 16a

In such diverse ways did the Ten-headed amuse himself until the day broke, when the lord of Laṅkā, fearless by nature and further blinded by pride, entered the council chamber.

Soraṭhā 16*b*

Though the clouds rain nectar upon it, the bamboo bears neither flower nor fruit; so the heart of a fool never learns, though he have Brahmā for his *guru*.

Caupāī 17

Meanwhile, Rāma woke at break of day and summoned his ministers to take counsel of them. "Make haste and tell me what course should be adopted." Jāmbavān bowed his head at

1. The word *Bhayamocanī* would seem to be here itself used in an obscure sense as an illustration of the ambiguous language to which the speaker refers. Its ordinary signification would be 'delivering from fear;' but it may also be interpreted as 'letting loose,' that is, 'causing' fear,' 'alarming.'

his feet and said ; "Hearken, O omniscient dweller in the hearts of all, perfection of wisdom, power, majesty, justice and every good quality! I thus advise you to the best of my ability : send the son of Bālī as an ambassador." Everyone heartily approved this good suggestion, and the All-merciful said to Aṅgada; "Son of Bālī, wise, strong and virtuous, go to Laṅkā, my son, in my service. Why should I give you any lengthy instructions ? I am aware of your distinguished ability. Frame your speech to the enemy in such a way that he will agree to my requirements."

Sorathā 17a-17b

Obedient to his Lord's command and doing reverence to his feet, Aṅgada arose, crying : "O Rāma, any one on whom you show favour becomes possessed of every virtue. You have graciously granted me, my Lord, your own good fortune for the accomplishment of this task of yours." At this thought the young prince exulted at heart and his whole body quivered with excitement.

Caupāī 18

After prostrating himself at his feet and imprinting the image of his majesty upon his heart, Aṅgada bowed to the assembly and went forth, the delighter in battle, the gallant son of Bālī, dauntless by nature and his heart all aglow with the might of his Lord. As he entered the city, he came across Rāvaṇa's son, who was playing there Words led to a struggle; both of unequalled strength and in the prime of their youth to boot. He raised his foot to kick Aṅgada, but Aṅgada at once seized him by it and swung him round and dashed him to the ground. All the demons, even the stoutest warriors among them, who saw the deed, dispersed hither and thither, but dared not give the alarm; they did not even whisper to one another, but remained silent when they saw his death. A rumour, however, was noised through the city : "The monkey who set Laṅkā on fire has come again; what has God in store for us now ?" Thus they all pondered in excessive dismay. Without being asked, they showed him the way : if he but looked at any one, he withered away.

Dohā 18

Then, with his thoughts fixed on Rāma's lotus feet, he entered the Council Hall, proud as a lion, glancing on this side and that, a bold and stalwart hero.

Caupāī 19

One of the demons was straightway despatched to report the news to Rāvaṇa. On hearing the tidings, the Ten-headed cried with a laugh : "Go and bring this strange monkey here." On receiving this order, a number of his messengers ran and fetched the monkey-chief. To Aṅgada the Ten-headed appeared like a living mountain of soot; his arms like trees, his head a rocky peak, the hair on his body as it were all kinds of creepers, and his mouth, nose, eyes and ears like caves and chasms in the rock. Without the slightest trepidation of heart he entered the Council Hall, the son of Bālī; most dauntless of heroes. The assembly rose at the sight of the monkey; but in Rāvaṇa's heart was ungovernable fury.

Dohā 19

Like a lion that goes among a herd of mad elephants, so, after bowing to the assembly he took his seat, his thoughts ever fixed on Rāma's power.

Caupāī 20

"Monkey, who are you ?" said the Ten-headed. "I am an ambassador from Rāma, O Rāvaṇa. There was friendship between you and my father; and on that account, brother, I have come to you to do you a service. Of high descent, the grandson of Pulastya, you duly worshipped Śiva and Brahmā, obtained your prayer of them, accomplished all you undertook and conquered the guardians of the eight quarters and every earthly sovereign. Now, under the influence of royal arrogance or some folly, you have carried off Sītā, the Mother of the world. Yet hearken to my friendly advice and the Lord will still pardon you. Put a straw between your teeth and an axe to your throat, and with all your family and your own wife and with Janaka's daughter placed reverently before you, go all of you in this way without any fear,

Dohā 20

Crying, 'O jewel of the race of Raghu, protector of the suppliant, save now me, even me'! When he hears your piteous cry, the Lord will set your mind at rest."

Caupāī 21

"Pooh! you wretched monkey! Take care what you say! Fool, do you not know that I am the declared enemy of the gods? Tell me your own name and your father's, friend, and through what relation you claim alliance," "My name is Aṅgada; I am the son of Bālī, with whom you once were on terms of friendship." On hearing Aṅagda's reply, he hesitated, "I admit monkey that it was so with Bālī : but if Aṅgada is that Bālī's son, he has been born as a fire-brand for the destruction of his race. The womb that bare you, forsooth, was not pregnant for nothing; who with your own mouth confess yourself a hermit's envoy. Tell me now, is all well with Bālī?" Aṅgada laughed and said, "Ten days hence go to Bālī and embrace your old friend and ask him how he fares. He will tell you the kind of welfare that results from fighting against Rāma. Hearken, fool; he is a man divided against himself whose heart is closed to the divine Raghubīra.

Dohā 21

Indeed, Rāvaṇa, I am the destroyer of my race, while you are the preserver of yours. Who can say that you are blind or deaf while you have twenty eyes and twenty ears ?

Caupāī 22

What ! I disgrace my family by acting as the envoy of one whose feet Śiva and Brahmā and all the gods and sages desire to serve ? Your heart should burst asunder for entertaining such an idea." When he heard the monkey's fierce rejoinder, the Ten-headed glared at him and cried : "Wretch, I suffer all your abuse because I understand the maxims of statecraft and religion." "Yes," said the monkey, "I have heard of the piety and virtue you showed in stealing away another man's wife; and how you were so good and patient that you did not drown yourself at the sight of your messengers and watchmen, and from pious motives forgave the wrong when you saw your sister with her nose and ears cut off. Your virtuous character is renowned throughout the world; I am most fortunate in being able to see you."

Dohā 22a-22b

"Prate no more, you stupid brute of a monkey ! Fool, look at my arms, you impudent monkey, very Rāhus as they have proved to eclipse the full-moon-like might of the Lokapālas: while Śambhu and Kailāsa in the palm of my lotus hand were but as the stately swan in the heavenly lake.

Caupāī 23

Hearken, Aṅgada; tell me what warriors there are in all your army fit to fight with me. Your Lord has lost strength through pining for his bride; younger brother too is all sad and forlorn; you and Sugrīva are each the curse of your family: while my brother is an utter coward. Your counsellor, Jāṁbavān, is so stricken in years that he can no longer enter the field of battle. True, Nala and Nīla are good architects, and there is one monkey of exceptional strength, he who came first and burnt the city." On hearing this, Aṅgada replied, "Tell me the truth now, O demon king; is it a fact that a monkey burnt down your city? A poor little monkey set Rāvaṇa's capital on fire ? Who, on hearing this said, could believe it true ? He, Rāvaṇa, whom you extol as so distinguished a champion, is only one of Sugrīva's inferior runners. He is a good one to go, but no fighter : we only sent him to get news.

Dohā 23a-23f

Did the monkey really set fire to the city without any order from his Lord ? This is why he did not go back to Sugrīva, but kept himself out of sight for fear. All that you have said, Rāvaṇa, is quite true, and I am not in the least angry at hearing it : there is not any one in our army who would be a fair match for you. Take your friends and enemies from among your equals is a good sound maxim : if a lion kills a frog, who thinks it a fine deed ? Though it is no glory to Rāma to kill you, however great your offence, still, mark me, Rāvaṇa, the fury of the Kṣatriya clan is hard to withstand." The monkey foe set his heart on fire with the arrows of speech shot from the bow of sarcastic eloquence, and it was, so to speak, only with a pair of pincers that the dauntless Rāvaṇa could get out a rejoinder. At last he laughed and cried : "A monkey has, at all events, one good quality; he will do anything to serve the man who feeds him.

Caupāī 24

Hurrah for a monkey who, regardless of shame, skips up and down in his master's service! Dancing and jumping about to amuse the people, he does his duty by his employer right well. All of your race, Aṅgada, are devoted to their lord; it is quite natural for you to speak of your master's good qualities in the way you do. But I am too sagacious in appreciating merit to pay any attention to your insolent tirade." Said the monkey; "Hanumān gave me a very true account of your generosity. Though he had laid waste your garden, killed your son and set fire to your city, still you would not do him any harm. It was in reliance upon your magnanimity, Ten-headed, that I have ventured to be so bold. Now that I am here, I see that whatever a monkey may say will neither put you to shame nor excite you to anger or resentment." "Your cleverness, monkey, is so great that it might well be the death of your father," so cried the Ten-headed and burst into a laugh. "After being the death of my father, I would now be the death of you too, had I not just thought of something. I look upon you as a monument of Bālī's honour and renown, and that is why I do not slay you, you wretched braggart. Come, Rāvaṇa, and tell me how many Rāvaṇas are there in the world ? Listen while I tell you how many I have heard of with my own ears. One went down into nether world to conquer Bali, where the children tied him up in the stable and made sport of him and buffeted him, till Bali took pity on him and let him go. Another again was discovered by Sahasrabāhu, who ran and secured him as a curiosity and took him home for a show, till the sage Pulastya came and rescued him.

Dohā 24

Another, as I am ashamed to say, was held tight under Bālī's arm. Do not be annoyed,[1] Rāvaṇa, but tell me the truth, which of all these Rāvaṇas are you ?"

Caupāī 25

"Hearken, you fool ! I am that mighty Rāvaṇa, the action of whose arms is well-known by Kailāsa and his valour by Śiva; for him I worshipped not with flowers but with my own heads, which I took off with my own lotus hands times innumerable, when I worshipped Tripurāri. The guardians of the eight quarters know the might of my arms; in their heart, you fool, is sore distress even today. The elephants of the quarters know the hardness of my chest; for whenever I grappled with them in bitter conflict their mighty tusks, though never broken before, broke off like radishes when they struck against my front. As I moved, earth quivered like a small boat when a wild elephant steps into it. I am that glorious and renowned Rāvaṇa; have you no ears to hear, you lying chatterer ?

Dohā 25

And that's the Rāvaṇa of whom you make light, while you exalt a mere man. Ah, vile monkey, infamous wretch, are you at last beginning to understand ?"

Caupāī 26

On hearing this, Aṅgada replied indignantly : "Give over

1. *Mānkhā* here stands for *māṣa*, which occurs elsewhere in the poem with the sense of 'anger.'

talking, you pitiful boaster. He, whose axe was like a fire to consume Sahasrabāhu's mighty forest of arms; whose sword was like the tide of the salt sea, in which kings innumerable have been drowned time after time; and at the sight of whose majesty every one took to flight, how can he be accounted a man, you wretched Rāvaṇa ? How can Rāma be mere man, you arrogant fool ? Is Kāmadeva an ordinary archer ? Is the Gaṅgā merely a river ? The cow of plenty only a cow ? The tree of Paradise only a tree ? Is charity only so much gain ? Is ambrosia only a liquid ? Is Garuṛ a mere bird or Śeṣanāga a serpent, or the philosopher's stone, Rāvaṇa, only a stone ? Hearken, O dull of understanding ! Is Vaikuṇṭha an ordinary world, or absolute faith in Rāma an ordinary blessing ?

Dohā 26

And was Hanumān a mere monkey, you fool, who escaped after trampling on the pride of you and your army, laying waste your garden, setting fire to your city and slaying your son ?

Caupāī 27

Hearken, Rāvaṇa, and have done with conceit and worship Rāma, the All-merciful. If you are foolish enough to provoke Rāma, neither Brahmā nor Rudra has the power to protect you. Do not puff yourself out with vain delusion; if you fight against Rāma, this will be your fate : smitten by Rāma's arrows, your many heads will fall to the ground, in front of the monkeys, and they and the bears will play polo with them, as if they were so many balls. When Rāma waxes wroth in battle, his arrows fly quick and terrible. Will you then persist in your vain boasting and not rather be wise and adore his clemency ?" On hearing these words, Rāvaṇa flared up afresh, like a blazing fire upon which butter has been cast.

Dohā 27

"Have you never heard of my brother Kumbhakarṇa," he cried, "and my renowned son Meghanāda and my own valour, by which I have conquered the whole universe ?

Caupāī 28

Fool, with the help of his monkey friends he has bridged the sea, but what is that to be proud of ? Birds innumerable traverse the ocean, yet they are no heroes. Now mark me, monkey : my arms are like a sea filled with a flood of strength, beneath which many gods, men and heroes have been drowned. What champion is there so strong that he can overcome these twenty unfathomable and boundless oceans ? I even made the Dikpālas draw water for me. You have told me, poor wretch, of your king's renown, but if your Lord is so valiant in battle as one would judge from the way in which you harp on his achievements, then why does he send an ambassador ? Isn't he ashamed of making terms with an enemy ? Just look at my arms, which could treat mount Kailāsa as a mere churning-stick, and then, foolish monkey, sing, if you will, the praises of your Lord.

Dohā 28

What hero is there equal to Rāvaṇa, who, with his own hands cut off his heads, and delighted to cast them into the fire, time after time, Śiva be my witness !

Caupāī 29

When I saw the skull burning with the letters traced on my forehead by the Creator, and read that my death was to be at the hands of a man, I laughed, for I knew the divine prophecy to be untrue. When I remember that I have no fear : Brahmā must have written it when he was old and stupid. Are you not then ashamed, you fool, to keep boasting of any warrior's strength as compared with mine ?" Aṅgada replied : "There is no one in the whole world, Rāvaṇa, as modest as you. Your modesty is so innate that you never speak of your own merits. You are always thinking of the old story of your heads and the mountain,[1] and that is the reason why you tell it me twenty times over. Bury deep in your heart the remembrance of that

1. That is to say, of how you cut off your ten heads as a sacrifice to Siva and how you uprooted mount Kailāsa.

strength of arm by which you overcame Sahasrabāhu and Bali and Bālī; but hearken, O dull-witted fool; enough of all this! If a man who cuts off his head is a hero, what a hero a juggler must be, who with his own hands cuts his whole body to pieces?

Dohā 29

A moth is infatuated enough to burn itself to death, and an ass bears any burden, but they are not called heroes : look, stupid, and understand.

Caupāī 30

Boast no more in arrogant speech, but listen modestly to my advice. I have not come, Rāvaṇa, as an envoy to make terms, but Raghubīra has sent me from another motive. In his mercy he has said again and again, 'It is no honour for a lion to kill a jackal.' Pondering at heart on my Lord's words, I have submitted, wretch, to your injurious speech; otherwise, I would have broken your head and carried off Sītā, the fair bride. I know all about your strength, vile enemy of heaven, how in Hari's absence you robbed him of his wife. Your pride, Demon King, is great, but I am only the envoy of Rāma's servant and if I were not afraid of displeasing him, I would as soon as look at you make you a perfect spectacle.

Dohā 30

After dashing you to the ground and routing your army and destroying your city, I would have carried off Sītā, fool, with all the ladies of your household.

Caupāī 31

If I had done so, it would still be no great matter; there is no valour shown in slaying the dead. Now, an outcast, a man mad with lust, a miser, a destitute beggar, a man in disgrace, a man in extreme old age, one who is always ill or always in a passion, a rebel against Viṣṇu, a hater of religion and the saints, a man who thinks only of his own body, a scandal-monger and a man thoroughly vicious, these twelve even while they live are no better than corpses. On this account, wretch, I do not slay you, but do not provoke me further." On hearing this, the Demon King bit his lips and rubbed his hands together and cried in a fury, "Though small of stature, you have spoken big words. O foolish monkey, he of whose might you vaunt so fiercely, has no might, or understanding, or glory at all.

Dohā 31a-31b

Seeing him to be of no worth or dignity, his father banished him, and this is a sorrow to him, as also is the loss of his wife; while his terror of me oppresses him night and day. Proud as you are of his might, there are numberless men like him whom my demons devour every day and night. Stop your obstinacy, fool, and come to your senses."

Caupāī 32

When he thus abused Rāma, the monkey prince grew furious; for those who open their ears to attacks upon Hari and Hara are as guilty as if they had killed a cow. The mighty monkey gnashed his teeth and taking him in his two arms hurled him furiously to the ground. The earth reeled, the assembly quaked and took to flight as if driven by a hurricane of terror. Rāvaṇa raised himself from his fall and sat up, but his magnificent diadems had fallen to the ground; part he took and re-arranged on his head, part Aṅgada despatched to his Lord. When the monkeys saw the crowns coming, they ran away, crying, "O God, here are stars falling in the day time, or Rāvaṇa in his fury has sent forth four thunderbolts that come with rushing speed." The Lord smiled and said, "Fear not at heart; here is no star, nor sword, nor either Ketu or Rāhu; those are Rāvaṇa's crowns that are arriving as despatched by Bālī's son.

Dohā 32a-32b

The Son of the Wind sprang forward and caught them in his hand and brought and laid them at his Lord's feet : the bears and monkeys gazed in astonishment at the sight, for their brilliancy was like that of the sun. On the other hand, Rāvaṇa in a paroxysm of fury shouted to one and all, "Seize the monkey, seize him and kill him." Aṅgada heard and smiled.

Caupāī 33

"In like manner, sally forth at once, all ye mighty men, and devour every bear and monkey wherever ye find one. Go and leave not a single monkey in the whole world, but take alive the two hermit brothers." The prince replied indignantly : "Are you not ashamed to brag and bluster like this ? Cut your throat and die, you shameless destroyer of your family ! Does not your heart crack at the sight of his power ? Ah ! villainous woman-stealer, compound of all that is mean and impure, sensual dullard, though at death's door, you still babble abuse; Fate has you in his toils, wretched cannibal. Hereafter you shall reap the fruit of this, when the bears and monkeys belabour you : but when you thus speak of Rāma as a man, I wonder your proud tongue does not drop off : and beyond a doubt, it will drop off to the ground, head and all, in the battle !

Soraṭhā 33a-33b

How can he be a mere man, Ten-headed, who slew Bālī with a single shaft ? you are blind with all your twenty eyes; a curse on your birth, you base-born fool. Rāma's arrows are all athirst to drink your blood: for fear of him I spare you, insolent babbler, contemptible demon !

Caupāī 34

I am quite capable of smashing your jaws, but Rāma has given me no order; otherwise I am so enraged that I would cleave asunder your ten heads and take up Laṅkā and drop it in the sea. Your Laṅkā is like a fig on a *gūlar* tree, and you the unsuspecting insect that lives in it. I, like a monkey, would lose no time in eating the fruit, but the gracious Rāma has given me no order." On hearing this simile, Rāvaṇa smiled : "Fool, where did you learn to tell such lies; Bālī never blustered like this; intercourse with the hermits has made you such a boaster."

"If I do not tear out your ten tongues, Twenty-armed, of a truth, I am a mere boaster." As he thought on Rāma's power, the monkey waxed furious; he planted his foot firm and offered the assembly this wager: "If you can move my foot, you wretch, Rāma will take to flight and I will accept the loss of Sītā." "Hearken, warriors all," cried Rāvaṇa, "seize this monkey by the leg and throw him to the ground." Indrajit and the other men of valour in their different ranks all got up with joy, but though they leapt on him with their full strength and with many a trick, his foot did not stir, and they bowed their heads and sat down again. Again the enemy of the gods rose to the contest; but the monkey's foot moved no more, Garuṛ, than the standard of selfishness planted in the soul of a hypocrite, which there is no shaking.

Dohā 34 a-34b

Myriads of warriors, Meghanāda's peers, arose with joy and essayed the wrestle; but the monkey's foot did not stir, and they bowed their heads and sat down again. The pride of the enemy was broken when they saw that the monkey's foot was moved from the ground as little as the soul of a saint abandons the maxims of morality, though assailed by a thousand difficulties.

Caupāī 35

When they saw the monkey's strength, they were all dispirited, till Rāvaṇa himself arose to try the test. On his grasping his foot, Bāli's son cried : "There is no safety in clinging to my feet ! why, fool, do you not go and clasp Rāma's feet ?" On hearing this, he turned away full sorry at heart, robbed of all his dignity, and his majesty clean gone from him, as when the moon shows faintly in the day-time. With bowed heads, he took his seat upon his throne, like one despoiled of all his possessions. How can there be any rest for an enemy of Rāma, the soul of the world, the Lord of life ? O Umā, the play of Rāma's eyebrows now creates a universe and now again destroys it. He makes a blade of grass into a thunderbolt and again a thunderbolt into a blade of grass; how could his messenger fail in his challenge ? Again the monkey gave him all kinds of sound advice; but he would not listen: his time had drawn near. When he had sufficiently crushed his enemy's pride and exalted his master's fame, the son of king Bālī departed, saying, "Why should I trouble myself any more about you now; I shall have the pleasure of killing you on the field." Rāvaṇa was despondent from the very first when he heard that the monkey had slain his son and the demons, when they witnessed Aṅgada's challenge, were all still more disturbed.

Dohā 35a-35b

Having crushed his enemy's might, the mighty monkey, the son of Bālī, his body quivering with emotion and his eyes full of tears, clasped in delight Rāma's lotus feet. When he saw it was evening, Rāvaṇa returned sadly to the palace, where Mandodarī again spoke words of warning and said :

Caupāī 36

"Reflect, my husband, and abandon evil counsel; it is not well for you to fight against Rāma. His younger brother drew a little line,[1] and even this you could not cross : such is your strength ! My beloved, you will never conquer him in battle, whose simple messenger has done such great acts. Having lightly leapt across the sea, the monkey like a dauntless lion entered your Laṅkā, killed your watchmen, laid waste your garden, slew Akṣa as soon as he looked at him, and then set fire to the whole of the city and reduced it to ashes. What place is now left you for pride of power ? Cease, my spouse, from idle vaunts and take my words a little to heart. Do not suppose that Rāma is a mere earthly king, but recognize in him the Lord of all animate and inanimate creation, of infinite power. Mārīca knew the force of his arrows; you, miserable wretch, regard not his voice. Janaka's court was crowded with kings, you too were there in all your valour; but it was he who broke the bow and wedded Sītā. Why did you not conquer him in battle then ? The son of Indra knew a little of his might when he had his life

1. This line was drawn round Sītā, as a barrier against the demons. The circumstance is told in the Sanskrit *Rāmāyaṇa*, and Tulasī Dāsa, who refers to it here, forgets that he had omitted to mention it in his own poem.

spared but lost one of his eyes; and you have yourself seen Śūrpaṇakhā's condition : yet still your heart continues absolutely uncowed.

Dohā 36

Know, Ten-headed, that this is he who slew Virādha and Khara and Dūṣaṇa; who with the greatest ease killed Kabandha and disposed of Bālī with a single arrow;

Caupāī 37

who bridged the ocean as a mere child's play and with all his army crossed over to Mount Suvela. But the Banner of the Solar race is full of compassion, and out of regard to you sent first an envoy; and even he in the very midst of the assembly trampled on your power, like a lion let loose upon a herd of elephants. Seeing that Aṅgada and Hanumān are his servants, such stout and lusty leaders of the fray, how can you, my spouse, persist in calling him a man; you are bewildered by the intoxication of pride and selfish arrogance. O my husband, when the quarrel is against Rāma, Doom prevents reason from working in the soul. It is not with uplifted club that Doom strikes, but by robbing a man of his piety, his strength, and his faculty of reason. Whenever, Sir, a man's Doom is near at hand, he becomes infatuated, as you are now.

Dohā 37

He has slain your two sons and set your city on fire; today, husband, let him have your answer. O my lord, adore the mercy of Rāma and thus win for yourself the highest renown."

Caupāī 38

He heard out his wife's speech, though it pierced like an arrow, and then arose and went into the council-chamber, for it was now dawn. As he took his seat on his throne, he swelled with excess of pride; all his terror was forgotten. Meanwhile, Rāma summoned Aṅgada, who came and bowed his head at his lotus feet, but he, with the utmost courtesy, seated him by his side and then said, with a smile, the gracious Kharāri: "O son of Bālī, I am full of curiosity, answer truly, my friend, when I ask you. Rāvaṇa is the chief of all the demon race, and the unbounded might of his arm is famous throughout the world—how then did you send me four of his crowns? Tell me, my friend, by what device you secured them?" "Hearken, All-wise protector of the humble, they were not crowns, but the four prerogatives of a king—conciliation, concession, subjugation, and division, which as the Vedas declare, abide in a king's soul. Having recognized the gracious feet of kingly polity and religion, they came of themselves to their Lord.

Dohā 38a-38b

Leaving the impious Rāvaṇa, the rebel against his Lord, the death-doomed, his kingly prerogatives—mark me, monarch of Kosala—have come to you." On hearing this most ingenious conceit, the gracious Rāma laughed, and the son of Bālī then proceeded to give him all the news from the fort.

Caupāī 39

When Rāma had received his report of the enemy, he called all his ministers to him: "Take counsel as to how we should attack the four great gates of Laṅkā." Then the king of the monkeys and the king of the bears and Vibhīṣaṇa, with their hearts fixed on the Glory of the Solar race, took counsel and settled a plan and divided the monkey army into four companies. After exalting their Lord's power, they issued their orders; and the monkeys no sooner heard them than they rushed forward, roaring like lions. Joyfully they first bowed their heads before Rāma's feet and then the heroes sallied forth, with peaks of mountains in their hands, roaring and leaping, bears and monkeys alike, and shouting, 'Victory to Raghubīra, the sovereign of Kosala!' Though they knew that Laṇkā was a most formidable stronghold, they went on undismayed in the strength of their Lord, spreading like a cloud over the whole horizon and making martial music with trumpets at their mouths.

Dohā 39

"Victory to Rāma! Victory to Lakṣmaṇa! Victory to the

monkey chief, Sugrīva !" Such was the lion-roar of the great and valiant monkeys and bears.

Caupāī 40

Laṅkā was full of the utmost confusion; but Rāvaṇa heard the news with his wonted arrogance. "See the impudence of these monkeys," he said with a smile and summoned his demon host. "These monkeys have come by the decree of fate; all my demons wanted a meal" — so saying, the wretch burst into a loud guffaw — "and God has provided them with one, without their going abroad to seek it. Sally forth in every direction, my warriors all, and seize these bears and monkeys and devour them." O Umā, Rāvaṇa's conceit was as great as that of the sandpiper, which goes to sleep with its legs in the air.[1] On receiving their orders, the demons sallied forth, grasping in their hands slings and mighty javelins, clubs, maces and trenchant axes, pikes, swords, bludgeons and masses of mountain rock. Like foul carnivorous birds that swoop down upon a heap of rubies which they have espied, and after breaking their beaks upon them find out their mistake, so these man-eating monsters rushed forth in their folly.

Dohā 40

Armed with bows and arrows and weapons of every description, myriads upon myriads of the stoutest and most valiant demons climbed up to the battlements of the fort.

Caupāī 41

The battlements of the fort looked like the peaks of Mount Meru amidst dense clouds. Drums and other martial instruments of music sounded for the fray, and the soul of the warriors was stirred to fighting frenzy. The trumpets and clarions brayed so fiercely that even a coward, on hearing them, would forget his fear. The throng of monkeys could not be seen for the mighty stature of the warrior bears. They rush on, making no account of the most precipitous passes, but tearing down the rocks and

1. And thinks that they help to support the sky.

so clearing a way for themselves. Grinding their teeth and biting their lips in their excess of fury, myriads of warriors shout aloud, there calling upon Rāvaṇa and here upon Rāma. 'Victory ! Victory !' they shouted, and the battle began. If the demons cast down any mountain crag, the monkeys with a bound would seize it and hurl it back.

Chand 1

The fearsome monkeys and bears catch the mountain crags and hurl them against the fort. They join in closer struggle, seizing an antagonist by one leg and dashing him to the ground, and if he takes to flight, challenging him again to the combat. With a bold dash and a vigorous spring they bound up the heights of the fort ; and every palace, into which the bears and monkeys penetrated, resounds with songs in praise of Rama.

Dohā 41

Again, each clutching a demon, the monkeys ran off and then dropped to the ground with the enemy beneath and themselves on the top.

Caupāī 42

Strong in the power of Rāma, the monkey host overcame the throng of demon warriors, and having climbed the fort, made it ring all over with shouts of glory to Raghubīra, the sun of majesty ! The demons fled headlong, like thunder-clouds driven by a strong wind. There was a grievous wailing throughout the city, children crying and women in dire distress. All agreed in abusing Rāvaṇa the king, who had thus invited ruin. When the king of Laṅkā heard that his forces had been routed, the Lord of Laṅkā indignantly rallied his captains : "If I hear of any one turning his back in battle, I will slay him myself with my terrible sword. After devouring all my substance and feasting as you pleased, you now on the field of battle think of nothing but your own safety!" On hearing these stern words, the chiefs were all frightened and ashamed. Working themselves into a fury, they sallied forth again crying, 'It is the glory of a warrior to die with his face to the foe,' and all desire to live entirely left them.

Dohā 42

Arming themselves with many a weapon, the gallant chiefs pressed forward to the fray, challenging the enemy, one after the other, and so wielding mace and javelin that they sorely discomfited the bears and monkeys.

Caupāī 43

Overcome with terror, the monkeys began to flee, although, Umā, they were going to win the day in the end. Said one : "Where are Aṅgada and Hanumān ? Where Nala and Nīla and the stalwart Dvivida ?" Hanumān heard that his troops were in distress, but the hero was kept at the western gate. There Meghanāda led the defence, nor was it possible to force the gate, so great was its strength. Then the Son of the Wind waxed furious with a terrible roar, as though the end of the world had come. The hero made a bound and sprang upon the top of Laṅkā; then seizing a rock, he rushed upon Meghanāda, shattered his chariot, hurled its driver to the ground, and struck the prince himself with his foot in the chest. Another charioteer, seeing him senseless, threw him on to his car and brought him home in haste.

Dohā 43

When Aṅgada heard that Hanumān had made his way into the fort alone, he too, that doughty warrior, bounded forward to join in his monkey sports.

Caupāī 44

Maddened by the battle and full of fury, the two monkeys, mindful at heart of Rāma's glory, rushed upon Rāvaṇa's palace, and shouting, 'The king of Kosala to the rescue!' overthrew the whole building, so that not a pinnacle was left standing. When the Demon King saw this, he was terrified; while the women all beat their breasts, crying, 'Now two of these pestilent monkeys have come.' After frightening them with their monkey tricks, and proclaiming the praises of Rāmacandra, they grasped each a golden column in their hands and cried, 'Let us now make a beginning of destruction.' With a roar, they rushed into the midst of the enemy's army, and began laying them low with mighty strength of arm, here a kick and there a blow; crying, 'Worship Rāma or take the consequences.'

Dohā 44

Crushing one against another, they smashed off their heads and hurled them away, so that they fell at Rāvaṇa's feet smashed in pieces like so many earthen pots.

Caupāī 45

Whenever they caught any great commander, they seized him by the foot and tossed him to the Lord. Vibbīṣaṇa mentioned their names and Rāma assigned them his own sphere in heaven. Thus man-eating monsters, who had devoured even the flesh of a Brāhmaṇa, obtain a translation such as even devotees desire. O Umā, Rāma is tender-hearted and full of compassion and bestowed salvation upon them for this reason, that the demons had him in mind albeit in a spirit of enmity. Tell me, Bhavānī, who else would be so merciful. Dull of heart indeed and utterly wretched are the men who, on hearing of such a Lord, do not abandon their errors and worship him. 'Aṅgada and Hanumān'—thus cried the lord of Avadh—'have forced their way into the fort and Lankā with the two monkeys makes a sight like the sea churned by two Mount Merus.'

Dohā 45

After crushing and destroying the host of the enemy with the might of their arms, they perceived that it was now the close of day, and forgetting all their fatigue, they both came bounding into the presence of their Lord.

Caupāī 46

They bowed their heads before their Lord's lotus feet, and he was glad at heart to see his champions again. Graciously he looked upon them both, and at once their fatigue passed away and they were completely refreshed. On learning that Aṅgada and Hanumān had left the field, many warriors among the bears and monkeys turned to follow them; while the demons, recovering their strength at nightfall, made a fresh onset, crying, 'Rāvana to the rescue!' At the sight of the demon army, the monkeys turned again; there was everywhere gnashing of teeth as the heroes closed in the fray. In both gallant armies, the leaders impatiently challenged the foe, and fought as those who will not admit defeat. The valiant demons were all black of hue; the huge monkeys of many different colours. Both armies were equal in strength, with equally matched champions, the passion with which they fought was a sight to see; as when in the rains, or the autumn, masses of cloud are driven against one another by the force of the wind. When the line began to waver, the chiefs Akampana and Atikāya had recourse to jugglery, and all in a minute it became pitch dark, and there was a shower of blood, stones and dust.

Dohā 46

Beholding the dense darkness all around, the monkey army fell into confusion; it was impossible to see one another; there was everywhere a great shouting.

Caupāī 47

But Rāma understood the secret of it all and summoned Aṅgada and Hanumān and explained to them what was going on. The mighty monkeys had no sooner heard it than they rushed forth in a fury; but the gracious Lord with a smile drew his bow and at once let fly a fiery arrow. Light shone forth, and there was no darkness anywhere; as when at the dawn of intelligence all doubts disappear. Having recovered the light, the bears and monkeys forgot all their fatigue and alarm and pressed on exultingly. Hanumān and Aṅgada thundered aloud on the field of battle, and at the sound of their roaring the demons fled; but the bears and monkeys, seizing them in their flight, dashed them to the ground, performing prodigies of valour, or catching them by their feet, hurled them into the sea, where alligators, serpents, and fish snapped them up and devoured them.

Dohā 47

Some were slain outright, some were wounded, some fled back

to the fort; the bears and monkeys shouted for joy over the rout of the enemy's strong force.

Caupāī 48

Seeing that it was now night, the four divisions of the monkey army returned to the Lord of Kosala. As soon as Rāma cast his gracious glance upon them, all their fatigue was at once forgotten. On the other hand, Rāvaṇa summoned his ministers and told them all how his champions had been killed; "the monkeys have destroyed half my army; tell me at once what counsel should be adopted." Thereupon Mālyavān, a very aged demon, who had been the sagacious consellor of Rāvaṇa's father and mother, delivered himself of a speech of the soundest policy; "Hearken, my son, to a few words of instruction from me. Ever since you carried off Sītā and brought her, there have been omens of ill, more than I can tell. No advantage can be gained by opposing him, whose glory is the theme both of Veda and Purāṇa.

Dohā 48a-48b

He is the incarnation of the compassionate Lord God, who slew Hiraṇyākṣa, with his brother Hiraṇyakaśipu, and Madhu and the monster Kaiṭabha. Who can contend with him whom Śiva and Brahmā adore, full of all grace and wisdom, but like the angel of death, a very fire to consume the forest of wickedness ?

Caupāī 49

Do not fight with him any more; give back Sītā and worship the All-merciful with loving devotion." His words stung like arrows : "Away, wretch, with your abominable suggestions; if it were not for your age, I would have killed you; but do not appear in my sight again." He thought within himself, 'He wishes to be killed by the gracious Lord,' and so rose and departde, uttering words of reproof. Then Meghanāda cried in fury : "See what feats I shall perform tomorrow; though I do not say much, I do a great deal." On hearing his son's speech,

Rāvaṇa's confidence returned and he took him lovingly into his lap. While they were still making their plans, the day broke, the monkeys again assailed the four gates and fiercely encompassed the precipitous citadel. There was a confused noise in every part of the town, as the demons snatched up their weapons of every description and hurried forward and began hurling down masses of rock from the ramparts.

Chand 2

They hurl down myriads of mountain-peaks; missiles of every kind are sent flying; the shock is as when a bolt falls from heaven and the thunderous noise like that of the clouds on the day of dissolution. The formidable monkeys join in close combat; their bodies are hacked in pieces, but though mangled they faint not; they seize the rocks and hurl them against the fort wherever the demons are.

Dohā 49

When Meghanāda heard that they had again come and seized the fort, he gallantly left his stronghold and sallied forth with beat of drum to meet the enemy face to face.

Caupāī 50

"Where are the two brother princes of Kosala, those archers, so famous throughout the universe ? Where are Nala and Nīla, Dvivida and Sugrīva, Aṅgada and Hanumān, most powerful of all ? Where is Vibhīṣaṇa, his brother's curse that I may slay the wretch at once, this very day ?" So saying, he made ready his terrible arrows, and in vehemence of passion drew the string to his ear. The multitudinous shafts that he let fly sped forth like so many winged serpents. Everywhere you might see monkeys falling to the ground; at that time there was not one that dared to face him. Everywhere bears and monkeys were taking to flight, and every wish to fight was clean forgotten. Not a bear or a monkey was to be seen on the field but those who had left their life there.

Dohā 50

At each flight he sent forth ten arrows; the gallant monkeys all bit the dust : with the roar as of a lion, Meghanāda shouted aloud, exulting in his indomitable might.

Caupāī 51

When Hanumān saw that the army was in distress, he rushed forth terrible as death and quickly tearing up an enormous crag, hurled it at Meghanāda with the utmost fury. Seeing it come, he mounted up into the air; chariot, driver, and horses were all lost to sight. Again and again Hanumān shouted a challenge; but he came no nearer and he then understood the mystery. Meghanāda appproached Rāma, and after assailing him with every kind of abuse, aimed at him weapons and missiles of every description; but the Lord with the utmost ease snapped them asunder and warded them off. On seeing this display of power, the fool was sore vexed and began to put in practice all kinds of magic; as if a poor little snakeling were to mock Garuṛ and frighten him by supping at him.

Dohā 51

The demon in the foolishness of his soul displayed his supernatural powers to baffle him whose mighty magic subdues Śiva and Brahmā and all both great and small.

Caupāī 52

Mounting up into the sky, he rained down a shower of sparks, while streams of water broke out from the earth. Goblins and witches of diverse form danced with uproarious shouts of "kill him, tear him in pieces." Now a shower of excrement, pus, blood, hair and bones, and now an overwhelming downfall of stones and ashes. The duststorm made it so dark that if you held out your own hand you could not see it. The monkeys were greatly dismayed at the sight of these apparitions and thought, 'at this rate we must all of us perish.' But Rāma smiled at the idle show; seeing, however that all the monkeys were alarmed, he with a single arrow cleft asunder the delusion, as when the sun disperses the thick darkness. With a glance full of compassion, he looked upon the bears and monkeys; at once they waxed so strong that there was no holding them back from the field of battle.

Dohā 52

Having obtained Rāma's permission, Lakṣmaṇa, taking with him Aṅgada and the other monkeys, sallied forth in fury, with bow and arrows in hand,

Caupāī 53

With bloodshot eyes[1] and mighty chest and arms and his body of reddish hue like Mount Himālaya. On the other side, the Ten-headed sent out his champions, who took up their armour and their weapons[2] and hastened forth. With mountains and huge trees for missiles, the monkeys rushed to meet them, shouting, 'Victory to Rāma !' They all closed in the fray, equally matched one with another, and both equally sanguine of success. After hurling the rocks and mountains at the foe; the monkeys next fell upon them with blows of the fist and kicks, and rendings of the teeth: 'Seize ! Seize ! Seize ! Kill, kill, kill, ! Strike off their heads! Rend off their arms !' Such were the cries which filled the nine continents of the world, while headless bodies still full of fury kept running to and fro. From the heaven above, the gods beheld the spectacle now in dismay and now in rapture.

Dohā 53

Blood filled every hollow in the ground, while clouds of dust flew overhead, like the ashes of a pyre that conceal a heap of glowing embers.

1. In Rām Jasan's edition, the one I habitually use, the reading is *chataja-nayan*, which may be translated 'with blood-shot eyes,' an epithet which appears appropriate to the context. In other editions is subtituted the more common expression *jalaja-nayan*, with lotus eyes.'

2. Here the reading that I translate is *giri-śila*, 'the rocks and mountains' mentioned above as the monkeys' missiles. Rām Jasan reads *jaya-sīla*, which would mean 'triumphant.'

Caupāī 54

The wounded heroes resembled so many kiṁśuka (ḍhāka) trees in flower. The two champions Lakṣmaṇa, and Meghanāda, grappled, with one another in excess of fury. Neither could singly conquer the other; the demon by force and by feint showing himself so wicked. At last Lakṣmaṇa became mad with rage, and with one blow he shattered both the chariot and its driver. He so smote him in various ways that the demon was left barely alive. Then the son of Rāvaṇa thought within himself, 'I am in a strait, he will take my life; and he let fly his spear, the destroyer of heroes, which struck Lakṣmaṇa in the breast with full force. So great was the shock that he swooned away. Then he went and drew near, no longer afraid.

Dohā 54

A hundred myriad warriors as mighty as Meghanāda tried to lift him; but how could Śeṣanāga, the supporter of the world, be thus lifted ? They went off mortified.

Caupāī 55

Hearken, Bhavānī; who can conquer him in battle, the fire of whose wrath would consume in a moment the fourteen spheres of creation, whom gods and men and all things animate and inanimate adore ? He alone can understand this mystery, on whom rests the favour of Rāma. As it was now evening, both armies left the field and began to muster their several forces. The All-merciful, the ubiquitous Supreme Spirit, the invincible Lord of the universe asked, 'Where is Lakṣmaṇa ?' Hanumān then brought him in. When the Lord saw his younger brother, he was much distressed. Jāmbavān said: "The physician Suṣeṇa is in Laṅkā, send some one to fetch him." Hanumān at once assumed a diminutive form and went and brought him, house and all.

Dohā 55

Suṣeṇa came and bowed his head before Rāma's lotus feet and bade Hanumān go and bring a herb from a certain mountain that he mentioned.

Caupāī 56

With Rāma's lotus feet impressed upon his heart, the Son of the Wind started in confident assurance. On the other side, a spy gave information. So Rāvaṇa went to the house of Kālanemi and told him. When he had heard the news, Kalanemi beat his head again and again, crying, "Who can stop his path who burnt your city before your very eyes. Have some regard for your own welfare and worship Rāma and desist, sire, henceforth from these vain endeavours. Lay upon your heart the delight of all eyes, whose form is dark and beautiful as the dark-blue lotus! Have done with pride, conceit, and arrogance, and rouse yourself from this slumber in a night of delusion. Is it possible that any one should ever dream of conquering him for whom the serpent, Time, is mere food to devour ?"

Dohā 56

When the Ten-headed heard this, he was exceedingly wroth. He then reasoned to himself : "It will be better for me to perish at the hands of Rāma's messenger, and not for this wretch to kill me."

Caupāī 57

So saying, he went and wrought an illusion on the way side constructing a lake, temple and fine garden. Hanumān beheld the charming spot and thought to himself, 'After asking the holy man's leave, I will drink of the water and relieve my fatigue.' For the demon showed himself in a false attire, and sought to delude the messenger even of the king of delusion. So the Son of the Wind went and bowed before him; and he began to recite Rāma's praises, saying. "A great battle is raging between Rāvaṇa and Rāma, but Rāma will win the day; of this there is no doubt. Though I have not moved from here, I have seen it all, my brother; my intelligence is remarkably clear-sighted." On his asking for water, he gave him some in a cup; the monkey said, "That is not enough to satisfy me." "Go then and bathe in the lake", said the demon, "and quickly come back, and I will then bestow upon you a gift, by which you may attain to understanding."

Dohā 57

As he stepped into the lake, a female crocodile seized the monkey by the foot. In his alarm he killed it. Whereupon it assumed a divine form, and mounting a chariot ascended to the heavens.

Caupāī 58

"By the sight of you, O monkey," she said, "I have become freed from guilt, and the curse of the great sage has been removed. This is no hermit, but a fierce demon; doubt not the truth of my words." So saying, the heavenly nymph went her way, and the monkey at once returned to the demon. Said the monkey, "Holy sir, first receive my offering and after that tell me the charm." He then twisted his tail round his head and threw him down. At the moment of his death, he appeared in his proper form, and with a cry of "Rāma! Rāma" breathed his last. On hearing this, Hanumān went on his way rejoicing. The monkey saw the mountain, but could not recognize the herbs; so without any hesitation, he tore up the hill by the root and went off with it. As he rushed through the night air with the mountain in his grasp, he passed over the city of Avadh.

Dohā 58

Bharata saw a huge shape overhead and thinking it to be some most monstrous demon, drew his bow to his ear and shot him with a headless arrow.

Caupāī 59

Struck by the dart, Hanumān fell swooning to the earth, crying, ' O Rāma, Rāma, prince of Raghu's line !" On hearing this beloved sound, Bharata started up and ran, and in the utmost haste drew nigh to the monkey. Seeing him wounded, he clasped him to his bosom and tried in every way to revive him, but without success. With a disconsolate face and sorrowing, he made this prayer, while his eyes streamed with tears : "God, who made me Rāma's enemy, has now caused me this additional distress. If in thought and word and deed, I have a sincere affection for Rāma's lotus feet, and if Rāma is kindly disposed to me, may your pain and fatigue, O monkey, all pass away." At the sound of these words, the monkey chief arose and sat up, crying, "glory, glory to the king of Kosala."

Soraṭhā 59

With quivering limbs and eyes full of tears, Bharata clasped the monkey to his bosom, invoking Rāma, the crown of the line of Raghu, in a transport of affection, which was more than his soul could contain.

Caupāī 60

"Tell me friend," he said, "is all well with the Fountain of joy and with his brother and the revered Jānakī ?" The monkey told him briefly all that had happened. He became sad of heart and began to lament : "Alas, my fate, why was I born into the world, if in nothing I can help my Lord." But seeing the unfitness of the time, he mastered his feelings the gallant prince, and again addressed the monkey: "Sir, you will be delayed in your journey, and your task will come to nought, for the day is now breaking. Mount my arrow, mountain and all, and I will send you straight into the presence of the All-merciful." On hearing this, the monkey's pride was aroused. "How", he thought, "can his arrow fly with my weight ?" But again reflecting on Rāma's power, he did reverence to his feet and cried with folded hands :

Dohā 60a-60b

"O my lord, I have only to cherish the thought of your majesty in my soul in order to travel quickly." So saying, Hanumān took leave and after doing obeisance to his feet set forth. As he travelled on, the Son of the Wind again and again extolled to himself the mighty arm and the amiable disposition of Bharata and his boundless devotion to his Lord's feet.

Caupāī 61

Meanwhile, Rāma was watching Lakṣmaṇa and using language after the fashion of a man. When half the night was spent, and still the monkey had not returned, Rāma raised his brother and clasped him to his heart. "O my brother, once you could not endure to see me in sorrow, your disposition was ever so affectionate. On my account, you abandoned father and mother and exposed yourself to the hardships of the forest, the cold, the heat and the wind. But where is now your old love, my brother, that you do not stir in response to my distress. If I had known that exile involved the loss of my brother, I would never have obeyed my father's commands.[1] Sons, riches, wives, house and kinsfolk come again time after time in a life, but a real brother is not so to be had; remember this, Lakṣmaṇa, and awake! As a bird is utterly miserable without wings, a serpent without its head-jewel, or an elephant without its trunk, so is my life without you, my brother. If cruel fate preserves me alive, with what face can I show myself at Avadh, after sacrificing a dear brother for the sake of a woman ? I would rather have endured the social disgrace; for after all, the loss of a wife is no great loss, and my heart is so hard and unfeeling that it can bear the sight even of this your anguish. Your mother's only son, my brother, you are the sole support of her life, but she took you by the hand and entrusted you to me, knowing what a comfort and what a friend I should find you. What answer can I go and give her ? Why do you not rise and advise me, brother ?" Thus grievously sorrowed the healer of sorrow and his lotus eyes streamed with tears; but O Umā, Rāma is one and unchangeable, and it was only in compassion to his worshippers that he played a man's part.

Soraṭhā 61

All the monkeys were sore distressed on hearing their Lord's

1. This lament over his want of foreknowledge and other similar passages, in which Rāma is represented as subject to human infirmities, are frequently quoted in Missionary polemics as fatal to the idea of his being a divine person and as clear evidences, even on the showing of the Hindu narrative itself, that he was only an ordinary human being. But it is very unwise to adopt such a line of argument, which might be retorted with equal force against the inspired records of Christianity. From the Hindu point of view, the answer given by Tulasī Dāsa sufficiently covers the difficulty and corresponds precisely with the explanation of S. Jerome: "Non quod personam Domini separemus, sed quod opera ejus inter Deum hominemque divisa sint."

lamentation, till Hanumān arrived, like an heroic strain in the midst of a dirge.

Caupāī 62

Rāma received Hanumān with exceeding joy, for the Lord is most grateful and supremely wise. Then quickly the physician applied his remedies, and Lakṣmaṇa gaily rose and sat up. The Lord affectionately clasped his brother to his heart and all the bears and monkeys were rejoiced. The physician was then conveyed home again in the same manner as he had been brought away. When Rāvaṇa heard what had happened, he was greatly disturbed and began beating his head. In his agitation, he went to see Kumbhakarṇa and with much trouble succeeded in awakening him. When the monster was roused, he showed like Death itself in visible form. He asked, "Tell me, brother, why is your face so sad." He told him the whole history of how in his pride he had carried off Sītā. "Brother, the monkeys have killed all the demons and routed my stoutest warriors, Durmukha and the man-devouring Suraripu; Atikāya and Akaṁpana, those valiant warriors, together with Mahodara and other valiant heroes, who have fallen on the field of battle."

Dohā 62

On hearing Rāvaṇa's report, Kumbhakarṇa cried out: "Fool, you have carried off the Mother of the universe and yet expect to prosper !

Caupāī 63

You have done ill. O Demon King; and now why have you come and awakened me ? At once, brother, abandon your pride and worship Rāma: so shall you prosper. How, Ten-headed, can Rāma be a man, when he has such a servant as Hanumān. Alas, brother, you have acted very foolishly; why did you not come and wake me before ? You have rebelled against the god who is adored by Śiva and Brahmā and every other divinity. The knowledge which the sage Nārada imparted to me, I now declare to you; for the time has come. Embrace me, my brother, for I go to rejoice my eyes with the sight of the dark-hued, lotus-eyed healer of every sorrow!"

Dohā 63

As he meditated on Rāma's beauty and perfection, he was for a moment unconscious, then demanded of Rāvaṇa a million jars of wine and a whole herd of buffaloes.

Caupāī 64

After he had eaten the buffaloes and drunk the wine, he roared aloud with a voice of thunder and sallied forth from the stronghold without any escort, maddened with drink, the war-loving Kumbhakarṇa. Vibhīsana, on seeing him, ran forward and fell at his feet and declared who he was. He raised his brother and clasped him to his heart, delighted to find him a worshipper of Rāma. "Brother, that wretch Rāvaṇa struck me with his foot for giving him the best possible advice. Resenting such treatment, I came to Rāma, and the Lord was glad at heart to accept me as his humble servant." "Mark me, brother, Rāvaṇa is under the influence of face and will listen to no advice, however good. Thrice blessed are you, Vibhīṣaṇa, the glory of all the demon race; you have shed a lustre on all your kinsfolk by your worship of Rāma, that ocean of beauty and felicity.

Dohā 64

You have guilelessly worshipped the heroic Rāma in thought, word and deed. But go now; I cannot distinguish here between friend and foe; I am a warrior destined to die."

Caupāī 65

On hearing his brother's words, Vibhīṣaṇa departed and presented himself before the jewel of the three spheres. "My Lord, Kumbhakarṇa approaches; a warrior huge of stature as a mountain." The monkeys waited to hear no more, but ran off jabbering, the stoutest of them, and plucked up trees and rocks, which they hurled against him, gnashing their teeth the while. Millions and millions of mountain peaks did the bears and monkeys hurl upon him one after another; but neither did his courage fail, nor did he stir from his position; like an elephant pelted with flower-seeds. At last the Son of the Wind gave him a blow with his fist; he fell to the ground and beat his head in dismay. Rising again, he gave Hanumān such a blow that he spun round and fell at once to the earth. Next he overthrew upon the plain Nala and Nīla and dashed down the chiefs, hurling them this side and that. The monkey host took to flight in an utter panic, nor were there any to rally.

Dohā 65

Having rendered Aṅgada and the other monkeys unconscious, and Sugrīva as well, he pressed the king of the monkeys under his arm and went off, in his illimitable might.

Caupāī 66

O Umā, when Rāma plays the part of a man, it is like Garuṛ sporting in company with snakes. If he but knit his brows, he annihilates Death himself, how then can he condescend to such a combat as this ? The answer is that the fame of it, when spread abroad, tends to the redemption of the world, and mortals, who make it their song, emerge safely from the ocean of existence. When he regained consciousness, the Son of the Wind awoke and began at once to look for Sugrīva. But Sugrīva, on recovering from his swoon, slipped out of Kumbhakarṇa's clutches, who had taken him for dead. Having bitten of his nose and ears, he with a shout ascended into the air; but the giant saw him and caught him by the foot and dashed him to the ground. With wonderful agility he rose and struck him back and then betook himself—the hero—to the presence of his Lord, crying, 'Victory, victory, victory to the Fountain of Mercy.' But he, when he became sensible of his mutilated nose and ears, turned in a flurry and with sore distress of soul. The monkey host were horror-stricken when they saw the terrible warrior thus earless and noseless.

Dohā 66

Raising a shout of 'Victory to Rāma,' the monkeys rushed forward, and all at once hurled upon him a volley of rocks and trees.

Caupāī 67

Maddened with the rage of battle, Kumbhakarṇa advanced, furious as Death, and seized and devoured myriads of monkeys, like locusts swallowed up in a mountain cave; myriads of others he crushed with his body, and myriads he ground to powder let mingle with the dust of the earth. But hosts of bears and monkeys escaped, by the passage of his mouth, or nostrils or ears. Drunk with the madness of battle, the demon was as boastful as though the whole universe had been made over to him to ravage. Every champion took to flight, and there was no turning them back; they could neither see with their eyes nor hear any cry. When they learnt that Kumbhakarṇa had utterly routed the monkey host, the demons all rallied. But Rāma saw his army in distress and the forces of the enemy coming on in full array.

Dohā 67

"Hearken, Sugrīva and Vibhīṣaṇa, and you my brother," said the Lotus-eyed, "collect your troops and let me test the might of these miscreants," thus cried the lotus-eyed.

Caupāī 68

With bow ready in hand and quiver fitted to his side, Raghunātha went forth to scatter the ranks of the enemy. The Lord gave his bow a preliminary twang; the hosts of the foe were deafened by the din. Then he let fly a million of arrows, he, the god ever faithful to his promise; the winged shafts sped like serpents of death. The terrible volleys flew in all directions; the mighty demon warriors were cut to pieces. Feet, trunk, head, and arms were shorn away: many a hero was cut into a hundred pieces. The wounded reel and fall to the ground, but gallantly recover themselves and rise again to renew the fight. The arrows as they strike give a thud like thunder: many fled when they saw how terrible they were. Headless bodies rush madly on; they cry resounds, 'Seize! Seize! Kill! Kill!'

Dohā 68

In a moment Raghubīra's arrows cut to pieces the terrible demons; and then his shafts all came back into the quiver.

Caupāī 69

When Kumbhakarṇa saw and perceived that the demon host had been routed in a minute, the mighty warrior waxed exceeding worth and roared aloud with the voice of a lion. In his fury, he tore up mountains by the root and hurled them upon the throng of monkey chiefs. The Lord saw the monstrous rocks coming and with his arrows shattered them into dust. Again Raghunāyaka indignantly strung his bow and let fly a volley of his terrible shafts. As they entered and passed through his body, they seemed like flashes of lightning stored in a dense thunder cloud. The streams of blood on his black frame resembled rivers of red ochre on a mountain of soot. Perceiving his discomfiture, the bears and monkeys rushed forward; he laughed when he saw them draw near.

Dohā 69

Roaring aloud he seized myriads and myriads of the monkeys, and dashed them to the ground like a lion, invoking the name of Rāvaṇa.

Caupāī 70

The bears and monkeys all fled, like a flock of sheep at the sight of a wolf; and in their flight, Bhavānī, they cried aloud in their distress with a piteous voice: "This demon is for the monkey race like a sore famine that threatens to devastate a whole country! O Rāma, Kharāri, rain-cloud of mercy, ever ready to relieve the distress of the suppliant, have mercy upon us, have mercy upon us." When the Lord God heard their piteous cry, he took his bow and arrows and went forth. His army he checked in the rear and went forth in his own might, full of indignation. He drew his bow and fitted a hundred arrows to the string; they flew forth and entered into his body. At their stroke he rushed forth enraged; the mountains reeled, the earth staggered. He tore up a rock, but Rāma shot away his arm. Again he rushed on, with a rock in his left hand; but that arm too Rāma cut off and it fell to the ground. The monster thus robbed of his arms resembled mount Mandara without its wings. With savage eyes, he glared upon the Lord, as though ready to devour the whole universe.

Dohā 70

Uttering a most terrible shriek, he rushed on with wide open mouth. The saints and gods in the heavens cried out in their terror, 'Alas! Alas!'

Caupāī 71

When the All-merciful saw that the gods were frightened, he drew his bow with its string to his ear. The flight of arrows filled the demon's mouth, yet he was so strong that he did not fall to the ground. With his mouth full of arrows, he still rushed upon the foe, like a living quiver of death. Then the Lord in his wrath took a keen shaft and struck his head right off his trunk. The head fell at the feet of Rāvaṇa, who was as dismayed at the sight as a snake that has dropped its crest jewel. The ground sank beneath the weight of the trunk, as it still ran madly on: till the Lord cut it in two. Then it fell to the earth like a mountain from the sky, crushing beneath it monkeys, bears, and demons. His spirit entered the Lord's mouth, to the astonishment of gods, saints, and all. The gods in their delight beat kettle-drums and hymned his praise, and rained down flowers in abundance. After paying homage, all the gods went their way. At that time came also the divine sage, Nārada, and extolled above the heaven Hari's infinite perfection. The Lord's soul was pleased by his stirring heroic strain. 'Make haste to destroy these miscreants' were the sage's words as he left. Rāma remained glorious on the field of battle.

Chand 3

All-glorious shone forth Raghupati on the field of battle, in his immeasurable might and manifold beauty, with the sweat of toil on his lotus face, with his lovely eyes and his body flecked with drops of blood, while in both hands he brandished his bow and arrows, with the bears and monkeys grouped all around him. Not Śeṣanāga with his many tongues could tell all his beauty, so says Tulasī Dāsa.

Dohā 71

Though the demons were so vile and very mines of impurity, he translated them to his own sphere. O Umā, how dull of understanding are the men who do not worship the divine Rāma !

Caupāī 72

At the close of the day both armies retired; the battle had thoroughly exhausted the stoutest warriors. But by Rāma's favour the monkey host gathered fresh strength, like as a fire blazes up when fed with straw; while the demons wasted away day and night, like the merit of a man's good deeds when he tells them himself. Rāvaṇa made great lamentation, again and again taking his brother's head in his lap. His wives also wept and beat their breast with their hands, while they told of his pre-eminent majesty and vigour. At this juncture Meghanāda arrived and with many words consoled his father : "Be witness tomorrow of my valiant deeds; what need now of boastful speeches ? I have received from my patron divinity a chariot of strength, the virtue; of which I have never yet shown you, father." While he was thus bragging, the day broke and swarms of monkeys assailed the four gates. On the one side were the bears, and monkeys terrible as death; on the other the demons; fiercest of warriors. Valiantly they fight, each thirsting for victory; the battle, Garuṛ, baffles all description.

Dohā 72

Meghanāda mounted his magic chariot and ascended into the air with a laugh like the roar of thunder, which struck the monkey army with terror.

Caupāī 73

Spears, lances, swords, and scimitars were hurled down, with weapons and missiles of every description; axes, hatchets, clubs and stones, and then a shower of innumerable arrows. The heaven was as dark all round with arrows as when the constellation Maghā[1] pours down its torrents. 'Seize, seize, kill, kill', were the cries that sounded in their ears, but none could tell who it was that struck them. Snatching up rocks and trees, the monkeys sprang into the air, but still they could not see him and fell back disappointed. Ravines, gorges, roads, and mountain-caves were turned by his magic power into arrowy cages. The monkeys were confounded and knew not where to turn, and fell to the ground like the mountains fallen in bondage to Indra.[2] Hanumān, Aṅgada, Nala, Nīla, and every other warrior he sorely distressed; then he assailed with his shafts Lakṣmaṇa, Sugrīva and Vibhīṣaṇa, piercing their bodies through and through again. Lastly he joined in combat with Rāma himself and let fly his arrows, which as they struck turned to snakes. Kharāri was rendered powerless by the serpents' coils, he, the great free agent, the everlasting, the one immutable, who like a juggler performs all sorts of delusive actions, but is ever his own master, Rāma, our Lord. It was only to enhance the glory of the battle that he allowed himself to be bound by the serpents' coils; but the gods were in a panic.

Dohā 73

Is it, O Umā, possible for him to be brought into bondage, by whose name when repeated in prayer the sages free themselves from the bonds of existence; who is the omnipresent centre of the universe ?

Caupāī 74

O Bhavānī, the actions of the incarnate Rāma are beyond the range of thought, or human strength, or speech. This is the reason why the wisest ascetics discard theological speculations and simply adore. Having thus thrown the army into confusion, Meghanāda at last manifested himself with words of reviling.

1. Maghā is reckoned as the tenth of the Nakṣatras and is the ascendant in the month of Bhādrapada, at the height of the rains. Hence the saying *mata ke parase aur Maghā ke barase.*

2. Indra, the wielder of the thunderbolt, is represented as the mountains' master, or jailor, the word *bandi* here is not the participle of the verb 'to reverence,' but the noun meaning a captive or 'slave'.

Jāmbavān shouted: 'Wretch, keep your place.' On hearing this, the demon waxed all the more furious. 'Fool, I only spared you on account of your age, I think scorn of your challenge.' So saying, he let fly his terrible trident; Jāmbavān caught it in his hand and then rushed on and gave Meghanāda such a blow on the chest that he. the scourge of heaven, fell swooning to the ground. Then in his wrath he caught him by the foot and swung him round and dashed him on the earth as a display of his strength. But he by virtue of the divine boon died not for all his killing; so he took him by the foot and tossed him into Laṅkā, while the gods and saints sent Garur, who came in haste to Rāma,

Dohā 74a-74b

And seized and swallowed the whole swarm of false serpents. The delusion was dispelled, and all the monkey host rejoiced again. Tearing up with their claws the trees and rocks of the mountain, they rushed forward, while the demons fled in utter confusion and climbed up into the fort.

Caupāī 75

When Meghanāda recovered from his swoon, he was greatly ashamed to look his father in the face, and arose and went off at once to a cave in the mountain, intending to perform a sacrifice that would ensure victory. But Vibhīsana gave the caution: "Hearken, O king of unbounded might and generosity, Meghanāda is preparing an unholy sacrifice—wretched sorcerer and scourge of heaven as he is—and if he bring it to completion, Sire, it will not be easy to overcome him." On hearing this, Raghupati was highly pleased and said to Aṅgada and the other monkeys: "Go, my brothers, you and Laksmana, and put a stop to his sacrifice. It is for you, Lakṣmaṇa, to slay him; in battle; I am distressed to see the terror of the gods. Kill him, either by open force or by stratagem; one way or another—mark me, brother—the demon must be got rid of. But you three, Jāmbavān, Sugrīva and Vibhīṣaṇa, remain with the army." When Raghubīra had finished his commands, the hero girt his quiver by his side and took his bow, and with the glory of his Lord impressed upon his heart, cried aloud with a mighty voice as of thunder: "If I return this day without slaying him, may I be no longer called Rāma's servant! Though a hundred Śivas give him help, I will slay him yet, in the name of Rāma."

Dohā 75

After bowing his head before Rāma's feet, Lakṣmaṇa went forth at once and with him Aṅgada, Nīla, Mayanda, Nala, and the valiant Hanumān.

Caupāi 76

When the monkeys arrived, they found him making an oblation of blood and buffalo's flesh. They all tried to interrupt the ceremony, but he would not stir; they then took to praising him.[1] When still he did not rise, they went and pulled him by the hair, upon which he kicked out so fiercely that they ran away. He pursued them with his trident as they fled, till they joined Laksmana. He came on in the wildest fury, striking and crying out again and again with a terrible roar. Hanumān and Aṅgada rushed fiercely at him, but he smote them on the breast with his trident and beat them to the ground. Then he shot forth his mighty spear at the Lord, but he warded it off and broke it in two. Meanwhile the Son of the Wind and the prince had risen again and smote him furiously; but his wounds had no effect upon him. The heroes fell upon him once more, but their enemy was not to be killed; again he came on with a terrible shriek. Then Lakṣmaṇa made up his mind; 'I have played with this miscreant long enough,' and seeing him advance, furious as hell, he let fly his terrible shaft. When he saw the arrow coming on like a thunderbolt, the wretch at once disappeared from sight and continued fighting under various disguises, now visible and now invisible. The monkeys thought him invincible and trembled. Then Lakṣmaṇa, the incarnation of the Serpent King, became exceeding wroth and directing his intention to the glory of the Lord of Kosala, fitted an arrow to

1. That is, they enlarged upon his strength and courage and wondered why he should turn from fighting to sacrifice.

the string and with all his might let it fly. It struck him full in the breast. In the moment of death he abandoned all falsehood,

Dohā 76

And invoking the names of Lakṣmaṇa and Rāma drew his last breath. 'Blessed, blessed indeed is thy mother', cried Aṅgada and Hanumān.[1]

Caupāī 77

Without an effort Hanumān lifted up his body and put it at the gate of the city and returned. When they heard of his death, the gods and Gandharvas mounted their chariots and came thronging the heaven, showering down flowers and beating drums and hymning the spotless renown of the Lord Raghubīra. 'Glory to Śeṣanāga! Glory to the world-supporter! You, O Lord, are the Saviour of all he gods.' Having thus hymned his praises, the gods and saints withdrew, while Lakṣmaṇa went and presented himself before the Lord of mercy. When the Ten-headed heard of his son's death, he swooned away and fell to the ground; Mandodarī made grievous lamentation, beating her breast and ever calling upon his name; the citizens too were all sorrowful and dismayed and with one consent upbraided the Ten-headed.

Dohā 77

Then Rāvaṇa set to comforting his wives in every way he could : "See and consider at heart how transitory is everything in this world."

Caupāī 78

Rāvaṇa gave them sound advice; though evil himself, his counsel was good and wholesome. There are many men who excel in giving advice, but the people who put it in practice are not very plentiful. When the night had passed and the day broke, the bears and monkeys again beset the four gates. Rāvaṇa summoned his warriors and thus addressed them: "If anyone's

1. For giving birth to such a gallant warrior and one who showed such faith in the hour of death.

heart fail him in facing the battle, he should better withdraw now and not incur disgrace by running away in the midst of the engagement. Relying on the strength of my own arms, I have continued the struggle, and can give an answer to any enemy who may challenge me." So saying, he made ready his chariot, swift as the wind, while every instrument of music sounded forth a strain of deadly combat. His stalwarts marched on in their peerless might, like the march of a whirlwind of soot. At that time occurred numberless omens of ill, but he heeded them not, in the overweening pride of the strength of his arms.

Chand 4

In his overweening pride, he took no heed of omens, good or bad. Weapons dropped from the hand; warriors fell from their cars: horses, frightened by the trumpeting of the elephants, ran out of the line: jackals, vultures and huge packs of dogs made a frightful clamour, and owls, like harbingers of dooms, uttered their most lugubrious notes.

Dohā 78

How was it possible for him to have prosperous omens of good fortune, or even to dream of peace of mind, when he was so infatuated that he desired the ruin of the whole world and was set upon opposing Rāma ?

Caupāi 79

The huge demon host marched on in countless number: elephants and chariots, foot and horse, line after line; equipages of every description, wagons and cars, with banners and standards of diverse colour; innumerable troops of infuriated elephants like autumn clouds when driven by wind; battalions of savage demons of different colours, inspired with all the frenzy of martial heroes: an army magnificent in every respect, like the mustered array of the gallant god of spring. As the host marched forth, the elephants of the eight quarters reeled, the ocean was stirred from its depths, the mountains shook. Dust rose in clouds that obscured the sun, the wind failed, and the earth was troubled. Drums and other instruments of music made an awful din, like the crash of thunder-clouds on the last day. Clarions. trumpets, and hautboys sounded the martial strain that gladdens the souls of heroes. With one accord they roared like so many lions, each extolling his own strength and manhood. Rāvana cried: "Hearken, my warriors; do you attack the common herd of bears and monkeys; I myself will slay the two brother princes." So saying, he ordered the army to advance to the front. When the monkeys heard the news, they all rushed on, calling on the name of Rāma.

Chand 5

The gigantic and terrible bears and monkeys rushed on like Doom; flying through the air like so many winged mountains of diverse colours. With talons and teeth and rocks and lofty trees for weapons, they all feel no fear, singing the glory of Rāma, the lion-like vanquisher of the wild elephant Rāvaṇa.

Dohā 79

With a cry of victory raised from both sides, the heroes selected each his match and closed in combat, these calling on Rāvaṇa.

Caupāī 80

When Vibhīṣaṇa beheld Rāvaṇa mounted on a chariot and Rāma on foot, he became apprehensive; his extreme affection made him doubtful of mind, and falling at his feet, he cried tenderly: "My Lord, you have neither a chariot nor shoes to your feet, how can you conquer so powerful a warrior ?" "Hearken, my friend," replied the Lord of grace, "a conqueror has a different kind of chariot. Manliness and courage are his chariot wheels; unflinching truthfulness and morality his banners and standards; strength, discretion, self-control and benevolence his horses, with grace, mercy and equanimity for their harness: prayer to Mahādeva his unerring charioteer; continence his shield, contentment his sword, alms-giving his axe, knowledge his mighty spear, and perfect science his stout bow. His pure and constant soul stands for a quiver, his pious practices of devotion for a sheaf of arrows, and the revenue he pays to Brāhmaṇas and his guru is his impenetrable coat of mail. There is no equipment for victory that can be compared to this, nor is there any enemy, my friend, who can conquer the man who rides upon this chariot of righteousness.

Dohā 80a-80c

He who owns such a powerful chariot as this is a hero who can vanquish even that great and terrible enemy, the world; hearken, friend, and fear not." When he had heard his Lord's exhortation, Vibhiṣaṇa clasped his feet in his joy and cried, "O Rāma, full of mercy and kindness, you have taken this occasion to teach me a lesson." On the one side Rāvaṇa's rabble, on the other Aṅgada and Hanumān, the demons against the bears and monkeys had joined in battle, each swearing by his own lord.

Caupāī 81

Brahmā and the other gods, with all the saints and sages, mounted their chariots to watch the fray, from the heaven above. I too, Umā, was with them, beholding Rāma's exploits on the field of battle. On both sides the leaders were triumphant through the might of Rāma. With shouts of defiance, they closed in single combat, each mauling his foe and beating him to the ground. They struck, they bit, they clutched, they fell; they tore off heads and used them for missiles; they tore out their stomachs, wrenched off their arms, and seizing by the leg dashed them to the ground. The bears bury the demon warriors in the earth and pile over them heaps of sand; the sturdy monkeys raging in the fight were like so many monstrous images of ravaging death to look upon.

Chand 6

The monkeys, their bodies all streaming with gore, stood forth like multiplied images of the god of death, crushing the mightiest champions of the demon host and roaring like thunder. They struck them, they cuffed them, they tore them with the teeth, they crushed them beneath the feet, uttering fierce cries, both bears and monkeys, and employing strength and stratagem alike, by which to reduce the miscreants. They seized and tore open their cheeks, they ripped up the belly and took the entrails and hung them round their own necks, as though the Lord of Prahlāda (Narasiṁha) had assumed a multiplicity of forms, and were disporting himself on the field of battle. 'Seize, strike, tear, overthrow,' were the savage cries, with which earth and heaven resounded. Glory to Rāma, who can make a straw a thunderbolt and again reduce a thunderbolt to a straw.

Dohā 81

When he saw his troops in confusion, Rāvaṇa mounted his chariot, with his twenty arms and ten bows, and essayed to rally them, crying, 'Turn! Turn!'

Caupāī 82

The Ten-headed rushed forth in wild fury, and the monkeys with a whoop advanced to meet him. Taking in their hands trees, crags and mountains, together they all hurled them upon him. But as soon as the masses of stone struck his adamantine frame, they were at once shattered into pieces, while he flinched not, but stood firm as a rock and stayed his chariot, he, Rāvaṇa, maddened with the battle and terrible in his fury. This side and that, he scattered and battered the monkey warriors in the fierceness of his wrath. Bears and monkeys all took to flight, crying, "Help, help, Aṅgada, Hanumān! Save, save, O Lord Ragbubīra! This monster, as sure as death, will devour us all!" When he saw the monkeys in flight, he fitted an arrow to each of his ten bows.

Chand 7

He strung his bow and let fly a volley of arrows; they flew on and struck them like serpents; the heaven and the earth were full of arrows; the monkeys fled in all directions. There was a terrible uproar, the monkey host and the bears were panic-stricken and cried in dismay; "O Raghubīra, fountain of compassion! O Hari, O friend of the forlorn, saviour of the faithful!"

Dohā 82

Seeing the distress of his army, Lakṣmaṇa slung his quiver by his side, took his bow in his hand and sallied forth in a fury, after bowing his head at Rāma's feet.

Caupāī 83

"Ah! vile wretch," he said, "you kill bears and monkeys; but now look at me, I am your doom!" "I have been searching for you, you murderer of my son, and today I will gladden my soul by your destruction." Thus he cried and let fly a storm of keen arrows; but Lakṣmaṇa shivered them all into a hundred pieces. Then Rāvaṇa hurled upon him myriads of missiles, but he warded them off as though they had been tiny sesamum seeds, and in turn assailed him with his own shafts, smashing his chariot and killing his charioteer. Each of his ten heads he transfixed with a hundred arrows, which seemed like serpents boring their way into the peaks of a mountain. With a hundred arrows more he struck him in the breast: he fell senseless to the ground. When the swoon had passed off, he rose again with his vigour renewed and let fly the bolt given him by Brahmā.

Chand 8

The mighty bolt, the gift of Brahmā, smote the incarnate Śeṣanāga full in the breast; the hero fell fainting; the Ten-headed tried to lift up his body, but failed to do so despite all the might of his unequalled strength. In his folly Rāvaṇa thought to carry him off, not knowing him to be the Lord of the three spheres, who supports on one of his heads the whole created universe, as though it were a mere grain of sand.

Dohā 83

When the Son of the Wind saw this, he rushed forward with a furious cry; but as the monkey came on, he struck him a violent blow with his fist.

Caupāī 84

The monkey dropped on the knee but did not fall to the ground and, on recovering himself, arose full of exceeding wrath, and smote him one blow; he fell like a mountain struck by a thounderbolt. When he recovered from the swoon and regained his consciousness, he marvelled greatly at the monkey's mighty strength. "Shame on my manhood, shame on myself, if you remain alive, you plague of heaven." So cried the monkey, as he carried Lakṣmaṇa away. At this sight Rāvaṇa was greatly astonished. Said Raghubīra, on finding his brother still alive: "You are indeed the destroyer of death and the saviour of the gods." On hearing these words, the gracious Lord arose and sat up, and the terrible bolt vanished into the heaven. Then again they took bow and arrows and rushed forward with the utmost impetuosity to meet the enemy.

Chand 9

Again, by their impetuous attack, they put him to confusion, smashing his chariot and slaying his charioteer. Rāvaṇa fell fainting to the ground, his heart transfixed by a hundred arrows. Another charioteer threw him on his car and carried him to Laṅkā, while Lakṣmaṇa in all his glory bowed before Rāma's feet.

Dohā 84

Meanwhile Rāvaṇa, on recovering, began to make preparations for a sacrifice; fool to oppose Rāma and yet hope to prosper; obstinate and ignorant indeed!

Caupāī 85

In Rāma's camp Vibhīṣaṇa, on learning the news, went at once and told Raghupati, "My Lord, Rāvaṇa is engaged in a sacrifice; if he completes it, the wretch will never die. Dispatch your valiant monkeys, sire, in all speed, to cut short his life." At early dawn, the Lord dispatched his warriors. Hanumān, Aṅgada, and all started forth. Bounding with glee, the monkeys climbed Laṅkā and boldly entered Rāvaṇa's palace. Finding him engaged in the sacrifice, they all became furiously angry and cried, "You run away home without shame from the battle and on getting here practise this hypocrisy!"[1] So saying, Aṅgada gave him a kick, but the wretch took no notice, so absorbed was he in his own purpose.

Chand 10

As he took no notice of them, the monkeys in a fury tore him with their teeth and kicked him with their feet; his wives, too, they seized by the hair and dragged them out of doors, till the poor wretches screamed again. Then at last he rose, terrible as death, and caught a monkey by the leg and hurled him away, but seeing that the monkeys had thus succeeded in interrupting the sacrifice, he was in deep despair.

Dohā 85

Rejoicing at having upset his sacrifice, the monkeys returned to Raghupati, while the demon went off in a fury, abandoning all hope of life.

Caupāī 86

Terrible omens of ill met him as he went, for vultures flew and settled on his heads. Destined to die, he paid no heed, but gave the order to sound the onset. There seemed no end to the demon host as it marched on, with its many elephants, chariots, foot-soldiers and horsemen. The miscreants hastened to confront the Lord, like a swarm of gnats when they fly into the fire. Meanwhile, the gods sang songs of praise and said, "He has caused us grievous trouble; play with him no longer, O Rāma, for Sītā is in sore distress." On hearing the prayer of the gods. Rāma smiled[2] and rose and made ready his arrows.

1. *Vak-dhyān*, literally, 'the contemplation of a crane,' *i.e.*, the affectation of being absorbed in divine contemplation, while really thinking only of worldly interests; like the crane, which seems lost in abstraction, but is only waiting for a fish to pounce upon.

2. Knowing that the gods were chiefly anxious on their own account, though they professed to be only thinking about Sītā.

He bound his hair tightly in a knot on his forehead, beautiful with the flowers that had here and there been caught (as they fell upon him from heaven). With his bright eyes and his body dark of hue as a rain-cloud, rejoicing the sight of every created sphere, he girt his belt and quiver on his loins and took in his hand his mighty bow, the bow of Viṣṇu.

Chand 11

With his Śārṅga bow in his hand and his beautiful quiver full of arrows slung by his side, with his muscular arms and fine broad chest adorned with the print of the Brāhmaṇa's foot, when the Lord—says Tulasī Dāsa—began to handle his bow and arrows, the elephants that support the world, the tortoise, the serpent and the earth itself with its mountains and seas, all reeled.

Dohā 86

The gods rejoiced at the sight of his splendour and rained down flowers in abundance, singing, 'Glory, glory, glory to the Lord of compassion, the storehouse of beauty, strength and perfection.'

Caupāī 87

Meanwhile, the demon hosts came rolling on in infinite number. The monkey warriors at the sight advanced to meet them, like the thunder clouds gathered at the last day. Spears, lances and swords flashed again, like gleams of lightning from every quarter of the heaven. The awful din of elephants, chariots and horses was like the thundering of a frightful tempest. The monkeys' huge tails as they stretched across the sky were like the uprising of a magnificent rainbow. The dust was borne aloft like a cloud, and the arrows fell like a copious shower. The mountains hurled from either side fell in continuous showers like thunderbolts. When Rāma in his wrath poured forth his arrows, the demon crew were sore smitten. At the smart of his shafts the warriors screamed with pain, and everywhere reeled and fell to the ground. The rocks streamed as it were with cascades in a river of blood, the terror of cowards.

Chand 12

A most loathsome river of blood, striking cowards with terror, flowed on between the two armies for its banks, with chariots for sand and wheels for eddies—a frightful flood—with elephants foot-soldiers, and horses for its aquatic birds; and vehicles of every kind, more than one could count, for its reeds and grasses; with arrows, clubs and lances for its snakes, bows for its waves, and shields for its shoals of tortoises.

Dohā 87

The fallen heroes were like trees on its bank, the marrow of their bones its scum. Cowards trembled at the sight, but the gallant were dauntless of soul.

Caupāī 88

Those who bathed in it were imps, demons and goblins, monstrous ghouls and horrible vampires. Crows and vultures flew off with human arms, which they tore from one another and seized and devoured. Said one, 'At such a time of plenty, you wretch, is your hunger still unsatisfied ?[1] Wounded champions, fallen on the bank, uttered groans like the dying left half in and half out of the water.[2] Vultures sat on the bank and tore the entrails of the dead, like fishermen intent on their rods. Many bodies floated down with birds upon them, as if they were boating in a river. Witches drew water in skulls; other female demons and goblins danced in the air, clashing the skulls of warriors for cymbals, while the infernal goddesses sang song after song. Herds of jackals snarled and growled and scampered about devouring till they were gorged. Thousands of headless bodies roamed the plain, while the heads fallen to the ground still shouted, 'Victory! Victory!'

1. That you must come and steal from me instead of foraging for yourself.

2. By *arddha jal*, 'half in the water,' is meant a dying man who has been taken by his friends and laid on the very edge of the river, so that he may breathe his last in the sacred stream.

Chand 13

The heads cried, 'Victory! Victory!' while the headless trunks rushed wildly about. Swords and skulls were inextricably involved, hero against hero, fighting and overthrowing. The monkeys trampled down the demon crew and triumphed through the power of Rāma. Smitten by Rāma's arrows the brave were sleeping on the field of battle.

Dohā 88

Rāvaṇa thought to himself, "The demons are routed ; I am alone, the bears and monkeys are many ; I must put forth all my magic power."

Caupāī 89

When the gods saw that the Lord was on foot, they were exceedingly disturbed in mind, and Indra at once despatched his own chariot. Mātali brought it gladly, a splendid chariot, divine, incomparable ; the king of Kosala was delighted to mount it. Its four beautiful and high mettled steeds, deathless and ever young, flew swift as thought. When they saw Raghunātha mounted on a car, the monkeys rushed forward with renewed vigour. Their onset was irresistible. Then Rāvana exerted his magic power. Raghubīra knew it to be a mere delusion, but Lakṣmaṇa and the monkeys took it for reality. They saw among the demon ranks many Rāmas and as many Laksmanas.

Chand 14

Seeing the multitude of Rāmas and Laksmanas, the monkeys and bears were greatly dismayed ; wherever they looked, they saw him standing, as in a picture, and Laksmana with him. The Lord of Kosala smiled to see the perplexity of his troops: Hari made ready his bow and in a moment destroyed the delusion ; all the monkey host rejoiced again.

Dohā 89

Then Rāma looked upon them all and cried with a mighty voice : "Watch now the combat between us two, for my captains are all a-wearied."

Caupāī 90

So saying, Raghunātha urged forward his chariot after bowing his head before the Brāhmaṇa's lotus feet. Then was the king of Laṅkā mad with rage and rushed to meet him, challenging him with a voice of thunder : "As for the warriors you have defeated in battle, mark me, hermit, I am not like them. The glory of Rāvaṇa's name is known throughout the world, and how he cast into prison the regents of the spheres. You forsooth have slain Khara and Dūsana and Virādha and killed poor Bāli, lying in ambush for him like a huntsman. You have routed the leaders of the demon host, and put to death Kumbhakarṇa and Meghanāda. But to-day I will make an end of all this fighting ; unless, indeed, you save yourself by flight from the field. To-day, wretch, I shall surely consign you to death ; you have now to deal with the mighty Rāvaṇa." On hearing this abusive speech, the All-merciful, knowing him to be death-doomed, smiled and answered: "True, true, I have heard all about your mighty power ; but no more boasting words, let me see your strength.

Chand 15

Do not destroy your reputation by bragging, but listen patiently to the lesson I give you. In this world there are three kinds of men, resembling respectively the *dhāk*, the mango, and the bread-fruit tree. The one has flowers, the second flowers and fruit, and the third only fruit. The one talks; the second talks and acts ; the third only acts, but says not a word."

Dohā 90

On hearing Rāma's speech, he laughed and said, "Now you are for teaching me wisdom, aren't you? You did not fear to challenge me ; but at last you begin to hold your life dear."

Caupāī 91

Having uttered this taunt, Rāvaṇa in a fury began to let fly his arrows like so many thunderbolts. The shafts of many shapes sped forth till every quarter of heaven and earth was filled with the cloud of them. Raghubīra discharged an arrow of fire, and in a moment the demon's bolts were all consumed. He gnashed his teeth and hurled forth his mighty spear ; the Lord turned it with as arrow and sent it back. Then he cast against him thousands of discs and tridents ; but the Lord without an effort snapped them and turned them aside. Rāvaṇas artillery was as unavailing as are always the schemes of the wicked. Then with a hundered arrows at once he struck the charioteer, who fell to the ground, crying, 'Victory to Rāma !" So the Lord had compassion upon him and raised him up again but a terrible fury then possessed him.

Chand 16

Full of fury and raging in the battle, Raghupati's very arrows were ready to jump out of his quiver. At the sound of the dreadful twang of his bow the man-eating monsters were seized with terror. Mandodarī's heart quaked : the sea, the great tortoise, the earth and its supporter trembled ; the elephants of the quarters squealed and grasped the world tight in their jaws, while the gods laughed to see the sport.

Dohā 91

He drew the bowstring to his ear and let fly his keen darts; they cleft the sky, quivering like so many serpents.

Caupāī 92

The arrows sped forth like winged serpents and at once laid low the charioteer and the horses, shattering the chariot and snapping the flagstaff. Though inwardly his courage failed him, he roared aloud and quickly mounted another car, and grinding his teeth let fly weapons and missiles of every description. But all his efforts were as fruitless as the thoughts of a man who delights only in harming others. Then Rāvaṇa hurled forth ten spears, which struck the four horses and felled them to the ground. Rāma was furious : he raised the horses and then drew his bow and let fly his arrows. The edge of Raghubīras shafts swept off Rāvaṇas heads as though they had been lotuses. He smote each of his ten heads with ten arrows : the blood gushed forth in torrents. Streaming with gore, he rushed on in his strength ; but the Lord again fitted arrows to his bow and let fly thirty shafts; his heads and arms all fell to the ground. Again and yet again Rāma smote away his arms and heads ; for they had grown afresh after being cut off. Time after time the Lord struck off his arms and heads, but they were no sooner smitten off than they were again renewed. Again and again the Lord shred off his heads and arms. The king of Kosala mightily diverted himself. The whole heaven was full of the demon's heads and arms, like an infinite number of Ketus and Rāhus.[1]

Chand 17

Like a multitude of Rāhus and Ketus they rushed through the air streaming with blood ; for Raghubīra's fatal arrows had such force that once they struck a thing it could not fall to the ground. Each arrow transfixing a set of heads seemed, as it flew through the sky, like a ray of the angry sun strung all over with moon-troublers.[2]

Dohā 92

As quickly as the Lord struck off his heads, they sprang up again without end, like the passions of a man devoted to the world, which increase ever more and more.

Caupāī 93

When Rāvaṇa saw this multiplication of his heads, he thought no more of death and waxed still more furious. He thundered

1. The demon Rāhu, having disguised himself as one of the gods, succeeded in securing a draught of the nectar which they had churned out of the ocean. The sun and moon, who had detected the impostor, gave information to Viṣṇu, who thereupon cut off the monster's head and two of his four arms. As he could not rob him of the immortality that the nectar had conferred, the severed head and tail were metamorphosed into heavenly bodies, under the names of Rāhu and Ketu, or the ascending and descending node, of which the former still wreaks vengeance on the sun and moon by now and again swallowing them.

2. *Vidhun-tuda*—literally 'the moon-troubler'—is another name for Rāhu.

aloud in his insane pride, and rushed forward with his ten bows all strung at once, raging wildly on the field of battle, and overwhelmed Rāma's chariot, with such a shower of arrows that for a moment it was quite lost to sight, as when the sun is obscured by a mist. When the gods cried out in alarm, the Lord wrathfully grasped his bow and parrying the arrows smote off his enemy's heads, which flew in all directions, covering heaven and earth. Severed as they were, they flew through the sky, uttering hideous cries of "Victory ! Victory ! Where is Lakṣmaṇa, where Sugrīva and Aṅgada? Where is Rāma, the prince of Kosala ?"

Chand 18

"Where now is Rāma ?" cried the throng of heads as they sped through the air. The monkeys saw and turned to flight ; but the jewel of the race of Raghu, with a smile, made ready his bow and with his arrows shot the heads through and through. It was as though innumerable troops of Kālī were assembled with rosaries of skulls in their hands and had bathed in the river of Blood and come to worship at the banyan of War.

Dohā 93

Again Rāvaṇa in his fury hurled forth his mightiest spear : like the bolt of death it flew straight for Vibhīṣaṇa.

Caupāī 94

When he saw the dread spear coming and realizing that he had sworn to relieve the distress of his suppliants, Rāma at once put Vibhīṣaṇa behind him and exposed himself to the full force of the missile. When it struck him, the Lord swooned for a while, a mimicry which filled the gods with dismay. When Vibhīṣaṇa saw his lord fainting, he seized his club in his hand and rushed on in a fury : "Ah, ill-starred wretch ! You fool ! You dullard! You are enemy alike of gods, men, saints and Nāgas ! Inasmuch as you devoutly offered your head to Śiva, you have received a thousand for one in return. This is the only reason why as yet you have escaped; but now death is dancing on your pate. Fool, to oppose Rāma and yet hope to triumph!" So saying, he struck him on the chest with his club.

Chand 19

At the hard dread stroke of the mighty club on the chest he fell to the ground with his ten heads all streaming with blood; but he again picked himself up and came on full of fury. The two closed with all their might in savage wrestle, each mauling the other : but Vibhīṣaṇa was inspired with the strength of Rāma, and fell upon him as though he were of no account whatever.

Dohā 94

O Umā, Vibhīṣaṇa would not have dared of himself to challenge Rāvaṇa face to face ; but now in the might of Rāma he fought with him like very Death.

Caupāī 95

When Hanumān saw that Vibhīṣaṇa was sorely exhausted, he rushed forward with a rock in his hand, with which he crushed the chariot, horses and driver, and gave the demon himself a kick in the ribs. He stood erect but trembled all over. Vibhīṣaṇa escaped into the presence of the saviour of his servants. Then Rāvaṇa fell upon the monkey, who spread his tail and flew into the air. He caught hold of his tail and so was borne aloft with the monkey, the mighty Hanumān, who again turned and closed with him. The well-matched pair continued fighting overhead, each furiously bruising the other, and putting forth all his strength and skill ; as though mounts Añjana and Sumeru had come into collision in the heaven. The demon was so astute that there was no throwing him, till the Lord came to the support of the Son of the Wind.

Chand 20

Supported by the Lord Rāghubīra, the valiant monkey struck Rāvaṇa a violent blow. He fell to the ground, but rose again to fight, so that the gods shouted 'Victory ! Victory !' to both. Seeing Hanumān in such a strait, the monkeys and bears advanced in furious passion ; but Rāvaṇā, battle-mad, crushed all their stoutest champions with the might of his terrible arm.

Dohā 95

Incited by Raghubīra, the bold monkeys came on again. Seeing them to be so strong, he took recourse to his magic power.

Caupāī 96

In a moment he became invisible and then again showed himself in a multitude of forms. Every bear and monkey in Rāma's army saw a separate Rāvaṇa confronting him. At the sight of such an infinity of Rāvaṇas, the bears and monkeys fled in all directions. Not one of them had the courage to stay, but all fled crying, 'Help, Lakṣmaṇa; help, Raghubīra.' Myriads of Rāvaṇas pursued them on every side, thundering aloud with harsh and terrible cries. The gods were all panic-stricken and betook themselves to flight, saying : "Now, brother, abandon all hope of victory. A single Rāvaṇa subdued the heavenly host and now there are many of them ! Make for the caves in the mountain !" Only Brahmā and Sambhu and the wisest of the sages stood fast, who had some understanding of their Lord's greatness.

Chand 21

Those who understood his power remained fearless ; but the monkey took the apparitions for real enemies and fled, monkeys and bears alike, crying in their terror, 'Help, god of mercy !' Only Hanumān, Aṅgada, Nīla and Nala, the leaders of the warriors fought bravely on against the delusive growth of giants and crushed thousands and thousands of Rāvaṇas.

Dohā 96

The king of Kosala smiled to see the panic of the gods and monkeys, and stringing his bow dispersed with a single arrow the whole host of ten-headed kings.

Caupāī 97

In a moment the Lord dispersed the whole phantom scene, as darkness is scattered at the rising of the sun. Seeing only one

Rāvaṇa, the gods turned again with joy and showered down many flowers upon the Lord. Rāma then raised his arms aloft and rallied the monkeys, who turned again, each shouting to his neighbour. Inspired by the might of their lord, the bears and monkeys rushed on and with renewed vigour re-entered the arena. When Rāvaṇa saw the gods exulting, he muttered: "They think I am now reduced to one ; fools, you have ever been my prey." So saying, he made a savage spring into the air, and as the gods fled screaming, he cried : "Wretches, whither can you go from my presence?" Seeing their dismay, Aṅgada rushed forward and with a bound seized him by the foot and threw him to the ground.

Chand 22

Having seized and hurled him to the ground, the son of Bāli gave him a kick and then rejoined his lord. The Ten-headed, on recovering himself, rose again and thundered with a terrible harsh voice. Proudly he strung his bow, and fitting ten arrows to the string, he let fly many volleys, wounding all his enemies ; at the sight of their confusion he gloried in his might.

Dohā 97

Then Raghupati cut off Rāvaṇa's heads and arms, his arrows also and his bow ; but they all sprang up again, like sins committed at a holy place.

Caupāi 98

Seeing the multiplication of their enemy's heads and arms, the bears and monkeys were mightily indignant and rushed on in a fury, crying, "Will the wretch never die, with his heads and arms all cut off?" The son of Bāli, with Hanumān, Nala and Nīla, the monkey king Sugrīva and the valiant Dvivida, hurled upon him trees and mountains ; but he caught each mountain and tree and threw them back upon the monkeys. One ripped up the enemy's body with his claws, another would run past and kick him. But Nala and Nīla clambered up on to his heads and set to tearing his face with their talons. When he saw the blood, he was sore troubled in soul and stretched up his arms to catch them, but they were not to be caught and sprang about over his hands, like two bees hovering over a bed of lotuses. At last with a savage bound he clutched them both, but just as he was about to dash them to the ground they twisted his arms and escaped. Then in his fury he took his ten bows in his hands and with his arrows smote and wounded the monkeys, so that Hanumān and all were rendered senseless. The approach of night had invigorated him. Seeing all the monkey chiefs in swoon, the valiant Jāṁbavān rushed forward, and with him the bears, armed with mountains and trees, which they began hurling upon him. The mighty Rāvaṇa was furious, and many of the heroes he seized by the foot and dashed to the ground. Their king was wroth to see such havoc among his troops and gave him a savage kick on the breast.

Chand 23

The blow smote him so heavily on the breast that he fell fainting from his chariot to the ground, grasping a bear in each of his twenty hands, like bees hiding by night in the folds of the lotus. Seeing him unconscious, the king of the bears again struck him with his foot and then rejoined the Lord. As night had now come, the charioteer lifted Rāvaṇa on to the car and made off as best he could.

Dohā 98

On recovering from their swoon, the bears and monkeys all returned to Rāma ; while all the demons crowded round Rāvaṇa in the utmost consternation.

Cāupaī 99

During the night Trijaṭā went to Sītā and told her the whole story. When Sītā heard of the multiplication of the enemy's heads and arms, she was sorely dismayed and thus addressed Trijaṭā, with downcast face and much anxiety of soul : "Why don't you tell me, mother, what is to be done and how can this plague of the universe be put to death ? He will not die even though Raghupati's arrows have shorn off his heads; of a truth, God is making everything turn out perversely. It must be my ill fortune which keeps me alive; for I too survive, though separated from Rāma's lotus feet. The same fate that created the false phantom of the golden deer is still cruel to me. The god that enables me to support such insupportable anguish which made me speak crossly to Lakṣmaṇa, which keeps me alive under such pain, pierced through and through as I am with the poisoned shafts of Rāma's loss, shafts with which Love has smitten me : it is this god, I swear, that keeps him alive." With many such words did Jānaki make piteous lamentation, as she recalled to mind the All-merciful: "Hearken, royal maid," said Trijaṭā; "the enemy of the gods will die if an arrow strike him in the breast. But the Lord will not smite him there, because the image of Sītā is imprinted on his heart.

Chand 24

Jānakī dwells in his heart and in Jānakī's heart is my home; in my heart are all the spheres of creation; if an arrow lodge there all will be undone." On hearing this explanation, Sītā's soul swayed between grief and joy; but seeing her still uneasy in mind, Trijaṭā continued: "Now this is the way the monster will be killed; hearken, fair lady, and cease to be so greatly disquieted.

Dohā 99

In the pain of having his heads severed your image will be forgotten and the sagacious Rāma will then smite him in the heart."

Caupāī 100

With such words, having done all she could to comfort her, Trijaṭā returned home again. But Sītā, reflecting on Rāma's loving nature, was a prey to all the anguish of bereavement and broke out into reproaches of the night and the moon: "The night will never be spent, though it has seemed already an age long." In her heart of hearts she made sore lamentation, sorrowing for Rāma's loss . When the pangs of bereavement were at their very height, her left eye and arm began to throb. Considering this to be a good omen, she took courage: 'I shall now see again the gracious Raghubīra.' Meanwhile Rāvaṇa awoke at midnight and began abusing his charioteer: "Fool, to bring me away from the field of battle; a curse on you for a vile dullard!" He laid hold of his feet and deprecated his wrath; and he, as soon as it was dawn, mounted his chariot and sallied forth again. When they heard of Rāvaṇa's approach, the monkey troops were greatly excited, and rooting up mountains and trees on every side the terrible warriors rushed to the onset, gnashing their teeth.

Chand 25

The huge monkeys and awe-inspiring bears rushed on, with mountains in their hands, which they hurled forth with the utmost fury; the demons turned and fled. Having thus scattered the army, the valiant monkeys next closed around Rāvaṇa, buffetting him on every side and tearing him with their claws, so that his whole body was mangled.

Dohā 100

Seeing the overwhelming might of the monkeys, Rāvaṇa took thought, and in a moment became invisible and created a magic illusion.

Chand 26 (*Tomara*)

By the magic that he wrought terrible beings were manifested; imps, demons and goblins with bows and arrows in their hands, witches clutching swords and in one hand a human skull, from which they quaff draughts of blood, dancing and singing many a song. Their horrible cries of 'Seize and kill!' echoed all around, while dogs with open mouth[1] rushed on to devour. Then began the monkeys to flee; but wherever they turned in flight, they saw a blazing fire. Monkeys and bears were

1. For *mukh bāyā*, 'with open mouth,' some books read *makh bāyā*, which would mean 'having scattered the sacrifice.' As no sacrifice has been mentioned, the former seems preferable, though the latter may also be understood as a general image of horror.

both in dismay. Then there fell upon them a shower of sand. They were routed on all sides and the Ten-headed roared again. Lakṣmaṇa, the monkey-king and all stalwarts were at their wits' end. The bravest of them wrung their hands, crying, 'Alas, O Rāma! Alas, Raghunātha!' After crushing all their might in this fashion, he next practised another kind of magic. A host of Hanumāns were manifested, who rushed forward with rocks in their hands and encircled Rāma in a dense mass on every side. With gnashing teeth and up-turned tail, they shouted, 'Kill him! Hold him fast! Don't let him escape!' Their tails made a complete circle all around with the king of Kosala in the midst.

Chand 27

In their midst the dark-hued king of Kosala shone forth as resplendent in beauty as a lofty *tamāla* tree fenced in by a hedge of gleaming rainbows. As they gazed upon the Lord, the heart of the gods was moved with mingled joy and grief, while they raised the cry of 'Victory! Victory!' In a moment and with a single arrow Raghubīra indignantly dispelled the delusion. As the phantoms vanished, the monkeys and bears rejoiced and all turned again, with trees and rocks in their hands. Rāma shot forth a volley of arrows and Rāvaṇa's heads and arms again fell to the ground. Though a hundred Śeṣanāgas, Śāradās, Vedas and bards were to spend many ages in singing the various achievements of Rāma in his battle with Rāvaṇa, they would never come to the end of them.

Dohā 101a-101b

(Tulasī Dāsa, poor clown, has described something of the wonder of their exploits, much as a fly mounts up into heaven in accordance with the capacity it possesses.) Though his heads and arms were cut off again and again, the mighty king of Laṅkā was not killed. Sages, adepts and gods were confounded by the agonizing sight, the pastime of their Lord.

Caupāī 101

No sooner were his heads cut off than a fresh crop grew,

like covetousness increased by gain.[1] For all his toil the monster died not and Rāma then turned and looked at Vibhīṣaṇa. O Umā, the Lord, whom Fate and Death obey, thus tested the devotion of one of his creatures. "Hearken," said Vibhiṣaṇa, "O omniscient sovereign of all things animate and inanimate, defender of the suppliant, delight of gods and sages, it is only, sire, by virtue of the nectar that abides in the depth of his navel that Rāvaṇa lives." On hearing Vibhīṣaṇa's speech the All-merciful was pleased and took his terrible arrows in his hand. Many inauspicious omens then began to present themselves: asses, jackals and packs of dogs set up a howling; birds screamed over the distress of the world and comets appeared in every quarter of the sky; fierce flames broke out on every side, and though there was no new moon, the sun was eclipsed. Maṇḍodarī's heart beat wildly and statues shed tears from their eyes.

Chand 28

Statues wept, thunderbolts crashed in the air, a mighty wind blew, the earth quaked, the clouds dropped blood, hair and dust: who could recount all the portents? At the sight of such unspeakable confusion the gods of heaven in dismay uttered prayers for victory. Perceiving their distress, the merciful Raghupati set arrows to his bow:

Dohā 102

And drawing the string to his ear, he shot forth at once thirty-one shafts. The bolts of Raghunāyaka flew forth like the serpents of death.

Caupāī 102

One arrow dried up the depths of his navel, the others struck off his heads and arms, and with such violence that they carried heads and arms away with them. The headless and armless trunk still danced upon the plain. The earth sank beneath the

1. In a covetous man no sooner is one desire cut off or satisfied than other desires spring up to take its place.

weight of the body as it rushed wildly on, till the Lord with his arrows smote it in twain. At the moment of death he thundered aloud with a fierce and terrible yell, 'Where is Rāma, that I may challenge and slay him in combat?' The earth reeled as Rāvaṇa fell; the sea, the rivers, the elephants of the eight quarters and the mountains were shaken. The two halves lay full length upon the ground, thronged by crowd of bears and monkeys. But the arrows deposited the heads and arms before Mandodarī and then returned to the Lord of the universe and dropped again into the quiver. Seeing this, the gods sounded their kettle-drums. His soul entered the Lord's mouth; Śiva and Brahmā rejoiced to see the sight. The whole universe resounded with cries of "Victory, Victory! Glory to Raghubīra the mighty of arm! Glory to the All-merciful! Glory to Mukunda!" while throngs of gods and sages rained down flowers.

Chand 29

"Glory to Mukunda, the fountain of mercy, the subduer of rebellion, our refuge, our health-giving Lord; the scatterer of the ranks of the impious, the great First Cause, the compassionate, the ever Supreme." All the gods in their joy rained down blossoms and the kettle-drums sounded aloud, while on the field of battle Rāma's every limb displayed the beauty of a myriad Loves. The crown on his coil of hair all besprinkled with blossoms emitted rays of splendour like flashes of lightning gleaming amidst the star-lit peaks of a dark mountain. With bow and arrows brandished in his arms, his body, spangled with specks of blood, seemed like a flock of spotted amandavas joyously perched on a *tamāla* tree.

Dohā 103

With a shower of gracious glances the Lord dispelled the fears of all the gods; and the bears and monkeys rejoiced and cried, "Glory to Mukunda, the abode of bliss!"

Caupāī 103

When Mandodarī saw her lord's heads, she fainted in her grief and fell to the ground. Her bevy of weeping maidens sprang up in haste and supported her and brought her to Rāvaṇa's body. When she saw her lord's condition, she cried aloud, her hair flew loose, and there was no strength left in her body. Wildly beating her bosom and weeping, she recounted all his glory: "Before your might, my lord, the earth ever reeled, fire, moon, and sun were bereft of splendour. The great serpent and tortoise could not bear the weight of your body, which now lies on the ground, a mere heap of ashes. Varuṇa, Kuvera, Indra and the Wind-god had never the courage to face you in battle. By the might of your arm, O my husband, you conquered death and fate, but to-day you have fallen like the poorest creature. Your magnificence was renowned throughout the world; while the strength of your son and your kinsmen surpassed description. But you fought against Rāma, and this is now your condition: not one of your stock is left even to make lamentation. The whole sphere of creation was in your power, my lord, and the frighted regent of the eight quarters ever bowed their heads before you; but now jackals devour your heads and arms; and rightly so, seeing that you opposed Rāma. Deathdoomed, my lord, you heeded not my words, and took the Lord of all things, animate and inanimate, for a mere man.

Chand 30

"You took for a man, Hari the self-existent, that fire to consume the forest of devildom; and you worshipped not, O my spouse, the All-merciful, to whom Śiva and Brahmā and all the gods do reverence. From birth you have delighted to injure others, and this your body has been one mass of sin, and yet Rāma has now raised you to his own abode: I bow before the blameless God.

Dohā 104

"Ah, my lord, there is none other so gracious as Raghunātha the great God, who has bestowed on you the liberation to which even the company of yogīs can hardly attain."

Caupāī 104

When they heard Mandodarī's lament, gods, saints and sages

were all enraptured. Brahmā, Śiva, Nārada, Sanaka and all the great seers who have preached the way of salvation gazed upon Raghupati with eyes full of tears and were overwhelmed with devotion. Seeing all the women making lamentation, Vibhīṣaṇa went to them, his heart heavy with grief, and was sorely pained to see his brother's condition. Then the Lord gave an order to Lakṣmaṇa, who did all that he could to console him. At last Vibhīṣaṇa betook himself to the Lord, who looked upon him with an eye of compassion and said, "Stop mourning and perform the funeral rites." In obedience to his command, he celebrated the obsequies, wisely bearing in mind the circumstances of time and place.

Dohā 105

Mandodarī and the other wives presented the dead with the prescribed handfuls of sesamum seed and the queen then returned to the palace, recounting to herself all Raghupati's excellences.

Caupāī 105

Then Vibhīṣaṇa came and bowed his head. The All-merciful sent for his younger brother and said, "Do you and the monkey prince and Aṅgada and Nala and Nīla, with Jāṁbavān and the sagacious Son of the Wind go all together in company with Vibhīṣaṇa and make the arrangements for his coronation," thus said Raghunātha, "I by reason of my father's commands may not enter the city, but I send the monkey and my younger brother to take my place." The monkey started at once, on receiving his Lord's order, and went and made ready for the installation. With due reverence they seated him on the throne, and after marking his forehead with the royal sign, they sang a hymn of praise and with folded hands all bowed the head before him. Then with Vibhīṣaṇa they returned to the Lord, and Raghubīra addressed the monkeys with such gracious words as made them all glad.

Chand 31

He made them glad with words that were sweet as nectar:

"It is by your might the enemy has been slain and Vibhīṣaṇa crowned king; your glory will live forever throughout the universe. Whoever with sincere devotion shall sing your glorious deeds in connection with me shall cross without an effort the boundless ocean of existence."

Dohā 106

The monkey army would never have been tired of listening to their Lord's words; again and again they all bowed their heads and clasped his lotus feet.

Caupāī 106

The Lord next addressed Hanumān. "Go to Laṅkā," said the god, "and tell Jānakī the news and bring me back word of her welfare." When Hanumān entered the city, the demons and demonesses heard of it and ran to meet him. They showed him every possible honour and pointed out Sītā to him. From afar the monkey prostrated himself and Jānakī recognized Rāma's envoy. "Tell me, friend," she said, "of my gracious Lord, and of his brother; is he well and all the monkey host?" "All is well, madam," said he, "with the king of Kosala; he has conquered Rāvaṇa in battle; Vibhīṣaṇa has been placed in secure possession of the throne." On hearing the monkey's reply, joy was diffused over her soul.

Chand 32

Sītā's soul was overjoyed, her body thrilled and her eyes streamed with tears, as again and again she cried: "What can I give you, monkey ? There is nothing in the three spheres of creation to be compared to your tidings." "Hearken, madam," he replied, "to-day of a truth I have alrady obtained the undisputed sovereignty of the world, when I see and adore Rāma with his brother triumphing over the ranks of the enemy."

Dohā 107

"Hearken, my son," said she: "every virtue finds a home in

your heart: may you live and prosper forever in the service of the king of Kosala and Lakṣmaṇa !

Caupāī 107

But now, my friend, devise some plan by which I may see with my own eyes his dark but comely form." Hanumān then returned to Rāma and told him of Sītā's welfare. When the jewel of the Solar race heard her message, he said to prince Vibhīṣaṇa, "Go you with Hanumān and respectfully escort Sītā here." They all went at once to the place where Sītā was. The demon ladies humbly did her service and, being sharply ordered by Vibhīṣaṇa, attended her to the bath with all formality and adorned her with ornaments of every description. Then they made ready and brought a handsome palanquin, which she mounted with joy, thinking ever of Rāma with the deepest affection. On all four sides were guards, with stavesin their hands, who marched with the greatest gladness of soul. The bears and monkeys all came to catch a glimpse of her, but the guards in a fury rushed to keep them back. Said Raghubīra, "Attend to what I say; bring Sītā on foot, friend; let the monkeys see her as they would their own mother." Thus said the great Raghunātha and smiled. The bears and monkeys were delighted to hear his commands, and from heaven the gods rained down a profusion of flowers. To begin with, he placed Sītā in the fire, for he wished the internal witness[1] to be revealed.

Dohā 108

For this reason the All-merciful spoke with seeming harshness. All the demonesses, when they heard it, began to grieve.

Caupāī 108

But Sītā bowed to her lord's command—pure as she was in thought and word and deed — and said, "Lakṣmaṇa, be

1. The meaning of the words *Antara Sākhi*, the internal witness or witness of the soul, would not be very obvious without a reference to the Sanskrit text, in which Sītā makes her prayer to the Fire-god, addressing him thus: "Thou, O Fire, knowest the secrets of the hearts (*śarīrāntara gocaraḥ*) of all living creatures; be thou my witness (*sākṣī*); assume a visible form and save me, O best of gods."

sharer in this pious rite; show me the fire and be quick." When Lakṣmaṇa heard Sītā's words, so full of detachment, discretion, piety and goodness, his eyes filled with tears and he folded his hands in prayer but could not speak a word to his Lord. Seeing that Rāma was displeased, he ran and kindled a fire with a quantity of wood that he brought. Sītā beheld the fierceness of the flame, but was glad of heart without a particle of fear. She said, "If neither in thought, word or deed I have ever abandoned Rāma or cherished any other, may the fire, which tests all men's actions, become as cooling as sandal-wood !"

Chand 33

The flame was cool as sandalwood, as Sītā entered it, meditating on her Lord and saying, "Glory to the king of Kosala, for whose feet, ever worshipped by Śiva, I cherish the purest devotion." Her shadow and the stain of social disgrace were alone consumed in the blazing fire. Such an action on the part of the Lord had never been seen before : gods, saints and sages all stood at gaze. The Fire assumed a bodily form and took her by the hand and led and presented her to Rāma, even as The Ocean of Milk presented Lakṣmī to her Lord. Resplendent with exquisite beauty she shone forth at the left side of Rāma's body, like the blossom of a golden lotus bud beside a dark lotus newley opened.

Dohā 109a-109b

The gods in their delight showered down flowers and made music in the air, while the Kinnaras sang and the nymphs of heaven danced, all mounted on their chariots. The beauty of Janaka's daughter reunited to her lord was beyond all measure and bound; the bears and monkeys, in rapture at the sight, shouted "Glory to Rāma the beneficent !"

Caupāī 109

Then came Mātali, having obtained Rāma's permission, and bowed his head before his feet. The gods, too, selfish as ever came and made this seemingly pious prayer; "Friend of the destitute, gracious Raghurāī, a god yourself, you have shown mercy to the gods ! This sensual wretch, who delighted to harass the whole world, has perished by his own wickedness in his sinful course. You are the Supreme Spirit, one and everlasting, ever unchangeable and unaffected by circumstances, without parts or qualities, uncreated, sinless, all perfect, invincible, unerring, full of power and compassion: incarnate as the fish, the tortoise, the boar, the lionman[1], and the dwarf; as Paraśurāma also and now as Rāma; whenever, O Lord, the gods have been in trouble, you have taken birth in one form or another to put an end to it: but this impure wretch, the persistent plague of heaven, given up to sensuality, greed, pride and passion, this monster of monsters, has been promoted to your sphere and thereat we marvel greatly. We gods are high masters, but in our selfishness we have forgotten the worship of our Lord, and thus we are ever involved in the flood of worldly passions; but now, O Lord, have mercy upon us, for we come to you for refuge !"

Dohā 110

With folded hands the gods and saints stood all round about him, thus making supplication, while Brahmā — his whole body quivering with excess of devotion — at last broke out into this hymn of praise:

Chand 34

"Glory to the immortal Rāma, the blissful Hari, the prince of Raghu's line, with his bow and arrows; the lionlike Lord to rend in pieces the elephant of earthly existence; the ocean of perfection, the all-wise, the all-pervading; in whose body is concentrated the incomparable beauty of a myriad Loves: whose virtues are sung by bards, saints and sages. Hero of unsullied glory, who in thy wrath didst seize Rāvaṇa, as Garuṛ might seize some monstrous serpent; delight of mankind; destroyer of grief and fear; ever unmoved by passion; Lord of supreme intelligence; beneficent incarnation of illimitable perfection; loosener of earth's burdens; quintessence of wisdom; everlasting,

1. *i.e.*, Narasiṁha.

all-pervading, alone without beginning; I rapturously adore thee, O Rāma, fountain of mercy. Glory of the line of Raghu, slaying Dūṣaṇa and making a king of the ever-faithful Vibhīṣaṇa: storehouse of virtue and wisdom; incomprehensible and unborn, I constantly adore thee, O Rāma, the passionless, the omnipresent. Mighty of arm, strong in renown, exterminator of the hordes of the sinful; pre-eminent in auspiciousness; friend and protector even of the undeserving suppliant; I worship the perfection of beauty, the spouse of Lakṣmī. Deliverer from birth and death, transcending cause and effect, soul-created destroyer of hideous sin; wielder of the arrows and bow and lovely quiver; lotus-eyed paragon of kings; temple of bliss, Lakṣmī's beautiful consort; subduer of pride, lust, lying and selfishness; irreproachable, imperishable, transcendent; all forms alike and yet no determinate form; like the light of the sun—thus the Vedas have declared[1], it is no mere cock-and-bull story—which is separate from it and yet not separate. How fortunate, my Lord, are all these monkeys who reverently gaze upon thy face ! A curse, Hari, on the life we gods enjoy; without devotion to you we have all gone astray in the world ! Now, as thou art compassionate to the suppliant, have mercy upon me; a lion to destroy the elephant-like inconstancy of my purpose; may I practise the reverse of my former way and live happy, esteeming that a happiness which was before a pain. Mercy, destroyer of the wicked, beautiful jewel, whose lotus feet are cherished by Śambhu and Umā ! O king of kings, grant me this boon, the blessing of a constant devotion to thy lotus feet !"

Dohā 111

As Brahmā made his humble prayer, his whole body quivered with excess of devotion and his eyes beholding the ocean of beauty refused to be satisfied.

1. *Nadanti* may be taken as the third person plural of the present tense of the verb *nad*, 'to declare,' like *vadanti* from *vad* and some scholars from the way that they have divided the words in the text, evidently so regarded it. But perhaps it is better to divide thus, *na dānti-kathā*, instead of *nadanti kathā*; 'danta-kathā' being a common colloquial expression for a verbal quibble, or an argument unsupported by authority.

Caupāī 110

Then too came Daśaratha (in his celestial form) and, when he beheld his son, his eyes were flooded with tears. The Lord and his younger brother did obeisance and their father gave them his blessing. "It is all due, sire," said Rāma, "to your religious merit that the invincible demon king has been conquered." On hearing his son's words, his affection increased still more; his eyes streamed and he trembled with emotion. Seeing his father thus overcome by love, Raghupati, after first taking thought, bestowed upon him absolute wisdom. He did not receive the boon of deliverance from existence, Umā, for this reason, that Daśaratha has grasped the mystery of faith. Worshippers of the incarnate are not rewarded with liberation, but Rāma gives them devotion to himself. Having again and again prostrated himself before the Lord, Daśaratha returned with joy to his abode in heaven.

Dohā 112

The Lord, the king of Kosala, rejoiced together with his brother and Jānakī. At the charming sight Indra, the king of the gods, in his delight chanted this hymn of praise:

Chand (*Tomar*)[1] 35

"Glory to Rāma, the home of beauty, the merciful, the refuge of the suppliant; equipped with quiver and bow and arrows, triumphing in his mighty strength of arm! Glory to the foe of Dūṣaṇa, the foe of Khara, destroyer of the demon host! When my Lord slew this last monster all the gods were happy again. Glory to the remover of earth's burdens, whose greatness is indeed vast and unbounded. Glory to Rāvaṇa's merciful foe, the discomforter of the demons! Outrageous was the pride of the King of Laṅkā, who had overthrown gods and Gandharvas; who relentlessly pursued saints and sages, men, birds and serpents; a malignant and implacable monster; but who now—the wretch—has obtained his reward. Hearken now,

1. In the Tomar metre each line of the quatrain should consist of an anapaest followed by two amphibrachs; but many licenses are allowed.

O protector of the suppliant, with the large lotus eyes; my pride was inordinate, there was no one to equal me. Now after seeing thy lotus feet, the arrogance that caused me so much misery has passed away. Let others adore the impersonal Absolute, the primary existence, whom the Vedas hymn; but my delight is in the king of Kosala, the divine Rāma in personal form. Together with Sītā and Lakṣmaṇa, make my heart thy abode! O spouse of Lakṣmī, recognize me as thy servant, and grant me faith!

Chand 36

Grant me devotion to your feet, O spouse of Lakṣmī, soother of terror, solace of the suppliant! Thee I adore, O Rāma, abode of bliss, prince of the house of Raghu, beautiful as a myriad Loves. Delight of the hosts of heaven, queller of strife; in form as a man of incomparable strength; object of the adoration of Brahmā, Śaṅkara and all the gods; thee I worship, O Rāma, gracious and benign!

Dohā 113

Now in thy mercy, O most merciful, look upon me and direct me what to do." On hearing this tender appeal the protector of the poor made answer:

Caupāī 111

"Hearken, king of the gods: my bears and monkeys, who lie on the ground slain by the demons, have lost their lives on my account; restore them all to life, wise king of heaven." Hearken, Garuṛ, this request of the Lord's is a mystery that only the greatest sages can apprehend. The Lord could himself destroy and recreate the three spheres; only he wished to do Indra honour. With a shower of ambrosia he restored the bears and monkeys to life. They arose with joy and all betook them to the Lord. The shower of nectar fell on both armies; but the bears and monkeys came to life, not the demons. The image of Rāma was impressed upon the demons' soul; thus they were loosed from the fetters of existence and became absorbed in the divine. The bears and monkeys were all in essence divine, and so were brought to life by the will of Raghupati. Who is there so kind to the destitute as Rāma, who granted final deliverance even to the host of demons, while that filthy and sensual monster Rāvaṇa obtained translation to the same sphere as the holiest of sages ?

Dohā 114a-114b

After raining down flowers, the gods mounted their splendid cars and withdrew. Then seeing his opportunity the sagacious Śambhu drew near to Rāma. Most lovingly, with folded hands, his lotus eyes full of tears and his body quivering all over, Tripurāri uttered this prayer with choking voice:

Chand 37

"Save me, O Lord of the house of Raghu, equipped with thy strong bow and graceful arrows in thy hand; dispeller of the murky clouds of delusion; fire to consume the forest of doubt; delight of the gods; unembodied yet embodied; glorious shrine of perfection; sun of vehement splendour to disperse the darkness of error; a very lion to attack the elephantine monsters, lust, anger and pride; take up thy abode for ever, as in some forest, in the heart of thy servant. Stern frost to wither up the lotus bed of sensual desires; gracious beyond all conception; Mount Mandara to churn up the ocean of life; dweller of the highest sphere; avert from me the stormy waves of the world and transport me across them. O king Rāma, dark-hued and lotus eyed, protector of the poor, soother of the sorrows of the distressed, dwell for ever in my heart with Lakṣmaṇa and Jānakī, delight of the sages, glory of the terrestrial sphere, uprooter of every terror, Tulasī Dāsa's own Lord.

Dohā 115

When your coronation, O my Lord, takes place in the city of Kosala, I will come, O ocean of grace, to see the glorious ceremony."

Caupāī 112

When Śambhu had finished his prayer and gone away, Vibhīṣaṇa approached the Lord. Bowing his head before his feet he cried in pleading tones: "Hearken to my prayer, O Lord, with bow in hand! You have slain Rāvaṇa with all his kindred and all his army and made your unsullied glory known throughout the three spheres. On me, your vile servant, without either sense or breeding, you have in every way shown compassion. Now, Lord, honour your servant's house and bathe and refresh yourself after the toil of the battle. Inspect my treasure, my palace, and my wealth, and by this condescension make all the monkeys happy. Consider, my Lord, everything that I have as your own and take me with you to Avadh." When the All-merciful heard this gentle speech, both his large eyes filled with tears.

Dohā 116a-116d

"Hearken, brother, he said, "all you say is true; your house and treasure are as my own; but thinking of Bharata's plight, every minute seems to me an aeon. In penitential attire, with emaciated body, he is ever repeating my name in prayer. I beseech you, friend, to make an effort so that I may soon be able to see him again. If at the end of the time I go and find him no longer alive"—at the remembrance of his brother's affection, the Lord's body quivered all over with emotion—"but may you reign for a full aeon, your soul ever fixed on me, and at the last enter into my sphere, where all the good go."

Caupāī 113

When Vibhīṣaṇa heard Rāma's words, he was overjoyed and clasped the feet of the All-merciful. All the bears and monkeys with equal joy clasped the Lords's feet and recited his glorious merits. Then Vibhīṣaṇa proceeded to the palace and loaded the chariot with jewels and attire in abundance. When he had brought the car Puṣpaka and set it before the Lord, the All-merciful smiled and said: "Hearken, friend Vibhīṣaṇa, mount the car, and when you have risen high into the air, throw down the dresses and jewels." Accordingly, Vibhīṣaṇa mounted aloft into the heavens and scrambled the raiment and jewels among them all. The monkeys picked up anything they fancied cramming the precious things into their mouth, while Rāma and his brother and Sītā laughed; so sportive is the All-merciful.

Dohā 117a-117b

He, whom the sages cannot reach by contemplation, whom the Vedas fail to fathom[1] even he in his infinite compassion made merry with the monkeys. O Umā, abstraction, prayer, charity, penance, the different forms of fasting, sacrifice and vows,—all move Rāma's compassion less than simple love.

Caupāī 114

After securing the dresses and ornaments, the bears and monkeys clothed themselves with them and appeared before Rāma. The king of Kosala laughed again and again to see the monkeys in their motley attire. As he looked upon them all, he was moved with pity, and said in gracious tones: "It is by your assistance that I have killed Rāvaṇa and thus secured the throne for Vibhīṣaṇa. Now return all of you to your several homes; remember me and fear no one." On hearing these words the monkeys were overcome with affection, and all with folded hands thus reverently addressed him: "What you say, my Lord, is all to your honour; but we are foolishly perplexed on hearing such words. Knowing the low estate of us monkeys, you gave us a leader; you, O Raghunātha, are the sovereign of the three spheres. When we hear our Lord's words we die of shame; is it possible for a mosquito to assist the mighty king of birds?" The monkeys were so charmed as they gazed on Rāma's face that in the depth of their devotion they had no longing for their own home.

Dohā 118a-118c

When the Lord had dismissed them, the bears and monkeys all went their way, cherishing Rāma's image in their heart, exulting with joy and making frequent prayer. The monkey king, Nīla, the king of the bears, Aṅgada, Nala, Hanumān, Vibhīṣaṇa also and all the other valiant monkey chiefs were so overcome by their feelings that they could not speak a word,

1. *i.e.*, they speak of him in negative terms, calling him 'Not thus, not thus'.

while their eyes, streaming with tears, were fixed upon Rāma's person so intently that they had no time to wink.

Caupāī 115

When Rāma beheld their ecstatic devotion he took them all up with him into his car and, after mentally bowing his head before the Brāhmaṇas' feet, he directed the car towards the north. A tumultuous noise accompanied the car on its way, all shouting 'glory to Raghubīra!' The throne on which the Lord and his consort were seated was very lofty and magnificent; there Rāma and his bride shone resplendent, like a dark cloud on Meru's peak with attendant lightning. The beauteous car sped swiftly on its way, while the gods in their joy showered down flowers. A delightful breeze breathed soft, cool and fragrant; the water of the sea and the Gaṅgā was without a speck; omens of good fortune occurred on every side: the heart was glad and all the expanse[1] of ether clear. "Sītā" said Raghubīra, "look at the field of battle; here Lakṣmaṇa slew Meghanāda; here the huge demons that strew the plain were slaughtered by Aṅgada and Hanumān; here fell the two brothers Kumbhakarṇa and Rāvaṇa, that plague of gods and sages.

Dohā 119a-119b

Here the bridge was built and the image of the blessed Mahādeva set up." The all-merciful Lord and Sītā here both did obeisance of Śaṁbhu. Every place in the forest wherever the gracious god had taken up his abode or rested, he pointed out to Jānakī and told her the names of them all.

Caupāī 116

Forthwith the chariot arrived at the charming Daṇḍaka forest, and Rāma visited the hermitage both of Agastya and all the other great sages. After receiving the blessing of all the holy men, the Lord of the world came to Citrakūṭa.. After gratifying

1. *Asa* here is not the common word *āsa*, hope (from *a-sans*), but is derived from the root *as* and has the meaning of 'space, region, expanse.'

the hermits there, the chariot again sped swiftly on. Rāma next pointed out to Sītā the Jamunā, that beautiful river that washes away all the impurities of this sinful age. After this he espied the holy Gaṅgā and bade Sītā do obeisance. "See also the queen of all holy places, Prayāga," he added, "the sight of which puts away all the sins committed in a thousand births. See again the most holy Triveṇī, the antidote of sorrow, the ladder of heaven. See also the holy city of Avadh, which heals all the three kinds of pains and the disease of mortality."

Dohā 120a-120b

The gracious Lord and Sītā both did reverence to Avadh. Rāma's body quivered with emotion and his eyes streamed as again and again he expressed his unbounded joy. Then went the Lord and with much delight bathed at Triveṇī and both he and the monkeys bestowed gifts of all kinds on the Brāhmaṇas.

Caupāī 117

The Lord then spoke and enjoined Hanumān: "Take the form of a young Brāhmaṇa and go into the city. Tell Bharata that all is well with us, and come back here yourself with the news." The Son of the Wind was off at once. Then the Lord visited Bharadvāja. The sage received him with all possible honour and after hymning his praises, gave him his blessing. The Lord prostrated himself at his feet, with his hands folded in prayer, and then mounted his chariot and went on again. When the Niṣāda heard that the Lord had come, he cried, 'A boat, a boat!' and summoned his people. The chariot crossed the sacred stream and then stopped on the bank, obedient to the Lord's command. Then Sītā worshipped the divine Gaṅgā and again and again threw herself at its feet. In gladness of soul the Gaṅgā blessed her: "Fair lady, may your happiness be without a break!" At the news, Guha ran in a transport of love and drew near, bewildered with excess of joy. At the sight of Sītā and the Lord, he fell flat upon the ground quite out of his senses. When Rāma perceived the vehemence of his love, he was glad and raised him up and took him to his bosom.

Chand 38

The all-merciful and all-wise Rāma, the spouse of Lakṣmī, took and clasped him to his heart and seated him close by his side and asked him how he fared. He was all humility. "Now is all well with me," he said, "for I have seen thy lotus feet, the adoration of Brahmā and Śankara: O Rāma, abode of bliss, fulfiller of every desire, thee, thee only do I worship." Though he was only a poor low Niṣāda, Hari clasped him to his bosom, as though he were Bharata himself. (Dull of soul, says Tulasī Dāsa, is he who is so infatuated as to forget such a Lord. Gods, saints and sages sing with delight these achievements of Rāvaṇa's foe, for they have a sanctifying effect, ever inspire devotion to Rāma's feet, destroy lust and other evil passions and inculcate true wisdom.)

Dohā 121a-121b

(The wise, who listen to the achievements of Rāma and his victory in the battle, God rewards for ever with victory, wisdom and renown. This Kaliyuga is the very home of defilement; think well on it, O soul! and understand that if you abandon the blessed name of Rāma, there is no other saviour.)

[*Thus endeth the book entitled* LAṄKĀ, *the bestower of pure wisdom; being the sixth descent into the Holy Lake of Rāma's Acts, that cleanses from every defilement of the world.*]

BOOK VII

THE SEQUEL

THE SEQUEL

Sanskrit Invocation

I worship without ceasing the adorable lord of Sītā, the noblest of the sons of Raghu, even Rāma as he appeared when mounted on the car Puṣpaka, bright of hue as the neck of a peacock; marked with the print of the Brāhmaṇa's lotus foot, which declared him the greatest of the gods, all beautiful; yellow-attired; lotus-eyed; ever gracious; with bow and arrows in hand; attended by a host of monkeys and served by his brother.

Beautiful and tender are the lotus feet of the lord of Kosala, worshipped by Brahmā and Śiva, caressed by the lotus hands of Jānakī, ever clustered about by the beelike souls of the devout.

I worship Śaṅkara, the annihilator of Love; beautiful and white with the brightness of the jasmine, the moon and the conch shell, the lord of Aṁbikā : the granter of desired success, the compassionate lotus-eyed.

Dohā

There remained but one day of the period of Rāma's exile; the people of the city, men and women alike, sorely distressed in mind and wasted in body by sorrow for Rāma's absence, were everywhere anxious. Auspicious omens of every kind occurred; at once every heart was glad and the city itself brightened up all round, as if to announce the Lord's coming. Kausalyā and the other royal dames were all as happy as if that minute expecting to be told 'the Lord is here, and with him Sītā and Lakṣmaṇa.' Bharata's right eye and arm throbbed again and again. Recognizing this as a good sign, he was glad at heart and yet began to ponder deeply.

Caupāī 1

"There remains but one day of the period on whose end I had set my hope. As I think thereon, my soul is full of anxiety. What is the reason that my Lord has not returned? God saw my evil nature when he passed me over. Ah ! how blessed and truly fortunate is Lakṣmaṇa in his devotion to Rāma's lotus feet. The Lord knew me to be false and perverse, and, therefore he did not take me with him. If the Lord were to consider my actions, there would be no redemption for me in a hundred million of ages. But the Lord never regards offences of his servants, being a very brother to the destitute and most tender-hearted. I am firmly persuaded of soul that Rāma will come ; the omens are so favourable. But if my life holds out after the term once expires, I shall be a more despicable wretch than any in the world."

Dohā 1a-1b

While Bharata's soul was thus drowning in the sea of separation from Rāma, the Son of the Wind, disguised in form as a Brāhmaṇa, came like a boat to his rescue. Seeing him seated on a mat of sacred grass, with matted hair for a crown, his body all wasted away, his lips muttering the names 'Rāma, Rāma, Raghupati,' and his eyes streaming with tears :

Caupāī 2

When he saw him, Hanumān was overjoyed, every hair on his body stood erect and tears poured from his eyes; he felt at heart an indescribable satisfaction and addressed him in words that were as ambrosia to his ear : "He, for whose loss you sorrow night and day, the catalogue of whose virtues you are incessantly reciting, the glory of the line of Raghu, the benefactor of the pious, the deliverer of gods and sages, has arrived safely. After conquering the foe in the battle, with the gods to hymn his praises, the Lord is now on his way with Sitā and his brother." On hearing these words he forgot all his sorrows, like a man dying of thirst who finds a stream of nectar. "Who are you, Sir, and whence have you come, who have told me such glad tidings ?" "I am the Son of the Wind, a monkey, Hanumān by name, O fountain of mercy, a servant of the beneficent Raghupati." On hearing this, Bharata rose and respectfully advanced to meet him. The affection with which he embraced him was too great for heart to contain ; his eyes streamed with tears and his body quivered all over. "O monkey, at the sight of you all my sorrows are gone, for to-day I have embraced a friend of Rāma's." Again and again he asked of his welfare : "Hearken, brother, what is there I can give you? after taking thought, I find nothing in the whole world to match this news. Otherwise, I should be your debtor. Now tell me of my Lord's adventures." Then Hanumān bowed his head at his feet and told him all Raghupati's great doings. "Tell me, monkey, did the gracious master ever remember me as one of his servants ?

Chand 1

Did the jewel of the race of Raghu ever make mention of me his servant ?" On hearing Bharata's modest speech, the monkey was in a rapture and fell at his feet. How can he be otherwise than humble and holy and an ocean of virtue, whose praises Rāma, Lord of all animate and inanimate creation, himself recites with his own mouth ?

Dohā 2a

"My Lord," he said, "you are as dear to Rāma as his own life ; that is the truth, master." Again and again he embraced Bharata, and his joy was more than his heart could contain.

Soraṭhā 2b

After bowing his head at Bharata's feet, the monkey swiftly returned to Rāma and told him that all was well. Then the Lord mounted his chariot and joyfully set forth.

Caupāī 3

Filled with joy, Bharata too returned to Ayodhyā and told his *guru* all the news. Then he published the fact in the palace that Rāma was approaching the city and was safe and sound. At these tidings all the dowager queens arose in haste ; but Bharata spoke and assured them of their Lord's welfare. When the citizens heard the news, men and women all ran out in their joy : the ladies formed in procession with stately gait, singing and bearing golden salvers laden with curds, sacred grass, the yellow pigment, fruit and flowers and fresh springs of the *tulasi* plant, all things of good omen. Each ran out just as she happened to be, without stopping to bring either children or old folk. Everyone was asking his neighbour, "Brother, have you seen the gracious Rāma ?" Directly it knew the Lord was coming, the whole city of Avadh became a quarry of delights. The water of the Sarjū flowed clear, as clear as it could be; the air was deliciously soft, cool and fragrant.

Dohā 3a-3c

Bharata went forth to meet the All-merciful, full of joy and affection, accompanied by his *guru*, his kinsmen, his younger brother and a company of Brāhmaṇas. Many of the women mounted the upper storeys of the houses to look for the chariot in the sky and, when they espied it, raised their sweet voices in auspicious songs of joy. As the waves of the sea rise and swell at the sight of the full moon, so poured forth the women of the city with a tumultuous noise at the sight of Rāma.

Caupāī 4

Meanwhile, the sun of the lotuses of the Solar race was pointing out the beauties of the city to the monkeys: "Hearken, Sugrīva, Aṅgad and Vibhīṣaṇa : this city is so holy and the country is so charming that although all men speak of Vaikuṇṭha, which is indeed famous in the Vedas and the Purāṇas and celebrated throughout the world, still it is not so dear to me as this city of Avadh : only here and there one can be found to comprehend this saying. Here is the delightful city, my birth-place, and to the north the sacred Sarjū, where every man that bathes obtains without further trouble a home near me. The dwellers here are very dear to me ; the city makes them my fellow-citizens both here and hereafter and is the city of perfect bliss." The monkeys rejoiced to hear the Lord's words : what a glory for Avadh to be praised by Rāma !

Dohā 4a-4b

When the All-merciful Lord God saw all the people coming out to meet him, he urged on his chariot close up to the city and there dismounted. Having alighted on the ground, he directed Puṣpaka to return to Kuvera.[1] On receiving Rāma's order it went its way, full of mingled joy and sorrow at parting.

Caupāī 5

With Bharata came the whole population, all emaciated in body by their mourning for Rāma. When the Lord saw Vāmadeva and Vasiṣṭha, chief of sages, he dropped his bow and arrows on the ground and ran to clasp his *guru's* lotus feet, both he and his younger brother, with every hair on their body erect. The great sage embraced them and asked of their welfare. "By your favour all is well with us." Then the champion of the faith, the king of the Raghu race, made obeisance to all the Brāhmaṇas. Next Bharatā embraced the Lord's lotus feet, ever worshipped by Śankara, Brahmā and all the gods and sages. He fell to the ground and refused to rise, till the All-merciful by force took and pressed him to his bosom, every hair standing erect on his dark-hued body, and his lotus eyes all streaming with tears.

Chand 2

Tears rolled down from his lotus eyes and his beauteous body quivered with emotion, as he lovingly clasped his brother to his heart, even he, the Lord of the three worlds. There is no similitude by which I can express the beauty of the meeting between the Lord and his brother; it was as though Love and Desire in bodily form had met together in a rapturous embrace. When the All-merciful asked of his welfare. it was with difficulty that Bharata found words to reply. Harken, Umā; such joy can only be felt, it is beyond speech or intelligence. "Now is all well with me, O Lord of Kosala; seeing your servant's distress, you have revealed yourself to him and have taken me by the hand, O All-merciful, when I was sinking in the sea of bereavement."

1. The car Puṣpaka had originally belonged to Kuvera and had been stolen from him by Rāvaṇa.

Dohā 5

Then the Lord smilingly embraced Śatrughna and took him to his heart, while Bharata embraced Lakṣmaṇa, his heart overflowing with love.

Caupāī 6

After that Śatrughna and Lakṣmaṇa embraced, remembering no more the intolerable sorrow of separation. Finally Bharata bowed his head at Sītā's feet, both he and his younger brother, with an intensity of delight. The citizens were so glad at the sight of the Lord, that all the sorrow caused by his absence was at once forgotten. Seeing all the people so agitated by affection, the gracious Kharāri practised an illusion and appearing at one and the same time in multiplied form, was thus in his benignity enabled to salute everyone with due ceremony. The look of compassion, with which Raghubīra regarded them all, made every man and woman supremely happy. Thus in a single moment the blessed Lord embraced them all; this, Umā, is a mystery that none can comprehend. When Rāma the perfection of amiability and every virtue, had in this manner made them all happy, he went on his way. Kausalyā and the other royal dames ran out to meet him, like cows that have lately calved at the sight of their little ones.

Chand 3

Like cows that have been driven by force to graze in the woods, leaving their little ones at home, when they draw near to the village at close of day, hurry on lowing and with dripping udders, so did all the matrons haste to embrace the Lord with the utmost affection, lavishing upon him every term of endearment. The cruel pangs of parting had past away and were replaced by unutterable happiness and delight.

Dohā 6a-6b

Sumitrā embraced her son, remembering his devotion to Rāma's feet; Kaikeyī too embraced Rāma, but with a heart sadly ill at ease. Lakṣmaṇa embraced the royal dames and with joy received their blessing; but though he embraced Kaikeyī again and again, her anguish of soul still continued.

Caupāī 7

Sītā the princess of Videha embraced each of her mothers-in-law and was overjoyed to kiss their feet. They asked of her welfare and invoked upon her the blessing: "May your happy wedded life last for ever." All gazed at Raghupati's lotus face and out of regard for the auspiciousness of the day checked the tears that rose in their eyes. They waved about his head their golden salvers and sacrificial lamps and again and again contemplated his divine person. They scatter all round him every kind of offering, their heart full of supreme felicity. Again and again Kausalyā fixed her gaze on Rāma, so pitiful and so valiant, and kept pondering within herself; "How can he have killed the king of Laṅkā? My two boys are so daintily delicate, is it possible they can have slain the demon's doughtiest champions?"

Dohā 7

As Kausalyā looked upon the Lord and upon Lakṣmaṇa and Sītā, her maternal heart was overwhelmed with supreme felicity and her every limb quivered with emotion.

Caupāī 8

Vibhīṣaṇa, Sugrīva, Nala and Nīla, Jāṁbavān and the high-minded Aṅgada, with Hanumān and all the other monkey chiefs assumed beautiful human forms. With most reverent devotion, everyone told the tale of Bharata's loving disposition, has penance and vow. When they saw the citizens' mode of life, they extolled them also for their attachment to their Lord's feet. Then Rāma summoned all his comrades and bade them kiss the feet of the sage. "The *guru* Vasiṣṭha," he said, "is highly to be reverenced by all my race; it is by his favour that we slew the demons in the battle. But hearken, holy Sir, all these my comrades were the raft that bore me safely out of the waves of the battle. For my sake they lost their lives and they are more dear to me even than Bharata." On hearing the Lord's words, all were greatly overcome. Every moment gave birth to some new rapture.

Dohā 8a-8b

Then they bowed their heads at Kausalyā's feet, who rejoiced to give them her blessing, saying, "You are as dear to me as Rāma." The sky was obscured with the showers of flowers as the Lord of bliss took his way to the palace, while all the fairest ladies in the city mounted the tops of the houses to see him.

Caupāī 9

They ornamented all kinds of golden bowls with various designs and set every one of these at their doors. They buried themselves with wreaths of flowers, flags and banners, all to make a glad show. The roads were all watered with perfumes, and innumerable mystic squares were drawn and filled in with the finest pearls. Every kind of festive preparation was taken in hand; the city was *en fete* and all sorts of music were heard. In different places women scattered their offerings on his path, invoking blessings upon him with their hearts full of joy. Girls wave over his head their golden salvers and festal lamps, singing sweetly the while, they wave their salvers about the head of him who banishes all woe, who is the sun of the lotus growth of Raghu's line. The beauty, the wealth, the magnificence of the city would be a theme for the Vedas, or Śeṣanāga, or Śāradā; but the spectacle was too much even for them; how then can any man, O Umā, be able to describe its glory?

Dohā 9a-9b

Rāma's absence, like the heat of the sun, had withered the lily-like women in the Avadh lake; but now at sunset they opened their blossoms again at the sight of Rāma, the full moon. Every conceivable auspicious omen occurred and music resounded in the sky, as the Lord God moved to the palace, a father restored to his people.

Caupāī 10

The Lord knew that Kaikeyī was ashamed; so he went to her

apartments first, Bhavānī. After comforting her and putting her thoroughly at ease, Hari went on to his own palace. When the All-merciful entered the palace, every man and woman in the city was happy once more. The *guru*, Vasiṣṭha, then called the Brāhmaṇas. "The day and the hour are now most auspicious: give the glad order, all ye Brāhmaṇas, that Rāmacandra to-day take his seat upon the throne." On hearing Vasiṣṭha's gracious address, the Brāhmaṇas were all highly pleased and the multitude of them made seemly response : "Rāma's coronation brings joy to the whole world. Now, best of sages, make no delay, but mark the king's forehead with the sign of sovereignty."

Dohā 10a-10b

The sage thereupon ordered Sumantra, who no sooner heard than he went with joy and speedily got ready a multitude of chariots, elephants and horses. Then he despatched messengers in every direction to borrow stores of all good things, and lastly came himself with joy and bowed his head at Vasiṣṭha's feet.

Caupāī 11

When the city of Avadh had been beautifully decorated, the gods rained down a continuous shower of flowers. Rāma summoned and directed his servants, "Go first and assist my comrades at their bath." On receiving this order, his people ran in every direction and quickly bathed Sugrīva and the rest. Next the All-merciful Rāma summoned Bharata and with his own hands untied his knotted coil of hair; the Lord then proceeded to bathe all his three brothers, even he the gracious Raghurāī, the cherisher of all pious souls. The blessedness of Bharata, the meekness of the Lord, not a thousand million Śeṣanāgas would be able to declare. Finally, Rāma unloosed his own matted hair and, after receiving the *guru's* permission, himself bathed. After his bath the Lord put on his ornaments, the beauty of his every limb outshining a myriad Loves.

Dohā 11a-11c

Forthwith the queens bathed Jānakī with all reverence and attired her in heavenly apparel with rich jewels for every part of her body. As she shone forth on Rāma's left side, the Goddess Lakṣmī herself, full of beauty and goodness, the queens were all overjoyed at the sight and though; their life had been well worth living. Hearken, king of birdst upon this occasion Brahmā, Śiva and all the gods and sages mounted their chariots and came to have a sight of the Blessed one.

Caupāī 12

The soul of the sage was enraptured as he gazed upon the Lord. At once he ordered a gorgeous throne to be brought. Then Rāma took his seat after bowing his head to the Brahmaṇas, his glory effulgent as the sun, defying description. As they looked upon Rāma and Sītā, the whole saintly throng was overjoyed. Then the Brāhmaṇas repeated their Vedic incantations: while in the skies above the gods and sages shouted 'Glory! Glory!' The sage Vasiṣṭha first himself made the *tilak* and then ordered the other Brāhmaṇas to do the same. His mother rejoiced as she looked upon her son and again and again waved the sacrificial lamp about his head. All kinds of presents were made to the Brāhmaṇas and not a beggar remained with a want unsatisfied. At the sight of the Lord of the three spheres seated on his throne, the gods beat their kettle-drums.

Chand 4

Drums sounded in the heavens; Gandharvas and Kinnaras sang and bands of heavenly nymphs danced before the enraptured assembly of gods and sages. Bharata and his other brothers, with Vibhīṣaṇa and Aṅgada and Hanumān and the rest, were there to be seen, some with umbrellas and whisks and fans, and some with bows, swords, shields and spears. With Sītā by his side, the glory of the Solar race outshone the beauty of unnumbered Loves; the soul of the gods was fascinated by his exquisite cloud-dark form in its yellow apparel, his diadem and bracelets and other ornaments that bedecked his every limb, his lotus eyes and stalwart chest and long arms, a blessed vision indeed for man to behold.

Dohā 12a-12c

The magnificence of the sight and the delight of the assembly all beggar description. Garuṛ, Sarasvatī, Śeṣanāga and the Vedas may tell it in part, but only Mahādeva has learnt all the sweetness of it. After they had all severally hymned his praises, the gods departed each to his own sphere. Then came the Vedas, in the disguise of bards, into the presence of the Divine Rāma. The omniscient and compassionate Lord received them with all honour, but no one else at all penetrated the mystery as they thus recited his excellent perfections:

Chand 5

"Hail, visible manifestation of the invisible, incomparable in beauty, jewel of kings; who by the might of thine arm hast slain Rāvaṇa and all the other terrible demons, monsters of iniquity; who, incarnate as a man, hast rid the world of its burdens and put an end to its grievous affliction; hail, protector of the suppliant, lord of compassion, thee we worship, and with thee thy spouse. O Hari, gods and demons, Nāgas[1], men, and all creation, animate and inanimate, have been overcome by thy marvellous delusive power, wearily wandering night and day in the paths of life, full of the mysteries of fate and necessity. If there be any, O Lord, whom thou regardest with compassion, they at once are freed from all their troubles; so prompt to cut short the weariness of existence; have mercy upon us, O Rāma,

1. "Many tribes assumed in modern and ancient times the name of snakes (Nāgas) whether in order to assert their autochthonic right to the country in which they lived, or because, as Diodorus supposes, the snake had been used as their banner, their rallying sign or crest. At the same time, Diodorus points out, people may either have chosen the snake for their banner, because it was their deity, or it may have become their deity because it was their banner. At all events, nothing would be more natural than that people who, for some reason or other, called themselves snakes should in time adopt a snake for their ancestor, and finally for their god. In India the snakes assume, at an early time, a very prominent part in epic and popular traditions. They soon became what fairies or bogies are in our nursery tales, and they thus appear in company with Gandharvas, Apsaras, Kinnaras &c. in some of the most ancient architectural ornamentations of India." — Max Muller's *Hibbert Lectures*.

we implore thee. They, O Hari, who, intoxicated with the pride of learning, despise that faith in thee which saves them from rebirth, may attain to a rank which even the gods might fail to secure, and yet I have seen them fall from it again. They who confidently abandon every other hope and continue thy servants, by repeating thy name cross the ocean of life without any difficulty; this is the Lord whom we invoke. O Mukunda, Rāma, spouse of Lakṣmī, we ever worship thy lotus feet, object of the worship of Śiva and Brahmā; by touching the dust of which the sage's wife obtained salvation; from beneath the nails of which flows the Gaṅgā, reverenced by the sages, sanctifier of the three spheres; feet that bear the marks of the flag, the thunderbolt, the elephant-goad and the lotus, sorely pierced by the thorns during thy wanderings in the forest. We adore the uncreated tree whose root is the Primordial germ; whose coats of bark are fourfold as the Vedas and Purāṇas declare; whose boughs are six in number and branchlets twenty-five; with innumerable leaves and abundant flowers; whose fruits are of two kinds, bitter and sweet; with a single creeper ever clinging to it; full of buds and blossoms and fruit, the everlasting tree of creation.[1] Let them preach in their wisdom, who contemplate thee as the Supreme Spirit, the Uncreated, the inseparable from the universe, recognizable only by inference and beyond the understanding; but we, O Lord, will unceasingly hymn the glories of thy incarnation. O merciful Lord, home of compassion, this is the boon we ask, that in thought, word and deed, and without any variableness we may maintain a devotion to thy feet."

Dohā 13a-13b

Thus, in the sight of all, the Vedas uttered this glorious prayer, then vanished and returned to their home with Brahmā. Hearken, Garur; then came Śambhu to Raghubīra and with a

1. The four coats of bark are the four Vedas; the six boughs are thought to be the six stages of existence, *viz.*, conception, birth, childhood, manhood, old age and death; or else the six natural impulses, *viz.*, hunger, thirst, excretion of both kinds, sleep, and sexual intercourse. The twenty-five branchlets are Prakṛti, Buddhi, Ahaṅkāra, the five Tan-māt-ras, the five Mahābhūtas, the ten Indriyas, Manas and Puruṣa. The two fruits are pleasure and pain and the creeper Māyā.

choking voice and every hair on his body erect he thus made supplication:

Chand 6 (Trotaka)[1]

"Glory to thee, Rāma, the spouse of Lakṣmī, the pacifier; have mercy on thy servant, harassed with the terrors and troubles of existence. Glorious Lord, sovereign of Avadh, sovereign of heaven, Lakṣmī's sovereign, have mercy on the suppliant, who has fled to thee for refuge and craves protection! Destroyer of the ten-headed and twenty-armed, remover of earth's sore burden, consumer of the moth-like demon host in the fierce flame of thy fiery arrows; most beauteous ornament of the terrestrial sphere; noblest of all that handle bow, arrows and quiver; radiant as the sun to disperse the thick darkness of the night of pride, ignorance and egoism; thou hast vanquished the God of Love,[2] who like a huntsman had smitten all men to the heart with the arrows of evil desire as though they were herd of deer; now, O Lord Hari, have mercy on us destitute wretches, who are lost in the wilderness of sensuality. The countless diseases and bereavements, with which the people are afflicted, are the fruit of this disregard for thy holy feet. The bottomless ocean of existence overwhelms all who cherish no love for thy lotus feet. Poor indeed and vile and wretched for ever are they who have no affection for thy lotus feet. They who take delight in making mention of thy name have the sages as their constant friends for ever, are eternally exempt from passion, greed and arrogance, and regard prosperity and adversity as both alike. Thus it is that thy servants are so happy; the sage abandons for ever all confidence in mortification and making simply a vow of perpetual love serves thy lotus feet with a pure heart. O Raghubira, mighty and invincible hero, indwelling as a bee in the lotus-like soul of the sages, thy name, O Hari, I repeat

1. In the Toṭaka, or Troṭaka metre, each line in the quatrain consists of four anapaests. Thus :—

Jaya Rāma Ramā-ramaṇam samanam.
Bhava-tāpa-bhayākula pāhi janam.

2. *Manajād*, 'man-eaters,' or 'demons,' is the word in the text; but, as it seems impossible to fit it into the rest of the passage, I propose to read instead *manajāt*, the 'mindborn,' *i.e.*, Kāmadeva, the god of love.

in prayer and adore thee, destroyer of vanity and pride, which are the diseases of life. Humbly I adore without ceasing the spouse of Lakṣmī, the supreme abode of goodness, generosity and compassion. O sun of Raghu, extirpate every animosity; O king of earth, regard thy humble servant.

Dohā 14a-14b

Again and again I beg of thee a boon—be gracious and grant it gladly, O Śrīraṅga[1]—an unwavering faith in thy lotus feet and constant communion with saints." After thus hymning Rāma's virtues, Śiva returned with joy to Kailāsa. The Lord then assigned the monkeys most delightful residences.

Caupāī 13

Hearken, king of birds; this sacred legend annihilates all the distresses and fear of rebirth. Anyone who hears this narrative of the royal installation obtains self-control and discretion. They who lovingly sing it or hear it sung, obtain every kind of happiness and prosperity; after enjoying in this world a bliss, to which the gods can scarce attain, they are admitted after death into Rāma's own presence. The finally emancipated, the detached from the world and the worldly, who hear it, obtain respectively faith, absorption into the divinity and ever-increasing prosperity. O king of birds, this story of Rāma that I have repeated is the delight of a good understanding : a remedy for anxiety and sorrow; a confirmation of detachment, discretion and faith : a splendid raft on which to cross the river of delusion. In the city of Kosala was ever some new festivity; the people were all happy, from the highest to the lowest. All felt an evergrowing affection for Rāma's lotus feet, the adored of Brahmā, Śiva and the sages. The poor had clothes, given them in abundance and the Brāhmans were presented with offerings of every description.

Dohā 15

The monkeys were all rapt in blissful ecstasy, devoted to their

1. Śriraṅga, Holy Raṅga, is one of Viṣṇu's epithets and gives its name to the city of Seringapatam (Śrīraṅgapaṭṭana), where is a great temple dedicated to the divinity under this title.

Lord's feet : day and night passed unnoticed till now six months had been spent.

Caupāī 14

They had forgotten their homes so absolutely that they never even dreamt of them, just as the idea of injuring another never enters the soul of a saint. At last Raghupati summoned all his friends before him. They came and made reverent obeisance. He seated them by his side with the greatest kindness and thus addressed them in gracious terms, which might well gladden their pious souls: "You have done me excellant service; but how can I praise you to your faces ? I hold you all most dear for having left the comforts of your homes solely on my account. My younger brother, my crown, my fortune, my wife, my life, my home and loving kinsmen all these are dear to me, but you are dearer still. I speak, as I always do, in all sincerity. It is customary for a man to cherish his own adherents, but I feel a special affection for those who do me service.

Dohā 16

Now, comrades, return to your homes and there worship me with steadfast faith and maintain your fervent devotion, knowing me to be the eternal and omnipresent benefactor of every creature."

Caupāī 15

When they heard the Lord's words, they were all so overwhelmed that they forgot who they were, or where they were, or where they had come from. With clasped hands and fixed gaze they stood before him, unable to speak from excess of devotion. The Lord perceived the intensity of their devotion and said all he could to teach them resignation. In his presence they could make no reply, but still turned their eyes to his lotus feet. Then the Lord called for jewels and robes of honour, of many colours, incomparably beautiful, and first Bharata with his own hands made ready a dress, with which he invested Sugrīva. By the Lord's command Lakṣmaṇa next invested the king of Laṅkā, to Rāma's great contentment. But Aṅgada remained seated and did not stir. Seeing his love, the Lord did not speak to him :

Dohā 17a-17b

But proceeded with the investiture of Jāṁbavān and Nila and the rest, who, with Rāma's image impressed upon their hearts, bowed their heads at his feet and departed. Then Aṅgada arose and made obeisance and with weeping eyes and clasped hands uttered his humble petition, impregnate as it were with the very essence of devotion.

Caupāī 16

"Hearken, all-wise, all-merciful and all-blessed, commiserator of the destitute, succour of the distressed! Bāli, my Lord, in his last moments placed me in your charge. To be the helper of the helpless is the character you support; benefactor of the faithful, do not abandon me. You, Sire, are my spiritual guide, my father and my mother; whither shall I go if I leave your lotus feet ? Consider yourself and tell me, O king of men, apart from my Lord, what is my home to me ? Extend to me your protection, O Lord, a mere child as I am without knowledge, wisdom, or strength, and regard me as one of the humblest of your servants. Let me perform the most menial office in your palace, if only I may see your lotus feet and thus traverse the ocean of existence." So saying, he fell at the Lord's feet, "O Sire, do not again tell me to go home."

Dohā 18a-18b

On hearing Aṅgada's humble prayer, the all-merciful Lord Rāma raised him from the ground and clasped him to his bosom, his lotus eyes streaming with tears. He clothed the son of Bāli in his own robe and jewels and the garland from his own neck, and then the Lord bade him farewell with many words of consolation.

Caupāī 17

Being greatly moved by his devotion, Bharata with his brother Satrughna and Lakṣmaṇa proceeded to escort him. But Aṅgada's heart was so overflowing with love that he turned again and again for one more look at Rāma. Time after time he prostrated himself upon the ground, crying. 'Thus would I stay, if Rāma would only let me.' Treasuring up in his mind Rāma's look and voice and gait, his smile too and his embrace, with a last glance at his face and many words of fervent prayer, he went forth, cherishing his lotus feet in his heart. After escorting all the monkeys with the utmost respect, Bharata and his brother returned. Then Hanumān clasped Sugrīva's feet and earnestly besought him: "Let me spend ten days more in Rāma's service and then I will return to your feet, my master." "O Son of the Wind, great is your merit; go, serve the All-merciful." So saying, the other monkeys went their way, but Aṅgada cried: "Hearken, Hanumān,

Dohā 19a-19b

With folded hands I beg of you to present my service to the Lord and frequently remind him of me." So saying, the son of Bāli started on his way, while Hanumān returned and told the Lord of his devotion. The great god was overjoyed. Now hard as adamant, now soft as the petal of a flower, such, O king of birds, is Rāma's heart; who can comprehend it ?

Caupāī 18

Next, the All-merciful Lord summoned the Niṣāda and graciously presented him with jewels and raiment, saying, "Return to your home, but ever remember me, and in heart, word and deed observe all the ordinances of religion. You, my companion, are as much my brother as Bharata; you must always be backwards and forwards here." On hearing these words, Guha was greatly delighted and fell at his feet, his eyes full of tears. With the image of his lotus feet impressed upon his heart, he returned home and related the Lord's generosity to all his kinsfolk. The citizens, on beholding Rāma's actions, shouted again and again, 'Blessed be he in whom is perfect bliss !' Under Rāma's sway the three spheres were full of joy, all sorrow was at an end; no one had a grudge against another, every variance was extinguished under Rāma's auspices.

Dohā 20

Devoted to duty, the people walked in the path of the Vedas, each according to his own caste and stage of life,[1] and enjoyed perfect happiness, unvexed by fear, or sorrow, or disease.

Caupāī 19

In the whole of Rāma's realm there was no one who suffered from bodily pains, ill fortune or evil circumstance. Every man loved his neighbour and contented with the state of life to which he had been born, conformably to the teaching of Scripture and sound morality. The four pillars of religion[2] were established throughout the world; no one even dreamt of sin. Men and women alike were devoted to Rāma's worship and enjoyed all the blessedness of highest heaven. There was no premature death and no sickness even, but everyone was comely and sound of body. No one was in poverty, in sorrow, or distress; no one ignorant or unlucky. All the men and women were unaffectedly good and pious, clever and intelligent. Everyone appreciated the merits of his neighbour and was himself learned and wise; everyone was grateful for kindnesses and guilelessly prudent.

Dohā 21

Listen. O king of birds, during Rāma's reign there was not a creature in the world, animate or inanimate, that suffered from any of the ills that ordinarily result from time or past conduct or personal temperament and character.

Caupāī 20

The world engirdled by seven seas had only one king, Rāma, the lord of Kosala. This was no great matter for him, every

1. The *āśramas*, or 'stages of life,' are not to be confounded by the English reader with what would be ordinarily designated 'states of life.' They are four in number: 1st, that of the Brahmacāri, or student; 2nd, that of the Gṛhastha, householder; 3rd, that of the Vānaprastha, or anchorite; and 4th, that of the Bhikṣu, or mendicant.

2. The four pillars of religion are truth, purity, mercy, and charity.

hair on whose body is one of the countless spheres of creation. To a man who rightly understands the greatness of the Lord this description will seem highly disparaging. But those who understand his divine majesty, Garuṛ, are the very persons who take supreme delight in these actions of his. They are the special rewards of such knowledge; so declare the greatest of sages and ascetics.[1] Not even Śeṣanāga or Sāradā could describe the bliss and prosperity of Rāma's realm. Everyone was generous and kindly disposed to his neighbour and submissive to the Brāhmaṇas. Every husband was faithful to his single wife and every wife was devoted to her husband in thought and word and deed.

Dohā 22

A rod was never seen, save in the the hands of as.etics; the words 'to beat' had no meaning except to mark the time for a dancer on the stage; and the only victory known was self-conquest, throughout all Rāmacandra's realm.

Caupāī 21

The trees in the forest were ever full of flowers and fruit; the elephant and the lion dwelt peaceably together. Birds and deer forgot their instinctive animosities and lived in the greatest harmony with one another. The cooing of the birds and the many herds of deer fearlessly roaming the woods made a charming scene. The air was cool, fragrant and exquisitely mild; bees laden with honey made a pleasant humming. Creepers and trees yielded their sweetness on being asked and the cows in sheer lightness of heart dropped their milk on the road. The earth was ever clothed with crops and every feature of the Golden Age was repeated in the Age of Silver. Mines of jewels of every description were disclosed in the mountains and the world acknowledged its king to be in truth the Universal Spirit. Every river flowed with an abundance of water, cool, pure and delicious to the taste and refreshing. The sea remained within its

1. For *barad susila*, given in Rāma Jasan's edition, the preferable reading seems to be *bar dam-silā*.

bounds, casting forth pearls on its shore for men to gather. The ponds were all thick with lotuses and every quarter and section of the world was supremely happy.

Dohā 23

The earth was suffused with the radiance of the moon; the sun gave as much heat as was required, and the clouds dropped rain whenever asked, in the days when Rāma was king.

Caupāī 22

The Lord celebrated millions of horse-sacrifices and conferred innumerable gifts upon the Brāhmaṇas, approving himself the defender of the Vedic usage, the pillar of the faith perfect in every virtue and the sworn foe of all sensuality. Sītā was ever obedient to her lord, incomparable in her beauty, her virtue and her meekness, sensible of the majesty of the Lord of grace and devotedly attached to his lotus feet. Though there were many man-servants and maid-servants in the palace, all well-skilled in their work, she discharged every domestic duty with her own hands, waiting on Rāma's orders. Any service that might please the gracious Lord she herself skilfully performed. Without the slightest pride or conceit she attended on Kausalyā and the other queen dowagers in the place. O Umā, Lakṣmī, the object of the adoration of Brahmā and all the divinities, the mother of the universe, the ever blameless,

Dohā 24

She whose glance of favour is coveted by the gods—but she looks not at them—forgot her own high estate and practised this devotion to Rāma's lotus feet.

Caupāī 23

Though she waited diligently on all the brothers, her devotion to Rāma was most conspicuous. She never ceased to watch his lotus face on the chance that he might be pleased to speak to her. Rāma on his part was most affectionate to his brothers and instructed them on all points of morality. The citizens lived happily, each enjoying a felicity to which the gods might scarce attain. Day and night they made their prayer to God, beseeching him to grant them a fervent devotion to Rāma's holy feet. Two comely sons were born to Sītā, Lava and Kuśa; so the Vedas and Purāṇas have declared; both glorious in battle, modest and accomplished and so beautiful that they seemed the very image of Hari. The other brothers also had each two sons, preeminent in beauty, virtue and all good qualities.

Dohā 25

The Supreme Spirit that is beyond all knowledge, speech and perception, the uncreated, transcending illusion or the workings of mind or the properties of things, even he it was—the sum of True Being, Thought and Bliss—who thus exhibited the exalted actions of a mortal man.

Caupāī 24

Early in the morning after bathing in the Sarayū he sat in his court, in the midst of Brāhmaṇas and nobles, while Vasiṣṭha recited the Vedas and Purāṇas; Rāma listening attentively, though he knew them all. He took his meals with his brothers, the royal matrons looking on with the utmost satisfaction. Then Bharata and Śatrughna, the two brothers, would take Hanumān to some grove, where they would sit down and ask him all about Rāma's doings and he would reply out of the depth of his wisdom. It was such a delight to them to hear the glorious narrative that they would beg him to repeat it again and again. In every single house the sacred legend was told of Rāma's marvellously holy deeds. Men and women alike joined in hymning his praises, and day and night passed unheeded.

Dohā 26

Not a thousand Śeṣanāgas could describe all the happiness and prosperity of the city of Avadh, when Rāma reigned as king.

Caupāī 25

Nārada and Sanaka and all the great sages came every day to Ayodhyā to see the king of Kosala. The appearance of the city made them forget all their asceticism. There were balconies inlaid with gold and jewels, splendid pavements laid in diverse colours, magnificent forts on every side of the city with their brightly painted battlements, as though the nine planets had been mustered in array to beleaguer Indra's capital, Amarāvatī, and floors so beautifully inlaid with coloured crystal that the soul of any saint would be distracted at the sight; the glistening palaces, were so lofty that they touched the sky with pinnacles that put to shame the brightness of sun and moon, while the lattices gleamed with jewels and the jewelled lamps shone in every room.

Chand 7

Beneath the light of jewelled lamps the houses shone with their thresholds of coral and pillars of precious stone and golden walls such as the Creator himself might have fashioned, all inlaid with emeralds and gems. The stately palaces were lovely with inworked crystal, and every gate was fitted with folding doors of gold embossed with diamonds.

Dohā 27

In every house was a beautiful and well-furnished picture gallery, where Rāma's achievements were so set forth that the soul of a sage would be ravished at the sight.

Caupāī 26

Everyone had a flower garden trimmed with the greatest care, adorned with every kind of lovely creeper, blossoming as though it were perpetual spring. There was ever a pleasant sound of the buzzing of bees, and the air was delightfully cool, soft and fragrant. Birds of all kinds, the children's pets, sweet of note and graceful in flight, peacocks, swans herons and pigeons, made a charming show on the tops of the houses, cooing and dancing in high glee at the sight of their own shadow. Children were teaching parrots and *maināṣ* to speak andrepe at the name of Rāma, Raghupati, and 'Saviour'. The palace gates were most magnificent, and the roads, squares and bazārs all elegantly laid out.

Chand 8

The elegance of the market-places was beyond all description, and things could be had without price. How is it possible to sing of the riches of the city where the spouse of Lakṣmī reigned as king ? Cloth-merchants, money-changers and grain-dealers sat at their stalls like so many Kuveras. Everyone was happy, everyone well-conducted and comely, men and women, young and old, alike.

Dohā 28

To the north flowed the deep and pellucid stream of the Sarjū, with a row of charming steps and no muddy bank anywhere.

Caupāī 27

At some distance was a fine spacious *ghāṭ*, where all the horses and elephants went to drink. There were also splendid *ghāṭs* for the citizens' drinking water, where no one was allowed to bathe. The most beautiful of all was the royal *ghāṭ*, which was frequented by men of all four castes. All along the banks were temples of the gods surrounded by pleasant groves. Here and there on the river bank hermits, sages and anchorites dwelt and meditated ; and many bushes of the fragrant *tulasi* were there, planted by sages. The beauty of the city surpassed all description; its outskirts also were most picturesque. Every sin was effaced by a sight of it, with its woods and groves, its lakes and ponds.

Chand 9

Its matchless lakes and ponds and large and beautiful wells were so charming, with their elegant flights of steps and limpid water, that gods and sages were fascinated by the sight. The many-coloured lotuses, the cooing of innumerable birds and the buzzing of the bees made the garden a delightful one, where the parrots by the clamour seemed to be inviting travellers to halt.

Dohā 29

How is it possible to describe the city of which Lakṣmī's Lord was king ? Aṇimā and all the supernatural powers had diffused through the whole of Avadh every happiness and prosperity.

Caupāī 28

Everywhere men were singing Rāma's praises and as they sat thus exhorted one another : "Worship Rāma, the defender of the suppliant ; the home of beauty and goodness, of comeliness and virtue; the lotus-eyed and dark-complexioned : who protects his servants as the eyelid does the eye, who is equipped with a lovely bow and arrows and quiver ; the champion of the battle ; a very sun to rejoice the lotus-like company of the sages ; a Garuṛ to consume the terrible serpent Death : whose loving kindness is over all who unselfishly worship Rāma ; a huntsman Kirāta to scatter the deer-like herd of ignorance and greed ; a lion to quell the wild elephant, Love ; the granter of happiness to his people ; a sun to scatter the thick darkness of doubt and grief ; a fire to consume the dense forest of demons; who can refuse to worship Raghubīra and Sītā, seeing that he is the breaker of earth's burdens; the frost that kills the insect swarm of manifold desires ; the ever uniform ; the uncreated and imperishable ; the delight of the sages ; the breaker of earth's burdens ; Tulasī Dāsa's own gracious Lord ?"

Dohā 30

In such wise the city sang Rāma's praises, while on his part the All-merciful was ever to them most gracious.

Caupāī 29

From the time, O king of birds, of the rising of the glorious sun of Rāma's power the three spheres were all suffused with light : many were happy, but many also were sad. First to enumerate the sorrowful : to begin with, the night of Ignorance was at an end; owl-like Sin slunk away out of sight ; Lust and Anger, like gamblers, were ashamed to show themselves; Formalism,[1] Phenomenal Existence, Time and Nature, were as ill at ease as the partridge; Envy, Pride, Infatuation and Conceit were like thieves, with nowhere a chance to display their skill. But the ponds of Piety blossomed with the lotuses of Knowledge and Understanding ; while Happiness, Contentment, Self-control and Discretion were like so many *cakavās* and *cakavīs* when their sorrow is over.

Dohā 31

When this glorious sun illumines a man's heart, these latter qualities grow and increase and the first mentioned die away.

Caupāī 30

One day Rāma and his brothers together with his special favourite Hanumān went to visit a beautiful grove, where every tree was bright with flowers and fresh leaves. Sanaka and his brother sages noted their opportunity and came also, a glorious band of pre-eminent virtue and goodness, ever absorbed in the rapture of transcendental felicity and still youthful to look at despite their immemorial years. One in appearance and without any distinctive mark, as it might be the four Vedas in bodily form, the sages had but this one hope, desire and ambition, to hear the recital of Rāma's actions. They stopped, Bhavānī, at the same place as the learned sage Agastya, who repeated to them the whole of Rāma's story, the source of true wisdom, as the fire-stick is of fire.

1. By *Karma*, which I here translate 'Formalism', is meant ceremonial as opposed to contemplative religion: the ordinary routine of fasts, sacrifices, ablutions and other outward observances as distinct from the interior and purely spiritual exercises of the soul, which it is the main object of this poem to recommend. It may also be taken in a wider sense as Necessity, the inexorable sequence of cause and effect, by which the whole world is governed. The ultimate result is the same; for the practice of external religious observances for the sake of the minor prizes attached to them — minor, that is, as compared with the reward promised to interior faith — is only one illustration of the belief in the general law, though the most important to Tulasī Dāsa, writing as a theologian.

Dohā 32

When Rāma saw the sages approaching, he rejoiced and prostrated himself before them ; then after giving them welcome, the Lord of the yellow robe made them sit down.

Caupāī 31

His three brothers made their obeisance and were greatly delighted, as also Hanumān. The sages, as they gazed on Rāma's incomparable beauty, were beside themselves with rapture. With folded hands they bowed the head before him and could not close their eyes for a moment so intensely were they fixed on the shrine of beauty, the conqueror of the world, with his lotus-eyes and dark-hued frame. When Raghubīra perceived their condition, his eyes streamed with tears and his body quivered with emotion. He took them by the hand and made them sit down and addressed them in these most gracious accents : "Hearken, reverend Sirs ; to-day I am indeed blessed ; at the sight of you sin is annihilated. The fellowship of the sages is the greatest of blessings : it at once effects a severance from the world.

Dohā 33

Association with the sages leads to final beatitude, but with the sensual to endless transmigrations : so say the sages themselves, the greatest of the poets, the Vedas, the Purāṇas and all the scriptures."

Caupāī 32

The four sages rejoiced to hear the Lord's words and with quivering body they raised this hymn of praise : "Glory to the Lord God, the everlasting, the unchangeable, the sinless, the multiform, the One, the All-merciful ! Glory to the unembodied ! Glory to the universal embodiment, the palace of bliss, the beautiful in his comeliness ! Glory to the spouse of Lakṣmī ! Glory to the supporter of the earth, peerless in his splendour ; the uncreated, and from everlasting : the fountain of wisdom ;

the immeasurable[1] ; the bestower of honour; whose holy fame is the theme of the Vedas and Purāṇas ; the all-wise, the all-generous ; the destroyer of ignorance ; the many-named, the nameless ; the emotionless ; the universe itself, the universal spirit ; the indweller of every heart ! Abide with us and protect us for ever. O Rāma ; dwell in our heart, tearing asunder the bonds of the world and its miserable contentions and destroying our lust and conceit !

Dohā 34

O holy Rāma, All-blessed and All-merciful, fulfiller of every desire of the soul, bestow on us the boon of constant love and devotion !

Caupāī 33

Bestow on us, O Raghupati, that purifying faith which annihilates every distress and worldly conceit. Be propitious and grant us this boon, O our Lord, a very cow of plenty, and tree of Paradise to satisfy the desires of the suppliant. O Raghunāyaka, Agastya to swallow up the ocean of mundane existence, the bestower of blessings which only your servants find it easy to acquire ; destroyer of the destroying tortures of love; friend of the friendless: diffuser of equanimity; preventer of wrong desire and fear, of envy and all passions; bestower of meekness, discretion and detachment ; jewel of earthly kings; glory of the world; grant us devotion to thee, the only raft on which to cross the floods of existence; immortal swan in the holy lake of saintly souls; whose lotus feet are adored by Brahmā and Śiva; banner of the line of Raghu; the protector of the Vedic bounds ; annihilator of time, destiny, nature and phenomenal existence ; ark of salvation ; healer of every sorrow ; glory of the three spheres ; Tulasī Dāsa's own Lord."

1. *Amān* is capable of two meanings: either 'immeasurable,' from the root *mā*, 'to measure;' or 'without pride,' from the root *man*, to think.' Either will suit the context equally well, and the jingle between it and the following word *māna-prad* is probably what chiefly suggested it to the poet.

Dohā 35

Having again and again hymned his praises and lovingly bowed the head, Sanaka and his companions returned to Brahmā's sphere, after obtaining the boon they had so vehemently coveted.

Caupāī 34

When Sanaka and his companions had gone their way to Brahmā's sphere, the three brothers bowed their head at Rāma's feet, but being too diffident themselves to put the question to the Lord, they looked to Hanumān, wishing to hear from the Lord's own mouth an explanation which would terminate all their doubts. The reader of the heart understood this perfectly and said, "What is it you wish to know, Hanumān?" Then replied Hanumān with folded hands, "Hearken, All-merciful Lord God; Bharata, Sire, wishes to ask something, but is too diffident to speak out." "Monkey, you know my feelings," said the Lord, "there are no secrets between me and Bharata." On hearing the Lord's words, Bharata clasped his feet and said, "Hearken, my Lord, reliever of all the anxieties of the suppliant;

Dohā 36

I have no doubts whatever, Lord: not a shadow of disquietude or distrust; and this all of your mercy, O All-merciful and All-blessed.

Caupāī 35

But if I may presume on your loving-kindness—for I am your servant and you the benefactor of your faithful people—the Vedas and Purāṇas, O Raghurāī, have sung in various ways the greatness of the sages; you too have exalted them with your blessed lips, declaring that the Lord has a special affection for them. I would fain hear, Sire, their distinctive marks, O gracious discerner of character and understanding. Instruct me, protector of the suppliant, in the qualities that distinguish the good from the wicked." "Hearken brother: the marks of the good as told in the Vedas and Purāṇas are innumerable. The conduct of the good to the wicked is like that of the sandal tree to the axe, for—mark it, brother—the fragrant sandal imparts its perfume to the very axe that fells it.

Dohā 37

For this reason sandal-wood is the desire of the world and has the honour of being put on the head of gods; while the axe, for its punishment, has its blade heated in the fire and is well hammered.

Caupāī 36

Without attachment to sensual objects; store-houses of virtue and generosity; sorrowing in the sorrow of others and finding joy in their joy; equable, devoid of animosity; sober, passionless; conquerors of greed and impatience, joy and fear; tender-hearted, compassionate to the poor; with a guileless devotion to me in thought and word and deed; giving honour to all, but claiming none for themselves—such, Bharata, are dear to me as my own life. They are unselfish, devoted to my name; happy abodes of tranquillity, continence and humility; models of contentment, simplicity, benevolence, piety and devotion to the Brāhmaṇas. Verily, brother, any heart in which these qualities abide is ever the heart of a saint. They swerve not from quietude, self-control, religious observances or from their moral principles; they never utter a harsh word;

Dohā 38

They regard praise and blame as both alike in their exclusive devotion to my lotus feet; such men are the treasurers of virtue, the compendiums of bliss, who are good and whom I love as my own soul.

Caupāī 37

Hear now the characteristics of sinners, with whom one should carefully avoid any dealings. Their company always leads to trouble, as when an ill-conditioned cow gets a gentle companion beaten like itself. The heart of the wicked is a consuming fire, which is ever ablaze at the sight of another's prosperity; but whenever they hear a neighbour abused, they are as glad as if they had picked up a treasure on the road. Devoted to lust, choleric, arrogant and greedy; censorious, treacherous, perverse and impure; cherishing causeless animosities against everyone: disliking anything that others like, false in taking, false in giving, false in great matters and false in small; speaking plausible words, but ruthless of heart, like the peacock that sings so melodiously and devours the biggest snake.

Dohā 39

Injurious to their neighbour, covetous of his wife and wealth and gloating over his misfortunes; such men are vile and abominable, ruthless incarnate fiends.

Caupāī 38

Coveting dress, coveting bed; addicted to lust and gluttony; with no fear of hell; catching their breath, as though they had got the ague when they hear of anyone's advancement; but as glad as though they had been made kings of the world, when they see their neighbour in distress; devoted to their own selfish interests, quarrelsome among their kinsfolk, dissolute, avaricious and choleric; disrespectful to father and mother, to *guru* and Brāhmaṇa: dragging down others into the same ruin with themselves: infatuated workers of other's ill: taking no pleasure in the company of the good or in the discourse about Hari: oceans of immorality, dull of understanding, lascivious, revilers of the Vedas, claiming a right to other men's property, special torment of the Brāhmaṇas and the gods, with deceit and treachery in their heart, though outwardly fair seeming.

Dohā 40

No such vile wretches of man existed in the first and second ages,[1] and only a few in the third, but in the fourth there are swarms of them.

Caupāī 39

O my brother, there is no religion like doing good to others

1. The four ages are: Kṛtayuga, Tretāyuga, Dvāparayuga, and Kaliyuga.

and no meanness like malevolence. What I now declare to you is the sum of the Vedas and Purāṇas and the verdict of the philosophers. Men who in the body cause suffering to others undergo an enormous series of transmigrations. Men are so infatuated that in their devotion to their own selfish interests they commit many sins and ruin their prospects for the next world. I reveal myself to them, brother, as Doom and apportion the reward of their deeds, whether good or evil. The truly wise consider the matter thus and worship me, regarding the world only as a burden; they discard action with its result, good or bad, and devoutly adore me, the king of gods and men and saints. Thus have I declared the characteristics of the good and the bad; they who remember them will not be submerged in the flood of existence.

Dohā 41

Hearken, brother; the multitudinous forms of merit and demerit are all the products of Māyā: discretion lies in noticing neither: to notice them is an imperfection of knowledge."

Caupāī 40

On hearing this speech from Rāma's holy lips, the brothers rejoiced and their heart overflowed with love. Again and again they paid him profound homage, while a boundless delight filled the soul of Hanumān also. Rāma then withdrew to the private palace; but every day there was some new incident of the same character. Nārada the sage came time after time and hymned Rāma's holy acts, every day finding something new to record. He then went to Brahmā's realm and there recited the whole story. The Creator on hearing it was so highly pleased that he urged him to repeat it again and again. Sanaka and his brother sages marvelled at Nārada; and the saints, though absorbed in the contemplation of the Supreme Spirit, forgot their abstraction on hearing his hymn of praise. The highest powers listened reverently.

Dohā 42

Though exempted from mundane existence and intent on the contemplation of the Supreme, they interrupted their meditations in order to hear his lay. Truly theirs must be a heart of stone who take no delight in Rāma's story.

Caupāī 41

One day summoned by Rāma all the *gurus* and Brāhmaṇas and people of the city came together, and when the priests and nobles had taken their seats in the assembly, the comforter of the pious made them this speech: "Hearken to my words, all ye people of the city. I speak without any selfish motive at heart, neither wronging another nor aggrandizing myself; listen and act as may seem good to you. He is my servant and my best beloved who accepts my commands. If I say anything that is iniquitous, brother, do not be afraid to correct me. All the Scriptures declare that it is great good fortune and a great difficulty surmounted to be born with the body of a man, which is a storehouse of opportunities, a gate of deliverance; and those who have received it and still attain not to heaven,

Dohā 43

They, I say, reap torment in the next world and beat their heads in vain despair, wrongly attributing the blame to time, fate and God.

Caupāī 42

But materialism, brother, is not the proper object of the human body; it is happiness for a very brief period, but ends in misery. The possessor of a human body who gives himself up to sensual delights is like a fool who chooses poison in preference to ambrosia. He is one of whom none can speak well; he throws away the philosopher's stone to pick up a worthless seed. Such a creature drifts for ever among the four modes of birth and the forty-eight lakhs of living species, perpetually changing at the will of Māyā and encompassed by Time, Fate, Nature and Phenomena. At some time or another God of his mercy and without any reason for the favour, gives him a human body, a raft on which he may cross the ocean of existence, with my grace as a fair wind to speed him on his course: with pious teachers at the helm he easily procures all the equipment of a stout ship, which would else be beyond him.

Dohā 44

If thus equipped he fails to cross the sea, he is an ungrateful wretch, bent on his own destruction.

Caupāī 43

Whoso desires happiness in this world and the next will hearken to my words and imprint them deeply in his heart. It is an easy and pleasant road, my brothers, that of my service, as the Vedas and the Purāṇas declare. Knowledge is difficult and beset with impediments; its appliances are cumbrous and it has no grasp on the soul. Though a man endures endless tortures, he is not dear to me if he lacks faith. Faith is all-powerful and a mine of every blessing; but men cannot attain to it except by the fellowship of saints. The saints are not won except by meritorious deeds; their fellowship causes the end of mundane existence. Now there is no other meritorious deed in the whole world than this one, *viz*., to worship Brāhmaṇas in thought, word and deed. Seers and gods are all in his favour who eschews guile and devotes himself to the Brāhmaṇas.

Dohā 45

One other mysterious doctrine I with folded hands reveal to you all; without prayer to Śiva no one can attain to the faith that I require.

Caupāī 44

Tell me, what are the difficulties in the way of faith? Neither abstract meditation is necessary, nor sacrifice, prayer, penance nor fasting; only simplicity of character, a mind void of forwardness and absolute contentment whatever may befall. If one who is called a worshipper of mine puts confidence in man, tell me where is his trust in me? But why protract my discourse to such a length ? These are the practices, brother, by which I am won: avoidance of enmity and rancour, of hope and fear; a constant atmosphere of perfect repose; passionless, homeless; without pride and without sin; placid, provident and wise; ever devoted to the fellowship of the good; lightly esteeming every object of sense and even heaven and final deliverance from the body; persistent in faith, innocent of wickedness, a stranger to impious scepticism.

Dohā 46

Devoted to my name, which is the sum of all my perfections; devoid of selfishness, conceit and vanity; such a man's happiness, be assured, is the very sum of transcendental felicity."

Caupāī 45

On hearing the gracious Rāma's ambrosial speech, they all clasped his feet: "Fountain of mercy, you are our father, our mother, or spiritual guide and our brother, and are dearer than our life. You, O Rāma, have blessed us in body, substance and house, and have removed all the sorrows of your suppliants. No one but you could teach us this lesson; for even father and mother are self-interested. The only two disinterested friends in the world are you yourself and your servants, O foe of demons. Every friend in the world thinks first of himself; no one, Sire, ever dreams of thinking of the highest object." When Raghunātha heard them all speak in such terms of devotion, he was rejoiced at heart, and they on receiving his permission returned to their several homes, making the Lord the glorious theme of all their talk.

Dohā 47

O Umā, every man and woman among the inhabitants of Avadh was the picture of satisfaction; the supreme felicity of heaven suffused the whole city when Rāma was king.

Caupāī 46

One day the sage Vasiṣṭha came to visit the blessed and glorious Rāma. The prince of the house of Raghu received him with most profound respect and washed his feet and drank of the water. "Hearken, Rāma," said the sage, clasping his hands, "Ocean of mercy, I have a request to make. After seeing your deeds, a boundless bewilderment possesses my soul. Your immeasurable greatness is beyond the comprehension of the Vedas. How, then, can I speak of it? The business of a family-priest is very contemptible; the Vedas and the Purāṇas and other Scriptures make small account of it. At first I refused it, but the Creator said to me, 'You will be a gainer hereafter, my son. Brahmā, the Supreme Spirit, will be born in human form as a king, the glory of the race of Raghu.'

Dohā 48

Then I thought to myself that if I shall thus attain to him who is the object of all contemplation, penance, charity and sacrifice, there could be no higher office than this.

Caupāī 47

Prayer, penance, pious observances and doing one's duty in life are different good actions based on the Scriptures. But knowledge, mercy, self-control, bathing at holy places and all the religious practices inculcated by revelation, as also the study of the Vedas and sacred traditions and numerous Purāṇas, are only means to a glorious end, viz., a constant devotion to your lotus feet. Can dirt be removed by cleansing with dirt? Is *ghi* to be obtained by churning water? Except, O Raghurāī, by the water of faith and love, the interior stain can never be effaced. He is all-wise, he the philosopher, the scholar, the thoroughly accomplished, the irrefutable doctor, the truly judicious and the possessor of every auspicious attribute, who is devoted to your lotus feet.

Dohā 49

My Lord, there is just one boon I crave; grant it, O Rāma, in your clemency. In all my future births may my love for my Lord's lotus feet never diminish !"

Caupāī 48

So saying, the sage Vasiṣṭha returned home and the All-merciful was greatly pleased at heart. Then, being ever gracious to his servants, he took with him Hanumān and Bharata and his other brothers and in his benignity went outside the city, where he ordered up the elephants, chariots and horses. After reviewing them he was pleased to praise them all and then distributed them, giving each person the one that he wished. The Lord, the remover of all weariness, grew weary and repaired to a cool mango grove, where Bharata spread his own raiment on the ground, and there the Lord took his seat, with all his brothers in attendance, while the Son of the Wind fanned him. At this his body quivered with emotion and his eyes filled with tears. There is no one so blessed as Hanumān, nor any so devoted to Rāma's feet, whose love and devotion, O Umā, have again and again been told by the Lord with his own mouth!

Dohā 50

At that time came the sage Nārada with his lute in his hand, and began to hymn Rāma's glorious renown, that pregnant theme.

Caupāī 49

"Look upon me, O Lotus-eyed, merciful of aspect, liberator from delusion; dark of hue as the blue lotus; conqueror of love; bee of the perfumed lotus of Śiva's heart; Hari, breaker of the might of the demon host; delight of the saints and the pious; exterminator of sin; beneficent to Brāhmaṇas as a rain-cloud to the new crops; help of the helpless; befriender of the humble; by the might of whose arm earth's grievous burden has been broken; ingenious slayer of Khara and Dūṣaṇa and Virādha; Rāvaṇa's antagonist; incarnation of beauty; noblest of kings. Glory to you, O moon to the lily of the house of Dasarath, whose glory is renowned in the Purāṇas, the Vedas and all the Scriptures, and sung by gods and patriarchs and all the company of the saints. O merciful Lord, destroyer of falsehood and pride, infinitely glorious, glory of Kosala, whose name corrects all the impurities of this sinful age and puts an end to the delusions of self, have mercy upon your humble adorer, even me Tulasī Dāsa."

Dohā 51

When the venerable Nârada had completed his loving recital of Râma's praises, he clasped the Ocean of Beauty to his heart and departed to the realm of Brahmâ.

Caupāī 50

Hearken, Umâ, to his glorious legend, the whole of which I have now told to the best of my ability. But Râma's acts are hundreds of millions in number and beyond all reckoning; not even the Vedas or Sāradā could recount them all. Râma is infinite and infinite his excellent perfections; infinite are his incarnations, his actions and his names. You may count the drops in a shower of rain or the dust on the earh, but Râma's doings defy enumeration. This holy story ensures translation to Hari's own sphere; whoever hears it acquires an imperishable devotion. The whole of the delectable story, which Bhusuṇḍi repeated to the king of the birds, has now, Umâ, been narrated to you. I have told you only a fraction of Râma's virtues; tell me, Bhavânī, what I am to recount next." Umā rejoiced to have heard the glorious narrative and in modest and gentle accents thus replied: "Blessed, yea, thrice blessed am I, Purāri, to have heard the virtues of Râma that put an end to all the terrors of rebirth.

Dohā 52a-52b

By your grace, O most clement, I have attained my desire and am no longer in doubt: I know the glory of Rāma, that he is the Lord, the sum of all knowledge and joy. Your lips, Sire, flow like the moon with the nectar of Râma's praises; my soul drinks them in through the pitchers of my ears, but refuses to be satisfied, O resolute of purpose !

Caupāī 51

They who can be satiated with hearing Rāma's deeds do not experience their peculiar savour. The great sages, who have been liberated from mundane existence, listen for ever to the praise of Râma's virtues. Whoever desires to ferry across the ocean of life finds in Rāma's story a sure ship. Even the worldly accept the praises of Hari as pleasant to the ear and grateful to the heart; for is there anyone in the world with ears to hear who takes no pleasure in Rāma's story ? They must be dull of soul indeed and self-destroyers to whom the acts of Raghupati give no pleasure. While you have been reciting your Rāma lay, I have listened, my lord, with boundless delight. But this delectable story that you have repeated was declared by Kākabhuśuṇḍi to Garuṛ.

Dohā 53

Now I marvel greatly how anyone in the body of a crow could be a votary of Rāma's, and possess such self-control and knowledge and wisdom and such staunch devotion to his feet.

Caupāī 52

Hearken, Purāri; among a thousand men there may perhaps be one who is steadfast in the practices of his religion; among millions of religious people there may be one who loathes sensuality and delights in asceticism; among a millon ascetics—so declare the scriptures—there may be one who attains to perfect knowledge; among a million of the truly wise, one may be liberated from mundane existence; among a thousand of these it is difficult to find the perfect bliss of philosophic absorption into the Supreme Spirit. But beyond the religious, the ascetic, the wise, the exempt from transmigration and the absorbed in the divinity, beyond all these persons, O king of the gods, there is one yet more difficult to find : a devoted believer in Rāma, superior to all vanity and illusion of the senses. Tell me, Lord of the universe, how a crow could attain to such faith.

Dohā 54

Tell me, Sire, if he were devoted to Rāma, enamoured of wisdom, full of all good qualities and resolute of purpose, what was the reason that he had the body of a crow?

Caupāī 53

Be pleased to inform me where the crow learnt this holy and

delectable history of the Lord's doings. Tell me also, O conqueror of Love, the strange mystery of how you heard it. Garuṛ, again, is very wise and accomplished and one of Hari's most intimate disciples; what was the reason for his leaving the company of sages and going to a crow to hear this story? Tell me the nature of the interview between these two servants of Hari, the crow and the serpent-eater." On hearing Gaurī's artless and charming speech, Śiva was pleased and made reverent reply: "A blessing, Sati, on your sanctifying scheme ! Great indeed is your devotion to Rāma's feet. Now listen to the all-holy story, the hearing of which puts an end to every sorrow and delusion; for from it there springs up an implicit faith in Rāma's feet and without any difficulty man crosses the abyss of existence.

Dohā 55

This was the very question that the king of birds went and put to the crow. As I will reverently explain it to you in full, hearken, Umā, with all attention.

Caupāī 54

Beautiful and bright-eyed, deliverer from the world, listen to the account of how I heard the story. You first took birth in the house of Dakṣa and the name you then bore was Satī. At Dakṣa's sacrifice you were insulted and in the violence of your indignation yielded up your life. My servants then broke up the sacrifice; but all this is a story that you know already. Afterwards I was sorely troubled at heart, sorrowing for the loss of you, my beloved, and wandered among the beautiful woods, and hills and rivers and lakes, admiring the scene, but a sworn ascetic. Far away to the north of Mount Sumeru is a huge and magnificent purple peak with four glittering pinnacles of gold, so lovely that my soul was enraptured. On each stood one enormous tree, a banyan, a *pīpala*, a *pākara* and a mango, and on the top of the mountain was a glorious lake, with jewelled steps which it was a delight to behold;

Dohā 56

Its water cool, pure and sweet; its lotuses abundant and of

many colours, while flocks of swans uttered their melodious notes and the bees made a delicious buzzing.

Caupāī 55

On this fair mountain dwelt a crow, outliving even the end of the world. All the virtues and vices that are born of illusion, together with Delusion, Love and the other errors of judgment which permeate the whole world, never came near this mountain. Hearken now, O Umā, with tender affection, while I tell how the crow passed his life here in the worship of Hari. Beneath the *pīpala* tree he practised meditation; beneath the *pākara*, prayer and sacrifice; in the shade of the mango he mentally performed the temple ritual, having no other occupation whatever save the worship of Hari; and beneath the banyan he recited the story of Rāma's exploits, which countless birds flocked to hear. With loving reverence he sang the varying details of Rāma's deeds, in the hearing of all the pure-souled swans that ever dwell in that lake. When I arrived there and saw the sight, an intense joy sprang up in my heart.

Dohā 57

Assuming for a time the form of a swan, I took up my abode there and after reverently listening to Rāma's praises again returned to Kailāsa.

Caupāī 56

I have thus told you, Girijā, the whole story of the circumstances under which I visited the bird. Hearken now to the explanation of the reason for Garuṛ's going to see him. When Raghunātha exhibited the battle phantasm, though I understood his action, I was ashamed that he should allow himself to be bound by Meghanāda. Nārada the sage then despatched Garuṛ, who cut his bonds and returned, the serpent-eater, but a grievous dejection possessed his soul, as he thought over the Lord's bonds and pondered the matter to himself: "The omnipresent and passionless Supreme Spirit, the Lord of speech, who is absolute master over the vanities of illusion, has, I hear, taken birth in the world, but I see no signs of his majesty.

Dohā 58

Can this be Rāma, by the repetition of whose name men escape from the bonds of existence, if a wretched demon can bind him in serpent coils?"

Caupāī 57

Though he did his best to re-assure himself, his understanding was not enlightened; error overshadowed his soul. Distracted by doubt and full of mental questionings, he became as subject to delusion as you yourself were. In his perplexity he went to the divine seer and told him the difficulty that he had in his mind. On hearing his tale, Nārada was moved with a great compassion. "Hearken, O bird," he said, "Rāma's delusive power is very strong. When he robs the wise of their sense, he makes their infatuation superlative. The same spectre that has often disturbed me has now, O king of birds, affected you. The mighty error that has taken root in your soul will not be readily removed by any words of mine. You must go to Brahmā, and do whatever he enjoins you."

Dohā 59

So saying, the divine seer went his way chanting Rāma's praises, again and again in his infinite wisdom insisting on the might of Rāma's delusive power.

Caupāī 58

The king of birds then went to the Creator and told him his difficulty. On hearing his story, Brahmā bowed his head to Rāma and, as he thought on his majesty, his heart was filled with love, and he thus mused within himself: "Poets and the wisest of philosophers are subject to delusion. The might of Hari's magic power is unbounded; many a time has it made me its puppet, though all things, animate and inanimate, are of my creation No wonder, then, that it has beguiled the king of birds." Then said Brahmā in gracious accents, "Śiva comprehends the sovereign power of Rāma. Go to him, O son of Vinatā, and ask no questions of any other. There you will find the solution of your doubts." On hearing Brahmā's advice, the bird went his way.

Dohā 60

Then came the king of birds in the utmost distress to me. At that time, Umā, I was on my way to Kuvera's palace and had left you at Kailāsa.

Caupāī 59

He reverently bowed his head at my feet and then told me his difficulty. On hearing his humble petition, I lovingly responded, Bhavānī: "You have met me, Garuṛ, on the road; how can I instruct you? Your doubts will not be settled till you have enjoyed for a long time the fellowship of the sages. There you must listen to the glorious story of Rāma, as sung in diverse manners by the seers, in which the beginning, middle, and end is the adorable Lord, the great God Rāma. I will send you, brother, to a place where the story of Rāma is told without ceasing; go there and listen. As you hear it, all your doubts will vanish; you will have a vehement affection for Rāma's feet.

Dohā 61

Except in the company of saints, there is no talk about Rāma, without that there is no overcoming delusion; till delusion is dispelled, there is no firm affection for Rāma's feet.

Caupāī 60

Without such affection Raghupati is not won, though you have recourse to meditation, prayer, sacrifice, and asceticism. In the region of the north is a beautiful purple mountain, where lives the amiable Kākabhuśuṇḍi, supremely skilled in the method of Rāma's worship, wise and full of all good qualities and very aged. He unceasingly recites Rāma's history and all the noblest of the birds reverently listen. Go there and hear all Rāma's excellent virtues; your distress born of delusion will then be removed." After I had given him full instructions, he bowed his head at my feet and set out with joy. I did not myself instruct him, Umā, for I understood the mystery of Rāma's grace. Perhaps he had shown pride on some occasion and the gracious Lord wished that he should cure himself of this defect.

There was also another reason why I did not detain him; being a bird, he understood the speech of birds. The Lord's delusive power, Bhavânī, is great; who is so wise as not to be led astray by it ?

Dohā 62a-62b

Even Garuṛ, the vehicle of the Lord of the three spheres, the very crown of philosophers and saints, was overcome by its deceptive influence; wretched man may well have his doubts. It beguiles Śiva and Brahmā; why speak of other poor creatures ? The sages know this at heart, when they worship the great God, Māyā's master.

Caupāī 61

Garuṛ went to Bhuśuṇḍi's abode, that sturdy-hearted and indefatigable votary of Hari's. At the sight of the rock his heart rejoiced; the trouble caused him by Māyā's wiles all passed away. After bathing in the lake and drinking of its water, he went under the banyan tree with exulting soul. There assembled flocks of aged birds to hear of Rāma's glorious acts. He was just on the point of beginning to recite, when Garuṛ, the king of birds, arrived. All were glad to see him approach, the crow no less than the rest of the assembly. They received him with the utmost politeness and asked of his welfare and conducted him to a seat. Then the crow, after paying him loving homage, addressed him in these winning words:

Dohā 63a-63b

"Now am I content, O king of birds, in that I have seen you; whatever you may order me, I am ready to do: what is the object of your visit, my lord?" "You have ever been the image of content," replied Garuṛ in gentle tones, "seeing that Śiva with his own mouth is ever reverently singing your praises.

Caupāī 62

Hearken, father; the object for which I came was attained as soon as I saw you. Directly I beheld your most holy hermitage, my delusion was at an end with all my distracting doubts. Now, father, recite for me with all solemnity the most sanctifying story of Rāma, which is ever delightful and a remedy for every ill: this, my lord, is what I urgently beg of you." On hearing Garuṛ's humble petition, so simple, sincere and affectionate, so graceful and pious, a supreme joy was diffused over his soul and he began the recital of Raghupati's glory. First, Bhavānī, he expounded with fervent devotion the motive of Rāma's acts. Then he told of Nārada's extraordinary infatuation and of Rāvaṇa's birth as a demon. After this he sang the story of the Lord's birth and then carefully recounted his doings as a child.

Dohā 64

After telling all the details of his childish performances with the utmost rapture of soul, he next told of the coming of the seer and of Raghubira's marriage.

Caupāī 63

Then came the narrative of Rāma's coronation, of the king's promise and abdication of royal state, the sorrow of the citizens at parting, the colloquy between Rāma and Lakṣmaṇa, the journey to the forest, the devotion of the boatman, the passage of the Gaṅgā and the stay at Prayāga. He described also the Lord's meeting with Vālmīki and how the Blessed Lord dwelt at Citrakūṭa, the coming of the Minister, the death of the king in the city, the arrival of Bharata and the greatness of his affection, how after performing the king's obsequies both Bharata himself and the citizens had gone to join the Lord blessed for ever, and how after he had said all he could to console them Bharata took his sandal back with him to Avadh. Next he related Bharata's mode of life, the mischief wrought by the son of Indra and the Lord's interview with Atri.

Dohā 65

Then he told of Virādha's death, of how Śarabhaṅga quitted his body, of Sutīkṣṇa's devotion and the Lord's pious meeting with Agastya.

Caupāī 64

He told him also of the purification of the forest of Daṇḍaka, of the friendliness of the vulture, of the Lord's stay in the woods of Pañcavaṭī, and how he put an end to the fears of all the hermits. Then came the incomparable exhortation to Lakṣmaṇa and the story of Śurpaṇakhā's mutilation. After this, he narrated to him the slaying of Khara and Dūṣaṇa, and how Rāvaṇa penetrated the mystery and all the particulars of his talk with Mārīca. Then he described the rape of the fictitious Sītā and gave an idea of Rāma's bereavement. After this, he told how the Lord performed the vulture's funeral rites and slew Kabandha and granted salvation to Śabarī. He told of Raghubīra's mourning and how he went to the shore of the lake;

Dohā 66a-66b

Of his conversation with Nārada, his meeting with Hanumān, his alliance with Sugrīva and his taking Bāli's life; of his making the monkey king and taking up his abode on the rock during the rains. He described also the rains and the autumn and Rāma's indignation and the monkey's alarm;

Caupāī 65

How the Monkey King sent out monkeys who ran in every direction in quest of Sītā; how they entered the cave and found Sampāti; how Hanumān, when he had heard all the circumstances, jumped over the mighty ocean; how he made his way into Laṅkā and bade Sītā be of good cheer; how he laid waste the garden, and lectured Rāvaṇa and set fire to the city and leapt over the sea again. How the monkeys all rejoined Rāma and told him of Sītā's welfare; how Raghubīra with his army went and encamped on the sea-shore; how Vibhīṣaṇa came to meet him, and how the sea was put in check;

Dohā 67a-67b

How the bridge was built and the monkey host crossed over to the further shore, and how the valiant son of Bāli went as an envoy. He described the various battles between the demons and the monkeys, the might and valour of Kumbhakarṇa and Meghanāda and their destruction ;

Caupāī 66

The different deaths of all the demons, the fight between Rāma and Rāvaṇa, the death of Rāvaṇa, the mourning of Mandodarī, the enthronement of Vibhīṣaṇa and the satisfaction of the gods; the meeting also of Rāma and Sītā and how the gods with folded hands hymned their praises; how the Lord of grace with the monkeys mounted the car Puṣpaka and set out for Avadh; and how Rāma arrived at his own city. All these glorious doings were sung by the crow. Then he told of Rāma's coronation and described the city and all its kingly polity. The entire history did Bhuśuṇḍi tell, as I have told it to you, Bhavānī. When the king of birds had heard it all, his soul was filled with rapture and he said:

Soraṭha 68a-68b

"My doubts are dispelled, now that I have heard Rāma's full story. By your grace, O best of crows, I feel a devotion to Rāma's feet. A mighty bewilderment possessed me when I saw the Lord in bondage on the battlefield : if Rāma be the sum of all knowledge and bliss, what can embarrass him ?

Caupāī 67

Seeing all his ways so entirely consistent with humanity, a very grievous doubt arose in my heart. But now I understand that my error was a favour which the Lord of grace was pleased to bestow upon me. To appreciate the blessing of a shady tree, one must first have suffered from the sun. If this great delusion had not befallen me, how should I have met you, father, and how should I have heard the delightful story of Rāma which you have told me so fully in all its details ? This is the doctrine of the Purāṇas and all Scriptures, the unhesitating assertion of all the seers and sages, that the company of good and holy men can only be attained by one on whom Rāma has looked with an eye of grace. By Rāma's grace I have had sight of you, and by your grace all my doubts are gone."

Dohā 69a-69b

On hearing Garuṛ's modest and affectionate speech, the crow

felt a thrill of joy; every hair on his body stood erect and his eyes streamed with tears. O Umā, when a good man finds an intelligent and well-disposed listener, who is pious and fond of religious reading and a worshipper of Hari, he reveals to him hidden mysteries.

Caupāī 68

Then answered Kākabhuśuṇḍi, who had no slight affection for the king of birds : "My lord, you are in every way entitled to my respect, as a vessel of Hari's grace. You had no doubts, infatuation, or delusion; it was only a pretext, Sire, for doing me a kindness. By sending you, Garuṛ, as a victim of delusion, Raghupati has conferred an honour upon me. Yet there is nothing wonderful, Sir, in that delusion of yours of which you tell me; for Nārada, Śiva, Brahmā, Sanaka and his brothers, with all the great sages who discourse of the soul, is there one of them whom delusion has not blinded,. or whom love has not made a puppet of, whom desire has not driven mad, or whose heart anger has not inflamed ?

Dohā 70a-70b

Is there any philosopher, ascetic, or hero in the world, or any learned and accomplished bard, whom greed has not buguiled; whom the pride of wealth has not perverted; whom power has not rendered deaf; or whom the glance of beauty has not smitten as an arrow ?

Caupāī 69

Is there any whom success has not corrupted; whom vanity and pride have not influenced; whom the fever of youth has not overcome; whose glory has not been ruined by possessiveness; whom envy has not besmirched; whom the blast of sorrow has not shaken; whom the serpent of care has not bitten; or whom delusion has not affected ? Is there any so well seasoned of frame that he has not been attacked by desire, as wood by the weevil ? The desire of family, of wealth and of renown is a threefold temptation; whose soul has it not sullied ? These all are the attendants of Illusion; who can describe in full her illimitable might ? Since Śiva and Brahmā stand in awe of her, why speak of other creatures ?

Dohā 71a-71b

Māyā's formidable host is spread over the whole world; Love and its fellows are her generals; Fraud, Deceit and Heresy her champions. Being the servant of Raghubīra, though known to be a delusion, she can only be dispersed by his favour; this, my lord, I assert with the utmost confidence.

Caupāī 70

This Māyā, that sets the whole world adancing and whose mysterious actions no one can understand, is herself set dancing with all her troupe, like an actress on the stage, O king of birds, by the play of the Lord's eyebrows. For Rāma is the sum or totality of existence, knowledge and bliss[1], the uncreated, the all-wise, the home of beauty and strength; the permeator and the permeated[2]; the indivisible, the eternal; the insoluble, the unerring; the primal energy, the Godhead; of whom no qualities can be predicated and no deceit; beyond the range of speech or perception; all-seeing,[3] irreproachable, unconquered; without per-

1. For *Ghan-Rāma* some books read *Ghan-Syama*, which, however, would seem to be only an evasion of the difficulty. *Ghan* by itself, meaning literally solid, material, substantial, might be intended to denote the visible world of phenomena, which is the converse of the ideal world indicated by the term *saccidānand*. But it is simpler to take *saccidānandghan* as one compound and translate as in the text.

2. The words in the text are *vyāpaka*, *vyāpya*, which are technical terms in the *Nyāya* philosophy, meaning 'the pervader', or 'invariably pervading attribute' and 'invariably pervaded.' They are employed in making a universal affirmation, or in affirming universal distribution; as, for example. 'Wherever there is smoke, there is fire;' 'Wherever there is humanity, there is mortality.' In such cases an Indian logician always expresses himself by saying that there is an invariably pervading concomitance of fire with smoke and of mortality with humanity; thus fire and mortality would be called the pervaders, *vyāpakas*; smoke and humanity the pervaded. *vyāpya*. See *Monier Williams' Indian Wisdom*. As employed by Tulasī Dāsa, the words might be adequately rendered by 'cause and effect,' 'subject and predicate,' or by any other similar phrase which would be equally inclusive.

3. For *sab-darsi*, 'all-seeing,' another reading is *samdarsi*, 'seeing alike,' *i.e.*, 'impartial.'

sonal interests, without form, without illusion; deathless, passionless, blessed for ever; transcending nature; the Lord that indwelleth every heart; the Supreme Spirit, effortless, passionless, imperishable; in him delusion finds no place, for can darkness ever face the sun ?

Dohā 72a-72b

For the sake of his faithful people, the very God, our Lord Rāma, has become incarnate as a king and for our supreme sanctification has lived as it were the life of an ordinary man. As an actor in the course of his performance assumes a variety of disguises and exhibits different characters, but himself remains the same;

Caupāī 71

Such, Garuṛ, is Rāma's divertisement, a bewilderment to the demons, but a delight to the faithful. Sensual libertines in their dullness of soul impute the delusion to the Lord, like as when, Sire, a man whose eyesight is in fault says that the moon is of a yellow colour; or when mistaken as to the points of the compass, affirms that the sun has risen in the west; or as one in a boat, who deludes himself with the idea that he is standing still.and that the land is moving. When children in play turn round and round, the house, or whatever else it may be, does not turn round, but they tell each other so, talking in an idle fashion. In this way only, O Garuṛ, can error be ascribed to Hari; never even in a dream is he really subject to illusion. The wretched dullards, who succumb to Māyā, have a thick veil over their soul, and these are the obstinate fools who raise doubts and lay their own ignorance on Rāma.

Dohā 73a-73b

How can these clowns understand Raghupati, addicted as they are to lust, wrath, pride and greed, absorbed in domestic affairs, pictures of misery, at the bottom of a well of darkness? The impersonal form of the Godhead is easy to understand, but who can comprehend the personal ? The soul of a sage is bewildered on hearing of all his actions, both natural and supernatural.

Caupāī 72

Hearken, Garuṛ, I will tell you to the best of my ability an agreeable story in illustration of Rāma's power, declaring to you in full all the particulars of a delusion which befell myself. You, my friend, are a vessel of Rāma's grace and cherish a special affection for Hari's actions and are moreover my greatest benefactor ; I will therefore conceal nothing from you in this exposition of a great and excellent mystery. Hearken, Rāma's natural disposition is such that he never lets pride possess his servants. Pride has its root in worldliness and is the cause of many pains and evey kind of vexation. That is why the All-merciful Lord doesa way with it in the greatness of his affection for his servants ; in the same way, Sire, as when a child has a boil on its body, its mother with seeming cruelty cuts it open.

Dohā 74a-74b

At first the poor child cries with the pain, but the mother pays no attention to it, her object being to cure the disease. In like manner Raghupati heals his servants of pride, doing it all for their good. Ah, Tulasī Dāsa, who would not forswear error and worship such a Lord as this ?

Caupāī 73

I will now tell you the story, Garuṛ, of Rāma's grace and my own stupidity ; listen attentively. Whenever Rāma assumes a human form and goes through his series of mimic actions for his votaries' sake, I always betake myself to Avadh and delight to watch his boyish doings. I go and attend the rejoicings at his birth and am glad to stay there for five years. The boy Rāma is my patron divinity, beautiful in form as a myriad Loves. Ever gazing on the face of my own Lord, O Garuṛ, I give my eyes a treat indeed, and being in the trivial form of a crow, I keep close to Hari and observe all his childlike sports.

Dohā 75a-75b

Whenever he rambles in his boyish play, I flutter about close at hand, and for my food I pick up the crumbs in the courtyard that fall from his table. One day Raghubīra played a very quaint frolic." "At the remembrance of his Lord's playfulness, every hair on his body stood erect with rapture.

Caupāī 74

Bhuśuṇḍi continued: "Listen, king of birds, to my story of Rāma's actions, which are ever the delight of his servants. The king's palace was exquisitely beautiful, with every kind of precious stone set in gold. The pleasantness of the courtyard, where the four brothers were always playing, surpasses description. In that courtyard Rāma roamed about, to the delight of his mother, diverting himself with childish amusements; his delicate frame dark of hue as a sapphire, with the beauty of countless Loves in every limb; his soft rosy feet like lotus buds, with lustrous nails that outshone the brightness of the moon, decorated with the four-fold stamp of the thunderbolt, the lotus, the elephant-goad and the flag, and circled with pretty bangles that made sweet music. Melodious, too, was the pretty girdle about his waist fashioned of gold and bossed with gems.

Dohā 76

With a belly having three pretty creases, a navel shapely and deep, and a broad chest gleaming with all the ornaments that befit a child's attire;

Caupāī 75

With roseate hands and lovely fingernails, with long arms richly braceleted and the shoulders of a young lion; with dimpled neck and rounded chin and face the perfection of beauty; with lisping speech and ruddy lips and two dear little pearly teeth above and below; with chubby cheeks and darling nose and a smile as winsome as that of the moon; with lotus eyes that undo the bonds of worldly existence and forehead gleaming with the mark of yellow pigment; with arched eye-brows and pretty ears; with curly hair black and beautiful: with a thin yellow jacket to set off his body, he fascinated me with his merry glance, as he sported in all his loveliness in the king's courts, dancing at the sight of his own shadow, and playing all sorts of antics with me, which I am ashamed to tell. When he laughingly ran to catch me, I flew away; then he showed me a piece of cake.

Dohā 77a-77b

When I came near, the Lord laughed; when I flew away again, he fell a-crying. I approached to lay hold of his feet, and he ran off, again and again turning round to look at me. Seeing him play like an ordinary child, I was overcome by bewilderment. Can these be the actions of the Lord who is the totality of intelligence and bliss?

Caupāī 76

This was what came into my mind, king of birds, for Rāma had sent forth his delusive power to entangle me. Yet that illusion was in no way painful to me. I was not so affected by it as other creatures. A special cause, my lord, was here at work, which I wish you, Garuṛ, to observe attentively. Sītā's spouse alone is absolute intelligence; every creature, animate, or inanimate, is subject to illusion. If all had the same perfect intelligence, tell me what would be the difference between God and his creature? The arrogant soul is subject to illusion. Illusion with all its phenomena is subject to God. The soul is dependent on others, God is self-dependent. Souls are many, Rāma is one. Though the distinctions made by illusion are false, without Hari's help they cannot be dispersed, whatever you may do.

Dohā 78a-78b

Even the wisest of men, who hoped for salvation without prayer to Rāma, is but a beast without tail and horns. Though the moon were to rise in the brilliance of its fullness and all the starry host and the forests on every mountain were set on fire, night would not yield except to the sun.

Caupāī 77

In like manner, O king of birds, without prayer to Hari, the troubles incident to existence cannot be dispelled. Ignorance has no power over a servant of Hari, for knowledge emanating from the Lord pervades his whole being. Therefore, O best of birds, there is no destruction for a believer: his faith as of a servant in his master is ever growing. Rāma smiled to see me reel in error, and hear what a strange course he adopted. The secret of his diversion neither his brother nor his father or mother ever knew. As he crawled on his hands and knees in a hurry to catch me—with his body so dark of hue and his rosy hands and feet—I took to flight, Garuṛ, and he stretched out his arms to lay hold of me. High as I flew into the air, I still saw his arms as close to me as ever.

Dohā 79a-79b

I flew off to Brahmā's sphere, but when I looked back in my flight, two fingers' breadth, O my friend, was all the distance between me and Rāma's arms. I cleft the seven folds of the universe and mounted to the utmost height that I could reach, still I saw the Lord's arms. Then was I again dumbfounded.

Caupāī 78

Terror-stricken, I closed my eyes, and when I opened them again I found myself in the city of Kosala. Rāma looked at me with a smile and as he laughed I jumped down his throat. In his belly (hearken, king of birds) I saw a cluster of multitudinous universes, with many strange worlds, each more wonderful than the other: with myriads of Brahmās and Śivas; stars and suns and moons innumerable: innumerable guardians of the world and gods of Death and Times; innumerable mountains and vast plains of earth; seas, lakes, rivers and forests without end, and all the complex machinery of creation: with gods, sages, saints, serpents and Kinnaras and the four classes of living things, both moving and motionless.

Dohā 80a 80b

Such as eye has not seen, nor ear heard, nor has entered

my mind, were all the marvels that I saw; how is it possible to describe them? In each universe I stayed a hundred years and in this manner made the round of all the multitudinous globes[1] having the shape of an egg.

Caupāī 79

Each sphere had its own separate Brahmās, its own Viṣṇu, Śiva and Manu and its own regents of the spheres; with men, Gandharvas, imps and evils spirits, Kinnaras and demons, cattle, birds and serpents, all the tribes of gods and giants, and every living creature, but differing in form; with lands, rivers, seas, lakes, and mountains, and the whole mechanism of creation also quite distinct. Each mundane egg had its own peculiar aspect and in all its manifold details was wonderful to behold. In each world was a separate city of Avadh with its own Sarjū; its own men and women, with Daśaratha and Kausalyā and the other queens, and Bharata and his brothers, each in their proper form. Each sphere had its own incarnate Rāma with all his child-like sports for me to see.

Dohā 81a-81b

While, O Garuṛ, I saw all these wondrous pageants separately repeated in my round of the innumerable worlds, I saw no other Lord Rāma. The same child-like ways, the same beauty, the same gracious Raghubīra were what I saw in each successive world that I visited, driven on by the blast of delusion.

Caupāī 80

Imagine a hundred aeons to have passed in my wanderings through the different spheres. At last after all my travels I came to my own hermitage and there I stayed some little time. When I heard of my Lord's birth at Avadh, I started up in an overwhelming ecstasy of devotion and went and witnessed the rejoicings at his nativity as I have already described to you. In

1. *Aṇḍa-kaṭāha*, which I translate 'globes,' is simply a synonym for *Brahmāṇḍa*, which occurs in the previous lines. It would be more precisely rendered 'half-globe,' *kaṭāha* here standing for the common Hindi *karahā*, a large shallow iron vessel used for boiling sugar, &c.

Râma's belly I saw many worlds, but what I saw is past all telling. Then again I saw the all-wise Rāma, the lord of illusion, the merciful God, and much I questioned within myself, for my understanding was obscured by the mists of delusion. In two hours I saw everything; I was a-weary and my soul was bewildered entirely.

Dohā 82a-82b

Seeing my distress, the all-merciful Raghubīra laughed, and as he laughed I issued from his mouth; hearken, O firm of faith; Râma again began his childish pranks with me. I reasoned with myself in every way I could; but my mind had no peace.

Caupāī 81

Seeing these miracles and remembering that grand spectacle, I lost all conscionsness. I fell to the ground and no word came to my mouth, but 'save me, save me O saviour of all distressed worshippers.' When the Lord saw that I was distraught with love, he at once checked the influence of his delusive power. The Lord laid his lotus hands upon my head and—ever merciful to the poor—healed me of all my pain. Râma, the gracious benefactor of his servants, thus dispelled my infatuation. As I reflected on his mighty power, there first arose in my heart a great transport of delight; and seeing his loving kindness to his worshippers my bosom heaved with an unutterable love. With streaming eyes and quivering frame and hands folded in prayer, I again and again made my humble petition.

Dohā 83a-83b

When he heard my loving words and saw me to be his own devoted servant, he made me this gracious, profound and tender speech: "Kākabhuśuṇḍi, ask of me a boon, for know that I am highly pleased with you; be it the supernatural powers of the saints, or fabulous wealth, or deliverance from further transmigration, the sum of all bliss;

Caupāī 82

Or knowledge and wisdom, detachment and mystic wisdom,

qualities which as all the world knows scarce the gods can attain unto. To-day I will grant you anything; doubt not, but ask whatever your soul desires." On hearing the Lord's words, I was greatly moved and began to reason thus within myself : "The Lord, it is true, has promised to give me every blessing, but has not said he would give me faith. Without faith what are any virtues or blessings? They are like any quantity of condiments wlthout salt. Of what avail is any blessing without devotion?" Having thus considered, O Garuṛ, I made reply: "If it be your good pleasure, my lord, to grant me a boon and if you wish to do me a favour and kindness, I will ask the boon, Sire, which my soul desires; you are generous and know the secrets of the hearts.

Dohā 84a-84b

A steadfast and sincere faith in your person, such as the Vedas and the Purāṇas hymn, such as the greatest ascetics and saints search after, but few only find and that by the Lord's grace: O my lord Rāma, tree of paradise to the pious, friend of the suppliant, all-merciful, all-blessed, of your clemency grant me this faith."

Caupāī 83

"So be it," said the prince of the house of Raghu and then added these most gracious words: "Hearken, O crow; you are very sagacious, and therefore no wonder that you ask this boon. You crave faith, the source of every blessing; there is none in the world so highly favoured as you; for the sages cannot grasp it after all their labours, though they consume their whole body in the fire of prayer and meditation. I am pleased to mark your prudence; your prayer for faith is most agreeable to me. Hearken, now, O bird, to the favours I bestow upon you: every good quality shall dwell in your bosom; faith, knowledge, divine wisdom, self-governance, the practice of mystic abstraction and all the secrets of esoteric love. You shall understand the mysteries of every science and with my favour shall need no other help.

Dohā 85a-85b

None of the errors born of illusion shall henceforth affect you;

you know me to be the Supreme Spirit, without birth or beginning, the immaterial root of all matter. Remember, O crow, that every believer is dear to me; hearken to my words and in thought, word and deed maintain an unalterable devotion to my feet.

Caupāī 84

Listen now to this most holy exposition of mine, which is both simple and true and is implied in the Vedas and other scriptures. I will reveal to you my own peculiar doctrine: apply your mind to listen and worship me only, abjuring all others. The world is the product of my illusion, with all its varieties of life, both moving and motionless. I love them all, for all are my creation; but man is the creature that delights me most. Of men, Brāhmaṇas; of Brāhmaṇas, those who study the Vedas; of these, such as follow the precepts of the sacred texts; of these again, celibates are my favourites, and yet more the wise; of the wise I love best the spiritually wise, and of these the best beloved of all are my own servants, who come to me and have no other hope. Again and again I tell you of a truth there are none so dear to me as my own disciples. If Brahmā had no faith in me, he would be no dearer to me than any other creature; while the meanest creature that breathes, if possessed of faith, is as dear to me as my own soul; this is my doctrine.

Dohā 86

Tell me, how is it possible that a pure, well-disposed and intelligent servant should not be held dear? That is a principle laid down both in the Vedas and the Purānas.

Caupāī 85

O crow, now listen attentively. A father has a number of children, each different in character, temper and occupation. One is a student, another a philosophic ascetic, another an accumulator of wealth, an open-handed soldier, a clever man of the world, or a devotee; the father feels the same affection for them all. Another, again, is in thought, word and deed entirely devoted to his father, never even dreaming of any other duty;

and this is the son whom the father loves as his own soul, though he be a perfect ignoramus. In like manner all animate and inanimate beings, including brute beasts, gods, men and demons, in short, the entire universe that I have created, is viewed by me with equal compassion; but, amongst them all, if there be one who forswears vanity and delusion and worships me only in thought and word and deed,

Dohā 87a

Whether he be man, eunuch or woman, whether animate or inanimate, if with all his heart and soul he sincerely worships me, he is most dear of all to me.

Soraṭhā 87b

O bird, I tell you truly that an honest servant is as dear to me as my own life. Remember this and worship me only, adjuring every other hope and assurance.

Caupāī 86

Time shall have no power over you so long as you meditate on me and worship me without ceasing." I should never have tired of listening to my Lord's ambrosial discourse; my body quivered all over and my soul rejoiced exceedingly. My mind and my ears experienced a delight, which it is beyond the power of tongue to tell. Only my eyes can experience the bliss of beholding my Lord's beauty, but how can they express it? They have no voice. After he had gladdened me by his manifold exhortations, he again began to sport like a child. With streaming eyes and mouth a little awry, he looked at his mother as if he were very hungry. Seeing this she started up in haste and ran and spoke to him with caressing words and clasped him to her bosom; then holding him in her lap she gave him to suck, singing the while of Rāma's charming deeds.

Soraṭhā 88a-88b

The citizens of Avadh were ever flooded with that bliss, to attain which the blessed Śiva assumes his awesome garb. They who have once realized even in a dream the least atom of that joy, think nothing, O Garuṛ, if they are good and sensible, of the joys of heaven.

Caupāī 87

After that I stayed some little time at Avadh, a spectator of his delightful boyish amusements. Then, by Rāmā's grace, having obtained the boon of faith, I kissed my Lord's feet and returned to my hermitage. Since then no delusion has ever affected me, after I had joined Rāma. I have now told you the whole of this strange story of how I was bewitched by Hari's delusive power. From my own experience I warn you, Garuṛ, that without prayer to Hari your troubles will not yield. Hearken, O king of birds; without Rāma's grace, there is no understanding his power; without understanding there is no confidence; without confidence there is no affection; without affection there is no consistency in faith; it slips away, Garuṛ, like oil on water.

Soraṭhā 89a-89b

How can there be knowledge without a *guru*? How can there be knowledge without detachment or (as the Vedas and Purāṇas declare) how can man attain to happiness without devotion to Hari? Without innate content, my friend, none can win peace of mind. A boat will not float without water, though you strain every nerve, enough to kill yourself.

Caupāī 88

Without contentment there is no cessation of desire; so long as desire continues, it is vain to dream of ease. Can desire be subdued without prayer to Rāma; can a tree ever take root without soil? Can equanimity be attained without knowledge, or can you have space without ether? Without faith their is no religion, as there can be no odour without the earth? Can fame spread without penance, any more than there can be moisture in the world without water? Can virtue be acquired without attendance on the wise, any more than vision can exist, Sire, without light? Can the mind be at rest when ill at ease, any more than the sense of touch is possible without air?[1] Without

1. The five elements, ether, earth, water, light and air and their several properties are here enumerated.

confidence there is no exercise of supernatural powers, and without prayer to Hari there is no victory over the terrors of existence.

Dohā 90a

Without trust there can be no devotion; without devotion Rāṃa is not moved; without the grace of Rāma no creature can dream of peace.

Soraṭha 90b

Thus consider, O stout of heart, and abjuring all doubt and criticism, worship Rāma, the heroic son of Raghu, the fountain of compassion, the beautiful, the beneficent.

Caupāī 89

Thus have I proclaimed to you, O lord and king of birds, according to my ability, the greatness of the Lord's power; nor have I anywhere had recourse to studied invention, for I have seen it all with my own eyes. Rāma's greatness, his names, his glory, beauty and perfection, are all boundless and infinite. Sages hymn his virtues, according to their several ability, but not even the Vedas, Śeṣanāga or Śiva can declare them fully. There is no winged creature, from yourself down to a gnat, who can reach to the end of the sky in his flight. In like manner, my friend, the greatness of Raghupati is unfathomable; none can sound the bottom of it. Rāma is beautiful of body as a myriad Loves; irresistible in the destruntion of his foes as a myriad Durgās; jocund as a myriad Indras; immeasurable in expanse as a myriad firmaments.

Dohā 91a-91b

Rāma is as masterful in might as a myriad winds; as bright as a myriad suns; as cooling as a myriad moons, soothing all the terror of existence; as impracticable, inaccessible and interminable as a myriad deaths; as irrepressible as a myriad fires, our very God.

Caupāī 90

The Lord is as unfathomable as a myriad nether worlds; as

terrible as a myriad gods of death; as immeasurably holy as a myriad places of pilgrimage whose name obliterates any accumulation of sin, Raghubīra is as immovable as a myriad Himālayas; as profound as a myriad oceans; as liberal in the fulfilment of every desire as a myriad cows of plenty, and is our very God. He is as illimitable in eloquence as a myriad Śāradās: as skilful in creation as a myriad Brahmās; as potent to save as a myriad Viṣṇus; as potent to destroy as a myriad Śivas; as abounding in wealth as a myriad Kuveras; as fertile in phenomena as a myriad Māyās; a supporter of the world like a myriad Śeṣanāgas. The Lord is illimitable, incomparable and sovereign of the universe.

Chand 10

Incomparable indeed is he and knows no equal; for, as the Vedas declare, Rāma alone is Rāma's peer, none else can compare with him. If one should compare the sun to a hundred myriads of fire-flies, it would be a slight to the sun. In like manner, the great sages have exercised their ingenuity in describing Hari, and the Lord, appreciating their intention, has of his great clemency listened kindly and approved.

Dohā 92a

Rāma is an unfathomable ocean of perfections; who can sound it to bottom? I can only tell you the little I have myself heard from the sages.

Soraṭhā 92b

Abjure then all selfishness, pride and conceit, and ever worship Sītā's spouse, the great God who is moved by sincere devotion, the all-blessed, the all-merciful."

Caupāī 91

On hearing Bhuśuṇḍi's delectable discourse, the king of birds was overjoyed and preened his wings. His eyes filled with tears and his soul was overcome with delight as he meditated on the might of the divine Rāma. He was ashamed to think of his former delusion, when he had taken the everlasting and Supreme Spirit for a mere man. Again and again he bowed his head at the crow's feet, whom in the greatness of his affection he regarded as a second Rāma. "Without a spiritual guide none can traverse the ocean of existence, though he be the equal of Brahmā or Śiva. Doubt like a serpent had crushed me in the painful coils of wordy scepticism; but Rāma appeared in your form as an antidote and restored me to life, beneficent as he is to all his votaries. By your favour I have overcome my delusion and have learnt the incomparable mystery of Rāma."

Dohā 93a-93b

After eulogizing him in every possible way and bowing the head before him with folded hands, Garuṛ proceeded in these humble, affectionate and winning terms: "In my ignorance, O my lord and master, I would ask you a question. In your infinite compassion be pleased to instruct me, regarding me as your own peculiar servant.

Caupāī 92

You are all-wise and a perfect philosopher, you are intelligent, amiable and upright in your dealings; a store-house of wisdom, sobriety and spiritual intuition; and one of Rāma's beloved servants: what, then, is the reason, my father, for your having received such a form? Explain this to me in full. Tell me also, venerable bird, where you learnt this excellent history of Rāma's deeds. Further, my lord, I have heard from Śiva that you do not perish at the time of the destruction of things. The god never utters an idle word, and therefore my mind is in doubt. For the whole universe, my lord, with all creatures moving and motionless, serpents, men and gods, is but a mouthful for Death. Death has swallowed up worlds without end and is ever irresistible and strong.

Soraṭhā 94a

How is it that so terrible a monster as Death has no power whatsoever over you? Be pleased to inform me whether it be the power of your intellect or the virtue of your mystical devotion.

Dohā 94b

Further, my lord, be so kind as to explain to me how it was that my delusion vanished as soon as I approached your hermitage."

Caupāī 93

When he heard Garuṛ's petition, Uma, the crow was pleased and answered him with the greatest possible kindness: "A blessing on your wit, Garuṛ! Your questions are most agreeable to me. As I listen to your affectionate and becoming enquiries, the recollection of many former lives comes back to me. I will tell you the whole of my story: listen, my son, with full and reverent attention. Prayer, penance, sacrifice, sobriety of mind, self-control, acts of devotion, charity, chastity, knowledge, mystical meditation and spiritual wisdom, all have their fruit in the love for Rāma's feet, without which none can attain to happiness. It was in this body that I learnt devotion to Rāma, and therefore I have a special liking for it. Everyone likes that by means of which he has gained his object.

Soraṭhā 95a-95b

This is a maxim, O Garuṛ, approved by the Vedas and declared by the pious that love should be shown to the meanest creature, if you know it to be your friend. Silk comes from a worm, but from it is made beautiful apparel; therefore, vile as the worm is, everyone tends it with the most sedulous care.

Caupāī 94

The most profitable end of every living creature is the love of the feet of Rāma, in thought and word and deed. The holiest and comeliest of bodies is the one in which he has been worshipped. An enemy of Rāma's, though in bodily appearance he rival Brahmā, will never be extolled by any poet or scholar. It was in my present bodily form that my devotion to Rāma first took root, and on that account, my master, I have a great affection for it. Though I can die when I like, I do not give up my body, for without a body, as the Vedas declare, I could not pray. At first delusion led me greatly astray; having Rāma against me, I was never happy even in my sleep. In different births I practised different courses of action, essaying mystical contemplation, prayer, fasting, sacrifice and almsgiving. Is there any womb in which I have not at some time taken birth, during my peregrinations of the universe ? In all my experience, O king of birds, I was never so happy as I am at present; and yet, my lord, I recollect many previous existences, in which, by the blessing of Śiva, no delusion oppressed my understanding.

Dohā 96a-96b

Listen, O king of birds, while I now tell you the story of a former birth. To hear it will increase your devotion to the Lord, which is the remedy for every ill. In a former aeon,[1] my lord, there was an iron age, the Kaliyuga, full of inequity; man and woman were devoted to impiety and all rebelled against the Vedas.

Caupāī 95

In that age I went to the city of Kosala and was there born as a man of the Śūdra class, a devoted worshipper of Śiva, but a scornful reviler of all the other gods, intoxicated with the pride of wealth, outrageously boastful, savage and swollen with arrogance. Although I lived in Rāma's capital, I had at the time no knowledge of his greatness. Now I understand the virtue of Avadh, as it has been sung by the Vedas, Purāṇas and all the scriptures, that everyone who in any birth has lived at Avadh will eventually become a disciple of Rāma's. A man then knows the virtue of Avadh when Rāma with bow in hand takes up his abode in his heart. It was an age, Garuṛ, of terrible wickedness; every man and woman was bent on crime.

1. A *Kalpa* or aeon is a period of time comprising a thousand *mahā-yugas*. Each *mahā-yuga* is the aggregate of four *yugas*, or ages of gradually diminished duration, named respectively Kṛta, or Satya; Tretā; Dvāpara and Kali; giving together a total of 4,320,000 years. The length of a Kalpa is thus 4,320,000,000 years. When it is over, the existing world is annihilated and another begins to run its course, and so on to all eternity.

Dohā 97a-97b

The sinfulness of that age stifled religion; the sacred books were all neglected and false teachers published endless heresies, which they had invented out of their own imagination. The people were all over-mastered by delusion, and greed stifled all acts of piety. Hearken, wise Garuṛ, while I describe some of the religious practices of those evil times.

Caupāī 96

No regard was paid to the rules of caste and the four orders of life; everyone was bent upon attacking the Scriptures. Brāhmaṇas sold the Veda; kings devoured their subjects; no one regarded the injunctions of revelation. The right road was any that most took the fancy; the greatest Pandit was the one who talked the loudest. Any who indulged in false pretences and hypocrisy was universally styled a saint. A wise man was he who plundered his neighbour; every boaster was thought a fine fellow, every liar a wit and was spoken of as a man of parts in those evil days. A reprobate who denied the doctrines of revelation was an enlightened philosopher; and any one with unkempt hair and nails was celebrated in that debased age as a model of mortification.

Dohā 98a-98b

To be dressed in the loathsome rags and ghastly adornments of a mendicant and feed indiscriminately on any kind of food was to be an ascetic, a saint, an object of veneration in that age of iniquity. All kinds of evil-doers were held in high honour and respect, and the idlest babblers were accepted as preachers in those miserable days.

Caupāī 97

Men, my lord, were everywhere subject to women and danced to their tune like an acrobat's monkey. Śūdras instructed the twice-born in theology and assuming the Brāhmanical cord took their infamous gains. Everyone was addicted to sensuality, avarice and violence, and flouted the gods, the Brāhmaṇas, the

Scriptures and the saints. Wives deserted their husbands, however handsome and accomplished, and adored instead any wretched stranger. Married women appeared without any ornaments, widows were bedecked with jewels. Teachers and pupils were of no more account than the deaf and blind; the one would not listen, the other had never read. A teacher who takes his pupil's money but does not rid him of his doubts falls into an awful abyss of hell. Father and mother call up their children and teach them the duty of filling their belly.

Dohā 99a-99b

People who are devoid of spiritual knowledge talk about nothing else. In their greed they would kill a Brāhmaṇa or their own *guru* to gain a cowrie. Śūdras dispute with the twice-born, "Are you any better than we are? Any one who knows Brahman is as good as the best of Brāhmaṇas." Thus did they insolently scoff.

Caupāī 98

Lecherous after their neighbour's wives, surpassingly clever only in trickery, clasped about with ignorance, violence and selfishness, these are the men who are reckoned as mystic philosophers. I have seen the practice of the Kaliyuga. Falling themselves and dragging down others who were keeping the path of virtue, they who trouble the world by their glosses on the Scriptures spend a whole Kalpa in each abyss of hell. People of low caste, such as oilmen, potters, dog feeders, kirātas, kolas, and distillers of spirituous liquors, who on the death of their wives or loss of their household goods shave their heads and turn religious mendicants, and make Brāhmaṇas bow down at their feet: such men by their deeds ruin themselves both for this world and also for the next. A Brāhmaṇa is unlettered, greedy and sensual, dissolute, stupid and the husband of an outcast. A Śūdra practises prayer, fasting and all the other duties of religion and taking the highest seat expounds the Purāṇas. Everyone practises the duties of some other state of life than his own, and the endless perversions of morality are beyond all description.

Dohā 100a-100b

In the Kaliyuga or the Iron Age different castes are confounded together and every one is a law to himself. Men practise sin and reap its reward in trouble, terror, sickness, sorrow, and bereavement. Overcome by delusion, they walk not on the path of faith in Hari, such as is approved by the Scriptures and conjoined with sobriety and discernment, but invent diverse ways of their own.

Chand (*Tomar*) 11

Devotees build themselves costly houses and are carried away by sensuality, forgetful of self-mortification. Ascetics amass wealth, mendicants become householders; the absurdities of the Iron Age, Sir, are beyond all description. They turn out a well-born and virtuous wife and bring home a servant-girl in violation of family usage. A son obeys his father and mother so long only as he sees not a woman's face; as soon as he takes a fancy to his wife's kinsfolk, he looks upon his own family as his enemy. Kings, devoted to criminal courses and with no regard for religion, oppress their subjects with unrighteous judgments. The meanest churl, if he is rich, is accounted noble; a Brāhmaṇa is known only by his cord, and any naked wretch is an ascetic.

Any one in the Iron Age who rejects both Vedas and Purāṇas is held a worshipper of Hari and a veritable saint. The world neither rewards nor even listens to a poet; a guru is universally reviled and there is not a single wise man to be found. In the Iron Age famines are of frequent occurrence and the people perish miserably for want of food.

Dohā 101a-101b

Hearken, Garuṛ; in the Iron Age the whole universe is saturated with hypocrisy, violence, pride, enmity, heresy, arrogance, ignorance, sensuality and every other evil passion. Men worship the powers of darkness with prayers, fasting, sacrifice, vows and alms-giving: the gods rain not upon the earth and the rice is sown but does not germinate.

Chand 12

A woman's only ornament is her hair and she is sorely

a-hungered; the poor are in distress, but are intensely selfish. Fools desire happiness, but have no regard for religion; their narrow mind is hardened and knows no compassion. Men burdened with disease find no rest anywhere, but only self-conceit and causeless wrangling. Life is short; man's age is only fifteen years, yet in their pride they reckon on outliving creation. The Iron Age has no unsettled mankind, that no one shows any obedience, neither younger sister nor daughter. There is no contenment, nor consideration, nor repose; ever caste is degraded to the condition of an importunate beggar; the world is full of envy, censoriousness and greed; placldity of temper is obsolete. Everyone is smarting with sorrow and bereavement: all thought of the duties connected with caste and stage of life is abandoned. Men are so niggardly that they ignore all self-denial, charity and kind-heartedness; torpor and dishonesty are multiplied exceedingly. Men and women alike all pamper their body and slanderers are sown broadcast.

Dohā 102a-102b

Hearken, Garuṛ; the Iron Age is a mine of impurity and iniquity; but it has one enormous advantage, escape from it is easy. In the Ages of Gold, Silver, and Brass solemn worship, sacrifice and mystical meditation were the appointed means; in the Iron Age those who attain salvation do so only by Hari's name.

Caupāī 99

In the Kṛtayuga or the Golden Age everyone was spiritua and wise and crossed the ocean of existence by meditating on Hari. In the Tretâyuga or the Silver Age men performed various sacrifices and dedicating their actions to the Lord so accomplished their course. In the Age of Brass (Dvāparayuga) men had no other expedient save the ritual worship of Rāma's feet. In the Iron Age men sound the depths of existence simply by chanting Rāma's praises. In the Iron Age neither spiritual abstraction, sacrifice, nor knowledge is of any avail; man's only hope is in hymning Rāma. Anyone who abjures all reliance on every other and prays devoutly to Rāma and sings his praises shall assuredly escape further mundane existence. The power of his name is the special revelation of the Iron Age. It is its one sanctifying influence by which the soul is purified and sin destroyed.

Dohā 103a-103b

There is no age to compare with the Age of Iron; in it, if a man has only faith and devotes himself to praising Rāma's spotless virtues, he escapes from the sea of birth and death without further trouble. Religion has been revealed with four feet; in the Iron Age one is of the most importance; to whomsoever God has given, let him practise almsgiving and prosper.

Caupāī 100

Every age has its own peculiar characteristics, implanted in the soul by Rāma's delusive power. Purity, truth, equanimity and wisdom, combined with joy of soul, are recognized as the outcome of the Golden Age. A great devotion to truth—though with some admixture of passion—and general happiness are the note of the Silver Age. Much passion, little truth and some ignorance, with mingled joy and terror of soul, are the marks of the Brazen Age. Great ignorance, less passion and universal antagonism are the outcome of the Iron Age. The wise understand the proper virtue of each age and forswearing iniquity devote themselves to religion. The influence of the Iron Age has no effect on him who cherishes a love for Rāma's feet. A juggler, Garuṛ, may practise the most wonderful deceptions, but he does not impose upon his own servants.

Dohā 104a-104b

The merits and demerits which are the creation of Hari's delusive power can only be dispersed by prayer to Hari: know this and worship Hari, forswearing all sensuality. In that particular Iron Age I lived, Garuṛ for many years at Avadh, till a famine occurred which compelled me to go to another country.

Caupāī 101

I went to Ujjain—mark me, O king of birds—a miserable

fellow, in a state of abject poverty and utter wretchedness. After some time I acquired wealth and as before practised devotion to Śambhu. There was there a Vedic Brāhmaṇa, who constantly worshipped Śiva and had no other occupation; a very saintly man learned in divine truth, who worshipped Śambhu, but at the same time showed no disrespect to Hari. I hypocritically attended upon this benignant philosopher, and he, my lord, seeing me outwardly so submissive, instructed me as his own son, teaching me the Śiva incantations and giving me every kind of good advice. I went to a temple of Śiva and repeated the spells with a heart full of pride and self-conceit.

Dohā 105a

An ignorant wretch that I was, with a soul full of impurity, low-born and enthralled by delusion, I flew into a passion if I saw any Brāhmaṇa votary of Hari and vented my spleen on Viṣṇu !

Soraṭhā 105b

My *guru* was distressed to see my behaviour and was always admonishing me; but I became exceedingly angry. Is pride ever pleased by sober counsel?

Caupāī 102

One day the *guru* sent for me and instructed me at length in the principles of right conduct: "The reward, my son, for serving Śiva is a steadfast faith in Rāma. Śiva and Brahmā both worship Rāma; why speak then of miserable man? Do you hope to secure happiness, you luckless wight, by persecuting him whose feet even Śiva and Brahmā adore?" When I heard the *guru* speak of Śiva as a worshipper of Hari, my heart, Garuṛ, was all on fire. Being such a low-born churl, after receiving education I became like a snake that has been fed on milk. Arrogant, perverse, ill-starred and ill-bred, I worried my *guru* day and night. But he was too tender-hearted to be angry and still continued his wise admonitions. The very person from whom a churl obtains promotion is the first for him to destroy. Hearken, friend; smoke is produced by fire, and yet when promoted to cloudship it puts the fire out. Dust while it lies on the road is held in contempt and submits to be trodden under foot of everyone. If the wind carries it aloft, it first darkens that and then gets into king's eyes or sullies his crown. Hearken, Garuṛ, and thus understand my parable; sensible people have no dealings with the mean. The wisest of the poets have declared this maxim, it is good neither to quarrel with a churl nor to make friends with him; never have anything to do with him at all, Sire; let him alone, like a dog. Churl as I was, with a heart full of falsehood and perversity, I paid no heed to the *guru's* friendly admonition.

Dohā 106a-106b

One day I was in a temple of Hara repeating the name of Śiva when the *guru* came in, and in my conceit I did not rise to salute him. He was too gentle to say anything, neither did he feel the slightest atom of resentment, but the grievous sin of slighting a spiritual teacher was more than Śiva could tolerate.

Caupāī 103

A heavenly voice proceeded from the temple: "You miserable, conceited churl! Though your *guru* shows no resentment, being so kind-hearted and of such sublime wisdom, yet I must pronounce a curse upon you, you wretch: for I cannot endure such a breath of morality. If I were not to punish you for your wickedness, my scriptural ordinance would be violated. Villains who bear malice against their *guru* are cast for a million ages into the most awful abyss of hell; then they take birth in the brute creation and suffer affliction in a myriad successive existences. As for you, you guilty wretch, whose soul reeks with impurity, since you kept your seat, as it were some unwieldy boa-constrictor,[1] you shall become a snake; enter into the

1. The *ajagar*, here translated 'boa-constrictor,' is supposed to be too unwieldy to move, and devours only such animals as of themselves fall into its mouth. Hence the popular couplet of Malūk Dās:

Ajagar kare na cākarī, pacchī kare na kāma.
Dās Malūkā yon kahe, sab ke dātā Rāma.

hollow of some huge forest tree and there remain, vilest of the vile, in the form of the vilest of creatures."

Dohā 107a-107b

When the *guru* heard Śiva's terrible curse, he cried, "Alas, alas!" and seeing me all in a tremble, a profound compassion moved his soul. Devoutly prostrating himself in Śiva's presence, with his hands clasped and his voice choked with emotion as he reflected on my awful fate, he uttered this prayer:

Chand (*Bhujaṅga-prayāta*)[1] 13

"I reverence the Lord of lords, the embodiment of salvation, the Omnipresent and All-pervading Absolute, the image of the Veda! I worship the self-contained, the unqualified, without distinction or desire, who dewelleth in the heavens and who has heaven for his garment! I bow before the formless germ of the mystic incantation, OM, the transcendental, the Lord that is beyond all speech, understanding, or faculty of the senses, the Himālayan king, terrible and the death of tyrant Death, and yet the All-merciful, the grace-abounding refuge of the world! Rugged and stern as the Snowy Mountains, yet radiant with the beauty of the myriad Loves, with the bright waters of the Gaṅgā springing from thy head, with the crescent moon gleaming on the brow and snakes on thy neck, with tremulous earrings and large eyes and shaggy brows, with benignant face and deep-stained throat, O All-merciful robed in a tiger's skin, with a necklace of skulls, I worship thee, the universal Lord, Śaṅkara whom I love! I adore thee, the vehement, the exalted, the intrepid, the Supreme Lord; the indivisible, the unbegotten, whose glory is that of a myriad suns; tearing up by the root every kind of trouble with the trident in thy hand; Bhavānī's lord, accessible only by meditation. Unchangeable and ever-blessed Purāri, consummator of earth's cycles, constant bestower of blessings on the pious, sum of all knowledge and felicity, dispeller of delusion, conqueror of Love, have mercy, O my Lord, have

1. In the metre called *Bhujaṅga-prayāta*, which means literally 'snake-like motion,' each line consists of four Bacchics, or, to use the language of Hindi prosody, four *ya-gaṇas*.

mercy. So long as they worship not the lotus feet of Umā's lord, neither in this world nor in the next is there any happiness for men, nor peace, nor cessation of misery; O my Lord, clothed about with all the elements, have mercy. I know nothing of meditation, or prayer, or ritual, but at all times and in all places I bow before thee, O Śambhu. Have mercy, O my Lord, on a wretch so sorely afflicted by old age and life's flood of troubles;[1] for thee only I worship, O my Lord Śambhu."

Śloka 2

To those who devoutly repeat the eightfold hymn to Śiva, as uttered by the Brāhmaṇa in his propitiation, Śambhu will show his favour.

Dohā 108a-108d

When the omniscient Śiva heard the Brāhmaṇa's prayer and marked his devotion, a heavenly voice was again heard in the temple: "O noble Brāhmaṇa, ask a boon." "If my Lord is well-pleased with me and will show favour to his servant, grant me first devotion to thy feet and then yet another boon. Overcome by thy delusive power, ignorant creatures ever wander astray: be not then wroth with him, O merciful Lord, O gracious Śaṅkara, be merciful to him. After a little time may thy kindness release him from the curse;

Caupāī 104

And the highest blessings attend him; bring it thus to pass, O fountain of mercy." On hearing the Brāhmaṇa's speech so pregnant with charity, the heavenly voice declared, "So be it! Although he has committed a grievous sin, and I in my wrath have cursed him, yet seeing your goodness I will visit him with a special favour. O Brāhmaṇa, those who are of a forgiving disposition and charitable to their neighbours are as dear to me as Kharāri himself. Yet, Brāhmaṇa, my curse, cannot be in vain; he shall of a certainty have a thousand lives. But the insupportable misery of birth and death shall not have the slightest effect

1. *Tātapyamānam* is the participle of the frequentative verb from the root *tap*, and thus signifies 'suffering excessive pain'.

upon him. In no birth shall his knowledge fail. Hearken, Śūdra, to my unfailing promise. You have been born in Rāma's capital and, further, you have done me service. By the blessing of the city and by my favour a devotion to Rāma shall spring up in your bosom. Now hearken, brother, to my solemn declaration: the way to please Hari is by fasting and ministering to the Brāhmaṇas. Never again insult a Brāhmaṇa; regard the saints in the light of the Everlasting. Indra's thunderbolt, my mighty trident, the road of Death and Viṣṇu's terrible discus, by all these a man may be smitten yet not die; but a Brāhmaṇa's wrath is a fire which shall burn him to ashes. Cherish this counsel at heart and there is nothing in the world too difficult for you to obtain. One other blessing I have still to bestow; your goings shall never be impeded."

Dohā 109a-109d

On hearing Śiva's promise, the *guru* rejoiced and replied, 'so be it!' Then after admonishing me, he returned home, with the image of Śambhu's feet impressed upon his heart. Driven by the doom decreed, I went to the Vindhya mountains and then became a snake, and again after some time quietly dropped that form. Whatever body I assume, Garuṛ, I readily drop again, like a man who puts off his old clothes and takes to him new. Śiva observed the ordinances of the Veda, while I suffered no pain; thus I assumed many different forms, but my understanding, Garuṛ, never left me.

Caupāī 105

Whatever form I assumed—brute or divine or human—I invariably retained the practice of prayer to Rāma. The one regret that never ceased to torture me was in the remembrance of the *guru's* mildness of temper and disposition. Finally I was born in the holy form of a Brāhmaṇa, a form to which—as the Vedas and Purāṇas declare—it is difficult even for a good to attain. So joining in play with other children, I enacted all Rāma's boyish sports. When I grew older, my father gave me lessons, but though I listened to them and understood what he taught and turned them over in my mind, I never found any pleasure in them; every other inclination clean deserted me, for I was wholly absorbed in my devotion to Rāma's feet. Tell me, king of birds, is there any one so foolish as to abandon the cow of plenty to tend a she-ass? I was so overwhelmed with love that naught else pleased me and my father was quite tired of trying to teach me. After my parents had succumbed to fate, I went into the forest, to adore the Saviour of his people. Wherever I discovered any great sages living in the woods, I frequently visited their hermitages and bowed before them, asking them all about Rāma's excellences and listening, Garuṛ, with delight to what they told me. I went about everywhere hearing the tale of Hari's goodness, for by the blessing of Śambhu there was no check to my movements. The three kinds of evil concern[1] had left me and I had only one great longing at heart: 'When I shall behold Rāma's lotus feet, then I shall account my life to have been worth living.' Every sage, whom I questioned, told me thus; "The Lord is present in all his creatures." This religion of the impersonal did not satisfy me; I felt an overpowering devotion towards the incarnation of the Supreme.

Dohā 110a-110d

I remembered my Guru's words, and with my mind fixed on Rāma's feet, I wandered about, hymning his praises, and my love every moment grew yet more and more. On one of the peaks of Mount Meru, under the shade of a banyan tree, sat the seer, Lomaśa. On seeing him, I owed my head at his feet and addressed him in most humble strain. No sooner, Garuṛ, had the beneficent sage heard my meek and submissive address than he graciously enquired: "Say, O Brāhmaṇa, with what purpose you have come." Thereupon I replied: "Fountain of mercy, you are omniscient and very wise! Teach, my Sire, how to worship the incarnate God."

Caupāī 106

Then, O Garuṛ, the holy sage spoke, briefly though reverently

1. The three kinds of excessive concern relate to family, wealth and worldly reputation.

of Rāma's excellent virtues; then, being himself a philosopher devoted to the mystery of the transcendental and thinking that I was fully qualified, he began a sermon on the name of the Absolute, the unbegotten, the indivisible, the immaterial, the sovereign of the heart; unchangeable, unwishful, nameless, formless; approachable only by analogy, indestructible, incomparable; beyond the reach of thought or sense, spotless, immortal, emotionless, illimitable, blessed for ever; identical with yourself, you and he being as absolutely one as a wave and its water: so the Vedas declare. The sage gave me the fullest possible instruction, but the worship of the impersonal laid no hold of my heart. Again I said, bowing my head at his feet: "Tell me, O holy sage, how to worship the Incarnate. Devotion to Rāma, O wisest of sages, is like the element of water and my soul—which is as it were a fish—how can it exist without it? Of your mercy so instruct me that I may see Rāma with my own eyes. When I have seen my fill of the Lord of Avadh, then I will listen to your sermon on the Unembodied." Again the sage discoursed of the incomparable Hari and demolishing the dogma of the incarnation expounded him as altogether passionless. But I rejected the theory of the abstract and with much obstinacy insisted on his concrete manifestation. For every answer I had a rejoinder ready. The sage at last showed signs of anger. Mark me, Sir; I was so disrespectful that resentment was aroused even in the breast of a philosopher. An excessive amount of friction will strike fire even out of sandal-wood

Dohā 111a-111b

Again and again the sage angrily expounded his theory of the way of knowledge, while I sat still and argued the matter from every point of view in my own mind: "Can there be anger without duality, or duality without ignorance? Can a soul, dull, circumscribed and subject to delusion, be identified with God?

Caupāī 107

When one desires the good of all, can pain under any circumstances be the outcome? Can the possessor of the philosopher's stone suffer poverty? Can the oppressor be free from fear or the sensualist remain without reproach? Can a man's line prosper if he persecute Brāhmaṇas? Can religious observances be practised by a man careful only of bodily comfort ? Can sound doctrine be acquired by intercourse with the wicked? Can an adulterer attain to the felicity of the Blessed? Can a searcher after the Supreme Spirit escape from transmigration? Can a reviler of Hari ever be happy? Can a kingdom stand without a knowledge of statecraft? Can sin coexist with a recital of Hari's virtues? Can spotless renown be acquired without religious merit? Can any one be disgraced except by sin. Is there any blessing to equal faith in Hari, as hymned by the Vedas, the saints and the Purāṇas? Is there any loss, Brother, in the whole world like that of being born as a man and yet not worshipping Hari? Is there any other vice so bad as detraction, or any virtue, Garuṛ, so great as compassion?" Thus I reasoned to myself with much ingenuity and could not listen with patience to the sage's instruction. Again and again I maintained the doctrine of the Incarnation, till at last the sage uttered these angry words: "Fool, I have given you the most advanced teaching, but still you are not convinced and persist in your replies and rejoinders. You have no confidence in my voracious discourse, but like a crow suspect everything. Wretch, as your soul is so exceedingly self-opinionated, you shall at once be changed into an unclean bird."[1] I took the curse on my head, but was neither alarmed nor humbled.

Dohā 112a-112b

I immediately became a crow. Then again, I bowed my head at the sage's feet and mindful of Rāma, the jewel of the line of Raghu, I joyfully flew away. O Umā, they who devote themselves to Rāma's feet and abjure lust, pride and choler, they see their Lord present in everything; with what then can they quarrel?

Caupāī 108

Hearken, king of birds; the seer was in no way at fault; it

1. There is here a play on the words *sva pacch*' 'self-opinionated, and *pachi*, 'a bird' which cannot be preserved in an English translation.

was Rāma who had stirred his soul. The All-merciful had confounded his intellect and thus made trial of my love. When the Lord God had proved the thoroughness of my devotion, he restored the sage his senses. On beholding my great amiability and pre-eminent confidence in Rāma, the holy man was overwhelmed with astonishment and remorse and courteously summoned me near. After consoling me in every possible way, he gladly taught me the spell by which Rāma is invoked, and in his infinite compassion told me how to meditate on the blessed child. The beauty and sweetness of this cult pleased me well. I told you all about it at the beginning. The sage kept me there for some little time and recited the whole of the poem, entitled 'the Lake of Rāma's Deeds'. When he had reverently completed the narrative, he finally adressed me in these gracious words; "By the blessing of Śambhu, my son, I discovered this secret and delectable fountain of song; I know you to be one of Rāma's most devoted servants and therefore I have told it all to you. Never repeat it, my son, in the presence of any whose heart is void of Rāma's love." The sage reiterated his instructions again and again, and I lovingly bowed my head at his feet. He touched my head with his lotus hands and gladly gave me his blessing; "Henceforth by my favour an unalterable devotion to Rāma shall dwell for ever in your heart.

Dohā 113a-113b

Be for ever beloved of Rāma, a store-house of all good qualities, free from pride, changing your form at will and choosing your own time to die, treasure-house of knowledge and asceticism. May every hermitage, where you hereafter abide and make your prayer to the blessed God, be unapproachable by the spirit of ignorance for the space of a league all round.

Caupāī 109

May neither time nor fate, merit, demerit nor nature ever cause you any vexation! May the unspeakably delightful mysteries of Rāma, the esoteric as well as the exoteric doctrines of the Chronicles and Purāṇas, be all comprehended by you without any difficulty, and may your affection for Rāma's feet never grow old! May every desire you form in your mind by the blessing of Hari be ever easy of attainment!" On hearing the sage's benediction—mark me, O resolute Garuṛ—this solemn response of Brahmā's came from heaven; "May your words come to pass, O wisest of sages; he is my votary in thought, word and deed." When I heard the heavenly voice I rejoiced and was so drowned in love that all my doubts vanished. After making humble petition I received the sage's commands, and bowing again and again at his lotus feet I took my leave and arrived with joy at this hermitage, having obtained by my Lord's favour an inestimable boon. During my stay here, mark me, king of the birds, seven and twenty cycles have elapsed. I incessantly repeat Rāma's praises, and the birds in their wisdom reverently listen. Whenever Raghubīra in behoof of his votaries takes upon him the form of a man at the city of Avadh, I go and stay at his capital and delight myself with the spectacle of the childish sports. Again, cherishing in my heart the image of the child Rāma, I return Garuṛ, to my own cell. I have now told you the whole story of how I was changed into a crow and have replied, my friend, to all your questions. The efficacy of faith in Rāma is truly marvellous!

Dohā 114a-114b

The reason why I love this form is that in it my devotion to Rāma's feet has been exhibited, in it I have been favoured with the sight of my Lord and all my doubts have been removed. For my obstinacy in upholding the doctrine of faith I was cursed by the seer, but eventually I obtained a boon which even the sages find difficult: see the efficacy of prayer.

Caupāī 110

Those who knowingly reject such devotion and strive merely to tread the way of knowledge, are fools, who would leave at home the cow of plenty and go out to look for *āka* plants to give them milk. Hearken, Garuṛ, all who abandon the worship of Hari and seek to prosper by any other means are wretched blunderers who would try to swim across the ocean without a boat. On hearing Bhusuṇḍi's speech, Bhavānī,

Garuṛ was glad and said in gentle accents: "By your favour, my lord, every doubt, anxiety, error and delusion has been removed from my breast. Through your clemency I have heard the holy tale of Rāma's achievements and have gained peace. There is still one matter, Sir, about which I would ask; in your infinite compassion be pleased to enlighten me. The saints and sages, the Vedas and Purāṇas, all say there is nothing so difficult of attainment as wisdom. But the sage told you, father, that there is nothing so estimable as faith. Explain to me, most gracious lord, all the difference between faith and wisdom." The sagacious crow was pleased to hear Garuṛ's question and courteously replied: There is no real difference between the ways of faith and knowledge, for both put an end to the troubles springing from the cycle of mortality. There is no discrepancy, Sir, in the sage's doctrine; give me your attention, O noblest of birds, while I explain the matter. Wisdom, asceticism, abstraction and science—mark me, Garuṛ—are all masculine. Now the masculine character is altogether strong, while the feminine is weak and naturally inferior.

Dohā 115a

Men who can forswear women must be self-restrained and resolute; not sensual voluptuaries without any regard for Hari's feet.

Soraṭhā 115b

Even a very learned sage or philosopher, Garuṛ, is distracted at the sight of a woman, with her fawn-like eyes and moon-bright face. Now creation's bride is manifested as Māyā.

Caupāī 111

Here I uphold no private theory of my own. I only declare the doctrine of the Vedas, the Purāṇas and the saints. That one woman is not fascinated by the beauty of another, is, O Garuṛ, a strange proceeding. But, mark me, Illusion and Faith are both feminine, as every one knows. Again, Faith is beloved of Rāma, while he regards Māyā as a mere dancing-girl. Rāma being thus amiable to Faith, Māyā is greatly afraid of her.

Rāma's Faith is incomparable and illimitable, and he in whose heart she abides is ever blessed. Māyā at the sight of her is confounded and can do nothing of her own power. Knowing this, the most enlightened sages attest Faith to be the source of every blessing.

Dohā 116a-116b

This mystery of Raghunātha's no one can grasp all at once; whoever, by his favour, does comprehend it is never even in sleep subject to any delusion. Now hearken with your best intelligence to the distinction between knowledge and faith, the hearing of which induces an imperishable devotion to Rāma's feet.

Caupāī 112

Attend, my friend, to this unutterable lesson, which is in truth incapable of expression though it may be understood. The soul is a particle of the divinity, immortal, intelligent, pure, and naturally blissful. But, my lord, being overcome by Māyā, it is trapped like a parrot or monkey.[1] The enfeebled intellect is bound with a knot, which though imaginary is difficult to untie. Thus the soul becomes worldly; there is no loosing the knot and it knows no happiness. The Vedas and Purāṇas have declared many remedies; but there is no getting free, the entanglement is rather increased. The interior of the soul is full of the darkness of delusion and it cannot see how the knot can be untied. When God brings about such a complication, escape is problematical. If by Hari's favour a spirit of sincere piety like a beautiful cow comes and dwells in the heart, the

1. The allusion is to two modes of catching parrots and monkeys, which, whether ever really practised or not, have at all events passed into a proverb. A stick with a bait at the end and a string attached to it is so set in the ground that it revolves from the weight of the parrot when it lights upon it, and the bird confused by the motion fancies it is entangled in the string, though it is really loose and might fly away if it tried. For the monkey a large jar with a narrow mouth is sunk in the ground full of grain; the monkey puts in his paw and clutches a handful, but being unable to draw out his closed fist on account of the smallness of the jar's mouth, he fancies himself caught, though if he opened his hand he could extricate it immediately. Two apt illustrations are thus afforded of the way in which man allows himself to be caught by delusive phenomena.

prayers, penance and fasts, and all the religious observances and acts of devotion which the Vedas have inculcated as meritorious practices are, as it were, a green pasture for the cow to graze in. The calf which fills her teats with milk is love; the heel-rope with which she is bound is the spirit of quietism, the milk bowl faith, and the herdsman who tends her a spotless soul. After drawing off the milk of sound religion, it is set to boil on the fire of continence. Forbearance then cools it with the breath of patience; and perseverance is the rennet that coagulates it into curds. Contentment is the maid who churns it in the bowl of discretion, with self-restraint for the stick, and truth and good words for the cord. By such churning is produced the butter of pure, excellent and holy asceticism.

Dohā 117a-117c

After kindling the fire of ascetic contemplation with the fuel of actions both good and bad, Reason allows the *ghi* of wisdom to cool, but burns all the scum of selfishness in the fire. Then Reason, master of highest wisdom, takes the unsullied *ghi*, and filling with it the lamp of intelligence sets it firmly on the stand of equanimity. Then, extracting from the cotton the soul's three conditions[1] and the three properties, it works up the clean fibre of the fourth state and fashions it into an excellent candle.

Soraṭhā 117d

In this manner is kindled the splendid lamp, ablaze with highest wisdom, in which the gnat-like swarms of vanity and other vices are consumed as soon as they approach it.

Caupāī 113

'I am that'—this unalterable persuasion (of the identification

1. According to the Vedantists, the three ordinary conditions of the soul are waking, dreaming and profound dreamless sleep. The fourth is the state of abstraction in which it is permanent indistinguishable from the Supreme Spirit. When awake, it has to do with the visible and material world; while asleep with the world of illusion; and when in dreamless sleep it is temporarily enfolded as it were in the soul of the universe.

of the self with God) is its pre-eminently brilliant flame, and the happiness that results from this knowledge of self is the light it diffuses, by which it destroys the erroneous distinctions which are born of the world. Illusion and all the other forms of darkness that attend upon tyrant Ignorance are utterly dispersed. Thus Reason having procured a light[1] sits in the chamber of the heart and tries to loosen the knot; should he succeed in untying it, the soul obtains its object. But when Māyā, O Garuṛ, sees him loosening the knot, she creates many difficulties and sends forth, Brother, innumerable elves and fairies to tempt the Reason to avarice. In some way or other, by force or by fraud, they get near and try to put out the lamp by a side puff. If Reason is altogether wise, he perceives their hostile intent and will not look at them. Should he escape free from this danger, the gods then proceed to attack him. The faculties of sense are so many portals, at each of which a god sits on guard. When they see any sensual air stirring, they at once throw the doors wide open. If the blast penetrates the chamber of the soul, it forthwith extinguishes the lamp of knowledge. When its light is put out, there is no untying the knot, for Intelligence is undone by this blast of sensuality. Neither the senses nor the gods approve of wisdom; they are always inclined to sensual enjoyment. When Intelligence has been thus fooled by the breath of sensuality, who can light the lamp again as before?

Dohā 118a-118b

Then, Garuṛ, the soul is again subjected to all the manifold miseries of transmigration. Hari's delusive power is a trackless ocean that none can traverse. Wisdom is difficult to describe, difficult to understand, difficult to master, and if by any lucky chance a right judgment be formed, still many impediments block the way.

1. This is a paraphrase of a passage in the *Vedāntasāra*. "When the understanding, free from the four hindrances (mental inactivity, distraction, passion and propensity to pleasure) and motionless as a lamp sheltered, from the wind, thus becomes the infinite intelligence only, then is realized that which is called undifferentiated meditation.

Caupāī 114

The way of knowledge is like the edge of a scimitar; for those who fall on it, Garuṛ, there is no escape. If any traverse the path in spite of its difficulty, they attain to the supreme sphere of beatitude. But this exalted felicity is immensely hard of attainment, as is declared by the saints, the Purāṇas, the Vedas and all the Scriptures. By the worship of Rāma, Sir, salvation comes freely of its own accord. As water cannot stay without some support, however much you may try to make it: in like manner, mark me, Garuṛ, the joy of final salvation cannot be secured without the worship of Hari. The wisest of Hari's worshippers know this, and thinking lightly of the soul's deliverance from the body crave rather for faith. By faith, without any trouble or difficulty, the ignorance that arises from mundane existence is utterly abolished. Eating is for the sake of satiety, but it is the heat of the belly that digests what is eaten; in like manner the worship of Hari gives immediate relief. A man must be a fool indeed who does not delight in it.

Dohā 119a-119b

'I am the servant and He my master'—without this relationship, Garuṛ, it is not possible for any worshipper to cross the ocean of birth and death. Worship then the lotus feet of Rāma, knowing this to be the end of all theology. With Raghunātha is the power to make the living dead and the dead alive; blessed are the souls that worship him.

Caupāī 115

I have thus stated and expounded the doctrine of knowledge; hear now the virtue of the jewel faith. Faith in Rāma is a glorious philosopher's stone; for him in whose heart it dwells, Garuṛ, night and day is an infinite splendour, a lamp that never requires to be fed with oil. Delusion and poverty come not near; no blast of covetousness ever extinguishes it. The gloom of overpowering ignorance is dispersed; the swarms of gnats are all destroyed. Neither vile lust nor any other vice approaches the soul in which faith abides. It changes poison to ambrosia, enemies to friends, and without this jewel no one can attain to happiness. Those grievous mental diseases, by the influence of which all living creatures are rendered miserable, have no effect upon him in whose heart is the jewel of faith; not even in a dream can he feel the slightest atom of pain. They truly wear the crown of wisdom in the world who labour persistently to secure this jewel. Though it be revealed on earth, without Rāma's grace none can find it. There is an easy device for finding it, but luckless wights go on wrangling. The Vedas and Purāṇas are the holy mountain, the legends of Rāma its many glorious mines: the pious are the discoverers, and good counsel is their pickaxe, while knowledge and continence, Garuṛ, are their eyes. Any creature who searches with a will can find the jewel, faith; in itself a mine of every blessing. I have in my mind persuasion of this, Sir, that one of Rāma's servants is greater than Rāma himself. Rāma is the sea, the good and pious are the rain-clouds. Hari is the sandal-tree and the saints are the winds that diffuse its perfume. Faith in Hari is a delight and the crown of all desire, but it cannot be had without the saints. Any one, Garuṛ, who understands this and communes with the saints will find faith in Rāma easy of attainment.

Dohā 120a-120b

The Supreme Spirit is the ocean, wisdom is mount Mandara and the saints are the gods, while the sacred legends are the nectar which they churn out having faith for its sweetness. Again, self-control is the shield, and wisdom the sword, with which faith in Hari slays his enemies, Pride, Greed and Delusion, and wins the victory; take thought, O king of the birds, and see if it be not so."

Caupāī 116

Then Garuṛ replied in loving tones: "Since, my Lord, you are pleased to be gracious to me, acknowledge me as your disciple and resolve me these seven questions. Tell me first, O staunchest of the faithful, what form is the most difficult of all to obtain. Next, consider and explain briefly what is the greatest pain and the highest pleasure. Tell me also the essential characteristics both of the good and of the evil, for this is a secret you understand. Tell me further what is the highest religious merit as made known in the Scriptures, and what the most awful sin. In your infinite wisdom and supreme compassion explain to me also the diseases of the soul." "Listen, my son, with the greatest reverence and devotion, while I briefly expound this scheme of doctrine. The human form is the most excellent of all, and the desire of every living creature, moving or motionless. It is the ladder to hell and heaven and final liberation and is the bestower of the blessings of wisdom, detachment and faith. Men who have attained to this form and yet do not worship Hari show themselves, in their infatuation for the world, greater fools than any fool living, clutching at bits of glass while they throw away the philosopher's stone which they had in their hands. There is no pain in the world so great as poverty and no pleasure to equal the communion with the saints. It is an essential characteristic of the good, O Garuṛ, to be charitable to others, in thought, word and deed. The good endure pain to give pleasure to their neighbours, but wicked wretches to trouble them. The good in their compassion resemble the birch tree[1] and constantly submit to the direst distress in order to benefit others. The wicked, like the hemp have their skin flayed off and perish in agony, merely to supply ropes to bind people. Hearken, Garuṛ; the wicked do mischief, even though they have no object of their own to gain, like snakes and rats. They would kill themselves to ruin another's prosperity, like the hail which dissolves after destroying the crops. The rising of the wicked is as much a cause of calamity to the world as that of the famous planet Ketu is known to be. The rise of the good is ever productive of happiness as when the moon rejoices the world by scattering away the darkness. The highest religious merit, as the Scriptures declare, is to do no harm to any creature: and there is no sin so heinous as censoriousness. He who abuses Hari or his *guru* becomes a frog and is born a thousand times in that form. He who abuses

1. The bark of which is employed as paper and for other useful purposes and after being torn off the tree is again renewed.

a Brâhmaṇa, after suffering in many hells, will be born into the world in the form of a crow. They who have the presumption to abuse the gods or the Scriptures will fall into the lowest hell. They who delight in abusing the saints will be changed into owls, as loving the night of error and hating the sun of knowledge. The fools who abuse everyone will be born again as bats. Hearken now, my friend, to the diseases of the soul from which all people suffer pain. Ignorance is the root of all ailments from which again spring many torments. The flatulence of lust, the phlegm of insatiable greed, and the bile of passion constantly inflame the breast, and when these three combine, Sir, there results a miserable paralysis of the whole system. Who can tell the names of all the diseases, represented by the various obstinate sensual cravings ? Such are the leprosy of selfishness, the itch of envy, the rheumatic throbs of joy and sorrow, the consumption that burns at the sight of another's prosperity, the horrible open sore of a malignant spirit, the excruciating gout of egoism, the sciatica of heresy, hypocrisy, vanity and pride, the terrible leprosy of greed, the violent tertian ague of the three kinds of covetousness,[1] the two fevers of jealousy and indiscrimination; but why continue the interminable list of diseases?

Dohā 121a-121b

Men die even of one disease; but these incurable diseases which constantly harass the soul are many in number, how then can it find rest ? Pious and religious observances, penance, meditation, sacrifice prayer and almsgiving are so many different remedies;[2] but the disease, Garuṛ, does not abate.

1. The three things not to be coveted are another man's wife, wealth and good name.

2. The pessimistic views, as expressed above, have been revived in an exaggerated form by Schopenhauer and the modern European Buddhists, who hold that life is necessarily a state of suffering. For the only reality is Will, *i.e.* blind force pervading the universe, the Greek *avarky*. This is primarily unconscious and only manifested in the species by actions, which tend to the conservation of the individual and serve to prolong the life of the species. Will is thus the will to live; life being that for which everything pants and labours. To will is, therefore, to strive, and to strive is to suffer. Our nature is thus a kind of insatiable thirst, a struggle for exis-

Caupāī 117

Thus every creature in the world is sick of these diseases, distracted alternately by sorrow and joy, by fear and love. I have mentioned only some of the diseases of the soul; everyone suffers from them, but few only detect them. On detection the wretches diminish somewhat, but these tormentors of the faithful are not completely destroyed. They spring up even in the soul of a saint, if fed on the unwholesome diet of materialism; how much more in that of an ordinary man ? By the grace of Rāma every disease is extirpated, if the treatment is conducted in the following manner, with a holy teacher for physician, faith for a prescription, contempt of the world for regimen, devotion to Hari for life-giving drug and a soul full of faith for the vehicle in which it is administered. By this treatment the disease is easily subdued: otherwise all your efforts go for nothing. You may know, Sir, that the mind is free from disease as soon as it gains strength in self-control, with a daily increasing appetite for good resolutions and disappearance of the weakness of material hopes. After bathing in the pure stream of divine knowledge, the whole soul is suffused with faith in Rāma. This, O king of the birds, is the doctrine of Śiva, Brahmā, Śukadeva, Sanatkumāra, Nārada and all the sages, who have been eminent in theological speculation; 'Practise devotion to Rāma's lotus feet.' The Vedas and Purāṇas and all the Scriptures declare that without faith in Rāma there is no happiness. It would be easier for hair to grow on the back of a tortoise, or for the son of a childless woman to commit murder, or for flowers of every description to bloom in the air, than for any creature to find peace in opposition to Hari. Sooner shall

tence with the certainty of being vanquished. Hence the deductions, first, that all pleasure is merely negative, suffering alone positive; and second, that increased intelligence is simply increased capacity for pain; the world being the worst possible world; if it were worse, it would cease to exist. The will to live ought therefore to be rooted out, and the means to this (as Tulasī Dāsa also says) are voluntary poverty, chastity, and the various practices of asceticism. But the spiritual faith and devotion, upon which the Hindu theologian insists as the crowning step in the process, are necessarily ignored by the modern school, with whom not only is the world of experience an unreality but the idea of God also is a mere dream.

thirst be satisfied by drinking of a mirage, or horns sprout on the head of a hare, or darkness vanquish the sun, than any creature find happiness if he has Rāma against him. Sooner shall fire appear out of ice than anyone at variance with Rāma find happiness.

Dohā 122a-122b

Sooner shall butter be produced by churning water, or oil come out of sand, than the ocean of mortality be traversed without prayer to Hari. This is an indisputable truth. The Lord can change a gnat into Brahmā, or make Brahmā himself even less than a gnat. A wise man will consider this and discard all doubt and worship Rāma.

Śloka 3

I declare to you as an established truth, and I have nothing to say against it, that they who worship Hari can alone traverse the impassable.

Caupāī 118

I have told you, my lord, of the unparalleled achievements of Hari, in full or in brief, as best I can, and this, Garuṛ, is the crowning dogma of the Scriptures to abandon sensuality and worship Rāma. Whom else should you worship but the Lord Raghupati, who was compassionate even to such a wretch as myself. You are wisdom itself and superior to delusion, but you showed me, my lord, a great kindness in that you asked me for Rāma's history, which is so holy that it delights the soul even of Śukadeva and Sanatkumāra and Śambhu. The company of the good is hard to get in the world, even for once only and for a single moment. See, Garuṛ, and consider for yourself; I am now a master in the worship of Raghubīra; though I was the vilest of birds and in every way abominable, the Lord has made me famous as a purifier of the world.

Dohā 123a-123b

Blessed, yea, blessed indeed am I to-day notwithstanding my

meanness; for Rāma has acknowledged me as one of his own faithful servants and has admitted me to the communion of the saints. I have spoken, my lord, according to my ability and have concealed nothing; but Rāma's doings are a very ocean; who can find the bottom of them ?"

Caupāī 119

As he pondered on Rāma's many excellent perfections, the all-wise Bhusuṇḍi was yet more and more enraptured. "He whose greatness the Scriptures have declared to be unutterable, whose might and majesty and lordship are unrivalled, whose feet are adored by Śiva, and Brahmā, even he, Raghurāī, has in his infinite compassion shown favour to me. Never have I seen or heard of such benignity; to whom, O king of birds, can I compare Rāma ? Miracle-working saints, deified anchorites, inspired bards and rigid ascetics, spiritualists, doctors, self-mortified divines and the wisest and most religious of philosophers, can none of them find salvation but by serving my Lord; again and again, and yet again, I bow myself before Rāma. I worship the Immortal, with whom all who take refuge are sanctified, though even guiltier than I.

Dohā 124a-124b

He whose name is an elixir of life, the healer of every kind of trouble, may he in his mercy remain ever gracious both to me and to thee." Hearing Bhusuṇḍi's propitious prayer and perceiving his admirable devotion to Rāma's feet, Garuṛ replied in loving tones and with every doubt at an end:

Caupāī 120

"By your discourse I have attained my end, now that I have learnt the delectable doctrine of faith in Rāma. My devotion to his feet increases ever more and more, and my troubles born of Māyā are clean gone. You have been my raft in the sea of delusion and have bestowed on me, my lord, the most exquisite delight. I can in no way requite you; but again and again I prostrate myself at your feet. Full to overflowing with love for Rama, you are so blessed, Sire, that none can equal you. Sages, trees, rivers, mountains and the earth, all operate for the good of others. The heart of the saints is like butter, so the poets say, but they have not grasped the truth of the matter; for butter melts of its own heat, but the saints are so good that they melt at others' trials. Now has my life become worth living, for by your favour my doubts have disappeared. Regard me ever as your servant." Again and again, O Umā, thus spake the noblest of birds.

Dohā 125a-125b

After affectionately bowing his head at Bhusuṇḍi's feet, the resolute Garuṛ proceeded to Vaikuṇṭha, with Rāma's image impressed upon his heart. O Girijā, there is no blessing like that of communion with the saints: it is a tainable only by Hari's grace; so the Vedas and Purāṇas declare.

Caupāī 121

I have now finished the all-holy history, by the hearing of which the bonds of birth and death are loosened, a very tree of Paradise abounding in mercies for all who approach it and stimulating devotion to Rāma's lotus feet. Sins engendered of thought, word and deed are all absolved in those who listen attentively to this legend. Pilgrimages to shrines, recourse to other religious practices, meditation, self-control, perfection in wisdom, works of religious merit, devotional practices, fasting and almsgiving, continence, temperance, prayer, penance and manifold sacrifices, tender-heartedness to all living creatures, ministering to Brāhmaṇas and *gurus*, learning, morality and exalted intelligence in short, all the forms of discipline which the Vedas have recommended, have but one aim, Bhavānī, *viz.*, devotion to Rāma. To such devotion—as the Scriptures describe it—scarce any has attained and then only by the grace of Rāma.

Dohā 126

But though the patriarchs found it scarce attainable, anyone can now easily acquire it, by the repeated hearin g of this story, if only he puts his trust in it.

Caupāī 122

He is all-wise, he is an accomplished scholar, he is renowned throughout the world for learning and beneficence, he is truly pious and his kinsfolk's saviour, whose soul is enamoured of Rāma's feet. He is perfect in morality and supremely intelligent; he has a thorough understanding of scriptural doctrine; he is an inspired bard and a man of fixed purpose, who without hypocrisy worships Raghubīra. Blessed is the land where the Gaṅgā flows! Blessed is the wife who is faithful to her husband! Blessed is the king who governs justly! Blessed is the Brāhmaṇa who swerves not from his duty! Blessed is the wealth which is dispensed in charity! Blessed is the creed which most conduces to works of piety! Blessed is the hour of communion with the saints! Blessed is the life perpetually devoted to the Brāhmaṇas!

Dohā 127

Blessed is the family, yea—mark me, O Umā—worthy of veneration throughout the world and truly holy, in which is born a humble worshipper of the divine Raghubīra!

Caupāī 123

Though at first I kept it secret, I have now to the best of my ability told you the whole story. I saw the extreme devotion of your soul, and it is for this reason that I have declared to you Rāma's history. It is not to be repeated to the wicked, who will not give his mind to understand the tale of Hari's sportive manifestations, nor to any covetous, choleric or sensual person, who worships not the Lord of all animate and inanimate creation. Neither must it ever be repeated to a persecutor of the Brāhmaṇas, even should he be as great a king as Indra. They are fit for instruction in Rāma's story who dearly love to commune with the saints, who have a great affection for the feet of their *guru* and the precepts of morality and are submissive to the Brāhmaṇas. These alone are fit recipients. He will derive a special delight from it who loves Rāma as he loves his own life.

Dohā 128

Whoever wishes to love Rāma's feet or to attain to final liberation should devoutly fill the pitchers of his ears with the water of this legend.

Caupāī 124

The story of Rāma, as I have now told you, O Umā, has power to wash away the impurities of the Kaliyuga and to cleanse the defilement of the soul. It is a healing remedy for every disease of life, as is declared by those learned in the Vedas. It has seven beautiful ghāṭs, being so many steps towards faith in him. Only he to whom Hari shows, special favour can set his feet on this road. They who guilelessly recite this story obtain success in everything their soul desires. They who hear, or repeat and gladly assent to it, pass over the sea of birth and death as they would a mere puddle." Umā was greatly pleased to have heard the whole story and cried in joyous tones: "By my Lord's favour my doubts have been dispelled, and my love for Rāma's feet has sprung up anew.

Dohā 129

Through your grace, O Lord of the universe, I have now attained my desire; an unswerving devotion to Rāma has resulted and all my troubles are at an end."

Caupāī 125

This blessed dialogue between Śambhu and Umā is fraught with bliss and destructive of sorrow; it loosens the bonds of birth and death and dispels all doubt; it delights the believer and is dear to all good men, there is nothing in the world equally dear to a worshipper of Rāma. By Raghupati's favour I have sung to the best of my ability his holy and gracious deeds. In this, the last age of the world, there is no other means of salvation, neither abstraction, sacrifice, prayer, penance, the paying of vows, nor religious ceremonial. Meditate only on

1. *Cf. Adhyātma Rāmāyaṇa*, Uttarakāṇḍa, 9, 68-73; *Vālmīkīya Rāmāyaṇa*, Uttarakāṇḍa, 111, 1-25.

Rāma, sing only of Rāma, give ear only to Rāma's infinite perfections. Let the soul give over its perversity and worship him whose special characteristic it is to sanctify the fallen, as is declared by saints and seers, by Veda and Purāṇas: is there anyone who has worshipped Rāma and not found salvation ?

Chand 14

Hearken, O stupid soul ! Is there any creature who has worshipped Rāma, the purifier of the fallen, and not found salvation ? The wretches whom he has redeemed are countless, such as the harlot Piṅgalā and Ajāmila, the huntsman Vālmīki, the vulture Jaṭāyu, and the elephant.[1] An Ābhīra, a Yavana, a Kirāta, Khaśa, a Cāṇḍāla[2] and all who are most defiled by pollution are purified if they but once repeat his name; O Rāma, I adore thee. Any one who reads, or hears, or recites this history of the glorious son of Raghu washes out the stains of the world and the stains of his own soul and without any trouble goes straight to Rāma's sphere in heaven. Anyone who, appreciating their beauty, learns by heart five or six stanzas is delivered by the blessed Raghubīra from all the disorders created by the five[3] monstrous kinds of ignorance. Rāma alone is All-beautiful, All-wise, full of compassion and of loving-kindness for the destitute, disinterested in his benevolence and the bestower of final deliverance; whom else can I desire ? There is no other Lord like Rāma, by whose grace, however slight, even I, the dull-witted Tulasī Dāsa, have found perfect peace.

Dohā 130a-130b

There is none so miserable as I am and no one so gracious to the miserable as you, O Raghuvīra; remember this, O jewel of the

1. See page 26, Note 1.
2. Ābhīras and Khaśas are hill-tribes, the former inhabiting the south-west coast in ancient times and the latter Assam; Kirātas are Bhīls and Cāṇḍālas pariahs.
3. In this antithesis between the five stanzas and the five members of council, who are not specifically designated, the latter would seem to stand for five senses.

race of Raghu, and rid me of the grievous burden of existence. As a lover loves his mistress and as a miser loves his money, so for ever and ever may Rāma be beloved by me!

Śloka 4

While in former days the holy Lord Śambhu, that excellent poet, wrote a *Rāmāyaṇa*, difficult to understand, for the attainment of unending faith in the lotus feet of the blessed Lord Rāma, Tulasī, considering that poem to be instinct with Raghunātha's name, has composed the *Mānasa* in the vulgar tongue for the enlightenment of his own inner self. He who plunges with faith into this Holy Lake of Rāma's Acts, a lake of merit, which destroys all defilements and ever blesses the soul and grants devotion and wisdom, washing away the impurities of ignorance and illusion, is not burnt by the scorching rays of the sun of worldly illusion.

[*Thus endeth the Book entitled* THE SEQUEL, *a provocative to steadfast faith in Hari, being the seventh descent into the Holy Lake of Rāma's Acts, that cleanses every defilement of the world.*]